D1576483

Encyclopedia of Caribbean Archaeology

UNIVERSITY PRESS OF FLORIDA

Florida A&M University, Tallahassee
Florida Atlantic University, Boca Raton
Florida Gulf Coast University, Ft. Myers
Florida International University, Miami
Florida State University, Tallahassee
New College of Florida, Sarasota
University of Central Florida, Orlando
University of Florida, Gainesville
University of North Florida, Jacksonville
University of South Florida, Tampa
University of West Florida, Pensacola

ENCYCLOPEDIA OF CARIBBEAN ARCHAEOLOGY

Edited by Basil A. Reid and R. Grant Gilmore III

UNIVERSITY PRESS OF FLORIDA

Gainesville Tallahassee Tampa Boca Raton Pensacola
Orlando Miami Jacksonville Ft. Myers Sarasota

Frontispiece: Magens House compound, Charlotte Amalie,
St. Thomas. Courtesty of Douglas V. Armstrong.

This book may be available in an electronic edition.

19 18 17 16 15 14   6 5 4 3 2 1

Library of Congress Cataloging-in-Publication Data
Encyclopedia of Caribbean archaeology /
edited by Basil A. Reid and R. Grant Gilmore III.
pages cm
Includes bibliographical references.
ISBN 978-0-8130-4420-0 (alk. paper)
1. Archaeology—West Indies—Encyclopedias. 2. Excavations
(Archaeology)—West Indies—Encyclopedias. 3. West Indies—
Antiquities—Encyclopedias. I. Reid, Basil A., 1961–, editor.
II. Gilmore, R. Grant, III (Richard Grant), editor.
F1619.E63 2014
972.9'01—dc23   2013029231

The University Press of Florida is the scholarly publishing agency
for the State University System of Florida, comprising Florida
A&M University, Florida Atlantic University, Florida Gulf
Coast University, Florida International University, Florida State
University, New College of Florida, University of Central Florida,
University of Florida, University of North Florida, University
of South Florida, and University of West Florida.

University Press of Florida
15 Northwest 15th Street
Gainesville, FL 32611-2079
http://www.upf.com

Contents

Figures

Acknowledgments

We are indeed grateful to the authors of this volume, whose seminal contributions made the *Encyclopedia of Caribbean Archaeology* a reality. Louise Mathurin, Alexandra Sajo, Onika Mandela, former archaeology research assistants in the Department of History at The University of the West Indies (UWI), St. Augustine, should be commended for assisting with the formatting of several entries. Thanks to John Agard, head of the Department of Life Sciences of UWI, St. Augustine, for granting us permission to use the photograph of "Banwari Man." We wish to thank Adrian Camps-Campins for allowing us use of one of the images of the "Magnificent Seven" historical buildings in Port of Spain, Trinidad and Tobago. Laleta Davis-Mattis, former executive director of the Jamaica National Heritage Trust, graciously provided us with a photograph of Hibbert House (the headquarters of the Trust), and Vivian Crawford, retired executive director of the Institute of Jamaica, kindly furnished us with a photograph of the institute. We thank them both for their generous assistance.

Thanks to Katherine Derrett and Pierre Chemin for their photography work at the St. Eustatius Center for Archaeological Research (SECAR). Courtney Linderman and Katrien Janin should be thanked for producing illustrations for the volume while at SECAR. Ruud Stelten, who was formerly employed at SECAR, deserves special commendation for producing a comprehensive Caribbean map that shows the major archaeological sites discussed in the volume. Thanks to Daren Dhoray and Christopher Thomas of Campus IT Services, UWI, St. Augustine, and Christopher A. Riley, a graphic artist in Trinidad and Tobago, for assisting with the conversion and improvement of several images. José G. Guerrero's entry on La Isabela (Dominican Republic) was translated into English by his wife, Raquel D. Vicini. L. Antonio Curet translated into English all of the entries of fellow contributor Clenis Tavárez María. We gratefully acknowledge the important work of these two individuals.

Scott M. Fitzpatrick helped with the editing of the Ground Sloths entry, while Arie Boomert assisted with the editing of the Palo Seco and La Brea Pitch Lake (Trinidad) entries. Both Fitzpatrick and Boomert are hereby thanked for their unselfish contributions. We are grateful to Douglas V. Armstrong and Corinne L. Hofman for agreeing, at such short notice, to co-author the introduction. Zara Ali, in the Department of History at UWI, St. Augustine, helped with the collating and formatting of citations in this chapter. She also assisted with the formatting of the glossary. Her indefatigable efforts are well appreciated. Jeffrey P. Blick contributed a number of entries, one of which he co-authored with colleagues working in the Bahamas. He deserves special mention because he kindly agreed to write these entries at short notice. We wish to thank Peter L. Drewett, Georgia L. Fox, Cheryl White, Benoît Bérard, and Maria A. Nieves-Colón for agreeing, also at short notice, to contribute entries to the volume. During the copyediting phase of the project, Professor Peter Drewett passed away. We use this opportunity to pay tribute to Professor Drewett for his seminal contributions to Caribbean archaeology, particularly the archaeology of Barbados. We are grateful to Alissandra Cummins, Clenis Tavárez María, Peter E. Siegel, Patricia E. Green, L. Antonio Curet, and Scott M. Fitzpatrick for suggesting additional topics for the encyclopedia and writers for these topics. Also thanks to James Robertson for editorially tweaking the Notes on Contributors.

We are especially grateful to Leiden University, The Reed Foundation Inc., and The University of the West Indies, St. Augustine, for providing much-needed financial support for the encyclopedia. We thank the staff of the University Press of Florida for actively encouraging this project from beginning to end. Many thanks to the peer reviewers for taking the time to read and provide constructive comments on the first and second drafts of the manuscript. Special thanks to Kate Babbitt for her competence and thoroughness as she copyedited the volume. Finally, we place on record our deepest appreciation to our families for their patience and unwavering support while we sometimes worked late at night and early in the morning to complete this major research publication.

Basil A. Reid and R. Grant Gilmore III

Contributors

E. Kofi Agorsah

Douglas V. Armstrong

Tracy Assing

Lesley-Gail Atkinson

Allison Bain

Emma K. Bate

Brian D. Bates

Zachary J. Beier

Benoît Bérard

Jeffrey P. Blick

Arie Boomert

Bridget Brereton

Richard T. Callaghan

John F. Cherry

Michael A. Cinquino

Roger H. Colten

Ivor Conolley

John G. Crock

Alissandra Cummins

L. Antonio Curet

Kathleen Deagan

Rudylynn De Four Roberts

Maaike de Waal

Mark C. Donop

Peter L. Drewett

Ryan Espersen

Kevin Farmer

Anne-Marie Faucher

Scott M. Fitzpatrick

Georgia L. Fox

Gertrudis J. M. Gehlen

Joanna K. Gilmore

R. Grant Gilmore III

Patricia E. Green

José G. Guerrero

Jay B. Haviser

Michele H. Hayward

Ainsley Henriques

Corinne L. Hofman

Lennox Honychurch

Menno L. P. Hoogland

Naseema Hosein-Hoey

Charlene Dixon Hutcheson

Jeremiah Kaplan

Quetta Kaye

K. O. Laurence

Elise V. LeCompte

Stephan Lenik

Margaret E. Leshikar-Denton

Neal H. Lopinot

George M. Luer

Onika Mandela

Kathy Martin

H. Gregory McDonald

Marco Meniketti

Reg Murphy

Lee A. Newsom

Maria A. Nieves-Colón

Winston F. Phulgence

Elizabeth Pigou-Dennis

Mark G. Plew

Basil A. Reid

Andrea Richards

James Robertson

Stéphen Rostain

Krysta Ryzewski

Alexandra Sajo

Brinsley Samaroo

Gerald F. Schroedl

Della A. Scott-Ireton

Peter E. Siegel

Harrold Sijlbing

Sherry-Ann Singh

Theresa Singleton

Frederick H. Smith

Ruud Stelten

Clenis Tavárez María

Joshua M. Torres

Marcie L. Venter

Gifford J. Waters

Cheryl White

Samuel M. Wilson

Jennifer Wishart

Ieteke Witteveen

Preface

Caribbean archaeological research continues to experience exponential growth, as each year, Caribbean, North American, and European scholars working in the region publish dozens of monographs, journal articles, and edited volumes. As a result, research topics have become increasingly diverse and cutting edge, extending beyond the usual questions of colonization, adaptation, artifactual analysis, evolution, social and political organization, and mythology (Ayubi and Haviser 1991; Keegan 2000; Seigel 1989) to embrace emerging issues such as historical ecology (Fitzpatrick and Keegan 2007), geoinformatics (Reid 2008), paleodemography (Curet 2005), environmental archaeology (Newsom and Wing 2004), seafaring simulations (Callaghan 2011), DNA (Lalueza-Fox et al. 2001), and archaeometry (Hofman et al. 2008). While this large body of information is generally available, researchers may often find it time consuming to locate specific data in disparate formats, locations, and languages. The *Encyclopedia of Caribbean Archaeology* is a response to a growing need for easily obtainable scholarly information on Caribbean archaeology.

The alphabetized entries in the volume are eclectic, accurately reflecting the many theoretical and methodological approaches that are fundamental to Caribbean archaeological research. The topics cover a broad span of time, from the Ortoiroid sites of Banwari Trace and St. John in Trinidad, which both date to 7,000 years ago, to the most recent topics in archaeological research, such as archaeological heritage management (Siegel and Righter 2011), and affiliate organizations of UNESCO in the Caribbean (International Council on Monuments and Sites 2006). A significant number of entries relate to the archaeological profiles of specific Caribbean and circum-Caribbean territories sites, areas of interest, historic architecture, and the biographies of luminaries of Caribbean archaeology, who are now deceased. Historic architecture is included, as anything man-made, above or below the ground, is considered archaeological (see Delle, Hauser, and Armstrong 2011). Many of the entries are cross-referenced, enabling readers to easily access data on a variety of related topics. The volume's diverse collection of drawings, maps, and diagrams; its extensive bibliographies; and its glossary of terms contribute additional layers of valuable resources.

Chronologies

The radiocarbon dates cited in the volume are calibrated. However, in those rare cases where there are uncalibrated C14 dates, these will be clearly stated in the respective entries. The usual dating abbreviations used in the encyclopedia are BC and AD. Readers will notice the occasional use of the dating abbreviation BP, a time scale used in archaeology, geology and other scientific disciplines to specify when events in the past occurred. Because the "present" time changes, the standard practice is to use AD 1950 as the origin of the age scale.

Naming Prehistoric and Contact Period Native Groups in the Caribbean

While some history books (Rogoziński 2000; Dookhan 2006) continue to refer to the Arawak and Carib as the two major native groups that colonized the Caribbean, the encyclopedia discounts this simplistic view by highlighting multiple cultural groups that migrated to the region or evolved autochthonously into new native communities. On the basis of artifact types, the major prehistoric groups identified by Caribbean archaeologists are Ortoiroid, Casimiroid, Saladoid, Huecoid, Barrancoid, Troumassan Troumassoid, Suazan Troumassoid, and Ostionoid. While the practice of identifying "cultures" from archaeological remains is seen by many as hopelessly inadequate (Jones 1997), there is presently no better alternative, given that we are dealing with nonliterate peoples who existed thousands of years ago and who did not leave behind any tangible information about their names or ethnic identities. Despite the significant challenges associated with ascribing names to contact period groups (Hulme 1993; Reid 2009), the volume attempts to clarify the use of the terms Arawak, Taíno, Ciboney, Guanahatabey, Island-Carib, and Kalinago in the context of Caribbean archaeology and ethnohistory.

Conclusion

The *Encyclopedia of Caribbean Archaeology* presents Caribbean archaeology as a rapidly expanding area of scholarship in which ideas are being actively deliberated, discussed, and contested. Although the topics in this volume pertain to the region, they are expected to have considerable resonance and applicability wherever archaeology is taught and practiced internationally. Although not exhaustive in its treatment of Caribbean archaeology, the encyclopedia provides a balanced representation of the region by showcasing the Anglophone, Spanish, Francophone, and Dutch Caribbean. Because the volume contains contributions by many of the region's leading experts, it will undoubtedly prove useful to archaeologists, heritage professionals, and archaeology graduate students.

Basil A. Reid and R. Grant Gilmore III

References Cited

Ayubi, E., and J. B. Haviser, eds. 1991. *Proceedings of the Thirteenth International Congress for Caribbean Archaeology.* Curaçao: AAINA.

Callaghan, R. T. 2011. "Patterns of Contact between the Islands of the Caribbean and the Surrounding Mainland as a Navigation Problem." In *Islands in the Stream: Migration, Seafaring, and Interaction in the Caribbean,* ed. A. Curet and M. Hauser, 59–72. Tuscaloosa: University of Alabama Press.

Curet, L. A. 2005. *Caribbean Paleodemography: Population, Culture History, and Sociopolitical Processes in Ancient Puerto Rico.* Tuscaloosa: University of Alabama Press.

Delle, J. A., M. W. Hauser, and D. W. Armstrong. 2011. *Out of Many, One People: The Historical Archaeology of Colonial Jamaica.* Tuscaloosa: University of Alabama Press.

Dookhan, I. 2006. *A Pre-Emancipation History of the West Indies.* London: Longman Publishing for the Caribbean.

Fitzpatrick, S. M., and W. F. Keegan. 2007. "Human Impacts and Adaptations in the Caribbean Islands: An Historical Ecology Approach." *Earth and Environmental Science: Transactions of the Royal Society of Edinburgh* 98: 29–45.

Hofman, C. L., M.L.P. Hoogland, and A. L. van Gijn, eds. 2008. *Crossing the Borders: New Methods and Techniques in the Study of Archaeological Materials from the Caribbean.* Tuscaloosa: University of Alabama Press.

Hulme, P. 1993. "Making Sense of the Native Caribbean." *New West Indian Guide* 67 (3–4): 189–220.

International Council on Monuments and Sites. 2006. *Thematic Study: Rock Art of Latin America and the Caribbean.* Paris: ICOMOS.

Jones, I. 1997. *The Archaeology of Ethnicity.* New York: Routledge.

Keegan, W. F. 2000. "West Indian Archaeology. 3. Ceramic Age." *Journal of Archaeological Research* 8 (2): 135–67.

Lalueza-Fox, C., F. Luna Calderon, F. Calafell, and J. Bertranpetit. 2001. "MtDNA from Extinct Taínos and the Peopling of the Caribbean." *Annals of Human Genetics* 65: 137–51.

Newsom, L., and E. Wing. 2004. *On Land and Sea: Native American Uses of Biological Resources in the West Indies.* Tuscaloosa: University of Alabama Press.

Reid, B. A., ed. 2008. *Archaeology and Geoinformatics: Case Studies from the Caribbean.* Tuscaloosa: University of Alabama Press.

———. 2009. *Myths and Realities of Caribbean History.* Tuscaloosa: University of Alabama Press.

Rogoziński, J. 2000. *A Brief History of the Caribbean: From the Arawak and Carib to the Present.* New York: Facts on File.

Siegel, P. E. 1989. *Early Ceramic Population Lifeways and Adaptive Strategies in the Caribbean.* Oxford: British Archaeological Reports.

Siegel, P. E., and E. Righter. 2011. *Protecting Heritage in the Caribbean.* Tuscaloosa: University of Alabama Press.

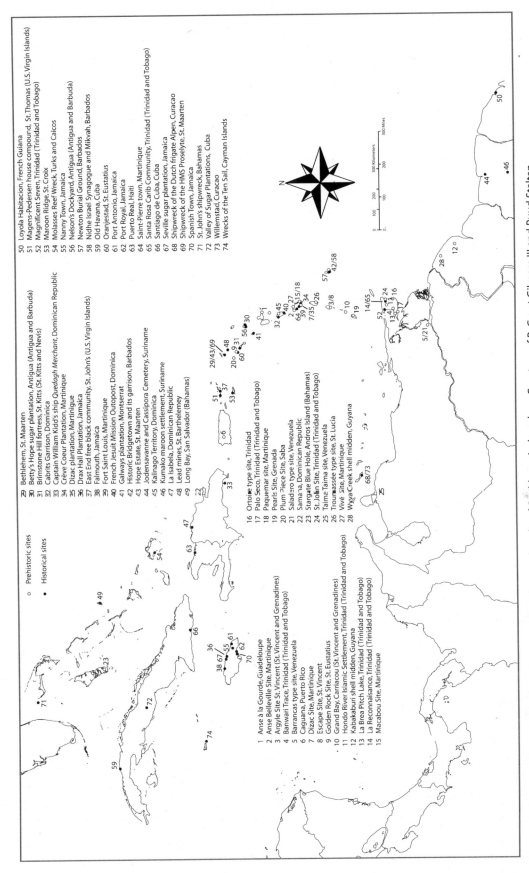

○ Prehistoric sites
● Historical sites

1 Anse à la Gourde, Guadeloupe
2 Anse Belleville Site, Martinique
3 Argyle Site St. Vincent (St. Vincent and Grenadines)
4 Banwari Trace, Trinidad (Trinidad and Tobago)
5 Barrancas type site, Venezuela
6 Caguana, Puerto Rico
7 Dizac Site, Martinique
8 Escape Site, St. Vincent
9 Golden Rock Site, St. Eustatius
10 Grand Bay, Carriacou (St. Vincent and Grenadines)
11 Hondo River Islamic Settlement, Trinidad (Trinidad and Tobago)
12 Kabakaburi shell midden, Guyana
13 La Brea Pitch Lake, Trinidad (Trinidad and Tobago)
14 La Reconnaisance, Trinidad (Trinidad and Tobago)
15 Macabou Site, Martinique

16 Ortoire type site, Trinidad
17 Palo Seco, Trinidad (Trinidad and Tobago)
18 Paquemar site, Martinique
19 Pearls Site, Grenada
20 Plum Piece Site, Saba
21 Saladero type site, Venezuela
22 Samana, Dominican Republic
23 Stargate Blue Hole, Andros Island (Bahamas)
24 St. John Site, Trinidad (Trinidad and Tobago)
25 Taima Taima site, Venezuela
26 Troumassée type site, St. Lucia
27 Vivé site, Martinique
28 Wya Creek shell midden, Guyana

29 Bethlehem, St. Maarten
30 Betty's Hope sugar plantation, Antigua (Antigua and Barbuda)
31 Brimstone Hill fortress, St. Kitts (St. Kitts and Nevis)
32 Cabrits Garrison, Dominica
33 Captain William Kidd's ship *Quedagh Merchant*, Dominican Republic
34 Crève Coeur Plantation, Martinique
35 Dizac plantation, Martinique
36 Drax Hall Plantation, Jamaica
37 East End free black community, St. John's (U.S. Virgin Islands)
38 Falmouth, Jamaica
39 Fort Saint Louis, Martinique
40 French Jesuit Mission Outpost, Dominica
41 Galways plantation, Montserrat
42 Historic Bridgetown and its garrison, Barbados
43 Hope Estate, St. Maarten
44 Jodensavanne and Cassipora Cemetery, Suriname
45 Kalinago Territory, Dominica
46 Kumako maroon settlement, Suriname
47 La Isabela, Dominican Republic
48 Lead mines, St. Barthélemey
49 Long Bay, San Salvador (Bahamas)

50 Loyola Habitacion, French Guiana
51 Magens-Pedersen house compound, St. Thomas (U.S. Virgin Islands)
52 Magnificent Seven, Trinidad (Trinidad and Tobago)
53 Maroon Ridge, St. Croix
54 Molasses Reef Wreck, Turks and Caicos
55 Nanny Town, Jamaica
56 Nelson's Dockyard, Antigua (Antigua and Barbuda)
57 Newton Burial Ground, Barbados
58 Nidhe Israel Synagogue and Mikvah, Barbados
59 Old Havana, Cuba
60 Oranjestad, St. Eustatius
61 Port Antonio, Jamaica
62 Port Royal, Jamaica
63 Puerto Real, Haiti
64 Saint-Pierre town, Martinique
65 Santa Rosa Carib Community, Trinidad (Trinidad and Tobago)
66 Santiago de Cuba, Cuba
67 Seville sugar plantation, Jamaica
68 Shipwreck of the Dutch frigate Alpen, Curacao
69 Shipwreck of the HMS Proselyte, St. Maarten
70 Spanish Town, Jamaica
71 St. John's shipwreck, Bahamas
72 Valley of Sugar Plantations, Cuba
73 Willemstad, Curacao
74 Wrecks of the Ten Sail, Cayman Islands

Figure 1. The Caribbean, showing major sites discussed in *Encyclopedia of Caribbean Archaeology*. Courtesy of R. Grant Gilmore III and Ruud Stelten.

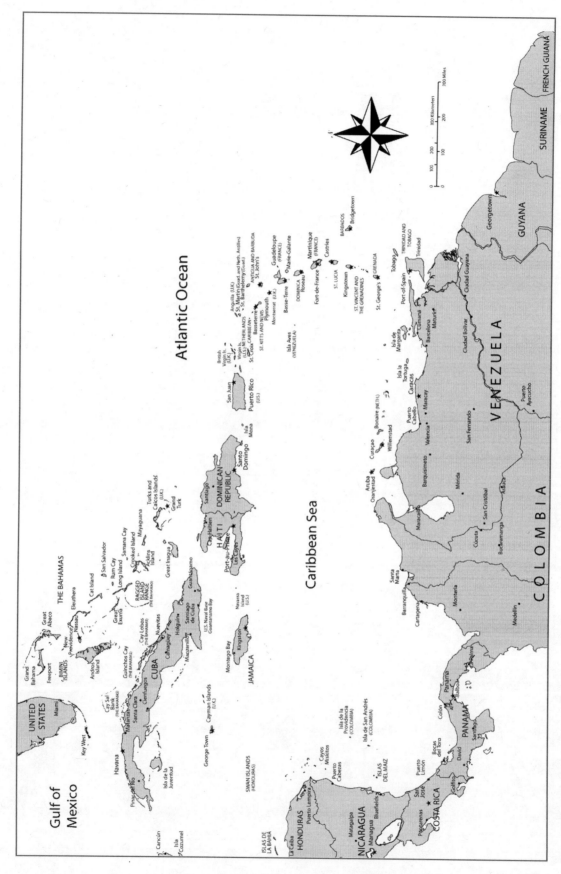

Figure 2. Topographic map of the Caribbean. Courtesy of R. Grant Gilmore III and Ruud Stelten.

Introduction

Caribbean Prehistoric and Historical Archaeology

Basil A. Reid, Corinne L. Hofman, R. Grant Gilmore III, and Douglas V. Armstrong

Caribbean archaeology can be broadly subdivided into two major time periods: prehistoric archaeology (5000 BC–1492) and historical archaeology (post-1492). Prehistoric archaeology includes studies relating to various Amerindian peoples and cultures: the Ortoiroid, Casimiroid, Saladoid, Huecoid, Barrancoid, Troumassan Troumassoid, Suazan Troumassoid, Ostionoid, and Taíno. Caribbean prehistoric archaeology is based on a rich mosaic of migrations, cultural interactions, and sociocultural complexities.

According to the traditional schema, prehistoric migrations to the region started about 7,000 years ago with the advent of Ortoiroid (Archaic) groups from South America, followed by movements by Casimiroid (Archaic) groups from Central America 1,000 years thereafter. The next wave of migrants were the Huecoid, Saladoid, and Barrancoid, who came from South America between 800 and 200 BC and AD 350, respectively, and, like their Archaic forerunners, established several indigenous communities in the Caribbean. However, recent revisions of this schema present a much more dynamic picture involving processes of intensive mobility from various parts of South and Central America, intercultural dynamics (competition over resources, marriage alliances), and local developments (Hofman and Bright 2010; Hofman and van Duijvenbode 2011; Rodríguez Ramos 2010). As such, Huecoid may have developed locally from Archaic groups, but this development may have included influences from Central America (the Isthmo-Columbian area) or may have been a separate migration from the Central or South American mainland (Rodríguez Ramos 2010). Similarly, around AD 600, the Ostionoid (who eventually evolved into the "Taíno") developed from a combination of Archaic and Saladoid-Huecoid cultural influences. The Troumassan Troumassoid, Suazan Troumassoid, Ostionoid, and Taíno were not migrants but were indigenous cultures that developed autochthonously in the region. Straddling the prehistoric and historic periods are contact period indigenous populations, such as the Taíno and Guanahatabey in the northern Caribbean and the Island-Carib in the southern Caribbean (Boomert 2000; Keegan 1992; Keegan and Rodríguez Ramos 2007; Petersen 1997; Reid 2009; Rouse 1992).

As elsewhere in the Americas, the focus of historical archaeology in the Caribbean begins with the arrival of Christopher Columbus in 1492. The combination of archipelagic insularity, geographic variation, and the cultural diversity of indigenous populations set the stage for extraordinary cultural complexity in the region during the historic period. In reviewing historical archaeology in the Caribbean, Douglas Armstrong and Mark Hauser define the region as a cultural "sea of diversity" and describe a "complex historical landscape in which local contexts punctuate global trends with unique material expressions" (2009, 583). This introduction explores ways that historical archaeology has been used to better understand the cultural contexts of the Caribbean that resulted from the convergence of European, Native American, African, and then Asian settlers in the Caribbean (see also Armstrong and Hauser 2009; Armstrong 2011a, 2011b). Although the specific historical path of each island is different, they share common themes that can be explored through archaeology. These themes include the decimation or assimilation of indigenous societies and the emergence of colonial societies; expressions of economic power and dominance that the materialization of substantial agro-industry and the shift to sugar- and coffee-based plantation systems involving the large-scale enslavement of African laborers created. Colonial societies were supported by massive fortifications, such as Brimstone Hill Fortress (St. Kitts) and Castillo San Felipe del Morro (Puerto Rico), that were designed to protect them from naval invasions, enforce the authority of each colonial power, and subjugate its laboring population. The inherent inequality in repressive labor systems also left their marks on the cultural land-scape in the form of sites of rebellion and struggles for freedom. The more subtle material records of life reflect the dynamic processes of cultural genesis and transformation in house sites and communities. Figure 1 shows a map of the Caribbean that indicates many of the major sites discussed in the volume.

However, before surveying the region's prehistoric and historical archaeology, it is important to examine Caribbean geography, given its significant role in both colonization and migration.

Caribbean Geography

The Caribbean region consists of the Caribbean Sea, its islands, and the surrounding mainland coasts. The latter is usually referred to as the circum-Caribbean (Figure 2). The island chain of the Caribbean is divided into three parts: the Greater Antilles, the Lesser Antilles, and the Bahamian Archipelago (Rouse 1992, 3). The Greater Antilles are large, mountainous, and mostly sedimentary islands in the northwestern portion of the Caribbean Sea. They include Cuba, Hispaniola (Haiti and the Dominican Republic), Jamaica, and Puerto Rico. The Lesser Antilles constitutes a long arc of smaller, mostly volcanic islands in the Caribbean Sea extending in a north-south direction from the Virgin Islands to Trinidad and in an east-west direction from Margarita to Aruba, off the northern coast of Venezuela. The north-south portion of the Lesser Antilles has been divided into the Windward and Leeward Islands, because of their geographical location in relation to the prevailing easterly trade winds. The Windward Islands range south from Dominica to Grenada; the Leeward Islands arc in a generally westerly direction from Guadeloupe to the Virgin Islands. Two groups of tiny coral islands make up the Bahamian Archipelago. The Bahamas lie north of Cuba, and the Turks and Caicos Islands are north of Hispaniola. The Leeward Antilles, an east-west chain of islands close to the South American coast, are arid because most of the precipitation from trade winds is concentrated on the Windward Islands of the Lesser Antilles. Three small islands (Margarita, Coche, and Cubagua) form the Venezuelan state of Nueva Esparta, and some seventy others, most of which are uninhabited, belong to Venezuela.

The circum-Caribbean area includes the zone along the Caribbean coast of Colombia, Venezuela, Guyana, Suriname, and French Guiana. These territories are considered to be important for Caribbean archaeology because the majority of early Caribbean indigenous peoples (the Ortoiroid, Saladoid, Huecoid, Barrancoid,

and later the Arawak and Island-Carib) migrated from South America. Over the years, the presence of several indigenous communities in the circum-Caribbean has provided useful ethnographic information that is helping to unlock the narratives of the precolonial past. Central America territories (especially Belize, the Yucatán Peninsula, and Nicaragua) are also part of the circum-Caribbean. Because of their cultural connections to the islands (as a result of prehistoric migration and trade), Central America also has an important place in Caribbean archaeology (Callaghan 1990, 1995, 2001; Hofman and Bright 2010; Murphy et al. 2000; Rodríguez Ramos 2010).

The topography of the Caribbean islands is very diverse because of variations in underlying geology (Wilson 2007, 9). The Caribbean is part of a tectonic plate that includes Central America and is creeping slowly westward at about 4 centimeters a year. The fault-block mountains of the Greater Antilles are continuations of the cordillera systems of Central America, and a tectonic plate boundary between the expanding Atlantic plate and the Caribbean plate accounts for the volcanism and uplift of the arc of the Lesser Antilles (Wilson 2007, 9–10).

Because of the region's tropical climate, oceanography, and proximity to various physiographically distinct land masses, the Caribbean possesses amazing biodiversity. The region's rich mosaic of natural environments supports a rich array of fauna and flora that offered a wide variety of resource habitats to early native inhabitants. It is home to 2.3 percent of the world's endemic plant species and 2.9 percent of endemic vertebrate species—enormously significant percentages considering that the Caribbean contributes only 0.15 percent of the earth's surface. In addition, there are over 1,500 species of fish, over 630 mollusk species, and numerous echinoderms, crustaceans, sea mammals, sponges, birds, and reptiles in marine, freshwater, brackish, and terrestrial environments (Fitzpatrick and Keegan 2007, 31–32).

In the Lesser Antilles, the people's diets were almost always linked to ocean resources, whereas in the interior of the large islands people often had a wholly terrestrial food supply (Wilson 2007, 9). All four islands of the Greater Antilles—Cuba, Hispaniola, Jamaica, and Puerto Rico—have fertile soils that were capable of supporting dense pre-colonial populations (Curet 2005; Rouse 1992). The two largest islands, Cuba and Hispaniola, have yielded remains of ground sloths, which the first settlers may have hunted to extinction (Harrington 1921, 165, 409; Veloz Maggiolo 1976, 25). The Bahamas are rich in marine resources but lack good agricultural soils

(Rouse 1992). The Lesser Antilles possessed resources rich offshore habitats; some of the shallow shelves and banks surrounding the islands were much larger than the islands themselves (Hofman and Hoogland 2011; Keegan et al. 2008; Wilson 2007, 9).

The Caribbean Sea is the second largest sea and the seventh largest body of water in the world. It encompasses an area of 2,754,000 square kilometers (1,063,000 square miles) and stretches 1,700 kilometers north-south from Florida to Panama and 2,300 kilometers east-west from the Antillean chain of islands to the Yucatán (Fitzpatrick and Keegan 2007, 31). However, the Caribbean Sea is small by the world's standards, and traversing it would not have posed a significant challenge for early natives from Central and South America. To put it in perspective, after 2000 BC, early Polynesians successfully crossed the Pacific Ocean, where islands are sometimes thousands of kilometers apart (Fagan 2005; Reid 2009). Most of the islands in the Lesser Antilles are within sight of each other, which would have facilitated island-hopping (Rouse 1992; Torres and Rodríguez Ramos 2008), but radiocarbon dates indicate there were also direct jumps, which Callaghan (2003) described as "chance discoveries," from the South American mainland to the northern Leeward Islands, the United States Virgin Islands, and eastern Puerto Rico (Keegan 1992; Haviser 1997; Hofman and Hoogland 1999; Petersen 1996; Reid 2009).

The currents and trade winds in the Caribbean favor travel from south to north and from east to west. A south equatorial current that flows across the South Atlantic from Africa is deflected northward along the coast of the Guianas. The Orinoco River, with its massive outpouring of fresh water at its mouth, helps divert part of the south equatorial current northward (Rouse 1992). The remainder of the south equatorial current continues in a westerly direction along the coast of South America and northward past Central America into the Gulf of Mexico and the Florida Straits. Trade winds, which blow steadily from the northeast during most of the year, reinforce the westward-moving currents (Rouse 1992). Columbus's first, second, third, and fourth voyages took advantage of these ocean currents and prevailing trade winds; they all entered the region from the northeast or east. A countercurrent moves eastward along the southern side of the Greater Antilles that would have facilitated travel from the Yucatán to the Greater Antilles. Callaghan's computer simulations, which use winds, currents, and other conditions of the natural environment as variables, suggest that while the route from the Yucatán to Cuba was possible for precolonial peoples, it was far easier to migrate from South America (Callaghan 1990).

Prehistoric Archaeology

While some history texts (Rogoziński 1999; Dookhan 2006) continue to refer to the Arawak and Carib as the two major Amerindian groups or peoples, Caribbean archaeologists have identified multiple cultural groups based on artifact types (Reid 2009). The practice of attaching an identity to particular artifacts or monuments, which are most frequently expressed in terms of the ethnic groups (or people) who produced them, has been the center of archaeological inquiry (Hides 1996; Reid 2004, 2009). While many see identifying cultures using archaeological remains and associating them with past ethnic groups as hopelessly inadequate (Jones 1997), there is no better alternative at present, given that we are dealing with nonliterate groups, communities, and societies that existed thousands of years ago, and left behind no tangible information about their names or ethnic identities. Caribbean archaeologists have sought to circumvent the problem of names by using artifactual assemblages relating primarily to pottery and lithic artifact types to identify the presence or absence of major cultural groups (Rouse 1992; Petersen, Hofman, and Curet. 2004). This is called the culture-historical approach and can be defined as an attempt to use approaches that traditional historians use or to simply project history back into periods when there was no writing (Drewett 1999). In other words, the culture-historical approach attempts to "reconstruct" the history of people based on detailed local sequences of artifacts and information about their geographic distribution (Drewett 1999).

Most research in the West Indies is structured by Irving Rouse's (1992) method of time-space systematics (Keegan 2000, 2007). In this system, the characteristic modes of pottery at a site have been used to identify a style that usually bears the name of the first site where it was described (Keegan 2000). Pottery and stone tools are the most ubiquitous artifacts found at Caribbean prehistoric sites, hence their importance in Rouse's time-space systematics. According to this classification, local pottery and lithic styles that share enough similarities are grouped into subseries (denoted by an -an suffix), and subseries are grouped into series (denoted by an -oid suffix) (Rouse 1992, 182; Keegan 2000). Rouse (1992, 182) used this classification to identify "peoples" and "cultures," which in his view were "two sides of the same coin, one consisting of a local population group and the other of the cultural traits that define the group. For example, Saladoid is a series and Cedrosan is a subseries of the Saladoid series. Despite minor adjustments through the years, this system of classification is an intrinsic part of scholarly research in the Caribbean (Reid 2011). But even as we adopt the series and subseries approach, we should always be mindful that within this broad classification, several local groups emerged throughout the Caribbean that are identified by their distinctive artifact styles (Hofman and Hoogland 2004; Reid 2009).

Archaic Age

In Caribbean archaeology, Archaic is generally considered to a developmental stage characterized by a marine-oriented subsistence followed by a terrestrial hunting-based economy (Goodwin 1978; Keegan 1994). Traditionally, Archaic sites are distinguished by an abundance of marine mollusks, the absence of pottery, and the use of ground stone, coral, and shell tools. Until recently, the absence of both pottery and agriculture was considered a major defining characteristic of Archaic peoples in the region. However, increasing evidence of pottery-making and plant manipulation among several Archaic Age communities has invalidated this idea. It is now generally agreed that pottery-making and incipient agriculture began in the Caribbean during the Archaic Age rather than the early Ceramic Age (Hung 2005; Rodríguez Ramos and Pagán-Jiménez 2006; Rodriguez Ramos 2007; Tabío 1984; Keegan 1994; Keegan and Rodríguez Ramos 2007; Reid 2009). Couri I and Pascade II in Haiti, the Playa Blanca and Jobos sites in Puerto Rico, El Caimito at the La Caleta site in eastern Dominican Republic, and La Luz, El Nispero and Catunda in Cuba are notable examples of pottery-bearing Archaic sites (Rouse 1941, 1952, 1992; Reid 2009; Keegan and Rodríguez Ramos 2007). Unlike Saladoid pottery, which has a highly formalized grammar (Roe 1989), the pots at Archaic sites seem to reflect a period of experimentation during which different pastes and decorative techniques were explored (Jouravleva 2002; Keegan and Rodríguez Ramos 2007). Botanical studies that investigate preserved starch grains on grinding tools have demonstrated that virtually all of the plants that were supposedly introduced during the Ceramic Age by the Saladoid or Huecoid were already being cultivated by their Archaic predecessors (Newsom 1993; Keegan 1994; Acevedo-Rodríguez et al. 1996, 50; Hung 2005; Curet, Dawdy, and La Rosa Corzo 2005; Tabío 1984; Pagán-Jiménez 2011; Rouse and Alegría 1990; Rodríguez Ramos 2007; Rodríguez Ramos and Pagán-Jiménez 2006; Ve-

loz Maggiolo and Vega 1982). Because of this evidence, a more appropriate characterization of the Archaic Age would be a combination of highly mobile and more sedentary communities with a mixed marine-terrestrial oriented subsistence that included plant management and incipient domestication of tubers. Mobility was often determined by resource availability and season, and the neolithization process on the islands was gradual rather than sudden.

Caribbean archaeologists commonly refer to the two earliest Archaic Age groups as Ortoiroid and Casimiroid. The Ortoiroid, who originated from northwest Guyana (Wilson 2007) and were assigned their name from the shell midden of Ortoire in southeast Trinidad (Rouse 1992), first settled Banwari Trace and St. John in Trinidad approximately 7,000 years ago, eventually moving to Puerto Rico. Callaghan's (1990) computer simulations, however, suggest that some Ortoiroid groups may have jumped directly from South America to the Greater Antilles. The artifacts from Banwari Trace and St. John include tools of bones and stone related to fishing and collecting, canoe building, plant processing, and general cutting and scraping (Boomert 2000; Wilson 2007). Many of the ground stone tools appear to have been used for pounding and processing hard and fibrous vegetable matter (Wilson 2007).

Taking their name from the archaeological type site of Casimira in southwestern Hispaniola (Rouse 1992), the Casimiroid migrated from Belize around 4000 BC and colonized Cuba and Hispaniola. Casimiroid stone tools, which are similar to those of the Ortoiroid, include sophisticated blades used as spear points to hunt sloths and manatees; conical pestles and mortars to prepare food; a variety of possible ritual implements such as stone balls, disks, and dagger-like objects; and elaborate stone beads and shell jewelry. Casimiroid sites, which date around 2660 BC, have been identified on the north and south coasts of Haiti (Keegan 1994). In the Dominican Republic, Casimiroid sites are located in river valleys and along the coast. It appears that Casimiroid ground stone tools in south-central Cuba were first shaped by flaking, then by pecking and grinding (Keegan 1994). There is growing evidence of interactions among Archaic Age communities inhabiting Puerto Rico to the northern Leeward Islands, with the sites of Maruca (Puerto Rico), Whitehead's Bluff (Anguilla), several sites on St. Martin, Plum Piece (Saba) and divers localities on Antigua cited as prime examples of such cultural exchanges (Bonnissent 2008; Crock 2000; Hofman, Bright, and Hoogland 2006; Wilson 2007).

Saladoid, Huecoid, and Barrancoid

Saladoid

Saladoid takes its name from the archaeological type site of Saladero in the Orinoco valley of Venezuela (Boomert 2000; Keegan 2000; Rouse 1992). In the Caribbean, the archaeological manifestations of agricultural expansion, known in the Spanish-language literature as an Agro Ceramic period, is associated with the Saladoid series (Allaire 2003). While their Archaic predecessors were engaged in incipient agriculture and experimental pottery-making, the Saladoid developed full-scale horticulture (based heavily on the cultivation of a variety of tubers) and a well-developed ceramic production (Rouse 1992; Veloz Maggiolo 1997). They also lived in large, permanent villages and interacted with their environments and neighbors in unique ways (Hofman and Hoogland 2004, 2011; Hofman et al. 2007; Wilson 2007).

The origins of the people of the Saladoid series have traditionally been traced to the Orinoco River in northeastern Venezuela (Rouse 1989; Reid 2009). As early as 2100 BC, villages of agriculturalists who used pottery vessels to cook their food had been established along the middle Orinoco. During the ensuing 2,000 years, they probably expanded downriver and outward along the Orinoco tributaries (Keegan 1992; Reid 2009). It was previously accepted that they moved into the islands of the Lesser Antilles in a stepping-stone fashion (Rouse 1992). However, recent research suggests that Saladoid communities entered the insular Caribbean between 800 and 200 BC in a far more dispersed way than was previously thought. While a significant number of Saladoid migrants may have island-hopped from South America into the Caribbean, archaeological evidence also points to the likelihood of direct jumps from South America to islands of the northern Caribbean such as Montserrat, St. Martin, Puerto Rico, and the Virgin Islands (Hofman and Hoogland 1999; Petersen 1996; Keegan 2000; Haviser 1997; Reid 2009). However, because of its close proximity to South America, Trinidad and Tobago would conceivably have been among the first places of contact in the Caribbean for many Saladoid groups. Radiocarbon dates obtained from the Palo Seco and Cedros sites of Trinidad suggest that communities of the Saladoid series occupied the island by the third to second century cal. BC (Boomert 2000, 131). In 2004, the Saladoid site of Lovers' Retreat (Tobago) yielded an early radiocarbon date of 770 to 380 years BC (Reid 2005). Saladoid interactions with Archaic Age peoples who were already living in the islands prob-

ably played an important role in shaping the Saladoid advance, their adaptation to the Caribbean environment, and their culture generally (Curet 2005; Hofman, Bright, and Rodríguez Ramos 2010; Keegan and Rodríguez Ramos 2007; Reid 2004; Wilson 2007).

Although the Saladoid experienced a veritable boom around AD 400, Saladoid culture in the islands came to an end between AD 600 and 800 (Hofman et al. 2011; Keegan 2000; Reid 2009). There are indications, however, that Saladoid in the northern Lesser Antilles might have existed beyond AD 800. The Saladoid site of Golden Rock in St. Eustatius, for example, was settled until around AD 900 (Versteeg and Schinkel 1992). Saladoid distinctive pottery styles of red, white-on-red, black and polychrome paint and zone-incised cross hatchings have been the primary benchmarks that archaeologists use to trace the migratory route of the Saladoid from northeast South America to the eastern extremity of the Greater Antilles, although most of the pottery in Saladoid sites in the region is undecorated (Keegan 2000), and there is much more heterogeneity between the different Saladoid assemblages than was previously thought (Hofman and Hoogland 2004).

The Saladoid peoples practiced a mixed broad-spectrum economy that included root crop horticulture, the hunting of land animals, fishing, and mollusk collecting (Keegan 1999; Petersen 1997). The presence of clay griddles suggests that bitter manioc was cultivated for cassava bread at this time, as it was at contact (Veloz Maggiolo 1997). However, recent starch grain research suggests that these griddles were used to prepare multiple root crops and plants (Pagán-Jiménez and Rodríguez Ramos 2007). Saladoid technology was simple and was apparently available to everyone (Keegan 2000). Besides pottery, there is evidence for wood-, stone-, bone-, and shell-working, as well as lapidary trade and weaving (Righter 1997; Keegan 2000). Particularly at the onset of this period, a vast network of semi-precious stone artifacts and raw material circulated through the archipelago (Hofman et al. 2007). Some settlements specialized in certain materials, exchanging them for goods from other locales. It is generally inferred that the Saladoid had an egalitarian or "tribally based" society (Curet 1996; Siegel 1992), but alternatives have been postulated that range from theories about Big Man societies to theories that suggest hierarchically more complex societies (Boomert 2000; Hofman and Hoogland 2004; Petersen 1996). Saladoid villages are characterized by thick middens with shell and crab remains. Dog burials are characteristic of the onset of the Saladoid period. In the Puerto Rico area and on Morel, Guadeloupe, numerous dogs have been found buried among humans with shell and stone para-phernalia as burial goods (Hofman et al. 2004).

Huecoid

Huecoid ceramics have been found in Puerto Rico, Vieques, the northern Lesser Antilles, as well as on Grenada. The series is named after the type site of La Hueca on the island of Vieques, immediately east of Puerto Rico. The main characteristics of Huecoid decorated pottery are curvilinear-incised zones, sometimes filled with punctation or cross-hatching. Huecoid potters did not paint their ceramics; instead, they rubbed white or red paint onto the zoned-incised or zoned cross-hatched designs. The latter is more predominant in Puerto Rican and Vieques Huecoid ceramics (Chanlatte Baik 1981, 1984; Hofman 1999). Ceramic vessels are characteristically shaped like the body of an aquatic animal (a fish or a turtle) and have a zoomorphic adorno on the head side and curvilinear incisions on the tail (Hofman and Jacobs 2000, 2001). Huecoid communities in Vieques and Puerto also produced unique carved-stone bird head pendants from semi-precious materials, such as serpentine (Chanlatte Baik and Narganes Storde 2005; Rodríguez Ramos 2010). Huecoid assemblages in the northern Lesser Antilles are often found mixed with Saladoid assemblages, and conflicting stratigraphic data and radiocarbon dates from these sites have led to the "La Hueca" debate about the origin and character of the Huecoid series and its relationship to the Saladoid series (Oliver 1999).

Recently, the Huecoid series has been interpreted as a separate development from the Archaic with potential influences from Central America (Rodríguez Ramos 2010). In the Caribbean, the Huecoid probably competed over resources with both Archaic and Saladoid communities (Hofman et al. 2011). This competition resulted in emulative behavior that is reflected in the rich middens of sites such as La Hueca and Punta Candelero. It has been suggested by Hofman et al. (2011) that an early interaction sphere between Archaic, Huecoid, and Saladoid communities existed in northern Lesser Antilles between 800 BC and AD 200 and that subsequently, all other islands of the Lesser Antilles were increasingly inhabited. A recent reevaluation of the ceramic assemblage from Pearls on Grenada confirmed that the site bears a Huecoid component, which suggests that this settlement may also been part of the early northeastern Caribbean interaction sphere.

Barrancoid

The people who manufactured Barrancoid pottery were named after the site of Barrancas on the banks of the lower Orinoco River in Venezuela (Drewett 1991; Rouse 1992). Like the Saladoid, the Barrancoid were villagers, potters, farmers of cassava and other root crops, and expert boat builders. The Barrancoid followed the Saladoid migrants and are thought to have developed out of a local Saladoid tradition in Venezuela between 1500 BC and 1000 BC (Reid 2009). The mechanisms by which Barrancoid influences appear on (or became associated with) Saladoid pottery remain poorly understood. The mixed occurrence of Saladoid and Barrancoid pottery in Venezuela, Guianas, Trinidad, the Windward Islands, and on some islands as far north as Puerto Rico and Vieques suggests that between AD 350 and 650 Barrancoid styles were widely adopted by Saladoid potters (Boomert 2003) or that the Barrancoid were able to successfully colonize much of the southern Caribbean as a result of intensive trade and seafaring activities. In many ways, Barrancoid ceramics are an elaboration of previous Saladoid ceramic styles. Barrancoid pottery has been characterized as the "baroque" phase of Saladoid stylistic evolution and is typically represented by modeled incised decoration on handles; adornos with anthropomorphic and zoomorphic hands, feet, faces; and incense burners (Reid 2009).

Troumassoid

Troumassan Troumassoid

Unlike the Ortoiroid, Casimiroid, Saladoid, Huecoid and Barrancoid series, the Troumassoid and Suazoid developed locally in the islands. Recently, the Troumassoid and Suazoid were relabeled as Troumassan Troumassoid and Suazan Troumassoid, respectively. The Troumassan Troumassoid, which is named after the type site of Troumassée in Saint Lucia, culturally evolved from the Saladoid in the Lesser Antilles and was culturally influenced by the Barrancoid. The Troumassan Troumassoid timeline is AD 500–1000. The best evidence for the initial transition from Saladoid to Troumassan Troumassoid comes from Martinique, where the L'Espérance style emerged (Allaire 1977). The major characteristic of this style is a sudden simplification of pottery shapes and decoration (Allaire 2003). Specific to this subseries is a type of flat clay griddle with a raised triangular rim, suggesting the continuity of root crop cultivation (Allaire 1977). For the most part, zoomorphic adornos and loop handles disappeared during this period. Vessels are fitted with legs, pedestals, or annular (or ring-shaped) bases (Hofman et al. 2011; Keegan 2000). These stylistic trends are well represented on Saint Lucia and on other Windward Islands (Bright 2011; Rouse and Allaire 1978;

McKusick 1960). Clay spindle whorls first appeared at this time, which suggests increased cotton cultivation. Local societies made specific adaptations to their islands that enabled the Troumassan Troumassoid to expand their territory.

Troumassan Troumassoid culture appears to have developed differently in the northerly Leeward and Virgin Islands than in the more southerly Windward Islands (Boomert 2003). In Guadeloupe and the Leeward Islands, a subseries named Mamoran Troumassoid (named after the type site Mamora Bay on Antigua) emerged in AD 800 and lasted until 1200 (Rouse 1992). Mamoran ceramics present some Cedrosan Saladoid elements, although these became less over time. The Troumassan Troumassoid did not extend to the Virgin Islands. In these islands, Magens Bay ceramics display striking similarities with the ceramics of eastern Puerto Rico, where Ostionoid societies were beginning to emerge (Allaire 1997). As a result, these ceramics are generally classified as the Elenan Ostionoid series (Allaire 1997).

Suazan Troumassoid

The Suazan Troumassoid (also called Suazey) take their name from the Savanne Suazey site on Grenada, which succeeded the Troumassan Troumassoid series in the southern Lesser Antilles around AD 1000. Suazan Troumassoid pottery is characterized by simple and bulky plain vessels, scratched surfaces, finger-indented rims, and finger-painted red and incised wares. They also occasionally contain flat adornos of human heads with flaring pierced ears (Allaire 1997; Bright 2011). Footed griddles, which were first introduced in the Troumassan Troumassoid subseries, are also common in the Suazan Troumassoid subseries. Other Suazan Troumassoid items include clay spindle whorls and loom weights, (female) figurines, roller stamps, stone pestles, shell celts and gouges, and clay tripods and cylinders; the latter may have been incense burners (Allaire 1997; Bright 2011; Bullen and Bullen 1968; Hofman et al. 2011; Keegan, Hofman, and Hoogland 2007).

The impression from the literature is that Troumassan Troumassoid and Suazan Troumassoid ceramics are crude (Allaire 1977; Rouse 1992; Keegan, Hofman, and Hoogland 2007) As a result, Suazan Troumassoid ceramics are sometimes viewed as representing a general decline in technological production and artistic style from the earlier Saladoid and Troumassan Troumassoid traditions, though continuities exist. However, the presence of fine ware in the Suazan Troumassoid subseries, which may be affiliated with what has been called the Caliviny style (which is characterized by red-painted bodies, finished surfaces, and repeated geometric designs in black and red paint over the shoulders and incisions) (Boomert 2000; Bullen 1965), challenges the notion of Suazey technological deterioration. The Suazan Troumassoid persisted in some of the southern Lesser Antilles until the contact period (Hofman and Bradford 2011). Cultural traits that are reminiscent of Suazey pottery can still be seen on contemporary Afro-Caribbean earthenware in the Caribbean (Hofman and Bright 2004).

Taíno

At the time of European contact in 1492, three major cultural groups were reported to be present in the Caribbean: Taíno, Island-Carib, and Guanahatabey. The Taíno (AD 1200–1500) inhabited much of the northern Caribbean (especially in the Greater Antilles) at the time of Spanish contact in 1492, They produced a variety of pottery styles relating to the Ostionoid series, the latter of which developed autochthonously in the northern Caribbean from AD 600–1200. The Ostionoid series was named after the type site of Ostiones in Puerto Rico (Rouse 1992; Keegan 2000). Various pottery subseries have traditionally been included in the Ostionoid series, namely Ostionan, Elenan, Meillacan, Chican, and Palmettan (Rouse 1992; Keegan 1992). However, this classification is being challenged by some scholars, who prefer an analysis of independent developments, which they refer to as Ostionoid, Meillacoid, and Chicoid (Rodríguez Ramos 2010). Settlement remains suggest that Late Ceramic Age groups in the Greater Antilles were active farmers, potters, and villagers and that they had socially complex societies based on extensive interaction networks (Curet and Stringer 2010; Hofman and Hoogland 2011; Rodríguez Ramos 2010).

In order to capture the plurality of Taíno society that existed at contact, Caribbean archaeologists have developed classifications such as Classic, Western, and Eastern Taíno (Rouse 1992). Taíno in both Puerto Rico and Hispaniola are called Classic Taíno. Their societies were characterized by the highest level of sociopolitical development, as evidenced by the presence of ball courts, stone-lined plazas, and *conucos*. Taíno communities of less social complexity that lived elsewhere in the northern Caribbean are referred to as Western and Eastern Taíno (Rouse 1992). It was generally assumed that the Ostionoid/Taíno evolved from the Saladoid (Rouse 1992; Wilson 1997) with some influences from the Casimiroid (Archaic) peoples in eastern Hispaniola (Rouse 1992; Keegan 1994). However, alternative theories that strongly underscore the role of Archaic Age groups in the development of the Ostionoid/Taíno have been gaining broad acceptance among Caribbean archaeologists (Curet 2005; Chanlatte Baik 1986; Keegan and Rodríguez Ramos 2007; Reid 2009; Rodríguez Ramos 2010). The name Taíno is currently under heavy scrutiny because the term often masks the diversity of peoples and cultures that inhabited the islands at the time of contact (Rodríguez Ramos 2010).

The Taíno lived a settled village life and practiced agriculture, supplementing their main food of root crops such as manioc, zamia, and sweet potato, maize, a variety of fruits plus fish, shellfish, birds, rodents, snakes, manatees, and sea turtles. Tobacco and cotton were important nonfood plant resources. The Classic Taíno practiced a sophisticated form of *conuco* agriculture, in which they heaped up mounds of earth in more permanent fields to cultivate root crops, such as cassava, in the soft alluvial soil (Rouse 1992). The primacy of cassava for the Taíno was illustrated by the fact that one of their two supreme deities was Yocahu, the lord of cassava and the sea, and the other was Atabey, the goddess of fresh water and human fertility and the mother of Yocahu (Arrom 1978; Bourne 1906; Petersen 1997). The presence of maize is often underestimated, but recent starch grain analysis reveals that maize was consumed in the Caribbean by Taíno, Saladoid, and Archaic Age communities in the region (Pagán-Jiménez 2011).

The Taíno are believed to have had chiefdom societies, known as *cacicazgos*, many of which were organized into district chiefdoms. Each chiefdom was ruled by one of the village chiefs in the district, and the district chiefdoms were in turn grouped into regional chiefdoms, each headed by the most prominent district chief (Wilson 1990). By the time Columbus arrived in the Caribbean in 1492, 100 Taíno polities were reported in the region and combined populations in the tens of thousands existed (Wilson 2007). The larger Taíno villages are reported to have had hundreds of communal houses that were occupied by extended families. They were arranged around a central plaza that was used for social and religious events, such as ceremonial dances called *areitos* and ballgames known as *bateys*. Recent excavations in the Dominican Republic have revealed that smaller community villages also existed without a central plaza and house trajectories. These house trajectories, characterized by a series overlapping structures, lasted for more than 500 years (Hofman et al. 2008; Samson 2010). Exchanges of exotic items, which helped build regional alliances among trading partners, were part of the chief's elite exchange networks. Ethnohistorical accounts mentioned items such as parrots, feathers, raw and woven cotton, carved wood, gold, and *guanin* (a gold alloy) (Lovén 1935; Reid 2009). The trade objects most prominent in the archaeological record are elaborate ceramics, such as anthropomorphic and zoomorphic effigy bottles, carved stone objects, shell objects, and ritual paraphernalia (Hofman and Hoogland 2011; Mol 2007; Ostapkowicz et al. 2011; Wilson 1990).

The Taíno were adept at constructing plazas or ball courts that typically were composed of earth embankments and stone slabs (Olazagasti 1997). In the Caribbean, ball courts varied in size. However, they were generally oval, rectangular, or long and narrow in shape and may have been used either as ball courts or dance grounds (Olazagasti 1997). Of all the stone-lined plazas in the northern Caribbean, probably the most elaborate and specialized complex of the ball and dance courts can be found at the Caguana site (also known as Capá) in the mountains northwest of the El Bronce and Tibes sites in Puerto Rico (Reid 2009).

Guanahatabey

Scholars have mistakenly called the western neighbors of the Taíno in Cuba by another name, Ciboney, but the term actually applies to a local group of Western Taíno in central Cuba (Alegría 1981; Reid 2009). The generally accepted Caribbean name among archaeologists for inhabitants of western Cuba at contact is Guanahatabey (Rouse 1992; Wilson 1990; Keegan 1992). Taíno inhabitants of Cuba who met the Spanish colonizers apparently mentioned a non-Taíno people called Guanahatabey, or Guanahacabibe.

The Guanahatabey were reported to have lived at the far western end of Cuba. They probably spoke a different language from their neighbors, since Columbus's Taíno interpreter was unable to converse with them (Rouse 1992). Archaeological research has not identified any Taíno sites in western Cuba. What has been unearthed is evidence of a preexisting hunting, fishing, and gathering culture marked by the presence of small coastal sites. These sites contain a scatter of debris from tools, shellfish, iguanas, land and sea crabs, larger sea animals such as manatee and turtles, and rodents such as the hutia (Rouse 1948; Reid 2009). The evidence suggests the presence of people who lived in caves, rock shelters, and open-air sites; relied heavily on shellfish, fish, and wild game; and were organized into small bands rather than villages. It has been argued, however, that these sites may have been formed by people who were ancestors of the Guanahatabey (Rouse 1948). The name Guanahatabey may, in fact, be a figment of Spanish or Taíno imagination, given the lack of sufficient evidence to support the belief that such a population survived in western Cuba until Spanish contact (Keegan 1992; Reid 2009).

Island-Carib

In order to differentiate the mainland Carib of South America from the Carib of the Windward Islands at contact, Caribbean archaeologists generally refer to the latter as Island-Carib or Kalinago. Ethnohistoric documents suggest that in the mid-fifteenth century, Carib from South America moved into the southern Caribbean, filling the vacuum left by communities of the Suazan Troumassoid subseries (Reid 2009). The Kalinago are thought to have colonized the Windward Islands of Dominica, Martinique, St. Vincent, Grenada, and Guadeloupe as well as Tobago and northern Trinidad. Douglas Taylor and Berend J. Hoff (1980) theorize that the Island-Carib warriors who conquered the Igneri (an ethnic group that preceded the Island-Carib in the Windward Islands) retained their mainland pidgin as a symbol of their origin, but they probably maintained their language to facilitate trade with their neighbors on the mainland.

Island-Carib societies have been interpreted as egalitarian (or tribal-based). The village community was ruled by a headman, but unlike the Taíno, no chiefs ruled over groups of villages or entire islands. For purposes of war, however, some individuals were able to assume leadership over warriors from various islands and to lead expeditions all the way to the coasts of Guianas or Venezuela (Allaire 1997).

Island-Carib communities were primarily agricultural, though not as extensive as those of the Taíno. They grew and consumed manioc, making it into cassava bread. They also ate a stew known as pepper pot. Details about Island-Carib subsistence suggest that land crabs and shellfish were supplemented by agouti, birds, lizards, manatees, sea turtles, and fish (Petersen 1997). As they were for the Taíno, tobacco and cotton were important for the Island-Carib. Gardens were placed in protected locales, sometimes at great distances from Island-Carib habitations. Because of their more aggressive postures toward the Spanish, French, English, Dutch, and anyone else who threatened their sovereignty, the Island-Carib of the Lesser Antilles were erroneously categorized as cannibals (Beckles 1992; Keegan 1992).

Historical Archaeology

Historical archaeology in the Caribbean benefits enormously from the availability of both documentary and archaeological data. Archaeological studies of the landscapes created, the material used, and the social relations expressed allow us to better understand the richness of each localized history. We have already discussed the dramatic and devastating impact that Europeans had and continue to have on indigenous populations. This was just the first of a series of world-changing interactions for which the Caribbean was a central theatre (Williams 1944/2005). Each island interacted differently in the global arena based on colonial and postcolonial affiliations, trade patterns, and social networks. The cultures that emerged on each island were influenced by external colonial governance and global change, including the impact of movement of peoples associated with the slave trade, changes in world markets and economic structures associated with the production of sugar and other crops such as tobacco and cotton, or the exchange of ideas resulting from expanding networks of trade and interaction. The tragic form of chattel slavery that emerged in Barbados and spread through the West Indies beginning in the 1640s had profound impacts on the demography and cultural landscape of Western and Central Africa and was transferred almost directly within the region to places such as Jamaica and beyond the region to settlements in South Carolina (Williams 1944/2005; Green 1987). The wealth generated from colonial enterprises had a significant impacts on the social economic landscapes of Europe, resulting in transformations of landscapes where the legacy of the vast wealth created on the backs of enslaved laborers produced massive country estates such as the Harewood House (Beckles 2013; Finch and Armstrong 2013). Archaeologists and social historians are just now beginning to look both ways at the Caribbean and Europe to explore the important influences of the Caribbean abroad. For example, at Harewood House in Yorkshire, England, if one looks closely one will see Caribbean legacies in the form of prints and paintings of Caribbean landscapes displayed on its walls, documents in its chests, tortoise shells above the sink in its kitchen, papayas and cycads growing in its gardens, and Caribbean-derived wealth in the financial accounts of its owners (see University College of London 2013; Finch and Armstrong 2013). In the world of art, the dramatic shift to nineteenth-century impressionist art, with its transformation in use of color palette, use of light, and choice of subjects, was dramatically impacted by Camille Pissarro, a painter of Danish West Indian and Dominican parentage who influenced French and ultimately global artistic expression (Armstrong 2011c).

Each island's history and cultural trajectory correlates with unique relationships tied to complex differences in colonial rule by the English (on islands such as Barbados, Jamaica and St. Kitts), the Spanish (on Hispañola and later in the eastern half of the island that is now the Dominican Republic, along with Puerto Rico and Cuba), the French (on Martinique, Guadeloupe, and Saint-Domingue, now Haiti), the Dutch (on islands such as Aruba, Bonaire, Curaçao, and St. Eustatius), the Danish (on St. Thomas, St. Croix, and St. John), and even the Swedish (who once held Saint Barthélemy).

Before the 1970s, historical archaeology tended to focus on sites associated directly with colonial development, such as forts, the residences of planters, ports, and merchant quarters. However, over the past forty years, studies have broadened to include thematic coverage of just about every aspect of life, from studies of the quarters and burial sites of enslaved laborer (Armstrong 1983, 1990, 2011a; Armstrong and Kelly 2000; Delle 1998; Handler and Lange 1978; Higman 1998; Gilmore 2006a, 2006b; Pulsipher and Goodwin 2000; Howson 1990, 1995; Wilkie and Farnsworth 1999, 2005; Petersen and Watters 1988); to studies of free persons of color living in both urban and rural areas (Armstrong 2003a, 2003b; Armstrong and Williamson 2011; Gilmore 2009). Archaeological studies have examined pubs in Barbados (Smith 2005, 2008; Smith and Watson 2009), Jewish cemeteries on Nevis (Terrell 2004), the wreck of a nineteenth-century cargo ship in Jamaica (Cook and Rubinstein-Gottschamer 2011), health care (Gilmore 2008; Nicholson 1995), and the material record of local pottery production and marketing of goods in sites from Barbados to Jamaica (Handler 1963a, 1963b; Hauser 2008). The entries in this volume illustrate the breadth of sites and the findings of historical archaeology in the region.

From island to island, structures and their material residue show differences that correspond to various forms of governance, fortification, and modes of economic production, including differences in the scale of plantations and the timing of slavery and emancipation. Moreover, each island was prone to forms of localized destruction by the natural forces of hurricanes, earthquakes, tsunamis, and volcanic eruptions, which had dramatic impacts on some islands but spared others in the region. These events led to the destruction of vibrant cities such as Port Royal, Jamaica (earthquake); St. Pierre, Martinique (the eruption of Mt. Pelée); and Oranjestad, St. Eustatius (the worst hurricane in Caribbean history).

Each island followed its own path to independence and nation building. Postcolonial reevaluation of these pasts has engaged archaeological explorations that follow a wealth of local and national themes. In the following discussion, we examine a few of the most prominent themes that historical archaeologists are currently exploring in the Caribbean.

Columbus and the Period of Initial Contact and Interaction

The historic period in the Caribbean begins with Christopher Columbus's somewhat accidental passage through the islands in 1492. The encounter between indigenous populations and European explorers had sweeping consequences that were ultimately devastating to the native peoples and changed the trajectory of European and global history (see Woodward 2011). Archaeologists have long sought out the sites of the initial points of encounter, including landfalls and interactions on San Salvador island in the Bahamas and the ruins of Puerto Real in Haiti (Deagan 1995), La Isabella in the Dominican Republic (Deagan and Cruxent 2002a, 2002b), and the settlement at Seville La Nueva in Jamaica (Woodward 2011; Cotter 1970).

Comparing prehistoric settlement data with the various routes of early European exploration led William Keegan (1996) to conclude that the first landfall must have been on present-day San Salvador and that Columbus continued in his travels to Rum Bay, Long Island, and Crooked Island before crossing to Cuba and then Hispaniola (Keegan 1996; Reid 2009). Efforts to recover evidence of Columbus's settlements have resulted in studies that have significantly improved our understanding of the lifeways of Europeans as they entered the New World and the impacts that they had on the indigenous populations of the region. Studies at La Isabella, the first successful European settlement in the New World, provided evidence of the layout of the settlement and the conditions that both indigenous peoples and the Spanish settlers faced (Deagan 1995; Armstrong and Hauser 2009, 594).

Archaeological investigations at the Spanish-period settlement at Sevilla la Nueva in Jamaica not only tell of changes in how historical archaeology is done but also demonstrate historical archaeology's potential for reconstructing lifeways that have been long forgotten. From 1915 to around 1938, William B. Goodwin described a series of possible Spanish sites in Jamaica and undertook a massive excavation of Don Christopher Cove at Drax Hall using a steam shovel in an unsuccessful effort to rediscover two of Columbus's caravels (Goodwin 1940, 1946). Goodwin drew a series of plans of his surveys and excavations in Jamaica and noted a continuing friendly debate between himself and Frank Cundall, then director of the Institute of Jamaica, regarding the cultural attribution of sites as Spanish or English (Goodwin 1946, 10). Amateur archaeologist Charles S. Cotter stumbled on the ruins of Seville la Nueva in the 1930s and proceeded to clear land to expose ruins of early structures (Cotter 1964, 1970). His findings, which included carved limestone blocks, foundations, and wells, invigorated interest in the site and led to the acquisition of Seville Estate as a heritage park by the newly independent government of Jamaica in the early 1960s. Recently, studies by Robyn Woodward have systematically examined ruins at Seville that provide details of early sixteenth-century industry, economy, and social relations (Woodward 2011, 23). Woodward's excavations of an early sixteenth-century mill site combined with her thorough examination of historical documents pertaining to the settlement provide data about a way of life that was deeply invested in feudal systems of production. The technology derived from medieval sugar-milling practices and a centuries-old agricultural system in which farmers grew crops on a series of small tenant *estancias* (farms). The proceeds of the milled product were split between the *repartidor* (the Crown representative), the miller, and the farmer. This sharecropping system replicated feudal production systems and provides evidence of a way of life that was significantly altered when the English brought their plantation system with them when they captured the island in 1655 (Woodward 2011, 38–40; Armstrong 2011a, 77–91).

Spanish settlers initially focused on mining and provisioning, but Spain quickly turned its attention to the vast potential for wealth that could be obtained by extracting resources from the mainland of Central and South America (Deagan 1995). They continued to expand their settlements, particularly on the larger islands of the Greater Antilles, but for Spain the primary roles of Caribbean settlements were as protective harbors and sources of provisions for fleets of ships laden with goods plundered from the Spanish Main.

During the late sixteenth and early seventeenth centuries, other European powers began to explore the Caribbean and establish beachhead settlements. From an archaeological standpoint, very little is known about these early outposts. It was not until the seventeenth century that England, France and the Netherlands began to establish permanent settlements in the region. St. Christopher and Barbados were settled by the English in the 1620s. Using GIS to orient a unique early plantation map for Barbados, the archaeologists researching the 1646 Hapcott Map have been able to identify the earliest plantation on Barbados, which was known as Fort

Plantation but now has been identified as Trents Plantation, located near the settlement at Holetown, Barbados (Armstrong, Watson, and Reilly 2012; Hapcott Map 1646). Excavation of this site has yielded data on early settlement, pre–sugar era farms, and the period of transition to sugar production and the rapid expansion of the use of enslaved labor on the island.

The French also established a colony on St. Kitts in the 1620s, splitting the island with the English. Both powers used the island to begin settlements on larger nearby islands. In the 1630s, the English established communities on Barbados, Anguilla, Antigua, Montserrat, Nevis, and Tortola and the French began settling on Guadeloupe and Martinique (Burns 1965). Dutch colonies were established on Aruba, Bonaire, Curaçao, Saba, St. Eustatius, and St. Maarten, primarily as trading centers (Goslinga 1971). The Dutch shared St. Maarten with the French, but the island was a Dutch dependency until 2010, when it, along with Curaçao, began the process of becoming independent.

In the 1960s and 1970s, historians, sometimes with the assistance of archaeologists, continued to document monumental historic properties (forts, estate works, and planter residences), but the real interest among archaeologists remained focused on defining the complex prehistory of the Caribbean region. The fact that insular variations occurred over time on each island and the material record was diverse, even among affiliated groups and islands, brought an understanding of the complexity and variability in the historic record that has been critical for later historical archaeologists in the region. Even a cursory examination of the insular nature of the region reveals the diversity of ethnic and social relations and the distinctive differences in the historical trajectories of each colonial domain and local polity. Historical archaeologists found distinctive differences in the material and cultural records from island to island and from colonial domain to colonial domain.

Samuel Wilson points out that there is a rich history of ethnographic, historical, and archaeological explorations of the early colonial era (Wilson 1990). Armstrong and Hauser link the interest of prehistoric archaeologists in the early colonial era to the theoretical groundings of the direct historical approach, whereby archaeologists tried to establish the location and context of sites associated with historic contact (2009, 583). They would then draw upon the rich ethnographic detail of the chroniclers of the interactions of indigenous people and colonizers in the historic period and work back to interpret the archaeological record of prehistoric peoples. Archaeologists who focused on the prehistoric era used historic sites as a starting point to establish a basis for defining the era of contact and the consequences of colonial encounters on local indigenous populations. Studies drawing on historic period sites and accounts are compiled in Julian Steward's *The Circum-Caribbean Tribes* (1948) and works by DeBooy (1919), Rouse (1939), Rainey (1940), Wilson (1990, 2007), Keegan (1994), Siegel (2005), and Rouse (1992). These works figured strongly in establishing the ethnohistorical basis for understanding more recently defined contact period sites such as Argyle, on St. Vincent (Hoogland, Hofman, and Boomert 2011).

In the Lesser Antilles, the period of historic contact is less formally documented than in the Greater Antilles, and many islands were essentially abandoned by the time of later colonial settlers with sanctions from England, France, Holland, or Denmark. One of the critical questions archaeologists have faced is how to define the ethnic identity of those who occupied the Lesser Antilles during the protohistoric and early historic periods. Armstrong and Hauser (2009, 586) note that one of the biggest interpretive problems has been that "until recently archaeologists continued to generalize the early contact era population as 'Carib' without solid evidence from well-defined archaeological contexts." This practice did not account for variations in material expression by island and the very diverse and temporally distinct trajectories of surviving, remnant, and resettled populations in the region (see Allaire 1980, 1984, 1991; Goodwin and Davis 1990). The term "Carib" became a catchall term that did not account for the diverse trajectories historians have defined (Paquette and Engerman 1996). The "Carib" issue is currently being studied on islands such as Dominica (Honychurch 1997), Saint Lucia (Hofman and Bright 2004), and St. Vincent (Hoogland, Hofman, and Boomert 2011). To date, the most well-defined example of a site with clear contact and early historic context is the Argyle site on St. Vincent that has been explored by Hoogland, Hofman, and Boomert (2011). The layout of the village with oval and round houses around a plaza matches the descriptions in the ethnohistoric sources. The associated Cayo pottery, now confirmed to be the ceramic tradition associated with the Island-Carib, was found commingled with early seventeenth-century European artifacts. Remarkably, the rims of some of the Cayo potsherds were inlaid with European seed beads. The excellent context of this site will provide a basis for comparing and contrasting contact period settlements throughout the region. For example, we will now be able to compare these findings with sites and lifeways that are defined as being "Carib" on Dominica. We will also be able to contrast the material record from this site with an array of contexts associated with refuge, Maroon, and entrepreneurial settlements by peoples of a wide range of African, European, and Native Caribbean ancestry before islands were formally colonized.

Manifestation of a Colonial Presence: Landscapes of Power and Authority

Well before the emergence of a field defined as historical archaeology, scholars and avocational archaeologists began to study the ruins of early settlements, massive forts, and abandoned plantation houses and lifeways associated with colonialism. Sir Hans Sloane, one of the most noted naturalists of the late seventeenth century, wrote detailed descriptive accounts of the early colonial landscape of many islands in the West Indies (Sloane 1707–25). Sloane set out to document the natural landscape of Jamaica and in the process recorded not only the flora and fauna but also the structural manifestations of an earlier colonial era. Sloane's observations at Seville la Nueva in Jamaica include details of the ruins of the surviving visible relics of an earlier Spanish era, including the art and architecture of a Catholic church and the unusual presence of a trench cut across the yard in front of the planter's house at the English colonial sugar estate at Seville plantation, which he described as a defensive trench designed to defend the estate from possible attack by the Spanish.

Armstrong and Hauser point out that these observations of monuments to early colonial rule "conflate 'moral' 'natural' and 'civil' aspects of history" (2009, 587). Most histories of the region include some description of the monumental architecture and archaeological ruins from this historic period; these descriptions are used to illustrate and reflect the power and authority of contemporary colonial enterprises or the vestiges of past colonial lifeways. For example, early works such as Richard Ligon's history of Barbados (1657) and Edward Long's history of Jamaica (1770) use descriptions of past and current structures to define and defend the emerging or established socioeconomics of slavery and the plantation system.

Historic sites archaeologists, both avocational and professional, have documented the monuments of the colonial era. Moving beyond abstract or casual description to detailed archaeological investigation, they began to focus on forts and great houses as soon as the social systems that had supported large-scale naval forces and massive plantation works began to collapse. For example, as early as 1859, Jeremiah D. Murphy described the abandoned ruins of Fort James in Jamaica (Mayes 1972, 9). Much of this early literature took a perspective that mourned the passing of the colonial era.

Archaeologists documented and explored historic forts soon after they were abandoned. Massive fortresses such as Brimstone Hill on St. Kitts, El Morro in Puerto Rico, the Citadel in Haiti, and Fort Shirley in Dominica (Beier 2011), and Nelson's Dockyard in Antigua literally dominate the landscape and remained a strong presence even after they were abandoned. In the years before colonial powers transferred control to local rule, there was a keen interest among sectors of the population in heralding the might of European imperial power. Hence, historians and archaeologists began a process of documenting and preserving these sites (see Mathewson 1971). In recent years, archaeologists have renewed their interest in these sites as a means of exploring the use of power and to illuminate details that initially were overlooked, including the involvement of enslaved and indentured laborers in the construction of forts, the lifeways and conditions of soldiers, and the role black soldiers and enslaved laborers played in the specific living and working contexts associated with these fortifications (Ahlman, Schroedl, and McKeown 2009; Schroedl and Ahlman 2002; Honychurch 2011; Murphy 2011).

As in North and South America, Caribbean plantation great houses or "big houses" were often built in locations where owners of enslaved laborers could project their power literally and symbolically on the landscape. Plantation owners or their proxies could often observe every aspect of plantation life from their elevated locations. Caribbean archaeologists have analyzed the spatial distribution of plantations on island landscapes (e.g. Delle 1998, 2008; Leech 2007). Over time, as the sugar industry gave way to the oil and tourism industries in the last half of the twentieth century, the plantation landscapes were often swallowed up by development or nature. The industrial buildings associated with sugar production were often large and were the most significant private investment in the Caribbean. The substantive architecture involved in these structures has ensured that windmills, aqueducts, sugar factories, curing facilities, and rum distilleries still dot island landscapes. They have proven to be a strong attraction to archaeologists studying the manifestations of the industrial revolution in the Americas. The lives of the enslaved and free people have also been the focus of much research in the region.

Moving sugar, rum, and people throughout the region required the development of an extremely efficient interisland and regional trade network. This network was serviced by thousands of ships both large and small. The ports these vessels called upon were places where news, information, contraband, and ideas were imported along with manufactured goods. Ports were thus very important to the functioning of Caribbean social and economic frameworks. Three primary trading centers have been studied in some detail by historical archaeologists: Port Royal in Jamaica, Charlotte Amalie on St. Thomas, and Oranjestad on St. Eustatius have each been analyzed by archaeologists for several decades.

Explorations of the African Diaspora

In the period 1950–1970, many Caribbean nations gained independence from former colonial powers and began the process of nation building under local control. A new field of study quickly emerged as archaeologists and other scholars began exploring the rich topic of postcolonial identity. At the same time the direction of archaeological studies shifted direction. Archaeologists had been primarily engaged in the study of prehistoric sites and contact period sites that helped define questions of the region's prehistory. With the emergence of new nations, attention shifted to learning more about the heritage of persons of African descent in the region and the diversity of cultural backgrounds of peoples of the Caribbean (see Delle, Hauser, and Armstrong 2011). For this shift in focus to occur, it was necessary to conceptualize the African Diaspora in the Caribbean. The shift was strongly influenced by the emergence of the historical archaeology of Diaspora contexts in North America, but some of the initial examinations of African Caribbean contexts emerged somewhat independently based on explanations of findings associated with port towns (Mayes 1970), elite colonial housing in Jamaica (Mathewson 1971), and ethnographic studies of pottery production in Barbados (Handler 1963a, 1963b).

Early studies of locally produced earthenware were completed as part of more broadly defined studies of the colonial period at Port Royal and the Old King's House in Jamaica (Mayes 1970, 1972; Mathewson 1971, 1972a, 1972b, 1973). These studies led to the realization that archaeology could provide significant information about the majority population of African-descended laborers in the Caribbean. Persons of African descent and the cultural landscapes of plantations quickly emerged as a significant focus for Caribbean research. Geographer and historian Barry Higman organized excavations at the well-documented ruins at Montpelier in Jamaica (1974, 1998), and Jerome Handler and Frederick Lange began an effort to locate and excavate village sites associated with enslaved laborers in Barbados. A significant result of their study was their identification of the burial ground for enslaved people at Newton Plantation (Handler and Lange 1978).

Information from Handler and Lange's efforts to

locate enslaved laborer settlements in Barbados was used to help model Armstrong's archaeological studies at Drax Hall and Seville Plantations in Jamaica (Armstrong 1983, 1985, 1990, 1992, 2011a). The archaeological investigation of Drax Hall Plantation examined the households of both enslaved laborers and planter/managers and focused on the bilateral expressions of continuity and change in African and European lifeways (Armstrong 1990). In Jamaica, plantation studies focused on the material record recovered from domestic spaces, including discrete houses and yards, and went on to examine social relations, power relations, and ethnic identity as expressed in laborer contexts (Armstrong and Kelly 2000; Armstrong and Fleischman 2003; Armstrong 2011a) In Montserrat, Jean Howson explored enslaved laborers' houses and social relations expressed in the material record on Galways Plantation, and Conrad Goodwin and Lydia Pulsipher explored plantation management and the spatial manifestation of managerial controls (Goodwin 1987; Pulsipher 1986, 1991, 1993; Pulsipher and Goodwin 1982, 2000). Pulsipher also gathered detailed and irreplaceable ethnographic studies of houses, yards, and gardens in an area that was destroyed by the eruption of the Soufrière Hills volcano in 1995 (Pulsipher 1991).

Armstrong's study of Seville Plantation initially focused on two temporally and spatially discrete settlements of enslaved laborers (Armstrong 1991, 1992, 1999; Armstrong and Kelly 2000), but expanded to contrast findings from the enslaved laborer settlements with data from sites representing three distinct levels of plantation management (Armstrong 1998). This study also explores the plantation landscape to examine how plantation managers expressed their control over enslaved laborers in the positioning of housing and buildings on the estate (Armstrong and Kelly 2000). An important aspect of this study was the recovery of burials in the yards of houses associated with the early (1670–1770) enslaved laborer village at the site (Armstrong and Fleischman, 2003). A significant accidental discovery was the identification of the site of a nineteenth-century house that was built and occupied by East Indian contract laborers (Kelly and Armstrong 1991; Armstrong and Hauser 2003, 2004; Kelly, Hauser, and Armstrong 2011).

Since the early 1980s, archaeological studies of plantation contexts have been the most prominent form of historical archaeology studies in the region. Such studies have now been carried out in virtually every part of the Caribbean. These studies have concentrated on illuminating lifeways associated with the majority population of African and African-descended enslaved laborers.

They have examined the local social and economic systems, legacies of emergent societies, landscapes of power, and the relationship of local sites to a globalized world in the context of the rise of capitalism under a wide range of local conditions and colonial polities. Archaeologists have done plantation studies on the Anglophone islands of Barbados (Handler 1963a, 1963b, 1964, 1965, 1972, 1997; Handler and Lange 1978; Loftfield 2001), the Bahamas, (Farnsworth 1992, 1996, 1999, 2000, 2001; Wilkie 1995, 2000a, 2000b; Wilkie and Farnsworth 1999, 2005; Wilkie and Bartoy 2000), Nevis (Hicks 2008; Meniketti 1998; Platzer 1979), Montserrat (Petersen and Watters 1988; Pulsipher 1986, 1991, 1993; Pulsipher and Goodwin 2000; Watters 1987, 1994a, 1994b; Watters and Petersen 1988), Antigua (Handler 1964; Murphy 1996, 2001), Trinidad and Tobago (Clement 1997; Lopinot and Venter this volume), and, most significantly, Jamaica (Agorsah 1992, 1993; Armstrong 1983, 1990, 1991, 1992, 1998, 1999, 2011a; Armstrong and Fleischman, 2003; Armstrong and Hauser 2004; Armstrong and Kelly 2000; Bonner 1974; Delle 1999, 2000a, 2000b, 2001, 2008, 2009; Delle, Hauser, and Armstrong 2011; Farnsworth 1992; Goucher 1990; Hamilton 2006; Hauser 2001, 2006, 2008, 2011; Hauser and DeCorse 2003; Higman 1975, 1976, 1986a, 1987, 1996, 1998, 1999, 2002, 2005; Kelly and Armstrong 1991; Kelly, Hauser, and Armstrong 2011; Mathewson 1972a, 1972b, 1973; Mayes 1972; Priddy 1975; Reeves, 1997, 2011; Robertson 2005).

Other than the island-wide archaeological surveys Haviser conducted in the early 1980s, few detailed analyses of plantation life have been conducted in the Dutch islands outside of St. Eustatius. Barka (1996), Haviser (2001), and Hofman et al. (2008) have done some work on St. Maarten. On St. Eustatius, four plantations have been excavated, primarily by Gilmore (2005). This work combined with detailed documentary analyses has revealed a plantation landscape unlike that found anywhere else in the Americas. Over ninety plantations were distributed over the island's 22 square kilometers—about the same size as Thomas Jefferson's Monticello in Virginia. The research has shown that the plantations served primarily as centers for subversive activities in the region that significantly impacted the mercantile systems of France and England. French and English islands secretly exported a significant proportion of their sugar production to the island throughout the latter half of the eighteenth century. Testimony before the British Parliament in 1779 indicates that perhaps half the sugar produced on Jamaica during that year was sent to St. Eustatius to be reprocessed into more profitable white sugar and then reexported as "St. Eustatius" sugar (Gilmore forthcoming). The function of plantations as social centers was particularly important on St. Eustatius. Agricultural pursuits were not the primary focus of discussion at these country seats; international trade was the main issue. Owners earned their profits not from the plantations but from the trade that passed through their warehouses on Statia's Oranje Bay. As a consequence of this focus on trade, plantation landscapes on the island were significantly different from those on other islands in the region. On most Caribbean sugar plantations, the enslaved village was easily observable from the plantation seat. However, on every plantation on St. Eustatius, the industrial complex obscured the view of the enslaved laborer village. This was a reflection of the high value owners of enslaved laborers placed on the ultimate product of their enslaved laborers—capitalist trade. Enslaved Statians were literate and consummate traders themselves. They plied the surrounding sea conducting interisland commerce themselves as well as their owners (Equiano 1789; Gilmore 2006a, 2006b, 2009).

Dan Hicks has suggested a redefining of the meaning of landscapes for their residents in the eighteenth century. Previous post-medieval landscape studies in the Caribbean, North America, and England sought to define estates as illustrations of their owners' power to subjugate land, labor, and the economy. Hicks (2008) suggests that the focus of plantation owners was to attempt to "improve" the land, the environment, and society through a transformational process of carefully managed labor and agricultural pursuits.

Plantation archaeology on Spanish colonial sites included several studies in the Dominican Republic (Ortega and Fondeur 1978a, 1978b, 1979). Arrom and García Arévalo (1986) focused on industrial works and production systems associated with mining and sugar production. Several ethnohistorical and archaeological studies have focused on marronage (Cimarrons) (García Arévalo 1986; Arrom and García Arévalo 1986). In Cuba, as with many studies in the British Caribbean, plantations studies tend to examine the role of labor in the capitalist colonial plantation context and to focus on power relations. These studies found distinct differences linked to time period, crop production, and labor systems (Domínguez 1978, 1989, 1991; La Rosa Corzo 1988, 1991, 2003; La Rosa Corzo, Dawdy, and Curet 2005; La Rosa Corzo and Gonzalez 2004; Lugo Romera and Menendez Castro 2003; Prat Puig 1980; Singleton 2001, 2006; Singleton and de Souza Torres 2009). In contrast to most British colonial sites, Cuban plantations often involved the use of large-scale barracks, and in the mid-nineteenth century, plantations that had very large en-

slaved labor forces organized around large-scale works powered by steam engines grew rapidly (see Armstrong and Hauser 2009, 598).

The rapid growth of Cuban plantations in the nineteenth century can be attributed to the fact that the Spanish continued to use enslaved laborers into the era of industrialization, when plantations began using steam power to process sugar. Cuba was building new estates and was still importing enslaved and contract labor after the British, French, Danish, and Dutch Caribbean had abolished slavery. Theresa Singleton's recent studies of coffee estates in Cuba provide new examples of diverse forms of plantation management and social controls (Singleton 2001, 2006). Singleton's study shows examples of the construction of walled villages to control and restrict outsiders' access to laborers. The presence of locally made artifacts and items that were reworked using local materials is a consistent pattern in studies of enslaved laborers throughout the Caribbean (Singleton 2001; see also Armstrong and Hauser 2009, 598).

Sugar plantations in Puerto Rico have been studied, but the focus there has been on the industrial complexes on plantations, and archaeologists have not examined contexts associated with the island's African and African-descended populations and their heritage (Armstrong 2006).

Plantation studies have also been carried out in the Dutch Caribbean (Barka 1996; Delle 1989, 1994; Gilmore 2005, 2006a, 2006b, 2008; Haviser 1999a, 1999b; Haviser and DeCorse 1991; Heath 1988, 1991, 1999), the former Danish West Indies (Armstrong 2003a, 2003b; Armstrong, Hauser, and Knight 2005; Gartley 1979; Hauser and Armstrong 1999; Lenik 2004), and the French Antilles (Delpuech 2001; Kelly 2002, 2004, 2005; Kelly and Gibson 2003; Kelly et al. 2008a, 2008b; England 1994; Hauser, Kelly, and Armstrong 2007). Kelly's studies demonstrate the significance of differences in the trajectory of plantation slavery on the islands of Guadeloupe and Martinique.

Studies of cultural landscapes in relation to settings of authority, power, and control have been done for virtually every part of the Caribbean (for Jamaica see Delle 1998, 1999, 2001; Armstrong and Kelly 2000; Higman 1986a, 1986b, 1987, 1988, 1998; for the United States Virgin Islands see Armstrong 2003a; for Barbados see Handler and Jacoby 1993). Archaeological studies have also explored African Caribbean identities as expressed in the material record. Laurie Wilkie and Paul Farnsworth have explored how access to local and regional markets enabled enslaved Africans in the Bahamas to become active in the selection and consumption of the materials they used in their daily lives (Wilkie and Farnsworth 1999).

Studies of African Diaspora contexts include sites associated with resistance and freedom. Kofi E. Agorsah has researched Maroon communities in Jamaica (Agorsah 1992, 1993) and Suriname (Agorsah 2006), and examinations of sites in places such as Dominica and St. Vincent have explored possible refugee and Maroon sites. Port town contexts have also been important for studies of free blacks (see Hamilton 2006). Studies of rural settings where persons of African descent gained freedom prior to emancipation include Armstrong's detailed exploration of the East End maritime community on St. John (Armstrong 2003a) and a follow-up GIS study that demonstrated the presence of a series of free black settlements on lands that were marginal to sugar production on the island (Armstrong et al. 2008, 2009).

Underwater Explorations

Underwater sites in the Caribbean have been a catalyst for the broad expansion of archaeological explorations of nautical and inundated sites. When Port Royal, Jamaica, then the largest British settlement in the Caribbean, was struck by a devastating earthquake in 1692, much of the city sank into Kingston Harbour, and the damage was so great that its role as a vibrant port town was permanently altered. Rapid expansion of the plantation economy had already outpaced the scale of trade in the port town, and in the aftermath, the center of commerce quickly shifted to the land-based side of Kingston Harbour. Immediately after the earthquake, Port Royalists engaged in large-scale salvage operations to recover ships' cargoes and lost possessions, but a substantial portion of the town simply settled into the bay and was not seen again until the advent of scuba technology.

The well documented destruction of Port Royal and the visual access to ruins on the shallow shoreline off shore made this site an excellent laboratory and training ground for underwater archaeology. Excavations at Port Royal began in the 1950s at a time when the island was beginning a process of nation building and self-identification based on its distinct insular heritage. From the early 1950s to the 1980s, a near-continuous flow of archaeologists worked at the site and helped develop the emerging field of underwater archaeology. Beginning with excavations by Mr. and Mrs. Alexi DuPont (1954) and continuing with studies by Edward Link (1960), Robert Marx (1967, 1968a, 1968b, 1968c, 1973), Philip Mayes (1970), and Anthony Priddy (1975), researchers studied both submerged sites and waterlogged land-based sites. In 1960, Marian Link's study appeared in

National Geographic in a format that demonstrated the great potential for archaeological reconnaissance (Link 1960). The richness of the material record, the illustrations of whole vessels and artifacts from the seventeenth century, and the reconstructive drawings of the city did much to popularize historical archaeology and underwater archaeology. Subsequent studies gathered what is still the most wide-ranging collection of seventeenth-century material culture in the Americas. The most extensive excavations were carried out by Robert Marx (1967, 1968a, 1968b, 1973) using rather crude dredging techniques that allowed him to gather a large collection, albeit without very good excavation controls and at the expense of many smaller objects. This rather crude data gathering was followed by a series of studies that began to set the standard for underwater reconnaissance. Philip Mayes carried out very careful and detailed excavations on land and in the water (Mayes 1972; Mayes and Mayes 1972). The publications are well illustrated and are among the best-illustrated sources for the range of seventeenth-century material culture.

In the 1980s, Port Royal became a center for excavation and field training for Texas A&M's Institute of Nautical Archaeology (INA). Under the direction of Donny Hamilton, the site was used to refine underwater excavation and material conservation techniques. The careful excavations Hamilton directed produced an array of publications (Brown 1996, 2011; Darrington 1994; Dewolf 1998; Franklin 1992, 2011; Fox 1998; Gotelipe-Miller 1990; Hamilton 1986, 1988, 2006; Hamilton and Woodward 1984; Hailey 1994; Heidtke 1992; McClenaghan 1988; Smith 1995; Trussel 2004). These studies set in motion a Caribbean-wide effort to recover historic period archaeological sites from submerged contexts (see Downing and Harris 1982 for underwater studies of Bermuda; Leshikar-Denton 1991 for studies of the Cayman Islands; Cook and Rubinstein-Gottschamer 2011 for studies of a commercial sloop; and Nagelkerken 2000 for an overview of work done by him and the College of William and Mary during the 1980s in Oranje Bay, St. Eustatius).

Port Towns, Merchants, and Trade

The importance of port towns and trade has been well demonstrated by the extensive studies on land and underwater at Port Royal, Jamaica. Caribbean port towns were sites of commodity production and were central to trade routes and transshipment of merchandise. They have been well documented in archaeological studies throughout the region (see Armstrong and Williamson 2011). Norman Barka explored the Dutch trading center and port town at St. Eustatius in the early 1980s (Barka 1985, 1990, 1991, 1996; Dethlefsen et al. 1982). These studies examined the waterfront associated with the eighteenth-century Dutch trading center and began the process of documenting the distribution of domestic sites and plantations across the island. The archaeological studies Barka and his team began were followed up under the leadership of Netherlands Antilles archaeologist Jay Haviser and are currently being carried out by the St. Eustatius Center for Archaeological Research established and formerly directed by Grant Gilmore (http://www.secar.org/). In addition, merchant shops and an array of port town facilities, including rum bars, have been the focus of a series of archaeological studies on Barbados conducted by Frederick Smith and Karl Watson (2009).

Houses associated with merchants in the nineteenth-century port town of Charlotte Amalie on St. Thomas in what was the Danish West Indies demonstrate the complexity of local and global trade (Armstrong and Williamson 2011). The Magens House compound in Charlotte Amalie provided a material record that demonstrated use of a wide range of locally produced materials, including ceramics from the region. The labor quarters at the site offered evidence of an in situ cottage industry that made bone buttons for sale in the port. The site also illustrates the global nature of trade; the owners had warehouses throughout the Caribbean, in England, in South America, and even in Australia and New Zealand. The Danish global trade network had distinctive patterns, as illustrated by the presence of overglaze Imari-style porcelain from Japan. The presence of Royal Copenhagen lace-decorated porcelain illustrates the use of distinctive Danish products in Charlotte Amalie.

In light of the complexity of the Caribbean trade networks further work should be conducted in other trading centers that developed on other islands. Gustavia on Swedish/French Saint Barthélemy became a thriving port after the French increased taxation on St. Eustatius in 1795 effectively ending the dominance of the modern world's first free trade port. Falmouth on Jamaica was also a significant trading center for the island and although it has been studied as a townscape more work could be completed to integrate these results into regional and Atlantic World contexts. Local trading centers such as Sandy Ground on St. Kitts served a localized inter-island trade with a dozen warehouses that operated until quite recently. Operating as a virtual extension of Oranjestad on St. Eustatius, provisions and water were imported and exported directly to St. Eustatius. Additional examples abound across the Caribbean region that warrant further study to understand the complex economic dynamics that built the Atlantic World trading machine.

New Directions

Prehistoric Archaeology

New methods and techniques that have been successfully applied elsewhere in the world are increasingly being used in prehistoric archaeology in the Caribbean. Primary examples are archaeometric techniques for the study of artifacts and skull and dental morphology to determine origins and migration patterns (Coppa et al. 2008; Ross and Ubelaker 2010). Isotopic research has been used to study human mobility and nutrition. Other recent research strategies include starch grain analysis, dental calculus, use wear analysis (Hofman et al. 2008; Knippenberg 2006; Pagán-Jiménez 2011; Mickleburgh and Pagán-Jiménez 2012), and geoinformatics (Reid 2008). The application of chronometric hygiene to hundreds of radiocarbon dates of the Caribbean has provided rich insights into insular chronology (Fitzpatrick 2006; Rodríguez Ramos, Torres, and Oliver 2010). Computer simulations (Callaghan 2003) and social network analysis (Hofman et al. 2011) are additional new approaches. The near-absence of DNA research in the region has limited our understanding of the origin and ethnic diversity of various prehistoric populations in the Caribbean (Lalueza-Fox et al. 2003; Schurr 2010). DNA research is a fertile ground for expansion, given its unique ability to determine the origins, mobility patterns, and social relationships of various cultural and linguistic groups in the region.

The prehistoric archaeological record of the Caribbean continues to be threatened by climate change, earthquakes, hurricanes, and volcanic eruptions. In addition, tourism has caused considerable damage to much of the region's fragile archaeological record. In the Caribbean, heritage management legislation is either woefully inadequate or is not properly enforced (Siegel and Righter 2011). More effective cultural resource management is required to protect and preserve prehistoric sites in the Caribbean.

Too often, Caribbean prehistoric archaeology and Caribbean historical archaeology are still regarded as two distinctly different fields, when in fact there is much overlap between the two fields of inquiry. There is little cooperation between the two fields, limiting our understanding of cultural transformations Amerindian societies experienced during early European colonization (Hoogland, Hofman, and Boomert 2011; Valcárcel Rojas et al. 2011). Greater levels of collaboration between prehistoric and historical archaeologists, whose research agendas intersect, would significantly improve our understanding of dynamic interactions between native and early colonial societies.

Historical Archaeology

Now that we have a well-developed baseline of archaeological studies for the region for the sixteenth through nineteenth centuries, we can expect to see regional comparison on a wide range of topics. Already comparative analyses have begun to explore topics such as the range and variation in the production of earthenware from island to island. Studies of locally produced earthenware are defining the sources and composition of locally produced goods. The study of earthenware studies has moved toward refined petrographic, and element analyses that provide a basis for understanding production systems and regional variation.

In the Caribbean, archaeologists have struggled to interpret local and regionally produced ceramics (see the critique in Hauser and Armstrong 1999). In 1979, Gartley described a group of Afro-Cruzian wares for St. Croix. Soon after, Armstrong found an array of low-fired earthenware from the households of enslaved laborers at Drax Hall and pointed out the island-wide distribution of pottery in Jamaica made by African Jamaicans (1985). Soon, various forms of locally made earthenware were being reported from nearly every island in the Caribbean. For example, Jim Peterson and David Watters used data from local earthenware found at the Harney Cemetery site in Montserrat as part of their attribution of the human remains as enslaved Africans (Watters 1994a). They also suggested that these wares represented regionally produced material. Heath (1999) and Gilmore (2005) have completed petrographic analyses for St. Eustatius. Heath's work indicated that interisland trade was likely. Gilmore found strong evidence for a range of sources for low fired earthenware excavated on St. Eustatius. Over the past ten years, a number of archaeologists have tackled research questions related to the extent and diversity of interisland and local trade using elemental analyses. Mark Hauser has been at the forefront of these studies. His work includes the beginnings of comparisons of chemical and elemental analysis of regional earthenware using neutron activation analysis (Hauser, Descantes, and Glascock 2008; Kelly et al. 2008).

Conclusion

There was a time when Caribbean prehistoric archaeology was seen as peripheral to what was described as New World mainstream archaeology, which heavily focused on the "high cultures" of South America, Central America, the American Southwest, and the American Southeast. Happily for us, that time has long passed (Reid 2007). Since the late 1930s and 1940s, when Irving Rouse first introduced his cultural histories of series, subseries, and complexes, generations of archaeologists have developed new research techniques and approaches that are specific to but not necessarily unique to the Caribbean (Hofman et al. 2008; Reid 2007). This survey of Caribbean prehistoric archaeology reflects many of these positive trends, which are largely the result of the internationalization of Caribbean archaeology; scholars from the Caribbean, Latin America, North America, and Europe have brought a multiplicity of new ideas and perspectives to the archaeological discourse of the region.

Over the past several years, historical archaeology in the Caribbean has expanded to address a wide range of issues on practically every island. As a result, a wide body of data has been generated that is presently being used in comparative studies. Examples of the range of studies now being done include the examination of settings defined by specific cultural and religious expression, such as John Chenoweth's study of an estate in the British Virgin Islands that was owned by Quakers (Chenoweth 2011) and the recent excavations of the protohistoric contexts of the site of Argyle on St. Vincent (Hoogland, Hoffman, and Boomert 2011). Studies are also beginning to address sites and contexts relating to the more recent past. The significant impact of military sites associated with World War II is just beginning to be explored (Haviser 2011; Watters 2011). Although military installations made a significant material impact on the landscape, the cultural implications of interaction associated with these sites had a major impact on later twentieth-century Caribbean life. It is expected that in the near future studies of these sites will become a significant theme in regional research. Soon historical archaeologists will begin to explore the broader contexts of twentieth-century change, including sites associated with union and labor movements, independence, and nation building, themes that were significant to the creation of the modern cultural landscape, much as the transition from slavery was for earlier eras in the Caribbean.

Future archaeological study of prehistoric and historic contexts in the Caribbean has great potential for interpretations that project the diversity expressed in the local setting of each island. New research in the theory and methodology of the region is becoming increasingly important. It is clear that although the Caribbean occupies a small geographic space, it offers a rich, dynamic, plural, and complex archaeological heritage. The *Encyclopedia of Caribbean Archaeology* is designed to showcase this rich panoply of the region's archaeology and to point to areas where future research efforts should be usefully invested.

References

Acevedo-Rodríguez, P., et al. 1996. *Flora of St. John, U.S. Virgin Islands*. New York: New York Botanical Garden Production Department.

Agorsah, E. K. 1992. "Archaeology and Maroon Heritage." *Jamaica Journal* 22: 2–9.

———. 1993. "Archaeology and Resistance History in the Caribbean." *African Archaeological Review* 11: 175–95.

———. 2006. "The Other Side of Freedom: The Maroon Trail in Suriname." In *African Re-Genesis: Confronting Social Issues in the Diaspora*, ed. J. B. Haviser and K. C. MacDonald, 191–203. Walnut Creek, CA: Left Coast Press.

Ahlman, Todd, Gerald F. Schroedl, and Ashley McKeown. 2009. "The Afro Caribbean Ware from Brimstone Hill Fortress, St. Kitts, West Indies: A Study in Ceramic Production." *Historical Archaeology* 43 (4): 22–41.

Alegría, Ricardo E. 1981. "El uso de la terminologia ethno-historic para designer las culturas aborigines de las Antillas." *Cuadernos Prehispanicas*, Seminario de Historia de Amerrica, University of Valladolid.

Allaire, L. 1977. "Later Prehistory in Martinique and the Island-Caribs: Problems in Ethnic Identification." PhD diss., Yale University.

———. 1980. "On the Historicity of Carib Migrations in the Lesser Antilles." *American Antiquity* 45 (2): 238–45.

———. 1984. "A Reconstruction of Early Historical Island-Carib Pottery." *Southeastern Archaeology* 3: 121–33.

———. 1991. "Understanding Suazey." In *Proceedings of the Thirteenth International Congress for Caribbean Archaeology*, ed. E. N. Ayubi and J. B. Haviser, 715–28. Curaçao: Archaeological-Anthropological Institute of the Netherlands Antilles.

———. 1997. "The Lesser Antilles before Columbus." In *The Indigenous People of the Caribbean*, ed. S. M. Wilson, 177–85. Gainesville: University Press of Florida.

———. 2003. "Agricultural Societies in the Caribbean: The Lesser Antilles." In *General History of the Caribbean*, vol. 1, *Autochthonous Societies*, ed. Jalil Sued-Badillo, 195–227. Paris and London: UNESCO.

Armstrong, D. V. 1983. "The 'Old Village' at Drax Hall Plantation: An Archeological Examination of an Afro-Jamaican Settlement." PhD diss., University of California, Los Angeles.

———. 1985. "An Afro Jamaican Slave Settlement: Archaeological Investigations at Drax Hall." In *The Archaeology of Slavery and Plantation Life*, ed. Theresa Singleton, 261–87. New York: Academic Press.

———. 1990. *The Old Village and the Great House: An Archaeological and Historical Examination of Drax Hall Plantation, St. Ann's Bay, Jamaica*. Urbana: University of Illinois Press.

———. 1991. "Recovering an Early 18th-Century Afro-Jamaican Community: Archaeology of the Slave Village at Seville, Jamaica." In *Proceedings of the Thirteenth International Congress for Caribbean Archaeology, Curaçao, Netherlands Antilles*, ed. E. N. Ayubi and J. B. Haviser, 344–62. Curaçao: Archaeological-Anthropological Institute of the Netherlands Antilles.

———. 1992. "Spatial Transformations in African Jamaican Housing at Seville Plantation." *Archaeology Jamaica* 6: 51–63.

———. 1998. "Cultural Transformation among Caribbean Slave Communities." In *Studies in Culture Contact: Interaction, Culture Change, and Archaeology*, ed. James Cusick, 378–401. Carbondale: Center for Archaeological Investigations, Southern Illinois University.

———. 1999. Archaeology and Ethnohistory of the Caribbean Plantation. In *"I, Too, Am America": Archaeological Studies of African-American Life*, ed. Theresa Singleton, 173–92. Charlottesville: University of Virginia Press.

———. 2001. "A Venue for Autonomy: Archaeology of a Changing Cultural Landscape, the East End Community, St. John, Virgin Islands." In *Island Lives: Historical Archaeologies of the Caribbean*, ed. P. Farnsworth, 143–64. Tuscaloosa: University of Alabama Press.

———. 2003a. *Creole Transformation from Slavery to Freedom: Historical Archaeology of the East End Community, St. John, Virgin Islands*. Gainesville: University Press of Florida.

———. 2003b. "Social Relations in a Maritime Creole Community: Networked Multifocality in the East End Community of St. John, Danish West Indies." In *Proceedings of the Nineteenth International Congress for Caribbean Archaeology*, ed. L. Alofs and R.A.C. F. Dijkhoff, 195–210. Oranjestad: Archaeological Museum of Aruba.

———. 2006. "East End Maritime Traders: The Emergence of a Creole Community on St. John, Danish West Indies." In *African Re-genesis: Confronting Social Issues in the African Diaspora*, ed. J. Haviser and K. C. MacDonald, 145–59. London: Routledge.

———. 2011a. "Reflections on Seville: Rediscovering the African Jamaican Settlements at Seville Plantation, St. Ann's Bay." In *Out of Many, One People: Historical Archaeology in Jamaica*, ed. J. Delle, M. Hauser, and D. V. Armstrong, 77–101. Tuscaloosa: University of Alabama Press.

———. 2011b. "Epilogue: Explorations in Jamaican Historical Archaeology." In *Out of Many, One People*, ed. J. Delle, M. Hauser, and D. V. Armstrong, 258–71. Tuscaloosa: University of Alabama Press.

———. 2011c. "Paradox in the Renderings of Paradise: Camille Pissarro and Changing Esthetics in Art and Depiction of the Cultural Landscape of the Danish West Indies." In *Proceedings of the Twenty-Third Congress of the International Association for Caribbean Archaeology*, ed. S. A. Rebovich, 362–78. Antigua: International Association for Caribbean Archaeology.

———. 2013. "New Directions in Caribbean Historical Archaeology." In *The Oxford Handbook of Caribbean Archaeology*, ed. William Keegan, Corine Hofman, and Reniel Rodriquez Ramos, 525–41. Oxford: Oxford University Press.

Armstrong, D. V., and M. Fleischman. 2003. "House-Yard Burials of Enslaved Laborers in Eighteenth-Century Jamaica." *International Journal of Historical Archaeology* 7 (1): 33–65.

Armstrong, D. V., and M. W. Hauser. 2003. "An East Indian Laborer's Household in 19th Century Jamaica." In *Proceedings of the XIX International Congress for Caribbean Archaeology*, ed. Luc Alofs and Raymundo A.C.F. Dijkhoff, 2:195–210. Aruba: Archaeological Museum of Aruba.

———. 2004. "An East Indian Laborers' Household in 19th-Century Jamaica: A Case for Understanding Cultural Diversity through Space, Chronology, and Material Analysis." *Historical Archaeology* 38 (2): 9–21.

———. 2009. "A Sea of Diversity: Historical Archaeology in the Caribbean Region." In *International Handbook of Historical Archaeology*, ed. T. Majewsky and D. Gaimster, 583–612. New York: Springer.

Armstrong, D. V., M. W. Hauser and D. Knight. 2005. "The Early Shoreline Settlement at Cinnamon Bay, St. John, USVI: Before Formal Colonization to the Slave Rebellion of 1733." In *Proceedings of the Twentieth International Congress for Caribbean Archaeology*, ed. G. Tavares María and M. García Arévalo, 743–50. Santo Domingo: Museo del Hombre Dominicano.

Armstrong, D. V., M. W. Hauser, D. Knight, and S. Lenik. 2008. "Maps, Matricals, and Material Remains: Archaeology of Late Eighteenth Century Historic Sites on St. John, Danish West Indies." In *Archaeology and Geoinformatics: Case Studies from the Caribbean*, ed. Basil A. Reid, 99–126. Tuscaloosa: University of Alabama Press.

———. 2009. "Variation in Venues of Slavery and Freedom: Interpreting the Late Eighteenth-Century Cultural Landscape of St. John, Danish West Indies Using an Archaeological GIS." *International Journal of Historical Archaeology* 13 (1): 94–111.

Armstrong, D. V., and K. G. Kelly. 2000. "Settlement Patterns and the Origins of African Jamaican Society: Seville Plantation, St. Ann's Bay." *Jamaica Ethnohistory* 7 (2): 369–97.

Armstrong, D. V., K. Watson, and M. Reilly. 2012. "The 1646 Hapcott Map, Fort (Trents) Plantation, St. James, Barbados: A Significant Resource for Research on Early Colonial Settlement in Barbados. *Journal of the Barbados Museum and Historical Society* 58: 97–115.

Armstrong, D. V., and C. Williamson. 2011. "The Magens House, Charlotte Amalie, St. Thomas, Danish West Indies: Archaeology of an Urban House Compound and Its Relationship to Local Interactions and Global Trade." In *Islands at the Crossroads: Migration, Seafaring, and Interaction in the Caribbean*, ed. L. A. Curet and M. W. Hauser, 137–63. Tuscaloosa: University of Alabama Press.

Arrom, José, trans. and ed. 1978. *Relación acerca de las antigüedades de los indios by Fray Ramón Pané*. Mexico: Siglo Veintiuno.

Arrom, J. J., and M. García Arévalo. 1986. *Cimarron*. Santo Domingo: Fundación García Arévalo.

Barka, N. F. 1985. *The Archaeology of St. Eustatius, Netherlands Antilles: An Interim Report on the 1981–1984 Seasons*. Williamsburg, VA: Department of Anthropology, College of William and Mary.

———. 1990. "The Potential for Historical Archaeological Research in the Netherlands Antilles." In *Actas del undecimo Congreso, Asociación Internacional de Arqueologia del Caribe (Proceedings of the Eleventh Congress of the International Association for Caribbean Archaeology)*, ed. A.G.P. Tekakis, I. V. Arenas, M. S. Obediente, 393–99. Puerto Rico: La Fundación Arqueológica, Antropológica e Histórica de Puerto Rico.

———. 1991. "The Merchants of St. Eustatius: An Archaeological and Historical Analysis. In *Proceedings of the Thirteenth International Association for Caribbean Archaeology*, ed. E. N. Ayubi and J. B. Haviser, 384–92. Curaçao: Archaeological-Anthropological Institute of the Netherlands Antilles.

———. 1996. "Citizens of St. Eustatius, 1781: A Historical and Archaeological Study." In *The Lesser Antilles in the Age of European Expansion*, ed. R. L. Paquette and S. L. Engerman, 223–38. Gainesville: University Press of Florida.

Beckles, Hilary McD. 1992. "Kalinago (Carib) Resistance to European Colonization of the Caribbean." *Caribbean Quarterly* 38 (2–3): 1–14.

———. 2013. *Britain's Black Debt: Reparations for Caribbean Slavery and Native Genocide*. Cave Hill, Barbados: University of the West Indies Press.

Beier, Z. J. 2011. "Initial Feasibility and Reconnaissance at the Cabrits Garrison, Dominica." In *Proceedings of the Twenty-Third Congress of the International Association of Caribbean Archaeology*, ed. S. A. Rebovich, 233–42. Antigua: International Association for Caribbean Archaeology.

Bonner, T. 1974. "Blue Mountain Expedition: Exploratory Excavations at Nanny Town by the Scientific Exploration Society." *Jamaica Journal* 8 (2/3): 46–50.

Bonnissent D. 2008. "Archéologie précolombienne de l'île de Saint-Martin, Petites Antilles (3300 BP–1600 AD)." Thèse de doctorat. Aix-en-Provence: l'Université Aix-Marseille I.

Boomert, A. 2000. *Trinidad, Tobago, and the Lower Orinoco Interaction Sphere: An Archaeological/Ethnohistorical Study*. Alkmaar: Cairi Publications.

———. 2003. "Agricultural Societies in the Continental Caribbean." In *The General History of the Caribbean*, vol. 1, *Autochthonous Societies*, ed. Jalil Sued-Badillo, 134–94. Paris and London: UNESCO.

Bourne, E. G. 1906. "Columbus, Ramón Pané, and the Beginnings of American Anthropology." *Proceedings of the Antiquarian Society* 17: 310–48.

Bright, A. J. 2011. *Blood Is Thicker Than Water: Amerindian Intra- and Inter-Insular Relationships and Social Organization in the Pre-Colonial Windward Islands*. Leiden: Sidestone Press.

Brown, M. J. 1996. "An Archaeological Study of Social Class as Reflected in a British Colonial Tavern Site in Port Royal, Jamaica." MA thesis, University of Texas, San Antonio.

———. 2011. "Evidence of Port Royal's British Colonial Merchant Class as Reflected in the New Street Tavern Site Assemblage." In *Out of Many, One People*, ed. J. Delle, M. Hauser, and D. V. Armstrong, 56–75. Tuscaloosa: University of Alabama Press.

Bullen, R. P. 1965. Archaeological Chronology of Grenada. *American Antiquity* 31 (2): 237–41.

Bullen, R. P., and A. K. Bullen. 1968. "Salvage Archaeology at Caliviny Island, Grenada. A Problem in Typology." In *Proceedings of the Second International Congress for Caribbean Archaeology*, ed. R. P. Bullen, 31–46. Barbados: Barbados Museum.

Burns, S. A. 1965. *History of the British West Indies*. London: Allen and Unwin.

Callaghan, R. T. 1990. "Mainland Origins of the Pre-Ceramic Cultures of the Greater Antilles." PhD diss., University of Calgary.

———. 1995. "Antillean Cultural Contacts with Mainland Region as a Navigation Problem." In *Proceedings of the Fifteenth International Congress for Caribbean Archaeology*, ed. R. E. Alegría and M. A. Rodríguez López, 181–90. San Juan, Puerto Rico: Centro de Estudios Avanzados de Puerto Rico y el Caribe.

———. 2003. "Comments on the Mainland Origins of the Pre-Ceramic Cultures of the Greater Antilles." *Latin American Antiquity* 14 (3): 323–39.

———. 2001. "Ceramic Age Seafaring and Interaction Potential in the Antilles: A Computer Simulation." *Current Anthropology* 42 (2): 308–12.

Chanlatte Baik, L. A. 1981. *La Hueca y Sorcé (Vieques, Puerto Rico): Primeras migraciones agroalfareras antillanas. Nuevo esquema para los procesos culturales de la arqueología antillana*. Santo Domingo, Dominican Republic: Published by author.

———. 1984. *Arqueología de Vieques*. Santo Domingo, Dominican Republic: Editora Corripio.

———. 1986. "Cultura Ostionoide: Un desarollo agroalfarero antillano." *Homines* 10: 1–40.

Chanlatte Baik, L. A., and Y. M. Narganes Storde. 2005. *Cultura La Hueca*. San Juan, Puerto Rico: Museo de Historia, Antropología y Arte.

Chenoweth, J. 2011. "Religion on the Plantation: Quakers and the Enslaved in the 18th-Century British Virgin Islands." Paper presented at the Twenty-Fourth International Association for Caribbean Archaeology, Martinique.

Clement, C. O. 1997. "Settlement Patterning on the British Caribbean Island of Tobago." *Historical Archaeology* 31 (2): 93–106.

Cook, G. D., and A. Rubenstein-Gottschamer. 2011. "Maritime Connections in a Plantation Economy: Archaeological Investigations of a Colonial Sloop in St. Ann's Bay, Jamaica." In *Out of Many, One People,* ed. J. Delle, M. Hauser, and D. V. Armstrong, 23–40. Tuscaloosa: University of Alabama Press.

Coppa, A., A. Cucina, M.L.P. Hoogland, M. Lucci, F. Luna Calderón, R.G.A. M. Panhuysen, G. Tavarez María, R. Valcárcel Rojas, and R. Vargiu. 2008. "New Evidence of Two Different Migratory Waves in the Circum-Caribbean Area during the Pre-Columbian Period from the Analysis of Dental Morphological Traits." In *Crossing the Borders: New Methods and Techniques in the Study of Archaeological Materials from the Caribbean,* ed. C. L. Hofman, M.L.P. Hoogland, and A. L. van Gijn, 195–213. Tuscaloosa: University of Alabama Press.

Cotter, C S. 1964. "The Jamaica of Columbus." *Jamaica Historical Society Bulletin* 3 (16): 252–59.

———. 1970. "Sevilla Nueva, the Story of an Excavation." *Jamaica Journal* 4 (2): 15–22.

Crock, J. G. 2000. "Interisland Interaction and the Development of Chiefdoms in the Eastern Caribbean." PhD diss., University of Pittsburgh.

Cundall, F. 1915. *Historic Jamaica*. London: Institute of Jamaica.

Curet, L. A. 1996. "Ideology, Chiefly Power, and Material Culture: An Example from the Greater Antilles." *Latin American Antiquity* 7 (2): 114–31.

Curet, L. A. 2005. *Caribbean Paleodemography*. Tuscaloosa: University of Alabama Press.

Curet, L. A., S. L. Dawdy, and G. La Rosa Corzo. 2005. *Dialogues in Cuban Archaeology*. Tuscaloosa: University of Alabama Press.

Curet, L. A., and L. M. Stringer. 2010. *Tibes: People, Power, and Ritual at the Center of the Cosmos*. Tuscaloosa: The University of Alabama Press.

Darrington, G. 1994. "Analysis and Reconstruction of Impermanent Structures in the 17th and 18th Centuries." MA thesis, Department of Anthropology, Texas A&M University, College Station.

Deagan, K. A., ed. 1995. *Puerto Real: The Archaeology of a Sixteenth-Century Spanish Town in Hispaniola*. Gainesville: University Press of Florida.

Deagan, K. A., and J. M. Cruxent. 2002a. *Archaeology at La Isabella: America's First European Town*. New Haven, CT: Yale University Press.

———. 2002b. *Columbus's Outpost among the Taínos: Spain and America at La Isabella, 1493–1498*. New Haven, CT: Yale University Press.

DeBooy, T. 1919. "On the Possibility of Determining the First Landfall of Columbus by Archaeological Research." *Hispanic American Historical Review* 2: 55–61.

Delle, J. A. 1989. "A Spatial Analysis of Sugar Plantations on St. Eustatius, Netherlands Antilles." MA thesis, College of William and Mary, Williamsburg, VA.

———. 1994. "The Settlement Pattern of Sugar Plantations on St. Eustatius, Netherlands Antilles." In *Spatial Patterning in Archaeology: Selected Studies of Settlement*, ed. D. W. Robinson and G. G. Robinson, 33–61. Williamsburg, VA: King and Queen's Press.

———. 1998. *An Archaeology of Social Space: Analyzing Coffee Plantations in Jamaica's Blue Mountains*. New York: Plenum Press.

———. 1999. "The Landscapes of Class Negotiation on Coffee Plantations in the Blue Mountains of Jamaica, 1797–1850." *Historical Archaeology* 33 (1): 136–58.

———. 2000a. "Gender, Power, and Space: Negotiating Social Relations under Slavery on Coffee Plantations in Jamaica, 1790–1834." In *Lines That Divide: Historical Archaeologies of Race, Class, and Gender,* ed. J. A. Delle, S. A. Mrozowski, and R. Paynter. Knoxville: University of Tennessee Press.

———. 2000b. "The Material and Cognitive Dimensions of Creolization in Nineteenth-Century Jamaica." *Historical Archaeology* 34 (3): 56–72.

———. 2001. "Race, Missionaries, and the Struggle to Free Jamaica." In *Race and the Archaeology of Identity,* ed. C. E. Orser, 177–95. Salt Lake City: University of Utah Press.

———. 2008. "An Archaeology of Modernity in Colonial Jamaica." *Archaeologies: The Journal of the World Archaeology Congress* 4 (1):87–109.

———. 2009. "The Governor and the Enslaved: Archaeology and Modernity at Marshall's Pen, Jamaica." *International Journal of Historical Archaeology* 12 (4): 488–512.

———. 2011. "Excavating the Roots of Resistance: The Significance of Maroons in Jamaican Archaeology." In *Out of Many, One People: Historical Archaeology in Jamaica,* ed. J. Delle, M. Hauser, and D. V. Armstrong, 122–43. Tuscaloosa: University of Alabama Press.

Delle, J, M. W. Hauser, and D. V. Armstrong. eds. 2011. *Out of Many, One People: The Historical Archaeology of Colonial Jamaica.* Tuscaloosa: University of Alabama Press.

Delpuech, A. 2001. "Historical Archaeology in the French West Indies: Recent Research in Guadeloupe." In *Island Lives: Historical Archaeologies of the Caribbean,* ed. P. Farnsworth, 21–59. Tuscaloosa: University of Alabama Press.

Dethlefsen, E., S. J. Gluckman, R. D. Mathewson, and N. F. Barka. 1982. "Archaeology on St. Eustatius: The Pompeii of the New World." *Archaeology* 35 (2): 8–15.

Dewolf, H. C. 1998. "Chinese Porcelain and Seventeenth-Century Port Royal, Jamaica." PhD diss., Department of Anthropology, Texas A&M University, College Station.

Domínguez, L. 1978. "La transculturacion en Cuba (s. 16–17)." *Cuba Arqueologica* 1978: 33–50.

———. 1989. *Arqueología Colonial Cubana: Dos Estudios.* Havana: Editorial de Ciencias Sociales.

———. 1991. *Arqueología del Centro-Sur de Cuba.* Havana: Editorial Academia.

Dookhan, I. 2006. *A Pre-Emancipation History of the West Indies.* London: Longman Publishing for the Caribbean.

Downing, J., and E. Harris. 1982. "Excavations at Her Majesty's Dockyard, Bermuda." *Post-Medieval Archaeology* 16: 201–16.

Drewett, P. L. 1991. *Prehistoric Barbados.* London: Institute of Archeology, University College.

———. 1999. *Field Archaeology: An Introduction.* London: University College London Press, Taylor and Francis Group.

England, S. 1994. "Acculturation in the Creole Context: A Case Study of La Poterie Martinique." PhD diss., Cambridge University.

Equiano, Olaudah. 1789. *The Interesting Narrative of the Life of Olaudah Equiano, or Gustavus Vassa, the African.* London: Printed for the author.

Fagan, Brian. 2005. *World Prehistory: A Brief Introduction.* 6th ed. Upper Saddle River, N.J.: Pearson Prentice Hall.

Farnsworth, P. 1992. "Comparative Analysis in Plantation Archaeology: The Application of a Functional Classification." Paper presented at Twenty-Fifth Annual Meeting of the Society for Historical Archaeology, Kingston, Jamaica.

———. 1996. "The Influence of Trade on Bahamian Slave Culture." *Historical Archaeology* 30 (4): 1–23.

———. 1999. "From Past to Present: An Exploration of the Formation of African-Bahamian Identity during Enslavement." In *African Sites: Archaeology in the Caribbean,* ed. J. Haviser, 94–130. Kingston: Ian Randle.

———. 2000. "Brutality or Benevolence in Plantation Archaeology." *International Journal of Historical Archaeology* 4 (2): 145–58.

———. 2001. *Island Lives: Historical Archaeologies of the Caribbean.* Tuscaloosa: University of Alabama Press.

Finch, Jonathan, and Douglas V. Armstrong. 2013. "Preliminary Archaeological Investigations at The Mount, Barbados." Paper presented at the Society for Historical Archaeology, Leicester, England, January.

Fitzpatrick, S. M. 2006. "A Critical Approach to 14C Dating in the Caribbean: Using Chronometric Hygiene to Evaluate Chronological Control and Prehistoric Settlement." *Latin American Antiquity* 17 (4): 389–418.

Fitzpatrick, S. M., and W. F. Keegan. 2007. "Human Impacts and Adaptations in the Caribbean Islands: An Historical Ecology Approach." *Earth and Environmental Science: Transactions of the Royal Society of Edinburgh* 98: 29–45.

Fox, G. L. 1998. "The Study of the Kaolin Clay Tobacco Pipe Collection from the Seventeenth-Century Archaeological Site of Port Royal, Jamaica." PhD diss., Department of Anthropology, Texas A&M University, College Station.

Franklin, M. 1992. "Wrought-Iron Hand Tools in Port Royal, Jamaica: A Study Based upon a Collection of the Tools Recovered from Archaeological Excavations and Listed in the Probate Records of Colonial Port Royal, c. 1692." Master's thesis, Department of Anthropology, Texas A&M University, College Station.

———. 2011. "Port Royal and Jamaica: Wrought-Iron Hand Tools Recovered as Archaeological Evidence and the Material Culture Mentioned in Probate Inventories ca. 1692." In *Out of Many, One People,* ed. J. Delle, M. Hauser, and D. V. Armstrong, 41–55. Tuscaloosa: University of Alabama Press.

García Arévalo, M. A., 1986. *El Maniel de Jose Leta: Evidencias arqueologicas de un posible cimarron en el religion sud oriental de la isla de santo domingo.* Cimarron no 18. Santo Domingo: Fundación García Arévalo.

García Arévalo, M. A. 1990. "Transculturation in Contact Period and Contemporary Hispaniola." In *Consequences,* vol. 2, *Archaeological and Historical Perspectives on the Spanish Borderlands East,* ed. D. H. Thomas, 269–80. Washington, DC: Smithsonian Institution Press.

Gartley, R. T. 1979. "Afro-Cruzan Pottery: A New Style of Colonial Earthenware from St. Croix." *Journal of the Virgin Islands Archaeological Society* 8: 47–61.

Gilmore, R. G. 2005. "The Archaeology of New World Slave Societies: A Comparative Analysis with Particular Reference to St. Eustatius, Netherlands Antilles." PhD diss., University College London.

———. 2006a. "All the Documents Are Destroyed! Documenting Slavery for St. Eustatius, Netherlands Antilles." In *Afri-*

can Re-Genesis: Confronting Social Issues in the African Diaspora, ed. J. Haviser and K. C. MacDonald, 70–89. London: Routledge.

———. 2006b. "Urban Transformation and Upheaval in the West Indies: The Case of Oranjestad, St. Eustatius, Netherlands Antilles." In *Cities in the World, 1500–2000,* ed. A. Green and R. Leech, 83–96. Leeds: Maney.

———. 2008. "Geophysics and Volcanic Islands: Resitivity and Gradiometry on St. Eustatius." In *Archaeology and Geoinformatics: Case Studies from the Caribbean,* ed. B. Reid, 170–83. Tuscaloosa: University of Alabama Press.

———. 2009. "Blue Beads, Afro-Caribbean Wares, and Tumblers: International Trade by Enslaved Africans." In *Free Ports of the Caribbean,* ed. I. Witteveen, 42–53. Curaçao, Netherlands Antilles: National Archaeological Anthropological Memory Management.

———. 2013. "St. Eustatius—The Nexus for Colonial Caribbean Capitalism." In *The Archaeology of Interdependence,* ed. D. Comer, 41–60. New York: Springerlink.

———. Forthcoming. "European and African Vernacular Architecture in the Caribbean." In *Archaeology, Syncretism, Creolisation,* ed. T. Clack. Oxford: Oxford University Press.

González, N. L. 1988. *Sojourners of the Caribbean: Ethnogenesis and Ethnohistory of the Garifuna.* Urbana: University of Illinois Press.

Goodwin, C. M. 1987. "Sugar, Time, and Englishmen: A Study of Management Strategies on Caribbean Plantations." PhD diss., Boston University.

Goodwin, C. M., L. M. Pulsipher, M. R. Domurad Jones, and W. M Bass. 1992. "The Tschuh Chahd Burying Ground at Galways Plantation, Montserrat, West Indies." Unpublished manuscript in authors' possession.

Goodwin, R. C. 1978. "The Lesser Antilles Archaic: New Data from St. Kitts." In *Journal of the Virgin Islands Archaeological Society* 5: 6–16.

Goodwin, R. C., and D. Davis. 1990. "Island-Carib Origins: Evidence and Nonevidence." *American Antiquity* 55 (1): 37–48.

Goodwin, W. B. 1940. *The Lure of Gold: Being the Story of the Five Lost Ships of Christopher Columbus.* Boston: Meador.

———. 1946. *Spanish and English Ruins in Jamaica: A Brief History of That Tropical Paradise since the Discovery by Christopher Columbus, the Great Navigator, and Settled by His Son, Don Diego Colon in 1509 as Duke of Veragus.* Boston: Meador.

Goslinga, C. C. 1971. *The Dutch in the Caribbean and on the Wild Coast, 1580–1680.* Assen: Van Gorcum.

Gotelipe-Miller, S. 1990. "Pewter and Pewterers from Port Royal, Jamaica: Flatware before 1692." MA thesis, Department of Anthropology, Texas A&M University, College Station.

Goucher, C. 1990. "John Reeder's Foundry: A Study of 18th-Century African-Caribbean Technology." *Jamaica Journal* 23: 39–43.

Green, Jack, P. 1987. "Colonial South Carolina and the Caribbean Connection." *South Carolina Historical Magazine* 88 (4): 192–210.

Hailey, T. I. 1994. "The Analysis of 17th-, 18th-, and 19th-Century Ceramics from Port Royal, Jamaica, for Lead Release: A Study in Archaeotoxicology." PhD diss., Department of Anthropology, Texas A&M University, College Station.

Hamilton, D. L. 1986. "Port Royal Revisited." In *Underwater Archaeology: Proceedings from the Society for Historical Archaeology Conference,* ed. Calvin R. Cummings, 73–81. Pleasant Hill, CA: Society for Historical Archaeology.

———. 1988. "Underwater Excavations of 17th-Century Building at the Intersection of Lime and Queen Streets." In *Underwater Archaeology: Proceedings from the Society for Historical Archaeology Conference,* ed. Calvin R. Cummings, 9–12. Pleasant Hill, CA: Society for Historical Archaeology.

———. 2006. "Pirates and Merchants: Port Royal, Jamaica." In *X Marks the Spot: The Archaeology of Piracy,* ed. C. R. Ewen, 13–30. Gainesville: University Press of Florida.

Hamilton, D. L., and R. Woodward. 1984. "A Sunken 17th-Century City: Port Royal, Jamaica." *Archaeology* 37 (1): 38–45.

Handler, J. S. 1963a. "A Historical Sketch of Pottery Manufacture in Barbados." *Journal of the Barbados Museum and Historical Society* 30 (3): 129–53.

———. 1963b. "Pottery Making in Rural Barbados." *Southwestern Journal of Anthropology* 19 (3): 314–34.

———. 1964. "Notes on Pottery-Making in Antigua." *Man* 183–84: 150–51.

———. 1965. "Some Aspects of Work Organization on Sugar Plantations in Barbados." *Ethnology* 4 (1): 16–38.

———. 1972. "An Archaeological Investigation of the Domestic Life of Plantation Slaves in Barbados." *Journal of the Barbados Museum and Historical Society* 34 (2): 64–72.

———. 1997. "An African-Type Healer/Diviner and His Grave Goods: A Burial from a Plantation Slave Cemetery in Barbados, West Indies." *International Journal of Historical Archaeology* 1: 91–130.

Handler, J. S., and J. Jacoby. 1993. "Slave Medicine and Plant Use in Barbados." *Journal of the Barbados Museum and Historical Society* 41: 74–98.

Handler, J. S., and F. W. Lange. 1978. *Plantation Slavery in Barbados: An Archaeological and Historical Investigation.* Cambridge: Harvard University Press.

Hapcott, John. 1646. "Estate Plan of 300 Acres of Land Near Holetown, Barbados." Map housed in the John Carter Brown Library at Brown University. Available at http://www.brown.edu/Facilities/John_Carter_Brown_Library/mapexhib/describe.html. Accessed April 26, 2013.

Harrington, M. R. 1921. *Cuba before Columbus.* New York: Museum of the American Indian, Heye Foundation.

Hauser, M. W. 2001. "Peddling Pots: Determining the Extent of Market Exchange in Eighteenth-Century Jamaica through the Analysis of Local Coarse Earthenware." PhD diss., Syracuse University.

———. 2006. "Hawking Your Wares: Determining the Scale of Informal Economy through the Distribution of Local Coarse Earthenware in Eighteenth-Century Jamaica." In *African Re-Genesis: Confronting Social Issues in the Diaspora,* ed. K. C. MacDonald, 160–75. New York: University College London Press.

———. 2008. *The Archaeology of Black Markets, Local Economies, and Local Pottery in Eighteenth-Century Jamaica.* Gainesville: University Press of Florida.

———. 2011. "Of Earth and Clay: Locating Colonial Economics and Local Ceramics." In *Out of Many, One People,* ed. J. Delle, M. Hauser, and D. V. Armstrong, 163–82. Tuscaloosa: University of Alabama Press.

Hauser, M. W., and D. V. Armstrong. 1999. "Embedded Identities: Piecing Together Relationships through Compositional Analysis of Low-Fired Earthenwares." In *African Sites: Archaeology in the Caribbean,* ed. J. B. Haviser, 65–93, 313–64. Princeton: Markus Weiner.

———. 2012. "The Archaeology of Not Being Governed: A Counterpoint to a History of Settlement of Two Colonies in the Eastern Caribbean." *Journal of Social Archaeology* 12 (3): 310–33.

Hauser, M. W., and C. R. DeCorse. 2003. "Low-Fired Earthenwares in the African Diaspora: Problems and Prospects." *International Journal of Historical Archaeology* 7 (1): 67–98.

Hauser, Mark W., C. Descantes and M. Glascock. 2008. "Locating Enslaved Craft Production: Chemical Analysis of Eighteenth Century Jamaican Pottery." *Journal of Caribbean Archaeology* 8: 123–48.

Hauser, Mark W., K. Kelly, and D. V. Armstrong. 2007. "What to Do with 'Other Ceramics': Inter-Colonial Trade of French Coarse Earthenware." In *Proceedings of the Twenty-First Congress of the International Association for Caribbean Archaeology,* ed. Basil A. Reid, Henry Petitjean Roget, and L. Antonio Curet, 579–87. St. Augustine, [Trinidad and Tobago]: University of the West Indies, Trinidad.

Haviser, J. 1997. "Social Repercussions of Slavery as Evident in the African-Curaçaoan 'Kunuku' Houses." In *Proceedings of the Seventeenth Congress of the International Association for Caribbean Archaeology,* ed. John H. Winter, 358–75. Rockville Centre, N.Y.: Molloy College.

———. 1999a. *African Sites Archaeology in the Caribbean.* Princeton, NJ: Marcus Wiener; Kingston: Ian Randle.

———. 1999b. "Identifying a Post-Emancipation (1863–1940) African-Curaçaoan Material Culture Assemblage." In *African Sites Archaeology in the Caribbean,* ed. J. Haviser, 221–63. Princeton, NJ: Marcus Wiener; Kingston: Ian Randle.

———. 2001. "Historical Archaeology in the Netherlands Antilles and Aruba." In *Island Lives: Historical Archaeologies of the Caribbean,* ed. P. Farnsworth, 60–81. Tuscaloosa: University of Alabama Press.

———. 2011. "Archaeology at Tanki Maraka: Investigation of a World War II U.S. Military Base on Bonaire, Netherlands Caribbean." Paper presented at the Twenty-Fourth International Association for Caribbean Archaeology, Martinique.

Haviser, J. B., and R. C. DeCorse. 1991. "African-Caribbean Interactions: A Research Plan for Curaçao Creole Culture." In *Proceedings of the Thirteenth International Congress for Caribbean Archaeology,* ed. E. N. Ayubi and J. B. Haviser, 326–37. Curaçao: Archaeological-Anthropological Institute of the Netherlands Antilles.

Heath, B. J. 1988. "Afro-Caribbean Ware: A Study of Ethnicity on St. Eustatius." PhD diss., University of Pennsylvania, Philadelphia.

———. 1991. "'Pots of Earth': Forms and Functions of Afro-Caribbean Ceramics." In *Topics in Caribbean Anthropology,* ed. J. G. Cusick and K. Barnes, 33–50. Gainesville: University of Florida Anthropology Student Association.

———. 1999. "Yabbas, Monkeys, Jugs, and Jars: A Historical Context for African Caribbean Pottery on St. Eustatius." In *African Sites: Archaeology in the Caribbean,* ed. J. B. Haviser, 196–220. Kingston: Ian Randle.

Heidtke, K. 1992. "Jamaican Red Clay Pipes." MA thesis, Department of Anthropology, Texas A&M University, College Station.

Hicks, D. 2008. "'Material Improvements': The Archaeology of Estate Landscapes in the British Leeward Islands, 1713–1838." In *Estate Landscapes: Design, Improvement, and Power in the Post-Medieval Landscape,* ed. J. Finch and K. Giles, 199–207. London: Boydell and Brewer.

Hides, S. 1996. "The Genealogy of Material Culture and Cultural Identity." In *Cultural Identity and Archaeology: The Construction of European Communities,* ed. P. Graves-Brown, S. Jones, and C. Gamble, 25–47. New York: Routledge.

Higman, B. W. 1974. "A Report on Excavations at Montpelier and Roehampton." *Jamaica Journal* 8 (1–2): 40–45.

———. 1975. "Report on Excavations at New Montpelier, St. James, Jamaica, 22–24 March and 3–18 August." Manuscript, Department of History, University of West Indies, Mona, Jamaica.

———. 1976. "Report on Excavations at New Montpelier, St. James, Jamaica, 28 December 1975 to 10 January 1976." Manuscript, Department of History, University of West Indies, Mona, Jamaica.

———. 1986a. "Jamaican Coffee Plantations, 1780–1860: A Cartographic Analysis." *Caribbean Geography* 2: 73–91.

———. 1986b. "Plantation Maps as Sources for the Study of West Indian Ethnohistory." In *Ethnohistory: A Researcher's Guide,* ed. Dennis William Wiedman, 107–36. Williamsburg, VA: Department of Anthropology, College of William and Mary.

———. 1987. "The Spatial Economy of Jamaican Sugar Plantations: Cartographic Evidence from the 18th and 19th Centuries." *Journal of Historical Geography* 13 (1): 17–19.

———. 1988. *Jamaica Surveyed: Plantation Maps and Plans of the Eighteenth and Nineteenth Centuries.* San Francisco: Institute of Jamaica Publications.

———. 1996. "Patterns of Exchange within a Plantation Economy: Jamaica at the Time of Emancipation." In *West Indies Accounts: Essays on the History of the British Caribbean and the Atlantic Economy in Honour of Richard Sheridan,* ed. R. A. McDonald. Kingston, Jamaica: University of the West Indies Press.

———. 1998. *Montpelier, Jamaica: A Plantation Community in Slavery and Freedom, 1739–1912.* Mona, Jamaica: University of the West Indies Press.

———. 1999. *Methodology and Historiography of the Caribbean.* London: Macmillan Education.

———. 2002. "The Internal Economy of Jamaican Pens, 1760–1890." In *Slavery without Sugar: Diversity in Caribbean Economy and Society since the 17th Century*, ed. V. Shepherd, 63–81. Gainesville: University Press of Florida.

———. 2005. *Plantation Jamaica, 1750–1850: Capital and Control in a Colonial Economy*. Kingston, Jamaica: University of the West Indies Press.

Hofman, C. L. 1999. "Hope Estate: pottery." In *Archaeological investigations on St. Martin (Lesser Antilles). The Sites of Norman Estate, Anse des Pères, and Hope Estate with a Contribution to the "La Hueca Problem,"* ed. C. Hofman and M.L.P. Hoogland, 149–87. Leiden: Leiden University.

Hofman, C. L., A. Boomert, A. J. Bright, M.L.P. Hoogland, S. Knippenberg, and A.V.M. Samson. 2011. "Ties with the 'Homeland': Archipelagic Interaction and the Enduring Role of the South American Mainland in the Pre-Columbian Lesser Antilles." In *Islands in the Stream: Interisland and Continental Interaction in the Caribbean*, ed. L. A. Curet and M. W. Hauser, 73–86. Tuscaloosa: University of Alabama Press.

Hofman, C. L., and E. M. Bradford. 2011. "Lavoutte Revisited, Preliminary Results of the 2009 Rescue Excavations at Cas-En-Bas, Saint Lucia." In *Proceedings of the Twenty-Third International Association for Caribbean Archaeology*, ed. S. A. Rebovich, 690–700. English Harbour, Antigua: Dockyard Museum.

Hofman, C. L., and A. J. Bright. 2004. "From Suazoid to Folk Pottery: Pottery Manufacturing Traditions in a Changing Social and Cultural Environment on Saint Lucia." *New West Indian Guide* 78 (1–2): 5–36.

———. 2010. "Towards a Pan-Caribbean Perspective of Pre-Colonial Mobility and Exchange: Preface to a special volume of the Journal of Caribbean Archaeology." *Journal of Caribbean Archaeology* (Special Publication Number 3): i–iii.

Hofman, C. L., A. J. Bright, A. Boomert, and S. Knippenberg. 2007. "Island Rhythms: The Web of Social Relationships and Interaction Networks in the Pre-Columbian Lesser Antilles." *Latin American Antiquity* 18 (3): 243–68.

Hofman, C. L., A. J. Bright, and M.L.P. Hoogland. 2006. "Archipelagic Resource Procurement and Mobility in the Northern Lesser Antilles: The View from a 3000-Year-Old Tropical Forest Campsite on Saba." *Journal of Island & Coastal Archaeology* 1 (2): 145–64.

Hofman, C. L., A. J. Bright, W. F. Keegan, and M.L.P. Hoogland. 2008. "Attractive Ideas, Desirable Goods: Examining the Late Ceramic Age Relationships between Greater and Lesser Antillean Societies." *Journal of Island and Coastal Archaeology* 3 (1): 17–34.

Hofman, C. L., A. J. Bright, and R. Rodríguez Ramos. 2010. "Crossing the Caribbean Sea. Towards a Holistic View of Pre-Colonial Mobility and Exchange." *Journal of Caribbean Archaeology* (Special Publication Number 3): 1–18.

Hofman, C. L., A. Delpuech, M.L.P. Hoogland, and M. de Waal. 2004. "Late Ceramic Age Survey of the Guadeloupean Archipelago: Grande-Terre, La Désirade and Petite-Terre." In *Late Ceramic Age Societies in the Eastern Caribbean*, ed. A. Delpuech and C. L. Hofman, 159–82. Oxford: British Archaeological Reports.

Hofman, C. L. and M.L.P. Hoogland. 2004. "Social Dynamics and Change in the Northern Lesser Antilles." In *Late Ceramic Age Societies in the Eastern Caribbean*, ed. A. Delpuech and C. L. Hofman, 47–59. Oxford: British Archaeological Reports.

———. 2011. "Unravelling the Multi-Scale Networks of Mobility and Exchange in the Pre-Colonial Circum-Caribbean." In *Communities in Contact: Essays in Archaeology, Ethnohistory and Ethnography of the Amerindian Circum-Caribbean*, ed. C. L. Hofman and A. van Duijvenbode, 14–44. Leiden: Sidestone Press.

Hofman, C. L., and M.L.P. Hoogland, eds. 1999. *Archaeological Investigations on St. Martin 1993: The Sites of Norman Estate, Hope Estate and Anse de Peres*. Basse-Terre, Guadeloupe: Direction Régionale des Affaires Culturelles de Guadeloupe, Service Régionale de l'Archéologie.

Hofman, C. L., and L. Jacobs. 2000/2001. "The Dynamics of Technology, Function and Style: A Study of Early Ceramic Age Pottery from the Caribbean." *Newsletter of the Department of Pottery Technology* (Leiden University) 18/19: 7–43.

Hofman, C. L., and A. van Duijvenbode, eds. 2011. *Communities in Contact: Essays in Archaeology, Ethnohistory and Ethnography of the Amerindian Circum-Caribbean*. Leiden: Sidestone Press.

Honychurch, L. 1997. "Crossroads in the Caribbean: A Site of Encounter and Exchange on Dominica." *World Archaeology* 28 (3): 291–304.

———. 2011. *Archaeology of Dominica*. Roseau: Dominica.

Hoogland, M. L. P., C. L. Hofman, and A. Boomert. 2011. "Argyle, Saint Vincent: New Insights on the Island Occupation of the Lesser Antilles." Paper presented at the Twenty-Fourth International Association for Caribbean Archaeology, Martinique.

Howson, J. 1995. "Colonial Goods and the Plantation Village: Consumption and the Internal Economy in Montserrat from Slavery to Freedom." Ph.D. diss., New York University.

———. 1990. "Social Relations and Material Culture: A Critique of the Archaeology of Plantation Slavery." *Historical Archaeology* 24 (4): 78–91.

Hung, Ulloa. 2005. "Early Ceramics in the Caribbean." In *Dialogues in Cuban Archaeology*, ed. L. A. Curet, S. L. Dawdy, and Gabino La Rosa Corzo, 103–24. Tuscaloosa: University of Alabama Press.

Jones, S. 1997. *The Archaeology of Ethnicity: Constructing Identities in the Past and Present*. London: Routledge.

Jouravleva, I. 2002. "Origen de la alfarería de las communicadades protoagroalfareras del la region central de Cuba." *El Caribe Arqueológico* 6: 35–43.

Keegan, W. F. 1992. *The People Who Discovered Columbus: The Prehistory of the Bahamas*. Gainesville: University Press of Florida.

———. 1994. "West Indian Archaeology. 1. Overview and Foragers." *Journal of Archaeological Research* 2: 255–84.

———. 1996. "West Indian Archaeology. 2. After Columbus." *Journal of Archaeological Research* 4: 265–94.

———. 1999. "Archaeological Investigations on Ile à Rat, Haiti: Avoid the Oid." Paper presented at 18th International Congress for Caribbean Archaeology, Grenada.

———. 2000. "West Indian Archaeology. 3. Ceramic Age." *Journal of Archaeological Research* 8: 135–67.

———. 2004. "Islands of Chaos." In *Late Ceramic Age Societies in the Eastern Caribbean*, ed. A. Delpuech and C. L. Hofman, 33–44. Oxford: Archaeopress.

———. 2007. *Benjamin Irving Rouse 1913–2006: A Biographical Memoir*. Washington, DC: National Academy of Sciences.

Keegan, W. F., S. M. Fitzpatrick, K. S. Sealey, M. J. Febvre, and P. T. Senelli. 2008. "The Role of Small Islands in Marine Subsistence Strategies: Case Studies from the Caribbean." *Human Ecology* 36: 635–54.

Keegan, W. F., C. L. Hofman, and M.L.P. Hoogland. 2007. "Saint Lucia Archaeological Research Project: An Update." *Proceedings of the Twenty-First Congress of the International Association for Caribbean Archaeology*, ed. B. Reid, H. P. Roget, and A. Curet, 1:128–40. St. Augustine, Trinidad and Tobago: School of Continuing Studies, University of the West Indies.

Keegan, W. F., and R. Rodríguez Ramos. 2007. "Archaic Origins of the Classic Taínos." In *Proceedings of the Twenty-First Congress of the International Association for Caribbean Archaeology*, ed. B. Reid, H. P. Roget, and A. Curet, 1:211–17. St. Augustine, Trinidad and Tobago: School of Continuing Studies, University of the West Indies.

Kelly, K. G. 2002. "African Diaspora Archaeology in Guadeloupe, French West Indies." *Antiquity* 76: 333–34.

———. 2004. "Historical Archaeology in the French Caribbean." *Journal of Caribbean Archaeology* (Special Issue 1): 1–10.

———. 2005. "Historical Archaeology." In *Handbook of Archaeological Methods*, ed. H.D.G. Maschner and C. Chippindale, 2:1108–37. Lanham, MD: AltaMira Press.

Kelly, K. G., and D. V. Armstrong. 1991. "Archaeological Investigations of a 19th Century Free Laborer House, Seville Estate, St. Ann's Jamaica." In *Proceedings of the Thirteenth International Congress for Caribbean Archaeology*, ed. E. N. Ayubi and J. B. Haviser, 429–35. Curaçao: Archaeological-Anthropological Institute of the Netherlands Antilles.

Kelly, K. G., and H. R. Gibson. 2003. "Plantation Village Archaeology in Guadeloupe, French West Indies." In *Proceedings of the Twentieth International Congress of Caribbean Archaeologists*, ed. Glenis Tavarez and Manuel García Arévalo, 789–98. Santo Domingo: Museo del Hombre Dominicano and Fundación García Arévalo.

Kelly, K. G., M. W. Hauser, and D. V. Armstrong. 2011. "Identity and Opportunity in Post-Slavery Jamaica." In *Out of Many, One People*, ed. J. Delle, M. Hauser, and D. V. Armstrong, 243–57. Tuscaloosa: University of Alabama Press.

Kelly, K. G., M. W. Hauser, C. Descantes, and M. Glascock. 2008. "Cabotage or Contraband: Compositional Analysis of French Colonial Ceramics." *Journal of Caribbean Archaeology* 8: 1–23.

Knippenberg, S. 2006. "Stone Artefact Production and Ex-

change among the Northern Lesser Antilles." PhD diss., Faculty of Archaeology, Leiden University.

Lalueza-Fox, C., M.T.P. Gilbert, A. J. Martinex-Fuentes, F. Calafell, and J Bertranpetit. 2003. "Mitochondrial DNA from Pre-Columbian Ciboneys from Cuba and the Prehistoric Colonization of the Caribbean." *American Journal of Physical Anthropology* 121: 97–108.

La Rosa Corzo, G. 1988. *Los Cimarrones de Cuba: Historia de Cuba*. Havana: Editorial de Ciencias Sociales.

———. 1991. *Los palenques del oriente de Cuba: Resistencia y acoso*. Havana: Editorial Academia.

———. 2003. *Runaway Slave Settlements in Cuba: Resistance and Repression*. Chapel Hill: University of North Carolina Press.

La Rosa Corzo, G., S. L. Dawdy, and L. A. Curet. 2005. *Dialogues in Cuban Archaeology*. Tuscaloosa: University of Alabama Press.

La Rosa Corzo, G., and M. T. Gonzalez. 2004. *Cazadores de esclavos: Diarios*. Havana: Fundacion Fernando Ortiz.

Leech, R. 2007. "In What Manner Did They Divide the Land? The Early Colonial Estate Landscape of Nevis and St. Kitts." In *Estate Landscapes: Design, Improvement, and Power in the Post-Medieval Landscape*, ed. J. Finch and K. Giles, 191–98. London: Boydell and Brewer.

Lenik, S. 2004. "Historical Archaeological Approaches to Afro-Cruzan Identity at Estate Lower Bethlehem, St. Croix, U.S. Virgin Islands." MA thesis, University of South Carolina.

Leshikar-Denton, P. 1991. "Underwater Investigations of the Eighteenth-Century 'Wreck of the Ten Sail.'" In *Actas del Décimo-cuarto Congreso de la Asociación Internacional de Arqueologia del Caribe* (Proceedings of the Fourteenth Congress of the International Association for Caribbean Archaeology), ed. A. Cummins and P. King, 591–94. St. Michael, Barbados: Barbados Museum and Historical Society.

Link, M. C. 1960. "Exploring the Drowned City of Port Royal." *National Geographic* 117 (2): 151–82.

Loftfield, T. C. 2001. "Creolization in Seventeenth-Century Barbados." In *Island Lives: Historical Archaeologies of the Caribbean*, ed. P. Farnsworth, 207–33. Tuscaloosa: University of Alabama Press.

Lovén, S. 1935. *Origins of the Tainan Culture, West Indies*. Göteberg, Sweden: Elanders Boktryckeri Aktiebolag.

Lugo Romera, K. M., and S. Menendez Castro. 2003. *Barrio de Campeche: Tres estudios arqueologicos*. Havana: Fundacion Fernando Ortiz.

Marx, R. F. 1967. *Excavation of the Sunken City of Port Royal, December 1965–December 1966: A Preliminary Report*. Kingston: Institute of Jamaica.

———. 1968a. "Divers of Port Royal." *Jamaica Journal* 2 (1): 15–23.

———. 1968b. "Excavating Port Royal." *Jamaica Journal* 2 (2): 12–18.

———. 1968c. "Discovery of Two Ships of Columbus." *Jamaica Journal* 2 (4): 13–17.

———. 1973. *Port Royal Rediscovered*. New York: Doubleday.

Mathewson, R. D. 1971. "CCA Demonstration Project: Restoration of the Prince of Wales Bastion, Brimstone Hill, St.

Kitts." *Caribbean Conservation Association Environmental Newsletter* 2 (2): 34–36.

——. 1972a. "History from the Earth: Archaeological Excavations at Old King's House." *Jamaica Journal* 6: 3–11.

——. 1972b. "Jamaican Ceramics: An Introduction to 18th-Century Folk Pottery in West African Tradition." *Jamaica Journal* 6: 54–56.

——. 1973. "Archaeological Analysis of Material Culture as a Reflection of Sub-Cultural Differentiation in 18th-Century Jamaica." *Jamaica Journal* 7: 25–29.

Mayes, P. 1970. "The Port Royal Project." *Caribbean Conservation Association Environmental Newsletter* 1 (1): 37–38

——. 1972. *Port Royal, Jamaica: Excavations, 1969–1970.* Kingston: Jamaica National Trust Commission.

Mayes, P., and P. A. Mayes. 1972. "Port Royal, Jamaica: The Archaeological Problems and Potential." *International Journal of Nautical Archaeology and Underwater Exploration* 1:97–112.

McClenaghan, P. E. 1988. "Drinking Glasses from Port Royal, Jamaica c. 1630–1840: A Study of Styles and Usage." MA thesis, Department of Anthropology, Texas A&M University, College Station.

McKusick, Marshall B. 1960. "The Distribution of Ceramic Styles in the Lesser Antilles, West Indies." PhD diss., Yale University.

Meniketti, M. 1998. "The Port St. George Project: An Archaeological Assessment of a Sugar Plantation and Harbor Complex in Nevis, West Indies." MA thesis, Michigan Technological University.

Mickleburgh, H. L., and J. R. Pagán-Jiménez. 2012. "New Insights into the Consumption of Maize and Other Food Plants in the Pre-Columbian Caribbean from Starch Grains Trapped in Human Dental Calculus." *Journal of Archaeological Science* 39 (7): 2468–78.

Mol, A.A.A. 2007. *Costly Giving, Giving Guaízas: Towards an Organic Model of the Exchange of Social Valuables in the Late Ceramic Age Caribbean.* Leiden: Sidestone Press.

Murphy, A. R. 1996. "The Archaeology and Reconstruction of an Eighteenth-Century Windmill on Antigua, W.I." Paper presented at the Twenty-Ninth Annual Chacmool, University of Calgary.

——. 2001. "Plantation Systems on Antigua, W.I.: New Insights from an Archaeological Perspective." Paper presented at the UNESCO Experts Meeting, Slave Route Project, Paramaribo, Suriname.

——. 2011. "Preliminary Research at Shirley Heights, Antigua, an Eighteenth-Century British Military Outpost." Paper presented at the Twenty-fourth International Association for Caribbean Archaeology, Martinique.

Murphy, A. R., D. J. Hozjan, C. N. de Mille, and A. A. Levison. 2000. "Pre-Columbian Gems and Ornamental Materials from Antigua, West Indies." *Gems and Gemology* 36 (3): 234–45.

Nagelkerken, W. P. 2000. *Ceramics of Orange Bay, St. Eustatius, Netherlands Antilles.* Curaçao, Netherlands Antilles: Stichting Marien Archeologisch Onderzoek Nederlandse Antillen.

Newsom, L. A. 1993. "Native West Indian Plant Use." PhD diss., Department of Anthropology, University of Florida, Gainesville.

Nicholson, D. 1979. "The Dating of West Indian Historical Sites by the Analysis of Ceramic Sherds." *Journal of the Virgin Islands Archaeological Society* 7: 52–74.

——. 1990. "Afro-Antiguan Folk Pottery and Emancipation." *Actas del undecimo Congreso, Asociación Internacional de Arqueologia del Caribe* (Proceedings of the Eleventh Congress of the International Association for Caribbean Archaeology), ed. A.G.P. Tekakis, I. V. Arenas, M. S. Obediente, 433–37. Puerto Rico: La Fundación Arqueológica, Antropológica e Histórica de Puerto Rico.

——. 1995 "Blood and Mud: The Naval Hospital and Underwater Artifacts, English Harbour, Antiqua." In *Proceedings of the XV International Congress for Caribbean Archaeology*, ed. R. E. Alegría and M. A. Rodríguez Lopéz, 45–60. San Juan, Puerto Rico: Centro de Estudios Avanzados de Puerto Rico y el Caribe.

Olazagasti, Ignacio. 1997. "The Material Culture of the Taíno Indians." In *The Indigenous People of the Caribbean,* ed. S. M. Wilson, 131–39. Gainesville: University Press of Florida.

Oliver, J. R. 1999. "The La Hueca Problem in Puerto Rico and the Caribbean: Old Problems, New Perspectives, Possible Solution." In *Archaeological Investigations on St. Martin (Lesser Antilles). The site of Norman Estate, Anse des Peres and Hop Estate with a Contribution to the La Hueca problem,* ed. Corrine L. Hofman and Menno L. P. Hoogland, 253–97. Leiden: Leiden University.

Ortega, E., and C. Fondeur. 1978a. *Arqueología de los monumentos históricos de Santo Domingo.* San Pedro de Macorís: Universidad Central del Este.

——. 1978b. *Estudio de la ceramica del Periodo Indo-hispano de la Antigua Concepcion de la Vega.* Santo Domingo, República Dominicana: Fundacion Ortega Alvarez.

——. 1979. *Arqueología de la Casa del Cordon.* Santo Domingo: Fundacion Ortega Alvarez.

Ostapkowicz, J., C. Bronk Ramsey, A. Wiedenhoeft, F. Brock, T. Higham and S. Wilson. 2011. "This Relic of Antiquity: 5th-15th century wood carvings from the southern Lesser Antilles." In *Communities in Contact: Essays in Archaeology, Ethnohistory and Ethnography of the Amerindian Circum-Caribbean,* ed. C. L. Hofman and A. van Duijvenbode, 137–70. Leiden: Sidestone Press.

Pagán-Jiménez, J. R. 2011. "Early Phytocultural Processes in the Pre-Colonial Antilles: A Pan-Caribbean Survey for an Ongoing Starch Grain Research." In *Communities in Contact. Essays in Archaeology, Ethnohistory, and Ethnography of the Amerindian circum-Caribbean,* ed. C. L. Hofman, and A. van Duijvenbode, 87–116. Leiden: Sidestone Press.

Pagán-Jiménez, J. R., and R. Rodríguez Ramos. 2007. "Sobre el origen de la Agricultura en las Antillas." In *Proceedings of the Twenty-First Congress of the International Association of Caribbean Archaeology,* ed. ed. Basil A. Reid, Henry Petitjean Roget, and Antonio Curet, 1:252–59. St. Augustine, Trinidad: University of West Indies.

Paquette, R. L., and S. L. Engerman, eds. 1996. *The Lesser Antilles in the Age of European Expansion.* Gainesville: University Press of Florida.

Petersen, J. B. 1996. "Archaeology of Trants, Montserrat. Part 3. Chronological and Settlement Data." *Annals of the Carnegie Museum* 63: 323–61.

———. 1997. "Taino, Island-Carib, and Prehistoric Amerindian Economies in the West Indies: Tropical Forest Adaptations to Island Environments." In *The Indigenous People of the Caribbean,* ed. S. M. Wilson, 118–30. Gainesville: University Press of Florida.

Petersen, J. B., C. L. Hofman, and L. A. Curet. 2004. "Time and culture: chronology and taxonomy in the Eastern Caribbean and the Guianas." In *Late Ceramic Age Societies in the Eastern Caribbean,* ed. A. Delpuech and C. L. Hofman, 17–33. Oxford: British Archaeological Reports.

Petersen, J. B., and D. Watters. 1988. "Afro-Montserratian Ceramics from the Harney Site Cemetery, Montserrat, West Indies." *Annals of the Carnegie Museum* 67: 167–87.

———. 1995. "A Preliminary Analysis of Amerindian Ceramics for the Trants Site, Montserrat." In *Actas del undecimo Congreso, Asociación Internacional de Arqueologia del Caribe* (Proceedings of the Eleventh Congress of the International Association for Caribbean Archaeology), ed. A.G.P. Tekakis, I. V. Arenas, and M. S. Obediente, 131–40. Puerto Rico: La Fundación Arqueológica, Antropológica e Histórica de Puerto Rico.

Petersen, J. B., D. Watters, and D. Nicholson. 1999. "Continuity and Syncretism in Afro-Caribbean Ceramics from the Northern Lesser Antilles." In *African Sites: Archaeology in the Caribbean,* ed. J. B. Haviser, 157–220. Kingston: Ian Randle.

Platzer, E. 1979. "The Potters of Nevis." MA thesis, University of Denver.

Prat Puig, F. 1980. *Significado de un Conjunto Cerámico Hispano del Siglo XVI de Santiago de Cuba.* Santiago de Cuba: Editorial Oriente.

Priddy, A. 1975. "The 17th- and 18th-Century Settlement Pattern of Port Royal." *Jamaica Journal* 9 (2–3): 8–16.

Pulsipher, L. 1986. *Models to Guide the Study of West Indian Slave Villages.* Charleston, S.C.: American Society for Ethnohistory.

———. 1991. "Galways Plantation, Montserrat." In *Seeds of Change,* ed. H. J. Viola and C. Margolis, 139–59. Washington, DC: Smithsonian Institution Press.

———. 1993. "Changing Roles in Life Cycles of Women in Traditional West Indian Houseyards." In *Women and Change in the Caribbean,* ed. J. Momesen, 50–64. London: James Curry.

Pulsipher, L. M., and C. M. Goodwin. 1982. "A Sugar-Boiling House at Galways: An Irish Sugar Plantation in Montserrat, West Indies." *Post-Medieval Archaeology* 16: 21–27.

———. 2000. "'Here Where the Old Time People Be': Reconstructing the Landscapes of the Slavery and Post-Slavery Era on Montserrat, West Indies." In *African Sites Archaeology in the Caribbean,* ed. J. B. Haviser, 9–37. Kingston: Ian Randle.

Rainey, F. G. 1940. "Porto Rican Archaeology." *Scientific Survey of Porto Rico and the Virgin Islands* 18 (1): 1–208.

Reeves, M. 1997. "'By Their Own Labor': Enslaved Africans' Survival Strategies on Two Jamaican Plantations." PhD diss., Syracuse University.

Reeves, M. 2011. "Household Market Activities among Early Nineteenth-Century Jamaican Slaves: An Archaeological Case Study from Two Slave Settlements." In *Out of Many, One People,* ed. J. Delle, M. Hauser, and D. V. Armstrong, 183–209. Tuscaloosa: University of Alabama Press.

Reid, B. A. 2004. "Reconstructing the Saladoid Religion in Trinidad and Tobago." *Journal of Caribbean History* 38 (2): 243–78.

———. 2005. *Archaeological Excavations of Lovers' Retreat (TOB-69), Tobago (Phases 2&3), Final Report.* Conducted for Island Investment Limited (May 2005).

———. 2007. "Note from the Senior Editor." In *Proceedings of the Twenty-First International Association of Caribbean Archaeology,* ed. Basil A. Reid, Henry Petitjean Roget, and Antonio Curet, 1:ix–xiii; 2:v–ix. St. Augustine: School of Continuing Studies, The University of the West Indies.

———. 2008. *Archaeology and Geoinformatics: Case-studies from the Caribbean.* Tuscaloosa: University of Alabama Press.

———. 2009. *Myths and Realities of Caribbean History.* Tuscaloosa: University of Alabama Press.

———. 2011. "Passing of a Pioneer Researcher in Caribbean Archaeology." http://peabody.yale.edu/sites/default/files/documents/anthropology/Passing%20of%20a%20Pioneer%20Researcher%20in%20Caribbean%20Archaeology.pdf. Accessed April 3, 2013.

Righter, E. 1997. "The Ceramics, Art, and Material Culture of Early Ceramic Period in the Caribbean Islands." In *The Indigenous People of the Caribbean,* ed. Samuel Wilson, 70–79. Gainesville: University Press of Florida.

Robertson, J. 2005. *Gone Is the Ancient Glory: Spanish Town, Jamaica, 1534–2000.* Kingston: Ian Randle.

Rodríguez Ramos, R. 2007. "Puerto Rican Precolonial History Etched in Stone." PhD diss., Department of Anthropology, University of Florida, Gainesville.

———. 2010. *Rethinking Puerto Rican Precolonial History.* Tuscaloosa, Alabama: Alabama University Press.

Rodríguez Ramos, R., and J. Pagán-Jiménez. 2006. "Interacciones multivectoriales en el Circum-Caribe precolonial: Un vistazo desde las Antillas." *Caribbean Studies* 34 (2): 103–43.

Rodríguez Ramos, R., J. Torres, and J. R. Oliver. 2010. "Rethinking Time in Caribbean Archaeology." In *Island Shores, Distant Pasts: Archaeological and Biological Approaches to the Pre-Columbian Settlement of the Caribbean,* ed. S. Fitzpatrick and A. H. Ross, 21–53. Gainesville: University Press of Florida.

Roe, Peter G. 1989. "A Grammatical Analysis of Cedrosan Saladoid Vessel Form Categories and Surface Decoration: Aesthetic and Technical Styles in Early Antillean Ceramics." In *Early Ceramic Population Lifeways and Adaptive Strategies in the Caribbean,* ed. Peter E. Siegel, 267–382. Oxford: British Archaeological Reports.

Rogoziński, J. 1999. *A Brief History of the Caribbean: From the Arawak and Carib to the Present.* New York: Facts on File.

Ross, A. H., and D. H. Ubelaker. 2010. "A Morphometric Approach to Taíno Biological Distance in the Caribbean." In

Island Shores, Distant Pasts: Archaeological and Biological Approaches to the Pre-Columbian Settlement of the Caribbean, ed. S. M. Fitzpatrick and A. H. Ross, 108–26. Gainesville: University Press of Florida.

Rouse, I. 1939. *Prehistory in Haiti: A Study in Method.* New Haven, CT: Department of Anthropology, Yale University.

———. 1941. "An Analysis of the Artifacts of the 1914–1915 Porto Rican Survey." In *Scientific Survey of Porto Rico and the Virgin Islands*, vol. 18, part 2, 336–62, 442–53. New York: The New York Academy of Sciences.

———. 1948. "The West Indies: An Introduction to the Ciboney." In *The Circum-Caribbean Tribes*, vol. 4 of *Handbook of South American Indians*, ed. J. H. Steward, 497–503. Washington, DC: Government Printing Office.

———. 1952. "Porto Rican Prehistory: Introduction: Excavations in the West and North." In *Scientific Survey of Porto Rico and the Virgin Islands*, vol. 18, part 4, 463–578. New York: New York Academy of Sciences.

———. 1989. "Peoples and Cultures of the Saladoid Frontier in the Greater Antilles." In *Early Ceramic Population Lifeways and Adaptive Strategies in the Caribbean*, ed. P. E. Siegel, 383–404. Oxford: British Archaeological Reports.

———. 1992. *The Tainos: Rise and Decline of the People Who Greeted Columbus.* New Haven, CT: Yale University Press.

Rouse, Irving, and R. E. Alegría. 1990. *Excavations at Maria de la Cruz Cave and Hacienda Grande Village Site, Loiza, Puerto Rico.* New Haven, CT: Department of Anthropology, Yale University.

Rouse, Irving, and L. Allaire. 1978. "Caribbean." In *Chronologies in New World Archaeology*, ed. R. E. Taylor and C. W. Meighan, 431–81. New York: Academic Press.

Samson, A.V.M. 2010. *Renewing the House: Trajectories of Social Life in the Yucayeque (Community) of El Cabo, Higüey, Dominican Republic, AD 800 to 1504.* Leiden: Faculty of Archaeology, Leiden University.

Schroedl, Gerald F., and Todd M. Ahlman. 2002. "The Maintenance of Cultural and Personal Identities of Enslaved Africans and British Soldiers at the Brimstone Hill Fortress, St. Kitts, West Indies." *Historical Archaeology* 36 (4): 38–52.

Schurr, T. G. 2010. "Coastal Waves and Island Hopping: A Genetic View of Caribbean Prehistory in the Context of New World Colonization." In *Island Shores, Distant Pasts: Archaeological and Biological Approaches to the Pre-Columbian Settlement of the Caribbean*, ed. S. M. Fitzpatrick and A. H. Ross, 177–98. Gainesville: University Press of Florida.

Scott, M. F., and W. Keegan. 2007. "Human Impacts and Adaptations in the Caribbean Islands: A Historical Ecology Approach." *Earth and Environmental Science Transactions of the Royal Society of Edinburgh* 98: 29–45.

Siegel, P. 1992. "Ideology, Power, and Social Complexity in Prehistoric Puerto Rico." PhD diss., Department of Anthropology, State University of New York at Binghamton.

———. 2005. *Ancient Boriquen: Archaeology and Ethnohistory of Native Puerto Rico.* Tuscaloosa: University of Alabama Press.

Siegel, P. E., and E. Righter, eds. 2011. *Protecting Heritage in the Caribbean.* Tuscaloosa: University of Alabama Press.

Singleton, T. A. 2001. "Slavery and Spatial Dialectics on Cuban Coffee Plantations." *World Archaeology* 33 (1): 98–114.

———. 2006. "African Diaspora Archaeology in Dialogue." In *Afro-Atlantic Dialogues,* ed. K. A. Yelvington, 249–88. Santa Fe, NM: School for American Research.

Singleton, T. A., and M. A. de Souza Torres 2009. "Archaeologies of the African Diaspora: Brazil, Cuba, United States." In *International Handbook for Historical Archaeology*, ed. Teresita Majewski and David Gaimster, 449–69. New York: Springer.

Sloane, H. 1707–25. *Voyage to the Islands Madera, Barbados, Nieves, S. Christophers and Jamaica, with the Natural History of the Herbs and Trees, Four-Footed Beasts, Fishes, Birds, Insects, Reptiles, etc. of the Last of Those Islands.* London: Printed by B. M. for the author.

Smith C. W. 1995. "Analysis of the Weight Assemblage of Port Royal, Jamaica." PhD diss., Department of Anthropology, Texas A&M University, College Station.

Smith, F. H. 2005. *Caribbean Rum: A Social and Economic History.* Gainesville: University Press of Florida.

———. 2008. *The Archaeology of Alcohol and Drinking.* Gainesville: University Press of Florida.

Smith, F. H., and K. Watson. 2009. "Urbanity, Sociability, and Commercial Exchange in the Barbados Sugar Trade: A Comparative Colonial Archaeological Perspective on Bridgetown, Barbados, in the Seventeenth Century." In "Centering the Caribbean: Landscapes and Scale in Caribbean Historical Archaeology," ed. M. W. Hauser and K. G. Kelly, special issue of the *International Journal of Historical Archaeology* 13 (1): 63–79.

Steward, J. H. 1948. *The Circum-Caribbean Tribes.* Vol. 4 of *Handbook of South American Indians.* Washington, DC: Government Printing Office.

Tabío, E. 1984. "Nueva periodización para el studio de las communicadades aborigines de Cuba." In *Islas (Universidad Central de las Villas)* 78 (May–August): 37–52.

Taylor, D., and B. J. Hoff. 1980. "The Linguistic Repertory of the Island-Carib in the Seventeenth Century: The Men's Language—A Carib Pidgin?" *International Journal of American Linguistics* 46 (4): 301–12.

Terrell, M. M. 2004. *The Jewish Community of Early Colonial Nevis: A Historical Archaeological Study.* Gainesville: University Press of Florida.

Torres, J. M., and R. Rodríguez Ramos. 2008. "The Caribbean: A Continent Divided by Water." In *Archaeology and Geoinformatics: Case Studies from the Caribbean*, ed. B. Reid, 13–29. Tuscaloosa: University of Alabama Press.

Trussel, T. D. 2004. "Artifacts of Ambition: How the 17th-Century Middle Class at Port Royal, Jamaica, Foreshadowed the Consumer Revolution." MA thesis, Department of Anthropology, Texas A&M University, College Station.

University College of London Department of History. 2013. Legacies of British Slave Ownership. http://www.ucl.ac.uk/lbs/. Accessed April 26, 2013.

Valcárcel Rojas, R., M. Martinón-Torres, J. Cooper, and T. Rehren. 2010. "Turey Treasure in the Caribbean." In *Beyond the Blockade: New Currents in Cuban Archaeology*, ed. S. Kepecs, A. Curet, and G. de la Rosa, 160–25. Tuscaloosa: University of Alabama Press.

Veloz Maggiolo, M. 1976. *Medioambiente y adaptación humana en la prehistoria de Santo Domingo*. Vol. 1. Santo Domingo: Editorial de la Universidad Autónoma de Santo Domingo.

———. 1997. "The Daily Life of the Taíno people." In *Taíno: Pre-Columbian Art and Culture from the Caribbean,* ed. F. Bercht, E. Brodsky, J. A. Farmer, and D. Taylor, 34–35. New York: Monacelli Press.

Veloz Maggiolo, M., and B. Vega. 1982. "The Antillean Preceramic: A New Approximation." *Journal of New World Archaeology* 5: 33–44.

Versteeg, A. H., and K. Schinkel, eds. 1992. *The Archaeology of St. Eustatius: The Golden Rock Site*. St. Eustatius: The St. Eustatius Historical Foundation.

Victor, P. E. 1941. *La Poterie de Sainte-Anne (Martinique)*. Fort-de-France, Martinique: Impr. officielle.

Watters, D. R. 1987. "Excavations at the Harney Site Slave Cemetery, Montserrat, West Indies." *Annals of Carnegie Museum* 56 (18): 289–318.

———. 1994a. "Archaeology of Trants, Montserrat. Part 1. Field Methods and Artifact Density Distributions." *Annals of the Carnegie Museum* 63: 265–95.

———. 1994b. "Mortuary Patterns at the Harney Site Slave Cemetery, Montserrat, in Caribbean Perspective." *Historical Archaeology* 28 (3): 56–73.

———. 2011. "Is the Archaeology of World War II Now a Valid Field of Study?" Paper presented at the Twenty-Fourth International Association for Caribbean Archaeology, Martinique.

Watters, D. R., and J. Petersen. 1988. "Afro-Montserratian Ceramics from the Harney Site Cemetery, Montserrat, West Indies." *Annals of the Carnegie Museum* 57: 167–87.

Wilkie, L. A. 1995. "Magic and Empowerment on the Plantation: An Archaeological Consideration of African-American World View." *Southeastern Archaeology* 14 (2): 136–48.

———. 2000a. "Culture Bought: Evidence of Creolization in the Consumer Goods of an Enslaved Bahamian Family." *Historical Archaeology* 34 (3): 10–26.

———. 2000b. "Evidence of African Continuities in Material Culture of Clifton Plantation, Bahamas." In *African Sites Archaeology in the Caribbean*, ed. J. B. Haviser, 264–75. Kingston: Ian Randle.

Wilkie, L. A., and K. Bartoy. 2000. "A Critical Archaeology Revisited." *Current Anthropology* 41 (5): 747–77.

Wilkie, L. A., and P. Farnsworth. 1999. "Trade and the Construction of Bahamian Identity: A Multiscalar Exploration." *International Journal of Historical Archaeology* 3 (4): 283–320.

———. 2005. *Sampling Many Pots: An Archaeology of Memory and Tradition at a Bahamian Plantation*. Gainesville: University Press of Florida.

Williams, Eric. 1944/2005. *Capitalism and Slavery*. Chapel Hill: University of North Carolina Press.

Wilson, S. M. 1990. *Hispaniola: Caribbean Chiefdoms in the Age of Columbus*. Tuscaloosa: University of Alabama Press.

———. 2007. *The Archaeology of the Caribbean*. Cambridge: Cambridge University Press.

Wilson, S. M., ed. 1997. *The Indigenous People of the Caribbean*. Gainesville: University Press of Florida.

Woodward, R. P. 2011. "Feudalism or Agrarian Capitalism? The Archaeology of the Early Sixteenth-Century Spanish Sugar Industry." In *Out of Many, One People*, ed. J. Delle, M. Hauser, and D. V. Armstrong, 23–40. Tuscaloosa: University of Alabama Press.

Afro-Caribbean Earthenwares

R. Grant Gilmore III and Kevin Farmer

Afro-Caribbean earthenware is a ceramic type that is ubiquitous on many Caribbean historical archaeology sites. Produced by both enslaved and free blacks in the region, these low-fired coarse earthenwares were made from locally obtained clays and tempers and were sold in local and regional markets by their makers. As with the Afro-Colonoware (or Colonoware) found in North America, there is some debate about whether all these vessels were made by people of African heritage.

The environmental, economic, and social environments under which enslaved Africans produced these earthenwares differed across the West Indies, resulting in considerable variation in the degree of African cultural retentions in these ceramics. Research has shown that in Antigua and Barbuda, African material cultural retentions were freely expressed under the more oppressive conditions enslaved individuals endured there. Leland Ferguson (1992) was a pioneer in addressing possible West African characteristics found in the ceramics produced by the enslaved in South Carolina. Barbara Heath (1998) has documented vessel types and forms for Afro-Caribbean pots excavated on St. Eustatius. Heath observed contemporary potters on Nevis to compare their work with pots she analyzed on St. Eustatius and was able to successfully build a typology for St. Eustatius Afro-Caribbean wares and provide some ideas about the functions of the various vessel types. However, she was unable to establish specific relationships with potters or pottery on other West Indian islands.

Ceramic samples obtained from a range of West Indian islands have been compared using both petrographic analyses and vessel forms. A wide variety of vessel forms are found among Afro-Caribbean potters. Heath (1998) and Gilmore (2005) have both described the diversity of vessel forms found across the Caribbean. Vessel forms are defined according to several characteristics and can be classified as being derived from European designs, African forms, or a hybrid of both pottery traditions. Vessels with handles and flat bottoms can generally be considered to have derived from European designs. Round or globular bottoms are common in West African pottery traditions. Hybrid forms may incorporate elements of both, such as handles on a round or globular vessel. Round-bottom cooking vessels have been excavated on Antigua, Jamaica, and St. Eustatius. Both in West Africa and the West Indies, pots with rounded bottoms were placed directly in coals during cooking. Many of the vessels recovered from St. Eustatius were burned and coated in soot from this activity. Hybrid forms including flat-bottomed handle-less cooking or storage vessels have been found on St. Croix and St. Eustatius. Vessels with lids have been recovered archaeologically from Jamaica and Barbados.

Particularly noteworthy are jugs with handles and spouts known as "monkeys." Monkey jugs from various Caribbean territories are illustrated in Figure A.1. The cultural derivation of these vessel forms is not known; they may represent a design developed in the West Indies. Some have suggested that all of these vessels may date to the post-emancipation period, but their presence in eighteenth-century archaeological contexts suggests otherwise. In addition, they bear some similarity to the *hidroceramo* forms produced in Spain and Mexico. In Figure A.1, the jug from Barbados (BAR) has a distinct foot ring while the other two vessels have rounded bottoms. The jug from Montserrat tapers more sharply, in contrast to the more squat form characteristic of the St. Eustatius (EUS) jugs. Carafes (vessels with flared lips used for serving water) have also been found on both St. Eustatius EUS (g) and Jamaica JAM (h, j). Gilmore has also noted this on vessel forms from Barbados BAR (d). These are all European designs that exhibit no aspects of West African pottery traditions. Among the vessel forms seen in Figure A.1 from Barbados is a "flower pot" BAR (c), which Heath (1998) indicates also has been found on St. Eustatius. Although vessel forms exhibit a great deal of variation among the islands, they also provide evidence of the likely possibility of a shared corpus of pottery forms

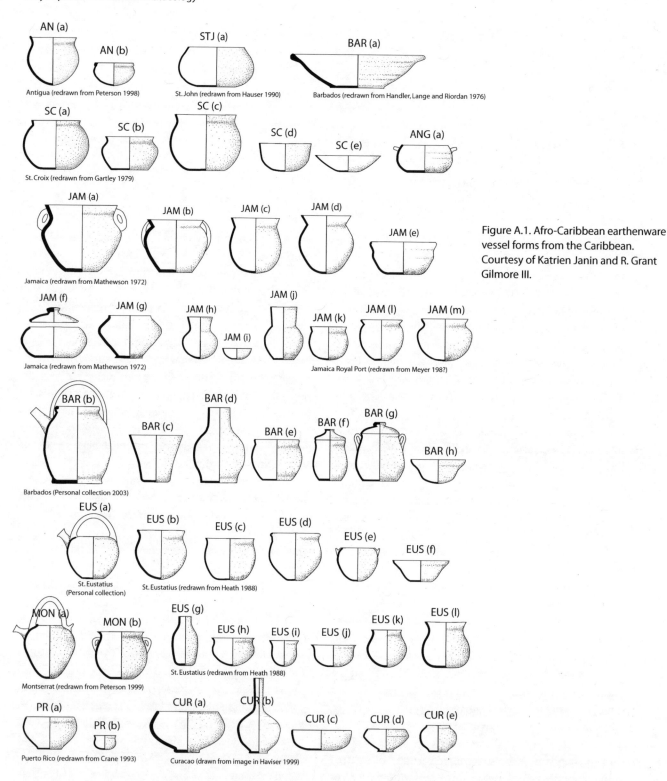

Figure A.1. Afro-Caribbean earthenware vessel forms from the Caribbean. Courtesy of Katrien Janin and R. Grant Gilmore III.

across the West Indies. This implies an exchange of ideas, pottery technologies, and material culture uses among people of African heritage both before and after emancipation.

Ongoing X-ray fluorescence, neutron activation, and petrographic work across the West Indies, especially in the French Islands and the Virgin Islands, also indi-

cate a strong interisland trade in ceramics among the enslaved. Islands in the region are in close proximity to one another and had well-established trade connections throughout the eighteenth century. The results of the petrographic analysis and analysis of vessel forms indicate that there was some cultural exchange between St. Eustatius, Antigua, St. Croix, and Nevis and probably among other islands, including Barbados and Jamaica. Even with current data, it is not possible to determine whether the enslaved or their masters were traveling between the islands with the express purpose of trading Afro-Caribbean earthenwares and/or their contents. However, two facts support the supposition that the enslaved themselves were traders. First, documentary evidence for St. Eustatius indicates that the enslaved were active participants in interisland trade for their owners by acting as tradesmen and by crewing and piloting vessels among these islands. Bermuda also had ships' crews comprised of the enslaved. Second, the product was produced almost exclusively by people of African heritage and most often by the enslaved. It is also possible that enterprising enslaved tradesmen acted as middlemen in an active trade economy of Afro-Caribbean earthenware vessels (and their contents) among many Caribbean islands. Research on Afro-Caribbean earthenware embodies a confluence of research themes relating to historical archaeology, archaeometry, foodways, rituals, and power relationships between dominant and subordinate groups.

Further Reading

Ferguson, L. G. 1992. *Uncommon Ground: Archaeology and Early African America, 1650–1800.* Washington, DC: Smithsonian Institution Press.

Gilmore, R. G. 2005. "The Archaeology of New World Slave Societies: A Comparative Analysis with Particular Reference to St. Eustatius, Netherlands Antilles." PhD diss., University College London.

Hauser, M. W. 2008. *An Archaeology of Black Markets: Local Ceramics and Local Economies in Eighteenth-Century Jamaica.* Gainesville: University Press of Florida.

Heath, B. J. 1998. "Yabbas, Monkeys, Jugs, and Jars: An Historical Context for African-Caribbean Pottery on St. Eustatius." In *African Sites Archaeology in the Caribbean*, ed. J. B. Haviser, 196–220. Princeton, NJ: Markus Weiner Publishers.

Kelly, K. G., with Mark Hauser and Douglas V. Armstrong. 2007. "What to Do with 'Other' Ceramics: Inter-Colonial Trade of French Coarse Earthenware." In *Proceedings of the Twenty-First Congress of the International Association for Caribbean Archaeology*, ed. Basil A. Reid, Henry Petitjean Roget, and Antonio Curet, 2:579–87. Trinidad: University of the West Indies.

Petersen, J. B., D. R. Watters, and D. V. Nicholson. 1998. "Continuity and Syncretism in Afro-Caribbean Ceramics from the Northern Lesser Antilles." In *African Sites Archaeology in the Caribbean*, ed. J. B. Haviser, 157–95. Princeton, NJ: Markus Weiner Publishers.

See also Archaeometry; Drax Hall Estate (Jamaica); Spanish Colonial Ceramic Types.

Agricultural Earthworks (The Guianas)

Stéphen Rostain

Today in Amazonia, most Indians cultivate with the slash-and-burn technique, which involves opening up of an area in the rainforest by cutting and burning trees. Ash has been used to fertilize poor Amazonian soils on occasion. There are many variations of shifting cultivation, including slash/mulch and agroforestry systems. It is often assumed that pre-Columbian Indians mainly used the same technique. However, various other elaborated agricultural techniques were developed during pre-Columbian times, such as those relating to *terra preta* (black earth), *várzeas* (fertile floodplains along the main Amazonian rivers), and raised fields. It is now accepted that the first agricultural inhabitants of the rainforest used complex farming techniques that left important and long-lasting modifications on the landscape.

Ancient Raised Fields

Ancient raised fields are known from various parts of South America, especially around the periphery of the Amazon rainforest. Most of these earthworks date back to the first millennium AD, but some were made as early as 1000 BC and were used until the period of European conquest and beyond. They are located in savannas, Andean valleys, and flooded areas generally. In fact, the main reason for building raised fields is to control excess water for agricultural purposes.

Pre-Columbian Indians also used the raised-field technique to cultivate in the coastal swamps in the Guianas, comprised of French Guiana, Suriname, and Guyana (Rostain 1994). This technique is based on building

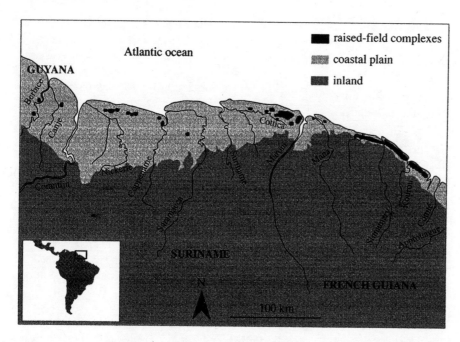

Figure A.2. Map of raised-field areas in the Guianas. Courtesy of Stéphen Rostain.

mounds above the water level. The goal is to concentrate fertile matter from the organic horizon level of the swamp. Raised fields were not always sufficient to protect cultivated plants from flooding, so canals and ditches were also dug for the purpose of controlling variations in water levels. Raised fields had two main functions: 1) to secure a dry location for cultivation; and 2) to concentrate fertile material.

Thousands of pre-Columbian raised fields surrounded by ditches are presently located in the coastal zone of the Guianas (McKey and Rostain 2010). Raised fields are classified on the basis of their size, shape, and topographical location (Rostain 2008). This last criterion is indicative of differences in adaptation to both hydrographical conditions and the nature of the soil. In French Guiana, raised fields have been recently dated for the first time to the eleventh and fourteenth centuries (McKey et al. 2010).

Raised-field complexes are found along the coast of the Guianas from central Guyana up to central French Guiana, which represents a distance of approximately 600 kilometers (Figure A.2). However, colonial and modern earthworks, especially Dutch and English polders, destroyed many sites during the eighteenth century.

Types of Raised Fields

Four types of raised fields have been identified:

1) Ridged fields are found in the Guianas (Figure A.3). They are elongated and narrow, measuring between 1 and 3 meters in width, 5 to 30 meters in length, and 30 to 80 centimeters in height. They take the shape of the slope between the sandy ridges and the swamp. Their distribution is related to both altitude and existing water levels. At the foot of the Quaternary sand ridges, elongated raised fields are positioned in the direction of the slope to allow for easy drainage. Near the top of the sandy bars, the ridged fields are arranged perpendicular to the slope for optimal water retention. In Suriname, two types of raised fields are distinguished: regular and irregular ones. On the western coast of Suriname, irregular raised fields are located near residential artificial mounds (Boomert 1980). They are distributed arbitrarily or arranged in groups of 2 to 15. They are oval shaped, measuring between 3 and 6.5 meters wide, 8 to 140 meters long, with an average of four to five meters wide and twenty to thirty meters long. In eastern Guyana, raised fields are mostly rectangular and are distributed in a linear configuration. They are associated with a residential mound between the Canje and Berbice Rivers.

2) Large raised fields, which range in size from 2 to 5 meters in diameter and from 30 to 100 centimeters tall (Figure A.4). These raised fields, generally round in shape, are found in eastern Suriname and around Kourou and Sinnamary in French Guiana, but they are more square or rectangular near Cayenne Island. On the eastern coast and in some areas of the western coast of Suriname, the regular raised fields have rounded-off rectangular or square shapes. Their size ranges from 3 to 4 meters wide, 4 to 30 meters long and 50 to 100 centimeters high. They are clearly visible on aerial photographs. These large raised fields are located in the most flooded areas, and their sizes are smaller in the deepest swamps.

Figure A.3. Ridged raised fields in the Lower Mana in western French Guiana. Courtesy of Stéphen Rostain.

Figure A.4. Large raised fields west of Kourou in French Guiana. Courtesy of Stéphen Rostain.

3) Medium-sized raised fields can be round, square, or rectangular and are found only in French Guiana. Their size ranges from 1.5 to 3 meters diameter and 20 to 30 centimeters tall. They occur in large clusters. They were originally placed in open areas, but vegetation has grown in these areas since the Indians left, and today they are sometimes under forest cover so it is not possible to see them on aerial photographs.

4) Small, rounded raised fields, which range in size from 50 to 100 centimeters in diameter and from 20 to 50 centimeters tall. They are found only in French Guiana and are almost invisible on aerial photographs at a scale of 1:10,000. Known cases were found during ground surveys. They cover the entire surface of the seasonally flooded savannas, which dried out in August.

Local Differences

A general study of the raised fields emphasizes local differences along the coast of the Guianas. In eastern Guy-

ana, elongated raised fields are distributed perpendicular to a river. In western Suriname, complexes are made of small groups of elongated raised fields. In eastern Suriname, rectangular and square raised fields are located along sandy bars. In the Lower Mana in French Guiana, parallel and ridged fields are in flooded depressions. Between the Organabo and Sinnamary Rivers, savannas are covered by a large number of rounded medium-sized raised fields. Between the Sinnamary and Kourou rivers, rounded or square raised fields, associated with ridged fields, are located in the savannas and along the edge of the sandy ridges. Between the Kourou River and Cayenne Island, rounded or square raised fields cover the savannas.

Along the French Guiana coast, raised fields are generally arranged roughly in squares, and the largest ones are often located in the deepest and wettest areas. The raised fields seem to be organized by homogeneous areas of an average size of 0.5 hectares each, placed side by side. A precise stereoscopic comparison of aerial photographs with field data shows that the raised fields were made and situated on the landscape according to the differences in water levels during the two annual seasons (Rostain 1994). In fact, water was the main physical constraint that determined both the shape and the topographical location of these structures. However, shape and location were not always sufficient to prevent the drowning of the raised fields. For this reason, it was necessary to surround some groups of raised fields with a belt ditch. In some cases, the checkerboard distribution of the ridged fields also reflected the need to control the water level. In some areas, such as in the Iracoubo surroundings, the whole surface of the lower area is covered by raised fields, and in other areas, such as in Kourou area, only the edge of the sandy ridges has raised fields.

Identification of Cultivated Plants

One of the important aspects of the raised field study is the proper identification of cultivated plants. Phytoliths, pollen, and starch grains have been collected and identified. Phytolith and pollen from raised fields were analyzed like starch grains from sherds of ceramic griddles from the nearby domestic dwellings. Based on the results of these analyses, the main plants cultivated on raised fields were maize (*Zea mays*), manioc (*Manihot esculenta*), sweet potato (*Ipomoea batatas*), and gourd (*Cucurbita*). Maize, manioc, and chili pepper were cooked on griddles, suggesting that these plants were both cultivated on raised fields and consumed in the villages.

The first raised fields were made in Suriname in AD 350 by the Barrancoid inhabitants of western Guyana. However, most of the earthworks are associated with Arauquinoid sites in Guyana, Suriname, and French Guiana (Rostain 2008). Along the coast of the Guianas, Arauquinoid culture spread from the middle Orinoco to the coast of the Guianas. The first Arauquinoid raised fields were made from AD 650. These became more common and eventually spread extensively along the coast up to Cayenne Island between AD 1000 and 1450. This represents a territory of approximately 600 kilometers long where the raised field technique was intensively used for almost 1,000 years prior to the European conquest.

Social Complexity

There is evidence for the emergence of chiefdoms on the coast of the Guianas during this period. The chiefdom is the prehistoric equivalent of a polity with centralized authority in this region. Such a polity could have been directly involved in the creation of the diversity of the landscape that is evident today. It is obvious that pre-Columbian Indians intensively transformed coastal savannas of the Guianas.

In the flooded savannas, raised fields seem to have been the best agricultural answer to population growth because this technique made intensive agricultural land use possible. Population density may have reached 50 to 100 persons per square kilometer in areas with raised fields. Arguably, from AD 650, the intensification of agriculture (based on raised fields) resulted in population growth, social complexity, intersocietal interactions, craft specialization, and long-distance trade. These factors led to the emergence of chiefdoms along the coast of the Guianas.

Further Reading

Boomert, A. 1980. "Hertenrits: An Arauquinoid Complex in Northwest Suriname." *Journal of the Walter Roth Museum of Archaeology and Anthropology, Georgetown* 3 (2): 68–104.

Iriarte, J., B. Glaser, J. Watling, A. Wainwright, J. Birk, D. Renard, S. Rostain, and D. McKey. 2010. "Agricultural Landscapes of Coastal Amazonia: Phytolith and Carbon Isotope Analysis of Raised Fields from French Guiana Savannah." *Journal of Archaeological Science* 37 (12): 2984–94.

McKey, D., and S. Rostain. 2010. "Les champs surélevés préhistoriques: Histoire, sols et impact sur le fonctionnement actuel des savanes côtières de Guyane." In *Amazonie, une aventure scientifique et humaine*, ed. Alain Pavé and Gaëlle Fornet, 132–34. Paris: Éditions Galaade.

McKey, D., S. Rostain, J. Iriarte, B. Glaser, J. Birk, I. Holst, and D. Renard. 2010. "Pre-Columbian Agricultural Landscapes, Ecosystem Engineers and Self-Organized Patchiness in Amazonia." In *Proceedings of the National Academy of Sciences of the USA* 107 (17): 7823–28.

Rostain, S. 1994. *L'occupation amérindienne ancienne du littoral de Guyane*. coll. Travaux et Documents Micro-fichés 129, Paris: Éditions de l'ORSTOM.

———. 2008. "Agricultural Earthworks on the French Guiana Coast." In *Handbook of South American Archaeology*, ed. Helaine Silverman and William Isbell, 217–34. New York: Springer.

See also Arawak versus Taíno; Archaeometry; The First Caribbean Farmers.

Alegría, Ricardo E. (1921–2011)

L. Antonio Curet

Ricardo E. Alegría was a Puerto Rican archaeologist, anthropologist, historian, folklorist, historical conservationist, and cultural activist. Many saw him as the defender of Puerto Rican culture. He was born in Old San Juan on April 14, 1921. In 1947, Alegría earned his master's degree in anthropology from the University of Chicago, and in 1954, he earned his PhD from Harvard University. In 1945, he was named instructor of history at the University of Puerto Rico and assistant director of the Museo de Historia, Antropología y Arte at the same institution. In 1947, he founded and directed the Centro de Investigaciones Arqueológica y Etnológicas of the University of Puerto Rico and began an ambitious research program that included excavations of several important sites of Puerto Rico and the Caribbean, including Monserrate (Luquillo), Hacienda Grande (Loíza), Cueva María la Cruz (Loíza), and the Caguana Ceremonial Center (Utuado). He also conducted an ethnographic study of the town of Loíza, which was composed primarily of the descendants of former enslaved Africans, and extensive research on early colonial ethnohistoric sources.

In the 1950s, he was instrumental in the formation of the Instituto de Cultura Puertorriqueña (ICP), and in 1955 he became its first executive director. During his directorship, the ICP maintained an anthropological view that integrated various fields, including folklore, history, art, literature, music, and theater. The ICP had the monumental task of defining, identifying, promoting, and preserving Puerto Rican culture, a topic that was never part of any aspect of the daily life of the island before. Using his anthropological background, Alegría began defining Puerto Rican culture as the historical product of the fusion of native, African, and European influences. Under his direction, the ICP implemented a series of programs to preserve and stimulate Puerto Rican culture through publications, exhibitions, conferences, and festivals. The institute also conducted the restoration of historical buildings, first in Old San Juan and later in Ponce, San Germán, and other towns. Alegría also established guidelines for the restoration of historic buildings that eventually were enacted as law. Perhaps the most influential and effective ways of disseminating and promoting Puerto Rican culture were 1) creating local museums throughout the island; 2) publishing popular books, especially on the least-known components of Puerto Rican culture, the influences of native and African cultures; and 3) adopting these ideas in textbooks and school curricula. These and other efforts helped developed a sense of a unified national identity that had repercussions in many other aspects of Puerto Rican (and, eventually, Caribbean) life. For example, the emphasis on the mixture of cultures led to a marked decrease in open racial discrimination in Puerto Rico. In 1976, Alegría founded and directed the Centro de Estudios Avanzados de Puerto Rico y el Caribe, a graduate school that specializes in social, cultural, artistic, economic, and historical research. Today, the Centro offers the first and only MA program in archaeology in Puerto Rico. Alegría retired from the Centro in 2001.

Among other things, Alegría made major contributions to the archaeology, ethnohistory, and historical preservation of and education about the Caribbean. His contributions to archaeology include discovering definite evidence of the presence of Archaic people in Puerto Rico; defining the ancient Puerto Rican cultures, including defining the Hacienda Grande style; and publishing a cross-cultural study of ball courts in the Caribbean. Most of his work was published in prestigious national and international media. His contributions in ethnohistory are as important as those in archaeology. He was responsible for transcribing and publishing a large number of early colonial documents from Puerto Rico. Many

of Alegría's publications included his commentaries on or analysis of these documents. He also used historical documents as the basis for articles and books on chiefdoms, indigenous religions, personal ornaments and other accessories among the late pre-Hispanic groups of the Greater Antilles, and harmful gases indigenous groups used as weapons. Alegría published several popular books, some of which were children's books. These include *Historia de Nuestros Indios* (History of the Indians of Puerto Rico), *Descubrimiento, Conquista y Colonización de Puerto Rico, 1493–1599* (Discovery, Conquest, and Colonization of Puerto Rico, 1493–1599); *La Fiesta de Santiago Apóstol en Loíza Aldea* (The Feast of the Apostle James in the Village of Loíza); and *El Fuerte de San Jerónimo del Boquerón* (The Fort of San Jerónimo del Boquerón). Some of them were eventually translated into English.

His efforts at historical conservation are probably the most visible of all his works. He was responsible for conserving and protecting individual sites by turning them in historical parks such as the Caguana Ceremonial Center (Utuado) or the Ruinas de Caparra, the first European settlement in the island. He also began a program for the restoration and renovation of Old San Juan. One key part of this program was Alegría's novel vision of turning Old San Juan into a living city rather than a static museum. Alegría's program for Old San Juan served as a model for similar projects throughout the Americas, including in the United States. As a result of his work, Old San Juan was declared a historical zone by the U.S. federal government.

During Alegría's lifetime he was recognized by a number of national and international institutions, including the Catholic University of Puerto Rico (1971), New York University (1971), Inter-American University (1986), and Hunter College of New York (1989). Alegría also received the History Prize (1941), the National Prize (1977), and the Prize of Honor (1981) from the Puerto Rican Athenaeum; the George McAneny Prize (1970) from the American Historical Preservation Society; and the Charles Frankel Prize (1993) from the National Endowment for the Humanities. In 1990, the Puerto Rican Endowment for the Humanities named him Humanist of the Year, and in 1998 he was honored by the Fernando Ortiz Foundation in Cuba. The government of the Commonwealth of Puerto Rico gave him the gold medal of the Order of the Fifth Centennial of the Discovery of the Americas and Puerto Rico. U.S. president Bill Clinton presented Alegría with the Charles Frankel Prize in 1993 for his contributions in the field of archaeology. He was a member of the Puerto Rican Academy of the Spanish

Language, the Puerto Rican Academy of Arts and Sciences, and the San Jorge Academy of Fine Arts in Barcelona, among other organizations.

Further Reading

Alegría, R. E. 1983. *Ball Courts and Ceremonial Plazas in the West Indies.* Department of Anthropology, New Haven, CT: Yale University.

———. 1986. *Apuntes en Torno a la Mitología de los Indios Taínos de las Antillas Mayores y sus Orígenes Suramericanos* (Notes on the Mythology of the Taíno Indians of the Greater Antilles and Its South American Origins). 2nd ed. Museo del Hombre Dominicano, Santo Domingo, Dominican Republic.

Alegría, R. E., H. B. Nicholson, and G. R. Willey. 1955. "The Archaic Tradition in Puerto Rico." *American Antiquity* 21 (2): 113–21.

Rouse, B. I., and R. E. Alegría. 1990. *Excavations at María de la Cruz Cave and Hacienda Grande Village Site, Loíza, Puerto Rico.* New Haven, CT: Yale Peabody Museum.

Anguilla

John G. Crock

Anguilla is a relatively small island (91 square kilometers) with a rich archaeological record. The majority of archaeology conducted in Anguilla has focused on the pre-Columbian Amerindian occupation; little research to date has been devoted to colonial and more recent historical and nautical archaeology. One exception is the documentation of numerous shipwrecks in Anguillan waters, including a limited survey of the *El Buen Consejo*, a ship carrying Spanish missionaries to Mexico that wrecked off Anguilla's south coast in 1772. More than 40 pre-Columbian Amerindian sites are known in Anguilla, with occupations cumulatively spanning 3,200 years or more (Crock and Petersen 1999)

(Figure A.5). Several smaller cays to the north and east of Anguilla, including Dog Island, located some 20 kilometers to the northwest, and Scrub Island, less than one km to the east, also preserve significant pre-Columbian sites.

Anguilla's limestone bedrock and low elevation (maximum of 65 meters AMSL) are largely responsible for its limited arable land (less than 3 square kilometers) and limited annual rainfall (ca. 100 centimeters/year), factors that limited colonial interest in the island and resulted in a comparatively short history of plantation agriculture. These conditions are partly countered by the abundance of maritime resources and a few permanent

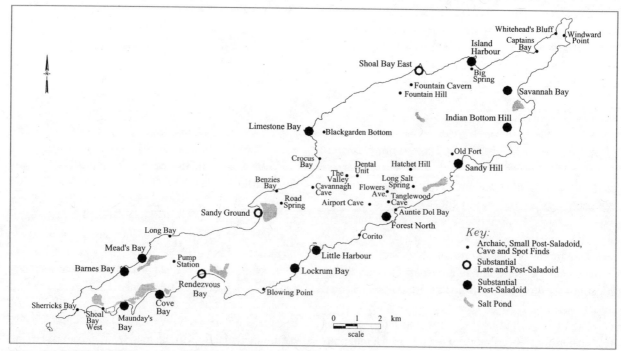

Figure A.5. Precolonial sites on Anguilla. Courtesy of John G. Crock.

water sources such as the freshwater spring in the pre-Columbian Fountain Cavern ceremonial site. The Anguilla Bank, which stretches eastward to St. Martin, Saint Barthélemy, and beyond, is one of the most productive reef systems in the Caribbean. Abundant fish and shellfish were a major factor in the use and settlement of the island by Amerindians. A reconstructed culture history for Anguilla is partially based on surface collections the Anguilla Archaeological and Historical Society (AAHS) has made since 1981 and on limited AAHS excavations (Crock and Petersen 1999; Douglas 1986). Various systematic excavations made by professional researchers have provided context for local collections and have addressed research questions related to the timing of occupation, participation in interregional systems of exchange, and the development of social complexity (Crock 2000; Crock and Petersen 1999; Watters 1991).

At least two Archaic period sites are known in Anguilla, including the Whitehead's Bluff and Flowers Avenue sites. The combined inventory from these sites includes shellfish food remains, shell axes and shell containers, and stone tools made from flint likely imported from Antigua. The Whitehead's Bluff site has been dated to cal. 1670–1430 BC. No evidence has yet been found in Anguilla of the very earliest Saladoid period (Early Ceramic Age), dating from 500 BC to AD 300. It is possible that Anguilla may have been the home to Archaic Amerindians at this time, that the earliest sites have been eroded/inundated, or that the island was temporarily abandoned. Paleoenvironmental data also indicate that this was the driest period during the span of Amerindian occupation in the Caribbean, and this may explain the absence of occupation on the low, dry island of Anguilla.

Fisher-farmers first colonized Anguilla by AD 300–400, and to date, only four of the many known sites in Anguilla have produced artifacts that are diagnostic of the late-terminal Saladoid period, which is estimated to extend from AD 300 to 900. These include three residential sites, including Rendezvous Bay, Sandy Ground, Shoal Bay East, and the Fountain Cavern ceremonial site (Watters 1991). More extensive Late Ceramic Age (Post-Saladoid) deposits overlie all of these earlier occupations and are found at numerous other sites in Anguilla, suggesting a substantial increase in local population after AD 600. In fact, between circa AD 900 and 1200, Anguilla apparently became an important center in a local hierarchy of settlements, based on its position within an interisland exchange network (Crock and Petersen 2004).

At least 14 substantial residential sites in Anguilla can be assigned to one or more portions of the Post-Saladoid period, circa AD 900–1500, along with other smaller sites. Sizeable collections exist from the majority of these sites, and field inspections suggest that originally all of these settlements probably exceeded two hectares in size. The largest sites are typically located near beaches, salt ponds and/or arable soils. Anguillan sites in this category include Rendezvous Bay, Sandy Ground, Island Harbour, Sandy Hill, Cove Bay, Mead's Bay, Barnes Bay, Indian Bottom Hill, Savannah Bay, Little Harbour, Shoal Bay, Forest North, Lockrum Bay, and Limestone Bay. Unfortunately, coastal development has resulted in the complete or partial destruction of several documented sites and continues to threaten archaeological resources on the island.

A total of four or perhaps five ceremonial cave sites have been recorded in Anguilla, all of which likely were used during the Late Ceramic Age. These sites include Fountain Cavern, Big Spring, Airport Cave, and Tanglewood Cave. The Cavannagh Cave site may have originally belonged in this category too, but historic mining activities completely destroyed the archaeological deposits contained therein. The subterranean Fountain Cavern site clearly was the most significant; it contains a carved stalagmite statue, numerous pecked petroglyph designs, and dense artifacts associated with a freshwater pool (Watters 1991). Twelve other sites, all attributable to the Late Ceramic Age, are characterized as smaller "hamlets," or special-purpose sites. These were occupied contemporaneously with the one to five more substantial sites mentioned above. Other sites in the AAHS inventory are spot finds or reported sites that have not been thoroughly investigated. Available information indicates that most, if not all, of these are also likely attributable to the Late Ceramic Age.

Petrographic and neutron activation analysis indicates that pottery and/or volcanic temper was imported into Anguilla from other nearby islands during this period. Volcanic material, such as greenstone and calcirudite, both of which originated in nearby St. Martin, also were imported in addition to materials from farther away. The greenstone was used to manufacture petaloid celts, and the calcirudite was used exclusively to produce three-pointed *cemí* idols. Evidence from other islands suggests that these artifacts also were exported from Anguilla.

The development of a hierarchy of settlements and more political centralization apparently took place in Anguilla, where there is also evidence for religious ceremonialism. These data link populations in Anguilla culturally with populations that have been documented ethnohistorically in the Greater Antilles. The timing and nature of the Amerindians' abandonment of Anguilla is not known. No mention of an Amerindian population was made when Columbus sailed by Anguilla on his second voyage in 1493, and no Amerindians lived in Anguilla when the first Europeans and Africans came in the 1650s.

Further Reading

Crock, J. G. 2000. "Interisland Interaction and the Development of Chiefdoms in the Eastern Caribbean." PhD diss., Department of Anthropology, University of Pittsburgh.

Crock, J. G., and J. B. Petersen. 1999. "A Long and Rich Cultural Heritage, 1992–1998." Report prepared for the Anguilla Archaeological and Historical Society, The Valley, Anguilla, British West Indies.

———. 2004. "Inter-Island Exchange, Settlement Hierarchy, and a Taino-Related Chiefdom on the Anguilla Bank, Northern Lesser Antilles." In *Late Ceramic Age Societies in the Eastern Caribbean*, ed. André Delpuech and Corinne Hofman, 139–56. Oxford: Archaeopress.

Douglas, N. 1986. *Anguilla Archaeological and Historical Society Review, 1981–1985*. Anguilla Archaeological and Historical Society, The Valley, Anguilla.

Watters, D. R. 1991. "Archaeology of Fountain Cavern, Anguilla, West Indies." *Annals of Carnegie Museum* 60 (4): 255–320.

Antigua and Barbuda (Archaic Sites)

Reg Murphy

Shell middens and debitage from the manufacture of stone tools typically delineate Archaic Age sites. They are mostly situated on the seafront in close proximity to marine ecosystems that are rich with shellfish, mangroves, and shallow grassy bottom bays that have a higher diversity of species (Rouse 1992). It appears that Archaic Age people did not make or use pottery and it is believed that they were highly mobile and lived in small family groups. Their apparent reliance on shellfish, which can be rapidly depleted from a habitat zone, adds to their classification as a fisher-forager society. However, the numerous mortars, pestles, and tools commonly associated with the processing of plants (seeds, roots, fruit, etc.) suggest that they were an early horticultural people who planted and foraged over a wide area, moving seasonally between the islands and sites to exploit a variety of resources.

To date, about 50 sites have been classified as Archaic Age on Antigua (see Figure A.6). Researchers do not know what these first seafaring people called themselves, but archaeologists refer to them as Archaic Age people because they did not make or use pottery, although some pottery-bearing Archaic sites have been found in the northern Leeward Islands and islands of the Greater Antilles such as Cuba, Hispaniola, and Puerto Rico. In addition, it is often stated that their material culture was not as complex as the Ceramic Age peoples who eventually displaced them. The earliest date of human occupation on Antigua is 3106 BC at the Little Deep Site, Mill Reef. Other early sites include Twenty Hill, Parham (2910 BC), Crabb's Peninsula (1770 BC), Deep Bay (1387 BC), Jolly Beach (1775 BC), and the Clover Leaf Site (383 BC) at Emerald Cove (de Mille 2005, 339). Archaic Age sites were densely situated along the northeast coast of Antigua, from Hodges Bay to Mill Reef (Davis 2000). Some underlay later Ceramic Age deposits, as at Blackman's Bay and Winthorpes Bay. On Barbuda, much of the west coast from Spanish Point south to the River Site comprises a single site several miles long known as the Strombus Line. The dates are similar to those of Antigua, ranging between 2000 and 1000 BC (Watters 1980).

Archaic Age peoples occupied Antigua until the arrival of Arawak-speaking, fully horticultural, ceramic-making Saladoid people in the middle of the first millennium BC. The area most extensively occupied was the east coast of the island, from Barnacle Point to Parham. Sadly, many of the best and largest sites have been lost to development, including Deep Bay and Jolly Beach. The only well-preserved large habitation site remaining on Antigua is located in the military compound at Crabb's Peninsula. On Barbuda, the once-spectacular Strombus Line and River sites have mostly been destroyed by recent land development, and only a few pockets remain intact. The transition from the Archaic Age to the Ceramic Age on Antigua and Barbuda remains a mystery to archaeologists, but it appears that the Archaic people

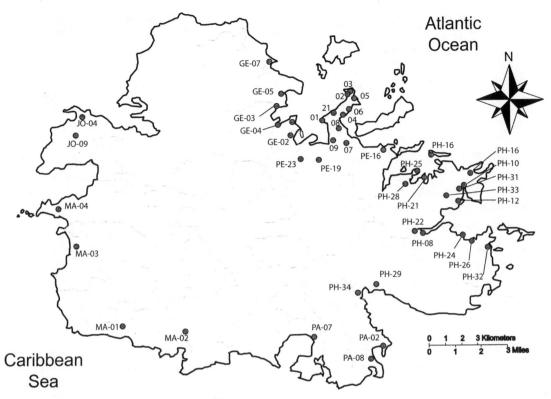

Figure A.6. Archaic sites on Antigua. Map by Reg Murphy.

were present on Antigua in significant numbers at a time when Ceramic Age settlements were being established on other islands such as Montserrat and St. Martin.

Further Reading

Davis, Dave D. 2000. *Jolly Beach and the Preceramic Occupation of Antigua, West Indies*. Yale University Publications in Anthropology, New Haven, CT: Yale University Press.

De Mille, C. N. 2005. "The Pre-Ceramic Occupation of Antigua, W.I." PhD diss., Department of Archaeology, University of Calgary.

Rouse, I. 1992. *The Tainos: Rise and Decline of the People Who Greeted Columbus*. New Haven, CT: Yale University Press.

Watters, D. R. 1980. "Transect Surveying and Prehistoric Site Locations on Barbuda and Montserrat, Leeward Islands, West Indies." PhD diss., University of Pittsburgh.

See also The Archaic Age.

Arawak versus Taíno

Basil A. Reid

It is impossible to write about the past without assigning names to the peoples about whom we write. Over the years, a variety of names have been used to designate the precolonial peoples of the Americas. Unfortunately, the names that were selected have in some cases led to confusion about cultural heritage and ethnic identity. The name Arawak is one that has resulted in such significant confusion that archaeologists working in the region have now abandoned the name, as it specifically relates to the

Caribbean. In order to distinguish the substantial cultural differences between Arawak societies in mainland South America and the peoples of the northern Caribbean at the time of Spanish contact, Caribbean archaeologists now use the name Taíno to refer to the latter. This term relates specifically to natives who lived in the northern Caribbean from AD 1200 to 1500 and who had evolved from the Ostionoid. Although the names Taíno and Arawak have been used interchangeably, from all accounts, they were two distinct ethnic/cultural groups: the former were located in northeastern South America, while the latter occupied much of the Greater Antilles and the Bahamas at the time of Columbus.

The Name Arawak

Neither Columbus nor any of his contemporaries came across the name Arawak. Essentially, the term Arawak does not appear in the literature until the exploration of the Guianas began in the late 1500s, almost a century after the arrival of Columbus in the New World. Sir Walter Raleigh, the famed English explorer, identified the Arawak and at least four Indian groups when he visited Trinidad in 1595. Centuries later, in 1894, Juan Lopez de Velasco noted the presence of people who called themselves Arawak on the Guiana coast and commented that a group of them had "intruded" into Trinidad. Although the Arawak of Trinidad have long ceased to be an identifiable ethnic group, there are numerous Arawak villages in Guyana, Suriname, northern Brazil, and French Guiana to this day.

In the past, some scholars used certain linguistic similarities between these native peoples of South America and those Columbus encountered in the northern Caribbean. In 1871, for instance, Daniel Brinton, after studying a few word lists that survived in the Greater Antilles with the modern language of the Arawak in the Guianas, came to the conclusion that the Amerindians in the Greater Antilles also conversed in the language the Arawak spoke. He applied the name "Island-Arawak" to the Antilleans in order to distinguish them from the peoples of the mainland. Unfortunately, this distinction was lost and the peoples of the Caribbean came to be known simply as Arawak. Subsequent authors such as Sven Lovén have demonstrated a preference for the terms Insular Arawak or Island-Arawak.

Linguistic and Cultural Differences between the Taíno and the Arawak

The Taíno, who inhabited the northern Caribbean at contact, spoke a different language and were culturally distinct from the South American Arawak. At a more general level, the languages of the Taíno and the Arawak share enough similarities to be classified as members of the Arawakan language family (Keegan 1992). However, this is not surprising as the languages of the Taíno, Arawak, and Island-Carib all originated from the Arawak family of languages, which extended from the Upper Amazon Basin to Venezuela, the Guianas, and the West Indies. But the differences between these languages were substantial, and whatever similarities that existed could be compared to those between English and Dutch within the Indo-European family of languages.

The Arawak language itself (now called Lokono) is better documented than the language of the Taíno. There is general consensus among linguists that the Taíno, Island-Carib, and Arawak languages diverged from the main line of Arawak development at the same time and that all three belong to the Maipuran family. However, scholarly research has shown that the Taíno language shared few cognates with those of its nearest neighbors at the time of European contact: the Island-Carib and Arawak. Therefore, its line of development branched off the trunk of the family tree earlier than the lines leading to the Island-Carib and the Arawak (Rouse 1992) (see Figure A.7).

The cultural differences between the Taíno and the Arawak clearly distinguished one group from the other. Although both worshipped ancestral spirits (*zemíes*) and used griddles to bake cassava bread, archaeological and ethnohistorical data indicate that the Arawak had a simpler culture. While the Arawak slashed and burned the forest to make temporary farms, the Taíno of the Caribbean, especially those in Hispaniola and Puerto Rico, practiced a sophisticated *conuco* agriculture that was based on mounds of earth in more permanent fields. In contrast to the Arawak of South America, the Taíno built much larger, permanent villages. The latter were characterized by an elaborate sociopolitical organization that included district and even regional chiefdoms as well as ballparks and plazas.

However, the notion that the Arawak were culturally inferior to the Taíno has been seriously questioned. According to Heckenberger (2009), several headwater basins of the southern Amazon show evidence of substantial pre-Columbian landscape modification, particularly in areas historically dominated by speakers of the Arawak language family. He and his team have unearthed evidence of early cultures going back to about AD 500 that had larger populations and were more advanced than previously imagined. Of special significance were elaborate pottery, ringed villages, raised fields, large mounds, and evidence of regional trade networks. All of these are markers of a sophisticated Arawak culture. There is also evidence that the early natives modified the soil using various techniques such as deliberate burning of vegetation to transform it into *terra preta*, or "black earth," which even today is

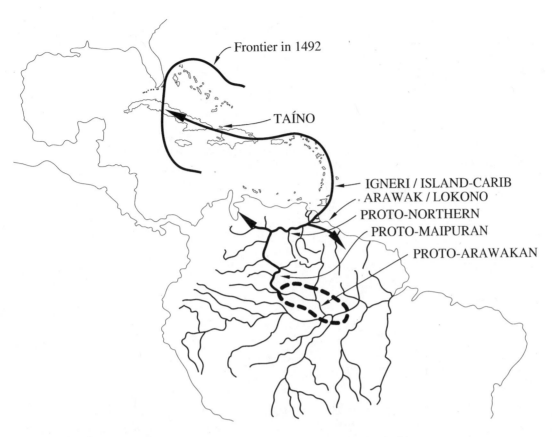

Figure A.7. Advance of Arawakan speech communities from Amazonia into the Caribbean. Reprinted from Rouse (1992, fig. 12) by permission of Yale University Press.

famed for its agricultural productivity (Heckenberger 2009). It is likely that this conception of a simpler Arawak culture was propagated by the first archaeologists to study this area (such as Betty Meggers and Julian Steward), who thought the region had been occupied by small bands of hunter-gatherers living in a world of scarcity.

Controversy

However, the use of the word Taíno has not been without controversy. Taíno purportedly means "good" or "noble," and several of this group's members allegedly used that word when speaking with Columbus's crew to indicate that they were not Island-Carib (Rouse 1992). This was documented in Peter Martyr D'Anghera's late-sixteenth-century account of an incident during Columbus's second voyage while Melchior Maldonado was exploring the coast of Hispaniola. But the authenticity of this account has been seriously questioned (Hulme 1993), considering that Peter Martyr was not an actual eyewitness to the event and never set foot in the New World.

The word Taíno may have first been used in an academic context by Constantine Samuel Rafinesque in 1836 in specific reference to the language spoken anciently in Haiti. Over time, Caribbean archaeologists applied the name Taíno to the ethnicity of natives in the northern Caribbean at contact. The word *nitayno*, which bears a striking similarity to the name Taíno, has cropped up in the Spanish literature as referring to Taíno nobility (Rouse 1992). Instead of being used as an ethnic label, *nitayno* referred to the Taíno ruling class. This was probably a reflection of how the natives were viewed through the prism of the Spanish class structure (Hulme 1993). It is likely that the islanders Columbus encountered on his first voyage did not have a specific self-designation, or if they did, Columbus made no mention of it. Columbus simply called them *indios*, as the admiral mistakenly thought that he had "discovered" natives of islands off the coast of Asia.

Taíno Heterogeneity

But even if we accept the use of the name Taíno for the northern Caribbean, the natives Columbus encountered were not homogenous because they had diverse phenotypes, languages, and cultural traditions. Columbus reported differences in physical appearance and material culture between the natives of northeastern Hispaniola and those elsewhere on the island (Dunn and Kelley 1989). Although there seemed to have been one dominant speech community, Las Casas and other writers of the early 1500s clearly distinguished between a number of other aboriginal languages in the Greater Antilles, such as Macorix, Ciguayo, and Guanahatabey. The most reasonable explanation for this is that the Taíno language of the Greater Antilles, which had many monolingual speakers and was the numerically dominant language of the Greater Antilles, also served as a language of interchange, even with the speakers of other languages. Thus, it served much the same purpose as Norman French did in post-1066 England (Granberry and Vescelius 2004). However, language uniformity does not necessarily indicate the presence of an ethnic group, because a single speech community may be the result of colonization or assimilation. For example, English has been the official language of the Anglo-Caribbean for centuries because of British colonial rule. However, the extensive use of English belies the many ethnic and cultural differences that exist in specific territories in the region.

To further compound the issue, a number of Taíno subdivisions relating to both geography and cultural development are being used in Caribbean archaeology, namely Classic, Western, and Eastern Taíno. These names are more reflective of broad regional classifications than of localized differences and represent an effort by some Caribbean archaeologists to capture the level of indigenous plurality that existed at contact. Caribbean archaeologists refer to the Taíno in Puerto Rico and Hispaniola with the highest level of sociopolitical development (including ball courts, stone-lined plazas, and *conucos*) as Classic Taíno, while they refer to the less-developed members of the Taíno community who lived elsewhere in the northern Caribbean as either Western or Eastern Taíno (Rouse 1992). In addition to being called Western Taíno, the natives of the Bahamas have also come to be known as the Lucayans (Keegan 1992). The Spanish called the islands to the north of Hispaniola "Las Islas de Los Lucayos"; therefore, all peoples of the Bahama archipelago are referred to as Lucayans, or more accurately Lucayan Taíno (Keegan and Carlson 2008).

Conclusion

Whether or not the natives of the Greater Antilles and the Caribbean actually identified themselves as Taíno is still a subject of considerable debate. Despite the controversy surrounding the word Taíno, it is generally accepted that there were significant linguistic and cultural differences between the contact period natives of the northern Caribbean and the Arawak of South America, although the notion of a "simple Arawak culture" may have been overplayed. It is therefore grossly inaccurate to refer to the inhabitants of the Greater Antilles and the Bahamas at the time of Spanish contact as Arawak. The jury is still out on whether the word Taíno is entirely accurate as it is presently used. Suffice it to say that Caribbean archaeologists will continue to use it until they find a better alternative.

Further Reading

Dunn, O., and J. E. Kelly Jr., eds. 1989. *The Diario of Christopher Columbus's First Voyage to America, 1492–1493.* Abstracted from Bartolomé de las Casas. Norman: University of Oklahoma Press.

Granberry, J., and G. S. Vescelius. 2004. *Languages of the Pre-Columbian Antilles.* Tuscaloosa: University of Alabama Press.

Heckenberger, M. 2009. "Biocultural Diversity in the Southern Amazon." *Diversity 2010* 2 (1): 1–16.

Hulme, P. 1993. "Making Sense of the Native Caribbean." *New West Indian Guide* 67 (3–4): 189–220.

Keegan, W. F. 1992. *The People Who Discovered Columbus: The Prehistory of the Bahamas.* Gainesville: University Press of Florida.

Keegan, W. F., and L. A. Carlson. 2008. *Talking Taino: Caribbean Natural History from a Native Perspective.* Tuscaloosa: University of Alabama Press.

Reid, B. A. 2009. *Myths and Realities of Caribbean History.* Tuscaloosa: University of Alabama Press.

Rouse, I. 1992. *The Tainos: Rise and Decline of the People Who Greeted Columbus.* New Haven, CT: Yale University Press.

See also Ciboney versus Guanahatabey; Origins of Indigenous Groups in the Northern Caribbean; Taíno Settlement Ethnohistory.

The Archaeological Committee of Trinidad and Tobago

K. O. Laurence

The Archaeological Committee of Trinidad and Tobago came into being in 1979 as a result of a proposal by Wilfred Laurier University to carry out archaeological work at Lovers Retreat in Tobago. The government of Trinidad and Tobago was pleased to approve the project, but it recognized that there was no trained archaeologist in the country or any organization that could monitor such proceedings. The Cabinet therefore agreed to fund a post for an archaeologist at The University of the West Indies at St. Augustine on the condition that the appointee would act as technical liaison officer for the project and for any other similar undertakings that might arise. The Cabinet also appointed a Committee to co-ordinate the preparations for the Tobago project and to act as an Advisory Committee to the Minister of Education and Culture in Archaeological Matters that included the archaeologist. Thus was born the Archaeological Committee, which contained representatives of the Planning Authority, the National Cultural Council, and a number of special interests including tourism, forestry, conservation, and the National Commission for UNESCO. Tobago later acquired its own special representative. Although the Wilfred Laurier University's Lovers Retreat project never materialized because of funding problems, Trinidad and Tobago thus established both an Archaeological Committee that worked closely with the ministry responsible for culture and planning authorities, and a professional archaeologist (whose time was divided between work as a university research fellow and work as the committee's technical advisor).

Provided with access to infinitesimal resources through the ministry responsible for culture, the committee set out to accumulate an archaeological information bank and advise on the archaeological implications of construction projects. The committee thus has always worked very closely with Trinidad and Tobago's planning authorities. The archaeologist appointed in 1981, Dr. Arie Boomert, concentrated his attention in the early years on listing and classifying the archaeological sites that had been reported in the country over the years while noting new ones that came to light. The archaeological material that was found in the process, and sometimes in the possession of private citizens, was stored at The University of the West Indies, but studying it was deemed to be less important than producing a register and inventory of known sites, a task that was largely completed by the late 1990s, by which time some 300 sites had been listed. The committee was also able to closely monitor the activities of a series of visiting archaeologists, some of whom the committee was able to assist with small grants from the very limited budget the ministry allowed it from 1999 onward. The most important project the committee has been involved with is the exploration of an Amerindian settlement complex at Manzanilla that a team from Leiden University first investigated in 1997. The Archaeology Committee ceased to function in 2009, and in 2011 was replaced by the Archaeological Sub-Committee of the National Trust of Trinidad and Tobago.

Further Reading

Reid, B., and V. Lewis. 2011. "Trinidad and Tobago." In *Protecting Heritage in the Caribbean,* ed. Peter E. Siegel and Elizabeth Righter. Tuscaloosa: University of Alabama Press.

See also The National Trust of Trinidad and Tobago; Trinidad and Tobago.

Archaeological Conservation

Georgia L. Fox

Overview of Archaeological Conservation

Scientific conservation in archaeology provides for the stewardship of cultural property through the care and preservation of archaeologically recovered materials. A full program of archaeological conservation begins with the planning and budgeting for conservation as part of a project's overall research design, which includes both field and laboratory conservation. In the twenty-first century, conservation refers to the examination, documentation, assessment, analysis, cleaning, and stabilization of cultural heritage in the form of objects, on-site architectural features, shipwrecks, and other forms of human-made or modified material culture, including the conservation of rock art, which has been addressed for the Caribbean region by Hayward, Atkinson, and Cinquino (2009).

Archaeological conservation also addresses the processes of deterioration that affect chemical, biological, and physical archaeological remains. Restoration refers to the process of restoring an object to an assumed previous state through the repair or replacement of missing and non-original parts. This process is done with caution and judicious consideration (AIC 2012). Most conservation efforts currently focus on preventative care, which includes a fully integrated program of proper handling, storage, monitoring, transportation, and mitigation of the deterioration of archaeological collections to preserve them for posterity, research, and exhibition.

The special needs of archaeological conservation require a holistic approach, particularly in being able to recognize diagnostic features and attributes that are associated with the history of an object. These include elements that indicate materials and methods of construction, use wear, function, archaeological context, and cultural context. All of these provide information about an object's unique history and significance. Artifact conservation should not detract from an object's natural appearance or alter its scientific attributes. Having a treatment plan is part of a broad spectrum of ethical practices and standards that are implemented when conservation treatments for archaeological materials are being considered. Other factors to consider include the competence of the conservators, the ability of conservators to provide informed respect for the integrity of the object, and the presence of proper facilities to carry out conservation treatments that take into account the health and safety of the conservators.

Caribbean Examples

A variety of organic and inorganic materials may be encountered in an archaeological context in the Caribbean. Often organic materials do not survive unless they are well preserved in an anaerobic environment, such as well-sealed contexts like the sunken city of Port Royal, Jamaica. Some of the most commonly encountered materials from Caribbean archaeological sites include objects made of iron, glass, ceramics, wood, bone, and copper alloys. Materials recovered from prehistoric contexts include low- and high-fired pottery and objects made of stone, shell, clay, and bone. Care must be taken when considering any scientific testing such as DNA analysis, isotope analysis, or chemical analysis. Any preliminary intervention may contaminate an object, and even the simple act of mechanical cleaning can potentially affect scientific testing results. Common cleaning methods include removing dirt, repairing ceramics and glass with adhesives, removing soluble and insoluble salts, and consolidating archaeological bone.

The choice of materials and methods used in treatment can impact an object's long-term stability. This is where the principle of reversibility guides the conservator, particularly if a treatment proves ineffective or threatens an object's long-term stability. In such cases, other treatment options need to be considered. An example of this is the use of polyvinyl acetate resins used in repairing ceramics from Caribbean collections. These resins have proven to be unstable in many instances, especially in storage environments that lack any climate control in the often humid and hot conditions of the region. This has caused reassessment of certain commonly accepted treatments that used in more temperate climates that are unsuitable for artifacts recovered from Caribbean sites. This is particularly relevant when considering that once an object is removed from its archaeological context, the in situ equilibrium is disturbed, setting in motion deterioration processes that are exacerbated by atmospheric oxygen, moisture, and temperature, particularly for organic materials. This is why planning and budgeting for conservation in the field and in the laboratory is essential. For example, the recovery of waterlogged artifacts from marine sites require that objects remain wet until they can be properly stored, documented, and assessed for treatment. For field conservation, it is important to anticipate the types of material remains that might be encountered. This means preparing for the on-site removal of artifacts, on-site temporary storage, and the subsequent transportation of artifacts to a laboratory facility equipped with trained staff, supplies, and equipment in the controlled environment that is necessary for proper documentation, cleaning, and further analyses.

One of the more significant efforts in the conservation of Caribbean artifacts has been the conservation of hundreds of objects recovered from the sunken city of Port Royal, Jamaica. An array of imported ceramics, pewter plates, tankards, and utensils as well as numerous "onion" glass bottles have been cleaned, desalinated, and conserved at Texas A&M University's Conservation Research Laboratory in College Station, Texas, directed by D. L. Hamilton. One of the most challenging materials to conserve in the Caribbean is archaeological iron. Because iron is prone to corrosion, the deterioration processes both on land and underwater often result in loss of iron from the artifact. In some instances, iron objects recovered from Port Royal lost most of their remaining metal, leaving an encrusted calcium carbonate shell of the object's original shape. In one example, an iron butcher's cleaver was reproduced from a one-part epoxy resin mold of the missing metal. The original wooden handle of the cleaver survived and was conserved separately, then joined to the epoxy facsimile, resulting in a composite rendition of the original artifact, with details of the metal cleaver well preserved in the epoxy cast.

Excavated objects from Betty's Hope Plantation have been conserved at the Heritage Resources Conservation Laboratory (HRCL) at California State University, Chico, and were subsequently returned to be exhibited at the Museum of Antigua and Barbuda. Objects such as metal coins, iron padlocks and implements, parts of a cast-iron stove with the manufacturer's name intact, and small copper-alloy sewing notions are among a number of artifacts recently conserved from the plantation. An iron coffin plate recovered from another site on Antigua was carefully reconstructed and repaired at HRCL and returned to Antigua along with the artifacts from Betty's Hope. Finally, over the past three decades, an extraregional conservation partnership between St. Eustatius and Curtis Moyer's Conservation Laboratory at the College of William and Mary in Virginia has facilitated the conservation of hundreds of metallic and glass artifacts recovered from sites on St. Eustatius.

Further Reading

American Institute for the Conservation of Historic and Artistic Works (AIC). 2012. "Definitions of Conservation Terminology." http://www.conservation-us.org/index.cfm?fuseaction=page.viewPage&PageID=620&E:\ColdFusion9\verity\Data\dummy.txt. Accessed October 26, 2012.

Appelbaum, B. 2007. *Conservation Treatment Methodology*. Oxford: Butterworth-Heinemann.

Cronyn, J. M., and W. S. Robinson. 1990. *The Elements of Archaeological Conservation*. London: Routledge.

Hayward, M. H., L. Atkinson, and M. A. Cinquino. 2009. *Rock Art of the Caribbean*. Tuscaloosa: University of Alabama Press.

Sease, C. 1994. *A Conservation Manual for the Field Archaeologist*. 3rd ed. Los Angeles: UCLA Institute of Archaeology.

See also Archaeometry; Betty's Hope Plantation (Antigua); DNA and Caribbean Archaeology; Ferrous and Nonferrous Metals; Port Royal (Jamaica).

Archaeological Heritage Management

Peter E. Siegel

Heritage is intimately linked to the core of community, which is frequently diverse. Every human group has a past within which fundamental notions of identity are centered. Historical memories link people to one another and to the ground (Shackel 2003). According to the International Committee on Archaeological Heritage Management (ICAHM), "'archaeological heritage' . . . comprises all vestiges of human existence and consists of places relating to all manifestations of human activity, abandoned structures, and remains of all kinds . . . together with all the portable cultural material associated with them" (ICAHM 1990, Article 1). "Protection and proper management [of archaeological heritage] is . . . essential to enable . . . scholars to study and interpret it . . . on behalf of . . . present and future generations" (ICAHM 1990, Introduction). The following entries review the status of heritage management for specific Caribbean nations. They are abstracted from chapters in *Protecting Heritage in the Caribbean* (2011), edited by Siegel and Righter.

Antigua and Barbuda

Heritage resources in Antigua and Barbuda are considered under several regulations "spread through different ministries and government agencies" (Murphy 2011, 74). Because of poor oversight, many resources have been destroyed. Among all the government agencies on Antigua and Barbuda, "the National Parks Authority and the Development Control Authority have the strongest legislation and Acts of Parliament granting them clear authority to declare, manage, and protect heritage sites" (ibid., 75).

The Bahamas

Heritage management in the Bahamas is based on the Antiquities, Monuments, and Museums Act of 1998, which provides for "the preservation, conservation, restoration, documentation, study and presentation of sites and objects of historical, anthropological, archaeological and paleontological interest [and] . . . establish[ed] a National Museum" (quoted in Pateman 2011, 4). The Antiquities Act centralized heritage management initiatives into one agency, facilitating better regulatory oversight. A permitting process was instituted for "the excavation and/or removal of antiquities . . . [and the] lev[ying of] fines against the destruction of antiquities without prior approval" (ibid., 5). One limitation of the Antiquities Act is the "lack [of] significant enforcement . . . , [especially] when dealing with multimillion-dollar development projects." In addition, the act "does not cover the protection of underwater heritage resources" (ibid., 8).

Barbados

There is strong legislation in Barbados but little enforcement. The Town and Country Planning Act of 1985 is a regulatory and permitting process developers must follow before projects may proceed if it is anticipated that impact of the project will affect listed heritage resources (Farmer 2011). The Amended Physical Development Plan of 2003 addressed "cultural heritage in a systematic and deliberate manner with a view toward protecting it . . . , including both the built heritage and areas of archaeological significance" (ibid., 117). The Barbados Museum and Historical Society, a nongovernmental organization, maintains "the list of archaeological sites, [which] in the past has been shared with the Town Planning Depart-

ment" (ibid., 116). "Archaeological protection becomes the activity of the Barbados Museum and Historical Society and The University of the West Indies, Cave Hill Campus, two institutions acting out of . . . responsibility but not supported by a legislative framework" (ibid., 119).

Cuba

Heritage protection in Cuba stems from two laws enacted in 1977, the Law of Protection of Cultural Patrimony and the Law of National and Local Monuments. On paper, these laws require planning studies to document and preserve "structures, sites, and declared objects that are National or Local Monuments" (Torres Etayo 2011, 13). There is also oversight of the issuance of permits to conduct archaeological investigations and the registration of cultural resources and sanctions for violations of heritage legislation.

Guantánamo Bay, Cuba

Since 1903, the U.S. government has maintained a military presence at Guantánamo Bay, located along the southeastern coast of Cuba. In 1994, the U.S. Department of Defense implemented Final Governing Standards (FGS) for environmental protection on Cuba (Larson 2011, 19). Heritage resources are included in the mandate of environmental protection. The FGS addressed "historic and cultural resources . . . designed to be consistent with the [U.S.] National Historic Preservation Act. . . . The sole intent is to be compatible with host nation regulations and provide U.S. forces with a consistent approach to achieving the goal of stewardship of host nation cultural resources" (ibid., 19–20).

Dominican Republic

Heritage management has evolved from no protection of patrimony during colonial occupations to formal legislation with inadequate enforcement. The State Secretary of Culture, which was created in 2000, mandates coordination "across state institutions that deal with cultural issues" (Prieto Vicioso 2011, 37). This legislation promoted a strategy to "protect the tangible and intangible patrimony of the Nation against exploitation by others, and to protect the traditional ways of life of the Dominican people" (quoted in ibid., 37). The problem with Dominican heritage protection is nonexistent enforcement of relevant legislation: "protection of Dominican cultural heritage has not been a priority for recent government administrations. . . . Agencies charged with heritage preservation do not receive the necessary support to . . . carry out their mandates" (ibid., 45).

French West Indies

The French West Indies include Basse-Terre, Grande-Terre, Île des Saintes, Marie-Galante, La Désirade, Martinique, St. Martin, and Saint Barthélemy. Since 1946, they have been integrated into France as overseas departments, and national laws apply (Bérard and Stouvenot 2011, 80). Despite French legislation, "heritage management . . . has been slow to develop" in the FWI. One problem is the poor fit between the "French homeland" and the islands, and "development of an Antillean-centered perspective" is needed (ibid., 89). The heritage legislation applicable to the French West Indies is called the Code du Patrimoine (ibid., 80).

Jamaica

Heritage resources protection falls within the purview of the Jamaica National Heritage Trust, which was formed in 1985 as a statutory agency (Richards and Henriques 2011, 26–27). The trust is mandated "to promote the preservation of national monuments and anything designated as protected national heritage for the benefit of the island" (ibid., 27). The act has been implemented slowly, and in some cases it has been misinterpreted.

The Dutch Caribbean (Formerly the Netherlands Antilles)

"After October 10, 2010, the Netherlands Antilles ceased to exist, presenting interesting challenges for the future" of heritage management on Aruba, Bonaire, Curaçao, St. Eustatius, Saba, and St. Maarten (Haviser and Gilmore 2011, 134). Bonaire, St. Eustatius, and Saba (the BES islands) have become municipalities of the Netherlands, while "Curaçao and St. Maarten [have] become autonomous entities [like Aruba]" (ibid., 140). The Kingdom of the Netherlands now consists of the Netherlands, Aruba, Curaçao, and St. Maarten. In 1968, the Archaeological-Anthropological Institute of the Netherlands Antilles (AAINA) was formed to further "scientific archaeological research and public awareness" (ibid., 136). In the 1990s, AAINA became a government foundation called the National Archaeological Anthropological Museum (NAAM) and its mission shifted to heritage management "with a primary focus on the island of Curaçao." The Netherlands Antilles ratified the Malta Convention in 2007, "ensur[ing] application of the treaty standards for the individual islands

until such time as they make island-level revisions" (ibid., 137). Curaçao "has the most effective heritage management program" in the Dutch Caribbean; it includes a Monuments Foundation and a Monuments Plan, which registers heritage resources in a master inventory (ibid.).

The Bonaire Archaeological Institute was established in 2003 as an educational, research, and heritage management foundation. Later, a Monuments Ordinance was formed that registers archaeological sites as heritage resources, although "enforcement has been weak" (ibid.). A Monuments Ordinance was formed on St. Maarten in 2000 "for the identification, regulation, and protection of historical monuments . . . [and] in 2005 the . . . Ordinance was revised to include archaeological sites" (ibid., 138). In 2007, the St. Maarten Archaeological Center was formed "for documenting, conducting research, and regulating archaeological sites and properties on the island," although developers are not required to conduct archaeological investigations (ibid.). Some developers have voluntarily sponsored investigations in advance of their projects. Saba established a Strategic Development Plan 1998–2002, which addressed some "aspects of cultural heritage management" (ibid.).

On St. Eustatius, a Monuments Foundation was established in 1990 and a Monuments Ordinance was legislated in 2008. St. Eustatius made a commitment to heritage protection by creating a position for a professional archaeologist, who is employed by the St. Eustatius Center for Archaeological Research (SECAR). "In the Netherlands, commercial archaeology conducted prior to development is the only option . . . [and that] archaeology is paid for by the developer" (ibid., 13). In 2007, the Netherlands Antilles ratified the European Convention on the Protection of the Archaeological Heritage, also known as the Valetta Treaty; it became effective on the BES islands in 2010. The treaty requires that archaeological work be conducted before any construction is undertaken. On St. Eustatius, SECAR is responsible for archaeological assessments. SECAR partners with SABARC in conducting archaeological work on Saba and Bonaire.

Puerto Rico

Cultural heritage in Puerto Rico is considered at one of two regulatory levels: U.S. federal or local commonwealth. Who owns the land, what sources of project funding are available, and which agencies issue permits determine the level of regulatory oversight. The U.S. National Historic Preservation Act (NHPA) was approved by Congress in 1966. Every state, territory, and commonwealth in the United States has an agency called the State Historic Preservation Office (SHPO), funded by the National Park Service, an agency in the Department of the Interior. SHPOs are responsible for commenting on work performed within the framework of federal historic preservation law. Many development projects in Puerto Rico do not receive federal funds, take place on non-federally administered lands, and do not require federal permits. As such, the NHPA is not applicable, the Puerto Rico SHPO has no regulatory oversight, and local legislation applies. Commonwealth Law 112 of 1988 created the Consejo para la Protección del Patrimonio Arqueológico Terrestre de Puerto Rico, or Consejo, an organ attached to the Instituto de Cultura Puertorriqueña. Law 112 specifies broad powers of enforcement: "obligations regarding every excavation, construction and reconstruction work that is carried out in Puerto Rico" (quoted in Siegel 2011, 49). In 1992, the Consejo published rules that must be followed when conducting archaeological research associated with development projects. Included are statements about ultimate disposition of collections and associated documentation.

St. Kitts and Nevis

In 1987, the National Conservation and Environmental Protection Act was created, which governs heritage management on St. Kitts and Nevis. However, "there are no explicit standards of cultural resource regulations . . . guid[ing] the government or developer on . . . cultural resource investigations." Additional measures are "outlined in the National Environmental Action Plans of 1994 and National Environmental Management Strategy and Action of 2005–2009." Other legislation requires the completion of environmental impact assessments "prior to any development of more than three structures," which includes consideration of heritage resources, "but no specific guidelines are available . . . [that] address the way . . . heritage studies are to be conducted." Challenges in protecting heritage are exacerbated by rivalries between the two islands and "economic dependency . . . on tourism [leading to] unregulated development [produce] a constant threat to the nation's cultural heritage" (Ahlman and Scudder-Temple 2011, 66). Heritage management will be enhanced if St. Kitts (St. Christopher National Trust) and Nevis (Nevis Historical and Conservation Society) cooperate with common initiatives.

Saint Lucia

Heritage protection on Saint Lucia falls within the jurisdiction of the Saint Lucia Archaeological and Historical Society (SLAHS), which was recognized by the govern-

ment of Saint Lucia in 1968 (Branford 2011, 91). In 1975, the Saint Lucia National Trust was created to serve as an additional heritage agency. Between these two entities, "heritage . . . preservation; protection; and management of . . . architectural and historic buildings [are carried out]. . . . Since 2003, salvage archaeology has been undertaken on sites designated for development and recommendations for protection . . . [are] submitted to the government and developers. Developers are required to pay for reconnaissance and salvage archaeological investigations associated with their projects. Artifacts collected during these studies are curated by the SLAHS" (Branford 2011, 92).

St. Vincent and the Grenadines

There are a number of heritage-protection laws for St. Vincent and the Grenadines. These include the St. Vincent and the Grenadines National Trust Acts; the Preservation of Historical Building and Antiquities Act; the Botanical Gardens Act; the Marine Parks Act; the National Parks Act; the Plant Protection Act; the Fisheries Act; the Wild Life Act; the Forest Resources Conservation Act; and the Town and Country Planning Act. However, "implementation . . . in heritage protection is questionable . . . [owing to the] lack [of] trained manpower and finances to enforce such legislation" (Lewis 2011, 101). Although enforcement is spotty, Callaghan observed that the National Trust is taking a proactive stance to "identify priorities and meet . . . developers to . . . convince them to set aside . . . portions of sites for the future even if they are not currently listed in the PNH" (2011, 110). Legislative Act 37 of 2007 "provides the National Trust with the authority to 'declare as "Protected National Heritage" any place, building or object, which should be . . . protected on account of its national interest, or the archaeological, historic, artistic, architectural, scientific or traditional interest'" (quoted in ibid.).

Trinidad and Tobago

Heritage protection falls within the purview of the National Trust of Trinidad and Tobago; the Archaeological Committee of Trinidad and Tobago; the Advisory Committee on Historic Wrecks; the Archaeology Centre of the Department of History, University of the West Indies; and the World Heritage Convention (Reid and Lewis 2011, 126–30). Heritage resources managers face challenges, including the lack of enforcement: "Mandates requiring archaeological investigations in advance of development are ignored." Poor interagency coordination is a problem, and there is no centralized plan for regulatory oversight. As a result, consideration of heritage resources on Trinidad and Tobago is less than adequate (ibid., 130–31). The way forward for heritage protection is through productive dialogue among stakeholders, including "policy makers, archaeologists, museologists, heritage managers, developers, and members of the public" (ibid., 133).

United States Virgin Islands

Despite the fact that the U.S. National Historic Preservation Act applies to projects that receive federal funding, require federal permits, or take place on federal land, regulatory oversight on federally mandated archaeological projects in the United States Virgin Islands is inadequate (Righter 2011, 61–62). The Antiquities Act, the local heritage legislation, applies to projects without a federal link. "The goals of the Antiquities Act are lofty, and, as is frequently the case . . . local law does not provide staff or adequate funding for the additional workload involved with implementation of the law" (ibid., 63). Volunteer organizations and historical societies maintain interest in heritage preservation with uneven results (ibid., 64).

Heritage Protection in the Caribbean

One might ask, "Why are things of the past important to protect, conserve, manage, or consider when things of the present are increasingly dire?" Is heritage preservation a nicety of the global North? Consideration of Caribbean heritage resources ranges from seemingly strong and enforced legislation that is backed by government oversight to no apparent interest in preserving the past to instances of purposely obliterating a past associated with painful memories. The people of each nation must decide if cultural heritage is worthy of consideration in the face of development and, if so, what measures will be taken to achieve that goal.

Further Reading

Ahlman, T. M., and K. Scudder-Temple. 2011. "St. Kitts and Nevis." In *Protecting Heritage in the Caribbean*, ed. P. E. Siegel and E. Righter, 65–72. Tuscaloosa: University of Alabama Press.

Bérard, B., and C. Stouvenot. 2011. "French West Indies." In *Protecting Heritage in the Caribbean*, ed. P. E. Siegel and E. Righter, 80–89. Tuscaloosa: University of Alabama Press.

Branford, M. E. 2011. "Saint Lucia." In *Protecting Heritage in the Caribbean*, ed. P. E. Siegel and E. Righter, 90–95. Tuscaloosa: University of Alabama Press.

Callaghan, R. T. 2011. "St. Vincent and the Grenadines: Recent Efforts in Protecting Heritage." In *Protecting Heritage in the Caribbean*, ed. P. E. Siegel and E. Righter, 106–11. Tuscaloosa: University of Alabama Press.

Farmer, K. 2011. "Barbados." In *Protecting Heritage in the Caribbean*, edited by P. E. Siegel and E. Righter, 112–24. Tuscaloosa: University of Alabama Press.

Haviser, J. B., and G. Gilmore III. 2011. "Netherlands Antilles." In *Protecting Heritage in the Caribbean*, ed. P. E. Siegel and E. Righter, 134–42. Tuscaloosa: University of Alabama Press.

International Committee on Archaeological Heritage Management. 1990. *A Charter for the Protection and Management of the Archaeological Heritage Management.* Paris: International Council on Monuments and Sites.

Larson, B. J. 2011. "United States Naval Station, Guantánamo Bay, Cuba." In *Protecting Heritage in the Caribbean*, ed. P. E. Siegel and E. Righter, 15–25. Tuscaloosa: University of Alabama Press.

Lewis, P. E. 2011. "St. Vincent and the Grenadines." In *Protecting Heritage in the Caribbean*, ed. P. E. Siegel and E. Righter, 96–105. Tuscaloosa: University of Alabama Press.

Murphy, R. 2011. "Antigua and Barbuda." In *Protecting Heritage in the Caribbean*, ed. P. E. Siegel and E. Righter, 73–79. Tuscaloosa: University of Alabama Press.

Pateman, M. P. 2011. "The Bahamas." In *Protecting Heritage in the Caribbean*, ed. P. E. Siegel and E. Righter, 1–8. Tuscaloosa: University of Alabama Press.

Prieto Vicioso, E. 2011. "Dominican Republic." In *Protecting Heritage in the Caribbean*, ed. P. E. Siegel and E. Righter, 35–45. Tuscaloosa: University of Alabama Press.

Reid, B. A., and V. Lewis. 2011. "Trinidad and Tobago." In *Protecting Heritage in the Caribbean*, ed. P. E. Siegel and E. Righter, 125–33. Tuscaloosa: University of Alabama Press.

Richards, A., and A. Henriques. 2011. "Jamaica." In *Protecting Heritage in the Caribbean*, ed. P. E. Siegel and E. Righter, 26–34. Tuscaloosa: University of Alabama Press.

Righter, E. 2011. "U.S. Virgin Islands." In *Protecting Heritage in the Caribbean*, ed. P. E. Siegel and E. Righter, 58–64. Tuscaloosa: University of Alabama Press.

Shackel, P. 2003. *Memory in Black and White: Race, Commemoration, and the Post-Bellum Landscape.* Walnut Creek, CA: AltaMira Press.

Siegel, P. E. 2011. "Puerto Rico." In *Protecting Heritage in the Caribbean*, ed. P. E. Siegel and E. Righter, 46–57. Tuscaloosa: University of Alabama Press.

Siegel, P. E., and E. Righter, eds. 2011. *Protecting Heritage in the Caribbean.* Tuscaloosa: University of Alabama Press.

Torres Etayo, D. 2011. "Cuba." In *Protecting Heritage in the Caribbean*, ed. P. E. Siegel and E. Righter, 9–14. Tuscaloosa: University of Alabama Press.

See also The Archaeological Committee of Trinidad and Tobago; The Dutch Caribbean; The Jamaica National Heritage Trust; The National Trust of Trinidad and Tobago; Rescue Archaeology.

The Archaeological Society of Jamaica

Lesley-Gail Atkinson

The Archaeological Club of Jamaica, the predecessor of the Archaeological Society of Jamaica (ASJ), was formed in February 1965. The club was founded by Dr. James W. Lee and nine archaeologists and archaeological enthusiasts. Five years later, the Archaeological Club expanded, and on September 5, 1970, The Archaeological Society of Jamaica was established with a total of 40 members.

The ASJ is administered by the Executive Committee, which consists of the following ten positions: president, vice-president, secretary and treasurer, and the floor members. The most prolific president of the ASJ has been Dr. James W. Lee, a Canadian geologist who lived and worked in Jamaica from 1951 to 1986. Dr. Lee served as president for 17 years. The constitution has since then been revised so that the president cannot serve more than three consecutive years.

The ASJ and its members have played an integral role in the development of Jamaican archaeology. Its central objective is to research, preserve and promote Jamaica's archaeological heritage. The functions of the society include discovering new sites, doing site surveys, conducting and participating in fieldwork, promoting awareness, and preserving Jamaica's archaeological resources. As early as 1959, James Lee began mapping all the known Taíno (formerly known as Arawak) sites on the island. Thus, for the first 20 years, the society's primary focus was on the island's prehistory. During this period, Dr. Lee and the ASJ located and mapped 265 sites on the island. A number of members of the society conducted excavations, such as Father Osborne, who excavated Bengal (1962) and Cinnamon Hill (1974), and John Wilman, who conducted excavations at Rodney's House (1978 and 1979). In 2000, James Lee donated his collection of Jamaican prehistoric artifacts to The University of the West Indies, Mona Campus. The analysis of this collection was published in Philip Allsworth-Jones's *Pre-Columbian Jamaica* (2008). In addition to research on Taíno sites, members of the ASJ conducted excavations at Spanish sites such as Sevilla La Nueva (New Seville). Lieutenant Commander J. S. Tyndale-Biscoe worked on excavations there in the 1950s and 1960s, and Captain Charles S. Cotter excavated the site for almost 40 years until his death in 1977. During the 1990s, Afro-Jamaican,

Maroon, and Jewish archaeology became important research areas within the ASJ. Currently, the interests of the society are more diverse and have tended to reflect research trends on the island.

In attempts to encourage the preservation of archaeological sites, the ASJ has collaborated with several interest groups and organizations such as the Jamaica National Heritage Trust (JNHT), The University of the West Indies (Mona), and the Jamaica Historical Society. Presently, members of the Archaeological Society of Jamaica sit on the board of the JNHT, represent Jamaica's position on the ratification of the UNESCO Convention for Underwater Cultural Heritage Committee, and Jamaica's UNESCO World Heritage Sites Nomination Committee. One special preservation project was at Mountain River Cave, St. Catherine, the most prominent rock art site on the island; it has over 200 pictographs (rock paintings) and several petroglyphs (rock carvings). The site, which was initially discovered in the late nineteenth century, was lost until it was rediscovered in 1954 by James Lee and Robert Cooper. In 1976, the ASJ bought two acres of land that housed the rock art site. With the assistance of the Jamaica Defence Force, the society built a protective grill to shelter the cave from the elements and vandals. In May 1982, the ASJ handed over the management of the Mountain River Cave to the JNHT.

The main avenue for promoting the work of the ASJ and current research on the island is the society's newsletter, *Archaeology Jamaica*, which was first published in January 1965. The newsletter was initially produced monthly, but it is now an annual publication. Members of the ASJ have sought to highlight research in Jamaica by presenting papers at the International Congress of Caribbean Archaeology (IACA) and other archaeology conferences. The society has placed considerable emphasis on developing student awareness of Jamaica's archaeological heritage by hosting essay/poster/photo competitions and archaeological field schools and participating in exhibitions and expositions. Over the years, the society has hosted conferences for the Society for Historical Archaeology (January 1992) and the World Archaeological Congress Inter-Congress (May 2007), and since April 2002 it has held its own annual symposium.

Further Reading

Allsworth-Jones, P. 2008. *Pre-Columbian Jamaica*. Tuscaloosa: University of Alabama Press.

Cotter, C. S. 1970. "Sevilla la Nueva: The Story of Excavation." *Jamaica Journal* 4 (2): 15–22.

Keegan, W. F., and L. Atkinson. 2006. "The Development of Jamaican Prehistory." In *The Earliest Inhabitants: The Dynamics of the Jamaican Taíno*, ed. L. Atkinson, 13–33. Kingston: University of West Indies Press.

Lee, J. W. 1980/2006. "Jamaican Redware." In *Proceedings of the Eighth International Congress for the Study of Pre-Columbian Cultures of the Lesser Antilles, St. Kitts, 1979*, ed. S. M. Lewenstein, 597–609. Tempe: University of Arizona. Reprinted in *The Earliest Inhabitants: The Dynamics of the Jamaican Taíno*, ed. L. Atkinson, 153–60. Kingston: University of the West Indies Press.

See also Jamaica (Prehistory of); The Jamaica National Heritage Trust.

Archaeometry

Corinne L. Hofman

Archaeometry is the application of a variety of scientific methods and techniques in order to chemically and physically analyze archaeological materials. Archaeometric research uses analytical techniques from biology, earth sciences, chemistry, and physics to measure or quantify parameters in order to determine the ages of sites and artifacts, identify human mobility, provide insights into paleodietary exploitation and consumption patterns, establish the provenance of raw materials, and reconstruct the manufacturing processes of various materials. Among the main archaeometric methods and techniques are unstable (carbon-14) and stable isotope analysis (e.g., carbon, nitrogen, strontium, oxygen, lead, and sulfur), X-ray fluorescence, instrumental neutron activation analysis (INAA), X-ray diffraction, and ancient DNA analysis. These geophysical and geochemical analyses are often combined with a range of other "softer" technological approaches that include microscopic use-wear analysis and starch residue, phytolith, and pollen analysis. Experimental and ethnoarchaeological research can later be used to conceptualize the sociocultural behavior behind the technological sequence in the manufacture of artifacts.

Many of these approaches have long proven to be very successful in the study of archaeological materials elsewhere in the world. However, in the Caribbean, these techniques were less common and were not applied systematically until recently. The following examples illustrate some of the most recent advances in the application of archaeometric techniques in the Caribbean. These are only a few of the many methods and techniques from the archaeological sciences that have been successfully applied over the past decades to the study of archaeological materials from this region (for an overview see Hofman et al. 2008).

The most commonly used archaeometric technique is radiocarbon dating. Recently, "chronometric hygiene" has been applied to sets of Caribbean radiocarbon dates in order to eliminate unreliable and contaminated dates. This involves calibrating marine and terrestrial samples and correcting for the "marine reservoir effect" (Fitzpatrick 2006). Stable carbon and nitrogen isotope analysis has contributed to our understanding of prehistoric diet during the past decade. This technique is continuously being refined and combined with other isotopes. Recent applications of strontium, lead, and sulfur isotopes have provided insights into the mobility of precolonial insular communities (Laffoon et al. 2012). Although in its infancy, the analysis of ancient mitochondrial DNA in the Caribbean has also revealed some interesting patterns in precolonial migrations into the Caribbean islands from South America. Provenance studies of stone and pottery artifacts have been achieved through the use of archaeometric techniques such as thin sectioning and petrographic analysis, X-ray diffraction, and X-ray fluorescence, among others (e.g., Descantes et al. 2008).

Microscopic use-wear analysis and experimental archaeology have led to a better understanding of how Caribbean artifacts made of stone, ceramic, shell, bone, antler, and coral were manufactured and handled during domestic activities (Lammers-Keysers 2007). Both phytolith and starch grain analyses have identified plants and organic materials on precolonial lithic plant-processing tools, ceramics and dental calculus (Mickleburgh and Pagán-Jiménez 2012). The combination of wear patterns and starch residues reveal that many artifacts had multiple functions. This finding offers insights into the subsistence system of various Caribbean populations and provides information on intra- and interregional human-plant interactions through time and space.

Further Reading

Descantes, C., R. J. Speakman, M. D. Glascock, and M. T. Boulanger. 2008. "An Exploratory Study into the Chemical Characterization of Caribbean Ceramics." Special publication #2, *Journal of Caribbean Archaeology*.

Fitzpatrick, S. M. 2006. "A Critical Approach to 14C Dating in the Caribbean: Using Chronometric Hygiene to Evaluate Chronological Control and Prehistoric Settlement." *Latin American Antiquity* 17 (4): 389–418.

Hofman, Corinne L., M. L. P. Hoogland, and A. van Gijn, eds. 2008. *Crossing the Borders: New Methods and Techniques in the Study of Archaeological Materials from the Caribbean.* Tuscaloosa: University of Alabama Press.

Laffoon, J. E., G. R. Davies, M. L. P. Hoogland, and C. L. Hofman. 2012. "Spatial Variation of Biologically Available Strontium Isotopes (87Sr/86Sr) in an Archipelagic Setting: A Case Study from the Caribbean." *Journal of Archaeological Science* 39 (7): 2371–384.

Lammers-Keysers, Y. 2007. *Tracing Traces from Present to Past: A Functional Analysis of Pre-Columbian Shell and Stone Artefacts from Anse a la Gourde and Morel, Guadeloupe, FWI.* Leiden: Leiden University Press Academic.

Mickleburgh, H. L., and J. Pagán-Jiménez. 2012. "New Insights into the Consumption of Maize and Other Food Plants in the Pre-Columbian Caribbean from Starch Grains Trapped in Human Dental Calculus." *Journal of Archaeological Science* 39 (7): 2468–78.

See also The First Caribbean Farmers; Grindstones.

The Archaic Age

Basil A. Reid

The Archaic Age in the Caribbean spans from 5000 BC to 200 BC and is generally considered to be a developmental stage characterized by a marine-oriented subsistence followed by a terrestrial hunting-based economy. The two major groups associated with this period are the Ortoiroid (5000 BC–200 BC) and the Casimiroid (4000 BC–400 BC) (Figure A.8). The Archaic people were formerly referred to as Ciboney in popular literature and in some scholarly writings. However, the term Ciboney is a misnomer, because it specifically refers to a local Taíno group in central Cuba (Reid 2009).

The Ortoiroid, who originated from northwest Guyana and took their name from the shell midden of Ortoire in southeast Trinidad, first settled Banwari Trace and St. John in Trinidad approximately 7,000 years ago, eventually colonizing the entire swath of the eastern Caribbean region as far north as Puerto Rico. However, Richard T. Callaghan's computer simulations suggest that some Ortoiroid groups may have jumped directly from South America to the Greater Antilles. The artifacts from Banwari Trace and St. John include tools made of bones and stone related to fishing and collecting, canoe building, plant processing, and general cutting and scraping (Boomert 2000). Many of the ground stone tools appear to have been used for pounding and processing hard and fibrous vegetable matter.

Taking their name from archaeological type-site of Casimira in southwestern Hispaniola, the Casimiroid migrated from Belize around 4000 BC and colonized both Cuba and Hispaniola. Casimiroid stone tools, which are similar to those of the Ortoiroid, include sophisticated blades, which they used as spear points to hunt sloths and manatees; conical pestles and mortars to prepare food; a variety of possibly ritual implements such as stone balls, disks, and dagger-like objects; and elaborate stone beads and shell jewelry. Casimiroid sites, which date to around 2660 BC, have been identified on the north and south coasts of Haiti. In the Dominican Republic, Casimiroid sites are located in river valleys and along the coast. It appears that Casimiroid ground stone tools in south-central Cuba were first shaped by flaking, which was then followed by pecking and grinding (Reid 2009). There is growing evidence of interactions between the Ortoiroid and the Casimiroid from Puerto Rico and the northern Leeward Islands; the sites of Maruca (Puerto Rico) and Jolly Beach (Antigua) are cited as prime examples of such cultural exchanges (Wilson 2007).

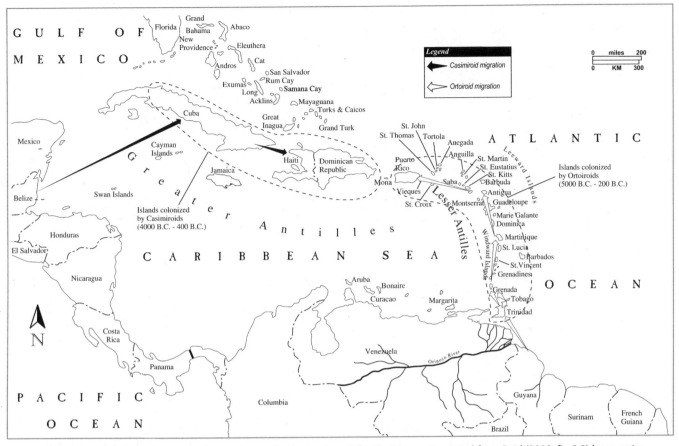

Figure A.8. Ortoiroid and Casimiroid migration and colonization of the Caribbean. Reprinted from Reid (2009, fig.2.2) by permission of the University of Alabama Press.

Archaic Age sites are also typically characterized by shell middens and waste material (or debitage) from the manufacture of stone tools. They are mostly situated in close proximity to marine ecosystems that are rich with shellfish, mangroves, and shallow grassy bottom bays that have a high diversity of species. Archaic stone technology was based on the reduction of flint cobbles to produce blades and usable flakes. The reduction process used a hard percussor to remove the outer layers or cortex of the cobbles, creating a core and platform from which flakes could be removed or struck off. At times, the larger blades were retouched to make specialized tools, such as backed knives, scrapers, and burins. Excellent examples of these have been recovered at a number of sites on Antigua. Ground stone tools are also represented but are comparatively rare. Bowls, mortars, pestles, and axes are the most common of these items.

For years, the Archaic Age was defined by the absence of pottery and agricultural practices. However, increasing evidence of pottery-making and horticultural practices at Archaic sites has now invalidated the idea

that neither the Ortoiroid nor the Casimiroid practiced pottery-making and agriculture. It is now generally accepted that pottery-making and incipient agriculture began in the Caribbean during the Archaic rather than the Saladoid period. Notable examples of pottery-bearing Archaic sites are Couri I and Pascade II in Haiti, the Playa Blanca and Jobos sites in Puerto Rico, El Caimito at the La Caleta site in eastern Dominican Republic, Krum Bay in the United States Virgin Islands and La Luz, and El Nispero and Catunda in Cuba. Unlike Saladoid pottery, which has a highly formalized grammar, the pots in Archaic sites seem to reflect a period of experimentation during which different pastes and decorative techniques were explored (Keegan and Rodríguez Ramos 2007). Botanical studies of preserved starch grains on grinding tools have demonstrated that virtually all of the plants that were supposedly introduced by the Saladoid were already being cultivated by their Archaic predecessors. Numerous Archaic Age grindstones and pestles and tools commonly associated with the processing of plants (seeds, roots, fruit, etc.) suggest that both the Ortoiroid and Casimiroid were part of early horticultural societies who planted and foraged over a wide area, moving seasonally within and between the islands and sites to exploit a variety of plant resources. Given these realities, a more appropriate definition for the Archaic Age in the Caribbean would be a period of marine-oriented subsistence followed by a terrestrial hunting-based economy, coupled with transition from a highly mobile hunting and gathering life to a more settled agricultural life.

Further Reading

Boomert, A. 2000. *Trinidad, Tobago, and the Lower Orinoco Interaction Sphere: An Archaeological/Ethnohistorical Study.* Alkmaar: Cairi.

Keegan, W. F., and R. Rodríguez Ramos. 2007. "Archaic Origins of the Classic Taínos." In *Proceedings of the Twenty-First Congress of the International Association for Caribbean Archaeology*, vol. 1, ed. B. Reid, H. P. Roget, and C. Antonio, 211–17. St. Augustine, Trinidad and Tobago: School of Continuing Studies, University of the West Indies.

Reid, B. A. 2009. *Myths and Realities of Caribbean History.* Tuscaloosa: University of Alabama Press.

Wilson, S. M. 2007. *The Archaeology of the Caribbean.* New York: Cambridge University Press.

See also Antigua and Barbuda (Archaic Sites); Ciboney versus Guanahatabey; The First Caribbean Farmers; Grindstones.

The Association of Caribbean Historians

Bridget Brereton and Sherry-Ann Singh

The Association of Caribbean Historians (ACH) is an independent, nonprofit, professional association of persons who research, write about, and teach the history of the Caribbean region. Its several hundred members are based in the region and in other parts of the Americas, Europe, Africa, and Asia. They include academic and public historians, archaeologists, graduate students, archivists, librarians, museum curators, secondary and tertiary level teachers, members of local historical societies, and others.

The origin of the ACH and of the annual Conferences of Caribbean Historians can be traced to 1969. In that year, Jacques Adelaide-Merlande of the Centre Universitaire des Antilles et de Guyane asked the Department of History of The University of the West Indies (UWI) if some of its members could join him in a small colloquium in Guadeloupe on the theme "From Slavery to Emancipation." Three members of the multi-campus History Department attended (Woodville Marshall, Carl Campbell, and Neville Hall), as did a few of Adelaide-Merlande's colleagues. Nine papers were presented and discussed. As the result of discussions in Guadeloupe and later discussions, UWI historians organized the second conference in 1970 at the Barbados campus of UWI. Continuing informal discussions on a wider basis led to conferences at the University of Guyana in 1971 and at the Jamaica and Trinidad campuses of UWI in 1972 and

1973, respectively. Thanks largely to the efforts of Douglas Hall of the Jamaica campus of UWI and Marshall, the decision was made to establish the ACH as a formal body at the Trinidad conference in 1973. As a result, at the sixth conference in 1974 at San Juan, Puerto Rico, the ACH constitution was adopted and the organization came into being, with Marshall as its first president and Campbell as its first secretary/treasurer.

Since 1974, each annual conference has included an annual general meeting of the ACH. Up to the time of writing (2011), fifteen persons have served as president for consecutive terms of from one to three years. Two persons, Adelaide-Merlande and Marshall, have served for two separate, nonconsecutive terms. Most of the presidents have come from universities or national archives throughout the region, but they have also included historians based in the United States. The Executive Committee consists of the president, the vice-president, the secretary/treasurer, and four other members, who are elected by the membership. The ACH does not have a fixed physical location; in effect, its base is the location of the current secretary/treasurer, who runs the organization between conferences and helps organize the conferences in collaboration with the host institution (usually a university in the particular Caribbean country chosen). In 1974, the ACH adopted as its logo the Birdman, a Jamaican Taíno carving found in the late eighteenth century that is now located in the British Museum.

The main aims of the ACH, according to its constitution, are to promote historical studies of the Caribbean, to facilitate regular communications and exchange of information among historians working on the region, and to keep under review the state of history teaching in the different countries of the region. The ACH produces two bulletins a year for its members, which are now posted online on the ACH Web site. The bulletins and the Web site provide information about the ACH and its conferences and about many other activities, conferences, publications, and so forth of interest to its members. The ACH awards two prizes, which are announced every two years. The most prestigious is the Elsa Goveia Book Prize, which was established soon after 1980 and is named for the distinguished Guyanese-born, UWI-based historian who died in that year. It is awarded for the best book on Caribbean history published over a two-year period, and a special committee makes the selection. The Andrés Ramos Mattei-Neville Hall Article Prize, which was established in 1995 to commemorate two active ACH members who had died, is awarded for the best article on Caribbean history published in a journal over a two-year period; it is also selected by a special committee.

The most important activity of the ACH, however, continues to be the organization of the annual conferences held in different Caribbean countries. Starting in 1969, before the ACH existed, these conferences have been held every year without a break; the 43rd conference was in 2011 in Puerto Rico. Conferences have been held (up to 2011) in Guadeloupe, Martinique, Guyane, Guyana, Suriname, Colombia, Trinidad and Tobago, Barbados, Curaçao, St. Thomas, the Bahamas, Jamaica, Puerto Rico, Cuba, and the Dominican Republic. At the first small meeting in 1969, nine papers were presented; at the 43rd conference in 2011, 57 papers were presented, grouped in 17 panels.

From time to time, papers on particular aspects of Caribbean archaeology are presented. For instance, at the 1978 conference in St. Thomas, a paper was presented on prehistoric rock art in Guyana and the Antilles, and at the eighteenth Conference in 1986 in the Bahamas, a paper was presented on the archaeological record of early nineteenth-century plantations on San Salvador, Bahamas. At the 1983 conference in Jamaica, a panel on archaeology included papers on nautical archaeology, Port Royal, and the surface collections of the Seville Heritage Park. In 1988, at the 20th conference in St. Thomas, a paper was presented on the first phase of archaeological research on the village of enslaved individuals at Seville, Jamaica. At the 22nd conference, in Trinidad, a paper was presented on archaeology in the teaching of history at the secondary school level in the English-speaking Caribbean, and at the 24th conference, held in the Bahamas, there was a panel on archaeological research in that country.

Further Reading

Association of Caribbean Historians. 2011. "The ACH." http://www.associationofcaribbeanhistorians.org. Accessed January 8, 2013.

See also The International Association for Caribbean Archaeology (IACA).

The Bahamas and the Turks and Caicos Islands

Jeffrey P. Blick

Prehistoric Archaeology in the Bahamas and the Turks and Caicos Islands

Prehistoric archaeology in the Bahamas and the Turks and Caicos Islands began in the 1880s with work conducted by William Brooks. Later, after collecting notable artifacts, including wooden paddles, *duhos*, stone carvings, and human skeletal remains, Theodoor de Booy was able to place the cultures and peoples of the Bahamas and the Turks and Caicos Islands in their proper relationships to other Native American cultures on mainland Florida, in the Caribbean, and in Central America. Archaeologists such as John Goggin (1939) (on Andros) and Julian Granberry (on Bimini and the Gordon Hill site on Crooked Island) continued the early work in the Bahamas and the Turks and Caicos Islands (Granberry 1955, 1957, 1978). Granberry also wrote extensively on Lucayan toponyms and linguistics. Avocational archaeologist Ruth Durlacher-Wolper discovered numerous prehistoric sites and founded the New World Museum on San Salvador.

Modern excavations in the Bahamas began with the work of Charles A. Hoffman Jr. on San Salvador, where he did work at Palmetto Grove. Hoffman's (1967, 1970) large-scale excavation was the first to identify Palmetto Ware as a major ceramic type in the Bahamas. Hoffman's work was also one of the first in the Bahamas to offer a systematic typology of Caribbean-area shell tools; this work was recently updated by Sharyn Jones and William Keegan (2001). While there has been some discussion of possible early (even Archaic) occupation in the Bahamian Archipelago, evidence for such early occupation is sparse and is only vaguely implied by early radiocarbon dates that are likely contaminated or problematic. Dates of 1880–1730 BC from North Storr's Lake and AD 120–260 from Minnis Ward, both based on charcoal from San Salvador, suggest that an earlier occupation in the Bahamian Archipelago is an unlikely scenario. The occupation of the Bahamas and the Turks and Caicos Islands dates to the Post-Saladoid/Early Ostionoid period, circa AD 600–900. Berman refers to this period as the Antillean expansion period, during which Ostionoid peoples migrated from the Greater Antilles into the Bahamian Archipelago, where they underwent in situ development to become the Lucayan Taíno. The Taíno in the Bahamas are referred to as Lucayans, derived from "*lukku cairi*," the Lucayan Taíno word for "people of the island."

Early period sites include Three Dog on San Salvador, Preacher's Cave on Eleuthera, and Coralie (AD 700–1170) on the Turks and Caicos Islands. Three Dog, which dates to AD 600–1030, is one of the earliest occupations in the Bahamas. It was excavated by Mary Jane Berman and Perry Gnivecki (1995). Early ceramics from Three Dog are similar to Cuba's Arroyo del Palo pottery, while John Winter and team (Winter and Gilstrap 1991) demonstrated ceramic ties between San Salvador, Hispaniola, and Cuba. Recent identification of Crooked Island Ware at Minnis Ward, San Salvador, suggests that Minnis Ward may also have an early component coeval with Three Dog and Preacher's Cave.

The intermediate prehistoric period, circa AD 900–1200, is sometimes called the Late Ostionoid or the Early Lucayan period. Recent settlement pattern studies on San Salvador (Figure B.1) by Blick, Hopkins, and Oetter (2011) suggest that sparse early occupation expanded from a few sites to virtually the entire island, indicating a period of relatively robust population growth. Further evidence of population growth and dispersal throughout the Bahamas around AD 1200 was detected by Eric Kjellmark (1996) on Andros Island vegetation, which suggests either human arrival or an increase in slash-and-burn cultivation. A human tibia from Sawmill Sink, Abaco, dates to the beginning of this period, AD 900–1030. Evidence of population growth during the intermediate period is reflected in the abundance of sites throughout the Bahamas, including Pink Wall (AD 850–1150), Clifton Pier (AD 1000–1200), and Alexandra (AD

Figure B.1. Prehistoric archaeological sites on San Salvador, Bahamas. The Long Bay site (SS-9), SW portion of the island, is the probable landfall of Columbus in 1492. Other sites mentioned in the article are indicated. Map drawn by Katrien Janin.

990–1310) on New Providence Island; McKay (AD 1200–1300) on Crooked Island; Pigeon Creek Dune 2 on San Salvador (AD 895–1170); and GI-12 (AD 1040–1270) on Great Inagua. Minnis Ward (AD 970–1430) and North Storr's Lake (AD 860–1310), both on San Salvador, also have components from this period.

The late prehistoric period, circa AD 1200–1492, called the Taíno period, the Taíno florescent period, or the Late Lucayan period, exhibited major population growth in many parts of the Bahamas, especially on San Salvador and areas of the northern Bahamas. This period continued until and just beyond the arrival of the Spanish into the Bahamas. Kjellmark (1996) demonstrated agricultural intensification on Andros based on the rise of charcoal particles in blue-hole sediments and concomitant changes in plant communities and an increase in disturbance indicators from AD 1210 to 1520. Perhaps the most spectacular late prehistoric site in the Bahamas is Deadman's Reef on Grand Bahama, which Berman and Gnivecki excavated. Large quantities of wooden remains with vestiges of anthropomorphic and zoomorphic carvings and designs have been dated to AD 1400–1485. Berman believes these wooden carvings and designs are suggestive of hallucinatory imagery that may have been inspired by the use of *cohoba* snuff (*Anadenanthera peregrina*). Grace Turner (2006a) reports a tiny charred corn cob from Preacher's Cave on Eleuthera dated to AD 1430–1570, around the same time period.

Late radiocarbon dates are reported from Barker's Point Shell Midden (AD 1170–1510), North Storr's Lake (AD 1520–1550), Pigeon Creek (AD 1435–1635), and Three Dog (AD 1492, lead shot) on San Salvador. The end of the late prehistoric period in the Bahamian Archipelago is marked by the arrival of Columbus in 1492, the best evidence for which is the intermingling of Lucayan and Spanish artifacts in the same strata at Long Bay, San Salvador. Lucayan occupation may have persisted in the Bahamas into the 1520s and 1540s and perhaps as late as the 1550s, as indicated by a number of radiocarbon dates from artifacts found from Eleuthera to San Salvador.

Although early archaeological interest in the Turks and Caicos Islands was spawned by the work of De Booy and others, modern systematic surveys and excavations were first carried out in the Turks and Caicos by William H. Sears and Shaun Sullivan (Sullivan 1981). This work was followed by that of William Keegan and associates (Carlson 1999; Keegan 1992). Coralie, Grand Turk, dated to AD 705–1170, is one of the earliest sites in the Turks and Caicos and is best known for its massive quantity of sea turtle (*Cheloniidae*) remains and for the presence of now-extinct fauna such as ground tortoises and birds, as reported by Betsy Carlson and W. Keegan (Carlson 1999; Carlson and Keegan 2004). Sea turtles outweighed all other animal taxa at Coralie, where the massive number of vertebrate fauna included some 6,500 pieces of sea turtles. Coralie has one of the largest samples of prehistoric sea turtle bones in the Bahamian archipelago, if not the entire Greater Caribbean. In the Turks and Caicos, Coralie (AD 1000–1200), Governor's Beach (AD 1000–1330), Kendrick (AD 1020–1240), and the MC-12 site on Middle Caicos (AD 1040–1280) date approximately to the intermediate period (ca. AD 900–1200). Governor's Beach, which Carlson (1993) has researched, probably has the largest collection of beads and bead manufacturing debris of any site in the pan-Caribbean region. The site, which has been dated to AD 1100–1200, contained thousands of whole beads, blanks, and bead fragments, and around 14,000 bead-making scraps and debitage. Governor's Beach was a Taíno site with connections to the Greater Antilles, rather than a Lucayan site. The Governor's Beach bead makers were obviously skilled artisans who fashioned red and white shell disc beads from *Chama sarda* (the cherry jewel box clam) and *Strombus gigas* (queen conch). The site was apparently a seasonal bead-making camp that was used for only a few months of the year.

Finally, Ia góra (MC-6) is an example of a late period site in the Turks and Caicos Islands. The site has been dated to circa AD 1200. Sullivan and Keegan described it as a chief's village with a ceremonial plaza or ball court between two groups of houses of differing social status. Interpretation of rock mounds on the site suggested that higher-status households may have been built on small platform mounds. More recently, MC-6 has been interpreted as a chiefly village that controlled access to salt resources of a nearby hypersaline pond. Keegan (1992) hypothesizes that salt was a high-value commodity that was traded throughout the pan-Caribbean because of its value as a dietary supplement and as a preservative for fish and other foodstuffs. Control and distribution of such necessary and desirable goods, including shell beads such as those from Governor's Beach, would have provided Taíno elites with opportunities to trade, travel, and expand their influence, thus increasing their social status. During this late period, which is rightly referred to as the Taíno florescent period, chiefdoms emerged in the Bahamas and the Turks and Caicos Islands before their development was curtailed by the arrival of the Europeans in the late fifteenth century.

Historical Archaeology in the Bahamas and the Turks and Caicos

Historical archaeology in the Bahamian Archipelago begins with the 1492 landfall of Columbus at Long Bay, San Salvador, and the contact between the Lucayans and Europeans. A small piece of evidence of Spanish contact on San Salvador includes an item that was not necessarily traded: a Spanish colonial lead *arquebus* (or pistol) ball that Berman and Gnivecki found about 2.7 kilometers south of Long Bay at the Three Dog site. The lead *arquebus* ball has been seen by very few, but that number includes Robert H. Brill, who tested lead scrapings from the ball (personal communication). The ball is similar in size to other lead *arquebus* balls of the time, such as those found at another Columbus-era settlement, La Isabela, in the Dominican Republic (1493–1498), and the Coronado expedition's 2nd infantry encampment in North America (1541). The lead from the *arquebus* ball has been sourced to the Sierra de Gador mining region in Spain and is compositionally similar to the lead in a small bronze buckle excavated at Long Bay. In his *Diario*, Columbus mentions several times the firing of an *espingarda*, a predecessor of the *arquebus*, musket, and rifle that was introduced in the mid-1400s but was superseded by the musket in Spain around 1520. It is clear that Columbus had weapons aboard that were capable of firing a lead *arquebus* ball, although some scholars believe that smaller shot was fired from *bomdardetas* (barrel-tube cannons) as scatter shot (Malcolm 1996).

The St. John's Bahamas Shipwreck Project is only one of several Spanish shipwreck recovery projects that have been conducted in the waters of the Bahamas and the Turks and Caicos. The St. John's wreck, located near the western end of Grand Bahama, contained one of the largest sixteenth-century maritime collections ever recovered (Malcolm 1996). Armaments from the ship, including various *versos* (swivel guns) and *bombardetas*, similar to weapons described aboard Columbus's 1492 vessels, indicate a 1550–1554 date. The Molasses Reef shipwreck in the Turks and Caicos, dated to circa 1520–1530, had a similar complement of weapons, olive jars, and other ceramics as the St. John's wreck. Weapons (e.g., sword hilts) from the St. John's wreck suggest dates overlapping between 1525 and 1550. A bowl-shaped Spanish helmet with a low comb and a down-turned brim from the St. John's wreck dates to 1520–1530 and is likely of Italian manufacture (Malcolm 1996). The Highborn Cay shipwreck from the early sixteenth century, with its 13 *versos* and two *bombardetas*, is another good example of the inherent perils of sailing the rocky and shallow Bahamian shoals during the late fifteenth through early seventeenth centuries. After the Spanish finished raiding the Bahamas for enslaved Lucayans to work on the Greater Antillean plantations and to dive for pearls in the lucrative pearl beds off the coast of northern Venezuela, the Spanish quickly turned their attention to the wealth to be found on the bigger islands of Puerto Rico, Hispaniola, and Cuba and mainland Mexico, Central America, and South America.

The fact that Spain's attention was diverted allowed the British to set their eyes on the colonization of the Bahamas and the Turks and Caicos, and they made claims to those lands as early as 1629. In 1648, during the time of the English Civil War, the vessel of a company of British colonists calling themselves the Company of Eleutherian Adventurers, the *William*, sank near the modern island of Eleuthera. Seventy souls went ashore on Eleuthera to establish a new colony based on freedom of religious conscience. Although archaeological evidence suggests that some of these Eleutherian Adventurers lived inside, stored goods and animals (such as cows and pigs), and may also have performed religious services in Preacher's Cave, the original 1648 settlement was soon deserted. The Eleutherians continued to receive political outcasts in the wake of the English Civil War and were forced to make a difficult living by scavenging shipwrecks (known as "wracking") and by harvesting braziletto dyewood and whale ambergris. Occasional shipments to and from the British mainland colonies of South Carolina and Massachusetts provide the inhabitants of Eleuthera with some needed financial support and survival necessities that were given as charity.

In 1787, William Wylly migrated to the Bahamas after being a Loyalist supporter during the American Revolution. Wylly became attorney general of the colonial Bahamas and a major plantation owner at Clifton Plantation on the western end of New Providence. Clifton Plantation is considered one of the best preserved plantations in the Bahamas today. William Wylly later became an abolitionist, and his abolitionist tendencies and advocacy for the enslaved from the Bahamas and former British colonies eventually resulted in his arrest for contempt (a series of events known as the Wylly Affair). Wylly apparently employed liberated African laborers at Clifton, and many freed Africans were allowed to serve in the Royal Navy and as apprentices for the standard seven-year period. New slave laws were implemented in 1824, and very soon thereafter, in 1824, the British Empire emancipated its enslaved. Numerous cotton plantations, many of which also raised cattle and sheep, dominated the economy of the Bahamas and the Turks and Caicos, but the peak British plantation period lasted only 50 years, from circa 1780 to 1834. Very few plantations of this period have been studied archaeologically and most of the plantation studies have focused on the bigger and better-preserved owner's houses rather than on more poorly built and smaller enslaved laborer quarters.

Several studies at plantations on New Providence and San Salvador indicate that in the wake of the collapsing slavery system and subsequent legal emancipation, the African population reused and modified the structure of main houses and storage buildings. For example, open doors and windows were blocked up, new interior room divides were added to existing structures, and generally the existing European-style architecture at many plantations was modified to meet the needs of the new African occupants. Although of uncertain dates and origins, many Bahamian plantation buildings have carved images of sailing ships, schooners, and other vessels scratched into the walls, usually in doorways and windows with ocean-facing views. Some have interpreted these ship drawings as accurate depictions of recognizable vessels that were regularly bringing supplies to the islands or simply as the drawings of children, likely boys, who were fascinated with the most common mode of transportation at the time, the sailing ship. Other interpretations of the ship drawings suggest that the illustra-tions may be related to the "wracking" industry that was common in the Bahamas and the Turks and Caicos from the seventeenth century. Other incidents of these drawings of sailing ships, known as "ship graffiti," have been found inside a cave on Abaco, on several plantations on San Salvador, on a Turks and Caicos hillside, and in prisons in Nassau and San Salvador in the eighteenth and twentieth centuries, respectively (Turner 2006a).

Recent work in the area is bringing the archaeology of the Bahamian Archipelago into the twenty-first century. Investigation of local reuse of older artifacts such as glass bottles by emancipated and recent peoples suggest that peoples at the end of fragile supply chains must reuse common materials at hand. Reinterpretations of ship graffiti and Bahamian cemeteries are using postmodern approaches and creating a transition from processual to postprocessual interpretations of archaeological materials in the Bahamian Archipelago (Baxter 2009; Baxter and Marshall 2009; Turner 2006b). The future of archaeology in the Bahamas and the Turks and Caicos is entering a new and exciting phase of research in the early decades of the twenty-first century.

Further Reading

Baxter, Jane. 2009. "Creating Community on 19th Century San Salvador: Ship Graffiti and Identity in the Bahamian Past." Presented at the Thirteenth Symposium on the Natural History of the Bahamas, Gerace Research Center, San Salvador, Bahamas, June 18–22.

Baxter, Jane, and Michael Steven Marshall. 2009. "Regional Variation in Historic Burial Practices on San Salvador, the Bahamas." Presented at the Thirteenth Symposium on the Natural History of the Bahamas, Gerace Research Center, San Salvador, Bahamas, June 18–22.

Berman, M. J., and P. L. Gnivecki. 1995. "The Colonization of the Bahama Archipelago: A Reappraisal." *World Archaeology* 26 (3): 421–441.

Blick, Jeffrey P., Jacqueline Hope Hopkins, and Doug Oetter. 2011. "Prehistoric Settlement Patterns of San Salvador, Bahamas." *Journal of Island and Coastal Archaeology* 6 (3): 421–41.

Carlson, Lisabeth Anne. 1993. "Strings of Command: Manufacture and Utilization of Shell Beads among the Taino Indians of the West Indies." MA thesis, University of Florida, Gainesville.

———. 1999. "Aftermath of a Feast: Human Colonization of the Southern Bahamian Archipelago and Its Effect on the Indigenous Fauna." PhD diss., Gainesville: University of Florida.

Carlson, L. A., and W. F. Keegan. 2004. "Resource Depletion in the Prehistoric Northern West Indies." In *Voyages of Discovery: The Archaeology of Islands*, ed. S. Fitzpatrick, 85–107. Westport, CT: Praeger.

Goggin, John M. 1939. "An Anthropological Reconnaissance of Andros Island, Bahamas." *American Antiquity* 5: 21–26.

Granberry, Julian. 1955. "A Survey of Bahamian Archaeology." MA thesis, University of Florida, Gainesville.

———. 1957. "An Anthropological Reconnaissance of Bimini, Bahamas." *American Antiquity* 22 (4): 378–81.

———. 1978. "The Gordon Hill Site, Crooked Island, Bahamas." *Journal of the Virgin Islands Archaeological Society* 6: 32–44.

Hoffman, Charles A., Jr. 1967. *Bahama Prehistory: Cultural Adaptation to an Island Environment.* Ann Arbor, MI: University Microfilms, Inc.

———. 1970. *The Palmetto Grove Site on San Salvador, Bahamas.* Gainesville, FL: University of Florida.

Jones O'Day, Sharyn, and William F. Keegan. 2001. "Expedient Shell Tools from the Northern West Indies." *Latin American Antiquity* 12: 1–17.

Keegan, William F. 1992. *The People Who Discovered Columbus: The Prehistory of the Bahamas.* Gainesville: University Press of Florida.

Kjellmark, E. 1996. "Late Holocene Climate Change and Human Disturbance on Andros Island, Bahamas." *Journal of Paleolimnology* 15: 133–45.

Malcolm, Corey. 1996. *St. John's Bahamas Shipwreck Project: Interim Report I: The Excavation and Artifacts, 1991–1995.* Key West: Mel Fisher Maritime Heritage Society. Available at http://www.melfisher.org/interimreport1.pdf. Accessed January 8, 2013.

Sullivan, Shaun D. 1981. "Prehistoric Patterns of Exploitation and Colonization in the Turks and Caicos Islands." PhD diss., University of Illinois at Urbana-Champaign.

Turner, Grace. 2006a. "Bahamian Ship Graffiti." *International Journal of Nautical Archaeology* 35 (2): 253–73.

———. 2006b. "Dark Visions from the Ocean: Lucayan Perspective on a Spanish Vessel." Presented at the 71st Annual Meeting of the Society for American Archaeology, San Juan, Puerto Rico, April 26–30.

Winter, John, and M. Gilstrap. 1991. "Preliminary Results of Ceramic Analysis and the Movements of Populations into the Bahamas." In *Proceedings of the Twelfth International Congress for Caribbean Archaeology,* ed. L. S. Robinson, 371–86. Martinique: International Association for Caribbean Archaeology.

See also Arawak versus Taíno; Beads; Columbus's Landfall; The Palmettan Ostionoid Series.

Banwari Trace (Trinidad)

Basil A. Reid

The 7,000 year old Banwari Trace, along with St. John—both situated in southwest Trinidad—are the two oldest sites in the Caribbean. The Banwari Trace deposit is located on the southern edge of the Oropouche Lagoon in southwest Trinidad, just west of the Coora River. The site occupies the top of a Miocene hillock that rises above the swamp. Irving Rouse classifies all of the Archaic sites in the Lesser Antilles and Puerto Rico, including Banwari trace, as belonging to the Ortoiroid Series, which gets its name from the type site of Ortoire in Trinidad. Peter Harris excavated Banwari Trace in the center of the midden in 1969/1970 and 1971. The observed change in shell-collecting habits of the Banwari Trace people closely reflects the alteration in the natural environment, which took place in the Oropouche Lagoon area during the period of midden formation in about 5000 BC.

The material culture of Banwari Trace suggests that its Ortoiroid inhabitants were actively engaged in hunting, gathering, and shell (mollusk) collecting. A considerable portion of the shellfish collected was deposited in the immediate surroundings of the site. Objects associated with hunting and fishing found at the site include bone projectile points, most likely used for tipping arrows and fish spears, beveled peccary teeth used as fishhooks, and bipointed pencil hooks of bone that were intended to be attached in the middle to a fishing line. A variety of ground stone tools were manufactured especially for vegetable foods processing, including blunt or pointed conical pestles, large grinding stones, and round to oval manos. In the absence of starch grain analysis, it is unclear what specific plant foods were processed at the Banwari Trace site, but they probably included edible roots, palm starch, and seeds. The midden has also yielded a large variety of small, irregular chips and cores manufactured from quartz, flint, chert, and other rock materials by percussion flaking. They include flake scrapers, cutters, small knives, blades, and piercers, which were probably used for a multitude of purposes, for example, cutting meat, scaling fish, prying open shells, scraping skins, finishing arrow shafts, and processing vegetable fibers for making baskets.

A significant discovery at Banwari Trace in 1969 was the remains of a human skeleton, dubbed "Banwari Man" (Figure B.2). Lying on its left side in a typical Amerindian

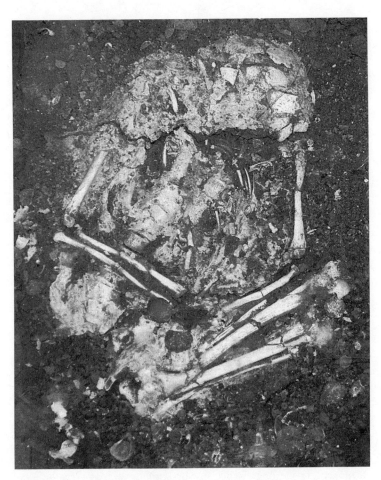

Figure B.2. Remains of "Banwari Man." Courtesy of the Department of Life Sciences, The University of the West Indies, St. Augustine.

tightly flexed "crouched" burial position along a north-west axis, Banwari Man was found 20 centimeters below the surface (Harris 1973). Only two items were associated with the burial, a round pebble by the skull and a needle point by the hip. The individual was apparently buried in a shell midden and was subsequently covered by shell refuse. Based on its stratigraphic location in the site's archaeological deposits, the burial can be dated to the period shortly before the site was abandoned, approximately 3400 BC, which makes it approximately 5,400 years old (Reid 2009). Plans are afoot to conduct more detailed research on these remains, which are currently in the custody of the Life Sciences Department at The University of the West Indies, St. Augustine. The gracile nature of the skeleton and pelvic structure both suggest that the famous "Banwari Man" could in fact be a woman (K. B. Tankersley, personal communication 2013). Upon examining its third upper molar teeth, physical anthropologist Alfredo Coppa noticed that all the roots were formed and that there was a slight wear on the occlusal portion. Subject to further verification, this suggests that "Banwari Man" or "Woman" was a 25- to 30-year-old adult. There is clear evidence of blunt force trauma (likely fatal) to the right parietal portion of the cranium. Evidence from the burial context suggests that the interment was made in the midden. An unfused portion of the sacrum appears to be pathological (Tankersley, personal communication, 2013).

The archaeological site of Banwari Trace was featured in the World Monuments Watch in 2004, an internationally acclaimed program that showcases the world's 100 most endangered sites.

Further Reading

Boomert, A. 2000. *Trinidad, Tobago, and the Lower Orinoco Interaction Sphere*. Alkmaar, The Netherlands: Cairi Publications.

Harris, P. O. B. 1973. "Banwari Trace: A Preliminary Report on a Preceramic Site in Trinidad, West Indies." In *Proceedings of the Fourth International Congress for the Study of Pre-Columbian Cultures of the Lesser Antilles*, ed. Ripley P. Bullen, 115–25. Castries, Saint Lucia: Saint Lucia Archaeological and Historical Society.

Reid, B. A. 2009. *Myths and Realities of Caribbean History*. Tuscaloosa: University of Alabama Press.

Rouse, I. 2006. *The Tainos: Rise and Decline of the People Who Greeted Columbus*. New Haven, CT: Yale University Press.

See also The Archaic Age; St. John Site (Trinidad); The Ortoiroid; Trinidad and Tobago.

Barbados

Kevin Farmer

Prehistoric Archaeology

Archaeological evidence suggests that the earliest settlement of the island by Archaic peoples took place sometime between 2300 and 3300 BC (Drewett 2000; Fitzpatrick 2011). This evidence was recovered from the Heywoods/Port St. Charles site located on the island's northwest coast. The site, located near a marine inlet, was first investigated in 1986 and later excavated in 1991 by Drewett. Interestingly, the recovery of two Archaic-type queen conch (*Eustrombus gigas*) lip adzes buried 1.5 meters in marsh clay suggests that there was an earlier settlement on Barbados. The deposit, which has been radiocarbon dated to around 2000 BC, was the first to demonstrate the possible presence of an Archaic occupation on Barbados. An Archaic age was later confirmed with the dating of one of the two adzes Drewett (2000) recovered and another associated juvenile conch shell that Fitzpatrick (2011) recovered to as early as 328–940 BC. If the earliest of the dates is confirmed, this would make Heywoods the oldest site in the Lesser Antilles. Although not much else is known about the daily activities of these Archaic groups on the island, Heywoods was probably a temporary foraging and fishing camp, similar to what has been seen on other islands, particularly in the northern Lesser Antilles such as Saba and Antigua. Questions still remain as to why the Archaic groups here did not exhibit the typical lithic toolkit seen at other similarly aged sites in the Caribbean.

Given the rise in sea level over the intervening period, many Archaic coastal sites on Barbados may either be below sea level or may have been washed away. The origins of the first settlers are currently unknown, but the site date corresponds to the earliest habitation of the region by the Ortoiroid people from Trinidad. These people, who originated from the Guianas, migrated to the region around 5000 BC and take their name from the Ortoire site in Trinidad. They settled the southern Caribbean region as far north as Puerto Rico. These native peoples were primarily subsistence hunters and gatherers who exploited both terrestrial and marine ecosystems. This is reflected in the stone tools they used to process vegetable matter.

The second wave of migrants to the island, the makers of Saladoid-style pottery, originated from lowland South America, although they may have traveled directly to the northern Caribbean islands and then moved south to the Lesser Antilles. Though Saladoid pottery is normally characterized by thin, hard, white on red or finely incised pottery, in Barbados elements of Barrancoid style are also seen, with its raised modeling and broad curvilinear incisions. The intertwined styles on the island can be referred to as Modified Saladoid (Drewett 2000). The earliest datable sherds of this type were excavated by Steven Hackenberger at the Goddard site, which provided radiocarbon dates of 400 BC to AD 450 and 400 BC to 170 BC. Hillcrest was excavated by Drewett and provides a date of AD 380 to 460 (Drewett 2000). The date range for Modified Saladoid on the island is therefore circa 400 BC and AD 650.

The Troumassan Troumassoid tradition (AD 650–1150) followed the Modified Saladoid tradition. This pottery is larger and thicker than the pottery of the Saladoid and has less decoration. Troumassan Troumassoid pottery also has simple rims, lugs, and incurved forms. It is uncertain whether this new style marked the arrival of new peoples or contact with the Troumassan Troumassoid peoples. The final pottery style on the island is the Suazan Troumassoid (ca. AD 1150 to 1450), which noted for its finger-scratched surfaces and finger-indented rims. Although normally associated with an undecorated tradition, the Suazan Troumassoid on Barbados shows some innovative individualistic pieces that include decoration bordering on the baroque. Pottery design is illustrative of life in the society, and in some cases it uses zoomorphic and anthropomorphic forms, such as octopus pots or a human face modeled on a griddle (Drewett 2000). All pottery made during the Modified Saladoid to Suazan Troumassoid is hand built using either a coiled or molded technique of manufacture. Lys Drewett, who has used petrological analysis to identify the clay source used in the production of pottery, highlights two main areas of source clays. The clays used during the Modified Saladoid period are obtained from the quartz-rich areas of the Scotland District on the island's northeast coast. Clays used during the Suazey period indicate an increasing dependence on nearby marsh clays, which feature a heavy concentration of calcareous debris. This change in resource gathering might be attributable to increased population, resulting in stricter access to the better clay sources and the search for and use of alternative (though poorer) clays (Drewett 2000).

These Ceramic Age peoples lived in a series of rectangular and round/oval houses while constructing other shelters for ancillary use. Most settlements were situated in coastal areas, although there were some inland settlements (Drewett 1991). Excavations at Port St. Charles, Goddard, and Chancery Lane have revealed the outlines of such buildings and, in the rare instance of Port St. Charles, posts in situ. The house types on the island coincide with the type of houses used by the migratory peoples who settled the island, from the large round houses associated with Saladoid settlement to the smaller round houses associated with Troumassan Troumassoid and Suazan Troumassoid occupation. Both types of houses were excavated at the Port St. Charles site, where excavation recovered the remains of seventeen posts and bases of posts in waterlogged holes.

Analysis of the wood revealed that the posts are false mastic (*Mastichodendron* sp.), and date to AD 650–1150 (Drewett 2000). The structure at Hillcrest, located on the promontory overlooking the east coast of the island, was a small D-shaped building, perhaps constituting a windbreak consisting of five postholes. A shell tool taken from the site was radiocarbon dated to AD 1420–1680, suggesting a late occupation for the island (Drewett 2000).

The scarcity of water on coral islands, such as Barbados, with few above-ground rivers or springs led to a need to sink shallow wells to access drinking water. Access to underground water was increased through lining holes with large ceramic pots. Such a system of pot stacks were excavated at a number of sites and illustrate the ingenuity of these early peoples in obtaining drinking water in a water-scarce environment. Twenty-three pot-lined waterholes were excavated at Port St. Charles. They have also been found at Goddard, Spring Garden,

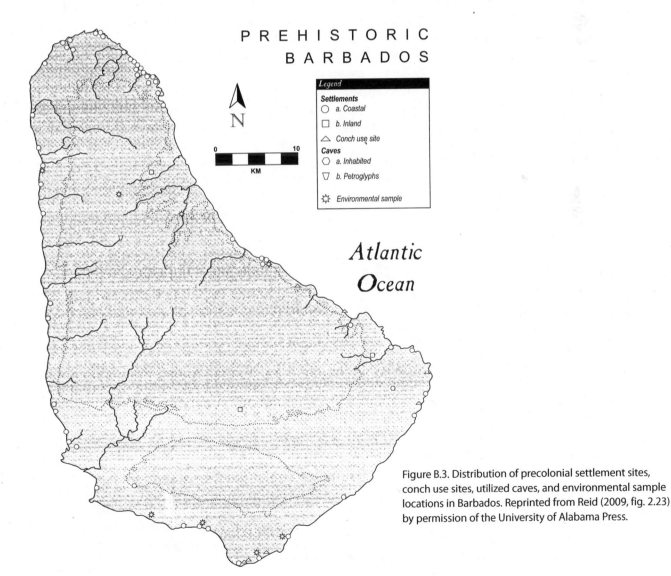

Figure B.3. Distribution of precolonial settlement sites, conch use sites, utilized caves, and environmental sample locations in Barbados. Reprinted from Reid (2009, fig. 2.23) by permission of the University of Alabama Press.

South Point, and Maxwell, suggesting they were widely used on the west and south coast of Barbados (Drewett 2000).

There is no naturally occurring hard rock on Barbados, which precludes a prehistoric local toolkit comprised of stone tools. Therefore, the presence of any stone tools on the island is assumed to be a consequence of trade (Drewett 1991). The toolkit on Barbados is predominantly comprised of shell technology. Early Amerindian settlers used the shell of the queen conch to fashion their major tools. Continued use of shell in the manufacture of tools developed during the Troumassan Troumassoid/Suazan Troumassoid period into a unique form of shell tool characterized by a distinctive twisted butt end and a scoop-like reverse side. This evolution in both form and style from the characteristic chipped lip with one end ground for cutting that was used during the Archaic Age to the smaller, better-shaped axes with a polished edge that were used during the modified Saladoid period perhaps takes a cue from the continental tradition of the stone toolkit in its appearance and application (Drewett 1991).

Such tools and their organic counterparts were used to plant cassava for harvest and aid in the hunting and fishing of many varieties of fauna. The Amerindian peoples of Barbados exploited their ecosystem for hunting and gathering a variety of species from nearshore reef fish, including the parrot fish and pelagic fish such as tuna; birds such as the ring-necked duck (*Aythya collaris*), the tree duck (*Dendrocygna* sp.), the purple gallinule (*Porphyrula martinius*), and the mocking bird (*Mimus* sp.); and even geckos. However, the primary protein source of the early natives came from the sea. More than 36 species of fish have been identified in the bone assemblages excavated at the key sites of Port St. Charles, Silver Sands, Hillcrest, and Chancery Lane. These include sharks, rays, moray eel, herring, flying fish, grouper, jack, grunt, hogfish, parrotfish, barracuda, mackerel, tunny, triggerfish, and trunkfish. By food weight, the assemblages are dominated by conch (*Strombus gigas*) and West Indian top shell, or whelk (*Cittarium pica*). Turtle bones, especially of the green turtle (*Chelonia mydas*), suggest that both the turtle and their eggs were eaten. Sea urchins, lobsters, and crabs were also found in the archaeological bone assemblages, indicating that virtually all marine life was eaten. Many of these foods are represented in stone, ceramic, and shell artifacts (Wing in Drewett 1991; Drewett 2000). The Amerindian presence on Barbados seems to have existed until the late fifteenth century; no contact pottery of the Island-Carib Cayoid pottery has been found on the island to date (Drewett 1991) (see Figure B.3).

Historical Archaeology

Historical archaeology research in Barbados has been directed at rural landscapes, burial sites (Handler and Lange 1978; Farmer 2004), enslaved villages (Handler and Lange 1978), sugar estates, the urban environment, and the creolization of pottery manufacture (Loftfield 2001). During the past thirty years, research has examined the lifeways of enslaved persons during the historic period in Barbados, primarily on plantations. This is in part the result of the primary thrust of Caribbean historiography of the region in the 1970s, which resulted in the seminal publication by Handler and Lange on the Newton Plantation Site (Handler and Lange 1978).

From the analysis of the Newton Burial Ground, it has been possible to reconstruct how enslaved people lived and died, what they ate, and certain pathologies in the enslaved population. The Newton site is a unique site in historical archaeology in the region, for it is the only excavated communal burial ground of enslaved individuals in the Caribbean. Notwithstanding their paucity, burial grounds of enslaved peoples offer an opportunity to examine the spiritual beliefs, concepts of cosmology, and afterlife beliefs of the enslaved community. The site, located within a half-acre site of land on a sloping field, has approximately 400 individuals interred within its grounds. Study of the site has made possible a detailed physical anthropological analysis of the effects of slavery on the enslaved population.

Because of the rapid rate of development of urban space, locating urban burial grounds of the enslaved takes on greater significance as we seek to piece together and understand the historic past. Burial sites can be used to reconstruct a people's cosmology, diet, and morbidity and the material culture they use in the ritual of death. Such practices might even be part of a new cultural shift brought about by deculturation, leading to the creation of other cultures. Research into enslaved persons living in urban Barbados has been undertaken by Smith and Farmer (Farmer 2004), and the excavation of burial spaces of enslaved individuals in urban Bridgetown has provided invaluable insight into the lifeways of enslaved persons living in this port city.

The Pier Head and Fontabelle sites are both situated on the seaside, one near commercial warehouses and the other on the periphery of the town. At Fontabelle, the interments were done in a uniform way. The burials were excavated at the same depth, indicating both a prescribed burial depth and knowledge of local conditions. Dateable material culture such as ceramics and pipe stems provide dates of 1670–1815 for the use of the site. Documentary evidence for the site underscores its use as a place of interment. In the seventeenth century, the Fontabelle area was an undeveloped area of beach and swamp land. Situated on the periphery of the northern end of Bridgetown, this area was noted as the West End in 1660. This place name was given in Poole's account, where he noted the burial ground for the enslaved of Fontabelle in 1748 (Farmer 2004).

In the 1990s, historical archaeological research was conducted on settlement sites in both rural and urban contexts (Farmer 2004). This research is ongoing in the context of limited cultural resource management (CRM) legislation. The continued development of historical archaeology in Barbados will further expand our understanding of this period and provide insight into the lifeways of members of both urban and rural communities who lived during the historic period.

Further Reading

Beckles, H. McD. 1990. *A History of Barbados: From Amerindian Settlement to Nation-State.* Cambridge, UK: Cambridge University Press.

Drewett, P. 1991. *Prehistoric Barbados.* London: Archetype.
———. 2000. *Prehistoric Settlements in the Caribbean: Fieldwork in Barbados, Tortola, and the Cayman Islands.* London: Archetype Publications for the Barbados Museum and Historical Society.
Farmer, K. 2004. "Human Skeletal Remains from an Unmarked Barbadian Burial Ground in the Fontabelle Section of Bridgetown, Barbados." *Journal of the Barbados Museum and Historical Society* 50: 84–90.
Fitzpatrick, S. M. 2011. "Verification of an Archaic Age Occupation on Barbados, Southern Lesser Antilles." *Radiocarbon* 53 (4): 595–604.
Handler, J. S., and F. W. Lange. 1978. *Plantation Slavery in Barbados.* Cambridge, MA: Harvard University Press.
Loftfield, C. T. 2001. "Creolization in Seventeenth-Century Barbados: Two Case Studies." In *Island Lives: Historical Archaeologies of the Caribbean,* ed. Paul Farnsworth, 207–33. Tuscaloosa: University of Alabama Press.

See also Historic Bridgetown and Its Garrison (Barbados); Newton Burial Ground (Barbados); *Strombus gigas* (Queen Conch).

Barbados Museum and Historical Society (BMHS)

Kevin Farmer

Incorporated in 1933 by an act of Parliament, the Barbados Museum and Historical Society (BMHS) is one of the oldest continuous-running museums in the English-speaking Caribbean; it celebrated its 75th anniversary in 2008. It is located in the precinct of the Historic Garrison Savannah in a military prison constructed in 1817 (Figure B.4). The BMHS is a general history museum that exhibits the natural history, prehistory, history, and art of the island. Its collection includes fine and decorative art, archaeology, photography, textiles, ethnography, manuscripts, and paper documents. The museum's mandate is to collect, interpret, and exhibit "all things Barbadian." It is also involved in cultural resource management on the island.

Founded in 1933 by elite members of Barbadian society, the BMHS was concerned with activities that would "collect, preserve and publish matter relating to the history and the antiquities of Barbados, and to gather and preserve appropriate articles for collection"

(Farmer 2008, 65). In the early period (1934–80), collections were mainly donated by members of the Historical Society, supplemented with purchases and actual fieldwork conducted in the acquisition of archaeological material. The systematic collection of archaeological material was a direct result of a research question posed at the first general meeting of the BMHS, during which a Committee of Archaeology was created to examine the origin of the precolonial inhabitants of the island. Early excavations that were carried out in the parish of Christ Church recovered native pottery and tools.

The Historical Society collected objects that interested its members. Thus, items such as Chinese export ceramics, silver, furniture, paintings, and maps were collected alongside native axes, pottery, African shields, arrows, and furniture. Such collecting informed an interpretative narrative that framed Barbadian history through the lens of empire and sought at the same time

Figure B.4. Front façade of the Barbados Museum and Historical Society. Photo by Barbados Museum and Historical Society. Courtesy of Kevin Farmer.

to highlight the economic, industrial, and aesthetic development of the island. This resulted in an impressive collection that included both commodified objects of high value and objects that spoke to the industriousness of Barbadian society in the fields of sugar, agriculture, and fishing. The eclectic nature of this collection changed during the museum's modern period (1980 to present).

A committee to inquire into the management and interpretation of the museum was formed in the 1980s, chaired by Professor Woodville Marshall. According to Marshall, the remit of the committee was to review the role of the BMHS and plan a way forward. The committee noted in its review that "the collection focuses mainly on one segment of society and culture and therefore does not present a coherent or complete story of Barbados in history" (Marshall 1982, 6). The result of its work was a move toward a professional museum organization and away from the institution's antiquarian roots. The shift is best embodied in the new mission statement of the institution, which appears on all of its publications: "The Barbados Museum is a nonprofit institution. Its mandate is to collect, document and conserve evidence of Barbados' cultural, historical

and environmental heritage and to interpret and present this evidence for all sectors of society."

This renewed mandate and policy focus led to focused projects such as the Barbados Archaeological Survey, undertaken from 1984 in conjunction with the University College London. The project was led by the late Professor Peter L. Drewett. The Drewett-led surveys of Barbados redefined the prehistory of the island: it was the first full-scale, systematic archaeological investigation of the island's prehistoric past since the introduction of professional archaeology in the island in the 1960s by Ripley and Adelaide Bullen. The museum was one of the founding institutions at a meeting of persons interested in prehistoric archaeology; this group evolved into the International Association for Caribbean Archaeology. The museum was also one of the founding members of the Museums Association of the Caribbean. Such change was brought about by the need to refocus the activity of the museum to include all community groups.

The development plan of the 1980s continues to guide the BMHS. It focuses on professional museum development and practice as it seeks to carry out its mandate and serve its community. Not only does the

BMHS serve as a place of interpretation of and a repository for the island's heritage, it also provides technical knowledge to both nongovernmental and governmental agencies in the areas of cultural resource management, museum development, and heritage preservation and interpretation. The museum houses the Documentary Heritage of the Enslaved Peoples of the Caribbean, which was inscribed on UNESCO's Memory of the World Register in 2003. It is also a component of Silver Men: West Indian Labourers at the Panama Canal, a documentary heritage project that was inscribed on the World Register in 2011. The museum continues to collect and interpret the history and ecology of Barbados as it serves as a custodian of Barbadian heritage.

Further Reading

Cannizzo, J. 1987. "How Sweet It Is: Cultural Politics in Barbados." *Muse* 4 (4): 22–26.

Cummins, Alissandra. 1998. "Confronting Colonialism: The First 60 Years at the BMHS." *Journal of the Barbados Museum and Historical Society* 42: 1–35.

Farmer, K. 2008. "From the Orient to Barbados: Seventy-Five Years of Collecting at the Barbados Museum." *Journal of the Barbados Museum* 54: 62–73.

Marshall, Woodville. 1982. "Final Report of the Museum Development Plan Committee." Unpublished document in author's possession.

See also The International Council of Museums (ICOM); The Museum of Antigua and Barbuda; Taíno Museum at White Marl (Jamaica).

Barka, Norman F. (1938–2008)

R. Grant Gilmore III

Born in Chicago, Illinois, in 1938, Norman Forthun Barka had a lifelong passion for archaeology, reflected in his numerous archaeological excavations across North America and the Caribbean. He is considered one of the founding fathers of the discipline of historical archaeology and was a primary founder of the Society for Historical Archaeology. "Sparky," as he was affectionately known, had a profound impact on the development of the discipline not only in the Caribbean but globally. Barka was educated at Beloit College and at Harvard University, where he earned his PhD in 1965. He worked extensively in Canada and Virginia during the first part of his career. After Thomas Jefferson, Barka was the first archaeologist hired by the College of William and Mary in Virginia, and it was here that his primary contribution to the discipline had the greatest impact. Dozens of students earned their MA and PhD degrees under his tutelage. Hundreds of graduate and undergraduate students participated in his field schools in Canada, Virginia, St. Eustatius, St. Maarten, and Bermuda. Although his publication record is not extensive, a significant proportion of his students have contributed to the teaching and practice of historical archaeology around the world. His sardonic manner, sarcastic asides, cheeky smile, and forceful nature kept students entertained in the classroom and in the field. His year-long artifact courses at William and Mary were legendary.

In 1979, Barka arrived on St. Eustatius with his colleague Edwin Dethlefsen. Shortly thereafter, their seminal article in *Archaeology Magazine* described Statia as "The Pompeii of the New World." He and his students spent the next 20 years recording standing structures and excavating a diverse array of sites on the island. He also worked on several sites in St. Maarten. Toward the end of the 1990s, Barka began working on Bermuda with his longtime friend and colleague, Edward C. Harris. He supported the development of the St. Eustatius Center for Archaeological Research until his death in 2008.

Further Reading

Barka, N. F. 2001. "Time Lines: Changing Settlement Patterns on St. Eustatius." In *Island Lives: Historical Archaeologies of the Caribbean*, ed. Paul Farnsworth, 103–41. Tuscaloosa: University of Alabama Press.

Dethlefsen, E., and N. F. Barka. 1982. "Archaeology on St. Eustatius: The Pompeii of the New World." *Archaeology* 35 (2): 8–15.

See also St. Eustatius; St. Eustatius Center for Archaeological Research (SECAR); St. Eustatius Historical Foundation.

The Barrancoid Series

Basil A. Reid

The Barrancoid series (AD 350–650) takes its name from the site of Barrancas on the banks of the lower Orinoco River in Venezuela. Barrancoid culture seems to have developed out of the local Saladoid tradition in Venezuela between 1500 BC and 1000 BC. Its peoples moved northward to the mouth of the Orinoco River delta, perhaps displacing or bypassing other Saladoid communities as they went. Like the Saladoid, they cultivated cassava, produced pottery, and lived in villages. Barrancoid influence was quite extensive throughout the Caribbean, reaching as far north as Puerto Rico. Like the Saladoid, the Barrancoid peoples were expert canoeists and appear to have been masters of long-distance trade. Archaeologists referred to sites such as Sorcé on Vieques and others in Montserrat and Tobago as Saladoid/Barrancoid ports of trade.

The Barrancoid peoples in eastern Venezuela and adjacent areas eventually settled Trinidad around AD 350. The mechanisms by which Barrancoid influences are associated with Saladoid pottery remain poorly understood, and the relationship between the two styles is problematic. A common tendency is to describe ceramics of this period as Saladoid with Barrancoid influences. Nevertheless, the discovery of Barrancoid pottery in Cedrosan Saladoid sites in Trinidad and Tobago and of typically Saladoid zone-incised cross-hatching pottery in the Lower Orinoco locations suggest that trade was an important mechanism. No independent Barrancoid settlements have been found on Trinidad or Paria (Venezuela), which further suggests that after AD 350 a significant element of the Barrancoid population went to live in Saladoid villages, where they interacted with the Saladoid.

The Barrancoid-influenced Saladoid pottery, referred to as the modified Saladoid tradition, differed little from the Saladoid pottery in terms of manufacture and choice of temper. However, striking differences are evident in vessel shapes and ornamentation. Barrancoid pottery has often been characterized as the "baroque" phase of Saladoid stylistic evolution, and it is typically represented by modeled incised decoration on handles; adornos with anthropomorphic and zoomorphic hands, feet, and faces (Figure B.5); and incense burners that were probably used for the ritual taking of hallucinogens. The Barrancoid culture faded in the Caribbean around AD 650. The reasons for this are unclear, and it is hoped that ongoing research will eventually provide more definitive answers.

Further Reading

Allaire, L. 1997. "The Lesser Antilles before Columbus." In *The Indigenous People of the Caribbean,* ed. S. Wilson, 20–28. Gainesville: University Press of Florida.

Boomert, A. 2003. "Agricultural Societies in the Continental Caribbean." In *General History of the Caribbean,* ed. J. Sued Badillo, 1:134–94. Paris and London: Autochthonous Societies, UNESCO.

Reid, B. A. 2009. *Myths and Realities of Caribbean History.* Tuscaloosa: University of Alabama Press.

See also The Saladoid; The Suazan Troumassoid (Suazey); The Troumassan Troumassoid.

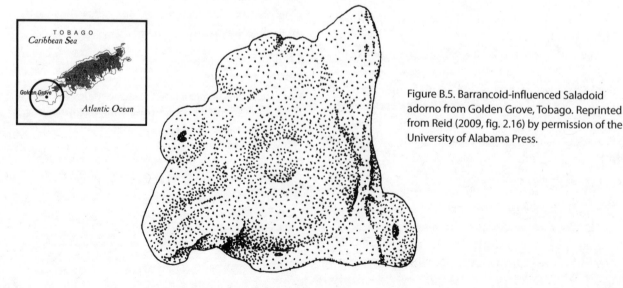

Figure B.5. Barrancoid-influenced Saladoid adorno from Golden Grove, Tobago. Reprinted from Reid (2009, fig. 2.16) by permission of the University of Alabama Press.

Beads

R. Grant Gilmore III

Beads have been used throughout much of human history for adornment and for exchange. Caribbean indigenous, colonial, and enslaved peoples are no exception. Stone, shells such as cowry and queen conch (*Strombus gigas*), coral, and seeds are all regularly found on Caribbean archaeological sites relating to precolonial societies and enslaved Africans. Glass, copper, gold and silver alloys, bone, and coral materials for beads are common on colonial sites.

Beads may be found in situ in human burials and ritual burials but the vast majority are found loose either on the ground surface or scattered across various archaeological contexts. Under fortuitous circumstances, entire necklaces may be recovered, such as in a privy context on St. Eustatius, where over 600 beads were found (Figure B.6). The necklace was likely lost while the owner was using the privy—thus they were not highly motivated to retrieve it despite its clear beauty.

Beads were valued primarily for aesthetics while some varieties have been ascribed intrinsic worth that is not related to the material they are made from. Beads have become a key interpretative artifact for archaeologists, providing insights into trade networks on local, regional, and global scales. Beads may also be reflective of religious beliefs. Certain bead types gain special meaning and obtain an almost cult status. This is true of the so-called Statia Blue Bead. Originally manufactured in Amsterdam, these wound cobalt glass beads were exported to many areas around the world. However, one type that is pentagonal in cross-section has been found only on St. Eustatius and at the factory site in the Netherlands. There is no mention of these beads in historical documents related to Statia, and thus their true use and value are unknown. However, tradition holds that these beads were thrown off the cliffs by the formerly enslaved when they were emancipated in 1863. Today, they are virtually a type of currency and command high prices on the island, especially for gullible tourists.

Because of a predominantly Catholic population, rosary beads are commonly found in the Spanish and French islands. Necklaces made from beads of precious metals and precious and semi-precious stones have also been found on wreck sites related to the Spanish colonial period.

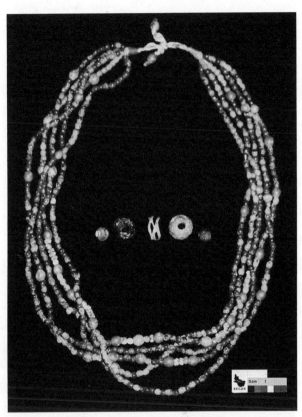

Figure B.6. A series of wound-glass trade beads (*center*). The restrung necklace surrounding these was found intact in an outhouse/privy in Oranjestad, St. Eustatius, and is made from glass and coral beads. The scale is 2 cm. Courtesy of R. Grant Gilmore III and SECAR.

Further Reading

Deagan, K. 2002. *Artifacts of the Spanish Colonies of Florida and the Caribbean, 1500–1800.* Vol. 2, *Portable Personal Possessions.* Washington, DC: Smithsonian Institution Press.

Handler, J. S., F. W Lange, and C. Orser. 1979. "Carnelian Beads in Necklaces from a Slave Cemetery in Barbados, West Indies." *Ornament* 4 (2): 15–18.

Karklins, K., and N. F. Barka. 1989. "The Beads of St. Eustatius, Netherlands Antilles." *Beads: Journal of the Society of Bead Researchers* 1 (1): 55–88.

Watters, D. R., and R. Scaglion. 1994. "Beads and Pendants from Trants, Montserrat: Implications for the Prehistoric Lapidary Industry of the Caribbean." *Annals of Carnegie Museum* 63 (3): 215–37.

See also Lapidary Trade; *Strombus gigas* (Queen Conch).

Betty's Hope Plantation (Antigua)

Georgia L. Fox

Betty's Hope, a former sugar plantation on Antigua, operated from the early 1650s until 1944. Betty's Hope is one of the oldest and best preserved plantation sites on Antigua and is currently managed by the nonprofit organization, Betty's Hope Trust. The site is currently being considered as a UNESCO World Heritage Site by Antiguan heritage societies.

The plantation was founded by Col. Chris Keynell in the early 1650s and was inherited by his widow Joan Hall in 1663. During the French occupation of 1666–1667, Hall fled the island and was denied ownership when she returned. The British Crown granted Betty's Hope to Christopher Codrington I in 1674, and the plantation remained in the Codrington family until its sale in

1944. This makes Betty's Hope one of the longest-running sugar estates in the Eastern Caribbean. Christopher Codrington I and Christopher Codrington II served as governors general of the Leeward Islands from 1689 to 1704.

The plantation, located in the fertile Central Plain region of the island, served as home to a large number of enslaved Africans. The estate continued to operate after 1834 (during the post-emancipation years in the Anglophone Caribbean), benefiting from the introduction of mechanization in 1853. Like many other sugar estates in the Caribbean, managers oversaw daily operations at Betty's Hope in the absence of landlords. Careful recording of the estate's operations has resulted in a substantial archive known as the Codrington Papers, which

Figure B.7. Students working at the Betty's Hope field project, summer 2008, directed by principal investigator Georgia Fox. Courtesy of Georgia Fox.

are housed in the National Archives of Antigua and Barbuda. Recent investigations at Betty's Hope have focused on restoration of one of the windmill towers (1990 to 1995 and 1993 to 1994). The University of Florida conducted an architectural study of the site's existing structures. More recently, Edith Gonzalez de Scollard (2008) from the City University of New York, Brooklyn, conducted an archaeological excavation of the nineteenth-century possible servants' area. Current investigations at the site are being conducted by Dr. Georgia L. Fox of the Department of Anthropology, California State University, Chico, under the direction of Antigua's archaeologist, Dr. Reginald Murphy (see Figure B.7).

Further Reading

Gonzalez de Scollard, Edith. 2008. "Raising Cane: Sugar, People, and the Environment in Nineteenth Century Antigua, West Indies." PhD diss., City University of New York.

Nicholson, D. 2005. *Heritage Landmarks of Antigua and Barbuda.* St. John's: Carib Press.

See also Nicholson, D. V. (1925–2006).

Bonaire (Dutch Caribbean; Former Netherlands Antilles)

Jay B. Haviser

In 1836, G. Bosch was the first person to mention an archaeological site on Bonaire; that year, he noted the rock paintings at the Onima site. Geologist K. Martin identified more rock paintings on Bonaire in 1888. In 1879 and 1880, Father A. J. van Koolwijk made extensive artifact collections from sites and private collectors on Bonaire. These artifacts were shipped back to the Museum voor Volkenkunde in Leiden, Holland, and were used to study Bonaire's archaeological research history. Although C. Leemans never actually visited the island, he wrote a summary of some of the van Koolwijk Bonaire artifacts in 1904, J. P. B. de Josselin de Jong published extensive descriptions of the van Koolwijk collection in 1918, 1920, and 1923.

During the 1930s and into the 1950s, Bonaire's rock painting sites became a research focus for various authors, newspapers, and amateur enthusiasts. The earliest well-organized work was done by Father P. Brenneker, who published numerous articles throughout the 1940s. However, the most scientific and professional analysis of the rock drawings was a four-volume research series by P. Wagenaar Hummelinck. His works, which were published during the period 1953 to 1972, were the standard for rock painting research on the Dutch islands until the late 1980s, when C. N. Dubelaar began reinvestigating the Hummelinck finds. H. Feriz also mentioned the Bonaire rock paintings in his 1959 book about Mexico and Peru. In 1957, Hartog wrote a review of Amerindian culture history, which included the listing of ten archaeological sites on Bonaire, all of which were rock painting sites.

Not until 1960, when the Dutch archaeologist H. R. van Heekeren visited for 12 days, was Bonaire subjected to its first systematic archaeological excavations. During this brief visit to the island, van Heekeren conducted a field survey to locate some archaeological sites and at least two test excavations, one at Wanapa and the other at Esperanza (Amboina). He published some of his results in 1961, 1963, and, with the help of C. J. Dury, 1962. While on Bonaire, van Heekeren encountered several persons who had made extensive artifact collections from the island, including Father R. Nooyen, Father P. Brenneker, and Father M. Arnoldo Broeders. Van Heekeren also noted that two other Dutch scientists, geologist P. de Buisonjé, and malacologist H. Coomans, had artifact collections from Bonaire. Coomans later conducted the shell species analysis for the excavated van Heekeren materials, which he reported in 1963.

In the 1960s and 1970s, little scientific archaeological research was conducted on Bonaire, except for the rock painting studies by Hummelinck and a cave investigation, also by Hummelinck, that was published in 1979. However, various amateur archaeological collections were made throughout this period, the most substantial by Father R. Nooyen, who eventually wrote about some of his finds in 1979. The 1969 edition of the *Encyclopedia van de Nederlandse Antillen* mentions archaeological research on Bonaire, primarily by J. Cruxent and I. Rouse. The work of E. Ayubi, E. Boerstra, and A. Versteeg is mentioned in the encyclopedia's 1985 edition.

In 1976, E. Ayubi, H. Kemperman, and J. Tacoma visited the Amboina site and collected human remains found there as well as some artifacts. No actual systematic excavations were conducted at this time, as the skeleton was taken to Holland by Tacoma, who published a report on it in 1980. In 1981, a listing of archaeological sites for Bonaire was written by F. Booi for the Department of Culture, Bonaire. In 1985, Father Nooyen wrote a book about the history of the people of Bonaire in which he made several references to archaeological sites, although most of the data were the same as those in his 1979 work.

Jay Haviser began work on Bonaire in 1987 with an island-wide field survey for the Archaeological-Anthropological Institute of the Netherlands Antilles (AAINA) and systematic excavations at the Wanapa, Amboina, Lagun, Gotomeer, North Lac, Den Bon, and Sorobon sites. In 1988, Haviser revisited the Sorobon site for more extensive excavations. The research resulted in the 1991 publication of an AAINA book by Haviser entitled *The First Bonaireans*, which is still the most comprehensive inventory of prehistoric research for the island. In 1990, Haviser conducted an anthropological interview program at various barrios on Bonaire. This study resulted in a paper presented at a seminar at Leiden University, Netherlands, and a subsequent publication in 1995 about the changing views of Amerindian heritage in the Caribbean.

Haviser conducted the first historical archaeology excavations on Bonaire at Fort Oranje in 1997; results of this research were published by Haviser and Arthur Sealy in 1999. In 2001 and 2002, Wil Nagelkerken, Raymond Hayes, and the Foundation for Marine Archaeology of the Netherlands Antilles (STIMANA) conducted underwater archaeological surveys in the Kralendijk, Bonaire, harbor anchorage and published the results via the STIMANA Foundation in 2002. In 2003 and 2004, the same team conducted more research in the Kralendijk harbor and at the Witte Pan shipwreck site on Bonaire; the results of both were again published via STIMANA (Nagelkerken and Hayes 2008). In 2002, Haviser helped the governments of Netherlands Antilles and Bonaire create the Bonaire Archaeological Institute (BONAI). One of the projects BONAI conducted was an investigation of the early wattle-and-daub vernacular architecture on Bonaire, called *kunuku* houses, which have African, European, and Amerindian elements of construction. This report was published by Haviser and F. Boi Antoin in 2003 and was presented at the IACA Congress in Santo Domingo that same year.

From 2003 to 2005, Haviser, with the help of BONAI students, conducted various archaeological surveys and excavations on Bonaire, from prehistoric sites at Lac Bay to historic city center sites in Kralendijk, the results of which were published by the BONAI Foundation. In 2005, Haviser investigated Bonaire's prehistoric rock art as a follow-up to his 1991 book on Bonaire prehistory. This research was presented at the IACA congress in Trinidad in 2005 and at the Society of American Archaeologists conference in Puerto Rico in 2006. The results were published in *Rock Art of the Caribbean* (Haviser 2009). In 2007, Haviser and the BONAI students conducted an archaeological survey and test excavations at the World War II military camp called Tanki Maraka on Bonaire; the report was published by the BONAI Foundation in 2008. In 2010, individuals from BONAI, Leiden University, and Stichting Nationale Parken Bonaire (STINAPA Bonaire) collaborated on an extensive archaeological survey and excavations at the Slagbaai and Gotomeer areas of the Washington Slagbaai National Park (Haviser 2010).

In October 2010, the islands of Bonaire, Saba, and St. Eustatius became municipalities of the Kingdom of the Netherlands, and the Netherlands Antilles ceased to exist as a country.

Further Reading

Farnsworth, P., ed. 2001. *Island Lives: Historical Archaeologies of the Caribbean*. Tuscaloosa: University of Alabama Press.

Haviser, J. 1991. *The First Bonaireans*. Curaçao: Archaeological-Anthropological Institute of the Netherlands Antilles.

———. 1995. "Towards Romanticized Amerindian Identities among Caribbean Peoples: A Case Study from Bonaire, Netherlands Antilles." In *Wolves from the Sea*, ed. Neil Whitehead, 139–56. Leiden: KITLV Press.

———. 2008. *Archaeological Research at the Tanki Maraka Site: A World War II US Military Base on Bonaire*. Willemstad: STIMANA.

———. 2009. "Prehistoric Rock Paintings of Bonaire, Netherlands Antilles." In *Rock Art of the Caribbean*, ed. M. Hayward, L. Atkinson, and M. Cinquino, 161–74. Tuscaloosa: University of Alabama Press.

———. 2010. *DROB Archaeological Report on Slagbaai-Gotomeer Bay*. Willemstad: STIMANA.

Haviser, J. B., and F. A. Antoin. 2003. "Observations of Vernacular Architectural Diversity between Curaçao and Bonaire." In *Proceedings of the Twentieth Congress of the International Congress for Caribbean Archaeology*, ed. C. Tavarez Maria and M. Garcia Arevalo, 759–68. Santo Domingo: Museo del Hombre Dominicano.

Haviser, J. B., and A. Sealy. 1999. "Archaeological Testing at Fort Oranje, Bonaire." In *Proceedings of the Seventeenth Congress of the International Congress for Caribbean Archaeology*, ed. John Winter, 340–57. New York: Molloy College Press.

Hayward, M., L. Atkinson, and M. Cinquino, eds. 2009. *Rock Art of the Caribbean*. Tuscaloosa: University of Alabama Press.

Heekeren, H. R. 1961. "A Survey of the Non-Ceramic Artifacts of Aruba, Curaçao and Bonaire." *Nieuwe West-Indische Gids* 40: 103–120.

———. 1963. "Prehistorical Research on the Islands of Curaçao,

Aruba and Bonaire in 1960." *Nieuwe West-Indische Gids* 43: 1–25.

Heekeren, H. R., and C. J. DuRy. 1962. "Study of the Relics of Indian Culture Present in Aruba, Curaçao and Bonaire." *Stichting Wetenschappelijk Onderzoek Suriname-Nederlandse Antillen* (WOSUNA): 31–33.

Hummelinck, P. Wagenaar. 1953. "Rotstekeningen van Curaçao, Aruba en Bonaire." -I, Uitgaven Natuurweteschappelijke Werkgroep Nederlandse Antillen, Curaçao 2 (41); -II, 1957 Uitg. 6 (33); -III, 1961 Uitg. 13 (43); -IV, 1972 Uitg. 21 (66).

———. 1979. *Caves of the Netherlands Antilles.* Utrecht: Foundation for Scientific Research in Suriname and the Netherlands Antilles.

Josselin de Jong, J. P. B. de. 1918. "The Precolumbian and Early Postcolumbian Aboriginal Population of Aruba, Curaçao, and Bonaire." *Internationales Archiv fur Ethnographie* 24 (3): 51–114.

———. 1920. "The Precolumbian and Early Postcolumbian Aboriginal Population of Aruba, Curaçao, and Bonaire." *Internationales Archiv fur Ethnographie* 25 (1): 1–26.

———. 1923. "Verslag van de Deensch-Nederlandse Expeditie naar de Antillen." *Bulletin van het Rijksmuseum voor Volkenkunde* 79: 3–8.

Nagelkerken, W. and R. Hayes 2002. *The Historical Anchorage of Kralendijk, Bonaire, Netherlands Antilles, including the Wreckage of the Dutch Brigantine Sirene (1831).* Willemstad: STIMANA.

See also Bonaire Archaeological Institute (BONAI); Cruxent, José María (1911–2005); The Dutch Caribbean; Foundation for Marine Archaeology of the Netherlands Antilles (STIMANA); Rock Art; Rouse, Benjamin Irving (1913–2006).

Bonaire Archaeological Institute (BONAI)

Jay B. Haviser

The Bonaire Archaeological Institute, called BONAI, is a nonprofit foundation assisted by the Bonaire Island Government. Founded in January 2003, the goal of BONAI is to work directly with the population of Bonaire, particularly teenage youth, to educate and train them in scientific methods and to conduct professional scientific research into the culture and history of Bonaire. The work of the institute is a response to a serious need for more Antillean youth to be inspired to pursue careers in the sciences so they can eventually become local leaders in eco-tourism and heritage/nature conservation on the islands. One of the more important aspects of this project is that 18 to 20 students from the Bonaire high school have been contributing to the planning, research, and archaeological work of the institute, in collaboration with its founder and president, Dr. Jay Haviser, and its secretary, Jackie Bernabela. The primary research focus of BONAI is the investigation of the science, history, and culture on Bonaire from the perspective of Bonaireans. Since their involvement in the 23rd Congress of the International Congress of Caribbean Archaeology in Trinidad and Tobago in 2005, BONAI participants have become a model for the broader Caribbean region, exemplifying the potential of individual islands to conduct their own cultural heritage research and reduce intervention by foreign specialists.

The BONAI Foundation is an after-school program that provides study credits from the high school of Bonaire, in conjunction with Bonaire's Dienst Ruimtelijke Ontwikkeling en Beheer (Monuments Section). The BONAI Foundation was also created to receive funds from organizations, such as the Stichting Antilliaanse Medefinanciering Organisatie and the Prince Bernhard Culture Fund. The BONAI office-laboratory-lecture facility has been established with the Bonaire Museum.

Both theoretical and practical applications are used in the BONAI program. The theoretical aspects include classroom lectures, group discussions, and presentations. There is also some practical work relating to archaeology, history, geography, anthropology, and other fields of science during the regular school academic year at the BONAI facility. The program also offers field projects in archaeology, history, geography, biology and anthropology for both students and community members. BONAI projects are given generous media publicity to promote the work of the local research heritage institute and develop more enthusiasm for history and culture within the Bonaire community. Indeed, the BONAI center has become a focal point for the Bonaire community in terms of heritage research and is a place where heritage artifacts from both public and private collections can be examined, identified, and stored.

See also Bonaire (Dutch Caribbean; Former Netherlands Antilles).

Bottles (Colonial)

Georgia L. Fox and R. Grant Gilmore III

Ceramic and glass bottles were used extensively in the Caribbean during the colonial period. Stoneware and coarse earthenware were the primary ceramic types used. The Westerwald region of what is now Germany produced a wide range of vessels for storing mineral water and alcohol in the period 1700 to 1775. Glass bottles were used primarily for decanting wine and spirits in taverns, homes, ships, and anywhere else alcohol might be served. On occasion, these bottles were also used for storing water. Some skill was required in glass bottle production and thus there is little evidence that production ever occurred in the Caribbean outside of early attempts that may have occurred at Spanish La Isabella on Hispaniola. Puebla (Mexico) was the primary production site for Spanish glass products exported to the Caribbean throughout the colonial period (Frothingham 1941, 121). Other European powers imported all of the bottles they used in the Caribbean.

The archaeological recovery of bottles in the Caribbean is largely limited to the contact/historic period, and most archaeological bottles are made of glass. Although glass was produced in ancient times, the more stable glass commonly encountered at historic sites is a relatively recent development in the history of glass. Archeologically recovered glass in the Caribbean includes glass used for windows, drinking vessels, trade beads, containers for holding liquids, and decorative objects. Regardless of age, the main constituent of glass and glass bottles is silica, to which is added an alkali or flux to lower the temperature during manufacture, such as soda or potash, and a stabilizer such as lime. Glass is affected by the various combinations and percentages of these raw materials and other internal constituents, such as the amount of impurities and colorants present in the glass. Over the centuries, experimentation with glass has resulted in various developments such as leaded glass, which was first developed in England in 1676 and became popular in the eighteenth century, particularly in stemware and leaded crystal.

Bottles recovered from Caribbean sites span several centuries, but the most common form of bottle is the liquor bottle, which was manufactured throughout Europe and America. Dating bottles is not a precise science, but certain features can be used to help date glass bottles such as mold seams, finish types, closures, and glass color. Generally, if a bottle lacks any mold seams,

is asymmetrical, or is not uniform, it dates before the 1860s.

Since the mid-nineteenth century, the successful combination of the basic materials mentioned above resulted in enough consistency for the mass production of glass bottles. Although most glass manufactured from the eighteenth century on has been produced from a stable glass formulation, most glass can deteriorate in an archaeological context, mostly affected by moisture in the burial environment. Under these conditions, water or surrounding moisture can leach alkali from the glass, leaving behind a distinct fragile, porous, and hydrated layer of silica. This causes the glass to craze, crack, flake, and pit and gives the surface of the glass a frosty appearance. In some cases, there is an actual separation of layers of glass from the body, resulting in iridescent and opalescent layers, an internal process known as devitrification. Archaeological glass is also affected by a variety of other factors such as pH, the chemical composition of the glass, temperature, and the presence of salts. Glass can also be recovered in a stable form, but it can deteriorate rapidly upon excavation. Glass recovered from seventeenth-century colonial sites is often unstable, particularly the commonly encountered "onion" bottles that were used for wine and spirits.

It is not always possible to provenience bottles, but an identifiable maker's mark stamped or labeled on the body or bottom of the bottle can be helpful. Following Noel-Hume's scheme, glass bottles are categorized in three types: glass liquor bottles, glass pharmaceutical bottles, and ceramic bottles, such as the Rhenish glazed stoneware Bartmann/Bellarmine bottles manufactured in Frechen (Germany) and early ceramic beer bottles from the nineteenth century. When examining bottles, the researcher might investigate the technological processes and techniques of manufacture, the bottle's place of manufacture, and the bottle's overall function. For example, glass bottles can be dated and grouped into typologies based on a variety of distinguishing features such as the shoulder of the bottle, the body, the base, the neck, and the lip and on the bottle's shape, color, and size.

Glass bottle technology ranges from mouth-blown glass with one-, two-, and multiple-piece molds to more recent machine-made glass. Typically, with the exception of soda bottles with rounded bottoms, most bottles have

Figure B.8. *From left to right*: 1750–60 English handblown; 1780 Dutch "onion" bottle often mistaken for a much earlier (1720s) English bottle; a ca. 1810 mold-blown bottle; a 1780s French bottle; a Westerwald stoneware bottle with a Selter maker's mark (all from St. Eustatius); a post-1872 Codd-neck bottle for mineral water from St. Kitts; and a Dutch case bottle from the 1780s. Courtesy of R. Grant Gilmore III and SECAR.

flat bases, although most bottle bottoms are indented or domed to lend workability during manufacture and to maintain stability during the life of the bottle. Until the 1860s, glass blowers used a steel rod attached to the bottom of the bottle using a small amount of molten glass to hold it in place while they applied the finish. Removal of the pontil often left a jagged piece of glass on the bottom of the bottle known as a pontil mark. English colonial bottles are often finished with the removal of the pontil mark, whereas this jagged piece is often visible on Dutch and French bottles. Pontil rods were not used in the manufacture of glass bottles after the 1860s.

In 1823, Henry Ricketts, a Bristol bottle manufacturer, invented a bottle-molding machine that produced uniformly manufactured bottles. The tops of the molds were left open so that the glass blower could access it to blow the glass. The necks and tops of the bottles were then added. In 1903, the automatic bottle machine was introduced, which produced a completely machine-made bottle. By the 1920s, bottles were being mass produced by machine. Mold lines that run down the sides of a bottle but stop short of the neck, therefore, indicate that a bottle was made in the nineteenth or early twentieth centuries. Bottles made before the introduction of the automatic bottle machine are usually less uniform in thickness and often have air bubbles. Pharmaceutical bottles, which include medicinal, apothecary, and per-fume bottles, are generally smaller than liquor bottles and come in a variety of shapes and colors.

All bottles may have an applied bottle seal that indicates the bottle's owner. After the advent of mold-blown bottles in the later eighteenth century, bottles had raised lettering that provided information about the manufacturer, the bottle's contents, or the owner of the bottle. Medicine bottles are commonly excavated on Caribbean sites and are generally identical in shape to those manufactured since Roman times. Leaded glass or cut crystal was primarily used to produce the decanters that are found on some archaeological sites in the Caribbean. Figure B.8 shows a sample of colonial bottles found at archaeological sites in the Caribbean.

Further Reading

Frothingham, A. 1941. *Hispanic Glass*. New York: Hispanic Society of America.

Jones, O., and C. Sullivan. 1989. *The Parks Canada Glass Glossary*. Ottawa: National Historic Parks and Sites, Canadian Parks Service Environment Canada.

Noël Hume, I. 1991. *A Guide to Artifacts of Colonial America*. New York: Vintage Books.

———. 2008. "Historic Glass Bottle Identification and Information Website." Society for Historical Archaeology. http://www.sha.org/bottle/index.htm. Accessed January 8, 2013.

See also Rum.

Brimstone Hill Fortress National Park (St. Kitts)

Gerald F. Schroedl

Introduction

Brimstone Hill Fortress is situated atop a 230-meter high volcanic extrusion on the northwest coast of St. Kitts, near the town of Sandy Point (Figure B.9). The hill is named for the sulfurous gases (brimstone) that vent just off shore. Built on three levels, the fortress covers nearly 20 hectares and includes over 50 structures, defensive walls, bastions, barracks, and other features relating to its occupation by the British military during the period 1690 to 1853.

History of Brimstone Hill Fortress

The British first recognized the hill's strategic importance in 1690 during the War of the Grand Alliance, when they attempted to direct cannon fire at the French, who had captured Charles Fort situated on the shore below. The fort's overall configuration was established in the 1720s, when defensive walls on the northeast, northwest, and southeast sides of the hill and a citadel known as the Mince Pye were constructed. The intention was to make the hill a place of refuge in time of foreign attack. Ad-

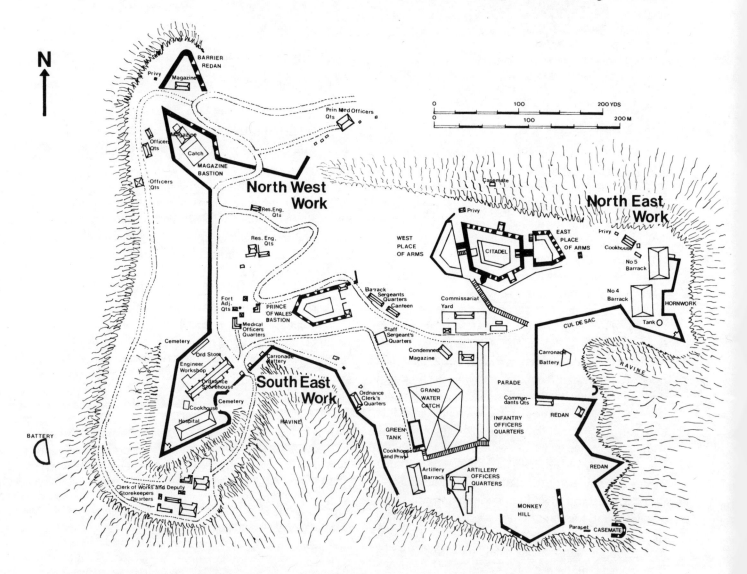

Figure B.9. Plan of Brimstone Hill Fortress in 1830 compiled from various sources. Reprinted with permission from Smith (1994).

ditional, but apparently only minor improvements were made to the fort through the 1770s. France declared war on Britain in 1778 during the War of American Independence and laid siege to Brimstone Hill in January 1782, capturing it a month later. Following the treaty of Paris in 1783, the fort was returned to the British, after which they embarked on a massive program of repairs, renovation, and construction to increase the number, size, and strength of the fort's defenses, support buildings, and associated facilities. This process continued into the early nineteenth century. The large and imposing Fort George replaced the Mince Pye citadel, and the Prince of Wales Bastion was built. A second citadel as imposing as Fort George was planned but never built. Although these structures were designed by British Royal Engineers, over 200 enslaved Africans who were conscripted from local plantations for a few weeks to several months did virtually all the construction and maintenance work. The British army also employed its own corps of enslaved African laborers at the site, known as the Corps of Black Military Artificers and Pioneers. After emancipation in 1834, the British military hired free blacks and whites for building and repair work. By the early nineteenth century, Brimstone Hill had largely achieved its modern appearance. The military maintained the fort until its abandonment in 1853, when most British troops were withdrawn from the Caribbean to fight in the Crimea.

At the height of its occupation, Brimstone Hill could accommodate about 800 soldiers, but rarely were this many ever posted at the fort, as troop levels fluctuated in response to the threat of invasion. Officers and enlisted men of twenty or more regiments were stationed at the fort during its history. Wives and children accompanied some men. The St. Kitts militia and enslaved Africans of the Corps of Embodied Slaves also served brief deployments, and beginning in the 1790s, black troops comprising the First, Second, Third, and Fourth West India Regiments were posted at the fort on separate occasions.

In 1853, the fortress was transferred to the local colonial government who sold whatever buildings and materials it could, including all the fort's cannons. In the early twentieth century, the government began to take a modest interest in the site and formed the Historic Sites and Records Committee, which was responsible for clearing brush and maintaining the buildings as time and money permitted. Active restoration and development of the site for tourism began in 1965 with the creation of the Society for the Restoration of Brimstone Hill. The site was designated a national park in 1983, and the Restoration Society was succeeded by the Brimstone

Hill Fortress National Park Society, which manages the site today. The fort was listed as a United Nations World Heritage site in 2000.

Archaeological Research

The archaeological potential of Brimstone Hill was recognized in the 1960s. From that time through the 1980s, rubble was cleared from buildings and occasional small excavations were made. In 1996, specific archaeological research goals were identified, and the University of Tennessee initiated a long-term excavation program at the site. The research design conceptualizes Brimstone Hill as a highly structured and frequently oppressive multiethnic community where the number, organization, and relationships of people differed with changing social, economic, and cultural circumstances. The Brimstone Hill community included colonial government officials; plantation owners; white militia; British army officers and enlisted men; wives, mistresses, and children of British soldiers; enslaved African laborers; black militia; and members of the West India Regiments. The goals of the investigations are to document the roles enslaved Africans played in the fort's construction and maintenance; to compare and contrast the archaeological records of enslaved Africans, British officers, and enlisted men; to excavate specific structures used or occupied by enslaved Africans, British officers and enlisted men; and to provide accurate information about architecture and associated archaeological assemblages at the site. These studies are intended to demonstrate that the heritage of Brimstone Hill is as much Afro-Caribbean as it is colonial British; generate information that the people of St. Kitts can use to better understand and appreciate their own cultural heritage; and place the study of enslaved Africans and British soldiers at Brimstone Hill in the comparative context of colonial Caribbean culture.

A 1791 military engineer's map showing how most structures were used has guided the placement of excavations in five areas. These are identified by BSH (for Brimstone Hill) followed by a site number. Contexts relating to the manufacture and storage of lime were conducted at BSH 1. At BSH 2, a hospital and workshop building where enslaved Africans lived and worked were excavated and a large assemblage of artifacts relating to the use of these structures was recovered. The headquarters of the Royal Engineers was investigated at BSH 3. Among the structures constituting this complex were a residence, a kitchen, an office building, a bath, three storage structures, connecting walls and walkways, a paved courtyard, and a quarter for enslaved laborers. Artifacts and faunal remains demonstrate that enslaved Africans and British army officers had different diets, and they also indicate differences between enslaved Africans at BSH 2 and BSH 3. These data document the use of imported beef and pork and the consumption of local goats and sheep. Imported fish such as cod and herring are present, as is a wide range of local fishes. Afro-Caribbean wares reflect food preparation, storage, and serving, while British-manufactured items include a wide range of food service and preparation vessels, personal items, uniform buttons and badges, military hardware, and construction materials. Data were recovered at BSH 5 relating to two enlisted men's barracks, a washhouse, two kitchens, a portable hospital, two privies, and other deposits. So far the investigations have recovered over 250,000 ceramic, glass, and metal artifacts; over 100,000 fish, bird and mammal bones; and human skeletal elements representing twenty-eight British soldiers.

Conclusion

In summary, the British occupied the Brimstone Hill Fortress for nearly 150 years. There is abundant documentary evidence attesting to the history of its construction, modification, renovation, and occupation by British soldiers and enslaved Africans. Archaeological studies have enhanced interpretation of the fort's plan and architecture and have produced significant knowledge of the lives and relationships of enslaved Africans and British soldiers.

Further Reading

Ahlman, T. M., G. F. Schroedl, and A. H. McKeown. 2009. "The Afro-Caribbean Ware from the Brimstone Hill Fortress, St. Kitts, West Indies: A Study in Ceramic Production." *Historical Archaeology* 43 (4): 22–41.

Klippel, W. E. 2001. "Sugar Monoculture, Bovid Skeletal Part Frequencies, and Stable Carbon Isotopes: Interpreting Enslaved African Diet at Brimstone Hill, St. Kitts, West Indies." *Journal of Archaeological Science* 28: 1191–98.

Klippel, W. E., and G. F. Schroedl. 1999. "African Slave Craftsmen and Single Hole Bone Discs from Brimstone Hill, St. Kitts, West Indies." *Post-Medieval Archaeology* 33: 222–32.

Schroedl, G. F., and T. M. Ahlman. 2002. "The Maintenance of Cultural and Personal Identities of Enslaved Africans and British Soldiers at the Brimstone Hill Fortress, St. Kitts, West Indies." *Historical Archaeology* 36 (4): 38–52.

Smith, V. T. C. 1994. "Brimstone Hill Fortress, St. Kitts, West Indies. Part One: History." *Post-Medieval Archaeology* 28: 73–109.

Wilson, B. 2012. "Geology and the Preservation of Historic Buildings: Cracking in the Walls of the Citadel, Brimstone Hill Fortress, St. Kitts." In *Caribbean Heritage*, ed. B. A. Reid, 306–14. Kingston, Jamaica: University of the West Indies Press.

See also Afro-Caribbean Earthenwares; The Cabrits Garrison (Portsmouth, Dominica); Historical Archaeological Sites (Types); Historic Bridgetown and Its Garrison (Barbados).

Bullbrook, John A. (1881–1967)

Arie Boomert

John Bullbrook, a resident of Trinidad from 1913 until his death in 1967, was an English avocational archaeologist and oil geologist who played an important role in Trinidad's archaeology for fifty years. He studied geology in his native Britain, where his interest in archaeology first developed. As a student, Bullbrook carried out archaeological fieldwork in both England and Sudan.

Bullbrook introduced modern stratigraphic excavation techniques to Trinidad when a government grant allowed him to excavate the Palo Seco shell midden site in April–September 1919. This ceramic site was being threatened due to the quarrying of shells as material for graveling roads. Following these excavations, Bullbrook successfully urged the colonial government to protect the site from further destruction by acquiring part of it as Crown lands. His finds were donated to the British Museum in London. Unfortunately, Bullbrook's pivotal work remained unnoticed until the 1950s, when his detailed report on the Palo Seco excavations was published. The report is considered exceptional for its discussion of the Palo Seco site's stratification and the reconstruction of prehistoric subsistence patterns.

In 1932, Bullbrook took up residence on Trinidad's south coast, close to the Erin shell midden. Between April 1934 and July 1935, he intermittently dug at the ceramic site nearby, donating his finds to the Royal Victoria Institute Museum in Port-of-Spain. Bullbrook and other avocational archaeologists subsequently established the Archaeological Section of the Historical Society of Trinidad and Tobago (hereafter called the Archaeological Section), which coordinated all archaeological work in the twin-island republic. The Archaeological Section received a small grant from the colonial government, which enabled Bullbrook to work intermittently at the Erin site from April 1941 to October 1942. The recovery of a complete Saladoid ceremonial vessel encouraged renewed investigations at Erin by the Archaeological Section from February to July 1945.

Bullbrook then coordinated a major excavation project under the direction of Benjamin Irving Rouse. This project, which was conducted under the joint auspices of the Archaeological Section and Yale University, New Haven, Connecticut in July–August 1946 and July–August 1953, led to the first relative chronology and prehistoric cultural classification of Trinidad. Over the years, until Bullbrook's death in 1967, there was considerable correspondence between Bullbrook and Rouse. In 1953, Bullbrook was appointed Associate Curator at the Royal Victoria Institute Museum, to which he donated his entire collection. This museum became the focal point of archaeological research in Trinidad. Bullbrook was also actively involved in research in Tobago. Following a survey of Tobago, which was carried out under the umbrella of the Trinidad and Tobago Tourist Board in 1960, Bullbrook and his assistant, Gloria Gilchrist, compiled a list of all known archaeological sites on the island. In October 1961, March 1963, and July 1964, under Bullbrook's guidance, Gilchrist carried out excavations at Tobago's Lovers' Retreat site.

Further Reading

Bullbrook, J. A. 1953. *On the Excavation of a Shell Mound at Palo Seco, Trinidad, B.W.I.* New Haven, CT: Yale University Press.
———. 1960. *The Aborigines of Trinidad*. Occasional Papers, Royal Victoria Institute Museum, no. 2. Port-of-Spain: Royal Victoria Institute Museum.

See also Palo Seco (Trinidad); Rouse, Benjamin Irving (1913–2006); Trinidad and Tobago.

Bullen, Ripley (1902–1976), and Adelaide Bullen (1908–1987)

George M. Luer

North American archaeologist Ripley Bullen did pioneering work in Florida and the Lesser Antilles and Greater Antilles. Adelaide Bullen was a physical and cultural anthropologist who also worked in archaeology. Each of them published independently, and they also coauthored 31 scholarly works. Much of their research focused on analyzing ceramic classification and seriation, analyzing lithic typologies, building culture histories, and detecting connections among regions and cultures. Adelaide is perhaps best known for her early recognition of the effects of treponemal infection in pre-Columbian Florida Indian skeletal remains.

The Bullens were married in 1929. Ripley was a mechanical engineer from 1925 to 1940. Changing careers, he joined Adelaide in graduate work at Harvard University in the 1940s, doing fieldwork in Massachusetts and New Mexico, at Chaco Canyon. In the 1940s, Ripley worked for the Peabody Foundation for Archaeology at Phillips Academy in Andover, Massachusetts. He also published prolifically about archaeology in Massachusetts during this period. In this decade, Adelaide and Ripley coauthored a notable study in historical archaeology, *Black Lucy's Garden* (1945).

In 1948, the Bullens moved to Florida, where Ripley worked for the Florida Park Service. In 1952, they began a long association with the Florida State Museum (now the Florida Museum of Natural History), where Ripley became chair of the Department of Social Sciences. In 1954, Adelaide was appointed as a research associate at the museum; she later became adjunct curator of anthropology there. During the 1950s, the Bullens' research focused on the central Florida Gulf coast and northeast Florida.

As the museum's research area expanded, Ripley began fieldwork in the Virgin Islands in 1959. In 1963, he examined pre-ceramic sites in Honduras and then did research through the Lesser and Greater Antilles. Early work focused on the Virgin Islands (Krum Bay), Grenada, Barbados, St. Vincent, the Grenadines, and Saint Lucia. By 1967, he had worked on St. Croix, Martinique, Marie Galante, Guadeloupe, St. Martin, Trinidad, Tobago, Curaçao, Aruba, Guyana, Suriname, Puerto Rico, Dominican Republic, Jamaica, and the Bahamas. Meanwhile, the Bullens maintained research in Florida and helped create a museum at the Crystal River site.

In 1967, the Bullens reorganized the International Congress for the Study of Pre-Columbian Cultures of the Lesser Antilles (renamed the International Association for Caribbean Archaeology in 1983). They edited and contributed to five of its *Proceedings* (1968, 1970, 1973, 1974, and 1976). In 1969, Ripley visited northern Columbia for research on origins of early fiber-tempered pottery in the southeastern United States. In the early 1970s, Ripley presented perspectives on a number of Antillean petroglyphs, and in 1974, he reviewed archaeological evidence for pre-Columbian contact (or the absence thereof) between Florida and the West Indies.

Throughout their careers, the Bullens published extensively and presented results at many meetings. They were well known for their accessibility to professional and avocational archaeologists. They shared information and gave editorial assistance to anyone seriously interested in archaeology. Their work encouraged research and preservation in many locations. In March 1976, Ripley was awarded an honorary Doctor of Science degree by the University of Florida. He died on Christmas Day, 1976. Adelaide survived him by eleven years.

Further Reading

Bullen, A. K. 1978. "Bibliography of Ripley P. Bullen." In *Proceedings of the Seventh International Congress for the Study of Pre-Columbian Cultures of the Lesser Antilles, Caracas, 1977,* 11–25. Montreal: Centre de Recherches Caraibes.

Bullen, A., and R. Bullen. 1945. "Black Lucy's Garden." *Bulletin of the Massachusetts Archaeological Society* 6 (2): 17–28.

Bullen, R. 1974. "Were There Pre-Columbian Cultural Contacts between Florida and the West Indies? The Archaeological Evidence." *Florida Anthropologist* 27 (4): 149–60.

Bullen, R. P., and J. B. Stoltman, eds. 1972. *Fiber-Tempered Pottery in Southeastern United States and Northern Columbia: Its Origins, Context, and Significance.* Gainesville: Florida Anthropological Society Publication 6.

See also The Florida Museum of Natural History; The International Association for Caribbean Archaeology (IACA).

The Cabrits Garrison (Portsmouth, Dominica)

Zachary J. Beier

The Cabrits Archaeological Research Project (CARP) is a long-term investigation of eighteenth- and nineteenth-century residential quarters, including enslaved laborers and soldiers of African descent, at the Cabrits Garrison, Dominica. In cooperation with the Dominica Forestry & Wildlife Division, this project is shedding light on the diverse nature of military life in the British Caribbean (Beier 2009). The fort is spread out on a hilly peninsula along the northwestern coast of the island, overlooking Douglas Bay to the north and Prince Rupert's Bay and the town of Portsmouth to the south. It encompasses an area of 200 acres that includes one fort, seven batteries, six cisterns, powder magazines, ordnance storehouses, and barracks and officers' quarters for 500 men and a company of artillery (Honychurch 1983). The first phase of excavations examined the enslaved village located in the valley between the Outer and Inner Cabrits Garrisons (CG-1) and the soldiers' barracks located in the northwest of the Outer Cabrits Garrison (CG-2). After its abandonment in the late nineteenth century, the site was overgrown by a dense dry forest, a process that has resulted in a lush wild landscape and historical structures in varying degrees of preservation. The area is the most recent addition to the Dominica National Parks Service, which was created in 1975. Restoration of the Fort Shirley battery has been under way under the direction of Dr. Lennox Honychurch since the early 1980s. In recent years, this portion of the fort has developed into a popular heritage destination with a number of modern facilities. Archaeological investigations offer aid to site interpretation and opportunities to engage the public through tours of excavations and hikes around the entire complex.

The development of the Cabrits headlands corresponded with the birth of colonial Dominica and with wider developments taking shape across the Atlantic World. The 1763 treaty of Paris marked the end of the Seven Years War and transferred Dominica to Britain. Dominica remained under British control until 1978 when the island achieved its independence (with the exception of a brief French occupation from 1778 to 1782). The first military post was established at the Cabrits in the 1770s, beginning a long process of intermittent construction until around 1813 (Honychurch 1983). Early administrative accounts state that "pioneers," "fort negroes," and "negro artificers" usually performed the required work. It is clear that the Cabrits Garrison was primarily built and maintained by enslaved laborers. In addition, in 1795, as a result of the high rates of mortality suffered by white soldiers, the British military began an active policy of raising black regiments from the local enslaved population and from men recently arrived from the west coast of Africa. It became common practice for black soldiers to replace white soldiers in garrisons around the Caribbean, including the Cabrits, until the British closed most of their colonial military installations in 1854 (Buckley 1998).

On April 9, 1802, enslaved African soldiers in the 8th West India Regiment mutinied. While the uprising was quelled by the British, this historic event, which was limited in duration but meaningful in scope, contributed to the Mutiny Act of 1807. This law freed some 10,000 enslaved soldiers and was one of the first acts of mass emancipation in the British Empire (Buckley 1998; Honychurch 1983).

Archaeological excavations have yielded detailed information relating to eighteenth- and nineteenth-century spatial and material practices in the enslaved village and a soldiers' barracks complex at the fort. Initial findings present the valley as encompassing numerous structures of varying architectural styles amid what appears to be a terraced landscape. A large sample of coarse earthenware sherds (both French and locally made) have been recovered, perhaps indicating a stronger connection between this area and the informal market(s) controlled by enslaved Africans (see Hauser 2011). Other findings include numerous tools that suggest the types of work fort laborers were engaged in and how they manipulated the volcanic bedrock to carve out their housing platforms. A 6th West India Regiment buckle was also recovered, direct evidence of the occupation of enslaved soldiers.

Further Reading

Beier, Z. J. 2009. "Initial Feasibility and Reconnaissance at the Cabrits Garrison, Dominica." Paper presented at the 2009 International Congress of Caribbean Archaeology, Antigua and Barbuda.

Buckley, R. N. 1998. *The British Army in the West Indies: Society and the Military in the Revolutionary Age*. Gainesville: University Press of Florida.

Hauser, M. W. 2011. "Routes and Roots of Empire: Pots, Power, and Slavery in the 18th-Century British Caribbean." *American Anthropologist* 113 (3): 431–47.

Honychurch, L. 1983. *The Cabrits and Prince Rupert's Bay*. Roseau: Dominica Institute.

See also Brimstone Hill Fortress National Park (St. Kitts); Cannon; Historical Archaeological Sites (Types); Historic Bridgetown and Its Garrison (Barbados).

Caguana/Capa Site (Puerto Rico)

Alexandra Sajo

Caguana, also known as Capa, is a Taíno site in central Puerto Rico that emerged between AD 1000 and AD 1450, spanning both the Ostionan Ostionoid and Chican Ostionoid periods. Caguana appears to have been a ceremonial center that developed an elaborate complex of decorated dance and ball courts, organized around the main central plaza where ceremonial activities took place (Figure C.1). The site's dance courts are partially paved with stone slabs and are bordered by vertically placed granite boulders or limestone slabs, most of which are decorated with petroglyphs that portray anthropomorphic and zoomorphic gods. Next to the dance courts are the ball courts, which are enclosed by lined undecorated stones. Rectangular buildings surround these courts. The site also includes a series of closely spaced and parallel raised earthen embankments.

Figure C.1. Aerial view of the Caguana dance and ball courts. Reprinted from Rouse (1992, fig. 28) by permission of Yale University Press.

The scarce evidence of residential structures at Caguana suggests that buildings positioned around the courts functioned as temples or as the chief's residence. The presence of single farm-like structures, which are dispersed in the countryside surrounding the site, suggests that Caguana acted not only as a ceremonial center but also as the political center for related chiefdoms. In this regard, Caguana may have been used as a regional ceremonial and political center.

The circumstances that led the Taíno inhabitants to desert the site around AD 1508 have not been thoroughly established. It appears that the Spanish did not know of Caguana's existence, since there are no historical or missionary documents that clearly refer to this site or its immediate surrounding areas. Also, no records of European materials have been found commingled with the Taíno artifacts recovered directly from the site. At present, the site has been reconstructed and designated as the Caguana Indian Ceremonial Park.

Further Reading

Rouse, I. 1992. *The Tainos: Rise and Decline of the People Who Greeted Columbus.* New Haven, CT: Yale University Press.

Wilson, S. M. 2007. *The Archaeology of the Caribbean.* Cambridge, UK: Cambridge University Press.

See also Plazas and *Bateys.*

Cannibalism (Anthropophagy)

Basil A. Reid

For centuries, the Island-Carib have been unfairly described as cannibals. Island-Carib are depicted in popular culture as fierce cannibals who fought unrelentingly against the Taíno, not only to subdue them but also to eat them (Figure C.2). Equally negative portrayals of Island-Carib are evident in more scholarly writings. Rouse (1992) contended that the Island-Carib men of the sixteenth and seventeenth centuries practiced ritualistic cannibalism as they "ate bits of the flesh of opposing warriors in order to acquire the latters' prowess" (1992, 22). Depictions of Island-Carib cannibalism in the 2006 Disney sequel *Pirates of the Caribbean: Dead Man's Chest*, which were vehemently denounced in 2005 by the chief of Dominica's Carib (Kalinago) Indians, underscore the extent to which these ideas still permeate popular culture. However, no evidence, whether archaeological or from first-hand observations by Europeans, conclusively proves that Island-Carib ever consumed human flesh (Reid 2009).

Cannibalism, or anthropophagy, can include drinking water-diluted ashes of a cremated relative, licking blood off a sword in warfare, masticating and subsequently vomiting a snippet of flesh, or celebrating Christian communion. Three major classifications of cannibalism have been cited. Endocannibalism refers to consumption of individuals within the group, exocannibalism indicates consumption of outsiders, and autocannibalism covers everything from nail-biting to torture-induced self-consumption (Arens 1979). Al-

Figure C.2. Illustration from *Nova Typis/Transacta Navigatio, Plautius* (1621), a fanciful account of what Benedictine missionaries saw as they arrived at the "Island of Cannibals" during Columbus's second voyage. (Caspar Plautius, 1621. *Nova Typis Transacta Navigatio: Novi Orbis Indiæ Occidentalis, Etc.,* [Linz].) Reprinted from Reid (2009, fig. 7.1) by permission of the University of Alabama Press.

though there is no clear definition of cannibalism, a practice that includes an extremely broad and sometime ambiguous range of behaviors, most researchers define cannibalism as the human consumption of human tissue, whether this is done in the context of warfare, as part of a funeral rite, or for gastronomic or survival purposes. The four lines of evidence important in the verification of cannibalism in the archaeological record are:

1. Similar butchering techniques in human and animal remains. The frequency, location, and type of verified cut marks and chop marks on human and animal bones must be similar, but we should allow for anatomical differences between humans and animals.

2. Similar patterns of long-bone breakage that might facilitate marrow extraction.

3. Identical patterns of post-processing discarding of human and animal remains.

4. Evidence of cooking. If present, such evidence should indicate comparable treatment of human and animal remains.

The Mancos case study in Colorado is perhaps the most important research that conclusively points to cannibalism in prehistoric America (Figure C.3) (White 1992). Based on a restudy of over 2,000 fragmented, burned, cut, and completely disarticulated human bones from an Anasazi pueblo, Tim D. White concluded that children, adolescents, and young adults of both sexes had been consumed at Mancos Canyon. The Mancos example has been cited as an excellent case of survival cannibalism. But even if we accept the survival cannibalism hypothesis for Mancos, it is simply not logical to apply this to the Island-Carib, given the latter's expertise as hunters and fishers in such a protein-rich environment as the Caribbean. Indeed, the Lesser Antilles possessed productive resources in the form of rich offshore habitats to which the Island-Carib had easy access. In fact, some of the shallow shelves and banks surrounding the islands that are populated by a diverse collection of aquatic foods are much larger than the islands themselves (Wilson 2007). Moreover, human beings from time immemorial have generally been able to successfully colonize environmentally unfriendly areas without necessarily resorting to cannibalism.

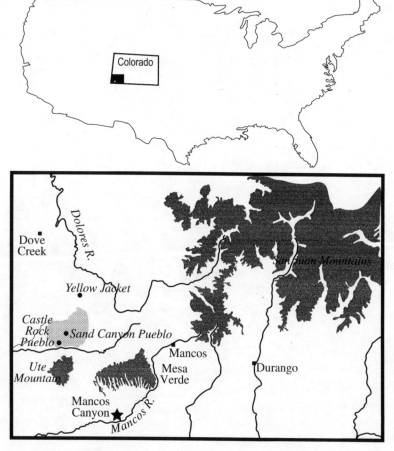

Figure C.3. Mancos Canyon in southwestern Colorado. Reprinted from Reid (2009, fig. 7.2) by permission of the University of Alabama Press.

To date, no hard archaeological evidence has been identified to suggest that the Island-Carib were cannibals. The very fact that the Island-Carib have largely been archaeologically invisible has no doubt complicated the issue (Keegan 1996). Proper site identification is necessary before any useful physical anthropological research can be conducted in the field. To date, Argyle in St. Vincent is the only fully investigated settlement site in the southern Caribbean that has been conclusively identified as Island-Carib. While the site has yielded a considerable number of Cayoid ceramic vessels, no evidence of human cannibalism has been forthcoming (Boomert 2011; Corinne Hofman personal communication 2013).

Clearly, claims of Island-Carib cannibalism are based on ethnohistory—that is, European accounts of native populations in the Island-Caribbean. Ethnohistorical sources cannot be entirely trusted as they are often laden with racial and cultural biases. A critical reading of Columbus's *diario* (most of which was actually written by Bartolomé de las Casas based on third-hand transcriptions) reveals a litany of half-truths, anecdotal descriptions, hearsay, and preconceived Eurocentric ideas about the native peoples of the Island-Caribbean. The following entry in Columbus's diary, dated November 4, 1492 has been interpreted as proof of the admiral's knowledge of cannibalistic practices among the Island-Carib: "He [Columbus] understood also that, far from there, there were one-eyed men, and others, with snouts of dogs, which ate men, and that as soon as one was taken they cut his throat and drank his blood" (quoted in Keegan 1996).

Although Columbus's *diario* has influenced in some way all discussions of the peoples of the Lesser Antilles, the admiral's first voyage never actually reached the Lesser Antilles. A critical analysis of this document reveals that both chroniclers and ethnohistorians have exhibited some confusion about the following mythical categories (Keegan 1996):

1. Cannibals: Natives who refused to submit to the Spanish were called cannibals. They were characterized as idolaters and consumers of human flesh who could not be converted into Christianity and were therefore suitable for enslaving.

2. Caribes: The Spanish understood Caribes to be real people when in fact they were creatures who existed only in Taíno mythology.

3. Caniba: Columbus's goals included having an audience with the Grand Khan of Cathay (China). He used the term "Caniba" to refer to the people he encountered because he mistakenly believed he was meeting subjects of the Grand Khan.

There was simply no merit to the allegations in item 1, as the so-called cannibals are essentially a legacy of the Spanish (Keegan 1992; Myers 1984). Since 1948, history writers have created a false dichotomy of the "peaceful Taíno" and the "man-eating cannibals"; this dichotomy first emerged in the *Handbook of South American Indians* series, where authors presented the Greater Antillean Taíno as noble, peaceful people and the Lesser Antillean Carib as savage or barbaric. In light of the regular skirmishes between the Taíno and the Spanish (which culminated with the battle of the Vega Real in 1495), it is clear that the notion of "peaceful Taíno" was considerably overplayed. Despite the experience of the Taíno with warfare, the Spanish were able to easily subjugate them in the northern Caribbean because they often attempted compromise and accommodation as an alternative to warfare (Reid 2009; Keegan 1992). The more militant Island-Carib of the Lesser Antilles, who adopted more aggressive postures toward the Spanish, French, English, Dutch and anyone else who threatened their sovereignty, were categorized as cannibals (Reid 2009; Keegan 1992). In fact, the word "Carib" soon became a general Spanish term for hostile natives. For example, from 1815 to 1820, an area on the coast of northeastern Luzon, Philippines, was labeled Negroes Caribes Bravos (González 1988). The Island-Caribs' aggressive responses to the European proved to be successful since they survived unconquered into the eighteenth century and beyond (Wilson 2007).

The Spanish distinctions between "peaceful" Taíno and "warlike" Island-Carib were not without self-interest (Reid 2009). At the outset, Columbus seemed to have in mind the development of a slave trade similar to the one Portugal was operating in Africa. The people Columbus believed could be converted to Christianity came to be known as the "peaceful Taíno," while those who resisted were pagans who deserved harsh treatment as enslaved people. In fact, agitation against slave-taking by priests who managed Spain's missionary efforts in the Greater Antilles caused the Crown to forbid slave-taking among Indians who were friendly to the Spanish. But in 1503, in response to economic interests, Queen Isabel excluded "all cannibals" from this ban. The Crown legally defined cannibals as barbaric people, enemies of the Christian, those who refuse conversion, and those who eat human flesh (Keegan 1992).

Further Reading

Arens, William. 1979. *The Man-Eating Myth*. New York: Oxford University Press.

Boomert, A. 2011. "From Cayo to Kalinago: Aspects of Island

Carib Archaeology." In *Communities in Contact: Essays in Archaeology, Ethnohistory and Ethnography of the Amerindian Circum-Caribbean*, ed. Corinne L. Hofman and Anne van Duijvenbode, 295–310. Leiden: Sidestone Press.

González, N. 1988. *Sojourners of the Caribbean: Ethnogenesis and the Ethnohistory of the Garifuna*. Urbana-Champaign: University of Illinois Press.

Keegan, W. 1996. "Columbus Was a Cannibal: Myth and the First Encounters." In *The Lesser Antilles in the Age of European Expansion*, ed. R. L. Paquette and S. L. Engerman, 17–32. Gainesville: University Press of Florida.

Myers, R. 1984. "Island-Carib Cannibalism." *New West Indian Guide/Neue West-Indische Gids* 58: 147–84.

Reid, B. A. 2009. *Myths and Realities of Caribbean History*. Tuscaloosa: University of Alabama Press.

Rouse, I. 1992. *The Tainos: Rise and Decline of the People Who Greeted Columbus*. New Haven, CT: Yale University Press.

White, T. D. 1992. *Prehistoric Cannibalism at Mancos 5Mtumr-2346*. Princeton, NJ: Princeton University Press.

Wilson, S. M. 2007. *The Archaeology of the Caribbean*. New York: Cambridge University Press.

See also The Cayoid Pottery Series; Island-Carib; Kalinago Descendants of St. Vincent and the Grenadines; The Kalinago Territory (Dominica).

Cannon

Ruud Stelten

Cannon, or guns, of all types were shipped to the Caribbean in large numbers during the colonial period because of the frequent conflicts and battles being fought in this part of the world. They were used on nearly all islands in the West Indies to repel attacks and to arm ships sailing through the region. Today, many cannon can still be found on countless military installations and shipwreck sites throughout the Caribbean. They are important artifacts because they can help date and/or identify particular sites (such as shipwrecks), shed light on historic trade patterns, and contribute to the study of military history of the Caribbean.

Throughout the sixteenth century, most cannon were made of bronze and wrought iron. Bronze was long considered the superior metal for ordnance manufacture. From the beginning of the seventeenth century onward, cast-iron guns were used extensively on merchant vessels and in the naval service in various countries. By the end of the 1600s, cast-iron ordnance had achieved such a high quality that the production of bronze guns was reduced, and by the 1770s most navies had abandoned them almost completely. There were three main advantages of cast-iron guns. First, they heated up more slowly and maintained their structural strength when fired frequently during battle. Second, they had greater longevity. Third, they were six to ten times cheaper to manufacture. The bronze ordnance on a ship could be more expensive than the entire vessel. As the principal maritime powers continued to increase the size of their navies in the

seventeenth century, this cost became excessively high. However, a number of factors made bronze guns preferable. Firing an iron cannon was a lot riskier than firing a bronze one: although bronze guns could deform and tear open, iron guns could burst without warning and fly to pieces, injuring or killing nearby personnel. Furthermore, bronze is a stronger metal, and bronze guns were thinner and lighter than their iron counterparts. Bronze was also easier to cast. Bronze guns were often heavily decorated and were considered true pieces of art.

The vast majority of cannon used in the West Indies were made of cast iron. The same guns that were used on ships were also used in fortifications in the colonies. There were often not enough gunners available on the garrisons in the West Indies to operate all the cannon in the various batteries. Ordinary soldiers would sometimes make up the shortfall. Aiming cannon at a moving ship was both a difficult and strenuous task. The gun crew had to maneuver the carriage by hand, and frequently it cracked or collapsed under the stress. Furthermore, aiming through a high embrasure provided a limited field of fire. These factors ensured that cannon in the colonies were rarely effective. Guns on ships were mounted on wooden carriages with wooden wheels (trucks) that would not damage the deck when the gun recoiled. Carriage hardware may be found on well-preserved wreck sites. Garrison guns could be mounted on larger wooden or iron carriages that had iron or wooden wheels. The iron carriage, introduced in 1810, was preferable in warm climates, where a wooden carriage would be vulnerable to rot. These iron carriages may be found at restored and abandoned fortifications throughout the region. For example, dozens of iron carriages that supported the guns at the Brimstone Hill Fortress on St. Kitts have been found. Guns could be elevated to desired heights by an elevating screw, which could raise or lower a wedge on which the end of the barrel rested. Carriages were stepped at the rear, so that a handspike could be inserted to lever up the heavy breech end and more wedges could be inserted.

The loading, firing, and cleaning of naval guns were described in great detail in several works from the eighteenth and nineteenth centuries. These were very structured activities that involved crews of up to thirteen people per cannon. Ordinary cannonballs were not the only type of projectile cannon would fire. A large variety of shot was available that was designed to serve specific purposes. Examples are cannonballs that were attached to each other by a chain (loose shot) or a bar (bar shot), small bits of iron put into a cartridge (case shot), and iron balls put into a thick canvas bag (grape shot). The first two types were used against ships, especially to damage rigging, masts, and spars, while the latter two were used specifically against people. All shot types are regularly found on Caribbean historical archaeological sites.

There were two main suppliers of cast-iron guns in the seventeenth and eighteenth centuries: Great Britain and Sweden. Apart from producing guns for its own navy, merchant ships, and trading companies, Great Britain also produced guns for export: it supplied the Dutch Republic, Spain, Sicily, Russia, Turkey, and Morocco. There were numerous gun foundries in England, the most famous of which was located at Woolwich. In general, there were two classes of cannon manufacturers: foundries that cast cannon for government establishments and those that supplied private organizations (e.g., merchant ships). Over time, armies and navies began standardizing the dimensions and calibers of their artillery. British manufacturers were expected to produce their guns to a government design, which resulted in a remarkable similarity of guns from different founders.

Toward the mid-seventeenth century, England was struck by an energy crisis that was the result of deforestation for the charcoal that was used in the furnaces that produced cast-iron goods. In addition, the English feared that the Dutch maritime empire would become too strong. After growing complaints, the House of Commons prohibited the export of cannon from England. Thus, Sweden came to dominate the European market for cast-iron guns from the middle of the seventeenth until the end of the eighteenth centuries. (After that, England recovered its leading position as a major exporter.) Swedish cannon were produced at a number of foundries, including those at Huseby, Stafsjö, Åker, and Ehrendal. The most important and famous Swedish foundry was located at Finspång. Swedish guns were exported through Amsterdam to Denmark, the Dutch Republic, England, Spain, and France, and to anyone else who would buy them.

France and Denmark (who had a number of furnaces in Norwegian lands), Norway, Spain, and some German states also had small cast-iron cannon industries, but this was not sufficient for large-scale export. In the eighteenth century, a number of local furnaces were set up in France; the main one was located at Indret near Nantes. The only cast-iron guns made by the Dutch were cast in Liege from 1817 to 1831, when Belgium was part of the Netherlands.

Cast-iron guns can be identified by their markings and shape. Most foundries and/or master gun founders put their maker's marks (such as an F for Finspång) on one trunnion and the date of casting on the other.

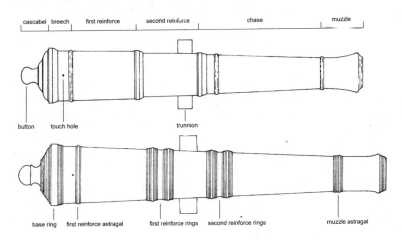

Figure C.4. Two cast-iron cannon. The top one is an English Borgard pattern gun, cast between 1716 and 1725. The bottom one is a so-called Finbanker, cast at Finspång, Sweden. The English cannon has few reinforce rings, while the Swedish type has many. Also note the different placements of the reinforce rings, the differences in the shape of the muzzle, the base ring, the cascabel, and the button and the stepped design of the English gun. Redrawn by Ruud Stelten after Nico Brinck.

On the trunnions, the muzzle face, or the barrel, one frequently finds the weight of the piece and its casting number along with other marks such as coats of arms of admiralties or a fleur-de-lis. Furthermore, many cannon display royal ciphers from the ruling monarch at the time of casting, such as GR2 for King George II of Great Britain and Ireland.

Guns are often classified by the weight of the cannonball they fired, for example "24 pounder." There are many differences in the shapes of guns cast in various foundries, especially in the seventeenth century. Figure C.4 highlights some differences between cannon cast in different countries.

When peace came to the Caribbean in the early nineteenth century at the end of the Napoleonic Wars, there was no longer a need for defense. Large numbers of guns were taken away from the area in this century to be put on display in museums and forts in the United States or simply to be sold as scrap metal. Although many guns have been recorded and island-wide surveys of artillery have been carried out on St. Eustatius and Barbados, new cannon are being found regularly on both terrestrial and maritime archaeological sites. Large numbers of guns still await discovery throughout the Caribbean region.

Further Reading

Caruana, A. B. 1994. *The History of English Sea Ordnance.* Vol. 1, *The Age of Evolution (1523–1715).* Rotherfield, UK: Jean Boudriot Publications.
———. 1997. *The History of English Sea Ordnance.* Vol. 2, *The Age of System (1715–1815).* Rotherfield, UK: Jean Boudriot Publications.
Hartland, Maj. M. 2010. *The Great Guns of Barbados.* St. Thomas, Barbados, West Indies: Miller.

See also Brimstone Hill Fortress National Park (St. Kitts); Historical Archaeological Sites (Types); Historic Bridgetown and Its Garrison (Barbados).

Carriacou

Scott M. Fitzpatrick

The island of Carriacou is located in the southernmost point of the Grenadines chain of the Lesser Antilles, approximately 200 kilometers north of Venezuela and 30 kilometers from Grenada, to which it belongs politically. The island is 32 square kilometers in area and is home to around 6,000 people. Geologically, it is fairly mountainous and is composed of a mixture of volcanic lava and fossiliferous limestone that dates to the Miocene. The mountains reach heights of 290 meters in both the northern and southern parts of the island, though the Grenadines in general are of low relief compared to other islands in the Antilles.

One of the first references to Carriacou was made by Jean-Baptiste du Tertre. When he described his 1656 visit to "Kayryoüacou" (the land of many reefs), he declared that the island was "the most beautiful of all the little islands . . . where I stayed long enough to be able to notice its special features" (Tertre 1667, 41). However, Du Tertre made no reference to any people inhabiting the island.

Originally settled by the French, Carriacou was ceded in 1763 to the British when they captured neighboring Grenada. The federation gained independence in 1974. Cotton was the leading export from the eighteenth to the early twentieth centuries, when lime production augmented the island's economy. The last lime factories closed in the mid-1980s, and the crumbling remains of lime kilns can be found scattered around the island, including a particularly well-preserved one at Sparrow Bay. On the northeastern side of Carriacou, people of Scottish and Irish ancestry continue traditional boatbuilding.

Recent research has revealed that Carriacou is one of the archaeologically richest islands in the southern Caribbean. In the early 1900s, Jesse Fewkes of the Smithsonian Institution visited the island and remarked that the pottery found here was some of the most beautiful he had seen in the Caribbean. Subsequent research by Ripley and Adelaide Bullen in the 1970s identified a number of important sites along the coast, though no systematic survey was carried out before 2003, when the Carriacou Archaeological Project was established under the direction of Quetta Kaye (University College London), Scott M. Fitzpatrick (then at North Carolina State University), and Michiel Kappers (QLC, BV, The Netherlands). This survey of almost the entire coastline and accessible flat inland areas helped identify over a dozen prehistoric settlement areas.

Two of the most intensively occupied and archaeologically important sites on Carriacou are Grand Bay (Figure C.5) and Sabazan, which are located on the windward (east) coast. Both sites display deep stratified deposits that form multilayered middens that extend up to several meters high. Much of the profile is evident through natural erosion that has been exacerbated by decades of sand mining by locals, a problem that persists in many parts of the Caribbean. The dense middens contain substantial cultural, botanical, and zooarchaeological materials. These include human burials; posthole features/household structures; midden refuse; stone, shell, and bone tools; shell and exotic stone beads; a wide array of pre-Columbian ceramics; and a variety of food remains. Prehistoric settlement has been dated by an extensive suite of over thirty-five radiocarbon assays, indicating that peoples lived here for over a 1,000-year period, from the late Saladoid (ca. AD 380) almost up to the time of European contact (AD 1400).

The ceramic material includes decorated and undecorated Saladoid-, Troumassan Troumassoid-, and Suazan Troumassoid–style pottery sherds. Troumassan Troumassoid ceramics display a simplification of the decoration of the Saladoid ceramics and Suazan Troumassoid ceramic ware developed from the earlier

Troumassoid and is characterized by a further simplification in shapes and decoration. The domestic ware includes rather thin griddle sherds: some of these are finely slipped on the upper side, some present upturned round edges, and others have wide feet. The latter were apparently used contemporaneously with those that were flat. Ceremonial ceramic artifacts such as inhaling bowls or spouts, incense burners, decorated body stamps, ceramic spindle whorls, and several three-pointed *zemíes* attest to past ritual activities at the site. Different tool assemblages that have been recovered from the various midden layers suggest a wide trade span, including the possible transport of heirlooms in the form of ceramic inhaling bowls used to ingest *cohoba*, which is thought to have been derived from the seeds of the yopo tree (*Anadenanthera peregrina*) (Fitzpatrick et al. 2008).

Zooarchaeological analysis of faunal remains found in the different layers of the middens indicates the presence of food from both the land and sea but with an emphasis on the exploitation of marine habitats that include both inshore and offshore environments. This evidence clearly suggests that marine foods were an important part of the diet of the inhabitants throughout their occupation of the island and that they developed

Figure C.5. Excavation and sand mining at Grand Bay, Carriacou. Photo by Scott M. Fitzpatrick.

different procurement strategies such as nets, hooks, lines, and wires to capture food. Faunal remains consist of numerous species of fish and shellfish remains, agouti, opossum, birds, iguana, land crab, sea urchin, and an abundant amount of turtles. Archaeological evidence further indicates that the island was a centerpiece for many economic activities in the southern Antilles during the Saladoid and post-Saladoid periods, reflected in part by the large number of animals that translocated to the island prehistorically.

Further Reading

Bullen, R. P., and A. K. Bullen. 1972. *Archaeological Investigations on St Vincent and the Grenadines, West Indies.* William L. Bryant Foundation American Studies, Report 8. Orlando: William Bryant Foundation.

Fitzpatrick, S. M., M. Kappers, Q. Kaye, C. Giovas, M. LeFebvre, M. H. Harris, S. Burnett, J. A. Pavia, K. Marsaglia, and J. Feathers. 2009. "Precolumbian Settlements on Carriacou, West Indies." *Journal of Field Archaeology* 34, no. 3: 247–66.

Fitzpatrick, S. M., Q. Kaye, J. Feathers, J. Pavia, and K. Marsaglia. 2008. "Evidence for Inter-Island Transport of Heirlooms: Luminescence Dating and Petrographic Analysis of Ceramic Inhaling Bowls from Carriacou, West Indies." *Journal of Archaeological Sciences* 36, no. 3: 596–606.

Fitzpatrick, S. M., Q. Kaye, and M. Kappers. 2004. "A Radiocarbon Sequence for the Sabazan Site, Carriacou, West Indies." *Journal of Caribbean Archaeology* 5: 1–11.

Tertre, J. B. du 1667. *Histoire Générale des Antilles.* Vols. 1 and 2. Paris: Thomas Jolly.

See also The Suazan Troumassoid (Suazey); The Troumassan Troumassoid.

The Casimiroid

Alexandra Sajo

Casimiroid culture emerged in the Greater Antillean islands of Cuba and Hispaniola (Haiti and Dominican Republic) from around 4000 to 400 BC. The culture is named after the Casimira site in the Dominican Republic, where the earliest stone tools were first found. All Casimiran period settlements are located inland and developed a marine and hunting oriented economy. Their tools were based on the flake-stone technique, which consisted of collecting flint or other fine-grained rocks and using a hammerstone, producing a series of irregularly shaped flakes used for different purposes such as knives and scrapers. It is generally accepted that the first inhabitants of these islands may have originally come from Belize in Central America, while evidence of a later occupation indicates a Venezuelan origin.

Casimiran tools recovered from Cuba and Hispaniola share strong similarities with lithic tools manufactured in Belize during the Archaic Age from 7000 BC to around 4000 BC, when the variations in the assemblages of flake-stone tools are due to the availability of raw material and the local style of working, while the later occupation of the islands by the Courian and Redondan cultures developed a tool assemblage that shares strong similarities with the Manicuaroid period of Venezuela, further suggesting that the Casimiroid may also have come from South America. Nonetheless, archaeological evidence strongly suggests a Central American origin for the population of these islands.

Well-known Casimiran workshop sites are Rancho Casimira, Berrera-Mordan in the Dominican Republic (which has been dated to around 2610 BC and 2165 BC), and Seboruco and Levisa in Cuba (which has been dated around 4190 BC). On the site of Levisa, archaeologists have been able to reconstruct aspects of the diet of the first inhabitants from cultural, botanical, and zoological deposits. The diet of these early groups of hunters consisted of big marine game, such as seals, manatees, and sea turtles, and land mammals, such as hutia and large sloths, which were probably hunted to extinction. There is no evidence indicating that these hunters practiced fishing, and the collection of shells was not as abundant or as important to their diet as it was during later periods (Keegan 1994; Rouse 1992; Wilson 2007).

On Hispaniola, people of the Courian culture succeeded the Casimiran and can be further divided into two local cultures, the El Porvenir in the Dominican Republic and the Couri in Haiti, which have been dated to between 2630 BC and AD 240. During this period, pottery developed and early agricultural activities emerged, together with fishing and shellfish collection, producing a shift in diet from large sea and land animals to coastal fish and shellfish resources, supplemented with small inland mammals and crops. The Courian people moved seasonally, exploited inland and coastal resources, and manufactured stone tools such as spearheads, backed knives, and end scrapers, which were used in hunting animals. During this period, single- and double-bitted axes, conical pestles, and mortars were used for food processing, and a variety of stone and coral balls, disks, and dagger-like objects were possibly used as ritual implements. Elaborate stone and shell beads and pendants have also been found at Courian period sites, and there is evidence for the use of red ochre both as body paint and as treatment for the dead.

The Redondan subseries succeeded the Casimiran on Cuba from 2050 BC to AD 1300. During this period, two local cultures emerged: Guayabo Blanco and Cayo Redondo. Both cultures share the unique manufacture of triangular shell gauges, which have also exclusively been found at the St. John's River site in Florida. During their occupation of the island, the Archaic inhabitants continued to make stone tools similar to those of the Courian period of Hispaniola, although they also developed a wide range of shell tools that included gauges, plates, cups, tips, and hammers.

Casimiroid settlements were located in both coastal and inland areas, occupying open-air sites and rock shelters, which they painted with geometric designs. Shell mounds left by Redondan culture are distributed along the coast and in marshes as well as on adjacent islets. Archaeological research indicates that the Casimiroid buried their dead in the caves they occupied and in the earth mounds they constructed. Occasionally, stone balls accompanied the dead.

Further Reading

Keegan, W. F. 1994. "West Indian Archaeology. 1. Overview and Foragers." *Journal of Archaeological Research* 2 (3): 255–84.
Pantel, A. G. 2003. "The First Caribbean People, Part II: The Archaics." In *General History of the Caribbean*. Vol. 1, *Autochthonous Societies*, ed. Jalil Sued Badillo, 118–33. London: Macmillan and UNESCO Publishing.
Rouse, I. 1992. *The Tainos: Rise and Decline of the People Who Greeted Columbus*. New Haven, CT: Yale University Press.
Wilson, S. M. 2007. *The Archaeology of the Caribbean*. Cambridge, UK: Cambridge University Press.

See also Antigua and Barbuda (Archaic Sites); The Archaic Age; The Ostionoid.

Cassava (Manioc)

Mark C. Donop

Cassava (*Manihot esculenta*) is a poisonous neotropical root crop from the Euphorbiaceae family that has become the staple for hundreds of millions of people worldwide. Cassava has been cultivated for thousands of years as a rich source of carbohydrates despite the fact it also produces cyanide. The approximately 5,000 varieties of *M. esculenta* are most often referred to as cassava, yucca, or manioc; the first two words are derived from the Amerindian Arawakan Taíno language of the Greater Antilles and the third from the Tupi-Guarani of South America.

Cassava is a drought-resistant, perennial shrub with starchy roots that can be produced in large quantities in marginal conditions. The nonpropagative roots of the cassava plant contain large amounts of carbohydrates because of a unique combination of C_3 and C_4 photosynthetic pathways but lack a balanced profile of nutrients, specifically protein. The leaves and peel of the cassava plant contain significant amounts of protein and vitamins A and C, but they also contain high levels of cyanogenic chemical compounds. Crop yields of up to 90 tons per hectare can be achieved even in harsh environments with acidic soils, depending upon the amount of effort invested.

All of the plants in the *Manihot* genus are cyanogenic, and cassava contains dangerous cyanogenic glucosides (CG) in all parts of the plant except the seeds. Cyanide is rapidly absorbed through the gastrointestinal tract and prevents cellular respiration in organic tissues, particularly the heart and the central nervous system, causing paralysis and death in extreme cases. Hydrogen cyanide (HCN), or free cyanide, is released when tissue disruption brings the CG linamarin in the cell vacuoles in contact with the enzyme linamarase found in the cell walls. This toxicity is most likely a chemical defense against predation in locations where herbivorous pressure in resource-poor environments is significant. Cassava is loosely divided into "bitter" and "sweet" varieties based on the amount of HCN they contain. Bitter cassava requires more intensive processing, but it is probably more pest resistant and starchy and is one of the few crops in the world for which more toxic varieties are preferred. While proper processing and cooking eliminates most of the toxicity, a small residue remains that is released during digestion. An adequate daily intake of protein that contains methionine is necessary to buffer the toxic residue to avoid permanent damage to the nervous system.

Cassava processing is dependent on the bitterness of the variety and the desired product. Cassava roots can be harvested within six to seven months, and its cylindrical stems, or "stakes," can be immediately replanted for clonal propagation, although the plant can be left unmolested for up to two years before the roots become largely inedible from lignification and infestation. Harvested cassava roots spoil within three days, although traditional methods can be used to store fresh cassava roots for up to two years. Peeled sweet cassava can be boiled and eaten, but bitter varieties must be processed more thoroughly to prevent cyanide poisoning. Grating the peeled bitter roots increases the surface area of the product and promotes activation of the cyanide. The grated product is then pressed or strained through woven bags or elastic basketry tubes called *matapi*. The collected starchy juice can be processed into a variety of products such as tapioca and cassava beer, and the solid flour can be dried and stored for long periods of time and it is often roasted and made into bread on flat ceramic or metal griddles.

Cassava originated in the Amazonian lowlands and spread into Central America and the Caribbean during prehistory. Antonio C. Allem identified *Manihot esculenta flabellifolia* as the wild, living ancestor of cassava in 1982, and subsequent genetic research has revealed that it probably originated in Brazil along the edge of the Amazon basin. The domestication of cassava may have taken place at multiple locations perhaps 8000–10,000 BP, although direct evidence for cassava in the archaeological record is limited because tubers generally carbonize poorly, they produce few pollen grains, and their phytoliths are few and largely unidentifiable. The oldest *Manihot* starch grains recovered thus far were collected from ground stone tools from Colombia and Panama that date to between 7000 and 7500 BP.

Caribbean peoples have used cassava for at least the last 3,000 years. The earliest evidence for cassava use in the Caribbean comes from starch grains taken from Archaic edge-ground cobbles from Puerto Rico and Vieques that date to between 2400–3300 BP, refuting two long-held assumptions: that cassava first entered the Caribbean with Amazonian Saladoid pottery makers around 2500 BP, and that ceramic griddles were needed to process the plant. The oldest macrobotanical cassava remains in the Caribbean were recovered by Kathleen Deagan from the Taíno site of En Bas Saline in Haiti that date to the Chican Ostionoid period (AD 1200–1500). The Taíno practiced a sophisticated form of *conuco* agriculture in which they constructed mounds of soft alluvial soil for planting cassava and other crops. The importance of cassava among the Taíno was reflected in the fact that Yucahú, the lord of cassava and the sea, was the highest-ranking masculine deity depicted on *cemís*. Cassava continues to be an important staple for many people living in the Caribbean today.

Further Reading

Arroyo-Kalin, M. 2010. "The Amazonian Formative: Crop Domestication and Anthropogenic Soils." *Diversity* 2 (4): 473–504.

Olsen, K. M., and B. A. Schaal. 1999. "Evidence on the Origin of Cassava: Phylogeography of *Manihot esculenta*." *Proceedings of the National Academy of Sciences of the United States of America* 96 (10): 5586–91.

Pagán-Jiménez, J. R., and R. Rodríguez Ramos. 2007. "Sobre el Origen de la Agricultura en las Antillas." In *Proceedings of the Twenty-First Congress of the International Association for Caribbean Archaeology*, vol. 1, ed. B. Reid, H. P. Roget, and A. Curet, 252–59. St. Augustine, Trinidad and Tobago: School of Continuing Studies, University of the West Indies.

Wilson, W. M., and D. L. Dufour. 2002. "Why 'Bitter' Cassava? Productivity of 'Bitter' and 'Sweet' Cassava on a Tukanoan Indian Settlement in the Northwest Amazon." *Economic Botany* 56 (1): 49–57.

See also Agricultural Earthworks (The Guianas); *Conucos*; The First Caribbean Farmers; Griddles; *Zemíes (Cemís)*

The Cayman Islands

Peter L. Drewett

There is currently no evidence for human occupation of the Cayman Islands prior to their accidental discovery by Christopher Columbus in 1503. Field surveys of Grand Cayman, Cayman Brac, and Little Cayman were undertaken in 1992 and 1995 (Drewett 2000), and a second survey of Grand Cayman was undertaken in 1993 (Stokes and Keegan 1996). These surveys, together with the fact that no record of European contacts with Amerindians on the islands exists and no casual finds have been made over some five hundred years of European activity on the islands, suggest fairly conclusively that the islands were never occupied in prehistory. The importance of the Cayman Islands in our understanding of the human occupation of the Caribbean therefore lies in the fact that humans did not modify the fauna until the historic period.

The excavation of three 1 × 1 meter test units in the Great Cave on Cayman Brac in 1995 (Drewett 2000) enabled the study of the natural fauna of one cave (Scudder and Quitmyer 1998). The fauna consisted of 30 taxa of vertebrates and invertebrates that represented a minimum number of 286 animals. Terrestrial snails accounted for 78.0 percent of the sample, and aquatic gastropods accounted for 10.5 percent. Crabs, lizards, birds, and mammals account for the remaining taxa. Two possible genera of hutia, *Capromys* sp. and *Geocapromys* sp., and the now-extinct insectivore *Nesophontes* sp. represent the prehistoric mammals in the assemblage. Bones from cats, mice, and rats that were also found in the cave represent introductions in the historic period, all animals that had a fatal impact on the indigenous fauna.

Although the Cayman Islands are on a hypothesized migration route from Mesoamerica to Cuba, there is no evidence that the islands were actually found by prehistoric peoples. If, however, the islands were simply used as a staging post, then the archaeological evidence may have been so slight as to leave little or no trace. It is unlikely that archaeological sites on the low-lying Cayman Islands were washed away during hurricanes, given the survival of bone deposits recovered from Great Cave.

Further Reading

Drewett, P. L. 2000. *Prehistoric Settlements in the Caribbean: Fieldwork in Barbados, Tortola, and the Cayman Islands.* London: Archetype for the Barbados Museum and Historical Society.

Scudder, S. J., and I. R. Quitmyer. 1998. "Evaluation of Evidence for Pre-Columbian Human Occupation at Great Cave, Cayman Brac, Cayman Islands." *Caribbean Journal of Science* 34 (1–2): 41–49.

Stokes, A. V., and W. F. Keegan. 1996. "A Reconnaissance for Prehistoric Archaeological Sites on Grand Cayman." *Caribbean Journal of Science* 32 (4): 425–30.

The Cayoid Pottery Series

Arie Boomert

The Cayoid series, named after the Cayo complex of St. Vincent, represents the ceramic tradition of the Island-Carib (Kalinago). Settlement sites associated with this series have been found on Grenada, St. Vincent, Dominica, and Basse-Terre (Guadeloupe), while individual finds have been found in Trinidad, Île de Ronde (Grenadines), Saint Lucia, and Martinique. Thus far, Argyle, St. Vincent, is the only fully investigated Cayoid settlement site. Excavations by Leiden University in 2009–2010 yielded elaborate post-mold patterns that made possible reconstruction of the entire village at this site, which has been dated to circa 1550–1650. The introduction of the Cayoid series into the Lesser Antilles apparently took place somewhat earlier, in late prehistoric times.

The identification of the Island-Carib ceramic assemblage—once referred to as the "Island-Carib Problem"—has been a major issue of debate throughout most of the second half of the twentieth century. For years, the Island-Carib were considered to be the makers of the Suazan Troumassoid series, but documentary evidence regarding their pottery repertoire has discredited this view. Recent research indicates that most of the Island-Carib vessel forms show a distinctive resemblance to the antecedents of the ceramics presently made by the Carib (Kalina) Indians of the Guianas. This accords well

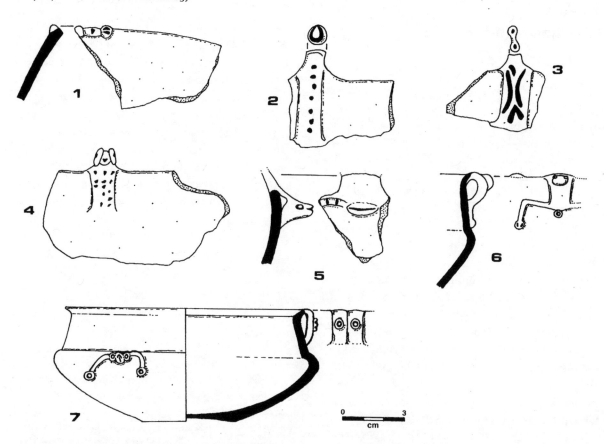

Figure C.6. Cayoid decorative techniques and motifs, St. Vincent. Courtesy of Arie Boomert.

with the Island-Carib origin myths, which suggest that the males in their society originally came from South America and were in regular contact with other natives on the mainland (such as Carib, Arawak [Lokono], and Nepoio) during the early colonial period.

The syncretism of the Island-Carib culture is accurately reflected in the Cayoid ceramics (Figure C.6). Several Cayoid vessel forms are clearly derived from the Koriabo complex, the late prehistoric pottery tradition of the Guianas that is closely related to the Polychrome Tradition of Amazonia. This complex was the precursor to the ceramic assemblages of present Carib and Palikur and possibly those of Arawak indigenes. Cayoid vessels include wide open bowls showing lobed rims, typically necked jars, and large containers or bowls with convex upper parts. In addition, the Cayoid series is characterized by bowls with decorative motifs that demonstrate a distinct relationship with the Chicoid Ostionoid/Taíno series of the Greater Antilles and Virgin Islands, suggesting that many Taíno relocated to the Lesser Antilles or that the Island-Carib captured women from these islands. The presence of Cayoid earthenwares with heavy scratching on vessel surfaces—primarily on griddles—suggests that Suazan Troumassoid women strongly in-

fluenced the male-dominated Island-Carib society in the domestic sphere.

A lively trade developed during the contact period between the Spanish and other European nations and the Island-Carib of the Windward Islands. The European sailors obtained foodstuffs and fresh water from the Island-Carib, while the Island-Carib received iron utensils, textiles, glass beads, and so forth from the Europeans. Cayo potsherds found at Argyle, St. Vincent, with European seed beads embedded in the vessel rims illustrate these trade contacts.

Further Reading

Boomert, A. 1986. "The Cayo Complex of St. Vincent: Ethnohistorical and Archaeological Aspects of the Island-Carib Problem." *Antropológica* 66: 3–68.
———. 2011. "From Cayo to Kalínago: Aspects of Island-Carib Archaeology." In *Communities in Contact: Essays in Archaeology, Ethnohistory, and Ethnography of the Amerindian Circum-Caribbean*, ed. Corinne L. Hofman and Anne van Duijvenbode, 295–310. Leiden: Sidestone Press.

See also The Chican Ostionoid Subseries; Island-Carib; Kalinago Descendants of St. Vincent and the Grenadines; The Kalinago Territory (Dominica).

Cemeteries

Naseema Hosein-Hoey

Cemeteries are important data sources because they can provide fascinating insights into the social lives of those who have been interred. The placement of grave goods and burial styles can provide information on religion, customs, and the social status of those who have been buried. Jerome Handler's and Frederick Lang's excavations on a burial ground for the enslaved located in Newton Plantation in Barbados are a classic example of the integration of traditional historical methods and archaeology in developing an understanding of Afro-Caribbean mortuary systems. Their research was based on the interpretation of material culture recovered from over 100 burials dating from the seventeenth to the early nineteenth centuries. Through the examination of these artifacts, it was concluded that there was a continuance of West African body ornamentation practices in the New World.

With the assistance of modern forensic anthropology, age, sex, stature, and some aspects of ancestry can be obtained through the examination of human remains. The bones and teeth derived from graves can furnish valuable information on injuries, degenerative diseases, disorders, physical stresses, infections, or the cause and manner of death of interred individuals; this research comprises an archaeological subfield known as osteoarchaeology. Evidence of surgical procedures on wounds can provide vital information about the historical treatment of wounds. Modern scientific analyses can also assist in the determination of individual or group diets. For example, Tamara Varney's stable isotope analysis of human remains from the Royal Naval Hospital in Antigua provided data that helped determine group membership. Varney excavated this site from 1998 to 2001 with the assistance of Reginald Murphy and the University of Calgary archaeological field school. Her research demonstrated that isotopic ratios of bone collagen samples may provide insights into different human ancestries.

With the goal of furnishing data on the life conditions and health issues relating to an enslaved community in Suriname, Mohammed Khudabux conducted fieldwork on graves that were uncovered due to coastal erosion. In 1984, a burial ground was found along the Atlantic coast in Suriname. Historical research indicated that this ground was once part of Plantation Waterloo, a thriving plantation during the nineteenth century. Khudabux and his team found fifty-seven graves in two concentrations located in the cotton beds near the coast. Even though these graves were under threat, he was able to obtain important information on the health and social conditions of those who had been buried.

Coffin types reflected the status of the enslaved as well as the preference for and accessibility of coffin burials. Thirty-two percent of the burials in Mohammed Khudabux's sample were interred with their heads to the west, while 68 percent were buried with their heads facing east. This change in burial practices may have been the result of the Christianization of enslaved individuals on the plantation.

Human skeletons can also give useful information about pathological bone changes, fractures, osteoarthritis, rickets, anemia, tuberculosis, leprosy, dentition problems, and other health anomalies. This kind of research is a subfield of osteoarchaeology known as paleopathology. Joanna Gilmore identified victims of Hansen's disease (leprosy) because their remains exhibited signs of secondary infections. Of note is the first paleopathological record of the pitting on the hyoid bone from leprosy. This has provided additional diagnostic evidence for both archaeologists and clinicians (Gilmore 2009).

Further Reading

Farmer, K., F. H. Smith, and K. Watson. 2007. "The Urban Context of Slavery: An Archaeological Perspective from Two Afro-Barbadian Slave Cemeteries in Bridgetown, Barbados." *Proceedings of the International Association for Caribbean Archaeology* 21 (2): 677–85.

Gilmore, J. K. 2009. "Leprosy at the Lazaretto on St Eustatius, Netherlands Antilles." *International Journal of Osteoarchaeology* 18 (1): 72–84.

Haviser, J. B. 1999. *African Sites Archaeology in the Caribbean.* Jamaica: Ian Randle/Markus Wiener.

Varney, T. 2005. "Does Diet Reflect Group Membership? A Stable Isotope Analysis of Human Remains from the Royal Naval Hospital Cemetery at English Harbour, Antigua, W.I." In *Proceedings of the Twenty-First Congress of the International Association for Caribbean Archaeology*, ed. Basil Reid, Henry Petitjean Roget, and Antonio Curet, Volume 2, 667–76. St. Augustine, Trinidad and Tobago: School of Continuing Studies, University of the West Indies.

See also Historical Archaeological Sites (Types); Hospitals and Leprosaria in the Colonial Caribbean; Newton Burial Ground (Barbados).

The Chican Ostionoid Subseries

L. Antonio Curet

The Chican Ostionoid subseries (originally known as the Chicoid series [Rouse 1964]), was first defined by Rouse (1992) in Hispaniola. The Chican subseries prevails in the Virgin Islands, Puerto Rico, the southern and eastern parts of Hispaniola, at least the eastern tip of Cuba, the Bahamas, and in the northern Leeward Islands, where some deposits have been identified. However, because of the highly elaborate and distinct styles of Chican pottery, Puerto Rico and Hispaniola are considered as the possible "center" or "core" of the Chican cultural development, leading Rouse to call these groups the Classic Taíno. The Chican from the rest of the islands are known as Eastern or Western Taíno, depending on their geographical location in relation to the Classic Taíno. Dates for the Chican subseries range from AD 800 to 1500, depending on the region. The material culture of these people is characterized by their ceramic styles and elaborate stone, shell, wood, and bone (manatee ribs) ritual paraphernalia.

According to Rouse, the Chican Ostionoid is represented by eight styles: the Magens Bay–Salt River II in the Virgin Islands (AD 1200–1500); the Esperanza style in the east and the Capá style in the west of Puerto Rico (both AD 1200–1500); the Atajadizo in Hispaniola (AD 800–1200), the Boca Chica (AD 1200–1500) and Guayabal (AD 1200–1500) styles in the east (Dominican Republic); the Carrier (AD 1200–1500) in the west (Dominican Republic); and the Pueblo Viejo style on the eastern tip of Cuba. In general, Chican pottery is characterized by the presence of incisions on the shoulders of *cazuelas* (incurving bowls) (Figure C.7). Paint is almost completely absent, although red- and white-slipped vessels are still observable in some areas. Strap handles are absent, but biomorphic, modeled-incised head lugs, or *adornos*, were still common among the decorated pottery. Prevailing ceramic forms include *cazuelas*, or ollas (incurving bowls), plain and highly decorated bottles (mostly in Hispaniola), plates, and *burenes* (cassava griddles). The incised designs include circles, triangles, parallel dashes, and lines ending in dots.

Other types of material culture include wood and stone idols, ornaments, and other high-status objects. Religious representation in Puerto Rico includes stone and wooden objects, the most common of which are the famous three-pointer idols, stone collars, elbow stones, and *dujos* (ceremonial stools). Wooden cohoba idols, three-pointers, Macorix heads made of stone, wooden dujos, and *potizas* (bottles) are more prevalent in Hispaniola. Other religious paraphernalia present in most islands are objects related to the *cohoba* ritual (in which the hallucinogen *cohoba* is snuffed in order to contact the supernatural world) such as inhalers and vomit spatulas (most of them made of wood or manatee ribs). Another artistic expression of the Chican Ostionoid subseries is the distinct rock art style. At the beginning of the Chican, petroglyphs and pictographs in Puerto Rico and Hispaniola became more elaborate and sophisticated

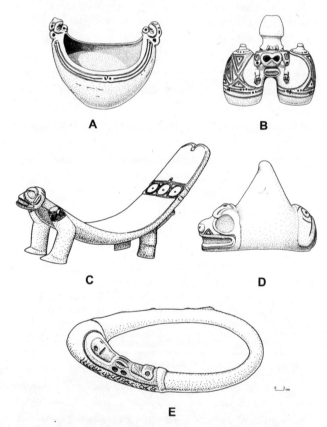

Figure C.7. Taíno (Chican Ostionoid) pottery and ceremonial objects. *A* and *B*, pottery from Hispaniola (postcards in possession of the author); *C, duho* from Hispaniola (after Kerchache [1994]); *D, zemí* from Puerto Rico (postcard in possession of the author); *E*, stone collar or belt from Puerto Rico (after Bercht et al. [1997]). All drawings by Jill Seagard. Courtesy of L. Antonio Curet.

than in previous periods and, at least in the case of the former, they shared some stylistic features with Chican pottery, including the use of circles, parallel lines, and triangles.

Chican Ostionoid funerary traditions seem to vary from island to island. In Puerto Rico, burials appear to be dispersed throughout settlements, in many instances in the context of the domestic unit. In contrast, on the island of Hispaniola, clusters of burials or cemeteries have been reported.

Chican settlement types included circular, nucleated villages; lineal sites along the coast or rivers; dispersed patterns of small sites, perhaps representing farmsteads or single households; and centralized settlement patterns with a large site in the center and smaller ones surrounding it. The few structures excavated in Puerto Rico and the Virgin Islands indicate that the Chican Ostionoid lived in small, round, nuclear family houses of 8–10 meters in diameter. Sites are found in a variety of ecological zones, including coasts, rivers, mangroves, foothills, and mountains.

The communal ritual tradition that began in the late Elenan/Ostionian periods for Puerto Rico is also present in the Chican Ostionoid, as indicated by the presence of larger and more elaborate ball courts, plazas, and ceremonial centers (sites with multiple ceremonial structures) such as are found at the site of Caguana, Utuado. Rectangular ball courts and square and small circular structures have been observed on Puerto Rico, eastern Hispaniola, the Virgin Islands, and possibly eastern Cuba. The highest number of structures has been found on Puerto Rico. Large circular plazas of 300 meters or more in diameter have been reported for central Hispaniola. Most of the structures from Puerto Rico, the Virgin Islands, and eastern Hispaniola are bounded by stone rows, some of which have petroglyphs. The large circular structures from central Hispaniola and the structures from eastern Cuba are delimited by earthen berms.

In the Greater Antilles, the Chican Ostionoid subseries has been related to the groups that inhabited these islands at the time of contact, particularly the group that has come to be known as the historic Taíno. At the time of contact, Hispaniola had several powerful paramount chiefdoms. According to early European accounts, the island was divided into five provinces, each of which covered over 1,000 square kilometers and was ruled by a single paramount chief. However, there is evidence that smaller polities coexisted in Hispaniola with these larger polities, strongly suggesting the presence of a wide variety of political structures and interactions. While no substantive data are available on population, the archaeological record and the evidence included in the ethnohistorical documents seem to indicate that Hispaniola was densely populated during this time. It is also clear from the documents and from the archaeological evidence that a number of "ethnic" groups coexisted on this island until the time of contact. Several researchers have argued that at this time Puerto Rico was divided among several paramount chiefdoms. However, considering that most of the chiefdoms mentioned in the chronicles tended to be located in valleys and that ball courts and plazas are widely distributed, Puerto Rico seems to have been divided instead into competing polities that were smaller than a paramount chiefdom. Interestingly, this island seems to have suffered a noticeable population decrease during this time.

Archaeological and ethnohistorical evidence strongly suggest that at this time in Cuba the Chican Ostionoid shared the island with hunting-and-gathering groups and other agricultural groups. While no clear archaeological boundaries are observable between the two types of groups, settlements of the former appear to have been concentrated in the eastern part of the island and settlements of the latter on the western side.

Further Reading

Bercht, F., E. Brodsky, J. A. Farmer, and D. Taylor. 1997. *Taíno: Pre-Columbian Art and Culture from the Caribbean.* New York: El Museo del Barrio and Monacelli Press.

Kerchache, J. 1994. *L'Art Taïno.* Paris: Musee du Petit Palais.

Oliver, J. R. 2009. *Caciques and Cemí Idols: The Web Spun by Taíno Rulers between Hispaniola and Puerto Rico.* Tuscaloosa: University of Alabama Press.

Rouse, I. 1964. "Prehistory of the West Indies." *Science* 144 (36): 499–513.

———. 1992. *The Tainos: Rise and Decline of the People Who Greeted Columbus.* New Haven, CT: Yale University Press.

Wilson, S. M. 1990. *Hispaniola.* Tuscaloosa: University of Alabama Press.

See also Arawak versus Taíno; Caguana/Capa Site (Puerto Rico); Chiefdoms (*Cacicazgos*); *Cohoba*; The Elenan Ostionoid Subseries; Jamaica (Prehistory of); The Ostionan Ostionoid Subseries; Plazas and *Bateys*; Taíno Settlement Ethnohistory; *Zemíes (Cemís)*.

Chiefdoms (*Cacicazgos*)

Joshua M. Torres and Basil A. Reid

Definitions of Chiefdoms

Chiefdoms are conventionally defined by the emergence of institutionalized social inequality and the formation of multivillage political units (or polities) under a centralized political authority. Because of this definition, the concept has come to represent a fundamental difference in the arrangement of human societies and a precursor to the state. According to Carneiro (1998, 19), the evolutionary significance of chiefdoms lies in the fact that it represented, for the first time in human history, the transcending of village autonomy and the establishment of a supravillage polity.

The concept of the chiefdom was first formally advanced by Kalervo Oberg in 1955, and the core of it was simply that a chiefdom is an aggregate of villages under a centralized rule of a paramount political leader. In other words, chiefdoms are regionally organized societies with a centralized decision-making hierarchy that coordinates activities among several village communities. Chiefdoms are considered intermediate-level or midrange societies, providing an evolutionary bridge between autonomous societies and bureaucratic states. For many researchers (Carniero 1998), "chiefdoms" are different from bands and tribes in both degree and kind.

Guided by neoevolutionary perspectives during the middle of the twentieth century, archaeologists traditionally viewed societal development as a series of progressive stages that were popularized by Elman Service in the 1960s and included bands, tribes, and chiefdoms. (The archaic state was added later.) These stages represented societal organization as a series of types whose inherent levels of complexity were tied to subsistence production strategies, regional organization, and degree (or scale) of social hierarchy. The process by which societies evolved, or became more "complex," was considered to be an "upward spiral of intensification primarily contingent on the systemic relationships between population and technology" (Johnson and Earle 2000, 29).

Several theories have been offered to explain the centralization of sociopolitical power and the emergence of institutionalized social inequality. Circumscription (involving imbalances in population resources) and/or warfare are among the popular explanations (e.g., Carneiro 1998). Another widely accepted perspective is based on political economies of staple finance in which surplus production funds the institutions of chieftaincy. In this political economy, local leaders attempt to expand the institutions of leadership and power through access to agricultural surplus. This is traditionally viewed as resulting from the intensification of agricultural technologies and/or attracting followers as a labor base for agricultural production. Both strategies inherently involve conflict in which local leaders contest for power in an attempt to control resources and ultimately the regional political economy. In this situation, hierarchical relationships are thought to develop from temporary resolution of this conflict.

As centralized political institutions, chiefdoms are founded on hereditary inequality and social stratification. Differences in prestige usually correlate with preferential access to wealth. For instance, chiefs and their families often have access to the best farmland or fishing places and to more food and more "exotic" items than the families of "commoners." In chiefdoms, control over production and exchange of subsistence and wealth creates the basis for political power. Characteristically, the chief operates some kind of redistributive system wherein food and/or goods from separate sectors of the chiefdom are brought together and then distributed according to fixed social rules. Although chiefdoms are highly variable, organization at this scale requires a political hierarchy for coordination and decision-making. Archaeologists generally use the presence and distribution of monumental constructions and prestige goods to document the evolution of chiefly societies (Johnson and Earle 2000). Chiefly positions of power are legitimized and perpetuated through access to and control over social history, ideology, and ritual knowledge.

Chiefdom Societies in the Caribbean

Many elements of Taíno societies in the Greater Antilles appear to be organized based on principles attributed to chiefdom-type societies, as previously defined. The contact-era Taíno villages of Hispaniola appear to have been loosely organized into district chiefdoms (*cacicazgos*), each of which was ruled by one of the village chiefs (*caciques*) in the district, and the district chiefdoms were in turn linked to broader social and political groupings.

Regional sociopolitical groups might have been delimited by geographical boundaries. However, the political boundaries were likely more fluid than the Spanish were able to discern and may have been based on disparate factors such as trade networks, marriage alliances, military leadership, and linguistic and ethnic affiliations (Wilson 1990). Both men and women are documented ethnohistorically as serving in the role of cacique. Chiefs lived in specially built houses (*bohios*), sat on throne-like stools (*duhos*), were carried around by their servants in litters and had access to specialized items that personified their social and ritual power. Caciques were likely polygamous, and some wives were from other communities. These arranged marriages were an important way for a cacique to acquire power and cement alliances with neighboring chiefs.

Each cacique presided over the village in which he or she lived. They organized the daily activities and were responsible for storing surplus commodities (which they kept in buildings constructed for this purpose) and redistributing exchanged goods. The power of the cacique extended to collective production. When Bartholomew Columbus demanded gold from the cacique Behecchío of Xaraguá in Hispaniola, the latter replied that although he did not have gold in the region, he could fill several Spanish caravels with cotton.

The chiefs acted as hosts when the villages received visitors, and they were the primary organizers of ceremonial feasting, ballgames, and trade relations with outside groups. There is strong evidence that the organization of Taíno society was ranked and that a small elitist group was in control of the society's social and ideological resources. In support of hierarchical social structures at varying levels of Taíno society, archaeological research (supplemented by ethnohistorical data) has suggested that status was divided between the elite *nitaínos* and the *naborias*, or commoners.

Another sign of the Taíno hierarchical social organization throughout much of the northern Caribbean is the presence of ball courts and stone-lined plazas. Many of these monuments could only have been constructed through the collective efforts of several workers coordinated by a centralized authority. This level of social organization can be compared cross-culturally to other ranked societies, such as the Mississippian mound builders in the American Bottom and the early Polynesians in the Tahitian, Hawaiian, and Easter Islands.

Research conducted by Rouse (1952, 468–70) suggests that there were at least nineteen caciques and *yacaciques* (subchiefs) in Puerto Rico. Fewkes mentions six chiefdoms as being paramount: Agueybana, Aymamon, Loiza, Urayoan, Guarionex, and Mabodamaca (Fewkes 1907/2009). Although there is considerable debate about the boundaries of the chiefdoms on Hispaniola and the identity of their principal caciques, six *cacicazgos* pertaining to the years before 1500 have been tentatively identified: Beheccio, Caonabo, Higüayo, Guarionex, Mayobanex, Guacangarí (Wilson 1990, 14–15). In 1730, based on the names of caciques, Pierre Charlevoix tentatively identified five chiefdoms in Hispaniola: Goacanagaric, Guacanagari, Behecchio, Caonabo, and Cayacoa (Wilson 1990) (Figure C. 8). However, it should be borne in mind that on Hispaniola—as elsewhere in the northern Caribbean—boundaries may have shifted between political communities and that the Spanish did not recognize a great deal of the island as the province of any of the major caciques (Wilson 1990).

Figure C.8. Reconstructed chiefdoms in Hispaniola based on the names of caciques, as interpreted by Pierre Charlevoix (1730). Reprinted from Wilson (1990, fig. 8) by permission of the University of Alabama Press.

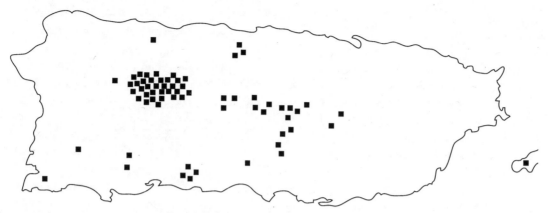

Figure C.9. Location of ball court sites in Puerto Rico. Reprinted from Wilson (1990, fig. 4) by permission of the University of Alabama Press.

Research suggests that ball courts in Puerto Rico were clustered on political boundaries, where they served to manage sociopolitical relations between regional polities (Figure C.9). It has been suggested that *cacicazgo* boundaries in Puerto Rico were likely flexible and permeable. Boundaries may have been influenced and delimited in large degree by geographic landforms and the development of multivillage communities. Several researchers have suggested that the inception of chiefly polities on the island of Puerto Rico is a product of a corporate mode of political economy that entailed a strategy of consolidation through persuasion and control over religious ideologies (Curet 1996).

While there is evidence for the presence of social inequality and regional power structures in the Greater Antilles at the time of European contact, evidence for centralized political formations is less apparent in the Lesser Antilles. Researchers in the northern Lesser Antilles have suggested that multi-island chiefdoms existed. While there is little settlement pattern data to support this, evidence for interisland interaction based on trade of goods and exotic items is amply demonstrated. The development and organization of chiefly societies in the Caribbean is a variable process that depended on historic contingencies related to a number of factors.

While the concepts of chiefdom and other societal typologies serve as useful heuristics, they tell us little about the historical circumstances and sociocultural processes that led to the emergence and organization of incipient political institutions. Simply put, while societal typologies provide some utility in *describing* complex phenomena and isolating some cross-cultural commonalities among societies of similar organizational scales, they possess little *explanatory* power.

Contemporary research on sociopolitical organization in the Caribbean (particularly the Greater Antilles)

uses modern social theory that stresses the importance of agency and history as central dimensions in the constitution and transformation of human societies and their various political forms. Future research related to the emergence of the *cacicazgo* in the Caribbean requires examination at multiple scales (e.g., from village to multivillage community to region) and dimensions (e.g., strategies of power and identity negotiation and multiple paths to power) to facilitate our understanding of incipient political institutions in the region.

Further Reading

Carneiro, R. 1998. "What Happened at the Flashpoint? Conjectures on Chiefdom Formation at the Very Moment of Conception." In *Chiefdoms and Chieftaincy in the Americas*, ed. E. M. Redmond, 18–43. Gainesville: University Press of Florida.

Curet, L. A. 1996. "Ideology, Chiefly Power, and Material Culture: An Example from the Greater Antilles." *Latin American Antiquity* 7 (2): 114–31.

Fewkes, Jesse. 1907/2009. *The Aborigines of Puerto Rico and Neighboring Islands*. Tuscaloosa: University of Alabama Press.

Johnson, A., and T. K. Earle. 2000. *The Evolution of Human Societies: From Foraging Group to Agrarian State*. Stanford, CA: Stanford University Press.

Oberg, K. 1955. "Types of Social Structure among the Lowland Tribes of South and Central America." *American Anthropologist* 57 (3): 472–87.

Rouse, I. 1952. *Scientific Survey of Porto Rico and the Virgin Islands*. New York: New York Academy of Sciences.

Wilson, S. M. 1990. *Hispaniola: Caribbean Chiefdoms in the Age of Columbus*. Tuscaloosa: University of Alabama Press.

See also Caguana/Capa Site (Puerto Rico); *Duhos (Dujos)*; Elite Exchange in the Caribbean; Lapidary Trade; Plazas and *Bateys*; Taíno Settlement Ethnohistory; *Zemíes (Cemís)*.

Ciboney versus Guanahatabey

Basil A. Reid

Introduction

A number of history and archaeology texts refer to the Ciboney as a native group inhabiting western Cuba at the time of Spanish contact. The term is also used to describe Archaic groups throughout the Caribbean. However, on both counts, the term Ciboney is misapplied, as it actually refers to a local Taíno group in central Cuba (Reid 2009). Guanahatabey, not Ciboney, is now the preferred term Caribbean archaeologists use for native inhabitants of westernmost Cuba at contact (Figure C.10). But even then, several questions remain about the actual existence of this group, and some argue that it was probably a figment of the Spanish or Taíno imagination.

Ciboney

For decades, many Caribbean historians and archaeologists asserted that the Ciboney lived in western Cuba at the time of contact. A variety of descriptions relating to Ciboney cultural traditions have been advanced. For example, according to Black, "In Haiti, Cuba and possibly Jamaica the Arawaks found an even more primitive tribe than themselves called Siboneys, or 'rock-dwellers.' These people who had made their way down from Florida were a simple fisher-folk. They lived mostly on the sea coast, made crude shell implements and, it is said, were used as servants by the Arawaks" (1983, 10). The Ciboney are also described as the original settlers of Cuba who had been largely replaced by the Taíno by the time of Columbus. Rouse (1992) argues the Ciboney had been pushed westward or absorbed by the encroaching Taíno and that they still lived on the southwestern Guacayarima peninsula of Hispaniola and the western end of Cuba when the Europeans arrived. Hung (2005) claimed that the term was allegedly coined by early Spanish chronicles for hunter-and-gatherer groups and was later developed as an archaeological cultural term by the North American investigator Mark H. Harrington. Caribbean archaeologists have geographically placed the Ciboney in Florida, the Bahamas, southwestern Hispaniola, and the United States Virgin Islands (Reid 2009).

However, the term Ciboney is a misnomer for the na-

Figure C.10. Guanahatabey in western Cuba. Reprinted from Rouse (1992, adapted from fig. 3) by permission of Yale University Press.

tives in western Cuba and elsewhere in the Caribbean, as the term actually applies to a local Taíno group in central Cuba (Reid 2009) and not to Archaic groups found throughout the Caribbean and circum-Caribbean, despite its continued use in this regard.

Guanahatabey

The generally accepted name used by Caribbean archaeologists for inhabitants of western Cuba at contact is Guanahatabey (Keegan 1992). Taíno inhabitants of Cuba who met the Spanish colonizers apparently mentioned some non-Taíno people called the Guanahatabey or the Guanahacabibes. The Guanahatabey were first described by Diego Velázquez de Cuellar as follows: "The life of these people is of the manner of savages, for they have neither houses or village quarters, nor field, nor do they eat anything else but the flesh they take in the mountains and turtles and fish" (quoted in Sauer 1966, 185).

Las Casas also provided an account of the natives of Cuba. In his 1516 memorandum to Cardinal Francisco Jiménez de Cisneros, he described four native groups who needed to be rescued: the peoples of the Jardines of both north and south Cuba; the Guanahacabibes of the Cape of Cuba; the Ciboney, who were the same as Jardines but were kept as servants by the other Cuban Indians; and any peoples left on the Lucayan islands who are described as having the same nature and ways as the Jardines (Keegan 1992). From this account, it is evident that Las Casas had two classificatory groups in mind: the Guanahatabey (i.e., the Guanahacabibes) and the people who have come to be called the Taíno (i.e., the Ciboney, the Lucayans, and the people of the Jardines) (Keegan 1992). Yet although both Las Casas and Velázquez lived in Cuba for some time, they never visited western Cuba and thus lacked firsthand knowledge of the Guanahatabey (Lovén 1935). When Pánfilo de Narváez entered the province of Habana he found caciques and conditions that were similar to those of eastern Cuba. In addition, five provinces of "chieftainships" have been identified in western Cuba from the reports of Diego Velázquez and Pánfilo de Narváez. These provinces bear the Taíno names (from west to east): Guanahacabibes, Guaniguanico, Marien, Habana, and Hanabana (Reid 2009). In sum, Las Casas's and Velázquez's reports of hunters and fishers who lacked houses and agricultural fields and lived in caves were apparently unsupported by firsthand observations of other Spanish officials (Keegan 1992).

The fact that the Guanahatabey allegedly spoke a different language than the Taíno also indicates that they formed a separate ethnic group (Rouse 1992). Archaeological research has not identified any Taíno sites in western Cuba. What has been unearthed is the presence of a preexisting nonagricultural culture based on mostly uniformly small coastal sites. These sites contain a scatter of debris from tools, shellfish, iguanas, land and sea crabs, larger sea animals such as manatee and turtles, and rodents such as the hutia. In a nutshell, the evidence suggests the presence of people who lived in caves, rock shelters, and open-air sites; relied heavily on shellfish, fish, and wild game; and were organized into small bands rather than villages. However, it has been argued that these archaeological data may in fact relate to native people who were ancestors of the Guanahatabey (Reid 2009). Interestingly, there may be no inherent contradiction between Pánfilo de Narváez's observations of a socially complex society that included caciques (chiefs) in the western province of Habana and the archaeological data found in western Cuba (Keegan 1992).

The Calusa, also called "the shell people," lived in southwest Florida from 1500 to 1800, and despite their nonagricultural lifeways, they had a socially complex society that was based on chiefdoms. It has been suggested that the Guanahatabey may have been culturally affiliated with natives of southern Florida because their archaeological remains show some resemblances, especially in shellwork and woodwork (Rouse 1992). To what extent these resemblances are the result of interaction or parallel adaptation to similar ecological conditions remains to be determined (Rouse 1992).

Conclusion

Even if Guanahatabey is the accurate name for the inhabitants of western Cuba at contact, there are still many gray areas concerning this native group, assuming of course, that such a group actually existed. It is unclear whether the Guanahatabey were a figment of the Spanish or the Taíno imagination or whether the archaeological materials found in western Cuba were generated by native forebears of the Guanahatabey who inhabited western Cuba long before Spanish contact. It is also unclear whether the Guanahatabey were culturally affiliated with the socially complex Calusa hunter-gatherers of southwestern Florida or to the pottery-making Casimiroid in Cuba. More intensive archaeology research should shed more light on issues of cultural affiliations and social complexity. What seems certain is that the Taíno did not occupy western Cuba at the time of contact, despite the evidence that the rest of the northern Caribbean was extensively inhabited by them (Reid

2009). The debate about who exactly occupied western Cuba may not be resolved any time soon, given the controversial nature of Spanish ethnohistorical records on the subject. However, while the presence of Guanahatabey in western Cuba is still somewhat controversial, it would be inaccurate to refer to these early natives as Ciboney. In addition, the term Ciboney has been misapplied in the vast majority of history books.

Further Reading

Black, C. V. 1983. *The History of Jamaica*. New York: Longman.

Hung, U. 2005. "Early Ceramics in the Caribbean." In *Dialogues in Cuban Archaeology*, ed. L. Antonio Curet, Shannon Lee Dawdy, and Gabino La Rosa Corzo, 103–24. Tuscaloosa: University of Alabama Press.

Keegan, W. F. 1992. *The People Who Discovered Columbus*. Gainesville: University Press of Florida.

Lovén, Sven. 1935. *Origins of the Tainan Culture, West Indies*. Göteborg: Elanders Bokfryckeri Akfierbolog.

Reid, B. A. 2009. *Myths and Realities of Caribbean History*. Tuscaloosa: University of Alabama Press.

Rouse, I. 1992. *The Tainos: Rise and Decline of the People Who Greeted Columbus*. New Haven, CT: Yale University Press.

Sauer, Carl O. 1966. *The Early Spanish Main*. Berkeley: University of California Press.

See also Arawak versus Taíno; Origins of Indigenous Groups in the Northern Caribbean.

Clay Tobacco Pipes (Bowls and Stems)

Naseema Hosein-Hoey

European and African tobacco smoking was probably copied from the Native Americans starting in the mid-sixteenth century. Tobacco was introduced in England in the late sixteenth century, and a domestic tobacco pipe industry was started by the early seventeenth century to satisfy the increasing demand. The principal shape of the clay tobacco pipe is seen throughout many generations, but there were many variations in pipe bowl and stem shapes that were determined not only by fashion but also by the specializations of tobacco pipe and mold makers (Figure C.11). Tobacco pipe bowl size and capacity was influenced by tobacco availability and cost at that time.

During the sixteenth century, the bowl became an effective tobacco consumption vessel with a barrel shape and a forward incline. The bowl base was often flat, and the stem ranged up to 100–150 millimeters long. The pipe

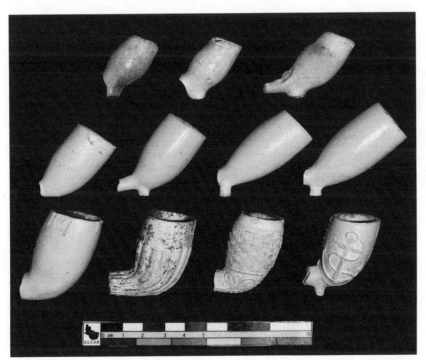

Figure C.11. Clay tobacco pipe bowls and stem diameters varied over time. All the pipes depicted here were excavated on St. Eustatius. Dating is based on bowl morphology that follows a known evolution over time. *Top row, left to right*: 1630–1640, 1640–1650, 1650–1660; *middle row, left to right*: 1750–1760, 1760–1770, 1770–1780, 1780–1790; *bottom row, left to right*: all 1790–1810. Image by Ruud Stelten and Alicia Caporaso at SECAR.

at that time was designed to rest on a table and to prevent the heat of the bowl from burning the polished surfaces of the table. These pipes were crudely made and small in comparison to later period tobacco pipes.

By the seventeenth century, the bowl diameter had increased to 9 millimeters and there was no increase in the length of the stem. A plain rim was common during this period, and except for the traditional maker's mark, these pipes were plain. During the eighteenth century, the pipes were made with more precise dimensions and a smoother finish. The bowl wall became considerably thinner and the stem was more slender. These improved clay pipe features illustrate the increasing specialization of the pipe and mold makers as well as improvements in firing techniques. These pipes had a flat-bottomed spur and some were even produced without a spur.

During the eighteenth century, long pipes became fashionable among the wealthy with stems as long as 600 millimeters. Pipe decorations, such as emblems, names, and motifs were more common. Decorative clay tobacco pipes continued to be produced throughout the nineteenth century. Pipes decorated with flowers, animals, fruit, fish, badges, and ships were most prevalent during this period. Bowl shape also evolved during the nineteenth century. Despite the popularity of designs on these pipes, members of the working class preferred the ordinary short clay pipe since this type was the least expensive.

Clay tobacco pipes also provide archaeological evidence for trade between Europe's colonial powers and the Caribbean colonies. As indicated earlier, tobacco pipe morphology is a great indicator for otherwise undatable contexts, while maker's marks may provide some additional dating information. Maker's marks must not be relied upon completely, as these marks could sometimes be used for extended periods of time (i.e., more than a century). Scotland, England, France, and the Netherlands produced the vast majority of clay pipes that were exported to the Caribbean colonies.

Further Reading

Ayto, E. 2002. *Clay Tobacco Pipes.* Buckinghamshire, UK: Shire.
Coleman, H. 1999. *The Art and Archaeology of Clay Tobacco Pipes.* CD. Devon, UK: Dawnmist Studio.

See also La Reconnaissance Site (Trinidad).

Cohoba

Joshua M. Torres

Cohoba (or *cohóbana*) refers to a psychotropic drug that is snuffed or inhaled through the nostrils and is also the vernacular name for the tree from which the seeds for the snuff are derived. Two species of the genus *Anadenanthera* (*A. peregrine* and *A. colubrina*) have historically been used by indigenous peoples of the Caribbean and South America to create this powerful drug for ritual ceremonies. Archaeological evidence for the plant has been recovered in the form of starch grains from a coral milling base from the habitation site of CE-11 in eastern Puerto Rico (Pagán-Jiménez 2011) and charred wood from archaeological contexts at the ceremonial center of Tibes in the south-central part of the island (Newsom 2010).

Preparation of the drug entails drying the seeds over a fire to remove the husks. The seeds are then ground and mixed with water and lime or calcium oxide. The lime serves as a chemical agent to promote the absorption of the drug in to the body. The resulting paste is dried and made into a powder that is placed on a plate or shallow bowl and inhaled through a hollow tube (Oliver 2009).

Cohoba inhalation induces a hallucinogenic trance-like state. Chagnon provides a detailed ethnographic account of the effects of the psychotropic *ebene* snuff used among the Yanomami of the central Orinoco Basin in northern Brazil that offers a potential point of comparison for the effects of *cohoba* on the individual (Chagnon 1968, 156–58). Ethnohistorical documents discuss the use of *cohoba* in ritual ceremonies, specifically in cases where the user communicated with spirits/gods also known as *cemís* (Pané 1999). *Cohoba* is thought to have been used primarily by shamans (*behiques*) and chiefs (*caciques*) in locales where communication with the spirit world was intimately linked to Taíno religion and politics (Oliver 2009).

Some of some of the earliest archaeological evidence for the use of *cohoba* in the Caribbean comes from Saladoid era (ca. 400 BC–AD 600) archaeological deposits on Puerto Rico in the form of specialized bowls and snuff tubes. Archaeological evidence for the use of *cohoba* in the Caribbean during the post-Saladoid era, especially the contact period Taíno era, is indicated by

Figure C.12. *Left*, reconstruction of Y-shaped *cohoba* snuff inhaler with bird bone tubes (with the corozo seeds at ends). Photograph by J. R. Oliver; snuff holder specimen from the Museo de la Fundación García Arévalo, Santo Domingo, Dominican Republic. The tubes are not original to the artifact, they were added by the photographer with Photoshop. *Center*, *cohoba* stand. The small platform at the top of the stand likely held a bowl or tray for *cohoba* (width 26.5cm, 7 kg). Photograph © Trustees of the British Museum. *Right*, vomiting spatula (b. Greater Antilles AD 1200–1500; 1.3 × 12.7 × 2.5 cm). Gift of Vincent and Margaret Fay, www.elmuseo.org.

several specialized items: *cohoba* trays, snuff tubes, and vomit spatulas.

The snuff tubes are generally Y-shaped; the split ends are inserted into the nostrils and the single tube is used for inhalation. Snuff tubes are carved into various zoomorphic and anthropomorphic shapes; the intake point is sometimes represented as an anus and the nostril tubes sometimes represent legs. Snuff trays are variable in form and composition, ranging from small elaborate shallow ceramic bowls and plates to carved wooden zoomorphic stands (Figure C.12).

Vomiting spatulas are typically made from bone or wood. These objects range in size and are characterized by a handle end (which is often carved or decorated) and a long curved, narrow shoehorn-shaped end used to induce vomiting. The handle end of the spatula is often carved with zoomorphic or anthropomorphic figures or incised with geometric designs. Vomiting was considered part of the *cohoba* ceremony and was conducted as part of purification prior to inhalation of the drug. Oliver (2009) posits that the self-induced vomiting process was part of an important symbolic association between purification and excrement. In this context, vomiting represents an inversion of the normal biological process of ingestion and excretion. Oliver suggests that through

this process a cacique can become an unpolluted vessel for the "divine excrement" of *cohoba* (Oliver 2009). Ritual paraphernalia used with *cohoba* have also been recovered from Late Ceramic Age archaeological contexts in both Hispaniola and Jamaica.

Further Reading

Arrom, José Juan. 1989. *Mitología y artes prehispánicas de las Antillas*. México: Siglo XXI.

Chagnon, Napoleon. 1968. *Yanomamo: The Fierce People*. New York: Holt, Rinehart and Winston.

MacManus, Jesús E., Irvine Rafael, Iván F. Méndez Bonilla, Carmen Dolores Hernández, and Lehman College Art Gallery. 2003. *Taíno Treasures: The Legacy of Dr. Ricardo E. Alegría*. Bronx, NY: Lehman College Art Gallery.

Newsom, L. A. 2010. "Paleobotanical Research at Tibes." In *Tibes: People, Power, and Ritual at the Center of the Cosmos*, ed. L. A. Curet and L. Stringer, 80–114. Tuscaloosa: University of Alabama Press.

Oliver, J. R. 2008. "El universo material y espiritual de los Taínos." In *El Caribe Precolombino: Fray Ramón Pané y el universo Taíno*, edited by J. R. Oliver, C. McEwan and A. Casas Gilberga, 136–221. Barcelona: Adjuntament de Barcelona-Institut de Cultura / Museo Barbier-Mueller / Ministerio de Cultura de Madrid / Fundación Caixa Galicia.

———. 2009. *Cacique Gods and Cemi Idols.* Tuscaloosa: University of Alabama Press.

Pagán-Jiménez, J. 2011. "Assessing Ethnobotanical Dynamics at CE-11 and CE-33 through Analysis of Starch Grains, Plant Processing, and Cooking Artifacts." In *Phase III Data Recovery Investigations at Three Prehistoric Archaeological Sites (CE-11, CE-32, and CE-33) Municipality of Ceiba, Puerto Rico,* prepared by L. Carlson and J. Torres, 325–74. Available at the Naval Facilities Engineering Command Southeast, Jacksonville, Florida.

Pané, F. R. 1999. *An Account of the Antiquities of the Indians.* Trans. S. C. Griswold. Durham, NC: Duke University Press.

See also Chiefdoms (*Cacicazgos*); *Zemíes* (*Cemís*).

Columbus's Landfall

Jeffrey P. Blick

According to Columbus's diary, on the morning of October 12, 1492, Cristoforo Colón stepped ashore in the New World. The Lucayans knew his landfall as Guanahani. As a sign of thanksgiving, Columbus christened the island San Salvador, or "Holy Savior." However, efforts to identify Columbus's first landfall are difficult, because there are competing claims for the honor of the "island of discovery." Ten of the islands in the Bahamas and on Turks and Caicos have been identified as the first landfall. Watling Island (present-day San Salvador) and Samana Cay (Figure C.13) are the leading candidates, with Grand Turk a distant third. In 1986, a team of National Geographic Society scientists, using computer simulations to reevaluate the data, concluded that Columbus had landed first at Samana Cay (even though they found no artifacts to support the claim). A year later, however, an oceanographer and computer scientist at Woods Hole Oceanographic Institute challenged the scientists' estimates of wind and water currents and placed Columbus within sight of San Salvador on the morning of October 12, 1492. Subsequent studies by Woods Hole scientists revised this earlier claim.

Columbus's *Diario*

A major challenge over the years has been the inconsistencies of Columbus's diary as a data source. Columbus

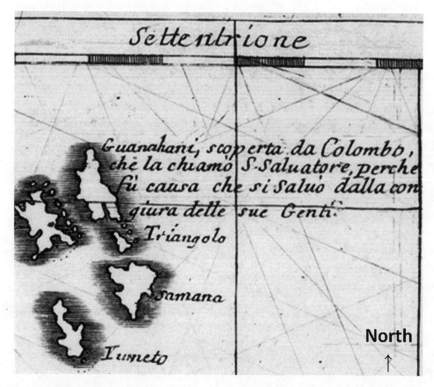

Figure C.13. Detail of *Isole Antili, La Cuba, e La Spagnuola*, a 1690 map drawn by Vincenzo Maria Coronelli that describes Guanahani as the island "discovered by Columbus, which he named San Salvador." Note that the toponym "Samana" is used to identify an island other than San Salvador. Reproduced by permission of Barry Lawrence Ruderman Antique Maps, Inc., La Jolla, California.

wrote an original diary with details of his first voyage. There were several copies of the original manuscript, including one onboard copy Columbus made to show his sailors that minimized the distance traveled and at least one copy of the original manuscript that was kept by his son, Diego Colon (Reid 2009). However, most of what we refer to today as Columbus's diary, or *diario de a bordo*, is a copy by Bartolomé de Las Casas.

In October 1492, Christopher Columbus sat down to compose in writing his first impressions of his New World landfall site. Columbus presented the original *diario* to Queen Isabel in 1493. She had a copy made for Columbus, but the location of the original is unknown, and all traces of the copy disappeared in 1545. A third-hand manuscript written sometime in the mid-sixteenth century by Bartolomé de Las Casas survived, but it remained unpublished until the end of the eighteenth century (Reid 2009). With the exception of one extensive first-person quotation of Columbus which covers the journey through the Bahamas (October 10–24, 1492), most of the *diario* consists of abstractions transcribed in the third person. It is unclear what Las Casas was copying, except that it almost certainly was not the original text. It has been argued that Columbus's *diario* bears comparatively little relationship to the text Columbus originally wrote, as this third-hand manuscript has numerous erasures, unusual spellings, confusing distance calculations (leagues vs. miles), brief passages that are questionable, and marginal notes. The ambiguities, errors, and omissions in this manuscript have been further compounded in modern-language translations (Dunn and Kelley 1989). Another version of the ship's diary was thrown overboard in a cask during a major winter storm on the return voyage in 1493 since Columbus believed his fleet would not survive the tempest.

Despite these shortcomings, Columbus's *diario* can be used in the search for Columbus's landfall in the New World because it provides the only historical accounts of the Lucayan Taíno in the Bahamas (Dunn and Kelley 1989). These accounts should enable (and have enabled) archaeologists to identify Columbus's route because the diary described the locations of seven Lucayan settlements on four separate islands. Lucayan sites are irregularly distributed, and only one route will have sites in the appropriate locations. The comparison of prehistoric settlement data along the various routes led William Keegan (1992) to conclude that the first landfall must have been on present-day San Salvador and that Columbus proceeded to Rum Cay, Long Island, and Crooked Island before crossing to Cuba and then to Hispaniola.

Archaeological Excavations on San Salvador (Bahamas)

Archaeological excavations conducted by Charles A. Hoffman Jr. at the Long Bay site on San Salvador, Bahamas, recovered early European colonial artifacts that match the descriptions of items traded to the local Lucayans in Columbus's *diario de a bordo*. These items included small green and yellow glass beads, a Spanish Henry IV *blanca* coin (Figure C.14), brass rings and buckles (Figure C.15), broken sherds of Spanish glazed pottery, and bits of metal recovered in the same strata with late Lucayan pottery. The Henry IV coin was minted from 1471 to 1474 and the glass beads are similar to other Spanish trade beads of the late fifteenth and early sixteenth centuries. Lead isotope analyses by Brill et al. (1987) on several artifacts identified elemental similarities with other artifacts and mineral ores from four separate areas in Spain, including the Río Tinto mining region located 70 kilometers inland from Palos de la Frontera, Columbus's port of embarkation. The coin's terminus post quem is 1471; minting of the coin was halted with Henry IV's death in 1474. The terminus ante quem, provided by the end dates of production of the Spanish glass beads, the brass buckle and D-ring, and the glazed pottery, is circa AD 1550, although one Spanish belt buckle may have been manufactured until 1485 (Brill et al. 1987). Finally, Blick's (2011) calculation of a mean artifact date of 1497.78, based on the published artifacts (Brill et al. 1987, Hoffman 1987, 1988), provides strong evidence that the Long Bay artifacts must have been deposited on San Salvador sometime in the late fifteenth century.

Columbus noted that the Lucayans traded cotton thread in balls (skeins), baskets of cotton, things to eat, fresh water, parrots, javelins (spears), dry leaves (tobacco), and other little things or trifles to his crew (Dunn and Kelley 1989, 65–93). His crew, in return, traded European goods to the Lucayans, including small green and yellow glass beads (on strings); small-denomination coins such as Spanish *blancas* and Portuguese *ceutis*, like those found at La Isabela by Deagan and Cruxent (2002); brass rings; broken pottery or pieces of clay bowls; fragments of glass (e.g., drinking cups); red cloth caps; hawk's bells or brass jingles; metal lace tips or aglets, like those found at La Isabela and Puerto Real; bread; honey; molasses; something to drink (water); and "other little things too tiresome to write down." Among these "tiresome little things," later scholars have added "shoe latchets"; mirror fragments; needles and pins; wine; and clothing.

The Spanish artifacts that have been found at Long Bay (SS-9) mirror the items Columbus mentioned as having

Figure C.14. Reverse and obverse of a Henry IV *blanca* minted in Burgos, similar to the Henry IV *blanca* found at the Long Bay site (SS-9), San Salvador, Bahamas. Diameter is 2.0 cm. Collection of Jeffrey P. Blick.

Figure C.15. Photographs of the bronze D-ring and small bronze buckle excavated from the Long Bay site (SS-9), San Salvador, Bahamas. Shank lengths are 2.7 cm and 2.0 cm, respectively. Images adapted from Brill et al. (1987).

traded to the Lucayans in his ship's log: seven green and yellow glass beads plus three glass bead fragments (10 glass beads in all, nine green and one amber or yellow), one copper Spanish *blanca* coin, one small bronze (shoe?) buckle, one bronze D-ring, thirty-eight potsherds of *melado* ware (honey-glazed ware), two potsherds of white glazed ware (majolica), many fragments of green glass, four metal (knife blade?) fragments, ten planking nails or spikes, one copper grommet, two metal hooks, one plain metal button, and many fragments of flat metal (Brill et al. 1987; Hoffman 1987). Although not necessarily traded, a Spanish colonial lead *arquebus*, or pistol ball, has been found about 2.7 kilometers south of Long Bay along the route Columbus would have taken if he had approached the west coast of San Salvador from the south after having rounded the southwestern corner of the island during the early morning and dawn hours of October 12, 1492.

Items in Columbus's *diario* that closely or exactly match the items recovered in archaeological contexts at the Long Bay site include small green and yellow glass beads; the Spanish *blanca*; brass rings (the bronze buckle and D-ring); broken pottery or clay bowls; fragments of glass (cups); and many "other little things too tiresome to write down" such as four metal (knife blade?) fragments; 10 planking nails or spikes similar to those found at 1493–1498 La Isabela and 1503 Puerto Real; one copper grommet; two metal hooks; one plain metal button; and many fragments of flat metal. The only nonperishable items mentioned in Columbus's *diario* that were traded but not found include hawk's bells or brass jingles, metal lace ends or lace tips, and items mentioned by later historians (mirror fragments, needles, and pins). Brill and colleagues and Hoffman (Brill et al. 1987; Brill 1988, 2005; Hoffman 1987) have been able to source several of these trade items to Spain based on lead isotope and stylistic analyses, including: two glass beads; one *blanca* coin; one bronze D-ring; one bronze buckle; one *melado* ware potsherd; two tin glazed earthenware (majolica) potsherds; and one lead pistol ball.

Lead in the San Salvador glass beads has been sourced to mines in the Sierra Morena region of south-central Spain. The glass beads appear to be of a style similar to beads produced in Puerto de Santa María near Cadiz on the southwest coast and/or Puebla de Don Fadrique north of Almería on the southeast coast of Spain (Brill et al. 1987). The history and chronology of glass-making in Spain are not well known, but cottage glass industries date back to the thirteenth and fourteenth centuries. Glass beads like those found on San Salvador are generally considered to date to circa 1490–1550.

The *blanca* coin (see Figure C.14) has been identified by four numismatists as a Henry IV *blanca* with a Segovia mint mark dating to the period 1471–1474, the last years of the reign of Henry IV of Spain (r. 1454–1474) (Brill et al. 1987). The coats of arms depicted on the coin provide a type of visual pun: on the obverse is a castle and on the reverse is a lion. The lead content of the coin is similar to that of other coins from the Segovia/Burgos area of north-central Spain (Brill et al. 1987). Henry IV *blancas* and Portuguese *ceutis* have also been found at another early Columbus settlement, La Isabela, Dominican Republic (1493–1498) by Deagan and Cruxent (2002, 195–96). The importance of this artifact is that the Spanish *blanca* provides the earliest possible date of deposition, the terminus post quem, of 1471 for the Spanish artifact assemblage at Long Bay.

The "brass" rings include a bronze buckle (similar in size to a shoe buckle) and a bronze D-ring (Figure C.15). These rings are similar to other bronze buckles and rings that date to circa 1401–1485 in Spain (Brill et al. 1987, 253). The lead from the bronze buckle has been sourced to a mine in the Sierra de Gador region of southern Spain near Almería, and the bronze D-ring has lead similar to that from the Sierra Morena mining region northeast of Seville (and similar to the lead from the glass beads previously described) (Brill et al. 1987). The bronze buckle and D-ring have strong similarities to buckles found at La Isabela dating to 1493–1498 (Deagan and Cruxent 2002, 157, Fig. 7.14).

The lead content of the *melado* (honey-glazed) ware and the tin-glazed white ware (majolica) pottery is similar to lead from the Río Tinto mining region of southwestern Spain (Brill et al. 1987). The pottery is also similar to types of pottery made in Triana, a suburb of Seville in southwestern Spain (Brill et al. 1987). Historical archaeologists have pointed out that one supplies a ship with goods from the nearest port, especially when it comes to fragile supplies such as ceramics and glass. The *melado* and white wares both have manufacturing production date ranges of circa 1401–1600; the plain white ware (Columbia Plain majolica) was more common before 1550.

Conclusion

The other artifacts found at the Long Bay site (SS-9), including fragments of green glass, four metal knife blade fragments, ten planking nails or spikes, one copper grommet, two metal hooks, one plain metal button, and many fragments of flat metal, have not yet been subjected to lead isotope analysis and their sources have not yet been determined, although their association with the other Spanish colonial artifacts at Long Bay is clear (Brill et al. 1987). While there is need for ongoing research, the weight of both ethnohistorical and archaeological evidence seems to point to San Salvador as the most likely location of Columbus's first landfall in the New World.

Further Reading

Blick, J. P. 2011. "The Case for San Salvador as the Site of the 1492 Columbus Landfall: Principles of Historical Archaeology Applied to Current Evidence." Paper presented at the Fourteenth Symposium on the Natural History of the Bahamas, Gerace Research Centre, San Salvador, Bahamas, June 16–20.

Brill, Robert H. 1988. "Glass Finds on Bahamian Island Open Up New World of Thought about Site of Columbus's Landfall." *The Corning Museum of Glass Newsletter* (Autumn): 1–2.

———. 2005. "Some Small Glass Beads from San Salvador Island." In *Glass Science in Art and Conservation: An International Conference Devoted to the Applications of Science to Glass Art and the Conservation of Glass Artifacts*, 135–36. [Lisboa]: ITN and Universidade Nova de Lisboa, Faculdade de Ciências e Tecnologia.

Brill, Robert H., I. L. Barnes, S. S. C. Tong, E. C. Joel, and M. J. Murtaugh. 1987. "Laboratory Studies of Some European Artifacts Excavated on San Salvador Island." In *Proceedings of the First San Salvador Conference: Columbus and His World*, ed. D. T. Gerace, 247–92. San Salvador: CCFL Bahamian Field Station.

Deagan, Kathleen, and José María Cruxent. 2002. *Columbus's Outpost among the Taínos*. New Haven, CT: Yale University Press.

Dunn, O., and J. E. Kelley Jr., eds. 1989. *The Diario of Christopher Columbus's First Voyage to America, 1492–1493*. Abstracted by Bartolomé de las Casas. Norman: University of Oklahoma Press.

Hoffman, C. A., Jr. 1987. "Archaeological Investigations at the Long Bay Site, San Salvador, Bahamas." In *Proceedings of the First San Salvador Conference: Columbus and His World*, ed. D. T. Gerace, 97–102. San Salvador: CCFL Bahamian Field Station.

Keegan, William F. 1992. *The People Who Discovered Columbus: The Prehistory of the Bahamas*. Gainesville: University of Florida Press.

———. 1992. "West Indian Archaeology. Vol. 2, After Columbus." *Journal of Archaeological Research* 4 (4): 265–94.

Reid, Basil A. 2009. *Myths and Realities of Caribbean History*. Tuscaloosa: University of Alabama Press.

See also The Palmettan Ostionoid Series.

Conucos

Ieteke Witteveen and Basil A. Reid

The mounded fields in which the Taíno people of the northern Caribbean planted their root crops were called *conucos*. The intense cultivation of root crops and other starches and other crops suggests a certain level of sedentism by these contact-period natives. Taíno production and use of cassava were recorded by the Spanish upon their arrival in the Caribbean. Petersen writes: "From the early accounts, it is obvious that the farm-ing technology was relatively simple, largely limited to a digging stick—a fact leading some to regard Taíno farming as horticulture, or gardening, rather than as agriculture proper. However, evidence suggests that sizeable earthen mounds, or *conucos*, were used for planting over extended periods and irrigation was practiced in arid areas such as southwestern Hispaniola" (1997, 128).

Figure C.16. A woman harvesting *maishi chiki* (the Papiamentu name for *Sorghum vulgare*) from a *conuco* in Curaçao, 1992. Courtesy of I. Witteveen.

The mounds, which were three feet high and some nine feet in circumference, were arranged in regular rows. They retarded erosion, improved drainage, and thus permitted more lengthy storage of the mature tubers in the ground. They also made it easier to weed and harvest the crops (Rouse 1992).

Agriculture is possibly one of the most influential factors in bringing about many of the social changes that occurred during the Taíno period. Root crop production may have provided enough surpluses to sustain individuals on longer travels and/or for military campaigns and may have allowed for public events, involving communal feasting and/or other large communal undertakings that required a specialized labor force.

Interestingly, the *conuco* is also a native cultural tradition on Curaçao, Aruba, and Bonaire and is currently utilized by the African-descended population of these islands (Figure C.16). *Conuco* (or *kunuku* in the Papiamentu language of Curaçao, Aruba, and Bonaire) refers to a plot for growing local food crops, or, as David Watts described it, "a system of shifting cultivation for the production of starch- and sugar-rich foods" (Watts 1987, 53). About 0.2 to 0.5 hectares of *conuco* land is required to provide each individual with adequate subsistence. The main crops are calorie-rich yucca (cassava/manioc, *Manihot esculenta*) and sweet potatoes (*Ipomoea batatas*) (Watts 1987, 55). Also planted in the *conucos* in these southern Caribbean islands are calabash gourd (*Crescentia cujete*), pumpkin (*Cucurbita moschata*), maize (*Zea mays*), beans (*Phaseolus vulgaris* and *Paseolus lunatus*), cactus (Cactaceae) fruit, and cocuy (*Agave* sp.) leaves. *Conuco* fields were prepared by heaping up mounds of soil (called *montones*, or *monte*). The custom of mounding may not have been universal, and the practice was usually avoided on well-drained sites.

In Curaçao, Aruba, and Bonaire, the *conuco* has survived both as a way of life and an important cultural identifier. This is the case despite slave-raiding expeditions against the indigenous population and the institution of African enslaved labor. *Conuco* agriculture in the Caribbean provided an exceptionally well-balanced form of land use, especially on the very dry islands of Curaçao, Bonaire, and Aruba, where a combination of shell-eating and dew-drinking was necessary to supplement the daily diet of Caquetío people who inhabited these islands at the time of European contact. The cultivation of *conuco* was encouraged by ecological factors such as unfavorable soil conditions and insufficient rainfall that hindered a commercial plantation economy. These factors made *conuco* agriculture an economic necessity. Cultural interactions between native peoples and Africans (through migration and marronage) may also be partly responsible for its persistence. People from Africa brought their own food crops with them, such as yams, that were planted in *conucos*. In Curaçao, food crops such as *maishi chiki* (Papiamentu for *Sorghum vulgare*) were also grown on *conuco* land. Some families in Curaçao, Aruba, and Bonaire still practice this traditional form of agriculture to this day.

For elderly people in Curaçao, the term *kunuku (conuco)* means life. Research in the rural western Curaçao by Weeber and Witteveen (2010) has shown that the principles of the *kunuku* way of life included:

Respect for nature and concern for the preservation of land resources

Knowledge of how to combine different calorie-rich crops

Reciprocal work involving family members and neighbors in tasks relating to the *conuco*, including sowing, planting, cleaning, and harvesting of the *maishi chiki*

Spiritual belief in a supreme being that was expressed in work songs (*kantika di trabou*) and the harvest celebration (*seú*)

Communal sharing of the products harvested from the *conuco*

Further Reading

Petersen, J. B. 1997. "Taíno, Island-Carib, and Prehistoric Amerindian Economies in the West Indies: Tropical Forest Adaptations to Island Environments." In *The Indigenous People of the Caribbean*, ed. S. Wilson, 118–30. Gainesville: University Press of Florida.

Rouse, I. 1992. *The Tainos: Rise and Decline of the People Who Greeted Columbus*. New Haven, CT: Yale University Press.

Watts, D. 1987. *The West Indies: Patterns of Development, Culture, and Environmental Change since 1492*. Cambridge, UK: Cambridge University Press.

Weeber, L., and I. Witteveen. 2010. *Banda Bou: Alma di Kòrsou: Kultura i Desaroyo den añanan 60 pa 90 di siglo binti*. Curaçao: KULDESPRO.

See also Arawak versus Taíno; Cassava (Manioc); Chiefdoms (*Cacicazgos*); The First Caribbean Farmers.

Crab/Shell Dichotomy

Joshua M. Torres and Basil A. Reid

The Crab Culture was first proposed by Froelich Rainey in 1935 after conducting archaeological excavations in Puerto Rico in the summer of 1934 (Rainey 1935). Rainey was the first to observe that early Saladoid deposits tended to consist mainly of land crabs and very few mollusks, while Ostionoid deposits were predominately mollusks with very few land crabs. According to Rainey, "This substratum proved to contain types of cultural material markedly different from those which have been previously found in Puerto Rico. The contrast between cultural types of this substratum, and those found in the superimposed shell level makes it clear that a distinct culture is represented by these remains" (Rainey 1935, 12).

Rainey noted that the ceramics of the Crab Culture deposits had fine grained paste with few aplastic inclusions, they were well fired, and they had painted surfaces (Rainey 1935, 1940). In contrast, pottery from the Shell Culture was coarse tempered and unpainted. He ultimately concluded that the distinct assemblages corresponded to two different migrations into the West Indies: a Crab Culture (Saladoid) that was replaced by a second group, the Shell Culture (Ostionoid).

After conducting his doctoral research in Haiti, Irving Rouse arrived in Puerto Rico to continue the work initiated by Rainey as part of the Scientific Survey of Puerto Rico and the Virgin Islands. On the basis of his pottery analyses, Rouse concluded that there was a continuum of ceramic modes between the Crab (i.e., Cedrosan Saladoid) and Shell (i.e., Ostionoid) cultures, suggesting that there was one migration of agro-potters to the Antilles and that the eventual development of this group resulted in the rise of the Taíno (Rouse 1989, 391). Rouse (1992) repeatedly argued that Rainey saw dramatic changes in the ceramic repertoire because he focused on decorated sherds and did not consider the gradual changes leading to the shift from fine Cedrosan Saladoid ceramics to the coarsely made Ostionoid wares (as noted in Rodríguez Ramos 2010).

There has been a great deal of debate about what this "Crab/Shell dichotomy" means in terms of the region's precontact social and cultural development. Traditional perspectives on the disparities between the faunal assemblages of these two periods have attributed them to land crab overexploitation or to climate change that produced drier conditions, which reduced the habitat of land crabs, limiting their availability (noted in Newsom and Wing 2004). Using optimal foraging theory, Keegan (1986) initially suggested that the dietary changes reflected what he termed a "diet breadth expansion," in which the increasing scarcity of terrestrial protein sources and an increasing demand for high protein necessitated the exploitation of other biotic sources. Susan deFrance (1989) suggested that the gradual decimation of the crab communities on the island led to the exploitation of other food sources such as mollusks.

Despite the current controversies regarding the efficacy of Rainey's Crab/Shell dichotomy, two important observations can be made. First, irrespective of the potential correlation between faunal remains and material cultural, it does appear that dietary patterns changed over time. Second, although land crabs were available during Archaic times, there is little evidence to indicate that they formed a substantive part of the Archaic people's diet. The greater frequency of mollusks in Ostionoid deposits has, in turn, been viewed as a continuity of the Archaic diet resulting from interaction between Puerto Rico's earlier Archaic inhabitants and subsequent Saladoid groups (Keegan 2006).

Further Reading

DeFrance, Susan D. 1989. "Saladoid and Ostionoid Subsistence Adaptations: Zooarchaeological Data from a Coastal Occupation on Puerto Rico." In *Early Ceramic Population Lifeways and Adaptive Strategies in the Caribbean*, ed. P. E. Siegel, 57–77. Oxford: British Archaeological Reports.

Keegan, W. F. 1986. "The Ecology of Lucayan Arawak Fishing Practices." *American Antiquity* 51 (4): 816–25.

———. 2006. "Archaic Influences in the Origins and Development of Taíno Societies." *Caribbean Journal of Science* 42 (1): 1–10.

Newsom, Lee A., and Elizabeth S. Wing. 2004. *On Land and Sea: Native American Uses of Biological Resources in the West Indies*. Tuscaloosa: University of Alabama Press.

Rainey, F. G. 1935. "A New Prehistoric Culture in Puerto Rico." *Proceedings of the National Academy of Sciences* 21 (1): 12–16.

———. 1940. *Porto Rican Archaeology*. Scientific Survey of Porto Rico and the Virgin Islands, vol. 18, pt. 1. New York: New York Academy of Sciences.

Rodríguez Ramos, R. 2010. *Rethinking Puerto Rico Precolonial History*. Tuscaloosa: University of Alabama Press.

Rouse, I. 1989. "Peoples and Cultures of the Saladoid Frontier in the Greater Antilles." In *Early Ceramic Population Lifeways and Adaptive Strategies in the Caribbean*, ed. Peter E. Siegel, 383–403. Oxford: British Archaeological Reports.

———. 1992. *The Tainos: Rise and Decline of the People Who Greeted Columbus*. New Haven, CT: Yale University Press.

See also The Archaic Age; Environmental Archaeology; The Ostionoid; Rainey, Froelich G. (1907–1992); The Saladoid.

Cruxent, José María (1911–2005)

Kathleen Deagan

José María Cruxent is acknowledged as the father of modern archaeology in Venezuela and as a pioneer in the historical archaeology of Latin America and the Caribbean. He is also recognized as an artist of international standing. Born in Barcelona, he studied archaeology and history at the University of Barcelona under Pere Bosch Gimpera. His studies were interrupted by the Spanish Civil War (1936–38), in which Cruxent served as a medic and cameraman with Republican forces fighting Franco. In 1939, he fled Spain and arrived in Venezuela with only the clothes he was wearing and ten dollars in his pocket. He did various jobs, including movie projectionist and fruit vendor, and eventually became a primary school art instructor. During his free time, he carried out archaeological surveys of the countryside (going by bus) and brought the resulting collections to the National Museum of Science in Caracas, where he became friends with Walter Dupouy and Antonio Requena. At that time, there were no formal academic or governmental programs of archaeology in Venezuela.

In 1944, Cruxent joined the staff of the museum, and by 1948, his passion for fieldwork and collections earned him the position of director of the National Museum of Science, a post he held until 1960. During his time as director of the museum, he established the first Department of Archaeology and relentlessly continued his programs of fieldwork. His programs included Paleo-Indian studies, working at El Jobo and Taima-Taima (some of the most influential sites for understanding the entry of people into the Americas) and at Nueva Cadiz on Cubagua, the first European settlement in South America and one of the first historical archaeology projects undertaken in the Caribbean. Cruxent also established close professional connections worldwide, bringing the museum (and Venezuelan archaeology) into the global arena.

One of his most fruitful collaborations was with Professor Irving Rouse of Yale University, with whom he collaborated on the pioneering monograph *An Archaeological Chronology of Venezuela* (1958, Pan American Union Monograph No. 6), later published as *Venezuelan Archaeology* (1963, Yale University Press). Another fruitful collaboration was with University of Florida archaeologist John Goggin, with whom he worked at the site of Nueva Cadiz, Isla Cubagua, in 1954. That program, as well as Cruxent's work during the 1950s in the early colonial sites of Panamá, was critical to the development of the classificatory system for Spanish colonial ceramics that is still used today by archaeologists in the Caribbean and beyond. Cruxent also engaged in collaborations with archaeological colleagues in Cuba, the Dominican Republic, and Puerto Rico and served as the president of the Roundtable Reunion of Caribbean Anthropologists held in Havana in 1950. The group established the Caribbean Anthropological Federation, a forerunner of the International Association for Caribbean Archaeology.

As director of the Museum of Science, Cruxent organized and participated in a number of exploratory expeditions into the unknown parts of the Amazon and Panamá, including the renowned Franco-Venezolano expedition of 1951 to find the source of the Orinoco. The successful seven-month expedition into the jungle fascinated and excited the press and the public, and Cruxent became a celebrity in Venezuela, where he offered frequent public lectures and media interviews. His celebrity was undoubtedly enhanced by his originality, simplicity, and lifelong lack of pretension. He preferred to appear with his pipe and wearing sandals, and he appeared only rarely wearing a tie.

Cruxent was one of the founders of the School of Sociology and Anthropology of the Universidad Central de Venezuela, created in 1952 through a formal agreement and professional exchange with the University of Wisconsin. His role as a teacher influenced archaeology in the circum-Caribbean region; he trained such archaeologists as Erika Wagner, Alberta Zucchi, Emiro Durán, and Eddie Romero. He further enhanced the professional standing of and training opportunities for archaeology in Venezuela in 1960 as the founder of the Department of Anthropology at the prestigious Instituto Venezolano de Investigaciones Ceintificas (IVIC; The Venezuelan Institute for Scientific Investigation), which had been founded the previous year by Marcel Roche. In 1963, Cruxent established the first radiocarbon dating laboratory in Latin America (supervised by Murray Tamers) at the IVIC. Cruxent remained at the IVIC, where he carried out his programs of teaching, fieldwork, and laboratory research, until 1976.

At the age of 65, Cruxent shifted his focus to Coro, in Falcón State in Venezuela, where he continued to pursue his two principal archaeological interests: the entry of humans into the Americas and the period of Spanish-American encounter. One of the earliest American proponents of the theory that people arrived in the Americas more than 10,000 years ago, Cruxent established the presence of lithic complexes dating to circa 14,000 BP at the site of Taima-Taima near Coro well before the contemporary research that corroborated his work. In 1987, he undertook the excavation of La Isabela in the Dominican Republic, the first European town in America. That project developed into an international collaboration among the Dominican Republic, Venezuela, the United States, Spain, and Italy, which Cruxent coordinated until 1996.

Throughout his archaeological career, Cruxent remained committed to his art. His mixed-media, textural works are featured not only in Venezuela but also in galleries and museums throughout Europe. His art, like his archaeology, is forward-looking, provocative, iconoclastic, and always impassioned. José Maria Cruxent died at the age of 94 in Coro, Venezuela.

Further Reading

Cabrero, F. 2009. *José María Cruxent: El espíritu de la materia.* Caracas: Instituto Venezolano de Investigaciones Científicas.

Cárdenas, M. L., and A. de Azcárate Wilson. 1992. *Homenaje a Cruxent: Siglo XXI: El hombre, cultura y desafíos.* Coro, Venezuela: Museo de Arte de Coro.

Wagner, E. 2006. "José María Cruxent: Padre de la arqueología moderna de Venezuela (1911–2005)." *Antropologica* 101 (2004): 9–12.

Wagner, E., and A. Zucchi, eds. 1978. *Undidad y variedad: Ensayos en homenaje a José M. Cruxent.* Caracas: Instituto Venezolano de Investigaciones Científicas.

See also The International Association for Caribbean Archaeology (IACA); Rouse, Benjamin Irving (1913–2006).

Cuba (Historical Archaeology of)

Theresa Singleton

Historical Background

Historical archaeology (a term used only recently in Cuba) designates the archaeological study of the period beginning with Spanish settlement of the island. It was initially referred to as colonial archaeology, and this term is still preferred by some practitioners today. The colonial period (1511–1898) continues to be the primary emphasis of this research, but Cuban historical archaeology has become more than the study of a time period; it is the study of the social processes involved in the making of Cuban society. Historical archaeology began taking shape in Cuba in the 1930s, and by the late 1960s it had become an integral part of Cuban archaeological research and practice.

Christopher Columbus landed on Cuba on October 28, 1492, and reputedly described the pristine landscape where he landed as "the most beautiful land the human eye has beheld." The colonization of Cuba began in 1511 under the command of Diego Velázquez y Cuellar, who wasted no time in subjugating the aboriginal population through violence and brute force. By 1515, the Spanish had founded seven settlements on the island, all of which are major cities today: Baracoa

(1511), Bayamo (1513), Sancti Spíritus (1514), Trinidad (1514), Havana (1515), Puerto Príncipe (1515; known as Camagüey today), and Santiago de Cuba (1515). The Spanish most likely established towns in these locations because of their close proximity to communities of aboriginals, who initially provided labor for the colonists. In each town, the central plaza, which featured a church, a town hall, and a garrison, was built first. Town dwellers received plots on which to build their houses and shared other plots used in common as forests, pastures, and watering places. Local representatives of the Spanish Crown, *vecinos,* distributed the remaining lands in the colony into smaller land portions known as encomiendas, based on the beneficiary's influence and position in the social hierarchy. Settlers were granted land in usufruct—they could profit from using the property, but the Spanish Crown retained all land ownership. Enslaved Amerindians, both native to Cuba and from nearby islands, supplied the work force for the encomiendas. Brutal treatment of Indian laborers drastically reduced their numbers, and in 1542, the encomienda system was abolished. By that time, many of the first Spanish immigrants to Cuba had left in search of gold in Mexico and Peru. For the next 200 years, Cuba developed into a sparsely populated colony of cattle and pig ranches and small-scale farms, some of which produced sugar and tobacco—staple crops that would later bring prosperity to the island. Enslaved Africans replaced enslaved Amerindians as the primary work force for many of these enterprises. Havana and Santiago flourished as port cities, servicing ships passing to and from mainland Spanish America.

During the second half of the eighteenth century, the Spanish Crown set in motion a series of reforms directed toward making Cuba a wealthy colony. Consequently, Cuba underwent major economic and social transformations that resulted in its emergence as the foremost nineteenth-century Caribbean plantation economy. These reforms permitted the breaking up of royal land grants into parcels for private land ownership, opened Cuba to free trade, and accelerated the importation of enslaved Africans. Immigrants, particularly French planters fleeing the Haitian Revolution, joined Cuban planters in the expansion of coffee and sugar production. By the 1830s, Cuba had become the world's leading producer of sugar; coffee and tobacco were important secondary crops. The explosion of Cuba's plantation economy boosted trade at port cities, and by 1850, Havana was among the ten busiest ports in the world. However, increased prosperity nurtured a growing desire for independence from Spain as Cuban taxpayers found themselves increasingly contributing to an empire that Spain was having difficulty financing. The Cuban struggle for independence lasted for thirty years (1868–1898), during which two wars took place. Finally, in 1898, after the United States intervened, Spain was forced to withdraw from Cuba.

Archaeological Research

Archaeologists have investigated diverse aspects of the 400-year Spanish colonial period in Cuba. Early studies of contact period sites, plantations, and significant historical buildings appeared in the journal *Revista de la Junta Nacional de Arqueología y Etnología* in the 1940s and 1950s. El Yayal in Hoguín province is an example of a contact period site that was originally thought to be near the location where Columbus first landed in Cuba. This area of interest was initially investigated in the 1930s and was restudied by Lourdes Domínguez in 1970 and 1981. She posited that the site was an aboriginal settlement with a large quantity of Spanish trade goods that was occupied during the first half of the sixteenth century. Whether or not Yayal was part of an encomienda is unclear, but it provides a glimpse of Cuban aboriginal life during the earliest period of Spanish colonization.

Plantation studies also contributed to the formation and development of Cuban historical archaeology. In 1930, Fernando Boytel Jambú began his study of La Isabelica, a French-owned coffee plantation outside Santiago, and in the early days of revolutionary Cuba (post-1959), archaeology was used to restore the site and develop it into a plantation museum that is still in operation today. Since that time, several plantations have been investigated on Cuba, including San Isidro de los Destiladeros (Figure C.17) and other sugar plantations in the UNESCO World Heritage Site of the Valley of Sugar Plantations near Trinidad in central Cuba on the south coast; coffee plantations in Sierra del Rosario in the Piñar del Rio; and coffee and sugar plantations in Havana and Matanzas provinces, including Taoro, La Manuela, Santa Ana de Biajacas, and La Dionesia. Plantation studies have primarily addressed questions about the spatial layout and built environment of slavery and (only recently) living conditions of the enslaved and the relationships between masters and enslaved peoples.

Complementing the study of plantations, investigations of sites where enslaved runaways settled have been undertaken in both eastern and western Cuba. These

Figure C.17. Bell Tower at San Isidro de los Destiladeros, a former sugar plantation near Trinidad, Cuba. Photo by Theresa Singleton.

sites are of two types: 1) *palenques*—substantial long-term settlements with evidence of horticulture; and 2) sites of *cimarrones*, small groups of runaways who were frequently on the move and lived in caves and overhangs, foraged for wild food, and raided nearby plantations for food and supplies. Gabino La Rosa has investigated both types of sites for over twenty-five years: *palenques* in the Sierra Maestra in eastern Cuba and *cimarrones* in the Sierra del Grillo in Havana province. At the *palenque* sites, La Rosa observed clusters of dwellings laid out to form inner squares and inner paths leading from one cluster of dwellings to another. These inner pathways may have facilitated communication and movement throughout the settlement without the knowledge of outsiders such as the slave hunters who were in constant pursuit of runaways.

The most ambitious project in historical archaeology has been the long-term study of Habana Vieja (old Havana), which has been continuously occupied since the relocation of the first site of Havana from the south coast to its present location on the north coast in 1519. Most of Old Havana was once enclosed within city walls measuring 1.4 meters (5 feet) thick, 10 meters (33 feet) high, and almost 5 kilometers long (3.1 miles) with nine gates. Building the walls took close to 100 years to complete, and in the nineteenth century the walls were almost completely demolished, except for a few remnants that are still standing today (Figure C.18). Systematic study of archaeological sites in Old Havana began in 1968, and in that same year historical archaeology became an established specialization throughout the country. Initial projects were baseline studies undertaken to salvage archaeological data from sites undergoing architectural restoration. These studies provided valuable information on the nature and stratigraphy of archaeological deposits in Old Havana and information that was used to identify and date artifacts. Since 1987, the Gabinete de Arqueología—a unit of the Office of the Historian for the City of Havana—has continued salvage archaeology within a research program designed to examine changing patterns of urban settlement, consumption, lifeways, and cultural interaction from the sixteenth to the twentieth centuries, among other topics. The work is done by multidisciplinary teams of archaeologists, historians, art historians, and architectural historians. Beginning in 2001, article-length studies from this research have been published in an annual journal, *Gabinete de Arqueología*. The journal quickly became the major publication of Cuban historical archaeology. The program in urban archaeology in Old Havana is unique and is the most comprehensive of its kind in the Caribbean and perhaps in all of Latin America. All historical archaeologists can learn from this extraordinary research program.

Conclusion

Cuban historical archaeology is a scholarly tradition of at least seventy to eighty years that continues to expand, despite the significant economic setbacks the country has endured over the past two decades. Most investigations are concentrated around Havana and Trinidad, two UNESCO World Heritage sites with strong heritage preservation programs, but other regions and provinces are also beginning more projects in historical archaeology. Publication based on this research is increasing, and the Web site www.cubaarqueologica.org provides up-to-date reports of ongoing projects. Collaborations between Cuban and expatriate archaeologists in long-term projects has further enhanced Cuban historical archaeology through cross-fertilization

Figure C.18. Portion of the wall that once enclosed Old Havana. Photo by Theresa Singleton.

of research ideas, approaches, and interpretations. This has resulted in greater visibility of Cuban research in archaeological venues outside Cuba. Once considered the pearl of the Spanish empire, Cuba is well on its way to becoming the jewel of the Caribbean in the area of historical archaeology.

Further Reading

Curet, L. A., L. D. Shannon, and G. La Rosa Corzo, eds. 2005. *Dialogues in Cuban Archaeology*. Tuscaloosa: University of Alabama Press.

Domínguez, L. 1995. *Arqueología colonial cubana: Dos estudios*. Havana: Editorial de Ciencias Sociales.

Hernández de Lara, Odlanyer. 2010. *De Esclavos y Inmigrantes: Arqueología Histórica en una Plantación Cafetalera Cubana*. Buenos Aires: Centro de Investigaciones Pre-Columbinas, Instituto Superior del Profesorado Dr. Joaquín V. González.

La Rosa Corzo, G. 2003. *Runaway Slave Settlements in Cuba: Resistance and Repression*. Trans. Mary Todd. Chapel Hill: University of North Carolina Press.

Singleton, T. A., and Marcos André de Souza Torres. 2009. "Archaeologies of the African Diaspora: Brazil, Cuba, United States." In *International Handbook for Historical Archaeology*, ed. T. Majewski and D. Gaimster, 449–69. New York: Springer.

See also Betty's Hope Plantation (Antigua); Historical Archaeological Sites (Types); La Reconnaissance Site (Trinidad); Magens House Compound, Kongens Quarters (Charlotte Amalie, St. Thomas); The Seville Sugar Plantation (British Colonial Jamaica); Spanish Town (Jamaica).

Cundall, Frank (1858–1937)

James Robertson

When Frank Cundall died in November 1937, a cable to the *New York Times* described him as "librarian at the Jamaica Institute and the leading historian of the British West Indies." He had served as secretary and librarian of the Institute of Jamaica for forty-six years. As secretary, Cundall led a cultural institution in a colony where such institutions were vulnerable during budget crises. He weathered cutbacks in the late 1890s; a legislators' proposal that the institute should be "shut down for the year" in 1904, and the challenges of rebuilding after the 1907 Kingston earthquake. He left an institutional legacy: in 1938 the colony's Legislative Council voted to fund the extension of the institute's buildings. While he was keeping the institute afloat, he developed an international reputation as an expert in Jamaican and West Indian history.

Cundall was a Londoner who came to Jamaica in 1891 at age 33 after a decade at the South Kensington Museum (today's Victoria and Albert Museum). The institute he joined had been established in 1879 and already had a library and museum. During his tenure, he built up both as major research centers. The West India Reference Library accumulated almost 11,000 books, maps, and documents covering not only Jamaica and the West Indies but also Central America and West Africa. During his tenure, the museum also accumulated substantial holdings, including prehistoric and geological collections. Cundall also established a Gallery of Historical Jamaican Portraits within the institute that acquired close to 900 portraits and views, with some originals and many photographs.

During the early 1890s, when the curator of the institute was J. E. Duerden, significant work was done to locate and excavate Taíno sites in Jamaica and publish on Jamaican prehistory. This period of vitality did not prevent the post from being frozen at the end of the decade. Cundall's achievements were secured on a shoestring budget with a negligible annual purchasing grant (though as a government department he did have free postage). Some acquisitions involved tracking down the officials who could let him examine such hoards as the manuscript records of eighteenth-century Kingston, which were stored in the back of an old fire station, and transferring them to the Institute. Today, the most immediate imprint of Cundall's work is that many original sources for West Indian history and prehistory are held at the Institute of Jamaica and the National Library of Jamaica rather than in metropolitan or North American collections.

Archaeologists will find Cundall's scholarly legacy not only in the survival of the Institute of Jamaica and its collections but also in studies prompted by his work as secretary of a committee to identify the island's historical monuments. He helped compile a provisional list of historic and archaeological sites meriting protection that was first published in a gazette in 1909. He wrote up many of them in articles that were later collected as *Historic Jamaica* (1915).

Figure C.19. A memorial plaque to Frank Cundall at the National Library of Jamaica. Photo by James Robertson.

Further Reading

Cundall, F. 1909. "Historic Sites, Ancient Buildings and Monuments in Jamaica." *Supplement to the Jamaica Gazette* 32 (December 23): 629–40.

———. 1915. *Historic Jamaica*, London: West India Committee for Institute of Jamaica.

Jacobs, H. P. 1968. "The Achievement of Frank Cundall." *Jamaica Journal* 1 (1): 24–28.

Robertson, J. C. 2005. "Frank Cundall's *Robert Sedgwick:* The Wartime Origins of a Colonial Research Project." *Jamaican Historical Society Bulletin* 11 (16): 436–48.

See also Duerden, J. E. (1869–1937); The Institute of Jamaica.

Curaçao (Former Netherlands Antilles)

Jay B. Haviser

Antonius J. van Koolwijk, a Catholic priest on Curaçao in the late nineteenth century, conducted the first archaeological investigations on the island as an amateur hobby. Van Koolwijk created his artifact collection on Curaçao during the period 1878–1880, after which he moved to Aruba. On Curaçao, van Koolwijk located numerous prehistoric sites at Knip Bay, Ascension, San Juan, and so on. He also conducted limited excavations at several sites, but his records were vague. He did send the artifacts to Holland, where they were analyzed and published by Conrad Leemans of the State University of Leiden from 1880 to 1904. Leemans and Johannes Schmeltz published these results in 1904, along with a thesis of Caribbean origins for the Amerindian populations. However, in 1914 Ten Kate reviewed the material in Holland and questioned the Caribbean origins theory and suggested a South American origin. J. P. B. de Josselin de Jong also reviewed the van Koolwijk collections in the Netherlands and published his comments in 1918, with an update in 1920. The van Koolwijk finds helped stimulate a 1923 expedition to the Caribbean by de Josselin de Jong, who excavated the San Juan site in Curaçao. In 1963, D. Hooijer published an article about the mammalian remains in the collection from de Josselin de Jong's research at the San Juan site in 1923.

In 1949, another amateur archaeologist, Aad Ringma, conducted extensive field surveys on the island to locate prehistoric rock art sites. It is to his credit that most of the rock art sites for the island have been identified. However, it was P. Wagenaar Hummelinck who, from 1953 to 1959, published the more extensive and precise descriptions of prehistoric rock art for Curaçao, based on formal excavations. In 1959, the first of a series of physical anthropology publications about prehistoric populations on Curaçao (and other Dutch islands) was published by the Dutch anthropologist Jouke Tacoma, whose 1985 publication on Curaçao skeletal remains is still the most extensive review of prehistoric human skeletal remains to date. One of the primary results of this research on Curaçao was the creation of the Archaeological-Anthropological Institute of the Netherlands Antilles (AAINA), which was founded and directed by Edwin N. Ayubi.

In the 1960s, a Dutch archaeological team led by H. R. van Heekeren and C. J. Dury produced three archaeological reports about Curaçao's prehistoric materials. Dutch shell specialist H. E. Coomans, who published his reports separately, augmented these investigations. One of the sites investigated was Rooi Rincon on Curaçao, which yielded the oldest known archaeological remains for the Netherlands Antilles; they have been dated to circa 4500 BC. Various other amateur archaeologists were making artifact collections on the island in the 1960s. The most prominent of these were Paul Brenneker and Elis Juliana, whose extensive collections are now at the National Archaeological Anthropological Museum (NAAM) on Curaçao (formerly AAINA). In 1964, a short visit by Dutch archaeologist P. Glazema provided oversight for rescue excavations at the Kintjan site. Glazema's report was published in 1964. In 1965, Venezuelan archaeologist José M. Cruxent conducted various test excavations on Curaçao to collect radiocarbon samples. These provided the first radiocarbon dating evidence for the island. Cruxent's results were published in 1965 through the Instituto Venezolano de Investigaciones Ceintíficas (IVIC) at Caracas. In 1969, Cruxent and Irving Rouse used the research on Curaçao in their contribution to the *Encyclopedia of the Netherlands Antilles*. In 1971, E. Boerstra and E. Juliana conducted an archaeological excavation at the Late Ceramic Age Santa Barbara site on Curaçao; their collections were deposited at AAINA. In 1980, a salvage archaeological excavation was carried out by E. Ayubi, J. Kemperman, and J. Tacoma at the Ceramic Age De Savaan site. The 1985 version of the *Encyclopedia of the Netherlands Antilles* includes a review compiled by E. Ayubi and A. Versteeg of all archaeological work done until 1983.

Beginning in 1982, Jay Haviser began work as the Netherlands Antilles archaeologist for AAINA. For much of the 1980s, he focused his research on excavations and inventories of archaeological sites on Curaçao. He submitted the first site inventory for the island to AAINA in 1983, which he subsequently published as part of an extensive inventory in his doctoral dissertation for Leiden University (the Netherlands) in 1987. Throughout the 1980s and 1990s, Haviser conducted archaeological surveys and excavations at the prehistoric sites of Sint Michielsberg (Archaic Age) and the Ceramic Age sites of De Savaan, San Hironimo, Kenepa, Santa Cruz, Santa Barbara, and Spaanse Water. He also carried out field activity at the historical sites of the Zuurzak slave camp, the Oost Seinpost site, the Midden Seinpost site, the Historic Punda city center, the Kenepa Plantation and *kunuku*-houses, the San Hironimo contact period site, the Daai Booi Bay site, and the De Tempel Dutch burial ground. In 1999, Haviser edited *African Sites: Archaeology of the Caribbean*, in which he defined a post-emancipation material culture assemblage for Curaçao from his research on the island. In 1995, Haviser published a textbook about prehistoric Curaçao for public schools.

During the 1980s and 1990s, underwater archaeological surveys and excavations were conducted around Curaçao by Wil Nagelkerken, and in the 1990s, he conducted research with the help of the Foundation for Marine Archaeology of the Netherlands Antilles (STIMANA). Some of the more important research Nagelkerken did included the Santa Ana Harbor survey and collections (1994), excavations at the eighteenth-century shipwreck *Alphen* (2009), and research on the nineteenth-century shipwreck *Mediator* (2003).

Since the 1990s and into the early twenty-first century, a team organized by the NAAM's former director, Ieteke Witteveen, called the Curaçao Archaeological Workgroup, has been documenting archaeological sites on Curaçao, with particular emphasis on the prehistoric rock art sites. The key figures involved in this early work-

group were Francois van der Hoeven, Eddy Batens, Andre Rancuret, and Jose DaCamara. The current director of the NAAM, Richenel Ansano, has followed up on this project. In 2005, Haviser conducted rescue excavations and collected material in Punda city center. University of Amsterdam professor J. H. G. Gawronski made a technical report of the results of this work for the NAAM. In 2007, Haviser conducted a short archaeological survey at the Rif Sint Marie plantation area. He and Miriam Sluis made minor artifact collections and submitted them to the NAAM. In 2008, Claudia Craan and Amy Victorina conducted rescue excavations for the NAAM that required the removal of historical period human skeletal remains from the Flor-de-Marie urban district of Curaçao. In 2008, a significant excavations campaign of a Leiden University team of archaeologists led by Corinne Hofman and Menno Hoogland conducted excavations at the Santa Barbara and Spaanse Water prehistoric sites.

In October 2010, Curaçao became an autonomous entity within the Kingdom of the Netherlands, as the Netherlands Antilles ceased to exist.

Further Reading

Farnsworth, P., ed. 2001. *Island Lives: Historical Archaeologies of the Caribbean*. Tuscaloosa: University of Alabama Press.

Haviser, J. 1987. *Amerindian Cultural Geography on Curaçao*. Utrecht: Natuurweteschappelijke Studiekring voor Suriname en de Nederlandse Antillen.

———. 1999. *African Sites Archaeology in the Caribbean*. Princeton, NJ: Markus Wiener Publishers.

Nagelkerken, W. 1994. "The 1993 Archaeological Research: Summary of the Report 'Underwater Archaeological Research of the Historical Refuse Dumpsite along the Handelskade in the Sta. Ana Bay, Curaçao.'" *Lanternu* 14 (March): 23–36.

———. 2003. *Rapport over de opgraving van het Engelse stoomschip Mediator gezonken in 1884 in de Haven van Curaçao*. Curaçao: Stichting Marien Archeologisch Onderzoek Nederlandse Antillen.

———. 2009. *De Noodlottige Geschiedenis van het Hollandse fregat Alphen; Geexplodeerd en gezonken in 1778 in de Haven van Curaçao*. Curaçao: STIMANA.

See also Cruxent, José María (1911–2005); The Dutch Caribbean; Foundation for Marine Archaeology of the Netherlands Antilles (STIMANA); The National Archaeological Anthropological Memory Management Foundation (NAAM); Rouse, Benjamin Irving (1913–2006).

D

De Boyrie Moya, Emil (1903–1967)

Clenis Tavárez María

Emil de Boyrie Moya was a civil engineer who also conducted studies in archaeology. He traveled throughout the Dominican Republic for his work as an engineer, and this provided him with the opportunity to find a large number of pre-Hispanic and colonial sites. He wrote the first law that banned the transportation of cultural heritage outside the Dominican Republic. He was also interested in the field of biology, and he reported 52 new species of flora and 34 new species of fauna.

On April 19, 1947, De Boyrie Moya founded the Instituto de Investigaciones Antropológicas (which today is known as the Instituto de Investigaciones Antropológicas Emile De Boyrie Moya), which is attached to the College of Philosophy of the Universidad Autónoma de Santo Domingo. This institute conducted many regional studies and other archaeological research, work that stimulated interest in archaeology among De Boyrie Moya's colleagues and family members, including engineer Elpidio J. Ortega Alvarez; Dr. Manuel Mañón Arredondo; Dr. Luis Chanlatte Baik; De Boyrie Moya's son, Andrés Emile; and De Boyrie Moya's nephews Bernardo and Wenceslao Vega de Boyrie, among others. E. Ortega and B. Vega became general directors of the Museo del Hombre Dominicano years later.

De Boyrie Moya participated in many national and international academic conferences. Among his most important works are studies conducted in the ceremonial plazas of Chacuey (Dajabón) and San Juan de la Maguana. He also published work on Punta Torrecilla (Santo Domingo), Fortaleza de Jánico (Santiago), the Casa de Juan Ponce de León, and the Anamuya site (La Altagracia Province). Furthermore, he worked at La Isabela de Puerto Plata, the first settlement in the New World, the old city of La Vega, the ruins of Jacagua (Santiago), and the sugar mills of Engombe (Santo Domingo) and Cepi Cepi (Azua).

He published a large number of articles in Dominican newspapers and in journals. But probably the most important of his publications is *Monumento megalítico y petroglifos de Chacuey, República Dominicana* (1955). This work is a detailed archaeological study of this pre-Hispanic ceremonial site that describes the complex, including the plaza, two causeways, and petroglyphs found in the nearby Chacuey River and in two stones from the plaza. Many scholars consider this book to be a classic of Caribbean archaeology.

De Boyrie Moya worked on expeditions with René Herrera Fritot and José María Cruxent and was a member of the Dominican Academy of History. He is seen today as the first Dominican archaeologist. Today, his archaeological collection forms part of the collections of the Museo del Hombre Dominicano and the Instituto de Investigaciones Antropológicas. Both institutions have exhibit halls named after De Boyrie Moya.

See also La Isabela (Dominican Republic); Museo del Hombre Dominicano.

De Hostos, Adolfo (1887–1982)

L. Antonio Curet

While Adolfo de Hostos began his archaeological career as a simple collector and never received any formal training in this discipline, he became an internationally recognized scholar who maintained strong relationships with archaeologists from both the United States and Europe. His work was published in internationally renowned publications such as *American Anthropologist*, *The Journal of the Royal Anthropological of Great Britain*, and *Proceedings of the Americanist Congress* as well as in local media. He conducted his work as a scientist with a theoretical framework that sought to understand the past and its people. It is for all these reasons that Adolfo de Hostos can be considered the first modern/scientific archaeologist from Puerto Rico, if not the entire Caribbean.

De Hostos was born in Santo Domingo, Dominican Republic, on January 8, 1887. He was the son of Eugenio María de Hostos, a renowned Puerto Rican educator and social philosopher, and Belinda de Ayala, a Cuban national. After a short stay in Chile and Puerto Rico during his early childhood, de Hostos returned to Dominican Republic in 1900, when the government of that country asked his father to reorganize their educational system. In the Dominican Republic Adolfo de Hostos came into contact with indigenous archaeological objects for the first time when a friend gave him a potsherd. In 1903, his family returned to Puerto Rico after the death of his father. He returned to Dominican Republic again in 1907 when his brother began a family farming business. They bought a farm in Boca Chica, close to the famous archaeological site of the same name, and it was here that de Hostos's interest in archaeology flourished. In 1909, he enlisted in the United States Army, and he was sent to Panama during World War I to guard the canal. There, he continued to cultivate his interest in archaeology by conducting research on the prehistory of the region and adding Central American artifacts to his collection. He returned to Puerto Rico in 1919 with a collection of ancient artifacts from Central America. In 1936, he was named the official historian of Puerto Rico. In 1938, de Hostos conducted his well-known excavations at the ruins of Caparra, the first European settlement in Puerto Rico. He retired in 1950, and for economic reasons he sold his collection in 1954, which was eventually donated to the Museo de Antropología e Historia of the University of Puerto Rico. He died in 1982.

De Hostos's contribution to Caribbean archaeology included works on theory, methodology, and interpretation. All of his work reflected an interest in understanding, explaining, and finding the reasons for the behaviors of ancient people. Although his ideas changed over time, from early on, he had a tendency to emphasize environmental factors, anticipating ideas developed decades later by cultural ecologists. Eventually, he combined these ideas with cultural evolutionism, although he did not follow the generic, universal stages European evolutionists had proposed in the nineteenth century. Instead, de Hostos proposed that cultural evolution is the product of environmental variables and cultural inventions,

emphasizing cultural differentiation and particularism. To understand the value of his contribution, it is important to understand that these ideas were published in the 1920s through the 1940s, when American scholars focused on collecting data and subscribed to what we now refer to as historical particularism and diffusionism. Both of these theoretical positions negated the need for general high-level theory and worked from an empiricist epistemology in which data informed theories and not the other way around.

De Hostos's contribution to Caribbean archaeology was also methodological. For example, he sought to understand the relationship between people and their environment. During his residence at his family farm in Boca Chica (1907–1909) he began to consider environmental variables such as slope, distance to the ocean, fresh water, access to firewood and other resources, natural plant resources, available marine and terrestrial fauna, and wind direction. He also noticed that the southern coasts of Hispaniola, Puerto Rico, and Jamaica have both larger densities of sites and some of the largest sites in those islands. He was also one of the first Caribbean archaeologists to use stratigraphic contexts to define archaeological cultures and organize them in chronological order, even before Rainey began his work in Puerto Rico. Another example of his contribution to the field is his use of functional criteria to classify his collections.

But perhaps the best example of de Hostos's contribution was the way he approached research problems, including his multidisciplinary approach and his final interpretations. It can be said with certainty that he was ahead of his time. In the foreword to his book *Anthropological Papers* (de Hostos 1941), where he republished many of his earlier articles, he emphasized the great need for archaeologists to work with zoologists, botanists, physiologists, geologists, psychologists, and even aestheticians and philosophers. This approach did not become common in archaeological research until after the 1960s. De Hostos's work included a long list of research projects and publications on West Indian hydrography, ceramic analysis, and interpretations of the meaning of native iconography in ceramics, *zemíes*, *dujos*, stone collars, elbow stones, prehistoric art, and ethnography.

In conclusion, it is clear that Adolfo de Hostos was a scholar in every sense of the word, and he was arguably the first modern archaeologist of the Caribbean. Because of its strong emphasis on theory and explanation, de Hostos's work can aptly be described as modern scientific archaeology. It is unfortunate that his contributions are so little known by many modern Caribbean archaeologists, and that many of his interpretations that are as valid today as when they were published are generally ignored.

Further Reading

de Hostos, A. 1919. "Prehistoric Puerto Rican Ceramics." *American Anthropologist* 21 (4): 376–99.

———. 1924. "Notes on West Indian Hydrography in Its Relation to Prehistoric Migrations." In *Annaes do XX Congreso Internacional de Americanistas*, vol. 1. Rio de Janeiro: Imprenta Nacional.

———. 1926. "Antillean Stone Collars: Some Suggestions of Interpretative Value." *Journal of the Royal Anthropological Institute of Great Britain* 56: 135–42.

———. 1938. *Investigaciones Históricas*. San Juan, Puerto Rico: Oficina del Historiador, Gobierno de Puerto Rico.

———. 1941. *Anthropological Papers: Based Principally on Studies of the Prehistoric Archaeology and Ethnology of the Greater Antilles*. San Juan, Puerto Rico: Oficina del Historiador, Gobierno de Puerto Rico.

———. 1967. "Plant Fertilization by Magic in the Taíno Area of the Greater Antilles." *Boletín de la Academia de Artes y Ciencias de Puerto Rico* 3 (14): 841–44.

DNA and Caribbean Archaeology

Maria A. Nieves-Colón

Archaeological research has benefited from the addition of genetic data, a valuable line of evidence in reconstructing ancient human societies. The relevant genetic markers for archeological inquiry are those that inform researchers about past evolutionary events. Mitochondrial DNA (mtDNA) and non-recombining Y (NRY) chromosome loci, for example, are inherited in a direct line from mother to daughter and father to son, respectively. This inheritance pattern allows these loci to accumulate high amounts of genetic diversity that can then be used to characterize population-specific mtDNA or NRY lineages. Thus, mtDNA and NRY markers can be instrumental in tracing and dating ancient population movement and in examining relationships between ancestral and descendant populations. Other frequently used loci are biparentally inherited autosomal DNA markers, such as short tandem repeats (STRs), which make individual and paternity identification possible. Additionally, small point mutations known as single nucleotide polymorphisms (SNPs) are useful for identifying ancestry and the presence of disease-associated mutations. The examination of any of these loci across living human groups allows the characterization of inter- and intrapopulation variation and diversity, thus providing important insights into population history and allowing archaeologists to infer ancient genetic patterns and relationships.

Archaeological research has also benefited from the analysis of ancient DNA (aDNA), the genetic material recovered from ancient biological remains. Ancient DNA can be extracted from a variety of sources, including bone, teeth, hair, tissue, plant material, and preserved fecal remains, or coprolites. In contexts that are ideal for DNA preservation (e.g., those with stable, dry, and cool temperatures such as the Arctic permafrost), aDNA can be preserved for more than 100,000 years. Thus, when aDNA is retrieved from archaeological contexts, it can provide researchers with the opportunity to reconstruct ancient biological relationships and yield valuable data for answering a variety of questions regarding ancient population movement, population structure and diversity, disease, diet, ecology, and the evolutionary relationships between ancient and living populations.

In the Caribbean, DNA research is used in archaeological inquiry to answer questions about the individual, community, and population history of Caribbean societies. For example, research using both ancient and modern DNA has contributed new knowledge to the debate about the initial peopling of the Antilles. Analysis of mtDNA data recovered from ancient skeletal remains found in Taíno sites in the Dominican Republic (n = 24) and Ciboney/Guanahatabey sites in Cuba (n = 15) has revealed mtDNA lineages among the skeletal samples that share strong affinity with modern South American Yanomami populations from the Amazonian region. This discovery supports the hypothesis of a South American origin for Arawak-speaking Caribbean Ceramic era groups (Lalueza-Fox et al. 2001, 2003). Genetic data from Puerto Rico have also been used to trace ancient migrations into the region. This is due to the discovery of mtDNA lineages among the modern Puerto Rican population that share strong affinity with modern South and Central American Amerindian groups. These lineages are estimated to have arrived on the island during the Archaic and Saladoid periods respectively, thus lending support to the hypothesis that successive waves of migration peopled the Caribbean (Martinez-Cruzado 2010).

The applications of ancient DNA in Caribbean archaeology can also be extended to the reconstruction of kin relations. Patterns of kinship and relatedness among individuals found in associated burials can be determined through the use of STRs to identify paternity and for genetic fingerprinting. Thus, genetic analysis of kinship can be used to test hypotheses bioarchaeologists have proposed about the presence of ancestor worship practices among early Caribbean natives. The hypotheses stem from multiple findings of individuals from Saladoid and post-Saladoid burial sites who were tightly holding skulls and other skeletal remains (Crespo-Torres 2011). Kinship analysis would allow an evaluation of the degrees of relatedness of the associated individuals and refute or support the hypothesis that these were close or distant relatives.

Other potential applications of aDNA analyses in Caribbean archaeology include the reconstruction of ancient diet through the examination of genetic signatures found in food remains. For example, genetic analyses can identify plant or animal taxa found in midden deposits or identify food residue on artifacts used for food preparation. Genetic traces of dietary remains can also be extracted from coprolites or preserved stomach contents. aDNA techniques can also be used to extract DNA from pathogens or parasites that may survive in small concentrations in skeletal remains or coprolites of humans and animals. Thus, genetic data can help identify skeletal pathology and provide information about ancient health patterns.

It is important to note that significant caveats accompany aDNA research in the Caribbean. Because of the effects of taphonomic damage and natural postmortem degradation, aDNA is extremely low in quantity and quality and tends to be very fragmented. Because of these problems, successful extraction, amplification, and analysis of aDNA becomes a difficult process, especially when samples have been subjected to the warm, humid climate of the Caribbean for hundreds or even thousands of years. The great potential for contamination of degraded samples by modern sources during handling and downstream analysis by archaeologists and DNA researchers is also a major problem. The limited quantity of skeletal remains recovered from archaeological contexts that are available for methods of analysis that would destroy samples can further restrict our ability to arrive at insights about ancient populations derived from aDNA. For these reasons, ancient DNA samples must be authenticated in order to validate results and

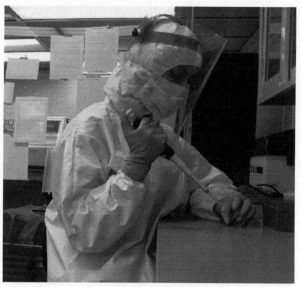

Figure D.1. Extensive personal protective equipment is needed to avoid introducing contamination when working with ancient DNA from archaeological samples. This researcher wears a full body suit, face shield, double gloves and face mask while working in a dedicated ancient DNA laboratory. Courtesy of Maria A. Nieves-Colón.

minimize the risk of false positives. This includes conducting all DNA extraction procedures in a clean-room environment; extensive personal protective equipment such as bodysuits, double gloves, and face shields; and independent replication of results (Figure D.1).

Further Reading

Crespo-Torres, E. 2011. "Bioarchaeological Evidence of Ancestor Worship from Paso del Indio: An Archaeological Site in the Island of Puerto Rico." In *Aportes universitarios: Antología de ensayos interdisciplinarios de las ciencias sociales*, ed. José R. Rodríguez-Gómez, 194–217. San Juan, Puerto Rico: Universidad de Puerto Rico.

Lalueza-Fox, C., M. Gilbert, A. Martínez-Fuentes, F. Calafell, and J. Bertranpetit. 2003. "Mitochondrial DNA from Pre-Columbian Ciboneys from Cuba and the Prehistoric Colonization of the Caribbean." *American Journal of Physical Anthropology* 121 (2): 97–108.

Lalueza-Fox, C., F. Luna Calderon, F. Calafell, and J. Bertranpetit. 2001. "MtDNA from Extinct Taínos and the Peopling of the Caribbean." *Annals of Human Genetics* 65: 137–51.

Martínez-Cruzado, J. C. 2010. "The History of Amerindian Mitochondrial DNA Lineages in Puerto Rico." In *Island Shores, Distant Pasts: Archaeological and Biological Approaches to the Pre-Columbian Settlement of the Caribbean*, ed. S. M. Fitzpatrick and A. H. Ross, 54–80. Gainesville: University Press of Florida.

See also Environmental Archaeology; Luna Calderón, Fernando (1945–2005); Origins of Indigenous Groups in the Northern Caribbean.

Drax Hall Estate (Jamaica)

Douglas V. Armstrong

The Drax Hall study examines the life of enslaved laborers at a plantation that was established circa 1690 on Jamaica's north coast, just east of St. Ann's Bay. The study is significant in that it represents the first comprehensive study of plantation slavery in the Caribbean based on evidence from an African Jamaican laborer settlement. The study began a survey and excavation of house sites associated with the settlement of enslaved African Jamaican laborers at Drax Hall in 1980 through 1982. It was then expanded to include excavation of the planter's residence, or "great house." The initial study of the households of enslaved laborers was the basis for Douglas Armstrong's dissertation at UCLA (1983b). That study was followed up with additional excavations within the enslaved settlement and excavations aimed at gaining a contrasting data set represented by the planter's residence and the cook house. The book *The Old Village and the Great House: An Archaeological Examination of Drax Hall Plantation St. Ann's Bay, Jamaica* (Armstrong 1990) was the major published result of these combined projects.

The Drax Hall Plantation study involved the combined use of historical documentary data to reconstruct a social history focusing on the lives of the enslaved at Drax Hall Plantation (Armstrong 1983a, 1990). The site was selected after an extensive archival and field survey that sought to locate a setting in which there was a high probability for the collection of a definitive body of data from discrete house sites. Data were initially compiled for hundreds of estates, and the list was initially narrowed down on the basis of the quality of historical documentation. Drax Hall and the Seville Plantation were initially selected from among twenty-one estates based on the combined quality of archival data (such as inventories, maps, and accounting records) and the integrity of the archaeological site (based on walking surveys and the identification of discrete ruins of houses on the landscape). Drax Hall was studied first, and several years later an investigation was carried out at the Seville Plantation.

The findings of the Drax Hall study included a wealth of information related to life in the village of enslaved laborers (Armstrong 1991a, 1991b). Nearly 50 house sites were identified (Figure D.2), and 1 × 1 meter testing at each of these sites made it possible to date each house and project temporal trends in the landscape. In the earliest years of Drax Hall, plantation houses were clustered up the hill behind the planter's residence (Armstrong

1991a). The houses were at a distance but close enough for surveillance by the planter. Even from the earliest period of occupation, houses were arranged in a cluster pattern that appears to have been organized as to maximize airflow into and around the houses. For example, doorways face into the prevailing winds.

Houses were nearly all built onto the slope of the hill and were relatively easily identified as platforms. The down-slope walls were built up with limestone cobbles, and in places where this angle faced the wind we were able to identify steps leading into each house (Armstrong 1990, 1991a). Houses varied in structure from one to three rooms and ranged in size from 3 × 4 meters to 3 × 8 meters. Several of the houses had flooring made of small cobbles of limestone and/or crushed limestone (marl). The foundations yielded indications of the presence of posts spaced out at even intervals with larger holes, suggesting larger posts in the corners and around the doorways. Internal partitions for room divisions were observable as smaller round postholes. We could also differentiate between the types of flooring used in each room.

While the house structures were where we began our investigations, excavation took place both inside and outside the houses. The result was the definition of definitive patterns in the use of houses and yard space. Much of the activities of each household took place in the yard behind the houses. Each yard had at least one hearth, marked by burned areas and sets of three or more stones grouped together to facilitate cooking using round-bottomed earthenware and (later) iron pots.

The material record from Drax Hall provided a pattern that reflected both continuity and change (Armstrong 1990). Elements of African-based knowledge were embedded in the use of locally produced earthenware cooking pots (Figure D.3) and in communal eating practices involving soups and stews. Personal items included cowry shells and beads, and the configuration and use of external space in the house-yard compounds is loosely associated with West African living practices, in sharp contrast to European practices at that time both in Europe and the Caribbean. Even though the majority of manufactured artifacts found at the site were imports from Europe, what they used and how they used them were quite distinct. They bear evidence of reworking (for example, gun flints retouched into flints for strike-a-lights) and use based on local needs (Armstrong 1990).

Figure D.2. House Area 1 of the African Jamaican village at Drax Hall, Jamaica. Photo by Douglas V. Armstrong.

There was a preference for bowls over plates throughout the history of the site (again a reflection of the consumption of stews, or "pepper pot" dietary practices). Local reuse of goods included reworked European and local pottery to create pieces used in games of chance. The Drax Hall study clearly demonstrated an array of local practices and lifeways that reflected the emergence of a locally based and internally defined African Jamaican community.

One of the initial problems of the study was the absence of data sets from the Caribbean that we could use for comparison. Thus, our interpretation of the significance of what we found was phrased as a "probability of specific practices." Now that a wide body of comparative data exists, nearly all of these initial observations have been confirmed as definitive expressions of life and internal social dynamics in African Jamaican and Caribbean enslaved communities. Perhaps the most significant element of the study (yet one that is often overlooked) is the detailed dietary analysis that combines historical records and archaeological findings to report on unusual aspects of the slave diet. (Elizabeth Reitz assisted with this study.) We identified a diet that included imported cod fish (evidence found only in the account books for the estate) and cattle culled from the planta-

tion's stock (evidence found in the archaeological record that was confirmed by account books that showed both the purchase of cattle and the practice of culling cattle for food). After emancipation, those who remained on the estate felt the loss of estate provisions (cod and cattle). Their diet shows evidence of a diverse starvation-style use of all available local marine shellfish (including a wide range of small mollusks that included many species of nerites). These dietary data indicate not only the range of diet, the cuts of meat that were consumed, and food preparation practices but also the fact that after emancipation the laborers had a difficult time finding enough food to eat.

While there are many other key findings, I will conclude with an observation made on changes in the cultural landscape that appear over time in the archaeological record. By the mid-eighteenth century, ownership of the plantation had changed hands and William Beckford had become the absentee owner. Soon thereafter, there was a major change in the organization of space on the estate. The works, along with the manager's house, were moved to the center of the cane fields and an aqueduct was built to carry water to this central industrial location. With this shift, the workers were less directly supervised, and over time many moved their houses down

Figure D.3. Afro-Jamaican earthenware from Drax Hall, Jamaica. Photo by Douglas V. Armstrong.

the hill and adjacent to the aqueduct and its supply of fresh water. As a result, we find that this later period is marked by larger yard areas and greater distances between houses. After emancipation, the village was gradually abandoned, but the relatively newer houses adjacent to the aqueduct were the last to be abandoned.

When the initial study of the enslaved laborer settlement was completed, Armstrong returned to Jamaica to direct a combined project that included participants from The University of the West Indies, the Jamaica National Heritage Trust field school, and the University of California, Los Angeles (UCLA). This project, which was known as the First African Jamaican Archaeological Field School, took place in January and March of 1983. Of note was the composition of this field program. Armstrong brought fellow UCLA doctoral student Kofi Agorsah to co-direct the program. E. Kofi Agorsah returned to Jamaica after the project to join the Department of History and Archaeology at The University of the West Indies, Mona (Jamaica) as its first archaeologist. Project staff included Paul Farnsworth and Christopher DeCorse (both then doctoral students at UCLA) and George A. Aarons and Roderick Ebanks (both of the Jamaica National Heritage Trust). The University of the West Indies faculty who participated on the project included Barry Higman, Patrick Bryan, and Neville Hall from the Department of History. Among the students who participated were Verene Shepherd, Dorrick Gray, and Basil Reid, all of whom have

gone on to have distinguished careers in Caribbean archaeological and historical studies.

Further Reading

Armstrong, D. V. 1983a. "The Drax Hall Slave Settlement: Site Selection Procedures." In *Proceedings of the 9th International Congress for the Study of Pre-Columbian Cultures of the Lesser Antilles, Santo Domingo, Dominican Republic*, 431–42. Montreal: Centre de Recherches Caraibes, University de Montreal.

———. 1983b. "The 'Old Village' at Drax Hall Plantation: An Archaeological Examination of an Afro-Jamaican Settlement." PhD diss., University of California, Los Angeles.

———. 1985. "An Afro-Jamaican Slave Settlement: Archaeological Investigations at Drax Hall." In *The Archaeology of Slavery and Plantation Life*, ed. Theresa Singleton, 261–87. New York: Academic Press.

———. 1990. *The Old Village and the Great House: An Archaeological and Historical Examination of Drax Hall Plantation, St. Ann's Bay, Jamaica*. Urbana: University of Illinois Press.

———. 1991a. "The Afro-Jamaican House-Yard: An Archaeological and Ethnohistorical Perspective." *Florida Journal of Anthropology Special Publication* 7: 51–63

———. 1991b. "An Archaeological Study of the Afro-Jamaican Community at Drax Hall." *Jamaica Journal* 24 (1): 3–8.

See also Afro-Caribbean Earthenwares; La Reconnaissance Site (Trinidad); The Seville Sugar Plantation (British Colonial Jamaica).

Duerden, J. E. (1869–1937)

Ivor Conolley

James Edwin Duerden, usually referred to in texts as J. E. Duerden, was born in Yorkshire, England, in 1869. He received his academic qualifications in zoology from the Royal College of Science, London, in 1889 and was appointed a Bruce Fellow at John Hopkins University, Baltimore, Maryland, in 1901. Duerden took positions in Ireland, the United States, Jamaica, South Africa, and England. He developed an interest in marine biology research from his first appointment, at the Royal College of Science in Dublin, where he served as a demonstrator in biology and paleontology. This interest continued in Jamaica, where he held the position of curator of the Institute of Jamaica Museum from 1895 to 1901, where he made benchmark contributions to Jamaican archaeology (Figure D.4).

During his tenure as curator of the Museum of the Institute of Jamaica, Duerden conducted research and published journal articles on actinians, hydroids, polyzoa, and corals. His outstanding work in marine biology in Ireland and Jamaica earned him recognition as an authority on the subject. His work in archaeology at the Institute of Jamaica became a valuable legacy to Jamaican archaeology, as he was engaged in island-wide surveys and studies of the native Jamaicans, the Taíno. Following this research, Duerden mounted the first known exhibit of precolonial "aboriginal Indian" artifacts in Jamaica. The publication associated with this exhibition, "Aboriginal Indian Remains in Jamaica" (Duerden 1897), was not just a report of the exhibit but was also the culmination of this island-wide research, which Duerden had been given a year to conduct. In 1900, the colonial government in Jamaica reviewed the operations and expenditures of the Institute of Jamaica and eliminated the full-time post of curator. This resulted in Duerden's release when his contract expired the following year.

Subsequently, the Carnegie Institute of Washington granted him facilities for research in recognition of the value of his marine expertise. His next position was that of associate professor at the University of Michigan, but soon after, in 1905, he took up a professorial appointment at Rhodes University, South Africa, where he remained for twenty-seven years, until his retirement in 1932. In South Africa, Duerden focused his research on ostriches and sheep, once again becoming recognized as an authority for his contributions to the field. During this time, he commenced pioneer work on the skin and

Figure D.4. James Edwin Duerden (1869–1937). Courtesy of Professor J. Peires.

fleece of South African Merino sheep, which he continued on his retirement in Leeds, England. He was active up to his death in 1937.

Further Reading

Daily Gleaner. 1896. "Institute of Jamaica." November 18. Institute of Jamaica Letter Boxes and Press Clippings, National Library of Jamaica.

Duerden, J. E. 1897. "Aboriginal Indian Remains in Jamaica." *Journal of the Institute of Jamaica* 2 (4): 1–52.

Jamaica Post. 1896. "The Missing Brochure." November 16. Institute of Jamaica Letter Boxes and Press Clippings, National Library of Jamaica.

Nature. 1937. "Prof. J. E. Duerden." *Nature* 140 (October 2): 576. http://www.nature.com/nature/journal/v140/n3544/abs/140576a0.html. Accessed November 14, 2012.

See also The Institute of Jamaica; Jamaica (Prehistory of).

Duhos (Dujos)

Joshua M. Torres

Duhos are ceremonial or ritual seats (Ostapkowicz 1997) that are primarily constructed of wood or stone. *Duhos* are represented as anthropomorphic and zoomorphic figures in which the leg appendages serve as the legs of the stool and the heads often protrude from the center of the front of the stool and the genitalia are on the underside of the back of the stool. *Duhos* were status items imbued with powerful symbology, personalities, and histories that set their owners apart from the rest of the community and were a central part of the *cohoba* ritual repertoire (Oliver 2009) As such, these items were generally attributable to the elite and represent the materialization of social practices associated with the veneration of those of status and rank. *Duhos* are primarily associated with Taíno groups in the northern Caribbean.

Two major types of *duhos* have been identified: those with backs and those without backs (Figure D.5). The use of *duhos* (without backs) as seats is questionable, as they may have actually functioned as elaborate serving platters. Geographically, the highest frequency of documented *duhos* comes from Puerto Rico and Hispaniola, although several examples have been recovered from the Turks and Caicos and the Bahamas and a few rare specimens have been recovered from Cuba and Jamaica. The largest number of *duhos* was recovered from Cartwright Cave on Long Island in the Bahamas.

Most *duhos* are carved from wood, although some are made from coral or stone. In the Dominican Republic, wooden examples are prevalent. Wooden *duhos* are often made of dense wood known as Guayacan (*Lignum vitae*). In Puerto Rico, stone *duhos* dominate the archaeological record, although many wooden examples have also been recovered from the island. The facial features and shoulders of *duhos* are often deeply carved to allow for inlays of gold or bone.

Further Reading

Oliver, J. R. 2008. "El universo material y espiritual de los taínos." In *El Caribe precolombino Fray Ramón Pané y el Uni-*

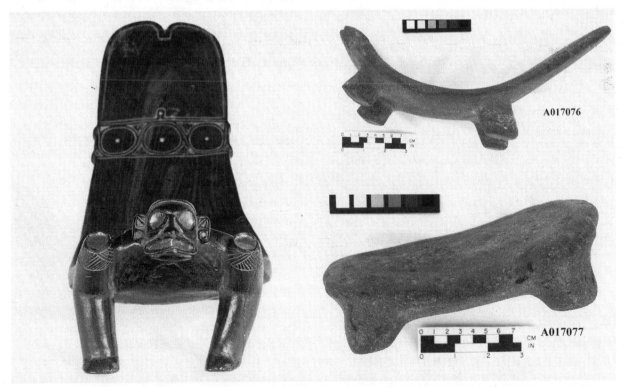

Figure D.5. *Left*, classic wooden *duho* with inlays of gold. Height: 22 cm; width: 43.8 cm; Dominican Republic. Photo © Trustees of the British Museum. *Top right*, profile of stone *duho* recovered from Puerto Rico. Photo: cat. A17076, Department of Anthropology, Smithsonian Institution. *Bottom right*, profile of a small stone backless *duho*, also from Puerto Rico. Photo: cat. A17077, Department of Anthropology, Smithsonian Institution.

verso *Taíno*, ed. J. R. Oliver, C. McEwan, and A. Casas Gilberga, 136–201. Barcelona: Ministerio de Cultura.

———. 2009. *Caciques and Cemí Idols: The Web Spun by Taíno Rulers between Hispanola and Puerto Rico.* Tuscaloosa: University of Alabama Press.

Ostapkowicz, J. M. 1997. "To Be Seated with 'Great Courtesy and Veneration': Contextual Aspects of the Taíno Duho." In *Taíno: Pre-Columbian Art and Culture from the Caribbean*, ed. F. Bercht, 56–67. New York: Monacelli Press.

See also Chiefdoms (*Cacicazgos*); *Cohoba*; Zemíes (*Cemís*).

The Dutch Caribbean

Jay B. Haviser

L. E. Bosch's 1836 descriptions of rock art at Fontein, Aruba, constitute the oldest records of prehistoric remains in the Dutch Caribbean. The most important research in the nineteenth century was completed by Father A. J. van Koolwijk, who assembled a rich collection of artifacts in the period 1870–1886 in the Leeward Islands of Curaçao, Aruba, and Bonaire. During that period, he found Amerindian shells, earthenware fragments, and stone artifacts. He also examined native rock art. His collection was sent to Leiden University in the Netherlands. Van Koolwijk's collection drew the attention of Prof. J. P. B. de Josselin de Jong, the curator of the National Museum for Ethnology at Leiden. In 1923, De Josselin de Jong was the first to identify prehistoric locations in St. Maarten, St. Eustatius, and Saba. During his time, his work was the best example of applied archaeological research in the Dutch Caribbean. In the 1920s, De Josselin de Jong conducted surveys on all six Dutch Caribbean islands; some of this work involved excavations. His published works provided well-documented descriptions of all of the sites and artifacts he encountered. However, he avoided making any interpretations of the lifeways of the prehistoric peoples whose remains he described. The majority of the artifacts De Josselin de Jong recovered were shipped to Leiden University in the Netherlands, while a few returned to the Antilles in the 1980s.

The early 1940s to about 1960 marked a transitional period for the field of archaeology in the Americas, which was becoming more anthropological in nature, and was placing greater emphasis on new contextual-functional approaches. In the Dutch Caribbean, this period was ushered in by a Dutch archaeological team led by H. R. van Heekeren and C. J. Du Ry in 1960. Wagenaar Hummelinck (a rock art expert), J. Tacoma (a physical anthropologist), and Du Ry and Van Heekeren were the primary archaeologists working in the Dutch Antilles at this time. Toward the end of the 1960s, José Cruxent and Irving Rouse published an overview of the status of archaeological research in the Netherland Antilles. Cruxent visited Curaçao and Aruba in 1965 and identified some historical archaeological sites. In 1965, he processed the first radiocarbon dates for historical archaeology sites on Curaçao, providing a date of 1610 for the Spanish-period Gaito site.

During the 1950s and 1960s, P. Brenneker, E. Juliana, and C. Engels made extensive amateur collections of ethnographic materials relating to Curaçao. The Engels collection forms the basis for the Curaçao Museum exhibits, while the majority of the Brenneker and Juliana collections are currently in the possession of the National Archaeological Anthropological Memory Management Foundation (NAAM). To date, the Brenneker and Juliana collections are the largest ethnographic artifact collections for the island. These collections remain an important reference for material culture research in Curaçao.

Beginning in the 1960s, archaeology in the Dutch Caribbean changed from a descriptive to a more analytical science. During the 1960s and 1970s, P. Glazema, P. Wagenaar-Hummelinck, J. Cruxent, and E. Boerstra were engaged in scientific archaeology in the Dutch Caribbean. In 1967, the Archaeological-Anthropological Institute of the Netherlands Antilles (AAINA) was founded, with Edwin N. Ayubi as director. In 1976, E. Boerstra was hired, and W. Nagelkerken and J. Haviser were both hired in 1981. This led to an expansion of the archaeological institute, and the department for cultural anthropology was placed under the leadership of Rosemary Allen. The institute made major contributions to scientific research and increased public awareness of archaeology in the Dutch Caribbean. During these decades, AAINA began to implement a more multidisciplinary approach involving the integration of geology, biology, and physical anthropology into archaeological research. Major scholars involved in this methodology included P. de Buisonje, H. Coomans, S. Gould, D. Hooijer, J. Tacoma, and E. Wing. During the 1980s, AAINA assisted with the founding of the Curaçao Rock Drawings Working Group, a group of amateur archeologists.

On St. Eustatius, a College of William and Mary archaeological research program under the direction of Norman Barka continued both general historical archaeology field schools and specific historical archaeology excavation programs from 1981 to 1998. Archaeological researchers from the University of South Florida had initiated investigations in 1981 but discontinued participation after the 1982 field season. AAINA collaborated with Jay Haviser from 1982 to 1985 in land surveys and mapping. W. Nagelkerken conducted underwater surveys and artifact recovery in Orange Bay. In 1984, AAINA also began research on the prehistory of St. Eustatius. This was jointly undertaken by Aad Versteeg of the Instituut voor Prehistorie of Leiden University, the St. Eustatius Historical Foundation (SEHF), and Jay Haviser of AAINA.

Given that the focus on historical archaeology began on St. Eustatius in 1981, it is ironic that Sint Maarten was given such little attention, considering that one must travel through Sint Maarten to reach St. Eustatius. Eventually, various historical archaeology sites were recorded on Sint Maarten: M. Sypkens-Smit worked there in 1981 and Haviser worked there in 1987. Both of these site listings were part of an overall prehistoric site survey. In 1987, the first extensive historical archaeology excavations were conducted at the Fort Amsterdam site by J. Baart (the city archaeologist for Amsterdam) in collaboration with AAINA. In 1989, Baart conducted further excavations at the Fort Amsterdam site again and did additional surface collections at the Bishop Hill site. In 1989, researchers from the College of William and Mary under the direction of Norman Barka conducted a survey and mapping of the Welgelegen Estate on Sint Maarten. This was followed by surveys and mapping of various historical sites on the Dutch side of the island from 1990 to 1992. Most of these sites were plantation estates of the eighteenth and nineteenth centuries. Underwater survey and mapping directed by K. Bequette was conducted at the *Proselyte* shipwreck site off the coast of Sint Maarten in 1994 and 1995. During the 1994 field season, Bequette and S. Sanders were called upon to make an emergency soil profile drawing of historic burials that were eroding

from a road cut at the Bishop Hill cemetery site. In 1996, Jay Haviser of AAINA conducted an archaeological survey and excavations at the Belvedere Plantation for the government of St. Maarten. In 2006, Menno Hoogland, Corinne Hofman, and Grant Gilmore conducted surveys and excavations at the Bethlehem Plantation site for the property owners. From 1996 to 2010, Jay Haviser conducted numerous historical archaeology investigations on St. Maarten. Since 2007, he has conducted field activity in his capacity as the government archaeologist for St. Maarten.

In 1983, Haviser conducted an island-wide archaeological survey of Saba for AAINA that identified both prehistoric and historic sites (outside the developed residential areas). This survey of Saba included the location and mapping of numerous historical sites and abandoned historic village complexes of the eighteenth through the twentieth centuries. Most had never been mapped before, for example, Mary's Point. Into the late 1980s and 1990s, Corinne Hofman and Menno Hoogland of Leiden University conducted significant prehistoric archaeological investigations at numerous sites on Saba, for which they acquired radiocarbon dates and new site pattern data for the island's prehistory. Both Hofman and Hoogland eventually published their doctoral dissertations at Leiden University based on their Saba research. In 2009, Ryan Espersen conducted archaeological research at the Mary's Point settlement on Saba.

The types of sites investigated on Curaçao using historical archaeology in the 1980s and 1990s were quite variable. Professional archaeological research on Curaçao was primarily conducted by AAINA, beginning in 1982 with an island-wide land survey of prehistoric and historic sites. One result of this investigation was the eventual publication in 1987 of a doctoral dissertation by Jay Haviser at Leiden University on prehistoric sites of Curaçao. The historic sites Haviser first reported in this survey were mostly of the protohistoric period. AAINA conducted excavations at the San Hironimo site on Curaçao. In 1990, Haviser and N. Brito conducted archaeological tests over much of the urban Punda district on Curaçao. This was followed in 1991 by excavations at the Zuurzak site by Haviser. Zuurzak is believed to be a Dutch slave camp from the late seventeenth century. In 1995, Haviser conducted a historical archaeology field survey and excavations at a slave period and post-emancipation African settlement in the Kenepa area of Curaçao for AAINA. Beginning in 1988, W. Nagelkerken conducted various underwater historical archaeology investigations on Curaçao for AAINA. These studies included general underwater surveys of the bays on the south coast, underwater mapping and excavations of the 1778 shipwreck *Alphen* in Santa Anna Bay, and underwater surveys and excavations along the wharf area of Handelskade in the commercial Punda district. Since the creation of the NAAM in 1999, various archaeological investigations have taken place on Curaçao. Since 2003, under the direction of Ieteke Witteveen of the NAAM, an amateur Archaeology Work Group, led by Andre Rancuret, Jose DaCamara, and Francois van der Hoeven, has recorded archaeological site locations on the island. In 2010, researchers from Leiden University conducted surveys and excavations of prehistoric sites at Spaanse Water, under the direction of Corinne Hofman and Menno Hoogland.

On Bonaire, archaeology was initially conducted by Haviser for AAINA in 1988 as part of a larger study of the cultural history of Amerindians. AAINA conducted an extensive historical archaeology investigation at Fort Oranje, Bonaire, in 1997, and Haviser and A. Sealy published the results of this research. In 2007, archaeological excavations were conducted by the Bonaire Archaeological Institute (BONAI) at a World War II military camp on Bonaire under Haviser's supervision. The most recent archaeological work on Bonaire, which was done in 2010, is the result of collaboration between BONAI and Leiden University.

In 1998, AAINA was shifted from full government service to become a government-sponsored foundation called the National Archaeological Anthropological Museum. The artifacts, which had hitherto been in AAINA's custody, were transferred to the museum. The decentralization of archaeological research in the Dutch Caribbean started with the creation of the Archaeological Museum of Aruba in 1981.

Beginning in 2000, archaeological research on St. Eustatius was done by the St. Eustatius Center for Archaeological Research (SECAR). In 2004, R. Grant Gilmore published his doctoral dissertation on the historical archaeology of St. Eustatius, and since 2004, Gilmore has led the SECAR project. In order to stimulate local involvement in archaeology, especially that of young people, Jay Haviser founded BONAI in 2003. In 2005, Haviser founded the Sint Maarten Archaeological Center (SIMARC) on St. Maarten, and in 2012 he founded the Saba Archaeological Center (SABARC) on Saba.

In October 2010, the Netherlands Antilles were dismantled and reformulated into four autonomous entities within the Kingdom of the Netherlands: The Netherlands, Aruba, Curaçao, and St. Maarten. The smaller islands of Bonaire, St. Eustatius, and Saba were absorbed into the Netherlands and given the status of municipalities.

Further Reading

Ayubi, E., E. Boerstra, and A. Versteeg. 1985. "Archeologie." In *Encyclopedie van de Nederlandse Antillen II*, ed. J. de Palm. Zutphen: Walburg Pers.

Haviser, J. 1987. *Amerindian Cultural Geography on Curaçao*. Amsterdam: Natuurweteschappelijke Studiekring voor Suriname en de Nederlandse Antillen.

———. 1991. *The First Bonaireans*. Curaçao: Archaeological-Anthropological Institute of the Netherlands Antilles.

Hofman, C. 1993. "In Search of the Native Population of Pre-Columbian Saba (400–1450 AD)." PhD diss., Leiden University, the Netherlands.

Hofman, C., and M. Hoogland, eds. 1999. *Archaeological Investigations of St. Martin (Lesser Antilles)*. Leiden: Faculty of Archaeology, Leiden University.

Versteeg, A. H., and S. Rostain, eds. 1997. *The Archaeology of Aruba: The Tanki Flip Site*. Oranjestad, Aruba: Archaeological Museum Aruba.

Versteeg, A. H., and K. Schinkel, eds. 1992. *The Archaeology of St. Eustatius: The Golden Rock Site*. St. Eustatius: St. Eustatius Historical Foundation.

See also Bonaire Archaeological Institute (BONAI); Curaçao (Former Netherlands Antilles); Foundation for Marine Archaeology of the Netherlands Antilles (STIMANA); The National Archaeological Anthropological Memory Management Foundation (NAAM); Saba; Sint Maarten (Former Netherlands Antilles); St. Eustatius; St. Eustatius Center for Archaeological Research (SECAR); St. Eustatius Historical Foundation.

Dutch Colonial Ceramic Types

R. Grant Gilmore III

Dutch ceramics are dominated throughout the colonial Caribbean by two types—tin-glazed earthenwares and lead-glazed coarse earthenwares. Dutch tin-glazed earthenwares suffer the same nomenclature identity crises as those produced elsewhere in Europe and thus have been mislabeled "Delftware" by many practitioners. In reality, these tin-lead oxide-glazed, soft-bodied, refined earthenwares were produced in many areas in the Netherlands other than Delft, including Amsterdam, Den Haag, and Haarlem. The rarest but most widely known Dutch tin-enamel ceramic types on Caribbean archaeological sites are tiles that were produced starting in the sixteenth century. They continue to be produced today. These tiles varied in size and were most often square in shape. Decorations were hand painted using cobalt blue but could also be polychrome. The decorative motifs varied but included nautical themes, hunting scenes, children at play, religious themes, and floral patterns. Similar tiles were also produced in England and are generally discernible from those made in the Netherlands. Dutch tin-enamelware plates, tea cups, and bowls are also commonly found on Caribbean archaeological sites. Another common Dutch tin-enamel vessel type is the chamber pot. These were generally left undecorated and have been found in sizes ranging from those for children to those for adults.

Dutch coarse earthenwares (Figure D.6) have not been studied extensively in the Netherlands or in the Caribbean. In both New York/New Amsterdam and in Cape Colony/South Africa, archaeologists have completed detailed analyses of vessel forms and functions. Coarse earthenwares produced in the Netherlands were primarily utilitarian and are directly descended from Roman types. Cooking pots, storage vessels, *kookpotten* (pipkins), and bowls are common in the Dutch Caribbean and are found occasionally on other islands. Absent from Caribbean collections are dairy wares that are quite commonly found in the Netherlands. This follows the patterns for both New Amsterdam and Cape Colony sites. As with other European coarse earthenwares, surface treatments include slip decoration, lead glazes, and *englobe*. The Dutch *kookpot*, a type of saucepan, is perhaps the most distinctive form found on Caribbean sites. The low cylindrical *kookpot* is larger in diameter than the bulbous seventeenth-century English pipkin and has a pronounced lip that permits a lid to be fitted tightly. Both vessels have three small legs on the bottom surface for keeping the pot above the coals.

Further Reading

Bartels, M. 1999. *Cities in Sherds: Finds from Cesspits in Deventer, Dordrecht, Nijmegen, and Tiel (1250–1900).* Amersfoort/Zwolle: ROB/SPA.

Gaimster, D., ed. 1999. *Maiolica in the North: The Archeology of Tin-Glazed Earthenware in North-West Europe, c. 1500–1600.* London: British Museum Press.

Schaefer, R. G. 1994. "A Typology of Seventeenth-Century Dutch Ceramics and Its Implications for American Historical Archaeology." PhD diss., University of Pennsylvania.

Wilcoxen, C. 1987. *Dutch Trade and Ceramics in America in the Seventeenth Century.* Albany, NY: Albany Institute of History and Art.

See also Afro-Caribbean Earthenwares; English Colonial Ceramic Types; French Colonial Ceramic Types; Spanish Colonial Ceramic Types.

Figure D.6. Dutch earthenwares. Courtesy of R. Grant Gilmore III and SECAR.

East End Free Black Community (St. John)

Douglas V. Armstrong

The archaeological study of the East End Community on St. John, Danish West Indies, provides a detailed examination of the emergence of a Caribbean free black community. Freedom, land ownership, and self-employment (in the maritime trades and in cottage industries) are the dominant life themes the East End Community archaeological studies project (Armstrong 2003a, 2003b). The free black community took advantage of ambiguities in the organization of the Danish colonial structure to gain land ownership in St. John's arid east end. This rural setting contrasts sharply with the conditions of slavery associated with the dominant economic and social structures of the Caribbean during the late eighteenth and early nineteenth centuries. The community developed when a group of five extended families of blacks and whites were forced off Virgin Gorda, British Virgin Islands, in 1754 because they lacked formal title to lands that others wished to develop into sugar estates. They were able to secure communal land ownership on the nearby island of St. John, at Hansen Bay and at Newfound Bay Estates. Perhaps the most significant finding pertains to the multifocal kinship and residential networks of this community (rather than the matrilineal relationships that are often described for the region). The East End community's multifocal social organization was identified through a combination of archaeological and historical analysis (Armstrong 2001, 2003a, 2003b).

By the 1790s, the East End community had emerged as a phenotypic black free settlement that was surviving through a combination of subsistence farming and fishing. They also sold provisions and construction materials to neighboring estates and to the growing port town of Charlotte Amalie, St. Thomas. This community thrived on the margins of plantation society through participation in the maritime trades, boat building, transporting interisland cargoes, and producing fine embroidery work. The fact that they owned the lands on which they lived provided them a safe base for self-employment. Children of community members were allotted small parcels on the community-owned lands to establish their own households. Archaeological evidence indicates the presence of fifty such house sites on the hills above Hansen Bay and Newfound Bay. East Enders had a close affiliation with the Moravian Church, and they placed so high a value on education that they gave land for the construction of a school that became a focal point in their community. Following the transfer of the Danish West Indies to the United States, the new administrators of the islands removed the school, and gradually the small "Tortola sloop"–type sailboats that East End carpenters built and East End mariners used were replaced by motor craft. The fine needlepoint of East End seamstresses was replaced by mass-produced wares and the fast stitchery of the mechanical sewing machine. New industries emerged, including basket production; but the distance that had once insulated this free black community at the far east end of St. John ultimately led to its demise, as its population used their skills in industry and education to take up new lands and trades. By the second decade of the twentieth century, this community was all but abandoned, and the significance of the ruins of small house sites (Figure E.1) that dot the hills of St. John's East End was lost from common memory (Armstrong et al. 2007; Armstrong et al. 2008.

When the island was surveyed for potentially significant historic sites in the 1970s and 1980s, the significance of the East End Community was completely missed. The archaeologists who conducted the surveys were looking for the more substantial ruins of large-scale plantations that related to the dominant form of sugar and the slavery-based economy for the island and region. When archaeologists encountered East End house sites, they misinterpreted what they saw as inconsequential estates. In fact, what they saw was only a small part of the landscape. What they did not consider was the fact that something other than a sugar estate

Figure E.1. East End Windy Hill ruins, St. John. Courtesy of Douglas V. Armstrong.

could have or would have been in operation on the island, and certainly they did not consider the possibility of a free black community.

In 1995, in response to an invitation from Mr. Guy Benjamin, who was born in the East End and who was later a teacher and superintendent of Virgin Islands schools, researchers from Syracuse University initiated a new survey of the area. The initial walk through the area identified at least fifteen distinct house platforms and living areas that included sites that had been old cotton estates from the early 1700s and a large number of small house sites spread out across the hillsides. Formal detailed walking surveys of the hillsides identified fifty of these house sites dating from the mid-eighteenth to the mid-twentieth centuries. The basic core of the community remained in place and thrived through the last years of slavery and into the period of freedom. The community withstood the trauma of a cholera outbreak that affected it and the rest of St. John in the 1750s and 1760s and was able to draw upon the strength of its base and maritime skills to maintain and even expand the community after the epidemic. A key factor in the community's survival in the late nineteenth century was the construction of the East End School. Education was a priority within the community, and all community children were enrolled and in attendance at the school at Emmaus Estate prior to the cholera outbreak of the mid-

1850s. When travel was restricted because of the epidemic, the community built a school on their own lands. The school, along with the maritime activities in Hanson Bay, became the center of activities in the community. The settlement was gradually abandoned after the Danish Islands were transferred to the United States, and the local school was closed. Many St. Johnians today trace their ancestry and their history of freedom to this community.

Further Reading

Armstrong, D. V. 2001. "A Venue for Autonomy: Archaeology of a Changing Cultural Landscape, the East End Community, St. John, Virgin Islands." In *Island Lives: Plantation Archaeology in the Caribbean*, ed. P. Farnsworth, 142–64. Tuscaloosa: University of Alabama Press.

———. 2003a. *Creole Transformation from Slavery to Freedom: Historical Archaeology of the East End Community, St. John, Virgin Islands*. Gainesville: University Press of Florida.

———. 2003b. "Social Relations in a Maritime Creole Community: Networked Multifocality in the East End Community of St. John, Danish West Indies." In *Proceedings of the XIX International Congress for Caribbean Archaeology*, ed. Luc Alofs and Raymundo A. C. F. Dijkhoff, 194–210. Aruba: Archaeological Museum Aruba.

———. 2006. "East End Maritime Traders: The Emergence of a Creole Community on St. John, Danish West Indies." In *African Re-Genesis: Confronting Social Issues in the Diaspora,*

ed. Jay Haviser and Kevin MacDonald, 146–59. London: University College.

Armstrong, D. V., and M. Hauser. 2005. "Reassessing the Cultural Landscape of St. John, USVI, Using GIS." In *Actas del XX Congreso International de Arqueologia del Caribe*, ed. Manuel García Arévalo and Clenis Tavárez María, 515–20. Santo Domingo, Dominican Republic: [Museo del Hombre].

Armstrong, D. V., M. W. Hauser, D. W. Knight, and S. Lenik. 2008. "Maps, *Matricals*, and Material Remains: Archaeology of Late Eighteenth-Century Historic Sites on St. John,

Danish West Indies." In *Archaeology and Geoinformatics: Case Studies from the Caribbean*, ed. Basil A Reid, 99–126. Tuscaloosa: University of Alabama Press.

Armstrong, D. V., M. W. Hauser, S. Lenik, and K. Wild. 2007. "Estate Consolidation, Land Use, and Ownership: A GIS Archaeological Landscape Survey of St. John." In *Proceedings of the Twenty-Fourth Congress of the International Association of Caribbean Archaeology*, ed. Basil Reid, Henry Petitjean Roget, and Antonio Curet, 1:69–80. St. Augustine, Trinidad and Tobago: School of Continuing Studies, University of the West Indies.

The Elenan Ostionoid Subseries

L. Antonio Curet

The Elenan Ostionoid subseries, originally known as Elenoid series (Rouse 1964), was defined by Rouse (1992) as the first post-Saladoid subseries for eastern Puerto Rico and the Virgin Islands. Rouse also includes the Leeward Islands as far south as Antigua in this subseries, but not everyone agrees with this categorization. A general trend in simplification of the pottery assemblage began toward the end of the Saladoid series, eventually leading to the Elenan Ostionoid subseries. The most observable change in Elenan ceramics is a marked decrease in aesthetics (both in stylistic complexity and aesthetic priority) and in craftsmanship (Figure E.2). Saladoid ceramics tend to have finer paste, thinner walls, and a more refined appearance than Elenan Ostionoid ceramics. Another change was the gradual loss of paint and slip from the Saladoid to the Elenan Ostionoid, to the point that by the end of the latter period, the main forms of decoration were plastic in nature, including vertical incisions perpendicular to the rim of the vessels, biomorphic adornos or handles, and appliqués. Thus, the tendency in ceramics is of workmanship degradation and a reduction in the use of symbolic decoration in pottery designs. These gradual but significant changes have been described as a "de-evolution" by Roe, and the later ceramic styles as the "Dark Ages" of the Greater Antilles by Rouse (Roe 1989; Rouse 1982). Although post-Saladoid pottery is less appealing to the eye, physical analysis suggests that its manufacture is better suited for utilitarian uses. The traditional dates for this subseries as defined by Rouse are AD 600 to 1200, but recent evidence suggests that it may have lasted longer than that.

In Puerto Rico, while the Elenan subseries of the Ostionoid is composed of only one style named Magens

Bay-Salt River I, in Puerto Rico it is traditionally divided into the Monserrate (AD 600–900) and Santa Elena (AD 900–1200) styles. However, the ceramic trends of the Magens Bay-Salt River I mimic the trends observed in Puerto Rico (Lundberg 2007). During the early style of this subseries (that is, the Monserrate style) some of the technology and vessel forms of the final Saladoid pottery were retained, including the tabular lugs, strap handles, and red-painted and slipped ceramics, while a limited number of other kinds of decoration were added. The persistence of a few Saladoid traits into the early part of the Elenan Ostionoid subseries makes the assignment

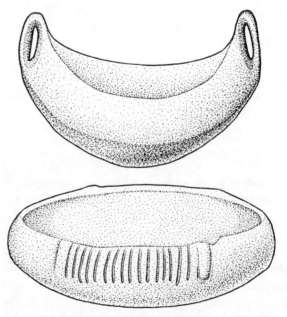

Figure E.2. Example of Elenan Ostionoid pottery. Drawings by Jill Seagard. Courtesy of L. Antonio Curet.

of this pottery to one or the other series very difficult, since there is no clear break in the ceramic trend. The distinction between the series becomes clearer at a later date, when the Monserrate style is characterized by large amounts of plain and red-slipped pottery, in contrast to the more varied and prevalent decoration of the previous Saladoid series. In general, the Monserrate ceramics are thicker, coarser, and rougher and the shapes are simple. Vessels tend to have outcurving sides, although incurving shapes start to increase in number. In addition, incised designs become less common and red-painted designs are still present. Black, negative, and smudging designs can also be found. Biomorphic modeled handles are common, especially the "monkey" heads that actually represent bat heads.

During the second half of this series (i.e., the Santa Elena style), more drastic changes in ceramic decoration and technological attributes occurred. Perhaps the most significant change is that the Santa Elena style shows a return to the practices of modeling and incision, including zoomorphic (especially bat heads) and anthropomorphic handles. The style also shows a gradual increase in the number of thicker, coarser, and rougher ceramics; the almost complete absence of red paint and slip; and simpler shapes (incurving bowls). Most of the decoration is restricted to crude, vertical, rectilinear incisions close to the rims of bowls, frequently accompanied by appliqué strips.

Other than ceramics, the material culture of the Elenan Ostionoid subseries includes the presence of religious and high-status objects made of stone and shell. The three-pointed *zemíes* found first in the Saladoid series are still present at this time, but many of them are larger. This has been interpreted as an indication that this type of idol was being used not only at the individual or household level but also in larger communal ceremonies. Other shell and stone objects include personal ornaments/idols and (according to some scholars) possible stone collars. Moreover, inhalers and vomit spatulas made of bone have been found in Elenan deposits. These, combined with the discovery of wood of the *cohoba* at the Elenan ceremonial center of Tibes, strongly suggest that the *cohoba* ceremony for contacting the supernatural, as described in early European documents, was also an important component of religious rituals during this time.

Other dramatic changes are observed in the archaeological record of the Elenan Ostionoid subseries of eastern Puerto Rico. During this time there were obvious changes in settlement patterns and a sharp increase in the number of sites and in population size, mostly during the second half of the period, or the Santa Elena style. As a matter of fact, the Elenan subseries seems to have had the largest population in pre-Hispanic times in Puerto Rico. Moreover, while some Elenan sites are circular, nucleated villages (similar to Saladoid settlements); other types of settlements were also present, such as medium and small sites (e.g., farmsteads and homesteads) and ceremonial centers. This period also shows a more diverse distribution of sites, including lineal sites along the coasts or rivers; dispersed settlement patterns of small sites, perhaps representing farmsteads or single households; and centralized settlement patterns that featured a large site in the center and smaller ones surrounding it. Interestingly, while most Saladoid sites were located close to the coasts and water streams, Elenan people seem to have diversified their exploitation of resources to other habitats, including mangroves, savannahs, foothills, and mountain forests.

Although few houses belonging to this subseries have been unearthed, there are indications that house size decreased through time, suggesting a shift from the multifamily structures reported for the Saladoid to single or

Figure E.3. Aerial view of the Tibes Indigenous Ceremonial Center, Ponce, Puerto Rico. Reproduced by permission of the Centro Indígena de Tibes, Ponce, Puerto Rico.

nuclear family houses. Furthermore, changes in mortuary practices have been reported, at least for Puerto Rico. Whereas clustered Saladoid burials have been found, especially around the central clearing of the settlement, Elenan Ostionoid burials seem to have been distributed throughout the site, in many instances within the context of the domestic unit. An increase in communal ritualism is also indicated by the development of ball courts and plazas. These are circular, rectangular, or square leveled areas that are bounded by stone rows or "causeways." Although single examples of these structures are found in many sites in southern Puerto Rico, some locations known as ceremonial centers show a multiplicity of them, as at the site of Tibes, Ponce (Figure E.3). In few cases, petroglyphs can be found in some of the stones in the structures, but these tend to be simpler and smaller than the ones of the next period (i.e., the Chican Ostionoid subseries).

The intensity and nature of all the changes observed in the archaeological record have led many archaeologists to argue that they are strongly related to sociopolitical changes from which institutionalized social stratification emerged. This may have set the foundations for the *cacicazgo* political system of the later Chican Ostionoid subseries (AD 1200–1500) that was reported by Europeans.

Further Reading

Curet, L. A. 1996. "Ideology, Chiefly Power, and Material Culture: An Example from the Greater Antilles." *Latin American Antiquity* 7 (2): 114–31.

Curet, L. A., and L. M. Stringer, eds. 2010. *Tibes: People, Power, and Ritual at the Center of the Cosmos.* Tuscaloosa: University of Alabama Press.

Curet, L. A., J. M. Torres, and M. Rodríguez. 2004. "Political and Social History of Eastern Puerto Rico: The Ceramic Age." In *The Late Ceramic Age in the Eastern Caribbean*, ed. A. Delpuech and C. Hofman, 59–85. Oxford: British Archaeological Reports.

Lundberg, E. 2007. "A Monserrate Component in the Virgin Islands in the Context of Inquiry into the Saladoid-Ostionoid Transition." In *The Proceedings of the Twenty-First Congress of the International Association for Caribbean Archaeology*, ed. B. Reid, H. Petitjean Roget, and L. A. Curet, 1:338–46. St. Augustine, Trinidad and Tobago: School of Continuing Studies, University of the West Indies.

Roe, Peter G. 1989. "A Grammatical Analysis of Cedrosan Saladoid Vessel Form Categories and Surface Decoration: Aesthetic and Technical Styles in Early Antillean Ceramics." In *Early Ceramic Population Lifeways and Adaptive Strategies in the Caribbean*, ed. P. E. Siegel, 267–382. Oxford: British Archaeological Reports.

Rouse, Irving. 1964. "Prehistory of the West Indies." *Science* 144 (3618): 499–513.

———. 1982. "Ceramic and Religious Development in the Greater Antilles." *Journal of New World Archaeology* 5: 45–55.

———. 1992. *The Tainos: Rise and Decline of the People Who Greeted Columbus.* New Haven, CT: Yale University Press.

See also The Chican Ostionoid Subseries; Chiefdoms (*Cacicazgos*); *Cohoba*; Duhos (*Dujos*); Origins of Indigenous Groups in the Northern Caribbean; Plazas and *Bateys*; The Saladoid.

Elite Exchange in the Caribbean

Basil A. Reid and L. Antonio Curet

Elite exchange can be defined as gift-giving among elite groups with the purpose of building alliances locally and regionally. This is an important strategy that many forms of leadership, including chiefdoms, use to acquire, solidify, and maintain power. In the Caribbean, elite exchange was part of an extensive and complicated network of interaction that included the movement of prestige and exotic goods, esoteric knowledge, and spouses from polity to polity and island to island. Trading of exotic items, for example, was part of the chief's elite exchange network, which helped to build regional alliances among trading partners. Only a few of the many trade goods that ethnohistorical accounts report as being traded in the Caribbean are preserved in archaeological contexts. Ethnohistorical accounts mention such items as parrots, feathers, raw and woven cotton, carved wood, shell "ornaments," stone carvings, gold, and *guanín* (a gold-copper alloy). Many of these objects were valued not only for the material they were made of or their craftsmanship but also because they were considered to be imbued with supernatural power. Objects of this kind were known as *zemíes*, and the general cult associated with them is known as *zemíeism*. Oliver (2009) argues that chiefs from the Greater Antilles gave portable *zemíes* to leaders from other polities as far south as the Lesser Antilles. The trade objects that are most evident archaeologically are the elaborate ceramics, such as anthropomorphic (or human-like) and zoomorphic (or animal-like) effigy bottles and carved stone objects (Wilson 1990). Elaborate ceramics, probably from Hispaniola, appear as trade items in Cuba, Jamaica, Puerto Rico and the Bahamas. They are often marked with repetitive and highly stylized artistic motifs, suggesting that the goods possessed a greater and more specific symbolic content than that of goods that simply marked social status (Wilson 1990).

In recent times, evidence from the Greater Antilles (Rodríguez Ramos 2011) suggests that elite exchange went well beyond the islands and points to the Isthmus-Colombian region as a place of regular contact. For example, objects made of gold and semi-precious stone found in the Caribbean seem to have been produced using the technology and styles found in regions such as Colombia and Costa Rica. Also, although the ethnohistorical evidence for contact with Mesoamerica is scant, there is some indication of contact between the Greater Antilles and its neighbors in Central America. For example, a version of Popul Vuh (the Mayan creation myth) mentions a possible attack by Caribbean Indians, and in Bernal Diaz's history of the conquest of Mexico there is mention of a Jamaican woman on Cozumel (Wilson 1990).

Contact with Mesoamerica is further suggested by the similarities in the ballgames played both in Mesoamerica and the Greater Antilles, although such games may have spread via South America. While the abundance of beads, pendants, and *zemíes* made from shells, carnelian, and diorite (all of local origin) clearly suggests that there was intra-island lapidary trade on the island of Antigua, the presence of amethyst, nephrite, serpentine, and turquoise (which are not local) imply that trade or exchange existed between Antigua and other parts of the circum-Caribbean and possibly the Americas during the Saladoid (Murphy et al. 2000). In fact, there is increasing evidence for the movement of precolonial peoples, goods, and ideas between the insular Caribbean and the Isthmo-Colombian area (Colombia, Panama, and Costa Rica). Jadeite axes from Antigua recently were sourced to the Motagua Valley in Nicaragua, gold objects have been traced to Colombia, and many of the personal adornments made from shell, stone, and bone have shapes and decorations that are identical to those found at the same time in this region.

The major native valuables exchanged in the southern Caribbean and beyond during European contact included *guanín* ornaments for the ear, nose, and breast; Amazon stones (i.e., animal-shaped, predominantly frog-like pendants and beads made of green-colored rock); and large strings of flat shell beads, known as *uruebe*, or *quiripá*. Pearls were collected at Cubagua and Margarita (Venezuela) and were traded in the interior and along the coast as far as Trinidad and the lower west coast of the Gulf of Paria.

Trading over such long distances was quite possible, given the seaworthiness of native canoes in the Bahamas and Cuba, which Columbus described as being able to comfortably hold 50 to 150 men. Although trade networks seem to have been present since Archaic times, elite exchange seem to have been more extensive during the Ostionoid period in all of the Greater Antilles, the Lesser Antilles, and mainland South and Central America.

Further Reading

Murphy, A. R., D. J. Hozjan, C. N. de Mille, and A. A. Levinson. 2000. "Pre-Columbian Gems and Ornamental Materials from Antigua, West Indies." *Gems and Gemology* 36 (3): 234–45.

Oliver, J. R. 2009. *Caciques and Cemi Idols: The Web Spun by Taíno Rulers between Hispaniola and Puerto Rico*. Tuscaloosa: University of Alabama Press.

Rodriguez Ramos, R. 2011. "Close Encounters of the Caribbean Kind." In *Islands at the Crossroad: Migration, Seafaring, and Interaction in the Caribbean*, ed. L. A. Curet and M. W. Hauser, 164–92. Tuscaloosa: University of Alabama Press.

Wilson, S. M. 1990. *Hispaniola: Caribbean Chiefdoms in the Age of Columbus*. Tuscaloosa: University of Alabama Press.

See also Chiefdoms (*Cacicazgos*); *Guanín*; Lapidary Trade; *Zemíes* (*Cemís*).

English Colonial Ceramic Types

R. Grant Gilmore III

Virtually all ceramic types produced in England during the colonial period can be recovered from Caribbean historical sites because of the consistent pan-Atlantic trade England encouraged. Utilitarian wares, primarily built from coarse earthenware clays, are commonly found. Forms include pipkins (saucepans with three feet and a handle), storage jars, and sugar processing vessels, including drip jars and sugar molds. It is not always common to find English coarse earthenwares at non-English sites because trade restrictions inhibited and sometimes prohibited the importation of these wares into other colonies. In addition, the low profit margins of utilitarian wares would have inhibited indirect trade to non-English colonies.

English stoneware vessel forms included jugs, plates, mugs, chamber pots, and bowls. So-called Fulham stoneware was imported throughout the colonial Caribbean colonies, starting in the 1670s. White salt-glazed stoneware is perhaps the most important English stoneware for dating archaeological sites. It is a very good marker ceramic because it was patented in the 1730s. During the 1750s, white salt-glazed vessels with incised decorations filled with cobalt begin to show up in Caribbean contexts, a form that has come to be known as scratch blue. Cof-

fee mugs and plates are the most common vessel forms recovered from sites. Other stonewares found on Caribbean sites include the dry-bodied red Rosso Antico and black basalts, which were primarily used as teapots.

Stoneware tablewares were eventually replaced by refined earthenwares, which include tin-enamel ware, Whieldon ware, creamware, and pearlware. Vessel forms included tewares, plates, bowls, coffee mugs, candy bowls, serving platters, chamber pots, and pharmaceutical types. The tin-enamel wares (Figure E.4) were produced in many areas of England but especially around London. Decorations sometimes echoed Dutch, French, and Mediterranean motifs, making specific origin attributions difficult without detailed clay body analyses. Whieldonware, creamware, and pearlware dominated refined earthenware production and importation to the Caribbean, beginning in the 1750s, surpassing any competition from other centers of production of European refined earthenware. Pearlware was especially popular during the period 1790–1810. After the 1820s, both whiteware and ironstone dominated the English refined earthenware types found on colonial Caribbean sites; this remained the case through World War II and the postwar independence period.

Figure E.4. Tin-enamel wares. Courtesy of R. Grant Gilmore III and SECAR.

Finally, although the vast majority of porcelains were imported from China (and, rarely, from Japan), English bone china shows up on Caribbean archaeology sites on a regular basis. Archaeologists should be aware of the differences between this china and that produced in France toward the end of the eighteenth century. English imports dominate most excavated Caribbean sites outside of the Spanish colonies. There are exceptions, such as on St. Eustatius, where a vast range of vessel forms and ceramic types reflect the flags of the thousands of trading ships that landed there during the eighteenth century. It is interesting to note that the cuisine on St. Eustatius was influenced by the cosmopolitan nature of their inhabitants and is reflected in the vessels recovered from many sites. Pipkins fell out of use on English sites during the early eighteenth century, evidence of both changing consumption patterns and the availability of iron cooking vessels. On St.

Eustatius, French and Dutch influences are evidenced both in kitchen architecture and the continued use of *koekpotten*/pipkin variants for meals that relied heavily on sauces and soups.

Further Reading

Barka, N. F. 1986. *Archaeology of the Government Guest House, St. Eustatius, Netherlands Antilles: An Interim Report*. Williamsburg, VA: Department of Anthropology, College of William and Mary.

Erickson, M., and R. Hunter. 2001. "Dots, Dashes, and Squiggles: Early English Slipware Technology." In *Ceramics in America 2001*, ed. Robert Hunter, 94–114. Milwaukee: Chipstone Foundation.

Hume, I. N. 1969. *A Guide to Artifacts of Colonial America*. New York: Alfred A. Knopf.

———. 2001. *If These Pots Could Talk: 2,000 Years of British Household Pottery*. Milwaukee: Chipstone Foundation.

Environmental Archaeology

Lee A. Newsom

Introduction

Environmental archaeology (EA) is a subfield of modern anthropological archaeology that emphasizes natural resources, ecology, environment, and related issues from a humanistic perspective. Four primary areas of specialization exist: zooarchaeology, archaeobotany, bioarchaeology, and geo- or pedoarchaeology. Caribbean EA has underpinnings in the research of individuals such as Jesse Fewkes, who wrote as early as 1914 about the potential significance of natural resources and island habitats for aboriginal peoples in the Lesser Antilles. By the 1930s, pathbreaking excavations and research in the Greater Antilles (Haiti, Puerto Rico, and Cuba) by Froelich Rainey (1940) and Irving Rouse (1941, 1986, 1992) included explicit observations about indigenous subsistence practices, based on recovered faunal remains. These scholars focused attention, in particular, on time-transgressive changes in the relative abundances of land crab and shellfish remains, which Rainey and Rouse interpreted as evidence of an apparent dietary shift. This "crab/shell dichotomy" was originally hypothesized to have been the result of food preferences or the cumulative effects of human overexploitation over time. The

faunal assemblages were eventually more fully explained by other scholars, particularly William Keegan (1985), using optimal foraging theory (diet breadth models), which better accounted for the complexity of human-resource interactions and decision making. The various efforts to clarify this issue during the 1960s through 1980s proved especially beneficial to the development of EA research in the region by stimulating some of the first detailed and ecologically informed considerations of foodways and the environmental circumstances of human economic patterns and settlement. This included the first systematic studies of plant and animal remains from Caribbean sites as various specialists became involved in projects to undertake identifications and analyses of the collections. Through this research, Elizabeth S. Wing (1969, 1989, 2008), who was originally trained as a zoologist, initiated scientifically oriented zooarchaeology, ultimately establishing a fully comprehensive program in Caribbean EA at the Florida Museum of Natural History that also incorporated archaeobotany and geoarchaeology. The museum remains an important center for EA research for the Caribbean region.

Zooarchaeology

Wing and others (e.g., Lisabeth Carlson, Susan deFrance, Sandrine Grouard, Yvonne Narganes Storde, Lourdes Pérez Iglesias, and Nathalie Serrand) have since clarified the essential relationship of marine faunal resources to Caribbean human existence throughout all periods of human occupation. They have identified the key foci of indigenous fishing—taxa such as groupers (Serranidae), snappers (Lutjanidae), parrotfish (Scaridae), and particular shellfish—and illuminated the variety and nature of fishing techniques and practices. Harking back to the former idea of a crab/shell dichotomy, this research has indeed revealed evidence of unsustainable practices, such as overfishing that led to adverse effects on land crab populations and predictable shifts in exploitation of fish taxa across trophic levels. However, Caribbean zooarchaeologists have also demonstrated that the fishing enterprise was only part of a much more complex and involved interaction with fauna. For example, muscovy ducks and turtles may have been managed, and capromid rodents (Capromyidae; also known as hutias) were apparently intentionally moved to islands where they were not originally found. Other small animals were evidently intentionally introduced from South America (e.g., agouti, *Dasyprocta leporine*; guinea pig, *Cavia porcellus*; opossum, *Didelphis marsupialis*; and armadillo, *Dasypus novemcinctus*) for reasons that are still debated. The potential significance and roles of these captive fauna in Caribbean indigenous social and economic systems, while still unknown, could certainly have served at least to enhance protein sources in this region, where terrestrial vertebrate fauna were impoverished. There is some suggestion that at least guinea pig presence involved exclusive use by elites, perhaps with ritual connotations, while the other animals may have been allowed to run wild in the islands, enhancing the availability of wild protein sources. Human interaction with domesticated animals besides guinea pig is clear from the presence of dogs; evidence includes dog burials and tooth modification (perhaps for a muzzle or other restraining device). Several additional types of animals, e.g. capuchin monkey (*Cebus* sp.) and macaw (*Ara autochthones*), may also have been kept as companions or pets.

Archaeobotany

Taíno staple crops and some aspects of indigenous *conuco* gardening practices have long been known from ethnohistoric documents. However, in the 1980s, Lee Newsom (1993) and Deborah Pearsall (1989) began to clarify details by initiating archaeobotanical research in the region. Although the first report and potential evidence of *conuco* crops—purported maize kernels (*Zea mays*) from the Sugar Factory site on St. Kitts—turned out to be incorrect, kernels and cob fragments have since been recovered from two late Ceramic (Ostionoid) sites: En Bas Saline, Haiti, and Tutu, St. Thomas, United States Virgin Islands. Intriguing suggestions that maize was multi-cropped exist in the presence of two distinct races at the former site, but there is no indication that maize ever attained the status of a staple food in the region. Root crops appear to have been the focus of food production; at least seven types of root crops are thought to have been grown in the Caribbean just prior to the arrival of Europeans. En Bas Saline is one of few sites to produce macro remains of these crops, including manioc (*Manihot esculenta*) and possibly also sweet potato (*Ipomoea batatas*). Seeds of chili pepper (*Capsicum* sp.), another of the ethnohistorically mentioned crops, were also recovered from En Bas Saline. Maize and the other crops previously mentioned plus a series of important arboreal taxa that have also been identified from Ceramic Age assemblages, including papaya (*Carica papaya*), guanábana (*Annona* sp.), achiote (*Bixa orellana*), and *cojóbilla* (*Anadenanthera* sp.), were introduced from outside the region. Undoubtedly in the Caribbean, as elsewhere, the significance and use of these botanical resources evolved over time. Nevertheless, their continued use in the Caribbean islands over the centuries demonstrates continuity with mainly South American traditions involving agricultural investments, home gardening, and a variety of ethnobotanical practices and ritual and belief systems.

In the 1970s, several Caribbeanists began to speculate in writing about whether plant cultivation and some degree of reliance on domesticated plants could possibly have occurred earlier than the Ceramic Age in the islands. Potential evidence from collections predating about 500 BC was known from the María de la Cruz rock shelter in Puerto Rico, which was excavated in the 1940s by Rouse and Ricardo Alegría, and from Krum Bay, St. Thomas. The rock shelter reportedly yielded wild avocado (*Persea americana*) and yellow sapote (*Pouteria campechiana*), both of which are native to Central America and have had long associations with indigenous home garden production there. Níspero, or sapote (*Manilkara* sp.), seeds from Krum Bay are morphologically consistent with *M. zapota*, a species from Central America that is cultivated for its edible fruit and "chicle" gum. Recently, Jaime Pagán-Jiménez (2009) has provided intriguing support for this hypothesis based on starch grain evidence from sites such as Maruca on

Puerto Rico. These data suggest history of maize and manioc that predates the Ceramic Age in the region and an early presence of common bean (*Phaseolus vulgaris*), sweet potato, and several other potential root crops from South America. The present consensus is that Caribbean subsistence economies before the middle of the first millennium BC extended beyond fishing and foraging to include plant management. Moreover, the relevant archaeobotanical assemblages imply two separate sources of original germplasm: Central America and South America. Pagán-Jiménez's analyses have also revealed the presence of the cycad *Zamia* (marunguey), another edible starch source and one that may represent in situ domestication of a native plant.

Zooarchaeologists and archaeobotanists have also been active with historic period contexts, revealing details of colonial or mestizo maize production, the fusion cuisine and foodways of enslaved peoples on Bahamian plantations, and the introduction of additional crops and domesticated animals from outside the region, for example, tomatoes (*Lycopersicon* sp.) from Mexico and pigs (*Sus scrofa*) from Iberia. Caribbean EA thus has also emerged as a way to elucidate the third major intercontinental transfer of biodiversity affecting the region, the so-called Columbian Exchange.

Recent technological refinements have made possible another relevant development: absorbed organic residues analysis to detect the presence of lipids and water-soluble compounds retained on or within items such as pottery, pipes, inhalers, and other bone or ceramic implements. This avenue of research is providing new insights into prehistoric food production and consumption practices, including feasting behavior, especially when combined with studies of vessel form and function. It is also a way to further elucidate ritual behaviors and practices, revealing both the history and variety of narcotic plants used by Caribbean Amerindians as smoking materials. These include tobacco (*Nicotiana*) and *cojóbilla* (*Anadenanthera*) snuff. Joanna Ostapkowicz (1997, 1998) and Elenora Reber (2012) have been at the forefront of this research. Genetic analysis is the latest addition to the analytical tool kit. One study presently under way involves ancient DNA (aDNA) analysis of bottle gourd (*Lagenaria*) remains.

Bioarchaeology

Bioarchaeology in the Caribbean has clear roots in the work of Adelaide Bullen, for example, her 1970 study of a burial on Saint Lucia. By the 1980s and 1990s, considerably more work was under way by others that incorporated increasingly sophisticated means of analyses. Research conducted on human remains from formal cemeteries (e.g., El Chorro de Maíta, Cuba; Maisabel, Puerto Rico; Anse à la Gourde, Guadeloupe; Malmok, Aruba; St. Michielsberg, Curaçao) and analyses of various isolated burials (e.g., Golden Rock, St. Eustatius) have provided details illuminating human health and nutrition and demographic and other issues, which are further contextualized with evidence for symbolic and ritual behavior, social inequality, and more. William Keegan originated osteochemical research in the region, using stable isotopes analyses of Lucayan Taíno remains from the Bahamas. Biogeochemical analyses have since been increasingly used to clarify information about diet for separate subregions, time periods, and cultures of the region. Most recently, work by Menno Hoogland (Hoogland, Hofman, and Panhuysen, 2010), Ann Ross and Douglas Ubelaker (Ross and Ubelaker 2010), and others involving analysis of skeletal morphometric traits and tooth wear patterns in combination with strontium isotope analysis has provided significant insights into human mobility and migration patterns. Genetic analyses have also been undertaken. Martínez-Cruzado (2010) has worked extensively on human mtDNA lineages in Puerto Rico. That and other research involving aDNA recovered from skeletal material from Hispaniola and Cuba was recently summarized by Schurr (2010). Along with the archaeobotany and zooarchaeology, this kind of research is providing a clearer picture of the shifting balance and baselines for human population in the region, including health and disease transmission, creating a better overall sense of the historical demographics of the region.

Geoarchaeology

Like the other pursuits, geoarchaeology, or pedoarchaeology, includes a range of techniques and scales of analyses. These may include basic soil and sediment research on a single site (e.g., Scudder's [2001] recent work at Tibes, Puerto Rico, which distinguished natural from culturally influenced deposits). On a larger scale, geoarchaeology may involve broader study of the surrounding landscape and regional environment (e.g., Waters and colleagues [1993] on Jamaica). Core sampling focused on discerning both paleoecological trends is increasingly being used in the region, as are Geographic Information Systems methods and technology. These have provided insights into drought history and freshwater availability, vegetation patterns, and various other concerns relevant to human occupation, such as the abandonment of particular islands or portions of islands at particular points in time. The multiproxy paleoecological record generated by Peros and colleagues (2007) from Laguna de la Leche, Cuba, is an outstanding example of modern practice. In this case, a team of EA specialists clarified the effects of relative sea level change and climate change in the context of human settlement dynamics.

Certainly Caribbean EA research has advanced considerably from the time when a crab/shell dichotomy was first discussed. A much-improved understanding of human behavioral ecology and a fairly expansive data base has done much to better contextualize the region's human cultures in terms of their environmental circumstances. Research examining the development of anthropogenic landscapes, including the role of past Caribbean peoples in trophic cascades, is especially relevant today because of the obvious implications for present conditions. We continue to seek a better understanding of the human decision-making process with respect to natural resources and the varied influences of human culture on the region's natural and agricultural biodiversity. EA is a vibrant and active area of research in the Caribbean and will continue to be so for years to come.

Further Reading

Bullen, A. K. 1970. "Case Study of an Amerindian Burial with Grave Goods from Grande Anse, Saint Lucia." In *Proceedings of the Third International Congress for the Study of Pre-Columbian Cultures of the Lesser Antilles, 1969*, 45–60. St. George: Grenada National Museum with the International Association of Caribbean Archaeology.

Fewkes, J. W. 1914. "Relations of Aboriginal Culture and Environment in the Lesser Antilles." *Bulletin of the American Geographical Society* 46 (9): 662–78.

Fitzpatrick, S. M., and A. H. Ross, eds. 2010. *Distant Shores, Distant Pasts: Archaeological and Biological Approaches to the Pre-Columbian Settlement of the Caribbean*. Gainesville: University Press of Florida.

Hofman, C. L., M. L. P. Hoogland, and A. L. van Gijn, eds. 2008. *Crossing the Borders: New Methods and Techniques in the Study of Archaeological Materials from the Caribbean*. Tuscaloosa: University of Alabama Press.

Hoogland, M. L. P., C. L. Hofman, and R. G. A. M. Panhuysen. 2010. "Interisland Dynamics: Evidence for Human Mobility at the Site of Anse à la Gourde, Guadeloupe." In *Island Shores, Distant Pasts: Archaeological and Biological Approaches to the Pre-Columbian Settlement of the Caribbean*, ed. S. M. Fitzpatrick and A. H. Ross, 148–62. Gainesville: University Press of Florida.

Keegan, W. F. 1985. *Dynamic Horticulturalists: Population Expansion in the Prehistoric Bahamas*. PhD diss., University of California, Los Angeles.

Martínez-Cruzado, J. C. 2010. "The History of Amerindian Mitochondrial DNA Lineages in Puerto Rico." In *Island Shores, Distant Pasts: Archaeological and Biological Approaches to the Pre-Columbian Settlement of the Caribbean*, ed. S. M. Fitzpatrick and A. H. Ross, 54–80. Gainesville: University Press of Florida.

Newsom, L. A. 1993. "Native West Indian Plant Use." PhD diss. University of Florida, Gainesville.

Newsom, L. A., and D. A. Trieu. 2011. "Fusion Gardens: Native North America and the Columbian Exchange." In *Subsistence Economies of Indigenous North American Societies: A Handbook*, ed. B. D. Smith, 557–76. Lanham, MD: Rowman and Littlefield.

Newsom, L. A., and E. S. Wing. 2004. *On Land and Sea: Native American Uses of Biological Resources in the West Indies*. Tuscaloosa: University of Alabama Press.

Ostapkowicz, J. 1997. "To Be Seated 'with Great Courtesy and Veneration': Contextual Aspects of the Taíno Duho." In *Taíno: Pre-Columbian Art and Culture from the Caribbean*, ed. F. Brecht, E. Brodsky, J. A. Farmer, and D. Taylor, 55–67. New York: Monacelli Press and Museo del Barrio.

———. 1998. "Taíno Wooden Sculpture: Duhos, Rulership and the Visual Arts in the 12th–16th Century Caribbean." PhD thesis, Sainsbury Research Unit, University of East Anglia, Norwich.

Pagán-Jiménez, J. R. 2009. "Recientes avances de los estudios paleoetnobotánicos en Puerto Rico: Nueva información obtenida desde la perspectiva del estudio de almidones antiguos." In *Encuentro de Investigadores de Arqueología y Etnohistoria*, no. 7, ed. Carlos A. Pérez Merced, 78–94. San Juan, Puerto Rico: Instituto de Cultura Puertorriqueña.

Pearsall, D. M. 1989. "Plant Utilization at the Krum Bay Site, St. Thomas U.S.V.I." In *Preceramic Procurement Patterns at Krum Bay, Virgin Islands* by E. R. Lundberg (Appendix C), PhD dissertation, University of Illinois, Urbana. University Microfilms, Ann Arbor.

Peros, M. C., E. G. Reinhardt, A. M. Davis. 2007. "A 6000-Year Record of Ecological and Hydrological Changes from Laguna de la Leche, North Coastal Cuba." *Quaternary Research* 67 (1): 69–82.

Rainey, F. G. 1940. *Porto Rican Archaeology*. New York: New York Academy of Sciences.

Reber, Eleanora A. 2012. "Absorbed Residue Analysis of 21 Sherds from the El Chorro de Maita Site, Holguin, Cuba." Papers of the UNCW Residue Lab 16, UNCW Anthropological Papers 21. Wilmington, NC.

Reitz, E. J., C. M. Scarry, and S. J. Scudder, eds. 2008. *Case Studies in Environmental Archaeology*. 2nd ed. New York: Springer.

Rouse, I. 1941. *Culture of the Ft. Liberté Region, Haiti*. New Haven, CT: Yale University Press.

———. 1986. *Migrations in Prehistory: Inferring Population Movement from Cultural Remains*. New Haven, CT: Yale University Press.

———. 1992. *The Tainos: Rise and Decline of the People Who Greeted Columbus*. New Haven, CT: Yale University Press.

Ross, A. H., and D. H. Ubelaker. 2010. "A Morphometric Approach to Taíno Biological Distance in the Caribbean." In *Island Shores, Distant Pasts: Archaeological and Biological Approaches to the Pre-Columbian Settlement of the Caribbean*, ed. S. M. Fitzpatrick and A. H. Ross, 108–26. Gainesville: University Press of Florida.

Schurr, T. G. 2010. "Coastal Waves and Island Hopping: A Genetic View of Caribbean Prehistory and New World Colonization." In *Island Shores, Distant Pasts: Archaeological and Biological Approaches to the Pre-Columbian Settlement of the Caribbean*, ed. S. M. Fitzpatrick and A. H. Ross, 177–97. Gainesville: University Press of Florida.

Scudder, S. J. 2001. "Soil Resources and Anthropogenic Changes at the Tibes Site, Ponce, Puerto Rico." *Caribbean Journal of Science* 37 (1–2): 30–40.

Waters, M., J. R. Giardino, D. W. Ryter, and J. M. Parrent. 1993. "Geoarchaeological Investigations of St. Ann's Bay, Jamaica: The Search for the Columbus Caravels and an Assessment of 1000 Years of Human Land Use." *Geoarchaeology* 8 (4): 259–79.

Wilkie, L. A., and P. Farnsworth. 2005. *Sampling Many Pots: An Archaeology of Memory and Tradition at a Bahamian Plantation*. Gainesville: University Press of Florida.

Wing, E. S. 1969. "Vertebrate Remains Excavated from San Salvador Island, Bahamas." *Caribbean Journal of Science* 9 (1–2): 25–29.

———. 1989. "Human Exploitation of Animal Resources in the Caribbean." In *Biogeography of the West Indies*, ed. C. A. Woods, 137–52. Gainesville, FL: Sandhill Crane Press.

———. 2008. "Pets and Camp Followers in the West Indies." In *Case Studies in Environmental Archaeology*, 2nd ed., ed. E. J. Reitz, C. M. Scarry, and S. J. Scudder, 405–25. New York: Springer.

See also Crab/Shell Dichotomy; DNA and Caribbean Archaeology; The Florida Museum of Natural History; Loyola (French Guiana).

F

Falmouth (Jamaica)

Patricia E. Green

Introduction

Historical archaeology draws upon research from many disciplines, including anthropology, history, geography, and folklore, to understand and interpret physical remains. Historical archaeologists consult both the historical record and the physical record in their efforts to discover the fabric of common everyday life in the past and seek to understand the broader historical development of their own and other societies. This approach has made possible fresh interpretations of the history and architecture of Falmouth, most notably through the Falmouth Façade Improvement Programme (FFIP) of the 1990s. This initiative helped define Falmouth as a Creole town, particularly because of the development of a residential architectural type there termed the Falmouth house, which evolved in the late eighteenth century and continues to be a part of Falmouth's townscape. Using

historic illustrations of the town, atlases, and maps, the FFIP delineated the boundaries of Falmouth's historic district and established the district as a priority area for the purposes of grants and awards.

In 1795, the port of Falmouth was declared the capital town of the parish of Trelawny, replacing the inland capital of Martha Brae. The parish vestry minutes state that it was the best-laid-out town on the island (Falmouth Restoration Company n.d.). The town was comprised of artisans and seafarers, freed people of color, freed Africans, and members of the plantocracy. By the early nineteenth century, it was a bourgeoning cosmopolitan port town and commercial center. Its harbor teemed with slaving vessels. From 1792 to 1808, Falmouth was the principal port of disembarkation in the Americas (Beeson 2002, 74), and in 1817, it was described as the second largest town in Jamaica (Lewis 1834, 170) (Figure F.1).

Figure F.1. Street in Falmouth, Jamaica, drawn by artist Henry Bleby (1809–1882). Originally published in Henry Bleby, 1868, *Death Struggles of Slavery: Being a Narrative of Facts and Incidents, Which Occurred in a British Colony, During the Two Years Immediately Preceding Negro Emancipation*, 3rd edition, W. Nichols, London.

Falmouth Houses and Falmouth's Townscape

By the end of the eighteenth century, the population of freed mulattoes and blacks on Jamaica had increased significantly, especially in the towns (Long 1774, 2:337). Many buildings in Falmouth were erected by Jamaican creoles (a group that included both ethnic whites and Africans [Braithwaite 1971]); freed mulattoes and Africans also owned buildings in the town.

A survey of the historic buildings in the Falmouth townscape revealed seven basic types: 1) civic buildings; 2) dwelling houses; 3) commercial buildings for manufacturing and warehousing goods; 4) military/naval structures (fortifications and barracks); 5) churches and temples; 6) shops (usually one story); 7) buildings that combined a shop and a dwelling (generally the shop below and the residence above in two-story structures). Although the Falmouth house falls within the residential category, some shop-dwellings are built in this style.

In the British Caribbean, the Falmouth style of housing developed alongside the Jamaica Georgian style of architecture, which is derived from the European Georgian tradition (Green 1997). Early buildings that were constructed in Falmouth followed this emerging creole trend. Falmouth houses are one- or two-story buildings (Figure F.2). They were built on a square plan and a three-bay street elevation, terminating with a very steep-pitched hip roof. Slate or wood shingles cover the entire structure. Today, roofs are covered with metal sheeting. Window types vary, combining glazed sash windows, wooden casement shutters, and/or movable jalousies in situ or as casements. Evidently, the windows of the wealthier residents were glazed and had triple-hung sashes.

Falmouth houses are decorated with wood shingle siding, and the foundation or lower floor is constructed of finished brick or limestone. Some houses have stucco on the exterior, which is sometimes scored to resemble a stone wall. The structural frame is made of stone, brick, or wood nogs or a combination of all three. The upper part is usually framed in timber. Sometimes the entire structure is framed in timber.

The entrances to Falmouth houses are generally located in three places: directly off a garden, off a narrow pathway between structures, and directly on the roadway (buildings with these entries are known as street-front buildings). Buildings in Falmouth are structured in three ways: detached buildings, row buildings (attached to each other and sharing walls on both sides), and semi-detached houses (sharing one wall). The Falmouth house is generally a street-front building in a row setting.

A unique feature of the Jamaica Georgian style is the integration of the piazza area of the dwelling under the roof covering. In the eighteenth and nineteenth centuries, piazzas were covered indoor-outdoor spaces between the principal rooms in the interior of the house and the street; they were in essence enclosed verandas. In the early eighteenth century, piazzas were tacked on like sheds to the core structure of buildings as part of the process of the creolization of Georgian architecture in the hot, humid climate of Jamaica. In the Transitional Georgian style, these attached piazzas have a separate roof, usually a shed roof. They appear on both the single- and double-story structures. On two-story Falmouth houses, the lower piazza is located directly on the street edge and is an extension of the public thoroughfare, providing continuous covered access between one building and the other.

One interesting observation is the intimacy of the town, which was laid out with discernible cardinal entrance features that the FFIP tied to the historic architecture; we called them "gateways." They acted as visual

Figure F.2. Restoration of Falmouth House. Courtesy of Patricia E. Green.

signposts and as end-stops for the small area defined as the historic core, which was planned on a grid. The FFIP identified four: people coming from Montego Bay entered the town through the western gateway, which we anchored at the St. Peters Parish Church on Duke Street between Victoria and Pitts Streets; those coming from the town of Martha Brae entered through the southern gateway at No. 25 Market Street; those who came from Kingston entered through the eastern gateway, located at the Falmouth Dome at the corner of Tharpe and Upper Harbour Streets; and those coming from the harbor and Fort Balcarrres came through the northern gateway, at No. 1 Market Street.

The core of the historic town plan is a six-by-eight-street grid west of a central square that is connected with a six-by-five-street grid located at a diagonal to the northeast of the first grid. The central square, called Market Square, was used historically for the sale of goods and persons. When Lady Nugent, the American wife of the governor of Jamaica, visited Falmouth in April 1802, she observed that the streets were crowded with people and that a Negro market where the Africans sold their food produce and wares was held in front of General Bell's house (Cundall 1907, 115). Falmouth boasts that it had piped water before New York City, the result of a petition that began in 1799 to erect a proper water system for the town. There was a circular water tank in the square, which became known as Water Square. By 1814, Falmouth held the distinction of having the first domestic water supply in the Americas. Water was pumped from the square until the 1950s (Dunkley 2011).

In the post-emancipation period (after 1834), a more decorative architectural style called Jamaica Vernacular developed on the Falmouth townscape. Its main feature is intricate fretwork with an interlaced pattern. Many of these buildings have a gable roof and are constructed of timber framing. An open veranda fronts these buildings instead of the closed piazza of the Jamaica Georgian style. Interestingly, some piazzas on the Falmouth houses were converted into opened verandas with slender chamfered posts, replacing the Doric pilasters of the Jamaica-Georgian style.

Further Reading

Brathwaite, E. 1971. *The Development of Creole Society in Jamaica, 1770–1820*. Oxford: Clarendon Press.

Besson, Jean. 2002. *Martha Brae's Two Histories: European Expansion and Caribbean Culture-Building in Jamaica*. Chapel Hill: University of North Carolina Press.

Cotter, J. L. 1974. "Above Ground Archaeology." *American Quarterly* 26 (3): 266–80.

Cundall, Frank. 1907. *Lady Nugent's Journal: Jamaica One Hundred Years Ago, Reprinted from a Journal Kept by Maria, Lady Nugent, from 1801 to 1815*. London: A. & C. Black for the Institute of Jamaica.

Dunkley, Daive A. 2011. "Falmouth." Jamaica National Heritage Trust Web site. http://www.jnht.com/site_falmouth.php.

Edwards, B. 1793. *The History, Civil and Commercial, of the British Colonies in the West Indies*. 2 vols. Dublin: Luke White.

Green, P. E. 1997. "Jamaica-Georgian." In *Encyclopaedia of Vernacular Architecture of the World*, ed. Paul Oliver, 1716–17. Cambridge, UK: Cambridge University Press.

———. 2000. "Architecture of the Caribbean: Colonial, Caribbean, and the Small-Scale Architectural Pieces." In *The Cultural Heritage of the Caribbean and the World Heritage Convention*, ed. Herman van Hooff, 285–304. Paris: Editions du CTHS, UNESCO.

Falmouth Restoration Company. N.d. "Falmouth, The 18th Century Commercial Capital of Western Jamaica." Falmouth: Falmouth Restoration Company.

Lewis, Matthew G. 1834. *Journal of a West India Proprietor: Kept during a Residence in the Island of Jamaica*. London: John Murray.

Long, E. 1774. *History of Jamaica, or a General Survey of the Antient and Modern State of That Island: With Reflections on Its Situation, Settlements, Inhabitants, Climate, Products, Commerce, Laws, and Government*. 3 vols. London: T. Lowndes.

See also The Magnificent Seven Mansions (Port of Spain, Trinidad); Port Antonio (Jamaica); Spanish Town (Jamaica).

Ferrous and Nonferrous Metals

Georgia L. Fox

Historic-period archaeological sites in the Caribbean, both terrestrial and underwater, often contain metal objects. The majority of metal artifacts recovered from Caribbean sites are those that were manufactured with consistent regularity. These include ferrous or iron metal objects and items made from nonferrous metals such as copper, lead, tin, silver, and gold and their alloys, such as weapons, tools, ornaments, hardware, and utilitarian objects. The physical properties of a metal artifact are determined by the internal structure of the metal, which is formed by a series of crystals known as grains, which, in turn, create internal lattice structures that meet at areas known as grain boundaries. Under the microscope, the internal structure of a metal artifact can also be seen in the form of phases that indicate the various stages of heating, cooling, and working of the metal at the various grain boundaries.

Ferrous (iron) artifacts can be distinguished by their carbon content. For example, wrought iron, which has a low carbon content, is formed and shaped by forging and welding. Wrought iron artifacts recovered from Caribbean archaeological sites include Iberian-manufactured cannons and anchors and European and American hand-forged nails. Another form of iron, cast iron, also known as pig iron, covers a large group of iron artifacts that have a carbon content of 2 percent or greater. The high quantity of carbon makes cast iron brittle, and the iron is workable only through casting or machining the metal. At Caribbean colonial sites, cast iron objects include cannon and other weapons, nails, tools, agricultural implements, cooking pots, building fixtures and hardware, and many other items. Steel, an alloy of iron that has carbon content of between 0.2 and 1.7 percent, is found on some archaeological sites that date from the mid-nineteenth century and later.

Metal artifacts recovered from Caribbean sites include objects that have metal parts, metal plating, or metal decorative elements and objects that are wholly metal. From the moment they are manufactured, with the exception of items made of gold, most metal artifacts react with their environment and begin a corrosion process that converts them to more stable compounds. In the Caribbean, a variety of archaeological environments can affect the stability of metal artifacts, which includes temperate, tropical, and arid environments, as well as marine and freshwater sites, which expose metal objects to aqueous corrosion. On many archaeological sites, iron objects recovered with a substantial metal core will survive, but more commonly, iron artifacts are found in varying stages of deterioration, and iron artifacts recovered from the sea are often found in the form of a concretion or encrustation (in which outer layers of calcium carbonate and other materials encase the iron object). In many cases, the iron has migrated into the surrounding environment, leaving little or no remaining metal in the core. In cases where the metal has completely corroded, the object's original shape can be preserved in the encrustation through the creation of a mold.

Nonferrous metals such as tin and lead and their alloys recovered from Caribbean historic sites include pewter tableware, tin cans, lead window frames, weights, and lead objects from shipwrecks such as fishing weights and sounding leads. As a rule, lead usually survives the archaeological record. Copper and its alloys, such as bronze and brass, can be found in the form of nails and fasteners, tools, fixtures, and decorative objects. Silver, which is a fairly noble metal, can corrode. Silver artifacts include jewelry, tableware, candlestick holders, buttons, threads, religious paraphernalia, and other objects. Only experienced and well-trained conservators should attempt to conserve ferrous and nonferrous metal artifacts. Caution should be exercised when removing metal artifacts from their archaeological contexts, as exposure to atmospheric moisture and oxygen can reactivate the corrosion process, setting in motion further deterioration.

Further Reading

Cronyn, J. M. 1990. *Elements of Archaeological Conservation*. London: Routledge.

Hamilton, D. 2000. *Methods of Conserving Archaeological Material from Underwater Sites*. College Station: Conservation Research Laboratory, Texas A&M University.

Pearson, C. 1987. *Conservation of Marine Archaeological Objects*. London: Butterworths.

Selwyn, L. 2004. *Metals and Corrosion: A Handbook for the Conservation Professional*. Ottawa: Canadian Conservation Institute.

See also Archaeological Conservation; Cannon.

The First Caribbean Farmers

Basil A. Reid

Definitions of Farming

Farming, or agriculture, has been defined in a variety of ways: the practice of cultivating the land or raising stock; production that relies essentially on the growth and nurturing of plants and animals, especially for food, usually with land as an important input; and the science or process of cultivating the soil to produce plants and animals that will be useful to humans in some way. Horticulture, which derives from the Latin *hortus,* meaning a garden space, in contrast to an agricultural space, is usually defined as the science and art of growing fruit, flowers, ornamental plants, and vegetables in small gardens. Ingold (1984, 5) has noted that anthropologists have the tendency to remove people from the category of foragers if they have any attributes of agriculture or pastoralism. There are really, however, three basic categories of human groups in terms of subsistence systems:

1) Those who subsist on uncultivated plants and wild fauna—foragers

2) Those who have a mixed subsistence economy, based partly on domestic and partly on wild resources: these can be subdivided further into two subcategories:

2a) foragers who farm; and (2b) farmers who hunt

3) Those who gain no significant subsistence from uncultivated plants and wild fauna—agriculturalists and pastoralists

In general, anthropologists have tended to view the universe of human subsistence economies as a binary set: those in category 1 and those in category 3 (Bogucki and Baker 1999). The root of the problem may be that the colonization of Africa, the Americas, Australia, and the Pacific in the eighteenth and nineteenth centuries essentially "froze" many societies as either foragers or food producers, depending on their circumstances at the time of European contact. The point of this frozen moment was then assumed to be fixed on the unilinear scale of progress from hunting and gathering to farming and stock-herding (Reid 2009). However, the evidence suggests that communities can be properly be described as farmers, even though agriculture was in fact part of a larger network of other food-getting strategies such as collecting, fishing, and hunting. This period is generally categorized as incipient agriculture, a process that is characterized by a gradual movement from food collecting to food producing. Incipient agriculture is one of the defining characteristics of the Archaic Age in the New World.

Archaic Farmers

Until recently, there was general agreement among Caribbean archaeologists that the Saladoid were the first horticultural Ceramic Age group. Saladoid sites are found in abundance from Trinidad and Tobago to Puerto Rico. The Saladoid, who arrived in the Caribbean in 500 BC, brought visible signs of their South American farming background, such as ceramic pots and cassava-like griddles as well as physical evidence of a settled village life, such as large middens and plazas. However, the idea that the Saladoid introduced pottery and agriculture to the islands is based on outdated models of cultural development and migration.

New evidence indicates that pottery-making and agriculture were already practiced in the islands by both the Archaic Casimiroid and Ortoiroid peoples at least 2,000 years before the Saladoid arrived. The discovery of crude pottery known as El Caimito at the La Caleta site in the eastern Dominican Republic was initially interpreted as evidence for transculturation between the Casimiroid of eastern Hispaniola and the Saladoid of western Puerto Rico (Keegan 1994). However, the ongoing discovery of a significant number of Casimiroid and Ortoiroid pottery-bearing sites points to the Archaic inhabitants, not the Saladoid, as the first potters and farmers in the region (Hung 2005). Abra del Cacoyoguin I, Santa Rosalia I, Vuelta Larga I, Corinthia III, La Herradura, La Linea, Mejias, Arroyo del Palo, Bitirí I, Solapa I, Catunda, La Escondida de Bucuey, Los Chivos, La Guira, Juan Barón, Punta de Peque, Benito, Belleza, La Luz, and Caimanes III are examples of Early Ceramic sites in eastern Cuba (Reid 2009).

Hunter-gatherers in the eastern woodlands of the United States cultivated a number of local plants that constitute the Eastern Agricultural Complex, and a similar "Caribbean agricultural complex" may have characterized the Archaic peoples of the region (Keegan 1994; Reid 2009). The presence of certain plant remains on Archaic sites suggests that many of the foods that were allegedly introduced by the Saladoid were already an established part of Archaic horticulture (Newsom 1993). Plants identified in Archaic deposits include zamia, or coontie (*Zamia pumila*), cupey (*Clusea rosea*), wild avocado (*Persea americana*), yellow sapote (*Pouteria campechiana*), primrose (*Oenothera* sp.), mastic bully (*Mastichodendron foetidissimum*), trianthema (*Trianthema portulacastrum*), and palms (Palmae) (Newsom 1993). Evidence for the use of palms such as corozo has been found in the macrobotanical and microbotanical record of Puerto Rico (Pagán-Jiménez et al. 2005). Recent analysis of starch grains in Archaic edge-ground cobbles from Puerto Ferro and Maruco in Puerto Rico showed many similarities with cobbles from early sites in the Isthmo-Colombian area that had been used for processing tubers such as manioc (*Manihot esculenta*), sweet potatoes (*Ipomoea batatas*), and cocoyam (*Xanthosoma* sp.). This suggests that the Archaic peoples in Puerto Rico may have used their ground stone tools in a similar manner and that these plants were part of Archaic horticulture on the island.

In the Dominican Republic, the site of El Caimito, which has been interpreted as a food preparation area, is located on the roof of a rock shelter and is characterized by the presence of highly fragmented ceramics in small quantities. Pollen analyses conducted on samples from the El Caimito midden produced no evidence of cultivation of plants such as manioc and corn, which are known to have been used by the Saladoid, the Ostionoid, and the Taíno. Instead, pollen evidence points to intensive

foraging based on the exploitation of *Zamia* sp., palm seeds (*Roystonea* sp.), and corozo (*Acrocomia* sp.) Fruit trees in the sapodilla family (*Sapotaceae*) (Figure F.3) are represented by seeds and wood fragments from Twenty Hill on Antigua and by seed remains from Hichmans' Shell Heap on Nevis. Other seeds from Archaic age sites derive from herbaceous or slightly woody plants. Seeds that are provisionally assigned to the genus *Siphonoglossa* sp. (Acanthaceae), cossie balsam, were recovered from Hichmans' Shell Heap (Newsom and Wing 2004; Reid 2009). This plant is documented among the flora of the northern Lesser Antilles, though it does not seem to have been recorded as part of the modern vegetation of Nevis (Newsom and Wing 2004). Its archaeological presence suggests that this plant was used by the Ortoiroid of Nevis, resulting in its occurrence on the island. Cossie balsam is potentially another species that had medicinal value (Acevedo-Rodríguez et al. 1996; Reid 2009). Because some of these seeds were introduced from outside the Caribbean and others present extensions beyond their present ranges, it is likely that at least some of these plants were managed if not cultivated outright (Newsom and Wing 2004; Keegan 1994; Reid 2009).

Emerging Trends in the Circum-Caribbean and New World Tropics

Rather than interpreting Archaic pottery-making and horticulture in the Caribbean region as an isolated phenomenon, it should be viewed as part of a much larger emerging trend in the circum-Caribbean and New World tropics (Reid 2009). The Caribbean coast of Colombia is one those areas where expressions of

Figure F.3. Sapodilla (*Sapotaceae*). Reprinted from Reid (2009, fig. 5.3) by permission of the University of Alabama Press.

early pottery have been reported. Shell middens such as Puerto Hormiga (Colombia) (5100–4500 BP or 3150–2550 BC), San Jacinto (Colombia) (5900–5200 BP or 4000 BC), and the contemporaneous Monsú (Colombia) seem to demonstrate the first attempts at village life in the region (Hung 2005). Their general characteristics suggest a transition from incipient agricultural practices and intensive gathering to a reliance on cultivated tubers such as manioc. This seems to be the case at other Colombian sites, such as Rotinet and Malambo, where the consumption of manioc in the form of cassava became habitual toward 2000 and 1200 BC, respectively. Sites studied in the region of Carúpano in Venezuela provide significant examples of the development reached by the foraging groups from this region of South America. These sites consist of large shell middens that provide evidence of surface ceramics and a mixed economy. The foragers of this area of Venezuela settled coastal areas near mangroves and lagoons in the Gulf of Paria and the Gulf of Cariaco. In Guyana, on the other hand, studies of late phases of the Archaic groups associated with shell middens (such as Hosororo Creek, which has been dated to 3975 ± 45 BP, or 2025 BC) document how communities with a basic gathering economy developed an undecorated pottery with very simple forms. In Central America, some shell middens such as Monagrillo in the Gulf of Panama (4500–3200 BP, or 2550–1250 BC), have evidence of a certain ceramic industry related to the use and exploitation of nearby resources in the mangrove swamp. The pottery at this site supports the impression that this location was home to an important phase in the dispersion and exchange of ceramic traditions in the Americas. In general, the shell middens with ceramics from Colombia, the coast of Venezuela, Guyana, and Panama reflect a phase of growth and intensification of foraging lifeways in the continental or riverine Caribbean that was characterized by experimentation with some horticultural practices and the manufacturing of wood-working instruments and tools.

Further Reading

Acevedo-Rodríguez, P. and collaborators. 1996. *Flora of St. John, U.S. Virgin Islands.* Bronx, NY: New York Botanical Garden.

Bogucki, P., and G. Baker, eds. 1999. "Early Agricultural Societies." In *Companion Encyclopedia of Archaeology,* 1:839–69. New York: Routledge.

Hung, U. 2005. "Early Ceramics in the Caribbean." In *Dialogues in Cuban Archaeology,* ed. L. Antonio Curet, Shannon Lee Dowdy, and Gabino La Roza Corzo, 103–24. Tuscaloosa: University of Alabama Press.

Ingold, W. K. 1984. "Time, Social Relationships, and the Exploitation of Animals: Anthropological Reflections on Prehistory." In *Animals and Archaeology,* vol. 3, *Early Herders and Their Flocks,* ed. J. Clutton-Brock and C. Grigson, 3–12. Oxford: British Archaeological Reports.

Keegan, W. 1994. "West Indian Archaeology. 1. Overview and Foragers." *Journal of Archaeological Research* 2 (3): 255–83.

Newsom, L. 1993. "Native West Indian Plant Use." PhD diss., Department of Anthropology, University of Florida, Gainesville.

Newsom, L., and E. Wing. 2004. *On Land and Sea: Native American Uses of Biological Resources in the West Indies.* Tuscaloosa: University of Alabama Press.

Pagán-Jiménez R., Miguel Rodríguez, Luis A. Chanlatte, and Yvonne Narganes. 2005. "La temprana introducción y uso algunas plantas domésticas, silvestres y cultívos en Las Antillas precolombinas." *Diálogi Antropológico* 3 (10): 1–27.

Reid, B. 2009. *Myths and Realities of Caribbean History of Caribbean History.* Tuscaloosa: University of Alabama Press.

See also Agricultural Earthworks (The Guianas); The Archaic Age; The Casimiroid; *Conucos*; The Ortoiroid.

The Florida Museum of Natural History

Elise V. LeCompte and Gifford J. Waters

The world-renowned Caribbean collections of the Florida Museum of Natural History contain both prehistoric and historical archaeological materials (artifacts, environmental remains, and the associated documentation) from over thirty-five sites throughout the West Indies, ranging in date from the ninth through the seventeenth century.

The Florida Museum of Natural History Caribbean Archaeology Program, founded in 1960 by Ripley P. Bullen, includes the prehistoric component of the museum's Caribbean collections. This segment of the museum's Caribbean collections is one of the largest systematic collections of precolonial artifacts from the West Indies in North America and contains collections from sites on Antigua, Aruba, the Bahamas, Barbados, Curaçao, the Dominican Republic, Grenada, Guadeloupe, Guyana, Haiti, Jamaica, Marie-Galante, Martinique, Puerto Rico, St. Kitts, Saint Lucia, St. Martin, St. Vincent and the Grenadines, Suriname, Trinidad and Tobago, the Turks and Caicos, the United States Virgin Islands, and Venezuela. The heart of the collection consists of materials recovered from excavations and surface collections carried out by Ripley P. and Adelaide K. Bullen, starting in the 1960s. The museum also curates a type collection composed of all the artifacts illustrated in Ripley Bullen's Caribbean publications. Another major component of this collection includes artifacts recovered during excavations directed by Charles A. Hoffman Jr. on the islands of Antigua and St. Kitts. Large contributions by private donors, such as Leon Wilder (1985) and Geoffrey Senior (1990s), round out the collection. Materials recovered during research directed by the present curator, William F. Keegan, remain in the host countries.

Some of the earliest historical archaeology collections from the Caribbean are found in the collections of the Florida Museum of Natural History. These collections can be credited to the work of John Goggin and his colleagues. During the 1940s and 1950s, Goggin began an ambitious historical archaeology program that generated a large collection of materials from sites throughout the Caribbean islands. In the course of conducting this research, Goggin collaborated with such researchers as Emile de Boyrie Moya of the Dominican Republic, José Maria Cruxent of Venezuela, and Irving Rouse of Yale. These collaborations resulted in the gathering of important historical archaeological data from the Caribbean and in the exchange of smaller comparative collections from throughout the region.

During the late 1970s through the 1980s, Charles Fairbanks and Kathleen Deagan conducted archaeological excavations in Haiti. These research projects generated two large historic-era collections that are currently being curated at the Florida Museum of Natural History on behalf of the Haitian government. These important holdings from the sites of Puerto Real and En Bas Saline make the museum one of the largest repositories of analyzed and documented archaeological materials from Haiti.

Since the late 1980s, research undertaken in the Dominican Republic under Deagan's direction has generated and illustrated large collections of materials from the Spanish colonial town sites of La Isabela (1493–1498) and Concepción de la Vega (1496–1562). The archaeological specimens from these sites are part of the collections maintained by the Dominican Republic National Park Service and are curated and maintained at the sites themselves. Photographs of many artifacts excavated from La Isabela and Concepción de la Vega, site backgrounds, and descriptions and lists of additional readings are available on the Florida Museum of Natural History Historical Archaeology Program's Web site (www.flmnh.ufl.edu/histarch/research.htm).

The majority of artifacts from historic-era sites in the Caribbean housed at the Florida Museum of Natural History are from the Dominican Republic and Haiti. These collections include sites that range in date from the protohistoric period through the late fifteenth and the sixteenth and seventeenth centuries. Artifacts from the Dominican Republic are primarily from Goggin's work in the 1940s and 1950s and are based on his collaborations with other Caribbean scholars. Artifacts from Haiti curated at the museum are from the excavations under the direction of Fairbanks and Deagan at the sites of Puerto Real and En Bas Saline.

The research conducted by museum curators, staff, and colleagues in the Caribbean has led to a greater understanding of the cultural development of indigenous Caribbean peoples such as the Taíno and of initial efforts at European colonization in the New World. Research at sites such as Paradise Park in Jamaica, the Coralie and

MC-6 sites in the Turks and Caicos, the Pearls Site in Grenada, and sites on Île à Rat in Haiti has shed light on the peopling of the West Indies by prehistoric populations, patterns of resource exploitation (including overexploitation) by early indigenous populations, and a clearer understanding of regional cultural patterns and evolution from the ninth through the fifteenth centuries. Research at sites such as La Isabela and Concepción de la Vega in the Dominican Republic and Puerto Real and En Bas Saline in Haiti have offered insights into the evolving policies and adaptations made by the Spanish in the early years of colonization. Examples of this can be seen in the modifications made in architectural style and town planning and layout from the late fifteenth through the sixteenth century.

Many scholarly works have been produced that are based on research conducted by the Florida Museum of Natural History in the Caribbean and its holdings of Caribbean materials. Clearing new ground in the study of prehistoric societies, Keegan published the first overview of the prehistory of the Bahamas, *The People Who Discovered Columbus: The Prehistory of the Bahamas* (1992). His scientific approach, called paleoethnography, links archaeological field data, artifact collections, and historical documents to determine how the Lucayans made their settlements, what they ate, how they organized in social groups, and how their population spread throughout the archipelago. Reanalysis of the ceramic assemblage that Ripley Bullen excavated at the Savanne Suazey type site on Grenada revealed that the Suazan Troumassoid ceramic series may represent prehistoric Amerindian groups that maintained individual identities within a sphere of cultural interaction. Other artifact-based research includes a study of shell bead manufacture and the comparative study of faunal remains to determine the effects of human colonization on the indigenous fauna across the southern Bahamian Archipelago. Perhaps the earliest work on the museum's Caribbean collections is John Goggin's 1968 work on Spanish

majolica found in the Americas. This work, along with Deagan's (1995, 2002) two volumes on artifacts of the Spanish colonies, has resulted in a much richer understanding of European goods brought to and produced in the New World and invaluable historic-era ceramic type collections that are housed at the Florida Museum of Natural History. These type collections are available for viewing online at the museum's Web site (www.flmnh.ufl.edu/histarch/gallery_types). Other artifact-based studies resulting from the museum's historical archaeology research include a detailed examination of Spanish coins and analyses of Colonoware and locally produced ceramics from sites such as Puerto Real and La Isabela.

Further Reading

Deagan, K. 1995. *Puerto Real: The Archaeology of a Sixteenth-Century Spanish Town in Hispaniola*. Gainesville: University Press of Florida.

Deagan, K., and J. M. Cruxent. 2002. *Archaeology at La Isabela: America's First European Town*. New Haven, CT: Yale University Press.

Ewen, C. R. 1992. *From Spaniard to Creole: The Archaeology of Culture Formation at Puerto Real, Haiti*. Tuscaloosa: University of Alabama Press.

Goggin, J. 1968. *Spanish Majolica in the New World*. New Haven, CT: Yale University Press.

Keegan, W. F. 1992. *The People Who Discovered Columbus: The Prehistory of the Bahamas*. Gainesville: University Press of Florida.

———. 2010. "Boundary-Work, Reputational Systems, and the Delineation of Population Movements in the Prehistoric Caribbean." In *Mobility and Exchange from a Pan-Caribbean Perspective*, ed. C. L. Hofman and A. J. Bright, special issue, *Journal of Caribbean Archaeology*, 138–55.

See also Bullen, Ripley (1902–1976), and Adelaide Bullen (1908–1987); Cruxent, José María (1911–2005); De Boyrie Moya, Emil (1903–1967); La Isabela (Dominican Republic); Puerto Real (Haiti); Rouse, Benjamin Irving (1913–2006).

Foundation for Marine Archaeology of the Netherlands Antilles (STIMANA)

Jay B. Haviser

The Foundation for Marine Archaeology of the Netherlands Antilles (STIMANA) was founded in 2000. The foundation was set up to continue maritime and underwater archaeological projects that had previously been conducted by the Archaeological-Anthropological Institute of the Netherlands Antilles (AAINA) after the termination of the latter in 1998. The research projects of STIMANA are primarily affiliated with the Curaçao Maritime Museum on Curaçao, the Maritime Archaeological and Historical Society of Washington, DC, and the cruise ship *Freewinds*. STIMANA projects are frequently under the direction of underwater archaeologist and marine biologist Wil Nagelkerken. Others who are closely associated with STIMANA research include Theo van der Giessen, Francois van der Hoeven, Eddy Ayubi, Dimitri Close, Mike Napier, Dennis Knepper, Raymond Hayes, and Edsel Jesurun. One the key results of STIMANA's research is a series of archaeological publications that includes investigations at the historical anchorages of Santa Anna Bay, Curaçao; Oranje Bay, St. Eustatius; Kralendijk, Bonaire; and Roseau, Dominica. STIMANA has also focused on the reconstruction of a nineteenth century frigate called *Negrita*; the removal, conservation, and care of cannons in the Santa Ana Harbor of Curaçao, excavations of the eighteenth-century Dutch frigate *ZM Alphen* on Curaçao; and excavations of the nineteenth-century coal ship *Mediator* off Curaçao's coast. Another important aspect of STIMANA's work is sensitizing the public to the importance of its underwater cultural heritage. After the disintegration of the Netherlands Antilles in 2010, this foundation was renamed STIMACUR, for Foundation for Marine Archaeology of Curaçao.

See also Bonaire Archaeological Institute (BONAI); Curaçao (Former Netherlands Antilles); Underwater Archaeology.

French Jesuit Mission Outpost (Dominica)

Stephan Lenik

In 1747, French Jesuits based in Martinique founded a mission outpost composed of a parish church and a plantation at Grand Bay on Dominica's south coast. The missionaries, who were under the direction of Antoine de La Valette, financial manager and later the Superior of the Jesuits in Martinique, found a receptive population of French-speaking Catholic settlers. These included a free person named Jeannot Rolle who had erected a stone cross on the bayfront after conflicts with the Kalinago in 1691. When the Jesuits arrived, Dominica was among the neutral islands of the eastern Caribbean. Agreements between Britain and France had determined that the territory was not to be inhabited by Europeans and would remain a Kalinago island. Many Europeans ignored these restrictions and exploited Dominica's fertile yet rugged landscape. La Valette justified this expansion as a mission among the Kalinago, though the parish church that was consecrated in late 1749 served the free and enslaved frontier population.

La Valette was most interested in Dominica's economic potential. Although excessive profit-making was forbidden for the Society of Jesus, La Valette organized a commercial empire that tested and at times overstepped the bounds of permissible commerce. Proceeds from his schemes funded the purchase of enslaved laborers and the construction of a factory at Grand Bay, where coffee, chocolate, cassava, and other crops were produced from 1748 to the early 1760s (Rochemonteix 1907; Thompson 1996). In 1755, a scandal exposed La Valette's activities, including the commercial activity in Dominica, when a shipment of products meant to repay debts in metropolitan France was captured at sea, sending a major lender to the Society of Jesus into bankruptcy. Creditors sought repayment through the courts, and eventually the cases were brought before the Paris *parlement*, which ordered the debt of 6.2 million livres to be repaid. When the society could not settle this debt, a series of judgments in the early 1760s dissolved the society in France and its colonies. This was part of a worldwide suppression of the society that culminated in its dissolution by papal decree in 1773 (Rochemonteix 1907; Thompson 1996). Thus, the mission outpost in Dominica played a major role in the demise of the French Jesuits.

Jesuit mission work in the Caribbean began in 1640. The society built administrative headquarters and churches in ports such as St. Pierre, Basse-Terre, Cap-Français, and Cayenne, and missionaries served as priests in parishes to which the Jesuits were assigned. To support these establishments the society owned plantations and enslaved laborers. These included sugar plantations in Martinique and Saint-Domingue and plantations with more diversified production in Guyane and Dominica. As an active Catholic presence in the colonies, Jesuit priests ensured that colonists attended Mass and observed religious holidays. A *curé des nègres* was assigned to oversee the conversion and practice of free and enslaved laborers who became Catholic. The society was integrated into Atlantic economic networks as full participants in the system of plantation slavery, though proselytizing rather than profit maximization was the priority. Consequently the spatial layout and management of Jesuit plantations diverges from patterns observed on secular plantations.

Remains of three buildings related to the Jesuit mission in Grand Bay were discovered during construction of a road in 2001. Excavations in 2007 and 2008 uncovered portions of the foundation of the church and two plantation buildings, including a factory. Stratigraphic layers dating to the Jesuit period include French *faïence blanche*, Huveaune, and Vallauris and Italian Albisola. Several earthenware fragments match Cayo and Koriabo types, which are associated with the Kalinago, suggesting either interaction with or emulation of indigenous pottery traditions (Lenik 2010).

When the Jesuits arrived, Dominica was settled by French inhabitants living on small plantations. Grand Bay was the first large-scale plantation investment in Dominica before the island became a formal British colony. Archaeological evidence and maps show that the site was placed in a flat coastal area between two hills that was near Jeannot Rolle's stone cross. This indicates efforts to attract gaze and to display the Jesuit prestige and mission work as a means of social control. The spatial layout reveals that maximizing efficiency and direct surveillance of enslaved laborers were reduced in importance (Lenik 2012). The Jesuits also founded one of Dominica's first parishes, which served a Catholic populace through the British colonial period and to the present day. A portion of the parish register from 1748 to 1755 lists twenty-two owners in addition to the Jesuits. Many of these surnames are listed in post-1763 British colonial records, as French families were permitted to remain in Dominica once certain conditions were met.

Further Reading

Lenik, S. 2010. "Frontier Landscapes, Missions, and Power: A French Jesuit Plantation and Church at Grand Bay, Dominica (1747–1763)." PhD diss., Syracuse University, Syracuse, New York.

———. 2012. "Mission Plantations, Space, and Social Control: Jesuits as Planters in French Caribbean Colonies and Frontiers." *Journal of Social Archaeology* 12 (1): 41–61.

Rochemonteix, P. C. de. 1907. *Le père Antoine Lavalette à la Martinique: d'après beaucoup de documents inédits.* Paris: Libraire Alphonse Picard et Fils.

Thompson, D. G. 1996. "The Lavalette Affair and the Jesuit Superiors." *French History* 10 (2): 206–39.

See also Island-Carib; Kalinago Descendants of St. Vincent and the Grenadines; The Kalinago Territory (Dominica).

French Colonial Ceramic Types

R. Grant Gilmore III

French potters were just as busy as their Dutch and English competitors. They turned out similar varieties, including a range of coarse earthenwares, *faïence* (French tin-enamelware), stonewares, and porcelain. Coarse earthenware forms can be quite similar to their Dutch counterparts, making distinctions between the two difficult. The primary production center for exported French coarse earthenwares was in the Saintonge province, which included the busy port of La Rochelle. La Rochelle's great position as a port coupled with the presence of good local clay sources provided adequate impetus for the development of a vibrant pottery trade in the region. These earthenwares have a distinct green-tinted lead glaze and are found throughout the Americas. A rather interesting example of a planting pot was found near Battery St. Louis on St. Eustatius (Figure F.4). It has two cartouches: a lion's head and a fleur-de-lis. Industrial forms expressly made for the sugar industry have been found in Martinique, Guadeloupe, and Haiti (the former Saint-Domingue). Locally produced coarse earthenwares echoing these vessels are also found on all of these islands. These ceramics are being studied by a number of practitioners, including Kenneth Kelly.

French tin-enameled refined earthenwares are generally known outside of France as *faïence*. Two types can be identified in Caribbean contexts—*faïence blanche* and *faïence brune*. The vast majority are platters, although creamers and other forms may be recovered. *Faience* may be identified through its pale pink to orange body, which is distinctive from the English and Dutch pale yellow clays used for tin enamelware. French *faïence blanche* is white on both the inner and outer surfaces, while *faïence brune*, the most distinct type, is dark purple brown on the exterior surface.

Although French stonewares have been identified in North American contexts, relatively few have been found in the Caribbean. The unique vessel forms, including jugs and beakers, were primarily produced in Normandy. On the French islands, the overwhelming influence of the Staffordshire potteries was not felt as deeply until the nineteenth century. Ceramics found on the French islands, especially Guadeloupe and Martinique, are usually locally produced items, while those of French origin were usually imported.

Further Reading

Hauser, M. W., K. G. Kelly, and D. V. Armstrong. 2005. "What to Do with 'Other Ceramics': Inter-Colonial Trade of French Coarse Earthenware." In *Proceedings of the Twenty-First Congress of the International Association for Caribbean Archaeology*, ed. B. A. Reid, H. P. Roget, and A. Curet, 2:579–587. St. Augustine, Trinidad and Tobago: School of Continuing Studies, University of the West Indies.

Kelly, K. 2008. "Creole Cultures of the Caribbean: Historical Archaeology in the French West Indies." *International Journal of Historical Archaeology* 12 (4): 388–402.

Loewen, B. 2004. "Céramiques francaises et réseaux de commerce transatlantiques, XVIe-XVIIe siècles." In *Champlain ou les portes du Nouveau-Monde*, ed. M. Augeron and D. Guillemet, 217–21. Paris: Gestes éditions.

Mock, K. 2006. "An Analysis of the Morphological Variability of French Ceramics from Seventeenth-Century Archaeological Sites in New France." Master's thesis, University of Maine.

See also Dutch Colonial Ceramic Types; Spanish Colonial Ceramic Types.

Figure F.4. French lead-glazed St. Onge ware flowerpot, late eighteenth century. Recovered on the surface near Battery St. Louis on St. Eustatius. Courtesy of R. Grant Gilmore III and SECAR.

G

Geoinformatics

Basil A. Reid and Joshua M. Torres

Introduction

Geoinformatics, a relatively new emphasis in archaeology, can be defined as an interdisciplinary field that develops and uses science and technology to address the problems of the geosciences. In order to achieve its objectives, geoinformatics uses a battery of integrative and innovative approaches to analyze, model, and develop extensive and diverse data sets. Several disciplines fall within the general purview of geoinformatics, including geographical information systems (GIS), global positioning systems (GPS), satellite imagery, aerial photography, photogrammetry, cartography, and geophysical surveys. Increasingly, geoinformatics is being used in Caribbean archaeology because of its usefulness in detecting sites and documenting them before their destruction. This is especially relevant in the face of the growing destruction of archaeological sites by flooding, land erosion, mining, and road and building construction, which often result in either partial or complete destruction of archaeological sites. The results generated by geoinformatics can also facilitate more targeted excavations of selected sites in the Caribbean, thus significantly reducing time and expense.

Reasons for Caribbean Geoinformatics

Although most publications on archaeology and geoinformatics revolve around North American and European case studies, an increasing number of research projects are being conducted in the Caribbean (Reid 2008). The Caribbean is fertile ground for several reasons. First, archaeological activity in the region since the 1980s has led to an increasing demand for state-of-the-art technologies. Research in the Caribbean is no longer based almost exclusively on conventional survey and reconnaissance methods such as trial trenching, shovel test pitting, field walking, and ground surveys. Indeed, the various papers presented at the 21st, 22nd, and 23rd congresses of the International Association for Caribbean Archaeology (IACA), held in Trinidad and Tobago (2005), Jamaica (2007), and Antigua (2009), underscored the extent to which research agendas are being increasingly informed by a holistic mix of archaeological data, field methods, and scientific techniques that include geoinformatics.

Another important reason for geoinformatics is the negative impacts on archaeological sites of sprawling urban growth, agriculture, mining, and land erosion in various Caribbean territories. These impacts have been particularly damaging to precolonial sites, since they tend to be generally less visible on the landscape than their historic period counterparts. For instance, since the first systematic archaeology was conducted on the island in 1985, Anguilla has experienced a dramatic loss of its Amerindian archaeological heritage by two decades of hotel development along the coastline where the sites are situated. In March and April 2003, eleven site locations in Carriacou were surveyed and mapped (Kappers 2004). Most sites in Carriacou were found to be endangered by erosion through waves, storm, tidal action, and sand dredging by the local population, with the site of Grand Bay being the primary example.

Caribbean geography is also well suited to the application of geoinformatics. Although the islands in the Caribbean are generally small, their myriad microenvironments such as river valleys, forested areas, grasslands, coastlines, plains, hills, and mountains often pose significant challenges to site visibility and accessibility. Low to nonexistent visibility due to dense vegetation cover is, of course, a common problem throughout the neotropics, which includes much of the Caribbean. Low site accessibility can be caused by difficult terrain or dense vegetation. In addition, recent landscape modifications in the Caribbean may have completely destroyed evidence of archaeological occupations or covered them entirely with large expanses of soil, water, or modern construction. Because of ongoing land erosion, much of Canoe Bay, a large Amerindian site on the southwest coast of

Tobago, has now been inundated by the sea, and much of the site is inaccessible to serious investigators (Reid 2008).

Geographic Information Systems

GIS is one of the major components of geoinformatics. The application of GIS technology in archaeological research of the Caribbean has primarily focused on analysis of settlement patterns. These studies have emphasized the role of the natural environment in the choice of settlement locations and the variations in settlement patterns in relation to environmental variables through time. More recent applications have examined line of sight analysis associated with navigation and spatial orientation in the Caribbean Sea. A prime example is the visual sight analysis of Joshua Torres and Reniel Rodríguez Ramos (2008), which demonstrates connectivity between Caribbean islands and between these islands and neighboring continental landmasses (Figure G.1). This study has serious implications for pre-Columbian migratory patterns and cultural interactions throughout the region, as it challenges notions of insularity and isolationism associated with the Caribbean archipelago.

GIS is also frequently used to facilitate archaeological heritage management. One of the central tenets of archaeological heritage management is predictive modeling. This practice is based on the simple assumption that patterns exist in the places where people locate their activities, camps, or settlements in the landscape. For example, Bheshem Ramlal and Basil A. Reid (2008) have studied the design and development of an Archaeological Information System (AIS) for the Archaeology Centre at The University of the West Indies, St. Augustine (Trinidad and Tobago). Considered to be far superior to conventional paper-based methods, this GIS AIS would provide both a means for accessing information and a digital database (Figure G.2) that can be maintained and updated with new information as it becomes available.

However, like all GIS operations, converting source material into spatial and attribute data for the sake of cultural resource management (CRM) can be very time consuming. Although GIS can be used to quickly make maps and tables, archaeologists, historians, and cultural

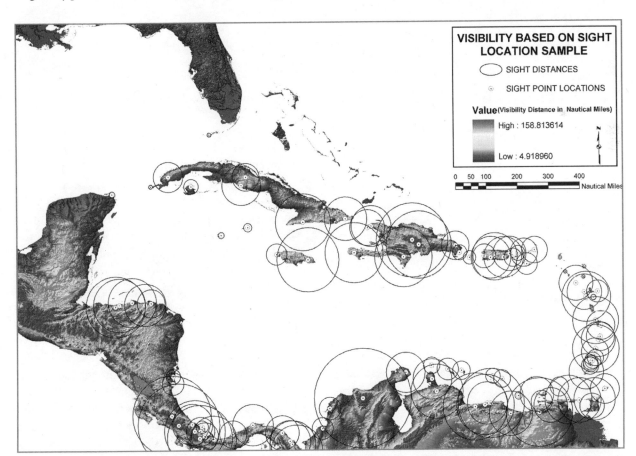

Figure G.1. Recalculated digital elevation model of the Caribbean using Bowditch's standard distance to the visible horizon formula. Map also shows sample points from/to which visibility is possible. Reprinted from Reid (2008, fig. 1.3) by permission of the University of Alabama Press.

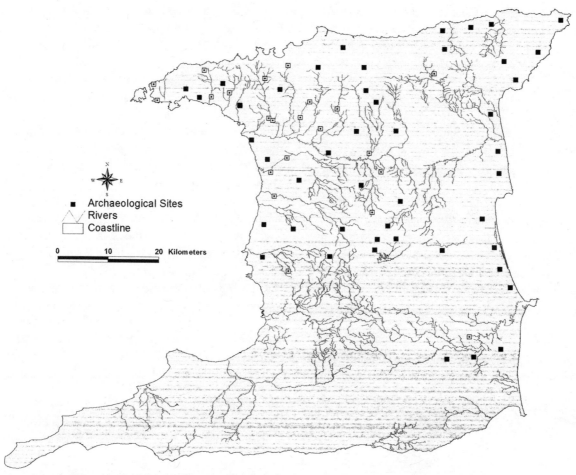

Figure G.2. Selected sites in Trinidad that are within 500 meters of a river and/or the coastline. Reprinted from Reid (2008, fig. 4.5) by permission of the University of Alabama Press.

resource managers should be prepared to invest considerable time in designing systems, acquiring data, and converting material from manuscript and print sources (including paper maps) into digital forms. GIS enables us to generate permanent records of sites, combine and jointly analyze diverse sources, understand how cultural heritage relates spatially to its surrounding natural and human environment, communicate knowledge and network databases, test proposed development models and conservation strategies, and facilitate monitoring and management of cultural resources.

Recent studies of St. Kitts's prehistoric settlement patterns used GIS-generated maps to supplement reconnaissance site visits and field surveys. These maps identified 500-meter buffer zones depicting possible site catchment zones (Farag and Ramlal 2005). Another example pertains to the system Landon and Seales (2005) created for building three-dimensional models of Caribbean petroglyphs based on reconstructions of Taíno petroglyphs at Caguana, Puerto Rico. These digital models were aimed at allowing digital access to and preservation of petroglyphs in remote areas that often remain unprotected from the elements. Another example is the work of Michiel Kappers, Fitzpatrick, and Kaye (2007), which combined aerial photographs with highly accurate survey techniques, large-scale area excavation, and a fully automated barcode-based computer system to create a three-dimensional model of the rapidly disappearing site of Grand Bay in Carriacou. The resulting GIS data set provided the means to construct 3D models of the site, a necessary step in developing future strategies for investigating and protecting archaeological sites on the island.

Caribbean archaeologists have combined GIS with other geoinformatics techniques. Through an eclectic mix of cartography, GPS, GIS, satellite imagery, aerial photography, and photogrammetry, Douglas Armstrong, Mark Hauser, David Knight and Stephan Lenik (2008) were able to reconstruct the social context of ownership and control in eighteenth-century St. John in the Danish West Indies. This was accomplished by utilizing an impressive collage of Peter L. Oxholm's historical maps, satellite imagery, archaeological data, documentary evidence, and tax records (*matricals*) in a GIS environment. Their research revealed the consolidation of sugar estates under a few key planters and the emergence of a free colored group who became owners of both land (cotton and provisioning estates) and slaves.

Aerial Photography and Photogrammetry

Aerial photographs are images of the earth's surface taken from a substantial height, often from either an airplane or satellite, that can provide rich insights into human impacts on cultural landscapes through space and time. Photogrammetry is the art, science, and technology of obtaining reliable information about physical objects and the environment through the processes of recording, measuring, and interpreting photographic images and patterns of electromagnetic radiant energy and other phenomena. A primary example of the use of both aerial photographs and photogrammetry in Caribbean archaeology is the ongoing aerial surveys by Stéphen Rostain of several raised agricultural field clusters along the entire French Guiana coast (Rostain 2008). Aerial surveys were made with photography from an ultra-light module to identify the clusters of raised fields. Then the entire French Guiana coastal area was studied by stereoscopic analysis of about 1,500 aerial photographs. Raised fields are generally easy to detect by stereoscopy unless they are hidden by alluvium or the forest. The analysis resulted in a complete map of the earthworks along the 200 kilometers of the western coastal area with detailed stereoscopic interpretations of several specific areas. Comparing 1947 and recent aerial photographs of the French Guiana coast also clearly shows the destruction of many raised fields for the past sixty years (Rostain 2008).

Parris Lyew-Ayee and Ivor Conolley (2008) used aerial photographs, photogrammetry, multispectral satellite imagery and three-dimensional images (in a GIS environment) to create a physical profile of Taíno locations in the parish of Trelawny, Jamaica. This was designed to produce predictive models of where Taíno sites are likely to be found in the parish. The use of remote sensed data, though useful, poses significant limitations because of Trelawny's thick forest canopy covers. A wide range of aerial photography products are available for the Caribbean, including several data sets for Puerto Rico and the United States Virgin Islands from the U.S. Geological Survey and the National Oceanic and Atmospheric Administration. Perhaps the most popular source of aerial photographs has been Google Earth.

Global Positioning Systems (GPS)

GPS uses triangulation to determine the location of features, relying on data from orbiting satellites. In archaeological fieldwork, GPS can be used for mapping find spots, earthworks, and other archaeological features without the need for conventional techniques (i.e., triangulation and offset grids). Because of the capacity of GPS for ground surveys and mapping, Lyew-Ayee and Conolley used it to locate Taíno sites in the field in their study of Trelawny, Jamaica (Lyew-Ayee and Conolley 2008). Realizing that using total stations and/or baselines and offsets would have been inappropriate for surveying many of the widely spaced features in the dense woodland of Nevis, Roger H. Leech (2008) successfully used navigation-grade GPS, which worked well in forested areas when supplemented by a hand-held aerial.

A similar success story comes from Saint Lucia, where an island-wide GPS survey was carried out in 2002 by a team of archaeologists, student assistants, and volunteers from Leiden University and the Florida Museum of Natural History. The project was highly successful, as several new sites were identified and mapped using GPS. What should be particularly encouraging for GPS users in the Caribbean is the excellent satellite coverage that is generally available in the region. The Wide Area Augmentation Service differential satellite is easily accessible in the Caribbean, and generally the satellite coverage seems much better than in Europe, possibly because of the defense interests of the United States in the Caribbean or because of the proximity of the equator. Further, the recent establishment of a Reference Station Network Web site by the Department of Geomatics Engineering and Land Management of The University of the West Indies, St. Augustine (Trinidad and Tobago) will undoubtedly provide better-quality post-processed data for the southern Caribbean.

Geophysics

Geophysics, the study of the various physical properties of the earth and the composition and movement of its component layers of rock, is increasingly being applied to detect archaeologically significant areas of interest. In 1998, geophysical surveys of a Jewish cemetery in Nevis resulted in the identification of at least forty-four possible burials in the cemetery in addition to the nineteen burials that are marked. R. Grant Gilmore III (2008) was able to use a fluxgate gradiometer in St. Eustatius to help identify the location of the slave village at English Quarter plantation. Dry soil and vegetation were the primary

English Quarter Plantation (SE 22)

Pleasures Estate Plantation (SE 57)

Figure G.3. Locations of Pleasures Estate Plantation and English Quarter Plantation on St. Eustatius. Image created by R. Grant Gilmore III, reprinted from Reid (2008, fig. 9.2) by permission of the University of Alabama Press.

deterrents to using the resistivity meter effectively at the Pleasures Estate on St. Eustatius. Despite this, however, this equipment was useful in identifying an enslaved village at English Quarter plantation, including quarters for the enslaved and sugar/rum processing buildings (Figure G.3). The results of geophysical surveys can help archaeologists focus their limited resources on specific areas of each site, thereby significantly reducing the cost of equipment and labor.

Conclusion

Geoinformatics as practiced by Caribbean archaeologists can include a rich array of technological, documentary, and cartographic data sets. Its noninvasive techniques, such as satellite remote sensing, cartography, aerial photography, photogrammetry, GIS, GPS, and geophysical surveys, have facilitated rapid reconnaissance of relatively large areas of archaeological interest. This has led to better site detection and more efficient data collection and management in the laboratory and in the field.

Further Reading

Armstrong, Douglas, Mark Hauser, David Knight, and Stephan Lenik. 2008. "Maps, *Matricals*, and Material Remains: An Archaeological GIS of Late-Eighteenth-Century Historical Sites on St. John, Danish West Indies." In *Archaeology and Geoinformatics: Case Studies from the Caribbean*, ed. Basil A. Reid, 99–126. Tuscaloosa: University of Alabama Press.

Farag, M., and B. Ramlal. 2005. "GIS Analysis on the Archaeological Sites on the Islands of St. Kitts." Paper presented at the Twenty-First Congress of the International Association for Caribbean Archaeology, Trinidad and Tobago.

Gilmore, R. G., III. 2008. "Geophysics and Volcanic Islands: Resistivity and Gradiometry on St. Eustatius." In *Archaeology and Geoinformatics: Case Studies from the Caribbean*, ed. Basil A. Reid, 170–83. Tuscaloosa: University of Alabama Press.

Kappers, M. 2004. "Grand Bay Project, July 2004." *IACA Newsletter*, August 8.

Kappers, M., S. Fitzpatrick, and Q. Kaye. 2007. "Automated Data Collection and 3D Modeling of Archaeological Sites: Examining the Prehistory and Destruction of Grand Bay in Carriacou." In *Proceedings of the Twenty-First Congress of the International Association for Caribbean Archaeology*, ed. B. Reid, H. P. Roget, and A. Curet, 1:81–90. St. Augustine: School of Continuing Studies, University of the West Indies.

Landon, G., and W. Brent Seales. 2005. "Bulking and Visualizing 3D Textured Models of Caribbean Petroglyphs." Paper presented at the Twenty-First Congress of the International Association for Caribbean Archaeology, Trinidad and Tobago.

Leech, Roger H. 2008. "Understanding Nevis: GPS and Archaeological Field Survey in a Postcolonial Landscape." In *Archaeology and Geoinformatics: Case Studies from the Caribbean*, ed. Basil A. Reid, 127–36. Tuscaloosa: University of Alabama Press.

Lyew-Ayee, P. and I. Conolley. 2008. "The Use of Imagery to Locate Taíno Sites in Jamaica in a GIS Environment." In *Archaeology and Geoinformatics: Case Studies from the Caribbean*, ed. Basil A. Reid, 137–52. Tuscaloosa: University of Alabama Press.

Ramlal, Bheshem, and Basil A. Reid. 2008. "Developing an Archaeological Information System for Trinidad and Tobago." In *Archaeology and Geoinformatics: Case Studies from the Caribbean*, ed. Basil A. Reid, 33–73. Tuscaloosa: University of Alabama Press.

Reid, Basil A., ed. 2008. *Archaeology and Geoinformatics: Case Studies from the Caribbean*. Tuscaloosa: University of Alabama Press.

Rostain, S. 2008. "Agricultural Earthworks on the French Guiana Coast." In *Handbook of South American Archaeology*, ed. Helaine Silverman and William Isbell, 217–34. New York: Springer.

Terrell, M. 1998. "What Are You Doing? Examining a Colonial Period Jewish Cemetery in the Caribbean." Paper presented at the Thirty-First Annual Meeting of the Society for Historical Archaeology, Atlanta, Georgia.

Torres, Joshua M., and Reniel Rodríguez Ramos. 2008. "The Caribbean: A Continent Divided by Water." In *Archaeology and Geoinformatics: Case Studies from the Caribbean*, ed. Basil A. Reid, 13–32. Tuscaloosa: University of Alabama Press.

See also Agricultural Earthworks (The Guianas); Archaeological Heritage Management; Nevis; Rescue Archaeology; St. Eustatius.

Golden Rock Site (St. Eustatius)

Joanna K. Gilmore

In 1923, Dr. J. P. B. de Josselin de Jong of Leiden University in the Netherlands found the first evidence for prehistoric people on St. Eustatius. The evidence was found on the Golden Rock sugar plantation, and thus the prehistoric site was named the Golden Rock Site, which now lies within the boundaries of the Franklin D. Roosevelt Airport. In 1984, Leiden University, the St. Eustatius Historical Foundation, and the Archaeological-Anthropological Institute of the Netherlands Antilles (AAINA) started a large-scale archaeological investigation at the site. The excavation continued until 1987; a total of 2800 square meters of earth were uncovered.

Dating from to AD 600 to 800, the Golden Rock prehistoric site is the largest and most important Saladoid site on St. Eustatius. This community of possibly 75 to 100 individuals who lived on the flat agricultural plain could access marine resources, clay sources, coral, wood, and groundwater from this central location. The group's diet mainly consisted of protein from marine resources (fish and shellfish) and was supplemented by occasional iguanas, rice rats, agoutis, birds, and land crabs. Using slash-and-burn agricultural techniques, they were able to cultivate cassava. Wood samples, preserved as charcoal, suggest that there was once a semi-deciduous forest on this flat plain.

The postholes from two circular structures were uncovered during excavations. One structure had an eight-meter diameter and nine postholes. This structure is thought to have been a one-family house, and it had a row of shallower postholes adjacent to the circular structure that may have formed a windbreak for cooking activities. The second structure was nineteen meters in diameter and had two circles of postholes (one inside the other) and evidence of windbreaks on either side. This larger structure may have been a *maloca*, a communal house for several families that is still used by natives in Venezuela today.

Archaeologists found a total of 14 structures, 9 burials, 4 caches, 3 hearths, 113 pits, and 2 middens at the Golden Rock Site. The pottery found at this site included earthenware with red and white slip designs, incisions, and rims that were modeled into human and animal forms. One-quarter of all the ceramics found were decorated; the rest were utilitarian wares that were used for cooking and storage. The ceramics found at the Golden Rock site were high quality. This information and the quality and complexity of the houses suggest that the community functioned on the level of a complex "tribe." Artifacts also included a wide variety of tools and decorative items made of bone, shell, stone, and coral. Faunal remains included fish, shellfish, birds, reptiles, and small mammals. The artifacts found at the Golden Rock site suggest that this was a self-supporting community because few trade items were found, with the exception of flint, which may have come from St. Maarten. The fact that the evidence of prestige items (such as quartz beads, which were found in one child's grave) is scant suggests that the community did not have important status differences or that evidence of status objects has been destroyed. The settlement was abandoned in AD 800 for unknown reasons. Fragments of charcoal found in the postholes of some structures imply that they may have burned down. However, the last *maloca* did not burn down and its posts were removed, which may indicate that habitation on the island continued.

A number of other prehistoric sites have been located

and excavated by archaeologists from Leiden University: these are situated at Corre Corre Bay and the Godet Site. The site at Corre Corre Bay is thought to date to the Archaic Age, several thousand years earlier than any other site on the island. An archaeological survey of the site in 1981 revealed a scatter of chert flakes, fire-cracked rock, and two hammer stones. No pottery or other prehistoric artifacts were found. Small prehistoric artifact scatters have been found across the island. These were documented in Eastman (1996).

Further Reading

Eastman, J. A. 1996. "An Archaeological Assessment of St. Eustatius, Netherlands Antilles." MA thesis, Department of Anthropology, College of William and Mary, Williamsburg, VA.

Josselin de Jong, J. P. B. de. 1947. *Archeological Material from Saba and St. Eustatius, Lesser Antilles*. Leiden: E. J. Brill.

Versteeg, A. H., and F. R. Effert. 1987. *Golden Rock: The First Indian Village on St. Eustatius*. St. Eustatius: St. Eustatius Historical Foundation.

Versteeg, A. H., and K. Schinkel. 1992. *The Archaeology of St. Eustatius: The Golden Rock Site, St. Eustatius*. St. Eustatius: St. Eustatius Historical Foundation; Amsterdam: Foundation for Scientific Research in the Caribbean Region.

See also The National Archaeological Anthropological Memory Management Foundation (NAAM); St. Eustatius Historical Foundation.

Grenada

Scott M. Fitzpatrick

Current archaeological research on Grenada suggests that the island was first settled sometime between 40 BC and AD 240, if not slightly earlier. The first attempt to systematically record prehistoric sites on the island was by Ripley Bullen. Beginning in 1963, Bullen's work was instrumental in forming early ideas about Amerindian settlements and technologies, particularly pottery manufacture and decorative techniques that later developed into a framework for ceramic classification. He conducted a salvage excavation on the small island of Caliviny, located along the southeast coast of Grenada, which eventually led him to name the Caliviny Polychrome style of pottery. Equally well known is his work at the Savanne Suazey site in northeast Grenada, which formed the basis for the well-known Suazoid series of pottery (now commonly referred to as the Suazan style). Other sites investigated by Bullen include Grand Anse, Westerhall Point, and Black Point Beach. However, most of Bullen's fieldwork focused on the Pearls Airport site on the northeastern part of the island, where he reported vast quantities of archaeological material spread over a large area. This research led to other ceramic classifications, including Pearls Cross Hatched.

Pearls is the largest and best known site from Grenada, but it also has the unfortunate distinction of being one of the most heavily impacted sites in the Caribbean due to looting and to the construction of the now-defunct airport by the Cuban government in the 1980s. Since Bullen's work in the 1960s, only limited archaeological research has been conducted by archaeologists on Grenada. The most recent work was in the late 1980s by the University of Florida, though other scholars have worked to record many of the beautiful petroglyphs found on the island along the major rivers and along coastal areas (Figure G.4).

Grenada was first sighted by Europeans during Columbus's third voyage in 1498 and named Concepcion in honor of the Virgin Mary, though it was known as Camerhogne by the native Amerindians. The island's name was changed two years later to Mayo, but in the 1520s it began to be referred to as Granada or variations thereof, which then became more common in usage. Although there were some minor attempts by Europeans to settle the island in the 1600s, it was not settled by Europeans until 1649, when the French landed troops in order to finally subjugate the island. Legend has it that in 1652, after years of conflict with the French, the last of the Island-Carib Indians committed suicide by leaping from the cliffs near the town of Sauteurs along the northern coast. Originally known as Leapers' Hill, it was later named Le Morne de Sauteurs. Over a century later, in 1762, during the Seven Years' War, the British captured Grenada and in 1763, the Treaty of Paris ceded the island to Britain. The French later recaptured Gre-

Figure G.4. Large stone with Amerindian petroglyphs located along one of Grenada's major river systems in the northern part of the island. Photo by Scott M. Fitzpatrick.

nada in 1779, but it was given back to the British in 1783 with the Treaty of Versailles. Today, many remnants of Grenada's historical past exist. One of the most prominent of these is Fort George, which was built between 1705 and 1710 and was used extensively in clashes between the French and British during their campaigns to take control of the island. Fort George is considered to be one of the best examples of Vauban-style masonry in the world, a style that was named after the great French military engineer.

Further Reading

Bullen, R. P. 1964. *The Archaeology of Grenada, West Indies.* Gainesville: University of Florida Press.

Bullen, R. P., and A. K. Bullen. 1972. *Archaeological Investigations on St. Vincent and the Grenadines, West Indies.* Orlando, FL: William Bryant Foundation.

See also Bullen, Ripley (1902–1976), and Adelaide Bullen (1908–1987); Island-Carib; The Suazan Troumassoid (Suazey).

The Grenadines

Scott M. Fitzpatrick

Like many tropical islands worldwide, the Grenadines have a rich array of marine resources (e.g., fish, shellfish) that was exploited extensively by humans in the past. However, they have an impoverished indigenous biota, particularly mammals, which are represented prehistorically in the Caribbean only by bats and rice rats. However, a number of animals were introduced to the islands by humans from South America before European contact. These include the agouti, the guinea pig, the armadillo, the peccary, the opossum, and possibly several others that were never brought in great numbers but probably were used for prestige or ritual foods. The island of Carriacou has the distinction in the Caribbean of having one of the most diverse assemblages of exotic animals that was translocated from South America.

Archaeologically, the Grenadines have been understudied compared to other parts of the Caribbean. In the early 1900s, Jesse Fewkes traveled through the Grenadine islands on behalf of the Smithsonian Institution, collecting samples of artifacts that he thought were best representative of the ancient cultures he found. A half-century later, I. A. Earle Kirby from the St. Vincent Archaeological and Historical Society and Ripley and Adelaide Bullen from the Florida Museum of Natural History (University of Florida) began archaeological research programs that involved more extensive surveying, recording, and small-scale excavation of precolonial locations. Through these efforts, a number of important sites were identified in the Grenadines that culturally and chronologically matched what was observed on the larger islands such as Grenada, St. Vincent, and Barbados.

It was not until 2003, however, that archaeologists began investigating the islands in the Grenadines in detail. In conjunction with the Carriacou Historical Society, Scott M. Fitzpatrick (then at North Carolina State University), Quetta Kaye (University College London), and Michiel Kappers (QLC, BV, ArcheoLINK, The Netherlands) surveyed much of the coastline and other accessible areas of Carriacou, the largest and southernmost island in the Grenadines. After relocating several known sites and discovering many others, excavation focused on the sites of Grand Bay and Sabazan. Over the course of six field seasons between 2003–2011, it became apparent through widespread area excavation at Grand Bay that despite the seemingly smaller and more peripheral nature of Carriacou, the island in fact held important clues to the nature of colonization and long-term settlement by native Amerindians.

Ongoing research indicates that the Grenadines were probably initially settled around AD 400, if not slightly earlier, and that settlement lasted for about 1,000 years. On many islands, including Carriacou, Union, Bequia, Mustique, and Balliceaux, there is evidence in the form of midden deposits, postholes, human burials, and a rich array of artifacts such as beautifully decorated Saladoid, Suazan-Troumassoid and Troumassan-Troumassoid pottery that testify to the vibrant cultures that existed on these smaller islands.

While Carriacou has received the bulk of attention by archaeologists in the Grenadines, a number of other prehistoric sites have been found throughout the islands and have been preliminarily investigated, including Chatham Bay and Miss Pierre on Union, Park Bay on Bequia, Banana Bay on Balliceaux, and Lagoon Bay on Mustique. Although very few radiocarbon dates exist for any of the islands (apart from Carriacou) with which to chronologically anchor these sites, the evidence thus far suggests that the Grenadines were settled during the terminal Saladoid period, a few hundred years later than other islands in the Antilles. Whether this is a result of poor survey coverage or it actually represents a settlement pattern that initially bypassed the Grenadines in favor of the larger islands first is a question currently under investigation.

Research on the Grenadines has helped fill in some of the geographical and chronological gaps in Lesser Antillean prehistory. Research indicates that even the smaller islands of the Caribbean had extensive Amerindian village sites that persisted for a millennium or more before European contact. Archaeological data also suggest that peoples in the Grenadines were actively engaged in trading with other islands, as demonstrated by pottery manufactured with nonlocal materials. They were influenced by peoples in the northern Antilles, as evidenced by the presence of spiritual objects such as *zemíes*. In addition, the discovery of a number of translocated animals and other lines of evidence indicate that the early natives of the Grenadines also interacted intensively with the South American mainland.

Further Reading

Bullen, R. P., and A. K. Bullen. 1972. *Archaeological Investigations on St. Vincent and the Grenadines, West Indies*. Orlando: William Bryant Foundation.

Fewkes, J. W. 1914. "Relations of Aboriginal Culture and Environment in the Lesser Antilles." *Bulletin of the American Geographical Society* 46: 667–68.

Fitzpatrick, S. M., M. Kappers, Q. Kaye, C. M. Giovas, M. LeFebvre, M. H. Harris, S. Burnett, J. A. Pavia, K. Marsaglia, and J. Feathers. 2009. "Precolumbian Settlements on Carriacou, West Indies." *Journal of Field Archaeology* 34: 247–66.

Keegan W. F., S. M. Fitzpatrick, K. Sullivan-Sealy, M. LeFebvre, and P. T. Sinelli. 2008. "The Role of Small Islands in Marine Subsistence Strategies: Case Studies from the Caribbean." *Human Ecology* 36: 635–54.

See also Barbados; Carriacou; Grenada; The Grenadines; St. Vincent.

Griddles

Mark C. Donop

The griddle is a plate-like utilitarian cooking vessel that has been used for thousands of years to prepare a variety of foods (Figure G.5). Griddles from the Caribbean are also known by the Arawakan words *burén* (Taíno), *budári* (Garinagu), and *boutálli* (Dominican Island-Carib). Griddles have traditionally been associated with the preparation of bitter cassava, although recent evidence suggests they may have served multiple purposes.

Ceramic griddles are flat, circular, ceramic vessels that tend to be large, thick, and heavy. Almost all griddles are smooth on the top working surface and rough or fabric-impressed on the bottom side. Griddles were slab-constructed by pressing clay on a flat surface to a suitable thickness and diameter and adding a coiled rim. The latter attributes are the most variable and easily identifiable griddle characteristics. Griddles were supported over fires with stones, clay supports (*topia*), or built-in tripodal legs; the latter innovation developed during the Troumassoid period (AD 500–1450) in the eastern Caribbean. Metal griddles introduced during European contact have almost entirely replaced ceramic ones in the circum-Caribbean.

Ceramic griddles were first produced in South America before the technology spread into the Caribbean with the Saladoid peoples. The earliest reported ceramic griddles have been recovered from the Agüerito site (5300–4000 BP) and various Saladoid sites (4500–3000 BP) in the Middle Orinoco in Venezuela, and they were certainly being produced throughout much of the Orinoco floodplain by 3000 BP. Griddles were brought into the Caribbean around 2500 BP by its earliest Cedrosan Saladoid colonizers, although it should not be assumed that their presence indicates the first use of cassava on the islands.

Recent evidence demonstrates that griddles were multifunctional tools used to process a variety of foods. It has often been assumed that griddles were used almost exclusively to prepare bitter cassava, based on ethnographic and ethnohistorical information. However, it should not be assumed that the absence of griddles at an archaeological site indicates that the people that lived there did not use cassava. The crop can be processed in a variety of ways that do not require the use of a griddle, including simply peeling, washing, cutting, and boiling the tubers in a pot. Additionally, griddles can be used to prepare numerous other foods. Recent starch grain evidence from Cuba showed that Late Ceramic Age people used griddles to process maize (*Zea mays*), beans (*Phaseolus vulgaris*), sweet potato (*Impomoea batatas*), maranta (*Maranta arundinacea*), malanga (*Xanthosoma sp.*), and Zamia (*Zamia pumila*). Animal fatty acids have also been found on griddle fragments.

Figure G.5. Griddle fragments from Savanne Suazey, Grenada, AD 1000–1450. Courtesy of the Anthropology Division of the Florida Museum of Natural History, 98008-09.

Further Reading

DeBoer, W. R. 1975. "The Archaeological Evidence for Manioc Cultivation: A Cautionary Note." *American Antiquity* 40 (4): 419–33.

Oliver, J. R. 2008. "The Archaeology of Agriculture in Ancient Amazonia." In *The Handbook of South American Archaeology*, ed. H. Silverman and W. H. Isbell, 185–216. New York: Springer.

Rodríguez Suárez, R., and J. R. Pagán-Jiménez. 2008. "The *Burén* in Precolonial Cuban Archaeology: New Information Regarding the Use of Plants and Ceramic Griddles during the Late Ceramic Age of Eastern Cuba Gathered through Starch Analysis." In *Crossing the Borders: New Methods and Techniques in the Study of Archaeological Materials from the Caribbean*, ed. C. L. Hofman, M. L. P. Hoogland, and A. L. van Gijn, 159–69. Tuscaloosa: University of Alabama Press.

See also Cassava (Manioc); The First Caribbean Farmers.

Grindstones

Joshua M. Torres and Basil A. Reid

Grindstones are culturally modified stone tools used for grinding. They are often used to process vegetal material in conjunction with the use of a grinding slab, or metate. Handheld grindstones are commonly referred to as manos (see examples in Figure G.6). In the Caribbean, one of the most ubiquitous handheld grindstone tools is the edge-ground cobble. This tool has a wide distribution ranging from Trinidad to Cuba and a broad temporal occurrence ranging from early sites in Trinidad to late Ceramic Age sites in Puerto Rico. From 2009 to 2013, four grindstones and three pestles were retrieved from the Ortoiroid site of St. John in southwest Trinidad. These artifacts clearly suggest the processing of plant materials and, by extension, early Ortoiroid farming in Trinidad. Recent work conducted by Rodríguez Ramos (2005) suggests that the tool represents a long tradition of practices of food production that connect Archaic peoples and later Saladoid–La Hueca and Ostionoid pottery makers in the Caribbean.

Further Reading

Rodríguez Ramos, R. 2001. "Lithic Reduction Trajectories at La Hueca and Punta Candelero Sites, Puerto Rico: A Preliminary Report." In *Proceedings of the Eighteenth Congress of the International Association for Caribbean Archaeology, Grenada, West Indies*, vol. 1, edited by Gerard Richard, 251–61. Guadeloupe, West Indies: International Association for Caribbean Archaeology.

———. 2005. "The Function of the Edge-Ground Cobble Put to the Test: An Initial Assessment." *Journal of Caribbean Archaeology* 6: 1–22.

Walker, J. B. 1985. "A Preliminary Report on the Lithic and Osteological Remains from the 1980, 1981, and 1982 Field Seasons at Hacienda Grande (12PSJ 7-5)." In *Proceedings of the Tenth Congress of the International Association for Caribbean Archaeology, Martinique*, ed. L. Allaire, 181–224. Montreal: Centre de Recherches Caraibe, Université de Montréal.

See also The Archaic Age; The Ortoiroid; St. John Site (Trinidad).

Figure G.6. *Left top and bottom,* pestle/edge-ground cobbles from Puerto Rico. Note the faceted lateral edges and worn ends. Photo: cat. A17066, Department of Anthropology, Smithsonian Institution. *Right,* possible grinding stone or small metate from Puerto Rico. Photo: cat. A231430, Department of Anthropology, Smithsonian Institution.

Ground Sloths

H. Gregory McDonald

Ground sloths in the Caribbean region during the late Pleistocene and early Holocene are represented by three families: Megalonychidae, Megatheriidae, and Mylodontidae. Megalonychidae is known in Cuba, Hispaniola, Puerto Rico, and Curaçao and in South, Central, and North America. The Megatheriidae and Mylodontidae are also present in countries bordering the Caribbean in South, Central, and North America. Currently five genera of late Pleistocene Caribbean megalonychid ground sloths—*Megalocnus, Parocnus, Neocnus, Acratocnus,* and *Paulocnus*—comprising fourteen species are recognized (see examples in Figure G.7). The family Megatheriidae is represented by a single species, *Eremotherium laurillardi*, which is distributed along the Atlantic coast of South America from southern Brazil through Mexico to Florida and as far north as New Jersey. The family Mylodontidae is represented by two genera, *Glossotherium* in Central and South America and *Paramylodon* in Mexico and the United States, but this family, especially species in the Caribbean region, requires further study.

Eremotherium is the largest genus; its estimated body mass was 3,960 kilograms. Its large size has facilitated its frequent discovery throughout the region. Some sites in Guatemala containing *Eremotherium* have been investi-gated as possible kill sites by humans, but the evidence is equivocal. Despite its wide geographic range, to date it has not been demonstrated conclusively that humans hunted *Eremotherium*, although the youngest radiocarbon date of circa 13,000 BP from a site in Brazil suggests that the species survived late enough in South America to have been encountered by humans.

Mylodont sloths, with a body mass of about 1,400 kilograms, are smaller than megatheres. While there is some evidence from Chile and Argentina that one species, *Mylodon darwinii*, may have been hunted by humans, there is no evidence to indicate that humans in the Caribbean region hunted members of the family. Compared to their mainland contemporaries, none of the Caribbean island sloths are large. The estimated body mass of the largest species, *Megalocnus rodens*, is 146 kilograms, while some species of *Neocnus* are considerably smaller with an estimated body mass of 8.4 kilograms.

Although the first ground sloth from Cuba, *Megalocnus rodens* (Figure G.8), was described in 1868 by Joseph Leidy, Mark R. Harrington (1921) was the first to propose the coexistence of humans and sloths in the Caribbean. His theory is based on his excavations at Cueva de la Caleta, Oriente Province, Cuba, and subsequent work

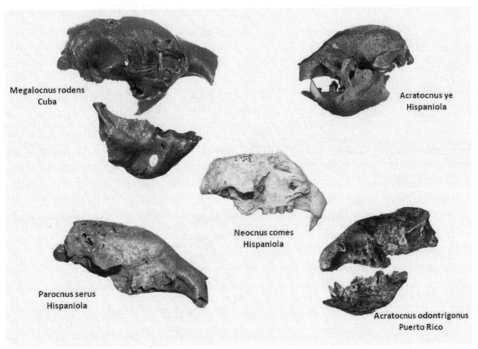

Megalocnus rodens
Cuba

Acratocnus ye
Hispaniola

Neocnus comes
Hispaniola

Parocnus serus
Hispaniola

Acratocnus odontrigonus
Puerto Rico

Figure G.7. Representative examples of skulls of West Indian Megalonychid ground sloths. *Megalocnus* from de Paula Couto (1959). *Acratocnus* from Anthony (1918). Other photographs courtesy of H. Gregory McDonald.

Figure G.8. Reconstruction of the appearance of *Megalocnus rodens* by Carl Buell based on mounted composite skeleton from Ciego Montero, Cuba, at the American Museum of Natural History, New York. Reproduced by permission of Carl Buell.

at Cueva de los Portales in Pinar del Río Province. The remains of the first ground sloths on Hispaniola were found in 1921, and the following year Gerrit S. Miller Jr. suggested that early humans and sloths had coexisted on Hispaniola based on the association of sloth remains with artifacts in caves near St. Michel, Haiti.

Recent radiocarbon dates of Caribbean ground sloths support Harrington's and Miller's contention that sloths survived into the Holocene well after the extinction of their counterparts in South, Central, and North America and coexisted with humans on both islands. *Parocnus browni* from the tar deposits of Las Breas de San Felipe, Cuba, has been dated to circa 5600 BP, while *Parocnus* sp. from Cueva de los Niños, Cuba, has been dated to circa 3500 cal BP and from Cueva del Túnel, Cuba, to circa 4800 BP. In Cuba, *Megalocnus rodens* from Caverna de Pío Domingo has been dated to circa 3000 BP, from Cueva Musulmanes to around 2500 BP, and from Cueva Beruvides to circa 7000 BP. *Megalocnus* from Solapa de Silex was dated at circa 4700 BP, but the human skeletal remains recovered there have been dated to 3200 BP.

A number of specimens of *Neocnus* from cave sites in Haiti have produced young dates, although none of the sites contained artifacts or evidence of human presence. The youngest date is from Trouing Ismays, which has been dated to circa 5000 BP. There are no radiocarbon dates for sloths from Puerto Rico or Curaçao.

The young radiocarbon dates for some sloth taxa on Cuba and Hispaniola clearly indicate their survival much later than sloths on the mainland. Given the earli-

est estimates for the arrival of humans on the islands at around 7,000–8,000 years ago, it appears that humans coexisted with sloths for about 3,000 to 4,000 years prior to extinction of the latter. Two cultural groups have been specifically identified as interacting with sloths in Cuba and Hispaniola: the Casimiroid (4000–400 BC), who may have hunted ground sloths in the northern Caribbean; and the Taíno (AD 1200–1500), who appear to have evolved from the Ostionoid.

The accumulation of adult and juvenile remains of *Megalocnus* from Solapa del Megalocnus, Cuba, were attributed to human hunting activity based on what were interpreted as cut marks on their bones. Other sloths, including *Parocnus browni*, *Miocnus antillensis*, *Neocnus gliriformis*, *N. minor*, and *Acratocnus* sp., were also reported from the site. While lithics recovered from the site were described as Archaic, a specific culture was not identified, and unfortunately no radiocarbon dates were reported. Bones of *Megalocnus* from Cueva del Chino, Cuba, have also been interpreted as having been intentionally fractured and burned by humans. Many of the Cuban archaeological sites with sloths were thought by Rouse to be associated with the Ciboney culture, though most Caribbean scholars now refer to this group as the Guanahatabey (Rouse 1992).

The production of large blades and projectile points by Casimiroid peoples in the Dominican Republic has led to the inference they hunted sloths. A date of circa 3000 BP for *Parocnus serus* recovered from a cave near Chinguela in the Cordillera Central was used to support this notion, although no artifacts were found in the cave, and it is more likely the site was used as a den instead of a kill site. If the inferred cut marks on bones from *Megalocnus* specimens at the Solapa de Silex and Cueva del Chino sites are valid, they would be some of the few to provide direct evidence of hunting and butchering by humans. More evidence is needed to assess if and how humans may have contributed to the extinction of the island taxa of sloths.

Further Reading

Anthony, H. E. 1918. "The Indigenous Land Mammals of Porto Rico, Living and Extinct." *Memoirs of the American Museum of Natural History* n.s. 2, part 2: 331–435.

Arredondo Antúnez, C. C., and R. Villavicencio Finalet. 2004. "Tafonomía del depósito arqueológico Solapa del Megalocnus en el noroeste de Villa Clara, Cuba." *Revista Biología* 18: 160–71.

De Paula Couto, C. 1956. "On Two Mounted Skeletons of Megalocnus rodens (Cuba)." *Journal of Mammalogy* 37 (3): 423–427.

Harrington, M. R. 1921. *Cuba before Columbus*. 2 vols. New York: Museum of the American Indian and the Heye Foundation.

MacPhee, R. D. E., M. A. Iturralde-Vienet, and O. Jiménez Vázquez. 2007. "Prehistoric Sloth Extinctions in Cuba: Implications of a New 'Last' Appearance Date." *Caribbean Journal of Science* 43: 94–98.

Miller, G. S., Jr. 1922. *Remains of Mammals from Caves in the Republic of Haiti*. Washington, DC: Smithsonian Institution.

Rouse, I. 1992. *The Tainos: Rise and Decline of the People who Greeted Columbus*. New Haven, CT: Yale University Press.

Steadman, D. W., P. S. Martin, R. D. E. MacPhee, A. J. T. Jull, H. G. McDonald, C. A. Woods, M. Iturralde-Vinent, and G. W. L. Hodgins. 2005. "Asynchronous Extinction of Late Quaternary Sloths on Continents and Islands." *Proceedings of the National Academy of Sciences* 102: 11763–68.

Veloz Maggiolo, M., and E. Ortega. 1976. "The Preceramic of the Dominican Republic: Some New Finds and Their Possible Relationships." In *Proceedings of the First Puerto Rican Symposium on Archaeology*, ed. L. S. Robinson, 147–201. San Juan: Fundación Arqueológica, Antropológica, e Histórica de Puerto Rico.

See also The Casimiroid; Ciboney versus Guanahatabey; Historical Ecology.

Guadeloupe (Eastern)

Maaike de Waal

Precolonial settlement patterns in eastern Guadeloupe (2000 BC–AD 400), specifically the easternmost tip of Guadeloupe, the Pointe des Châteaux peninsula, and the islands of La Désirade and Petite Terre, have been investigated through full-coverage surveys in the period 1998–2000. No evidence was found for Archaic or Early Ceramic A habitation, but it is possible that sites were once present in coastal areas, only to be eventually obliterated by land erosion. Because the area was ecologically diverse and relatively close to sources of good-quality chert (La Désirade) and flint (Antigua), it might have been attractive to Archaic and Early Ceramic A groups, and both periods have been hypothetically labeled as pioneer phases for eastern Guadeloupe.

The beginning of occupation in eastern Guadeloupe (AD 400–600/850) was coeval with a population increase on several other Caribbean islands with Early Ceramic A habitation sites, and with the occupation of islands that had previously been uninhabited. Settlement was concentrated in large permanent villages: five on Pointe des Châteaux and one on La Désirade. The villages were evenly distributed along the coasts in areas with easy access from the sea and good exploitation potential and observation facilities. The inhabitants probably exploited resource areas in close proximity to their settlements. To date, no ceremonial sites have been identified, and the discovery of only one possible temporary habitation site and a small quantity of off-site material suggests that most activities were centered in or near the settlements. No evidence has been found for the existence of any settlement hierarchy, although Les Sables (La Désirade) and Anse à la Gourde (Pointe des Châteaux) were the larger and most intensively occupied habitations.

During the Late Ceramic A period (AD 600/850–1200/1300), the open spaces in the landscape were gradually filled up with settlements, especially after AD 1000. During this period, the formerly uninhabited islands of Petite Terre were also being settled and exploited. People continued to live in large permanent villages, most of which continued to be situated in attractive coastal areas. Fifty-nine sites have been found, including twenty-two habitation sites, two ceremonial sites, one strategic outpost, and thirty-four sites that were used for temporary habitation, shelter, and other special activities. Site-type diversity had obviously increased, indicating that settlements no longer functioned as centers where all ceremonial, sociopolitical, and economic activities were carried out. Larger parts of the landscape gained importance, and the landscape was more intensively used. A settlement hierarchy began to develop, and Anse à la Gourde evolved into a central settlement.

The eastern Guadeloupe microregion became desolate during the Late Ceramic B period (AD 1200/1300–1493). Two small villages, Morne Cybèle 1 and Morne Souffleur, remained in formerly uninhabited, impressive, and well-defensible locations on La Désirade's central plateau. Their inhabitants exploited resources at quite some distance from their villages. One small Late Ceramic B component has been identified at Anse à la Gourde on Pointe des Châteaux. During this period, Petite Terre was abandoned, the landscape was less intensively used, and ceremonial activities were limited to the settlements once again.

Further Reading

De Waal, M. S. 1999. "The Pointe des Châteaux Survey 1998: A Preliminary Report." In *Actes du XVIII Congrès International d'Archéologie de la Caraibe* (*Proceedings of the XVIII International Congress for Caribbean Archaeology*), 2:268–76. Basse-Terre, FWI: l'Association Internationale d'Archéologie de la Caraïbe, Région Guadeloupe.

———. 2006. *Pre-Columbian Social Organisation and Interaction Interpreted through the Study of Settlement Patterns: An Archaeological Case-Study of the Pointe des Châteaux, La Désirade, and Les Îles de la Petite Terre Micro-Region, Guadeloupe, F.W.I.* Leiden: De Waal.

Hofman, C. L., A. Delpuech, M. L. P. Hoogland, and M. S. De Waal. 2004. "Late Ceramic Age Survey of the North-Eastern Islands of the Guadeloupean Archipelago: Grande-Terre, La Désirade, and Petite-Terre." In *Late Ceramic Age Societies in the Eastern Caribbean*, ed. A. Delpuech and C. L. Hofman, 159–81. Oxford: British Archaeology Reports.

Knippenberg, S. 2007. *Stone Artefact Production and Exchange among the Northern Lesser Antilles.* Amsterdam: Amsterdam University Press.

See also The Archaic Age; Martinique.

Guanín

Jeffrey P. Blick

Guanín is a metallic alloy, sometimes referred to as a base gold or low-grade gold, which is typically thought to have been a naturally occurring precolonial alloy of several metals, including copper, gold, and silver, with minor components of chromium, cobalt, manganese, zinc, and other elements (Stevens-Arroyo 2006, 68). *Guanín*, originally a Taíno word recorded by Columbus on his 1492 voyage, is found in the circum-Caribbean, the Andes, and Amazonia, including large areas of nearby Colombia and perhaps even as far south as the Southern Cone of South America. Sometimes *guanín* is referred to as a "manganese bronze," although it is typically considered by experts in precolonial metallurgy to be a gold-copper-silver alloy. In Colombia, this alloy was known as *tumbaga* (Figure G.9) and was traded far and wide, even toward the circum-Caribbean, and likely within the insular Caribbean itself.

Columbus transported a piece of *guanín* back to Spain for analysis, where it was found to be an alloy of gold (55 percent), copper (25 percent), and silver (19 percent), thus supporting the elemental characterization above. According to Roget (1997, 171) and Rouse (1992, 127), *guanín* objects were traded into the Caribbean islands by Cariban-speaking Island-Carib traders with objects ultimately derived from Central, South American, or Amazonian tribes familiar with metallurgy; the Caribbean groups were supposedly less sophisticated in their knowledge of metalworking. However, Caribbean Taíno metallurgists have been credited with the creation of precolonial works of art, including gold and/or *guanín* laminate or plates (probably hammered from alluvial gold dust), idols or *zemíes*, masks, nose rings, and earrings. A continuing trade in copper-

Figure G.9. A Sinú *guanín* (*tumbaga*) nose ring from northern Colombia similar to the nose ornaments worn by Taíno peoples of the Caribbean as reported by Columbus (ca. AD 800–1500, width 20 mm). Reproduced by permission of Edgar L. Owen (EdgarLOwen.com).

actually a linguistic reference to *guanín*. The word *guanín* has also been interpreted as a trade ornament made of low-grade gold that was typically worn in the noses and ears and as pendants by Taíno people as amulets of protection against illness (Roget 1997, 171). Columbus also noted *guanín* pendants on Jamaica on his second voyage in 1494, on Trinidad in 1498 and on the Paria Peninsula of Venezuela on his third voyage in 1498 (Rouse 1992, 148–49). Chiefs wore *guanín* ornaments on their chests as status symbols and apparently were buried with many of their high-status objects (Stevens-Arroyo 2006, 47).

The *guanín* ornament worn by the chief was a symbol of the multilayered universe in which health and sickness, good and evil, and the Rainbow Serpent (protection against disease) and its evil twin spirit (the cause of disease) all existed (Stevens-Arroyo 2006, 171). *Guanín* symbolized the chief's ability to mediate between different realms of the universe. Because of the general lack of knowledge about many of the *guanín* artifacts that have been recovered in the Greater Caribbean, new archaeometric techniques are being attempted by Corinne Hofman and associates to verify the source locations and manufacturing techniques of *guanín* artifacts and to infer their patterns of exchange across the greater pan-Caribbean region.

gold alloy objects from South America to the Caribbean was documented during the time of the Spanish conquistadors (ibid.). On Guanahani (San Salvador, Bahamas), Columbus recorded, "I saw that some of them had a small piece [of gold] fastened in a hole which they have in the nose" (Columbus in Markham 1893, 39 [entry for October 13, 1492]). Archaeological evidence of two copper fragments from North Storr's Lake, San Salvador, that included minor trace elements of silicon, aluminum, magnesium, and sodium supports the presence of a copper alloy, likely *guanín*, in the eastern central Bahamas.

There was a variety of words for "gold," or *guanín*, among the different linguistic groups of the Caribbean: it was called *nozay, nuzay, nuçay,* or *nosái* on San Salvador; *caona,* its most common name, throughout most of Hispaniola (Granberry and Vescelius 2004); and sometimes *tuob* (*twob*) in the more remote Ciguayo areas of Hispaniola, where that word was used synonymously for copper or poor-quality gold, probably *guanín*. One of the Island-Carib Columbus encountered on Hispaniola in January 1493 told a legend about an island named Goanin that contained large amounts of *tuob* (copper or base gold). It now appears that this fictional island was

Further Reading

Dunn, Oliver, and James E. Kelley Jr. 1989. *The Diario of Christopher Columbus's First Voyage to America, 1492–1493.* Norman: University of Oklahoma Press.

Granberry, J., and G. S. Vescelius. 2004. *Languages of the Pre-Columbian Antilles.* Tuscaloosa: University of Alabama Press.

Markham, Clements R., trans. 1893. *The Journal of Christopher Columbus (During His First Voyage, 1492–93).* London: The Hakluyt Society.

Plazas, Clemencia, ed. 1986. *Precolumbian American Metallurgy.* Bogotá, Colombia: Banco de la República.

Roget, H. P. 1997. "The Taino Vision: A Study in the Exchange of Misunderstanding." In *The Indigenous Peoples of the Caribbean,* ed. Samuel M. Wilson, 169–75. Gainesville: University Press of Florida.

Rouse, I. 1992. *The Tainos: Rise and Decline of the People Who Greeted Columbus.* New Haven, CT: Yale University Press, 1992.

Stevens-Arroyo, A. M. 2006. *Cave of the Jagua: The Mythological World of the Taínos.* Scranton, PA: University of Scranton Press.

See also Archaeometry; Elite Exchange in the Caribbean; Lapidary Trade.

Guano

Kevin Farmer

Guano is the name given to the excrement of bats and birds; it is used for fertilizer in agricultural production. The importance of this fertilizer facilitated the development of an international guano industry in the nineteenth century that enabled countries such as Peru to gain immense wealth from the harvesting and exportation of the resource to countries around the world. This fertilizer allowed nitrogen-depleted soils to be reinvigorated. It was also used to produce saltpeter, an important component in the manufacture of gunpowder.

During the 1800s, many planters in the Caribbean began to import guano to enrich the soil because of soil depletion caused by extensive sugar production. Initial shipments of guano originated from Peru and islands in the Pacific. In some instances, islands such as Barbados, which were dependent on Peruvian and Pacific island guano, were able to obtain supplies from islands such as Antigua, which developed a thriving guano industry.

Before European contact, guano was utilized as a fertilizer by the Amerindian peoples of the Americas. From as early as AD 500, the Moche people mined for *huano*, and the Incas did such mining in AD 1200. The Incas considered *huano* to be equivalent to gold and saw it as a gift from the gods. However, their use of the product as a fertilizer declined with the Spanish conquest. It was not until 1840, when Alexandre Cochet, a French scientist, successfully experimented with the effects of bird droppings on plant growth, that Europeans fully realized the potential of guano.

The English had early control of the guano market, but increased competition from the Americans began after the United States passed the Guano Islands Act in 1856. This act allowed the U.S. government to seize control of guano-producing islands such as Howland, Baker, and Jarvis islands in the Pacific and the Serranilla Bank, Navassa Island, and the Petrel Islands in the Caribbean. The latter islands are located in the northwestern Caribbean in close proximity to one other; the Serranilla Bank and the Petrel Islands (also called the Bajo Neuvo Bank) are located approximately 400 kilometers northeast of the Nicaraguan coast, while Navassa is located 52 kilometers west of Haiti.

The Age of Guano in Peru (1845–1880) resulted in revenue of $750 million and the excavation of some 11 million tonnes of guano. By the late 1870s, the resource had been overexploited, causing a decline in Peru's economy. This, coupled with the development of artificial fertilizers in the late nineteenth century, led to a sharp decline in the use of guano as an organic fertilizer in the early years of the twentieth century.

Further Reading

Gootenberg, P. 1989. *Between Silver and Guano: Commercial Policy and the State in Postindependence Peru*. Princeton, NJ: Princeton University Press.

Kaufman, W., and H. S. Macpherson. 2005. *Britain and the Americas*. Santa Barbara, CA: ABC-Clio.

Mathew, W. M. 1981. *The House of Gibbs and the Peruvian Guano Monopoly*. London: Royal Historical Society.

Pukrop, Michael E. 1997. "Phosphate Mining in Nauru." Ted Case Studies no. 412. http://www1.american.edu/ted/NAURU.htm.

See also The Cayman Islands.

H

Hematite

Joshua M. Torres

Hematite is a mineral form of iron oxide (Fe_2O_3). In powder form, hematite is red, and the name of the mineral derives from the Greek word for blood (*haima* or *haimatos*). Hematite naturally occurs in areas of banded iron formations as a consequence of thermal mineralized hot springs or in geologic formations associated with volcanic activity. The specific density of hematite is relatively heavy, and it is highly magnetic.

Hematite is present in various forms from an array of archaeological contexts in the West Indies. The local basalts of the Windward Islands contain high relative constituent percentages of the mineral. Hematite has been suggested as a primary pigment source for cave paintings on Curaçao and as a potential grave offering in association with red ochre in Archaic burials. Hematite rubbing stones are common prehistoric artifact types in the Lesser Antilles. Hematite occurs naturally in clays and is found in varying degrees in pottery pastes and paint throughout the Lesser Antilles, Puerto Rico, and Hispaniola. Hematite may also have been used by the native peoples of the Caribbean as body paint for rituals and warfare.

Further Reading

Haviser, J. B. 2001. "New Data for the Archaic Age on Curaçao." In *Proceedings of the Nineteenth Congress of the International Association for Caribbean Archaeology*, 288–300. Oranjestad: Archaeological Museum of Aruba.

Historical Archaeological Sites (Types)

Naseema Hosein-Hoey

Domestic Sites

Domestic sites can range from the smallest to the largest living structures. Structural evidence on domestic sites can assist in the reconstruction of domestic structures. The material culture recovered from habitation sites can inform us about trade, religion, and social hierarchy. It can demonstrate waste disposal patterns and can also provide evidence of elite and non-elite consumption patterns. In 1999, Brinsley Samaroo, Archibald Chauharjasingh, Kofi Agorsah, and a team of students from Portland State University and a team from the History Department of The University of the West Indies, St. Augustine, conducted excavations on the Hondo River Islamic settlement site at the foot of Trinidad's Northern Range. In examining the material remains and artifacts recovered from the site, the Hondo River research team was able to interpret the life conditions of the Islamic settlers. Objects recovered from the site include olive oil bottles, pharmaceutical bottles, metal objects, kaolin clay tobacco pipe stems and bowls, cooking utensils, utilitarian ceramics, chains, horseshoes, hammer heads, musket balls, machetes, and a variety of nails and spoons.

Another colonial Caribbean domestic site is Nanny Town, a Maroon site located in the Blue Mountains in eastern Jamaica. The site, which was excavated by Kofi Agorsah (1998) in the early 1990s, yielded mid-seventeenth-century Spanish coins, tin-glazed earthenwares, white and red clay tobacco pipes, glass and stone beads, locally produced terracotta and earthenware figurines, and a selection of precolonial native artifacts. The presence of these native artifacts suggests that there was a

Taíno occupation before or during the Maroon occupation, implying that the two populations possibly coexisted, traded, and interacted.

Douglas Armstrong conducted research on enslaved village spatial organization at the Seville Plantation in Jamaica in which he compared two village sites: one from the earlier part of the eighteenth century and the other from the latter part of the eighteenth century. He compared architectural evidence from these two villages and found that the linear organization of the village was influenced by the domination of the planter. The less formal layout of the later village sight indicated that the planter's powers were significantly relaxed as a result of creolization.

Industrial Sites

Industrial sites relate to the manufacture or production of goods for local, regional, or international trade. The study of industrial sites is known as industrial archaeology. Industrial archaeologists seek to record the remnants of industrialization, including transportation technology and the buildings associated with manufacturing or raw material production. Industrial archaeologists also concentrate on workers' social and economic conditions based on archaeological evidence and archival research. Xavier Rosseau and Yolande Vragar's research focused on the specialized production of indigo plants for production in Marie Galante, Guadeloupe. They proved that the French West Indies were the chief producers of sugar and indigo for France during the eighteenth century.

Reeder's Foundry in Jamaica has provided evidence of local metal production in the Caribbean. This foundry, based in Morant Bay (Jamaica), manufactured cannon balls and made and repaired metal objects during the eighteenth century. During peak production, 267 Africans were in charge of smelting and manufacturing iron and other metals. This site is an excellent example of the integration of traditional African iron smelting techniques and traditional African culture in the New World.

In the early 1980s, Lydia Pulsipher and Conrad Goodwin conducted investigations at Galways Plantation on Montserrat. Their research focused on the evolution of plantation systems, based on agricultural and industrial economies. Research at the Creque Marine Slipway in St. Thomas (United States Virgin Islands) revealed important data on the industrial landscape of the island. The presence of the Creque Marine Slipway Powerhouse and marine railway demonstrated that by the 1870s this slipway was a busy, important slipway that accommodated vessels hauling up to 1,200 tons.

Military Sites

Military sites relate to forts, batteries, blockhouses, earthworks, and battlefields. The study of fortifications in the Caribbean can provide insights into their physical infrastructure and into military engineering methods. The material culture present on these sites provides historical archaeologists with an understanding of the daily lives of those involved in warfare. Through the use of historical records, archaeologists can also study the strategies and tactics used in warfare.

Military sites also offer information on certain metals and how they were used on forts and fortifications. Excavations by Archibald Chauharjasingh, Candice Goucher, and Kofi Agorsah at the eighteenth- and early nineteenth-century blacksmith's shop at Fort George (Tobago) recovered metal artifacts, pottery, and large pieces of slag. There was also evidence at the fort of an African military presence known as the Black Jaegers. One of the objects found at the surface of the site was an intricately carved ornament, possibly a hip mask.

Gerald Schroedl has led a multiyear research program involving archaeologists from the University of Tennessee. This team has investigated the lives of soldiers, slaves, and civilians at Brimstone Hill on St. Kitts. During the 2000s, the team used geophysics, documentary evidence, and targeted excavations to analyze many dimensions of lifeways at the fortification complex, including health, foodways, the trans-Atlantic supply train, and the evolution of defensive works.

Maritime Sites

Maritime sites are areas where humans interacted with oceans, lakes, or rivers in the past. Maritime archaeology can assist in the interpretation of maritime trade routes, naval warfare, and nautical technology. It includes the study of objects and human remains that have been recovered from the remains of ships, boats, or other watercraft. Other types of maritime sites may include structures that were originally built either completely submerged in water or on shore. Bridges, piers, homes, port structures, and warehouses are all examples of maritime sites that are not shipwrecks.

Port Royal is perhaps the Caribbean's most well-known underwater archaeology site. However, several other maritime excavations have taken place throughout the region. In 1998, two groups in Cuba were principally involved in maritime archaeology: CARISUB and GEOCUBA. CARISUB was involved in underwater archaeological work for twenty years while GEOCUBA was involved for five years. During 1982 and 1988, the Archaeological Anthropological Institute of the Netherland Antilles (NAAM) and the College of William and Mary undertook archaeological research in the historical anchorage of St. Eustatius at Orange Bay. Both the size and location of this historical anchorage were identified and Dutch, British, and French material cultural remains were recovered. Port Royal was once the busiest port in the world.

By using the popular press in Trinidad and Tobago, Claire Broadbridge was able to encourage the government of the twin island republic to protect several French Louis XIV shipwrecks that were discovered buried in sediments on the coast of Tobago. Vel Lewis, the chair of the National Trust of Trinidad and Tobago, explained the importance of these seventeenth-century wrecks at the first meeting of the Technical Commission on Underwater Cultural Heritage in Santo Domingo. The Protection of Wrecks Act of 1994 is the primary piece of legislation used to safeguard underwater remains in Trinidad and Tobago.

Religious Sites

A wide range of religious sites have been investigated archaeologically in the Caribbean. Early Catholic Church sites in the Dominican Republic were excavated by teams led by Kathleen Deagan in the 1990s (Deagan and Cruxent 2002). Synagogue sites have been a special focus for Caribbean religious site specialists, and sites on St. Eustatius, Nevis and Barbados have been subjected to extensive scholarly research. Protestant churches have also been investigated in the Bahamas, on Jamaica, and on St. Eustatius. Military chapels in the former British colonies have also been examined during the past several decades. Bridgetown (Barbados) and Oranjestad (St. Eustatius) stand out in particular. The ruins of church sites reflect the great diversity of organized Christian religions established in the Caribbean. Lutheran, Catholic, Anglican, Dutch Reformed, and Methodist churches existed simultaneously in these cities during the late eighteenth century.

Burial Sites

Burial sites provide important information about past societies. Through physical anthropology, archaeologists are able to obtain useful information about the age, sex, and cause of death of buried individuals. Archaeologists are also able to obtain information about diet, the prevalence of disease, and the growth rates of children and adults. Although the study of these sites can be beneficial, ethical and religious issues may prohibit or inhibit archaeologists from studying these areas to their full potential.

Thomas Romon, Patrice Courtaud, and André Delpuech conducted archaeological investigations at three colonial cemeteries in Guadeloupe (Courtaud, Delpuech, and Romon 1998). Their research unearthed funerary artifacts that included bone buttons and copper needles. The Harney site in Montserrat provided insights into the possibility that malnutrition led to the death of enslaved males. Christopher Crain's study of fourteen individuals that were found in Bridgetown, Barbados, showed evidence of labor-intensive activities associated with the interred individuals. The grave goods recovered from these burials dated from the second half of the seventeenth century to the first half of the eighteenth century.

Special-Purpose Sites

Special-purpose sites are areas where individuals performed activities related to industrial production and military and domestic activities. Examples of special-purpose sites include taverns, churches, hospitals, and stores. Queen's Royal College, which was established in 1904 and is one of the oldest secondary schools in Trinidad, and Manning's High School in Jamaica, which was founded in 1738, are examples of special-purpose sites in the West Indies. During the 1980s and the 1990s, Norman Barka conducted excavations and research in areas where 600 seaside buildings, including warehouses, brothels, taverns, and homes, once stood on St. Eustatius (Barka 1985). His research furnished useful information on these structures, which were once the center of activity when St. Eustatius was the center for transshipment in the Atlantic World. In the 2000s, Grant Gilmore continued this work with the St. Eustatius Center for Archaeological Research on several sites on Oranje Bay, St. Eustatius, including the customs house, the offices of the Dutch West Indies Company, and a pauper/criminal burial ground adjacent to the gallows.

Multipurpose Sites

Multipurpose sites include areas where individuals carried out several important activities. These sites cannot be classified as special-purpose sites because various domestic and industrial tasks may have been performed in these spaces. One good example of a multipurpose site is Lime Street in Port Royal, Jamaica. The archaeological assemblage recovered from this site indicated multipurpose activities such as domestic duties, food preparation, and trade. A large portion of Port Royal was submerged due to a powerful earthquake in 1692.

Further Reading

Agorsah, E. Kofi. 1998. "Ethnoarchaeological Consideration of Social Relationship and Settlement Patterning among Africans in the Caribbean Diaspora." In *African Sites: Archaeology in the Caribbean*, ed. J. B. Haviser, 38–64. Princeton, NJ: Markus Weiner Publishers.

Armstrong, D., and E. Reitz. 1990. *The Old Village and the Great House: An Archaeological and Historical Examination of Drax Hall Plantation, St. Ann's Bay, Jamaica*. Urbana: University of Illinois Press.

Barka, Norman. 1985. *Archaeology of St. Eustatius, Netherlands Antilles: An Interim Report on the 1981–1984 Seasons*. Williamsburg, VA: College of William and Mary.

Courtaud, Paul, André Delpuech, and Thomas Romon. 1998. "Archaeological Investigations at Colonial Cemeteries on Guadeloupe: African Slave Burial Sites or Not?" In *African Sites: Archaeology in the Caribbean*, ed. J. B. Haviser, 277–90. Princeton, NJ: Markus Weiner Publishers.

Deagan, Kathleen A., and José María Cruxent. 2002. *Archaeology at La Isabela: America's First European Town*. New Haven, CT: Yale University Press.

Muckelroy, K. 1978. *Maritime Archaeology*. Cambridge, UK: Cambridge University Press.

Orser, C. E., Jr. 2004. *Historical Archaeology*. 2nd ed. Upper Saddle River, N. J.: Pearson Prentice Hall.

Palmer, M., and P. Neaverson. 1998. *Industrial Archaeology*. London: Routledge.

Ruppé, C., and J. Barstad. 2002. *International Handbook of Underwater Archaeology*. New York: Springer.

Singleton, T. 1999. *I, Too, Am America: Archaeological Studies of Africa-American Life*. Charlottesville: University of Virginia Press.

See also Hondo River Settlement (Trinidad); The Nanny Town Maroons of Jamaica; Newton Burial Ground (Barbados); Port Royal (Jamaica); The Seville Sugar Plantation (British Colonial Jamaica); Underwater Archaeology.

Historical Ecology

Scott M. Fitzpatrick

Introduction

Historical ecology can be defined as "the complex, historical interactions between human populations and the ecosystems they have inhabited" (Kirch and Hunt 1997, 2). This field of study, also referred to as human ecodynamics, combines paleoecology, archaeological investigation, land-use history, and more recent long-term (decadal) ecological research to help examine the life history of a region. Many researchers have been attracted to this multidisciplinary field of study because it provides a foundation for observing anthropogenic changes through time and how they relate to the environment. This perspective is not without its difficulties, however, as it is often challenging to document how and when environments change; they are rarely constant, and humans can adapt to these fluctuations in many different ways.

Despite these challenges, the interdisciplinary approach that historical ecology offers is particularly useful for examining island and coastal ecosystems. As research has shown for the Caribbean, the Pacific, and other island regions, these land forms were relatively stable before human arrival. Because the flora and fauna on islands reflect biogeographic distributions that typically limit the kinds of biota that cannot disperse easily by air or water, they have high rates of endemism (biological characteristics found exclusively in a given area). As a result, islands are particularly fragile ecologically, and the presence of omnivorous humans (and the things they brought with them) can dramatically disrupt these environments. As such, we should expect to see a number of changes to islands after humans arrive, though this is dependent on a number of factors that include population size and distance from islands to other land masses.

One of the main reasons scholars have moved toward a broader temporal perspective on human-environmental interaction on islands and elsewhere is the recognition that global climatic problems and human interference on land and sea is rooted in the ancient past. Historical ecology is needed to answer questions about how the environment changed or was impacted before and after human arrival. This approach is a result of the recognition by scholars that peoples in the past did not necessarily live in harmony with their environment but were active participants in exploiting resources, sometimes to the point of extinction. Archaeological research has shown that even relatively small groups of hunter-gatherers can have severe impacts on the environment, depending on the kinds of activities in which they are engaged. In general, it is becoming clear through archaeological and other lines of evidence that all humans can affect their environment in some fashion and that the levels of impact often intensify as populations grow.

One of the great benefits of archaeology is that it is the only discipline capable of revealing what has happened in antiquity from a deep time perspective. Because islands are ideal model systems for examining how humans impacted pristine environments, archaeology is providing useful information about changes that occurred to island ecologies because of clearing land for growing crops, (over)exploiting resources, and population expansion. This does not necessarily mean that all peoples were unaware of how they were (or might) impact their surroundings. It is likely that many human groups developed methods of conservation to prevent or reduce the degree of resource depletion and environmental impact. However, it can be difficult to observe in the archaeological record what these measures may have been and whether changing climates played a role.

Despite these difficulties, islands offer archaeologists and other scientists unique opportunities to observe the imprints humans left on the environment because they are surrounded by water and have biota that evolved over thousands or even millions of years without human interference. When compared to most continental areas, islands—including those in the Caribbean—were the last to be colonized by humans. In addition, peoples who first arrived on islands typically needed to bring with them plants and animals to survive, many of which were domesticated. Because humans transported non-native biota such as dogs, opossum, and agouti to the Caribbean, they began to disrupt the ecological balance of islands, and once they were entrenched, they outcompeted native flora and fauna. Archaeologists can gauge the effects that peoples had on islands by observing changes to the pollen and faunal record, for example.

A high degree of biological diversity exists among islands that is partly the result of geographical isolation (allopatry). The kinds of flora and fauna that existed before human contact allow researchers to measure the populations that were present before humans arrived and use this as a baseline for analyzing subsequent changes. Paleoclimatic studies worldwide demonstrate that climatic variability altered during the Holocene (roughly the last 10,000 years), including extended dry/wet periods and a gradually rising sea level. These climatic changes could have affected faunal composition and influenced human migration and settlement.

If we are to understand the degree to which humans influenced or impacted their island environments, it is critical to determine when they were first colonized using a combination of paleoenvironmental, archaeological, and chronological data. Information from the environment (including botanical remains taken from wet sites such as lakes or ponds) and the archaeological record can be analyzed to see what was present before and after humans arrived. Using an historical ecology approach, we can then attempt to tease out what may have caused these changes (e.g., climate, people). While historical ecology approaches have been quite popular in many parts of the world, researchers in the Caribbean are only now recognizing the utility of weaving these various lines of evidence together to more effectively examine landscape modification and altering patterns of resource use through time.

The Caribbean Islands

Archaeological research demonstrates that the Caribbean was settled by at least four major migratory groups with different levels of technology and economies:

1) Foraging "Lithic/Archaic" groups (sometimes referred to as "Casimiroid") settled Cuba and Hispaniola around 6000–3000 BP.
2) Other Archaic (or "Ortoiroid") peoples, who appear to have been mostly seasonal hunters and gatherers, began to occupy numerous islands in the Antilles as well as those islands adjacent to the South American mainland by circa 5000–4000 BP.
3) Saladoid horticulturalists settled the Virgin Islands, the Lesser Antilles, and Puerto Rico as early as circa 2500 BP.
4) Over two millennia later, Europeans arrived in the New World.

These multiple migrations of people from different parts of the world brought with them a host of plants, animals, parasites, diseases, and cultural behaviors that had profound effects on the landscapes, vegetation, and faunal composition of the Caribbean islands.

Although it is more difficult to discern what impacts early hunting-and-gathering groups had on the islands during the Lithic and Archaic, research shows that Archaic groups probably brought in plants from South America and may have even participated in small-scale gardening. There is also evidence that sloths in the Greater Antilles became extinct after humans arrived. The sloths' extinction was independent of any major climatic fluctuation, suggesting that people were the cause. During the Ceramic Age (ca. 2500 BP), we see populations expanding as Saladoid groups quickly spread throughout the Lesser Antilles and Puerto Rico and brought with them a horticultural lifestyle that included the cultivation of manioc, one of the their major food staples. Even on a small scale, this would have necessitated the clearing of land and an increase in erosion and sedimentation.

There is also evidence that terrestrial resources, such as land crabs and marine foods (e.g., fish, mollusks) were being overexploited on islands such as Puerto Rico, Jamaica, and Grand Turk. These types of impacts can be assessed in a number of different ways. For example, archaeologists can quantify the change in size of a particular taxon over time (a species of mollusk may get smaller over time if it was being continually overharvested since the juveniles could not grow to full maturity); look for observable trends of people switching resources from one that becomes less frequent over time to another that is more plentiful; document a group's effort to exploit a particular environment such as a lagoon to one with deeper waters if fish have been exhausted; or see an increase in charcoal particles in the soil that would indicate that fire was used to clear land.

Many instances of these activities have been documented in the Caribbean. In the Turks and Caicos Islands there is a curious case of a still-unidentified tortoise species that was found at a prehistoric site. This species was not seen historically, suggesting that it was driven to extinction by Amerindians. An apparent move from nearshore to offshore fisheries seems to have occurred on some islands, which was risky because it would have involved trolling with a boat and

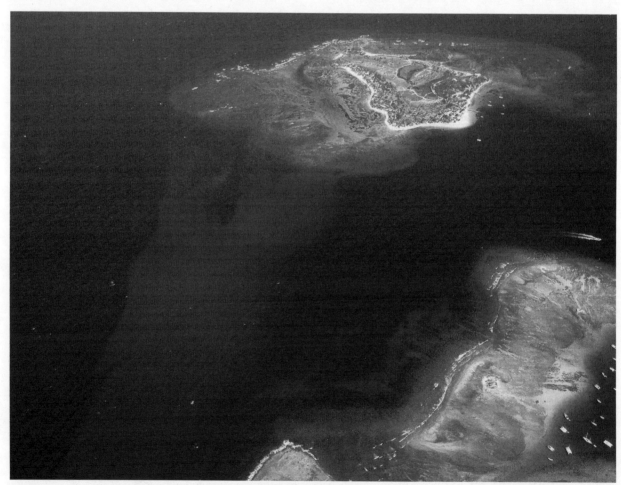

Figure H.1. View of some of the Grenadine islands showing the shallow reef banks and lagoons that have provided a rich source of food for inhabitants for several millennia. Photo by Scott M. Fitzpatrick.

Figure H.2. Excavation of many precolonial archaeological sites in the Caribbean such as this one at Grand Bay in Carriacou, Grenadines, shows intensive exploitation of the queen conch shells that were a primary source of food and an important material for making tools and other objects. Photo by Scott M. Fitzpatrick.

because success rates were likely lower than success rates in the reefs. This may have been the result of the overpredation of reef taxa that led to a heavier focus on horticultural food crops such as manioc or maize that needed to be supplemented by a protein source from the sea. Given the extensive reef systems in the Caribbean (Figure H.1), it is quite possible that mollusk and fish species such as the queen conch shell, which has been found at many precolonial sites, were overharvested (Figure H.2). With increased pressure to provide food to a growing population, clearing land to produce fuel and arable land would have also increased, and with it, erosion and the infilling of local embayments and the expansion of mangrove habitats.

While several good studies suggest that ancient Amerindians altered their environments over time, much of the more dramatic impacts came after Europeans arrived. The Columbian Exchange, a term coined by Alfred Crosby (1972), refers to the transfer of many nonnative biota from the Old World to the New World that effectively transformed landscapes in both major regions

of the world. In the Caribbean, this led to the widespread destruction of habitats from grazing animals and the clearing of native forests to grow sugarcane and other crops. The overharvesting of many animals, including whales, sea turtles, and manatees, as part of large-scale hunting efforts was widespread into the twentieth century. Many of these animals are now endangered, and the Caribbean monk seal—the region's only pinniped—is now officially extinct.

Despite a paucity of archaeological research into questions related to human impacts in the Caribbean prehistorically, scholars of historical ecology are now moving toward identifying questions that would enable us to better understand how people may have affected their island environments through time. This becomes an even more pressing issue given that the Caribbean islands are comprised of dozens of independent nations that bear responsibility for managing their resources. To effectively do this, a level of regional cooperation that utilizes an historical point of view is imperative so that the availability of and changes to marine and terrestrial ecosystems across time and space can be ascertained and used to help guide future conservation measures.

Further Reading

Crosby, A. W., Jr. 1972. *The Columbian Exchange: Biological and Cultural Consequences of 1492.* Westport, CT: Greenwood Press.

Crumley, C. L., ed. 1994. *Historical Ecology: Cultural Knowledge and Changing Landscapes.* Santa Fe: School of American Research Press.

Fitzpatrick, S. M., and W. F. Keegan. 2007. "Human Impacts and Adaptations in the Caribbean Islands: An Historical Ecology Approach." *Earth and Environmental Science: Transactions of the Royal Society of Edinburgh* 98: 29–45.

Keegan, W. F., R. W. Portell, and J. Slapcinsky. 2003. "Changes in Invertebrate Taxa at Two Pre-Columbian Sites in Southwestern Jamaica, AD 800–1500." *Journal of Archaeological Science* 30: 1607–17.

Kirch, P. V., and T. L. Hunt, eds. 1997. *Historical Ecology in the Pacific Islands.* New Haven, CT: Yale University Press.

See also Ground Sloths; *Strombus gigas* (Queen Conch).

Historic Bridgetown and Its Garrison (Barbados)

Kevin Farmer

Bridgetown is the capital of the island of Barbados. Founded in 1628, it is one of the older English port cities in the Western Atlantic world. Dominated by a large open bay on its southern side, it was protected by a series of batteries and main fortifications on the headlands. A major port was built on one of these headlands, around which a series of forts, batteries, and ancillary military buildings were constructed. This area became known as the garrison and served as the headquarters for the British army until 1905; prior to 1816, it was the headquarters for the British navy in the eastern Caribbean. The capital city and the garrison that protected it projected the British Empire's influence in the region.

The histories of Bridgetown and the garrison are intertwined. After the demise of tobacco production in the late 1630s, the need to find an attractive and profitable agricultural product to export to Europe for profit was of paramount importance to the early settlers. The selection of sugar as that crop and the resulting acceleration of the economy in the 1650s transformed both the island and its port city. The "sugar revolution" brought the island into the trans-Atlantic economy, including trade in enslaved Africans who were purchased for the sole purpose of producing and manufacturing sugar cane. The introduction of sugar altered the landscape, legislation, and economic prospects of Barbados within a decade. By the end of the seventeenth century, Barbados was the most valuable colony in the Americas to the British Crown (Newton 2008; Beckles 2000; Knight 1997; Watts 1987).

This wealth meant that the Crown had to safeguard Barbados by upgrading its defenses. The garrison and its forts that guarded the entrance to Carlisle Bay, the natural harbor bordering Bridgetown, were considered to be both strategic and effective. Because Barbados is located east of the Caribbean archipelago, the island was difficult to attack as ships had to sail into the prevailing trade winds. However, ships leaving the island could easily sail into the circum-Caribbean region, propelled by favorable trade winds and equatorial currents. This strategic location was very important during many conflicts between European powers. The establishment of the garrison in Barbados clearly reflected Britain's projection of its power in the region. The garrison enabled the British to quickly dispatch squadrons of marines and ships to attack neighboring islands possessed by their European rivals and, where possible, claim them for the Crown. They could also attack rivals from a safe harbor of an easily defended, fortified island.

The port city of Bridgetown served as a conduit through which goods, ideas, and people were transshipped. Ships were provisioned, repaired, and refitted for onward journeys into the Caribbean and across the Atlantic. The city was cosmopolitan in its demography and religious tolerance. The town in the eighteenth and nineteenth centuries was home to Sephardic Jews, who lived in the present-day areas of Swam Street and Synagogue Lane. They worshipped within the oldest Sephardic consecrated ground in the English Americas.

Figure H.3. Aerial view of National Heroes Square in Bridgetown, Barbados, showing radiating serpentine streets. Courtesy of the Ministry of Family, Culture, Sports and Youth, Government of Barbados.

They shared geographical space with other Christian denominational faiths such as the Anglicans, Methodists, Quakers, Moravians, Anabaptists, and Roman Catholics at a time when there was religious intolerance in the British metropole. Bridgetown has seen some 3,000 years of human occupation across the periods of its pre-Columbian, colonial, and postcolonial history. It rose to prominence during the 1650s, and remained an entrepôt well into the nineteenth century. The medieval town layout remains to this day; many historic buildings that were constructed by both enslaved and free labor can still be found within its historic core. Many of the buildings illustrate the Caribbean adaptation of European architectural forms, particularly Caribbean Georgian architecture.

Today, Bridgetown and its garrison constitute a thriving commercial hub, and living communities reside within their precincts (Figure H.3). Adaptive reuse of buildings coexists with new development. The historic city and its garrison were awarded World Heritage status in 2011.

Further Reading

Beckles, Hilary. 2000. *History of Barbados: From Amerindian Settlement to Nation-State.* Cambridge, UK: Cambridge University Press.

Knight, F. W. 1997. *The Slave Societies of the Caribbean.* Kingston: Macmillan Caribbean.

Ministry of Community Development, Government of Barbados. 2010. Historic Bridgetown and Its Garrison: Nomination Dossier of Barbados to UNESCO for World Heritage Status.

Newton, M. 2008. *The Children of Africa in the Colonies: Free People of Color in Barbados in the Age of Emancipation.* Baton Rouge: Louisiana State University Press.

Watts, D. 1987. *The West Indies: Patterns of Development, Culture, and Environmental Change since 1492.* Cambridge, UK: Cambridge University Press.

Welch, P. 2004. *Slave Society in the City: Bridgetown, Barbados, 1680–1834.* London: James Currey.

See also Barbados; Brimstone Hill Fortress National Park (St. Kitts); Cannon; Nidhe Israel Synagogue and Mikvah (Barbados).

Historic Trails (Jamaica)

Ainsley Henriques

The Taíno people were the first to settle the island of Jamaica. Taíno villages were located along the coast or on elevated lands near fresh water. These early immigrants must have established paths or trails to their villages or base camps for the purposes of collecting water and food. In fact, it is presumed that many of the roads that were developed by subsequent migrations and the introduction of more modern means of transport were based on these original pathways.

Horses arrived with the Spanish from the beginning of the sixteenth century, and the means of transportation were changed and trails were modified. The two famous trials used by the Spanish were Bluefields, or Oristan, on the south coast. This led to what is now Falmouth on the north coast. The other, Sandy Bay, went to Ocho Rios, or St. Ann's Bay. These two trails crossed the island in a north-south orientation. Many of the other trails were oriented along the coast. Trails were used instead of coastal shipping to trade products around the island. Another trail was the "spice trail," which was later used ostensibly to bring spices, pimento, and nutmeg from the north to the city of Kingston, which is situated on the large Kingston Harbour.

After the English captured the island in 1655, several Maroon settlements were established throughout Jamaica. These early free Jamaicans, of mainly African descent, lived outside English settlements and plantations. They established their own trails through the mahogany and montane forests of the island's plains and mountains. Perhaps the most frequently used today is the refurbished Maroon trail through the Cunha Cunha Pass from the Maroon village of Hayfield to Bowden Pen, a north-south orientation through the eastern Blue Mountains.

There are other trails oriented east to west that linked Maroon communities of the east with those in the west. These trails ran along the ridges of the Blue Mountains (in the east), joining up with other trails in western mountain ranges. These trails may have originated as the same trails their Taíno forebears used. Some of these trails are still in use. Others are hard or even impossible to find because of the subsequent development of roads and buildings.

Further Reading

Cundall, F. 1915/2010. *Historic Jamaica*. Ithaca, NY: Cornell University Library.
Padron, F. M. 2003. *Spanish Jamaica*. Miami, FL: Ian Randle.
Rouse, I. 1992. *The Tainos: Rise and Decline of the People Who Greeted Columbus*. New Haven, CT: Yale University Press.

See also Taíno Settlement Ethnohistory.

Hondo River Settlement (Trinidad)

E. Kofi Agorsah and Brinsley Samaroo

In 1998, the Department of History of The University of the West Indies (UWI) was able to secure the cooperation of Professor Kofi Agorsah, an archaeologist at Portland State University, Oregon, who came to Trinidad with a team of students. This group was joined by enthusiastic history students from the St. Augustine campus who excavated an African-American Islamic heritage site on the Hondo River in the Valencia forest of northeastern Trinidad in 1988. The site was occupied from 1819 to about 1843.

Historical Background

The end of the Anglo-American War of 1812–15 coincided with the cessation of the Napoleonic Wars. These two events presented the British Empire the major problem of what to do with free black soldiers who had fought on the British side during the War of 1812. At the same time, Britain had to settle hundreds of soldiers who had loyally defended Britain's Caribbean colonies against French attacks. When the British government requested assistance from West Indian governors, only Trinidad and British Honduras responded positively. Most of the other colonies were wary of accommodating free men in slave societies because of their potential to create mayhem on nearby slave plantations. Among the disbanded soldiers who came to Trinidad were east coast American Baptists who were settled in villages named after military companies in the southeastern corner of the island. Those among this group who were Muslims expressed a desire to be separately settled from the Christians, and Governor Woodford was pleased with this request since it gave him the opportunity to open up the colony's heavily forested east coast where colonial administration had not yet been established. Woodford wanted to see the Bande-de-L'Est opened up to both commerce and Christianity, at the same time securing the area from pirates and would-be possessors of that unguarded region. In mid-1819, the Muslims started arriving. In June and July of that year, the first contingent of 307 persons (233 men, 40 women, and 34 children) was transported to the banks of the Hondo River in the well-watered Quaré area, and in 1825 another 445 persons were introduced. The forests were cleared by native Amerindians, who showed no hostility to the newcomers. In 1820, in order to ease the problem of gender imbalance, the secretary of state ordered that free women from Antigua be brought to Trinidad. Some fifty-two women were "distributed to the men in the Hondo settlement" (Laurence 1963, 36).

Under the guidance of their leader, Imam Abu Bakar, the black Muslims continued to practice their faith. In true military style, the imam organized the settlers into regiments. He copied verses of the Qur'an on scraps of paper which he read to his jungle *jamaat* (Islamic society), whose members looked up to him "with the greatest reverence" (Henry Macleod to Lord John Russell, August 3, 1841, CO295/134, National Archives, London). The settlers produced rice, yams, moko, plantains, ginger, coffee, pigeon peas, and cocoa on the plots allotted to them. These crops were sold in the markets at Sangre Grande and Arima. However, an Islamic settlement could not be tolerated in a Christian society. Rev. J. H. Hamilton, the Anglican pastor for the East Coast, made a determined effort from the 1840s to convert these "mahometans" to his religion. This Christian campaign did much to bring about the disintegration of the settlement, and the administration that had brought the Muslim community to the island virtually abandoned it in the face of the pressure from Christians. Beginning in the 1830s, many of those who were determined to continue as Muslims relocated to join other Muslims in the suburbs of Port of Spain. Some moved to more developed areas, and others joined the constabulary which was willing to accept men with prior military experience.

Archaeological Excavations

The excavations that took place in 1998 were preliminary. Three full 2 × 2 and two half-meter-square units were excavated, varying in depth at 10-centimeter levels. These units contained glass and metal fragments, a kaolin pipe bowl and stem, and a few large quartz stones that researchers suspect marked the location of a temporary Muslim prayer area. On the southern edge of the central area there were four mounds that are presumed to be places of interment, since the graves were angled to face Mecca. Among the glass were light green bottles thought to be of French origin and to have contained olive oil; a clear glass with "gladiator" embossed decoration on the base; light pharmaceutical bottles embossed with "C.O. Bock, Trinidad, HR-1"; light green bottle fragments embossed on the broad side with the words "oriental Hair Tonic" and on the narrow side with "Inaman & Kemp"; and a rectangular light green bottle embossed on the front with "RR/WAY & Co, New York" and on the side with "ENTD ACCORD HR-3." Metallic artifacts included fragments of a cooking pot, a chain, a horseshoe, a hammerhead, a spike, a musket ball, a machete, a stirrup, a nail, and a spoon. All of these items were imported and date to the early nineteenth century, the period when disbanded service people arrived in Trinidad. That the location was a habitation area is confirmed by the presence of household cooking utensils, plates, and working tools such as machetes, nails, a stirrup, and a hammerhead. Unlike many archaeological sites of the period, which are characterized by green glass wine bottles, the bottles at the Hondo River site were mainly for olive oil and pharmaceuticals. The presence of these bottles that contained nonalcoholic substances is indicative of a Muslim presence in the area. It appears, however, that the site may have been too short lived for the residents to have been able to build an elaborate place of prayer. The stirrup indicates the Muslim tradition of horse riding on important religious occasions. Although the site was clearly an Islamic habitation, its extent is not clearly known. There is need for further work that might provide more data that would make possible a more comprehensive understanding of the Hondo River settlement.

Further Reading

Campbell, C. 1974. "Mohammedu Sisei of Gambia and Trinidad. "*African Studies Association of the West Indies Bulletin*, December 7.

Diouf, S. 1998. *Servants of Allah: African Muslims Enslaved in the Americas*. New York: New York University Press.

Laurence, K. O. 1963. "The Settlement of Free Negroes in Trinidad before Emancipation." *Caribbean Quarterly* 9 (1–2): 26.

Weiss, J. 1955. *Free Black American Settlers in Trinidad, 1815–16.* London: McNeish and Weiss.

Hospitals and Leprosaria in the Colonial Caribbean

Joanna K. Gilmore

Hospitals

At the beginning of the colonial era, the practice of medicine was based on medieval theories; it did not take the form of modern western medicine until the nineteenth century. The experiences of the military in the colonies certainly had an impact upon the development of medical practice, particularly because of the exposure of soldiers to new diseases in the Americas. Some of the first hospitals in the Caribbean were associated with the military, although this was not always the case. For example, on Curaçao a smallpox hospital was requested for the enslaved in 1642. At this time, there was no hospital for Dutch citizens or the military, but the economic value of healthy enslaved Africans was the biggest incentive to build a hospital. However, owners of huge plantations on the islands sometimes built their own hospitals. The enslaved were also often treated by visiting physicians in their own rooms. The style and architecture of plantation hospitals varied, but they were often built in a similar style to the main house. Public hospitals became more common by the end of the eighteenth century, although the wealthy and the enslaved were still usually treated at home.

Colonial hospitals were often described as dark, dirty, and foul-smelling spaces. A review of documentary sources from various islands gives the impression that most hospitals were poorly funded and poorly supplied and were either not completed or not fully maintained. For example, in Barbados the hospital in St. Michael's parish was started in 1848 but was not finished. It was difficult for European authorities to understand that far greater supplies were needed for the colonies than for hospitals in the homeland due to the new pathogens island residents encountered and the climate to which inhabitants were not accustomed. However, by the beginning of the nineteenth century, there was greater awareness of local conditions and modes of contagion and improvements in medical technology and diagnosis. In his *Practical Observations of the Diseases of the Army in Jamaica, 1799*, surgeon William Lempriere recommended that hospitals should be located in coastal locations for the fresh air and that they should also be built upon arched foundations to allow air to circulate beneath the building. The Old Naval Hospital in Port Royal, Jamaica, was built in the 1819. It is unique in that its cast iron sections were pre-fabricated in Bradford, England, and shipped to Jamaica for construction.

There have been very few studies of hospitals in the Caribbean. This may be partly explained by the fact that hospital buildings have been reused; for example the 1911 hospital on Barbados is presently used as the National Archives. Artifacts one can expect to find at a hospital site include typical domestic items, particularly those associated with the kitchen and dining areas; medical equipment; clothing; and items related to recreation. A trash pit associated with the Royal Naval Hospital in Antigua contained military buttons (deposited when clothing was burned after the patient's death); glass from containers for alcoholic beverages; artifacts associated with games and pastimes, such as an iron ring from the game of quoits; Jew's harps; counters; and clay tobacco pipes. Medically related artifacts included a small brown ceramic saucepan, which would have been used to prepare treatments. Scissors, pins, a glass bottle stopper, stirring rods, mortars and pestles, tin-glazed ointment pots, and chamber pots were also found.

Hospital cemeteries hold great potential for future research. Human skeletal remains excavated in hospital cemeteries can be studied to examine diet, ancestry, disease prevalence, average age at death, patterns of disease in relation to the tropical climate, and evidence of medical intervention. For example, using stable isotope analysis, Tamara Varney of Lakehead University, Canada, studied a sample of individuals buried at the Royal Naval Hospital cemetery at English Harbour, Antigua. By measuring levels of carbon and nitrogen, she was able to assess differences in diet, resource use, and allocation in relation to age, sex, and ancestry.

Leprosaria

It is believed that leprosy, now known as Hansen's disease, was bought to the Americas via the transatlantic slave trade. As early as the seventeenth century, leper colonies, or leprosaria, were established on the larger islands of the Greater Antilles, such as on Santo Domingo, Jamaica, and Cuba. By the late eighteenth century and during the nineteenth century, most islands had their own leprosaria to isolate people suffering from leprosy. These facilities also frequently housed people suffering from syphilis, yaws, elephantiasis, psoriasis, and tuberculosis as well as mental disorders and other disabilities. Leprosaria were usually located in remote areas, such as small coastal islands adjacent to the larger islands or on the periphery of towns in the smaller islands of the Lesser Antilles.

Records relating to the leper colonies do exist; these can be found in the form of laws regarding the establishment of facilities to isolate leprosy sufferers; administrative records, which state the number of in and out patients, including their sex, and occasionally, the reason for their isolation; the total annual expenditure or expenditure per patient; and the condition of the facilities. The living quarters' structure often separated patients by gender, for privacy and to discourage sexual intercourse and marriage between leprosy patients. Other structures included kitchens, dining areas, administrative offices, storage spaces, clinics, and chapels.

In 1846, the government of Barbados passed An Act to Provide Care and Maintenance of Persons Afflicted with Leprosy. Archival records indicate that a lunatic asylum and a leprosy asylum had been built by 1853 in St. Michael's Parish. A Lazaretto Land Plan that originated in the Public Works Office shows a single building divided into male and female quarters, a kitchen, seclusion cells, a wash stand, baths, a water tank, and a superintendent's house (Lazaretto Land Plan, 1891, Barbados National Archives). At Charles Fort on St. Kitts and the hospital at Morne Rouge on Grenada, there were stewards' and nurses' quarters, a dining hall and kitchen, spaces for exercise, and garden plots for growing produce. Male and female patients were separated; those who tried to escape were punished.

Gerald F. Schroedl (2000) of the University of Tennessee in Knoxville has investigated the leper colony at Charles Fort on St. Kitts. During this investigation, the site was surveyed and mapped and test excavations and documentary research were conducted. Charles Fort on St. Kitts was used as a leper colony, named Hansen Home, from 1890 to 1996. Surveying revealed that the home had separate areas for administration, food preparation, treatment and hygiene, and patient accommodation and a cemetery and a chapel area. Anderson (2005) wrote her MA thesis about the cultural history of the Hansen Home on St. Kitts.

Paola Schiappacasse (2011) wrote her PhD dissertation on the subject of the Lazaretto on Isla de Cabras, near San Juan, Puerto Rico. She focused on the administration buildings, the observation hospital, the convalescent hospital and infirmary buildings, and the cemetery. The study examined diet, architecture, medical treatments, sanitation, and the socioeconomic aspects of life at the hospital. Hospitals began with the earliest settlements on Puerto Rico in the 1540s, and these areas have only recently begun to be examined by archaeologists.

In the United States Virgin Islands, there was a leprosarium in the late nineteenth and early twentieth centuries and a yellow fever hospital on Hassel Island, near St. John. Mandy Barton, a graduate student at the University of Tennessee, Knoxville, conducted research at this site in 2008. During the research a cistern and three further structures were located. Artifacts recovered at the site included transfer-print table wares, stoneware bottles, wine and case bottle glass, beads, marbles, pipe bowls, and ceramic doll parts.

On St. Eustatius in the Dutch Caribbean, archaeologists from the College of William and Mary mapped and photographed the living quarters structure and two visible graves at the Lazaretto in 1989. In 2004, Joanna Gilmore of the Institute of Archaeology, University College London excavated the site. The primary focus of the investigation was a paleopathological study of the human remains. Excavation revealed five burials, and three individuals displayed evidence for leprous bone changes. The pathological changes in the bones of these individuals corresponded with examples of leprosy found in skeletons from medieval Europe, and potentially leprous bony changes were also found on the hyoid and cervical vertebra. Artifacts recovered included a variety of domestic ceramics, salve pots, glass used for alcoholic beverages and medicine, clay tobacco pipes, and marbles. Zooarchaeological remains were also recovered, including large quantities of fish and goat/sheep bones. Items that provide an insight into daily life included spectacles, a Bakelite dip pen, an ink bottle, and a slate pencil.

The architectural style of the Lazaretto on St. Eustatius and patients' housing in Charles Fort on St. Kitts reflected changing ideas described in manuals such as such as John Woods's *A Series of Plans for Cottages or Habitations of the Labourer* . . . (1781, 1792, and 1806) and Dr. Collins's *Practical Rules for the Management and Medical Treatment of Negro Slaves in the Sugar Colonies* (1803). The structures were raised off the ground to improve air circulation and had doors or windows at either side to encourage cross-ventilation. The dimensions of the building at the Lazaretto on St. Eustatius are also similar to houses for the enslaved at Estate The Williams on St. Croix (approximately 4.5 meters wide by 20 meters long, or 15 by 66 feet), and both have a linear row of rooms, each with their own exterior door leading directly to the outside (Chapman 1991, 114–15).

Through both historical and archaeological analyses of hospitals and leprosaria sites in the Caribbean, a great deal can be learned about cultural attitudes toward disease; disease patterns; interactions and prevalence; patient treatment; postmortem customs; the social status, diet, and ancestry of the sick; the development of medical technology, healthcare, and administration; and hospital architecture.

Further Reading

Andersen, N. R. 2005. "'It's Not Catching': Hansen Home and the Local Knowledge of Leprosy in the Federation of St. Kitts and Nevis, West Indies." MA thesis, University of Tennessee.

Chapman, W. 1991. "Slave Villages in the Danish West Indies: Changes of the Late Eighteenth and Early Nineteenth Centuries." *Perspectives in Vernacular Architecture* 4: 108–20. Columbia: University of Missouri Press.

Gilmore, J. K. 2008. "Leprosy at the Lazaretto on St Eustatius, Netherlands Antilles." *International Journal of Osteoarchaeology* 18: 72–84.

Nicholson, D. V. 1993. *Mud and Blood: English Harbour, Antigua, W.I.: Artifacts from Dredging and the Naval Hospital Site*. [St. John's, Antigua]: Museum of Antigua and Barbuda.

Prendes, M. A. G. 1963. *Historia de la lepra en Cuba*. Havana: Publicaciones del museo historico de las ciencias medicas.

Schiappacasse, P. A. 2011. "Archaeology of Isolation: The Nineteenth-Century Lazareto de Isla de Cabras, Puerto Rico." PhD diss., Syracuse University.

Schroedl, G. F. 2000. "Archaeological and Architectural Assessment of Charles Fort, St. Kitts, West Indies." Charles Fort Archaeological and Historical Project Report no. 1. Available at the Ministry of Tourism, Basseterre, St. Kitts.

See also Historical Archaeological Sites (Types).

I

The Institute of Jamaica

Andrea Richards

The Institute of Jamaica (Figure I.1) was established in 1879 by the island's governor, Sir Anthony Musgrave, for the encouragement of literature, science and art in Jamaica. The institute's major functions are centered on "researching, studying, encouraging and developing culture, science and history; and in the establishment of museums" (Institute of Jamaica Act 1978, amended 1995; Lewis 1967). The Crown colony government under Governor Musgrave was faced with a country devoid of basic structures for the educational advancement of the general populace, with the exception of Mico College, which was established in 1836 to train elementary school teach-

ers. Seeking to rectify this deplorable situation, Musgrave embarked on what was termed an educational "renaissance," and according to Section 4 (2) of the act, named some of the functions of the institute, including "the establishment and maintenance of an institution comprising a public library, reading rooms and collections . . . to make provisions for the reading of papers, delivery of lectures . . . and the establishment and maintenance of other institutions of learning, museums, galleries."

In addition to being instrumental in the evolution of social and cultural institutions in Jamaica, the institute played an important role in the development of Jamaican

Figure I.1. Headquarters of the Institute of Jamaica, East Street, Kingston. Reproduced by permission of the Institute of Jamaica.

archaeology and was responsible for all archaeological expeditions, surveys, and exhibitions from its inception to the mid-1980s. The institute's first major exhibition in 1895 showcased precolonial artefacts. During the 1890s, Frank Cundall and J. E. Duerden emerged as important figures. Cundall wrote many books on Jamaican history and was secretary and librarian of the institute from 1891 until his death in 1937. He realized that slavery had resulted in a people without any recorded history, and he made it his mission to correct this situation by building the West Indian Reference Library (now called the National Library of Jamaica by the 1978 amendment to the Institute of Jamaica Act), which now houses the largest collection on Jamaica's history, art, and culture in the Americas. Duerden served as curator of the institute's museum from 1895 until 1901. His 1897 study "Aboriginal Indian Remains in Jamaica" was the first general survey of its kind and was an essential reference for further work on the island. Notable investigations from this period included excavations at the Norbrook (St. Andrew) midden by Lady Edith Blake in 1890 and R. C. MacCormack's 1898 survey of seventeen caves and four sites in southern Vere and the Portland Ridge in Clarendon (Allsworth-Jones, 2008).

Realizing that education was not available to most Jamaicans, the institute provided tuition courses that were not available in the few educational institutions. Public lectures that were later reproduced in the public press were held in town halls or at the institute. The work of the West India Reference Library was central to this focus of the institute.

From its inception, the institute has fulfilled its functions in the areas of collections, and today it boasts a Natural History Division with an extensive herbarium and zoological collection. The Museums of History and Ethnography has developed a diverse collection of cultural objects that represent Jamaica's historical background, including extensive collections on Port Royal, the pre-emancipation period, the Taíno, and the Seville stones. It also manages museums in other parishes of Jamaica. Over the years, this division has increased the scope of its exhibition and has opened exhibitions such as *Quake, Xaymaca, Materializing Slavery,* and *Jamaica 50: Constructing a Nation.* Other entities that contribute to the institute's mandate are the African Caribbean Institute of Jamaica/Jamaica Memory Bank, which includes Liberty Hall (devoted to the legacy of Marcus Mosiah Garvey); the Junior Centre (which provides programs for children); the semi-autonomous National Library of Jamaica; the National Gallery of Jamaica; and the recently added Jamaica Music Museum. Each year, the institute awards the prestigious Musgrave Medals for achievements in the fields of literature, art, and science. The peer-reviewed *Jamaica Journal,* the institute's primary publication since 1967, is published twice each year and focuses on topics related to literature, science, and the arts.

Further Reading

Allsworth-Jones, P. 2008. *Pre-Columbian Jamaica.* Tuscaloosa: University of Alabama Press.

Duerden, J. E. 1897. "Aboriginal Indian Remains in Jamaica." *Journal of the Institute of Jamaica* 2 (4): 1–52.

Government of Jamaica. 1995. "Institute of Jamaica Act (1978, amended 1995)." http://www.moj.gov.jm/laws/institute jamaica-act. Accessed March 2, 2013.

Institute of Jamaica. 2013. "About." Institute of Jamaica Web site. http://instituteofjamaica.org.jm/?page_id=56. Accessed March 2, 2013.

Lewis, B. 1967. "History of the Institute of Jamaica." *Jamaica Journal* 1 (1): 4–8.

See also Cundall, Frank (1858–1937); Duerden, J. E. (1869–1937); Jamaica (Prehistory of).

The International Association for Caribbean Archaeology (IACA)

Basil A. Reid and Alissandra Cummins

Founded in 1961, the International Association for Caribbean Archaeology (IACA) is a group of professional and amateur archaeologists and interested individuals mostly from the Caribbean, North America, and Europe who work or have an interest in the archaeology of the Caribbean. The IACA's scope of interest includes the Greater and Lesser Antilles as well as countries bordering the Caribbean, whose prehistoric and historic cultures often interrelate with those of the islands. Following a congress in Martinique in 1961, an association was founded by Rev. Pere Pinchon and Dr. Jacques Petitjean Roget in 1962. The association was originally called the International Association for the Study of Pre-Columbian Cultures of the Lesser Antilles, but in 1985 it was incorporated under the name The International Association for Caribbean Archaeology. The corresponding names in French and Spanish are Association Internationale d'Archéologie de la Caraïbe (AIAC) and Asociación Internacional de Arqueología del Caribe (AIAC), respectively.

The association aims to promote good management of Caribbean archaeology at both the local and regional levels. It supports the preservation of sites and responsible archaeology throughout the region and acts as a point of reference for archaeologists. The association requires that its members subscribe to a code of professional practice, including compliance with the terms of the UNESCO Convention on the Means of Prohibiting and Preventing the Illicit Import, Export and Transfer of Ownership of Cultural Property (1970). This Convention includes clauses relating to prohibiting and preventing the illicit export and import of cultural heritage, the transfer of ownership as well as the destruction of cultural heritage through unscientific investigations, looting, or faking of archaeological and other cultural property, including underwater cultural heritage.

Congresses are held every two years in different Caribbean locations, and the proceedings of each congress function as a critical source of information on the current state of Caribbean archaeology. A newsletter is published at six-month intervals. The IACA also publishes a Directory of Caribbean Archaeologists. Recent congresses were held in Grenada (1999), Aruba (2001), the Dominican Republic (2003), Trinidad and Tobago (2005), Jamaica (2007), Antigua (2009), Martinique (2011), and Puerto Rico (2013). The twenty-fourth congress, which was held in Martinique in 2011, celebrated the fiftieth anniversary of the inaugural congress at that location.

Further Reading

International Association of Caribbean Archaeology. 2011. International Association of Caribbean Archaeology Web site. http://museum.archanth.cam.ac.uk/iaca.www/Eng_webset/iaca_eng.htm. Accessed January 14, 2013.

Keegan, William F., Corinne L. Hofman, and Reniel Rodríguez Ramos. 2013. "Introduction to the Archaeology of the Insular Caribbean." In *The Oxford Handbook of Caribbean Archaeology*, ed. William F. Keegan, Corinne L. Hofman, and Reniel Rodríguez Ramos, 1–20. New York: Oxford University Press.

Siegel, Peter E. 2013. "Caribbean Archaeology in Historical Perspective." In *The Oxford Handbook of Caribbean Archaeology*, ed. William F. Keegan, Corinne L. Hofman, and Reniel Rodríguez Ramos, 27–36. New York: Oxford University Press.

See also The Association of Caribbean Historians; Rescue Archaeology; Underwater Archaeology.

The International Centre for the Study of the Preservation and Restoration of Cultural Property (ICCROM)

Alissandra Cummins

The International Centre for the Study of the Preservation and Restoration of Cultural Property (ICCROM) was founded by UNESCO in 1956 to address the scientific, technical, and ethical issues relating to the conservation and restoration of cultural property. This autonomous, specialized intergovernmental organization contributes to the promotion and conservation of movable and immovable heritage through five main spheres of activity: training, information, research, cooperation, and advocacy.

The ICCROM is currently comprised of over 120 member states, including the Caribbean countries of Barbados, Cuba, the Dominican Republic, Guyana, Haiti, and Trinidad and Tobago, and more than 125 associate members from among the world's conservation institutions. Headquartered in Rome, the ICCROM serves as a clearinghouse for the exchange of conservation information among specialists and agencies worldwide. It collects and circulates information, institutes and coordinates research, and develops and implements conservation training programs. It seeks to improve the standards and practices of conservation, ultimately aspiring to ensure that cultural heritage benefits humanity.

The ICCROM also acts as technical consultant to the UNESCO World Heritage Committee and has developed and implemented projects for the restoration and protection of the sites inscribed on the World Heritage List. It has also developed training and education programs. Over the past ten years, the ICCROM has played roles in periodic reporting, the development of the Global Training Strategy, and the revision of World Heritage's Operational Guidelines. As the priority partner for training relating to cultural heritage, ICCROM has been contracted by the UNESCO World Heritage Centre to run national- and regional-level training courses on World Heritage topics.

The ICCROM has long been involved with the conservation and management of archaeological sites. This was its primary focus for many years. However, recent trends have changed the approach to work in this field in two important ways: an insistence on approaches to management that are based on identifying the value attached to a site; and the recognition that many archaeological sites should be viewed and actively managed as living sites. The ICCROM now emphasizes community-based education to support its management and conservation of heritage sites, and it continues to monitor developments in this field and publicize new thinking and solutions.

The ICCROM's institutional priorities include creating regional programs and training specialists in the restoration and conservation of cultural heritage, including archaeological sites and artifacts. Within the Caribbean, ICCROM training programs have largely been organized through associated institutions in Cuba and the Dominican Republic. More recently, the Centre launched the Conservation of Cultural Heritage in Latin America and the Caribbean Programme (LATAM; 2008–2019). The main objectives of the program are to improve and strengthen conservation capacity, enhance communication and exchange, and create a network of persons and institutions to improve the care of cultural heritage through innovative and sustainable collaboration mechanisms.

Further Reading

ICCROM. 2012. "LATAM Programme—2008–2019." http://www.iccrom.org/eng/prog_en/06latam_en.shtml. Accessed January 14, 2013.

Pye, E. 2001. *Caring for the Past: Issues in Conservation for Archaeology and Museums*. London: James & James.

Stanley-Price, N., ed. 1995. *Conservation on Archaeological Excavations: With Particular Reference to the Mediterranean Area*. 2nd ed. Rome: ICCROM.

Stovel, H. 1998. "Risk Preparedness: A Management Manual for World Cultural Heritage." http://www.iccrom.org/pdf/ICCROM_17_RiskPreparedness_en.pdf. Accessed January 14, 2013.

The International Council of Museums (ICOM)

Alissandra Cummins

Created in 1946, the International Council of Museums (ICOM) is a nongovernmental organization that maintains formal relations with UNESCO. ICOM is the international organization of museums and museum professionals committed "to the conservation, continuation and communication to society of the world's natural and cultural heritage, present and future, tangible and intangible." ICOM, which is based in Paris, is comprised of members in more than 150 countries who participate through national committees, including those in Barbados, Cuba, the Dominican Republic, Haiti, and Jamaica. ICOM is also affiliated with seventeen museum associations, including the Museums Association of the Caribbean.

ICOM's thirty specialist international committees represent various museum-related disciplines and types of museums that exchange scientific information, develop professional standards and best practices, and work with museum professionals abroad on international projects. ICOM's International Committee for Museums and Collections of Archaeology and History, which was established in 1946 at the very start of the organization, is dedicated to museums of archaeology and history that illustrate and interpret the complex relationship of humans to society and the environment.

In line with ICOM's Strategic Plan (2008–2010), its program responds to the challenges and needs of the museum profession and is implemented at the national, regional and international levels. Priorities include codifying and institutionalizing the ICOM Code of Ethics for museums, professional development workshops and training, the dissemination of knowledge through publications, twinning programs, and promoting museums through International Museum Day. ICOM also works in partnership with UNESCO and other professional organizations to promote the vision of a world "where the importance of the natural and cultural heritage is universally valued." Special initiatives include capacity building, community involvement, sustainable tourism, combating illicit traffic in cultural property, working with intangible heritage, and risk management. In the Caribbean, ICOM works primarily in conjunction with the Museums Association of the Caribbean in areas of capacity building, such as database development and risk preparedness.

The organization consistently stresses professionalism in both institutional and individual action and advocates adherence to the requirements of national and international legislation and treaty obligations, such as UNESCO's Convention on the Means of Prohibiting and Preventing the Illicit Import, Export and Transfer of Ownership of Cultural Property (1970). ICOM's code stresses the need for due diligence in establishing valid provenance for acquired objects; the duty of care in the conduct of excavations; the proper storage, care, and management of artifacts; and proper methods of documenting, exhibiting, and conserving archaeological materials. The code explicitly states that "museums should not acquire objects where there is reasonable cause to believe their recovery involved unauthorized, unscientific, or intentional destruction or damage of monuments, archaeological or geological sites" (ICOM 2006, 2–3). The code requires that respect be given to "the interests and beliefs of members of the community, ethnic or religious groups" and "the feelings of human dignity" associated with human remains or materials of sacred significance recovered in the field (ibid., 8).

ICOM's publications include *ICOM News*, a study series, conference proceedings, periodicals, and monographs on museum-related subjects. The council has consolidated its mission in the fight against illicit traffic in cultural property. This is being done through the development of both the Red List series and 100 Missing Objects series, both of which are intended to assist with the repatriation of these objects.

Further Reading

Askerud, P., and É. Clément. 1997. *Preventing the Illicit Traffic in Cultural Property: A Resource Handbook for the Implementation of the 1970 UNESCO Convention.* Paris: UNESCO. http://unesdoc.unesco.org/images/0011/001187/118783eo.pdf. Accessed January 14, 2013.

Hoffman, B. T. 2001. "ICOM Study Series: International Committee for Museums and Collections of Archaeology and History (ICMAH)." http://icom.museum/study_series_pdf/9_ICOM-ICMAH.pdf. Accessed August 9, 2011.

———, ed. 2005. *Art and Cultural Heritage: Law, Policy, and Practice.* Cambridge, UK: Cambridge University Press.

ICOM. 2006. *ICOM Code of Ethics for Museums.* Paris: ICOM.

———. 2012. ICOM Web site. http://icom.museum. Accessed January 22, 2013.

See also The Museums Association of the Caribbean (MAC).

The International Council on Monuments and Sites (ICOMOS)

Alissandra Cummins

Established in 1965, the International Council on Monuments and Sites (ICOMOS) is dedicated to the conservation and protection of cultural heritage and to the creation, promotion, dissemination, and application of theory, methodology, and scientific techniques for heritage conservation. Its members come from more than 110 countries, but to date, national committees have been established in six nations in the Caribbean: Barbados, Cuba, the Dominican Republic, Haiti, Jamaica, and Suriname. ICOMOS functions through a network of twenty-eight scientific committees, including the International Committee on Archaeological Heritage Management, which was established to promote international cooperation in the field of archaeological heritage management and to advise on the development of archaeological heritage management programs.

ICOMOS has developed and disseminated a series of international charters dealing with the conservation and protection of the cultural heritage, including the International Restoration Charter (Venice Charter, 1964); the International Charter for the Protection and Management of the Archaeological Heritage (1990), which lays down principles relating to different aspects of archaeological management; and the International Charter on the Protection and Management of Underwater Cultural Heritage (1996). ICOMOS has also defined an International Core Data Standard for Archaeological Sites and Monuments to facilitate assessments of monuments or sites with respect to planning, care, and management for academic or other purposes.

As one of three advisory bodies named in UNESCO's Convention concerning the Protection of the World Cultural and Natural Heritage (1972), ICOMOS is responsible for evaluating all nominations of cultural and mixed properties for the World Heritage List. To facilitate this process, ICOMOS undertakes comparative and thematic studies to provide a context for its evaluation of World Heritage nominations and to highlight the World Heritage potential in various regions.

ICOMOS has addressed the World Heritage Committee's 1994 Global Strategy for a More Representative, Balanced and Credible World Heritage List with *The World Heritage List: Filling the Gaps—An Action Plan for the Future*. Among its conclusions was the finding that "the category of archaeological properties is the best represented on the tentative lists of the Latin American and Caribbean region" (ICOMOS 2004, 60). Similar findings have been established for rock art sites in the region. The organization has facilitated regional World Heritage meetings at which archaeological sites were identified. At these meetings, archaeological sites were identified and categorized and issues relating to the outstanding universal value of cultural heritage in the Caribbean were addressed, as was the development of serial transboundary nominations of Caribbean cultural sites to the World Heritage List. Among the pan-Caribbean themes proposed were the Amerindian heritage, rock art, the contact period, and the African heritage. Thematic studies and reports have been produced for Caribbean rock art and archaeology sites.

Further Reading

Grenier, R., D. Nutley, and I. Cochran, eds. 2006. *Underwater Cultural Heritage at Risk: Managing Natural and Human Impacts.* Paris: ICOMOS.

ICOMOS. 2004. *The World Heritage List: Filling the Gaps—An Action Plan for the Future.* Paris: ICOMOS

———. 2006. *ICOMOS Thematic Study: Rock Art of Latin America and the Caribbean.* Paris: ICOMOS.

———. N.d. ICOMOS Web site. http://www.icomos.org.en. Accessed January 23, 2013.

See also Rock Art.

Island-Carib

Basil A. Reid

Ethnohistorians have added the prefix "Island" to distinguish the Carib peoples of the Caribbean from the Carib peoples who lived on the South American mainland. Beginning AD 1450, the Island-Carib occupied the Windward Islands, Guadeloupe, the neighboring islands at the southern end of the Leeward Islands, and northern Trinidad (Figure I.2). Island-Carib have long been associated with the Spanish arrival in the New World, although they were not encountered until Columbus's second voyage in 1493. If we are to believe Dr. Chanca's accounts (Hulme 1993) of Columbus's 1493 voyage, Guadeloupe was already in the hands of the ethnic Island-Carib at that time. Island-Carib appear by name in connection with enduring hostilities toward the Spanish colony in Puerto Rico throughout the sixteenth century, when they seem to have used the island of St. Croix as a base for their raids. The archaeological evidence indicates that Arawak-speaking "Island-Carib" moved into the vacuum left by the disappearance of the Suazan Troumassoid in the Lesser Antilles around AD 1450.

The seventeenth-century writings of French missionaries in Dominica, Guadeloupe, and St. Vincent have enabled scholars to learn more about the Island-Carib, or, as they called themselves, Kalinago (for the men) and Kalipuna (for the women). The chronicles of French missionaries describe the Island-Carib in the Lesser Antilles as essentially a farming people (Petersen 1997). They planted small gardens in the surrounding rain forest near their villages in which they grew manioc and sweet potatoes. Their villages consisted of a series of round huts for the women built around a larger rectangular men's house. Their settlements were found in the more humid and fertile islands, and although they fished and collected shellfish and trapped land crabs, they cannot be characterized as a society of fishermen.

Like their counterparts on the South American mainland, the Island-Carib baked cassava bread and prepared pepper pot. Beer drinking was a major activity, especially at intervillage gatherings. Their social organization was egalitarian. Although a headman ruled the village community, no chiefs governed over groups of villages or entire islands, as was the case among the Taíno. The Island-Carib villages are not reported to have contained plazas, ball courts, temples, or other public structures. The Island-Carib men of the fifteenth century emphasized warfare, including raiding Taíno villages to obtain additional wives. The men also undertook long-distance expeditions to South America. There were also considerable interisland interactions among the Island-Carib of the Lesser Antilles. The Island-Carib of Tobago, for example, kept close trade contacts with their counterparts in St. Vincent, Saint Lucia, and Grenada.

Although it was originally thought that Island-Carib made Suazey pottery, it now appears that Suazan Troumassoid pottery is not Island-Carib, as it is an entirely precolonial phenomenon that apparently disappeared after AD 1450 (Boomert 1986). Research has revealed that the Cayoid pottery style, named after Cayo in St. Vincent, may relate to the Island-Carib. At the end of precolonial times, the Cayoid pottery and other Guiana-related styles appeared in the Windward Islands of Tobago and St. Vincent. Characteristic features of the Cayoid pottery include incisions on a flat rim, cone-shaped necks, and bodies with appliqué decorations. Many of the Cayoid pots in Amazonia and the coastal Guianas are tempered with *caraipe* or *kwep* (burned tree bark). Cayoid pottery has been found in association with contact period materials such as glass and metals and has been tentatively associated with the Island-Carib occupation of the Windward Islands. It also shows some strong similarities in decoration and shape to the Kariabo pottery style of the Guianas, a group that may be culturally affiliated with the Island-Carib.

The Island-Carib are often portrayed as freedom fighters. They were savvy enough to manipulate relations between Spanish, English, French, and Dutch settlers to their own advantage. The Island-Carib's aggressive responses to Europeans proved to very successful: they survived unconquered into the eighteenth century and beyond. They tenaciously fought the attempts of Euro-

Figure I.2. Island-Carib colonization of the southern Caribbean. Reprinted from Reid (2009, fig. 2.22) by permission of the University of Alabama Press.

peans to colonize their islands for nearly two centuries, eventually making peace and living in reserved areas on Dominica and St. Vincent and in Central America. The Island-Carib sometimes allied themselves with a European power that shared their aim of preventing the colonization of the island by another national group. For example, in 1653, a party of Island-Carib, assisted and encouraged by the French, traveled 200 kilometers from Dominica to raid the English of Antigua (Wilson 2007).

The more militant Island-Carib of the Lesser Antilles, who adopted more aggressive postures towards the Spanish, French, English, Dutch, and anyone else who threatened their sovereignty, were inaccurately categorized as cannibals. In fact, the word Carib soon became a general Spanish term for hostile natives; between 1815 and 1820 an area on the coast of northeastern Luzon, Philippines, was labeled Negroes Caribes Bravos (Reid 2009). However, to date no concrete evidence has been found that would confirm claims of cannibalism.

Further Reading

Boomert, A. 1986. "The Cayo Complex of St. Vincent: Ethnohistorical and Archaeological Aspects of the Island-Carib Problem." *Antropologica* 66: 3–68.

Hulme, P. 1993. "Making Sense of the Native Caribbean." *New West Indian Guide* 67 (3–4): 189–220.

Petersen, J. 1997. "Taino, Island-Carib, and Prehistoric Amerindian Economies in the West Indies: Tropical Forest Adaptations to Island Environments." In *The Indigenous People of the Caribbean*, ed. Samuel Wilson, 118–30. Gainesville: University Press of Florida.

Reid, B. A. 2009. *Myths and Realities of Caribbean History.* Tuscaloosa: University of Alabama Press.

Wilson, S. M. 2007. *The Archaeology of the Caribbean.* New York: Cambridge University Press.

See also Cannibalism (Anthropophagy); The Cayoid Pottery Series; Kalinago Descendants of St. Vincent and the Grenadines; The Kalinago Territory (Dominica).

The Jamaica National Heritage Trust

Andrea Richards

The Jamaica National Heritage Trust (JNHT) is a statutory agency of the government of Jamaica. It is the leading government organization in Jamaica for the promotion, preservation, and development of the island's material cultural heritage resources (Figure J.1). The precursor of the JNHT was the Jamaica National Trust Commission, which was formed by law in 1958. Prior to the establishment of the commission, Governor Olivier asked the secretary of the Institute of Jamaica to prepare a list of the historic sites, buildings, and monuments of each parish. This list was included in a report on the preservation of historic sites and ancient monuments in the West Indian colonies (Cundall 1915). In 1985, a new law changed the commission's name to Jamaica National Heritage Trust and enlarged its functions. Its new objectives were to foster a sense of national pride and identity through heritage education, to identify and preserve the material cultural heritage resources of the Jamaican people, and to promote the sustainable utilization and management of Jamaica's material cultural heritage resources (Government of Jamaica 1985).

The JNHT's activities have focused on protecting sites that qualify as national monuments and protected national heritage through declaration and designation; managing and maintaining specific heritage sites; providing technical advice to owners of heritage sites; fa-

Figure J.1. Hibbert House, also known as Headquarters House, the head office of the Jamaica National Heritage Trust, Kingston, Jamaica. Reproduced by permission of the Jamaica National Heritage Trust.

cilitating research on archaeological and historic sites; developing heritage education programs for schools, facilitating the engagement of community groups in the protection of their heritage; providing information to the public on heritage sites; conserving archaeological objects; and facilitating the restoration of some historic sites, either through its own actions or in collaboration with others.

The trust carries out its functions through its five divisions: Archaeology; Heritage Protection, Research, and Information; Communications; Estate Management and Business Development (Sites and Monuments); and Corporate Services. More recently, a new unit has been created in the Archaeology Division which focuses on developing Jamaica's World Heritage Tentative List, preparing dossiers that nominate Jamaican sites for inclusion on the World Heritage List, and transforming national heritage sites into revenue-generating centers.

As the government agency responsible for regulating all archaeological research in Jamaica, the trust is often at the fore of rescue archaeology projects, archaeological impact assessments, and research on major development projects. The JNHT has an extensive collections management system for artifacts that includes a conservation program. Over 2 million objects have been recovered from numerous excavations over the years. It also maintains the Geographic Information Systems inventory of Jamaican archaeological sites. There is also an ongoing research program with various local and international institutions, such as the Texas A&M University and the Institute of Nautical Archaeology, for explorations at the underwater sunken city of Port Royal. The JNHT also monitors academic excavations, such as research projects of the Department of History and Archaeology at The University of the West Indies (UWI), Mona, and of overseas universities. During the late 1990s, there was renewed interest in Jamaican prehistory, and The University of the West Indies spearheaded research on sites such as Green Castle (1999–2001), Newry, Coleraine, and Wentworth (2002–2003), all located in the Annotto Bay area in St. Mary. This was a collaborative effort between The University of the West Indies and Murray State University of Murray, Kentucky.

The JNHT has embarked on a consultative process for reviewing and amending the Jamaica National Heritage Trust Act and has implemented an archaeological research permit to regulate all archaeological research in the country. Through its Archaeology Division, the JNHT has been involved in several large-scaled engineering projects, such as the North Coast Highway Development Project, through its provision of archaeological impact assessments. It has also monitored activities for other national projects, such as the Old Harbour Bypass, Highway 2000, and the Falmouth Pier. This is in keeping with the JNHT's role as a regulatory body. The staff at the trust stays abreast of changes in the field of cultural resource management and applies these standards to archaeological work conducted throughout Jamaica. The continuation of the development of infrastructure and housing across the island threatens prehistoric sites with no built structures, and the JNHT has conducted numerous rescue or salvage excavations at locations such as Prospect Pen, St. Thomas (1985); Mammee Bay, St. Ann (1986); Wentworth (Firefly), St. Mary (1988); Toby Abbott, Clarendon (2000); Barbican, Hanover (2000–2001); Long Mountain, St. Andrew (2001); and Mona Estate, St. Andrew (2010).

Further Reading

Acworth, A. 1951. *Buildings of Architectural or Historic Interest in the British West Indies.* London: His Majesty's Stationery Office.

Allsworth-Jones, P. 2008. *Pre-Columbian Jamaica.* Tuscaloosa: University of Alabama Press.

Cundall, F. 1915. *Historic Jamaica.* London: West India Committee.

Government of Jamaica. 1985. "Jamaica National Heritage Trust Act." http://www.jnht.com/jnht_act_1985.php. Accessed January 14, 2013.

Henriques, A. 2008. "JNHT: Reflections at 50." *Jamaica Journal* 31 (3): 6–11.

Jamaica National Heritage Trust. "About the Jamaica National Heritage Trust." http://wwwhttp://www.jnht.com/about_jnht.php. Accessed March 2, 2013

See also Archaeological Heritage Management; The Institute of Jamaica; Jamaica (Prehistory of); Port Royal (Jamaica); Rescue Archaeology.

Jamaica (Prehistory of)

Lesley-Gail Atkinson, Basil A. Reid, and Alexandra Sajo

History of Archaeological Investigations in Jamaica

During the eighteenth and early nineteenth centuries, the English made occasional references to the precolonial inhabitants of the island (Allsworth-Jones 2008). For example, in 1707, Sir Hans Sloane recorded that an English resident had "found a cave with human bones and potsherds attributed to the Indians" (Duerden 1897, 28). In 1774, Edward Long described the discovery of an Indian burial eleven years before by the side of the old road from Ocho Rios to St. Ann's Bay in what is now Carinosa Gardens (Allsworth-Jones 2008). It was not until the late nineteenth century that a more formal interest in precolonial Jamaica developed. This came about with the establishment of the Institute of Jamaica in 1879. The institute played an important role in the development of Jamaican archaeology; it was responsible for all archaeological expeditions, surveys, and exhibitions from its inception to the mid-1980s. The first major display of Jamaican precolonial cultural heritage was the institute's exhibition of pre-Columbian artifacts in 1895.

The early twentieth century was a crucial period for archaeological growth, commencing with J. F. Brennan's investigations at Knapdale, St. Elizabeth (1901) and Cundall and Lily Perkins's research at Liberty Hill, St. Ann (1902) (Keegan and Atkinson 2006). In this same period, Adolf Reichard (1904) and Dr. Bastian (1908–1909) explored caves and open-air sites in the parish of St. James. Interest in the anthropology and archaeology of the region surged during this period, and museums such as the Smithsonian Institute, the Heye Foundation, and the American Museum of Natural History funded expeditions to the Caribbean. Under the sponsorship of these American museums, Theodoor De Booy (1913) and G. C. Longley (1914) conducted research on various middens in the parish of St. Ann. The 1920s opened with the controversial discovery of seventy-five arrowheads by a Swedish sailor, who asserted that they were found in a mound near Old Harbour, St. Catherine (Lovén 1935). Eleven years later, Dr. Thomas Gann found flaked flint implements in Morant Bay, St. Thomas. Later it was believed that these implements possibly originated from a Mayan region in Belize, not from Jamaica. In 1933, Marion DeWolf conducted one of the most important Jamaican prehistoric excavations, at Little Nigger Ground Hill (Retreat), Windsor, and Little River sites in St. Ann. At the Little River site, she discovered a pottery style that resembled the pottery of the Cuevas and Ostiones of Puerto Rico.

The first Jamaican Spanish capital of Sevilla La Nueva (New Seville) and its environs in St. Ann have provided the opportunity to study a mixture of Taíno, Spanish, African, and English material culture. Capt. Charles S. Cotter commenced his research on New Seville in the 1930s, which he continued until his death in 1977. His investigations included excavations of prehistoric sites at New Seville, Seville Parson's Gully (1940s) Windsor Hill (1951) and Windsor (1952–1954). Jack Tyndale-Biscoe also excavated the Seville Parson's Gully site from 1951–1959. Tyndale-Biscoe, Jamaica's premier aerial photographer, was also a dedicated avocational archaeologist who researched the indigenous population of Jamaica for decades. Pedro, St. Elizabeth, Long Mountain, St. Andrew (1953), University Midden, St. Andrew (1953) and Bowden, St. Thomas (1960) are just a few of the sites Tyndale-Biscoe investigated.

The next phase of investigations in Jamaica took place in the late 1940s to the 1960s. This period was marked by the contributions of Robert Howard and Ronald Vanderwal. Howard was a product of the Yale University's special program in Caribbean Anthropology, headed by Professor Cornelius Osgood. This program also produced Irving Rouse and Froelich Rainey, who conducted research in Haiti, Puerto Rico, and Cuba. During the summers of 1947 to 1948, Howard performed a preliminary survey of the archaeology of Jamaica. In 1950, he completed his PhD dissertation, "The Archaeology of Jamaica and Its Position in Relation to Circum-Caribbean Culture." He listed seventy-five middens, twenty-seven caves, and nine localities with rock carvings (Allsworth-Jones 2008). His major research project was the White Marl site in St. Catherine, the Jamaican type site for the Meillacan Ostionoid. Vanderwal, who studied with Robert Howard, continued research at White Marl from 1965 to 1968. Vanderwal also conducted investigations on twenty-six sites across the island, which he discussed in his MA thesis, "The Prehistory of Jamaica: A Ceramic Study."

After the era of Howard and Vanderwal, and partly

overlapping with it, came the era of Canadian geologist James W. Lee and the Archaeological Society of Jamaica. In 1959, Lee embarked on a "project of mapping all known Arawak sites in Jamaica" (Allsworth-Jones 2008, 75). The net result is the precise listing of 265 middens and caves. In addition, Lee made note of seventy-seven other sites that he did not succeed in locating, thirty-six of which had been mentioned by previous authors such as Duerden, Cundall and Howard, and forty-one of which were known only on the basis of unverified reports. Lee founded the Archaeological Club of Jamaica in 1965, which evolved into The Archaeological Society of Jamaica in 1970. The society has conducted intensive investigations on the island since 1965 and has published several articles on Jamaican archaeology and artifacts and issues related to cultural resource management.

In 1958, the Jamaica National Trust Commission was established under the Institute of Jamaica. In 1985, the commission was separated from the institute and renamed the Jamaica National Heritage Trust. One of the main objectives of the trust is "to identify, research, record, interpret, regulate, protect and preserve the material cultural heritage resources of the Jamaican people" (Government of Jamaica 1985). The trust's Archaeology Division, in particular, has conducted numerous site visits, surveys, archaeological impact assessments, and rescue excavations on prehistoric sites.

Over the past two decades, Jamaican prehistory has sparked the interest of international researchers, as reflected in Elizabeth Rega's research on human skeletal remains from Sommerville Cave, Clarendon (1996–99). From 1998 to 2002, William F. Keegan conducted a comparative study of Redware and Montego Bay Style settlements at Paradise Park, Westmoreland. Also in 2002, Betty Jo Stokes analyzed the settlement patterns of the Jamaican Taíno at the Rio Nuevo site in St. Mary in an effort to identify evidence of Jamaican chiefdoms.

Prehistoric Archaeology

The earliest occupation of Jamaica took place with the arrival of the Ostionan culture, a subseries of the Ostionoid during the seventh century AD. This was thousands of years after the initial peopling of the Greater Antilles (4000–400 BC) by indigenous populations from the Yucatán. The earliest settlers moved into Cuba and Hispaniola and developed into the Archaic age Casimiroid peoples (Rouse 1992). To date, no evidence of Archaic cultures have been discovered in Jamaica, despite its proximity to Cuba and Hispaniola. Several reasons have been proposed for the late colonization of

Jamaica, including the island's southerly and isolated location and the probability that it was not visible from Cuba and Hispaniola. Richard Callaghan (2008) argues that because of the rough waters on the northern coast of Jamaica, Archaic groups in Cuba might have found it difficult to travel to that island. These environmental challenges would have delayed colonization until later indigenous populations, namely the Ostionan and Meillacan Ostionoid, developed the watercraft technology that was required to migrate to Jamaica from neighboring islands (Callaghan 2008).

Between AD 600 and AD 1000, Ostionoid from Hispaniola expanded south and west, migrating to Jamaica and the Bahamas. These were the first populations to colonize the island (Chanlatte-Baik 2003). Caribbean scholars have argued that the Ostionoid colonization took place in two migrations, the Ostionan (AD 650) and the Meillacan (AD 900). Little River, St. Ann, is regarded as the type site for the Jamaican Ostionan, or Redware, which is characterized by bright red ceramics that are made with fine-grained red bauxite clay and are decorated with zoomorphic figures and a red slip on the shoulders of pots (Rodney-Harrack 2006).

Associated with these pottery sherds are a number of shell beads and pendants; shell tools such as adzes, picks, and knappers; and a variety of lithic objects. Most of the Ostionan Ostionoid settlements occurred in locations near beaches and shallow fresh waters around the southern coastal areas. The faunal deposits mainly consist of conch shell and turtle bones. The arrival of the Meillacan Ostionoid around AD 900 is said to represent a second migration, possibly from Haiti where the Meillac type site is located. The Meillac style in Jamaica has been described as distinctive from other pottery styles found in the neighboring islands. Its pottery decoration consisted of various motifs that were impressed, incised, punctated, and modeled onto pots and vessels.

There are several differences between the Ostionan and Meillacan. First, unlike the coastal sites of the Ostionan, the Meillacan sites are found more inland and at higher elevations. The latter sites are more widely distributed and are located not only along the coast but also in the interior at elevations of up to 770 meters, such as Cooper's Hill, St. Andrew. In addition, there are noted differences in stone selection for lithic implements and their foraging practices that reflect cultural differences and/or changes in the marine environments near sites (Keegan, Portell, and Slapcinsky 2003). Botanical and faunal remains at sites in Jamaica show that the Ostionan practiced horticulture but were more dependent on marine resources than the Meillacan culture, which came later.

The Meillacan peoples practiced horticulture more intensively and relied mainly on agrarian resources, which they supplemented with marine resources such as reef fish and clamshells obtained from a mangrove environment.

Robert Howard identified a variant of the Meillacan Ostionoid in Jamaica, which he named the Fairfield Complex or the Montego Bay Style. This variant dates from AD 1100 to 1500 and is primarily located on the western coast in the parishes of St. James, Westmoreland, Trelawny, and St. Ann. The Montego Bay Style of pottery is distinctive from the White Marl style because of its thickness and coarseness and its incised decorations, which feature short horizontal parallel line incisions that are spaced just below the rim of the vessel.

The Taíno emerged from the Ostionoid people in the northern Caribbean around AD 1200. Rouse has subdivided the Taíno into Classic, Eastern, and Western Taíno. The contact period natives in Jamaica have been classified as Western Taíno, as have contact period indigenes of the Bahamas and central Cuba. Western Taíno culture is considered to be less developed than the Classic Taíno culture of Hispaniola and Puerto Rico, though Jamaican Taíno shared certain similarities with the Classic Taíno. Both groups practiced intensive horticulture based on various crops and used marine resources, and they both established a ranked sociopolitical system and had similar population densities. Rouse (1992) contended that the Jamaican Taíno may have been more socially complex than is generally assumed because indigenous Jamaicans had the greatest variety of ornaments among the Western Taíno, reflecting the existence of social rank. The Jamaican Taíno manufactured lithic tools, beads, pendants, and other implements from a wide variety of local stones and cultivated processed cotton into finished products that they traded to Cuba and Hispaniola (Rouse 1992; Atkinson 2006). Taíno pottery is represented in a variety of vessel forms. The most common include rounded and boat-shaped bowls for cooking and serving, griddles, body stamps, and effigy vessels. The surface decoration of Jamaican Taíno pottery is one of its distinguishing features. These features consist of anthropomorphic and zoomorphic representations (especially of turtles) and the use of incising, punctation, modeling, and other techniques to produce a variety of decorative motifs.

The Jamaican indigenous people produced exquisite wooden artifacts. For example, in 1792, three figures carved from dark, polished wood were discovered in a cave in Carpenter's Mountain in southern Jamaica. These figures are presently in the custody of the British Museum. In 1992, three wooden *zemíes* were discovered in Aboukir Cave, St. Ann. They are now on display at the National Gallery of Jamaica in Kingston, Jamaica. One of the figures is a ceremonial staff that features a carved male figure. It is 168.4 centimeters tall and has a maximum width of 28 centimeters and is probably made of mahogany (*Swietenia mahogoni*) (Saunders and Gray 1996).

During the mid- to late twentieth century, Jamaica's prehistory was primarily viewed as the backwater of

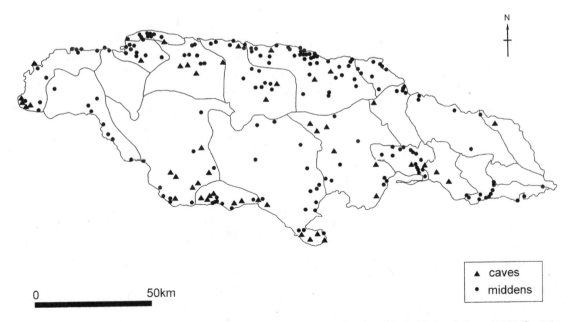

▲ caves
• middens

Figure J.2. All mapped prehistoric cave and midden sites in Jamaica. Reprinted from Allsworth-Jones (2008, fig. 17) by permission of the University of Alabama Press.

0   50km

Caribbean archaeology and there was a general lack of interest in the island's archaeology on the part of foreign archaeologists. Local researchers, however, have developed a model program of national archaeology through the combined efforts of the Institute of Jamaica, the Archaeological Society of Jamaica, the Jamaica National Heritage Trust, and The University of the West Indies. This investment has paid off, as over the past two decades there has been renewed interest in Jamaica's precolonial archaeology. (Figure J.2).

Further Reading

Allsworth-Jones, P. 2008. *Pre-Columbian Jamaica*. Tuscaloosa: University of Alabama Press.

Atkinson, L., ed. 2006. *The Earliest Inhabitants: Dynamics of the Jamaican Taíno*. Kingston, Jamaica: University of the West Indies Press.

Callaghan, R. T. 2008. "On the Question of the Absence of Archaic Age Sites on Jamaica." *Journal of Island and Coastal Archaeology* 3 (1): 54–71.

Chanlatte-Baik, L. 2003. "Agricultural Societies in the Caribbean: The Greater Antilles and the Bahamas." In *General History of the Caribbean*, vol. 1, *Autochthonous Societies*, ed. Jalil Sued-Badillo, 228–58. Paris: UNESCO Publishing.

Duerden, J. E. 1897. "Aboriginal Indian Remains in Jamaica." *Journal of the Institute of Jamaica* 2 (4): 1–51.

Government of Jamaica. 1985. "Jamaica National Heritage Trust Act." http://www.jnht.com/jnht_act_1985.php. Accessed January 14, 2013.

Keegan, W. F., and L. G. Atkinson. 2006. "The Development of Jamaican Prehistory." In *The Earliest Inhabitants: The Dynamics of the Jamaican Taíno*, ed. L. G. Atkinson, 13–33. Kingston, Jamaica: University of the West Indies Press.

Keegan, W. F., R. W. Portell, and J. Slapcinsky. 2003. "Changes in Invertebrate Taxa at Two Pre-Columbian Sites in Southwestern Jamaica, ad 800–1500." *Journal of Archaeological Science* 30 (12): 1607–17.

Lovén, S. 1935. *Origins of the Tainan Culture, West Indies*. Göteborg: Erlanders Boktryckerie Aktiebolag.

Rodney-Harack, N. 2006. "Jamaican Taíno Pottery." In *The Earliest Inhabitants: The Dynamics of the Jamaican Taíno*, ed. L. G. Atkinson, 146–52. Kingston, Jamaica: University of the West Indies Press.

Rouse, I. 1992. *The Tainos: Rise and Decline of the People Who Greeted Columbus*. New Haven, CT: Yale University Press.

Saunders, N., and D. Gray. 1996. "'Zemies,' Trees, and Symbolic Landscapes: Three Taino Carvings from Jamaica." *Antiquity* (December 1): 801–12.

See also Arawak versus Taíno; The Archaeological Society of Jamaica; Cundall, Frank (1858–1937); Duerden, J. E. (1869–1937); The Institute of Jamaica; The Jamaica National Heritage Trust; The Meillacan Ostionoid Series; Origins of Indigenous Groups in the Northern Caribbean; The Ostionan Ostionoid Subseries; Taíno Museum at White Marl (Jamaica); *Zemíes* (*Cemís*).

The Jodensavanne and Cassipora Cemetery (Suriname)

Harrold Sijlbing

The Jodensavanne settlement, or "Jews' Savannah," was established in the 1660s by the European Sephardic Jewish community. This was done under the leadership of Samuel Cohen Nassy and David Cohen Nassy (1612–1685), the patron of Jewish colonization in the New World. Jodensavanne is a phenomenon unique in the world and is the first and only example of a practically virgin landscape that New World Jews had the opportunity to design according to their needs, beliefs, and hopes. The site is considered to be one of the earliest and largest examples of a Jewish presence in the Americas. It is a historic point of entrance of the Jewish community in the New World. The site contains the remnants of the first synagogue of architectural significance in the New World and includes three historic cemeteries, two of which are over 300 years old and have hundreds of preserved gravestones.

Situated along the Suriname River some fifty kilometers from the capital city of Paramaribo, Jodensavanne was surrounded by dozens of Jewish plantations, most of which were devoted to the cultivation of sugar. The labor on these plantations was done by enslaved Africans. Under tolerant Dutch colonial authorities who succeeded the British Lord Willoughby from Barbados, Sephardim received rights, exemptions, and immunities as an ethnic minority and as burghers. This was the most liberal treatment Jews had ever received in the Christian world. By the end of the eighteenth century, the population from Jodensavanne had declined because of slave rebellions, Maroon attacks, soil depletion, and the general collapse of Suriname's economy. At that time, Suriname was home to the largest Jewish community in the Caribbean.

The Jewish community valued their settlement and named it Jerusalem by the Riverside (Figure J.3). Eu-

Figure J.3. *Gesigt van de Jooden savane, in de Colonie van Suriname* (A View of the Jewish Savanna in the Colony of Suriname), a late-eighteenth-century watercolor and pencil depiction by J. Hollinger. Now in the Edwin van Drecht Collection in Amsterdam. Courtesy of the Jodensavanne Foundation.

Figure J.4. Beth Haim Cemetery, Jodensavanne, Suriname. Courtesy of the Jodensavanne Foundation.

ropean Jews lived mostly in cramped quarters and, in some instances, in walled cities, where permission to build a synagogue was difficult to obtain and Jews were rarely given their choice of sites. In contrast, the Jews at Jodensavanne found themselves in a dense tropical forest landscape with full liberty to build their town, synagogue, and cemeteries.

The remains of the town plan and the synagogue and cemeteries are testimony to the longevity and wealth of the Jodensavanne settlement. Jodensavanne's significance for Caribbean history and archeology is most visible through its well-conserved rain forest cemeteries, of which the Cassipora cemetery is the oldest (*beth-ahaim velho*). The dates on its 216 gravestones range from 1666 to 1873 (Figure J.4). The cemetery, which covers around half a hectare, is located close to Cassipora Creek, where the first (wooden) synagogue was built, around two kilometers south of the Jodensavanne settlement. In 1671, the Joodse Burgerwacht Compagnie (Jewish militia) consecrated the Cassipora synagogue.

The Jodensavanne Jewish cemetery (*beth-ahaim*) covers roughly three-quarters of a hectare and has 462 gravestones that date from 1685 to 1873. Almost 700 European-fabricated marble and bluestone gravestones decorate the cemeteries of Cassipora and Jodensavanne. In order of frequency, the languages on the stones are Hebrew, Portuguese, Spanish, Aramaic, and Dutch. In the Cassipora cemetery, 92 percent of the grave markers were made from sedimentary stone, mostly limestone and bluestone, and 8 percent were made from white marble, all imported from Europe. Around 8 percent of the tombstones in the Jodensavanne and Cassipora cemeteries have iconography, but the artists of these icons are unknown in the majority of cases.

The third cemetery of the monumental site is the African/Creole cemetery, located some 400 meters east of the Jewish cemetery, in the "backside" of the Jodensavanne settlement. It is roughly half a hectare in size and has about 141 (mostly severely effaced) wooden grave markers that carry names of descendants of manumitted and emancipated slaves of dominantly of mixed Jewish-African background. The individuals buried in this cemetery had close connections to the Jewish village and the nearby Jewish plantations, and some may have been the offspring of Sephardim or Eurafrican Sephardim who were apparently not allowed to be buried in the Jodensavanne cemetery.

In 1685, the Beraha Ve Shalom (Blessing and Peace) synagogue was inaugurated. The synagogue, which was made of imported bricks, formed the central point of a rectangular village. The Jews of Jodensavanne sited their synagogue on a hill in accordance with Talmudic interpretation, making it the tallest building in the town. Beraha Ve Shalom was two stories (33 feet) high, and the roof was visible from the river. The building had two pointed gable walls on the short sides. The ruin measures 94 feet along its east-west axis and 43 feet across its north-south axis. In addition, the synagogue was adjacent to the river, which provided access to naturally flowing water used for purification rituals. The Jews established this synagogue despite many threats to their safety from raids and revolts by enslaved Africans, Maroons in the interior, rival European powers, and South American natives.

The monumental area mainly consists of the remnants of the synagogue and the three exceptional cemeteries. Yet to be surveyed and excavated are the remains of the old Jewish village that lie buried under thick vegetation. The Jodensavanne Foundation, the entity responsible for the conservation and management of the site, has been encouraging scholars and organizations to study the site and publish their findings. An international volunteer and intern program will be designed to support conservation goals. The archeological projects include baseline surveys to determine whether any archeologically significant areas exist in the monumental area and a geophysical survey in the Cassipora site to locate historic burials and the remains of the first synagogue, which was built in 1662. In 1998, the settlement of Jodensavanne and the Cassipora cemetery were submitted to the UNESCO World Heritage Site Tentative List. The site was declared a Surinamese National Archeological Monument in December 2009 and is fully protected under the Monuments Act of 2002.

Further Reading

Arbell, M. 2002. *The Jewish Nation of the Caribbean: The Spanish-Portuguese Jewish Settlements in the Caribbean and the Guianas.* Jerusalem: Gefen Publishing House.

Ben-Ur, A. 2004. "Still Life: Sephardi, Ashkenazi, and West African Art and Form in Suriname's Jewish Cemeteries." *American Jewish History* 92: 31–79.

Ben-Ur, A., and R. Frankel. 2009. *Remnant Stones: The Jewish Cemeteries of Suriname: Epitaphs.* Cincinnati: Hebrew Union College Press.

Frankel, R. 2001. "Antecedents and Remnants of Jodensavanne: The Synagogues and Cemeteries of the First Permanent Plantation Settlement of New World Jews." In *The Jews and the Expansion of Europe to the West, 1450 to 1800,* ed. P. Bernardini and N. Fiering. New York: Berghahn.

See also Nidhe Israel Synagogue and Mikvah (Barbados).

Kabakaburi and Wyva Creek Shell Mounds (Northwest Guyana)

Mark G. Plew

As defined by Rouse (1962), the Caribbean culture area includes portions of eastern and central Venezuela, the West Indies, the Guyana coastal plains, and portions of western Suriname. The Archaic littoral adaptations documented in the area are of considerable interest (Boomert 2000). Excavations at the Kabakaburi and Wyva Creek shell mounds provide further insights into the littoral tradition in general and Banwari origins and affiliations in particular.

Recent archaeological investigations in northwestern Guyana include test excavations of shell mounds at Kabakaburi and Wyva Creek near Santa Cruz, Guyana. These excavations were designed to address what are largely cultural historical questions: site dimensions, depositional histories, documentation of the range of material culture, site function (and whether site function has changed over time), and assessment of age. The site of Kabakaburi has been investigated by a number of amateurs and archaeologists, including W. H. Brett, Everard F. im Thurn, Clifford Evans, Betty Meggers, and Denis Williams.

Both Brett and im Thurn reported the recovery of a variety of faunal and human remains. Though unpublished, Williams's work is most detailed. Work at Kabakaburi determined the mound to be 20 × 30 meters, with a height of 2 meters. Excavation units and extensive shovel probes suggest that the Kabakaburi mound is different from other mounds in the region, such as Waramuri, Piraka, and Siriki. Kabakaburi appears to consist of multiple, but only periodic, accumulations of shell refuse on a natural slope, making the mound appear larger than it is. In contrast, other regional mounds represent extensive refuse deposits. Stratigraphic observations of the 2007 investigations mirror those of Williams's, though much disturbance is noted (Plew, Pereira, and Simon 2007). Historic nineteenth-century Dutch and English ceramics and metal artifacts are common in the upper levels of the site. Prehistoric remains include Alaka Phase celts, picks, and hammerstones. The pres-

ence of three quartz cores and numerous quartz flakes indicate on-site manufacture of lithic tools. The Kabakaburi ceramic assemblage is extensive: 66 percent of the assemblage consists of Wanaina Plain sherds. This contrasts with extensive evidence of Mabaruma Plain sherds reported by Denis Williams (unpublished notes). This apparent discrepancy may reflect multiple uses of the site area over time, as some Sand Creek, Hosororo Plain, and Kabakaburi Plain sherds were found in limited quantities, as were Mabaruma, Koriabo Incised, Akawabi Incised and Modeled sherds. Evans and Meggers (1960) describe an "incipient ceramic phase" in which Wanaina Plain co-occurs with the plain and decorated pottery of the Mabaruma Phase. Recent investigations by Plew, Pereira, and Simon (2007) appear to confirm the observations of Evans and Meggers. This bears upon the Williams-Roosevelt debate regarding the early pottery at Barabina Mound and the early occurrence of ceramics and horticulture. Though this issue is unresolved, Williams obtained a radiocarbon date of 5340 BP at the basal stratum of the Kabakaburi mound, which clearly indicates that ceramics occurred there earlier than Evans and Meggers thought.

Early investigators theorized that subsistence emphasized the use of the zebra nerite (*Neritina natalensis* sp.) supplemented with mussels, clams, mangrove oyster, crabs, fish, birds, and occasional mammals. Recent work suggests that the area was utilized seasonally or by preference and availability, so we now expect the presence or absence of different species in different locations in the mound. This is a departure from traditional interpretation that held that the mounds were used continuously over time. Though Williams estimated the nutritional values of the nerite to demonstrate the potential productivity of the shell mound resources, the food value of a few large fish may be seasonally more optimal than shellfish in cost-benefit returns.

A second mound, Wyva Creek shell mound, was first visited by staff of the Walter Roth Museum in

2009. The site, which had not been previously recorded, is being impacted by local commercial mining. Located on Wyva Creek off the Waini River near the village of Santa Cruz, the mound is very much like Piraka and Waramuri mounds and has a very conical form. A survey of the mound found that it measured 27 × 28 × 2.5–8 meters at its highest point. An existing cut into the western end of the mound was used to expose a stratigraphic profile. The height of the mound on its western edge was approximately 2.5 meters (Plew and Willson 2009). Three strata, consisting largely of nerites, were identified. A radiocarbon date of 6430 BP was obtained from a charcoal sample in what was described as feature A (an apparent fire hearth) at a depth of approximately 1.5 meters from the upper surface of the mound. Two 1 × 2 meter units were excavated near what appeared to be the base of the mound. Though no pottery was found, an extensive collection of chipped-stone tools (n = 72), including cores, choppers, a scraper, a whetstone, and fifty-four flakes, were recovered. Though the mound consists largely of zebra nerite remains, small and large mammal remains were recovered, as were fish bones and clam, conch, and crab remains. A number of large rib bones were recovered from the site area and from near the original surface of the mound. These remains have been identified as whale or large porpoise and a large rockfish. Notably, all are ocean species. While such species may occasionally find their way upriver into the interior, the age of the site may suggest a period of greater coastal inundation when ocean species were more common (Plew and Willson 2009). The radiocarbon date establishes Wyva Creek as one of the oldest shell mounds in Guyana. Because the date was obtained above the basal stratum of the mound, the mound could easily be as old as Piraka, which has been dated at 7280 BP, if not older.

The results of excavations at the Kabakaburi and Wyva Creek shell mounds provide further documentation of the localized Ortoiroid pattern that is known in northwestern Guyana as the Alaka Phase. Insights about subsistence variation, lithic assemblages, and the age of the Wyva Creek shell mound should prove important in further evaluations of the origins and cultural affiliations of the Alaka Phase sites and their importance to littoral adaptations in the southern Caribbean culture area.

Further Reading

Boomert, A. 2000. *Trinidad, Tobago and the Lower Orinoco Interaction Sphere: An Archaeological/Ethnohistorical Study.* Alkmaar: Cairi Publications.

Evans, C., and B. Meggers. 1960. *Archaeological Investigations in British Guiana.* Washington: Government Printing Office.

Plew, M. 2005. *The Archaeology of Guyana.* Oxford: Archaeopress.

Plew, M., G. Pereira, and G. Simon. 2007. *Archaeological Survey and Test Excavations of the Kabakaburi Shell Mound, Northwestern Guyana.* Georgetown: University of Guyana.

Plew, M., and C. Willson. 2009. *Archaeological Survey and Testing of the Wyva Creek Shell Mound.* Monographs in Archaeology no. 3. Georgetown: University of Guyana.

Rouse, I. 1962. "The Intermediate Area, Amazonia and Caribbean Area." In *Courses Toward Urban Life,* ed. Robert J. Braidwood and Gordon R. Willey, 34–59. Chicago: Aldine Publishing.

Williams, D. 2003. *Prehistoric Guiana.* Kingston: Ian Randle.

———. n.d. Unpublished notes on excavations at Kabakaburi.

See also Antigua and Barbuda (Archaic Sites); The Archaic Age; Banwari Trace (Trinidad); The Ortoiroid; St. John Site (Trinidad).

Kalinago Descendants of St. Vincent and the Grenadines

Kathy Martin

It is well known that the indigenous people of St. Vincent, along with those of Dominica, held out against all odds to defend their homeland against European aggression for over 300 years. These rugged islands, where "strike and sail" guerrilla warfare was conducted, were the only ones in the Caribbean to escape genocide. Some of the Kalipuna married African men who had escaped slavery and produced the line of people that the Europeans called Black Caribs. Adhering rigorously to Kalipuna cultural practices, they distinguished themselves from the enslaved black population. Thus, Garifuna were born. The Garifunas' vigorous defense of their land under the leadership of Paramount Chief Joseph Chatoyer resulted in their eventual deportation to the island of Roatan in Honduras in 1797 by the English. Only a small group in the village of Greiggs was left behind.

The remaining Kalinago peoples, who were of milder temperament, stayed in St. Vincent but were pushed further and further north as the voracious sugar planters sequestered the better lands. However, north of the dry Rabacca River, a new threat emerged. Eruptions of the La Soufrière volcano in 1812 drove the Garifuna from their villages and they fled south again, some as far as Santa Rosa, Arima, in Trinidad, where they mingled with members of colonial and postcolonial societies. But as Simon Smith (2011) points out, most returned to live in the primary hazard zone in the east of the country. This was no longer possible on the north leeward side, since the village of Morne Ronde was buried under ash and pyroclastic deposits.

The 2001 census indicates that the Carib population stands at 3,818 persons, or 3.6 percent of the total population of St. Vincent. This is an increase of 14.1 percent over the previous census. In contrast, the country's total population fell by 0.2 percent. Whether the increase is due to demographic change or self-perception is open to debate, but this population increase augurs well for the Kalinago community. Approximately 58.5 percent of the Carib population lives in Sandy Bay and another 11.6 percent lives in nearby Georgetown, both traditional Kalinago areas of the northeast. On the leeward side, people still identified themselves as Kalinago by selecting the Carib identity during the census in Rose Bank, Clare Valley, Chauncey, Questelles, and Camden Park (St. Vincent and the Grenadines Statistical Office. 2001) (Figure K.1).

Instructions from the British secretary of state contained in dispatches 133 of November 29, 1898, and 57 of April 4, 1899, required the colonial administration in St. Vincent to rehouse refugee Carib. The plans that were subsequently drawn up show 105 lots of land at Camden Park and 71 lots at Rose Bank for Carib resettlement. Fifty-four of the Rose Bank lots are recorded as being allocated to the Carib by name. The names of Lavia, Delpeche, Matthews, Pierre, Ashton, Edwards, Nanton, and Roberts were among those listed. Descendants of these refugees still live in Rose Bank today. For example, Lot 20 was allocated to James Augustus Roberts, who was referred to locally as a chief. Today his son Alfred still lives there in a small board house. He tells stories of the flight from Morne Ronde, where his father was born.

Traditional Kalinago lifeways have contributed substantially to the survival strategies of Vincentian residents, even in contemporary times. The crops they introduced, which include cassava, arrowroot, sweet potatoes, corn, peppers, cocoa, coffee, *mauby*, sapodilla, pineapple, pawpaw, soursop, guava, and avocado, remain staples in the diet. The Kalinago creatively prepared many of these foods to produce distinctive traditional dishes such as cassava bread, *ferein*, and potato pudding. Roucou, the plant that produced red body paint, can be used as a food coloring.

The maritime skills of the Kalinago have been passed down through generations of fisher folk and light craft operators. Other occupations such as basketry using whist and ping wing continue. Bamboo, roseau cane, and wattle-and-daub homes were once common and are now replicated as tourist attractions. The English spoken today is enriched with Carib and Arawakan words. A physical blow accompanied by an emphatic cry of "*boudow!*" reminds one of the heavy *boutou* club. When the calabash is used as a utensil, it is a "bowley," similar to the Garifuna "*bouli*." The *boyei*, or shaman, becomes the

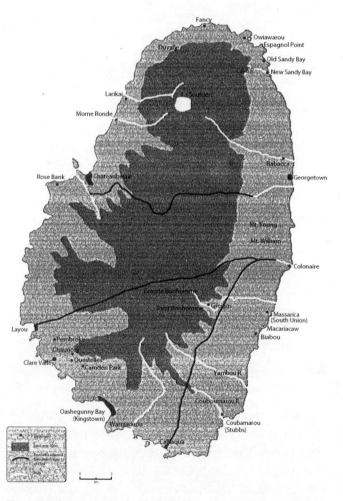

Figure K.1. Sites associated with the Kalinago on St. Vincent. Courtesy of Kathy Martin, 2011.

family name Boyea. Place names have also been inherited from the Amerindian, including Layou, Yambou, Biabou, Wallilabou, Wallibou, Wa-ra-cou. The Kalinago also reflect the culture of their old allies the French as they dance the intricate formations of the quadrille.

During the latter half of the twentieth century, people who claimed Yurumein (St. Vincent) as their motherland began arriving in St. Vincent. They were the Garifuna who had not only survived but had flourished as a people. An estimated 300,000 lived along the Caribbean coastlands of Belize, Honduras, Nicaragua, and Guatemala and in areas of the United States. They were strong in Garifuna cultural traditions and retained a living language that had developed from the Arawakan and Carib languages spoken by their Kalipuna and Kalinago grandparents. Garifuna was selected as a World Heritage Culture in 2002.

Garifuna representatives now make pilgrimages to the offshore island of Balliceaux, where their forebears were impounded prior to transportation to Roatan. They express pride in the rediscovery of their sixteenth-century Island-Carib village at Argyle, located between the Yambou River and the Atlantic Ocean. It was excavated by a University of Leiden team in 2010 and 2011. Initiatives are under way to involve their local kin in the rediscovery of their language, customs, and culture, especially sustainable livelihood projects involving members of the Rose Bank Kalinago community. In 2002, recognition

of the iconic achievements of the Kalinago in defending their homeland led the government to declare Paramount Chief Joseph Chatoyer as the first national hero of St. Vincent and the Grenadines.

Further Reading

Beckles, H. McD. 2008. "Kalinago (Carib) Resistance to European Colonisation of the Caribbean." *Caribbean Quarterly* 38 (2–3): 1–14.

Cayetano, E. R. 1993. *The People's Garifuna Dictionary/Dimureiágei Garifuna*. Dangriga, Belize: National Garifuna Council of Belize.

Ellis, G. 1997. *The Garinagu of Belize*. San Ignacio, Belize: Haman Belize Press.

Kirby, I. A. E., and C. I. Martin. 2004. *The Rise and Fall of the Black Caribs (Garifuna)*. 4th ed. Toronto: Cybercom.

Smith, Simon. 2011. "Volcanic Hazards in a Slave Society: The 1812 Eruption of Mount Soufrière in St. Vincent." *Journal of Historical Geography* 37 (1): 55–67.

St. Vincent and the Grenadines Statistical Office. 2001. *St. Vincent and the Grenadines: 2001 Population and Housing Census*. Kingstown, St. Vincent and the Grenadines: Statistical Office, Ministry of Finance, Planning and Development.

See also The Cayoid Pottery Series; Island-Carib; The Kalinago Territory (Dominica); The Santa Rosa Carib Community, or Santa Rosa First People's Community (Trinidad).

The Kalinago Territory (Dominica)

Lennox Honychurch

The largest concentration of the descendants of the last Amerindian group to occupy Dominica live in a community on the island's northeast coast known as the Kalinago Territory (Figure K.2). Although Kalinago descendants live among Creole communities all along the rugged east coast, the largest group lives within the territory. The Carib, now self-designated as the Kalinago people, once occupied some sixty settlement sites around the island but moved to this isolated area as European settlers took over more and more land. Since the mid-eighteenth century, this relatively isolated zone of scattered hamlets on the northeast coast of Dominica

has been generally referred to as the "Carib Quarter." This "Quarter" was formalized in 1776, when one lot of land amounting to 134 acres was set aside for the Kalinago during the British subdivision and sale of Dominica, after the British Crown secured the island in 1763 by the terms of the Treaty of Paris. The Crown expanded the area in 1777, and a piece was granted to the Roman Catholic Church in 1865.

Henry Hesketh Bell visited the area shortly after arriving to take up his post as administrator of Dominica in 1889 and formulated his ideas about the establishment of the reserve:

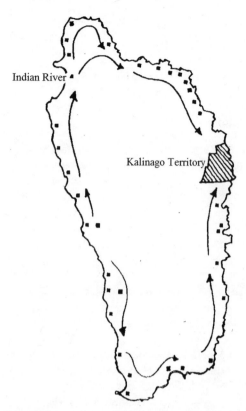

Figure K.2. Movement of Kalinago from former indigenous sites in Dominica in the eighteenth century. Courtesy of Lennox Honychurch.

No definite allocation of this land had ever been arranged, and it seemed to me highly desirable that the small remnant of the people, who once owned the whole island, should be permanently guaranteed the possession of their last homes. I decided therefore that their Reserve should be properly delineated and officially recognised. It was with the object of informing the Caribs of my decision that I was making my journey to their district. (Bell 1946, 19)

In 1902, Bell wrote a report on his ideas for the Carib to the secretary of state responsible for Britain's colonies, Joseph Chamberlain. Combining the philosophy of trusteeship with his own ethnological interests, he made a bid to reserve this land for the people. The letter included a basic historical outline of the Carib and his plans for their future, central to which was the establishment of a reserve of approximately 3,700 acres. In 1903, the British administrator of Dominica set out "the boundaries of their settlement or territory in the Parish of St. David." Notice was given that "with the approbation of the Secretary of State for the Colonies, the Government of Dominica desire to reserve to the Caribs for their use . . . the land so delineated and de-

scribed [which] will hereafter be taken and considered as the Carib Reserve and will be recognised accordingly" (*Dominica Official Gazette* [4 July 1903], 26).

This land was an area of roughly 5.5 square miles, or 2 percent of the entire island of Dominica. Bell officially recognized the first chief of the Carib (Francis Auguiste), and in 1916, he gave the second chief (Jules Benjamin Corriette) a silver-headed staff of office that is still used as a symbol of authority by chiefs. In 1952 the Kalinago Council was integrated into the local government system of village councils that operated across the island. In 1974, a seat in the national House of Assembly was created to represent the Salybia Constituency, which covered the Kalinago Territory. In 1978, a Carib Reserve Act was passed at the request of the Kalinago Council to further formalize the affairs of the territory before the island gained full independence from Britain. But the way that the reserve was established is now having serious consequences. Questions have been raised about individual land ownership, as opposed to the established tradition whereby land is held communally. Efforts are being made to institute regulations for land-use planning because there is now more intensive occupation of the territory by a growing population. Environmental issues such as soil erosion and housing distribution are high on the agenda.

In 2011, the population of the territory was 2,535; the ethnicity of most members is mixed with that of ethnic African Creole Dominicans. Since the 1970s, opportunities for further education beyond the two local primary schools have increased significantly. The main occupations in the territory are agriculture, fishing, and tourism, although many Kalinago work outside the territory in public- and private-sector jobs and professions. The main traditional skills that have been maintained are basketry, canoe building, and cassava processing.

Further Reading

Bell, H. H. 1902. *Report on the Caribs of Dominica*. London: HMSO.

———. 1946. *Glimpses of a Governor's Life*. London: Sampson Low, Marston.

Honychurch, L. 1984. "Community Development among the Caribs of Dominica." In *Training for Agriculture and Rural Development*, 8–86. Rome: Food and Agricultural Organization and International Labour Organization.

Taylor, D. M. 1938. *The Caribs of Dominica*. Washington, DC: Government Printing Office.

See also The Cayoid Pottery Series; Island-Carib; The Santa Rosa Carib Community, or Santa Rosa First People's Community (Trinidad).

Kirby, I. A. Earle (1921–2005)

Kathy Martin

Dr. Earle Kirby (Figure K.3) was viewed as an institution in his native St. Vincent and the Grenadines (SVG). As the island's sole veterinarian, his work took him all over the country, affording him the opportunity to examine numerous sites and artifacts that aroused his curiosity. As a result, he developed an interest in archaeology, to which he devoted a considerable part of his life. His first publication, *Pre-Columbian Monuments in Stone* (1969), brought local Amerindian rock art to the attention of the Vincentian public and emphasized its value. This monograph described over fifty sites with worked stones. He subsequently addressed the Congress of the International Association of Caribbean Archaeologists (IACA) on the topic in 1969.

The most common sign of prehistoric habitation sites in the Caribbean is the presence of pottery sherds, and most of Kirby's excursions yielded a full complement. Kirby said, "What I used to do at first was to take whatever artifacts I collected on any trip and clean them up and leave them at my work place. All of a sudden I was not having enough space for the vet business" (personal communication). He relocated the materials to the Botanic Gardens, where an archaeology museum was subsequently established under the auspices of the National Trust, which he chaired.

Figure K.3. I. A. Earle Kirby. Courtesy of Ashley Kirby.

His work with ceramics led him to wrestle with developing a chronology for St. Vincent and the Grenadines. At first he applied the Saladoid and Suazoid periods to the local assemblages, but he came to the realization that some pottery had distinctive characteristics that did not fit either of those classifications. He was in fact identifying material from the village of Sandy Bay. The valley of the Cayo River that flowed through this village became the type site for the Cayoid ceramic period. This Cayoid series is now generally accepted by Caribbean archaeologists as pottery produced by the Kalinago in the Eastern Caribbean during the contact period.

This was not Kirby's only contribution to restoring respect to the culture of the indigenous people of St. Vincent and the Grenadines. Together with C. I. Martin, he authored *The Rise and Fall of the Black Caribs (Garifuna)* (1972/2004). Joseph Chatoyer, the paramount chief of the Garifuna, was subsequently adopted as the first and only national hero of St. Vincent and the Grenadines, partly as a result of Kirby's research on SVG's native culture. Kirby left a record of archaeological sites that was hand drawn on 1:25,000 Ordnance Survey maps. Because of this meticulous documentation, the country had site registers of prehistoric habitation sites of different types and sizes. He also recorded the fast-disappearing fortifications and sugar-mill ruins. His work remains a primary source of information on the archaeology of St. Vincent and Grenadines to this day.

Kirby was well known and respected throughout the region. He was active in the early years of the IACA (1969–1979). During IACA conferences, he made seminal contributions on topics such as SVG petroglyphs, Cayoid pottery, the peopling of the Antilles, and the renowned Saladoid/Barrancoid bat stand from Arnos Vale. He served two terms as president of the IACA. For his outstanding investigative and conservation work in the insular Caribbean Earle Kirby posthumously received the 2007 McFarlane Environmental Leadership Award.

Further Reading

Kirby, I. A. E. 1969. *Pre-Columbian Monuments in Stone*. St. Vincent: St. Vincent Archaeological and Historical Society.
Kirby, I. A. E., and C. I. Martin. 1972/2004. *The Rise and Fall of the Black Caribs (Garifuna)*. 4th ed. Toronto: Cybercom.

See also The Grenadines; The International Association for Caribbean Archaeology (IACA); Kalinago Descendants of St. Vincent and the Grenadines; St. Vincent.

L

La Brea Pitch Lake (Trinidad)

Alexandra Sajo, Onika Mandela, and Basil A. Reid

The La Brea Pitch Lake is a bubbling lake of bitumen that is located in La Brea village in southwestern Trinidad. The pitch lake is situated at the end of a 45-meter high ridge that runs between the Rousillac Swamp to the northeast and the Vessigny River, which empties into Guapo Bay to the south of La Brea promontory. The existence of the lake was first reported by Sir Walter Raleigh in 1595. Raleigh himself used the asphalt to caulk his ship.

The pitch lake was well known to the Amerindians well before the arrival of the Spanish to the Americas. According to a popular Amerindian legend, the Chaima people offended the good spirits by killing hummingbirds, who they believe are the transformed souls of their dead. As a punishment for this act, the village sank into the earth, reemerging as asphalt or pitch lake, hence its name of Pitch Lake. This lake was of symbolic importance to Amerindian societies because it was a portal to the spirit world.

Chaima natives arrived in Trinidad from the coastal area of Cumaná in eastern Venezuela and settled in the central-west side of the island, mainly because Capuchin monks resettled them into missions located there. A variety of native tools from different periods have been found in the pitch lake and at a number of nearby sites, which suggests that the lake was used as a ceremonial site long before the arrival of the Chaima people. The artifacts recovered consist mainly of a variety of lithic tools of the Archaic Age, a small number of stone and wooden artifacts, and decorated and undecorated pottery sherds belonging to the Saladoid culture (specifically the local Palo Seco complex that developed in Trinidad). The Saladoid introduced the techniques of cassava cultivation, highly decorated pottery making, spinning, and weaving. Many of the Saladoid artifacts recovered from the pitch lake provide insights into these activities. The wooden artifacts retrieved are 1) a jaguar-shaped bench; 2) an oval seat, somewhat resembling a Taíno *duho* of the Greater Antilles (Figure L.1); 3) four paddles; 4) a bowl; 5) a container; 6) a mortar;

and 7) two weaving sticks. Given the discovery of so many precolonial wooden artifacts, the pitch lake holds a unique position in Caribbean archaeology, as it is one of the very few sites in the Lesser Antilles from which objects of organic materials have been recovered. Only one of these wooden artifacts (the jaguar-like bench) has been radiocarbon dated. The date provided is AD 500, which relates to the Saladoid Age.

It is possible that the pitch lake functioned as a burial and ceremonial site during the time of the Saladoid potters. It is believed that the small assemblage of wooden artifacts and pottery adornos recovered from the lake represent the gifts that specific native people were buried with. It is also possible that the Saladoid people used the resources of the lake to restore broken vessels and combined asphalt with porcellanite (naturally reddish-colored clay) to produce red pigment for decorating their pottery.

During the European occupation of Trinidad, the pitch was exploited as a natural source of asphalt, which was traded for salt and other goods on the mainland and other islands and was primarily used to caulk vessels. The pitch was exported to Europe in both its liquid and solid forms. Further attempts at commercial processing were made during the eighteenth and nineteenth centuries. Lake Asphalt of Trinidad and Tobago (1978) Ltd, a state-owned enterprise, presently mines and exports pitch mined from La Brea. The company has been involved in mining, processing, and exporting asphalt products for over 100 years.

The scenery and landscape near La Brea have undergone great changes: from rich luxuriant vegetation and abundant animal life to a desolate area with scarce vegetation. These changes were recorded in writings and paintings by missionaries, explorers, historians, and botanists who lived in and visited Trinidad, starting in the sixteenth century. The desolate panorama of the almost complete destruction of the original vegetation and animal life of the lake is mainly due to the centuries of asphalt extraction. Despite this, La Brea Pitch Lake is

CARIBBEAN SEA

Toco

Northern Range

PORT OF SPAIN

Arima

Chaguanas

GULF
OF
PARIA

Central Range

ATLANTIC
OCEAN

San Fernando

Rio Claro

La Brea

Guayaguayare

Figure L.1. La Brea Pitch Lake, Trinidad. *Inset*, drawing of a jaguar-shaped bench recovered from La Brea Pitch Lake. The bench is of the Late Palo Seco complex, Saladoid series, and dates to about AD 500. It is presently in the collections of the Yale Peabody Museum, New Haven, Connecticut. Courtesy of Arie Boomert.

one of the largest and most significant pitch lakes in the world and continues to attract tourists all year round.

Further Reading

Boomert, A. 1984a. "Aspects of Pitch Lake: The Pitch Lake in Archaeology." *Naturalist Magazine* 5 (11): 11–21.
———. 1984b. "The Pitch Lake in History: The Pitch Lake in Archaeology." *Naturalist Magazine* 5 (11): 21–28.

Boomert, A., and P. Harris. 1984. "The Pitch Lake in Amerindian Mythology: The Pitch Lake in Archaeology." *Naturalist Magazine* 5(11): 28–47.
Lake Asphalt of Trinidad and Tobago (1978) Ltd. 2011. "Company Overview." http://www.trinidadlakeasphalt.com/home/. Accessed January 14, 2013.

See also Archaeological Conservation; Palo Seco (Trinidad); Trinidad and Tobago.

La Isabela (Dominican Republic)

José G. Guerrero

La Isabela is located on the north coast of the Hispaniola, on the eastern half the island, which is currently occupied by the Dominican Republic (Figure L.2). Established in 1493, it was the first European town founded by Christopher Columbus, and its history is of great importance in understanding European colonization in the Americas. Historical and archaeological research over the past few decades has made reconstructing the lifeways of the approximately 1,500 Europeans who arrived with Columbus possible. The town was founded during his second voyage, to provide a base for the extraction of gold from the Cibao region in northern Dominican Republic. The Europeans

brought with them all the necessary supplies for settlement, including food, weapons, horses, cows, pigs, and sugar cane. They quickly built a stone church, a fort, a warehouse, and a hospital. The 200 domestic residences were built mostly from wood and straw. Soon after arriving, the settlers were celebrating Mass, gathering in the city hall, and (most significantly) coming into contact with local natives. Within four years, however, the settlement collapsed due to disease, hunger, death, hurricanes, fire, and internal conflicts, forcing the transfer of healthy settlers to the village of Santo Domingo early in 1498. La Isabella's stones were used as ships' ballast and in the construction of villas in the area. Despite

Figure L.2. Location of La Isabela, Dominican Republic. Reprinted from Deagan and Cruxent (2002, fig.1.1) by permission of Yale University Press.

from the Universidad de la Sapienza identified numerous additional skeletons, including one that exhibited sub-Saharan African features.

Historical Records

There are no reliable historical documents that support the presence of European women in this Spanish settlement. There is scant, indirect evidence from Hernando Colon and one communication from Fray Vicente Rubio relating to a 1511 royal order for the inspection of the ships in the Indies because some women had come without permission, dressed as men. After comparing old and new pieces of information, historian Amadeo Julián (1997) reported that white European women were present at La Isabela before Columbus's third voyage, a topic that Consuelo Varela (2010) has expanded upon. According to Julián:

> Some historians had suggested that the first Spanish women who came to America did so in Columbus' second trip. Documented to a certain extent, these women would be Catalina de Terreros, mentioned as having gone to America probably selling merchandise because many of the travelers owed her money according to a list dated March 1498. The existence of Maria Fernández has already been reported, who declared on February 22, 1497, that she was the admiral's maid. (Julián 1997, 59)

these calamities, La Isabela marked the beginning of European colonization of Hispaniola and the Caribbean.

Archaeological Research

From 1983 to 1985, an archaeological team from the Museo del Hombre Dominicano identified a range of occupants in a nearby cemetery, including the first white women who lived in a native settlement. The team exhumed sixteen skeletons that included twelve males (eleven adults and one child), three European women, and one native woman. One skeleton was facing downward with its hands behind the back; this may be Gaspar Ferriz, who was hanged by Columbus. The feet of each individual were facing east, and the arms were crossed on the chest (with the exception of the aforementioned individual). There was no evidence of clothing and they each had aboriginal grave goods, which may have resulted from burial fill contamination from an underlying Indian village or may be indicative of burial by indigenous peoples. In 2002, a team led by Kathleen Deagan and Jose Cruxent located another settlement containing Spanish ceramics, a pottery kiln, and a mill. Researchers

The fact that Columbus gave a native child to a Castilian woman in Guadeloupe is "enough to definitely state the presence of a Spanish woman in the second trip and suggests the possibility that one or more Spanish women came as well in that same trip" (ibid., 60). The number of Spanish women who arrived on Hispaniola from 1493 to 1496 must have been larger than officially reported because some women came as stowaways, including the "fourth part of the crew" during the second voyage. According to Hernando Colón, his father found "women and children" upon his return from El Cibao in 1495–1496 (Colón 1947, 201). After building the Santo Tomas fortress on March 29, 1494, Christopher Columbus found hungry, sick, and dying settlers in the village who were being forced to toil in public works, "*por lo que fue aborrecido por chicos y grandes*" (for which he was abhorred by young and old) (Las Casas 1985, 1:376).

During the tenure of Governor Nicólas de Ovando (1502–1509) and upon the arrival of Governor Diego Colón in 1509, other groups of European women came to Santo Domingo. The colonial policy promoted the presence of married men and their wives. Married Spanish couples were considered necessary for effective colonization. Because there were so few available Spanish women, many Spanish men formed unions with native women, giving rise to mixed races. The dearth of European women was seen as responsible for the failure of the Spanish colonial government. One difference between the Columbian settlement and the colonization efforts of Ovando was the fact that only a small number of married women or men were members of the former, even though Governor Ovando explicitly encouraged married couples to come to the New World.

References to Native Groups

Another goal of the investigation at La Isabela was to determine the degree to which the Spanish depended on the natives for sustenance. The first reference to native groups in La Isabela was made by Columbus himself, who, according to Bartolomé de las Casas, agreed to "jump on land in a village of natives" (1984, 1:362). Eyewitness reports of the town's construction by both Chanca and De Cuneo confirm this. Chanca stated that "many chiefs and natives come here constantly . . . and many native women as well, all carrying sweet potatoes" (quoted in Varela 1984, 173), and the De Cuneo holds that "they were one and even two miles away from us and they would come to see us" (quoted in ibid., 243).

Ortega (1988), Luna Calderón (1990), and Guerrero (2005) reported Chicoid ceramics, Mellacoid ceramics (Macorix), and a blend of these two at the same level at La Isabela. A mix of native and European materials was also found in the northern mountainous zone of the village (Guerrero and Veloz Maggiolo 1988; Ortega 1988). The archaeological record also contains evidence of the work activities and diet of native peoples. Research has also helped improve our understanding of some of the first native trails to the interior of the country and the settlement patterns that followed. Since the early 1980s, José Guerrero has undertaken an archaeohistorical research program on early Indo-European contacts, focusing on the participation of the Lucayans from the Bahamas in early native communities in both La Isabela and the rest of the island of Hispaniola. This research is based on the fact that Lucayan ceramics are a Mellacoid-Chicoid mixture and that the main guide and interpreter Columbus had on his trips was the Lucayan Indian D. Diego (Guerrero and Veloz Maggiolo 1988, 45; Rouse and Watters 1983).

Conclusions

The presence of a combination of Mellacoid *and* Chicoid ceramics at La Isabela and surrounding sites reveals a pre-

colonial interethnic process that has not received much scholarly attention until now. This complex interaction is the key to developing a better understanding of the early Indo-Hispanic contact and the later colonization of La Isabela, Hispaniola, and the Americas. It is now known that the Bahamas were inhabited by Taíno and Macorige from Hispaniola, as in Jamaica and Cuba. (Macorige were non-Taíno ethnic groups who mixed with the people inhabiting the east coast of Hispaniola.) Thus, the archaeology of La Isabela has contributed to an important archaeo-historical perspective of Hispaniola and the region.

Further Reading

Colón, Hernando. 1947. *Vida del Almirante don Cristóbal Colón.* Ed. and trans. R. Iglesia. Mexico: Fondo de Cultura Económica.

Deagan, K., and J. M. Cruxent. 2002. *Archaeology at La Isabela: America's First European Town.* New Haven, CT: Yale University Press.

Guerrero, J. G. 2005. "La Isabela, primera villa hispánica de América: Un patrimonio arqueo-histórico mundial." In *Arqueología del Caribe y Convención del Patrimonio Mundial (Caribbean Archaeology and [the] World Heritage Convention),* ed. Nuria Sanz, 185–94. Paris: UNESCO World Heritage Center.

Guerrero, J. G., and M. Veloz Maggiolo. 1988. *Los inicios de la colonización de América: La arqueología como historia.* San Pedro de Macorís: Editora Taller.

Julián, A. 1997. *Bancos, ingenios y esclavos en la época colonial.* Santo Domingo: Editora Amigo del Hogar.

Las Casas, Bartolomé. 1985. *Historia de las Indias.* Vol. 1. Santo Domingo: Editora Alfa & Omega.

Luna Calderón, F. 1990. "La Isabela: primera villa del Nuevo Mundo. Su importancia antropológica." In *Arqueología de rescate: Actas de la Tercera Conferencia del Nuevo Mundo sobre Arqueología de Rescate, Carúpano,* ed. G. Loyola and M. Sanoja, 332–341. Caracas: Editorial Abra Brecha.

Ortega, Elpidio. 1988. *La Isabela y la Arqueologia en la Ruta de Colon.* San Pedro de Macorís, República Dominicana: Universidad Central del Este.

Rouse, I., and D. R. Watters. 1983. "Environmental Diversity and Maritime Adaptations in the Caribbean Area." Paper presented at the annual meeting of the Society for American Archaeology, Pittsburgh, PA, April 30.

Varela, Consuelo. 1984. *Cristóbal Colón: Textos y Documentos Completos.* Madrid: Alianza Editorial.

———. 2010. *Cristóbal Colón y la Construcción de un Mundo Nuevo. Estudios 1983–2008.* Santo Domingo: Editora Búho.

See also Arawak versus Taíno; The Bahamas and the Turks and Caicos Islands; The Chican Ostionoid Subseries; The Meillacan Ostionoid Series; Puerto Real (Haiti).

Lapidary Trade

Basil A. Reid

A lapidary is an artisan who practices the craft of working, forming, and finishing stones, minerals, gemstones, and other suitably durable materials (amber, shell, jet, pearl, copal, coral, horn and bone, glass, and other synthetics) into functional, decorative, or wearable items.

The Saladoid who inhabited much of the Lesser Antilles and Puerto Rico from 500 BC to AD 600 participated in a lapidary trade. Excavations at Blanchisseuse in north Trinidad in March 2007 unearthed a stone derived from a fine-grained, acidic, extrusive igneous volcanic rock that is probably from the Lesser Antilles. While the function of this stone is unclear, the fact that it was imported into Trinidad from islands north of Trinidad in the Lesser Antilles suggests that it was of considerable cultural significance to the Saladoid inhabitants of Blanchisseuse. In the northern Lesser Antilles, information from excavated beads in Trants, Montserrat, strongly suggests that Trants was a prehistoric lithic bead manufacturing center that specialized in carnelian beads. It may be that certain islands in the Lesser Antilles such as Montserrat (carnelian) and Grenada (amethyst) specialized in the production of lithic beads primarily for offshore trade. However, not all of the stones used in lapidary trade were imported from outside specific island territories. Antigua is a stellar example of intra-island lapidary trade. Two archaeological sites that were excavated in Antigua in 1997 to 1999, Elliot's and Royall's, appear to have had flourishing lapidary industries (Figure L.3).

While the abundance of beads, pendants, and *zemíes* made from shells, carnelian, and diorite (all of local origin) clearly suggests that there was intra-island lapidary trade on of Antigua, the presence of nonlocal semiprecious stones, including amethyst, nephrite, serpentine, and turquoise, imply that trade or exchange existed between Antigua and other parts of the circum-Caribbean, and possibly the Americas, during the Saladoid period. In fact, there is increasing evidence that precolonial peoples, goods, and ideas moved between the insular Caribbean and the Isthmo-Colombian area (Colombia, Panama, and Costa Rica). Jadeite axes from Antigua recently were sourced to the Motagua Valley in Nicaragua, gold objects have been traced to Colombia, and many of the personal adornments made from shell, stone, and bone have shapes and decorations that are identical to those found at the same time in this region.

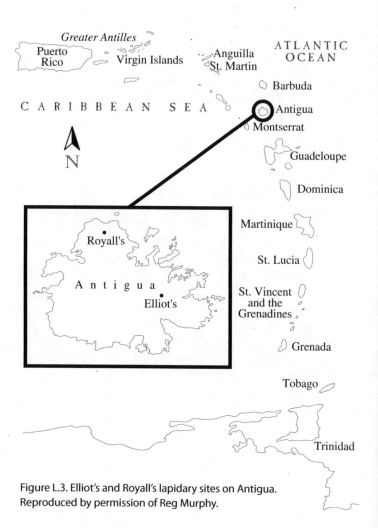

Figure L.3. Elliot's and Royall's lapidary sites on Antigua. Reproduced by permission of Reg Murphy.

Further Reading

Murphy, A. R., D. J. Hozjan, C. N de Mille, and A. A. Levinson. 2000. "Pre-Columbian Gems and Ornamental Materials from Antigua, West Indies." *Gems and Gemology* 36 (3): 234–45.

Reid, B. A. 2009. *Myths and Realities of Caribbean History*. Tuscaloosa: University of Alabama Press.

Watters, D. R., and R. Scaglion. 1994. "Beads and Pendants from Trants, Montserrat: Implications for the Prehistoric Lapidary Industry in the Caribbean." *Annals of Carnegie Museum* 63: 215–37.

See also Elite Exchange in the Caribbean; *Guanín*; The Saladoid; *Zemíes* (*Cemís*).

La Reconnaissance Site (Trinidad)

Neal H. Lopinot and Marcie L. Venter

La Reconnaissance is a multicomponent site in St. George County of the Northern Range of Trinidad. It is the location of the Lopinot Historical Complex, a national historic park. The La Reconnaissance estate (SGE34A) was established as a cacao plantation in 1806 by Charles Joseph Compte de Loppinot (1741–1819) and his wife Cécile (née Daunoy; 1752–ca. 1820). After fighting in a losing cause alongside the British for five years (1793–1798) in Saint Domingue (Haiti) while leading French Royalists who sought to restore the once-booming plantocracy way of life, the Loppinot family withdrew to Jamaica with seventy-five enslaved individuals for a few years before immigrating to Trinidad. The estate was home to 65–75 slaves until full emancipation in 1838. The slave population in 1813 consisted of six carpenters (all male), eight servants (five female, three male), thirty-nine laborers (twenty-six male, thirteen female), one mason (male), one washer (female), one "simstress,"

and fifteen children. The seventy-one slaves consisted of creoles from Trinidad (n = 14), Saint Domingue (n = 15), Louisiana (n = 3), and Jamaica (n = 1), as well as African-born individuals (n = 38) that represent at least thirteen ethnic groups.

After emancipation many former slaves left estates, creating an acute labor shortage in the cacao plantations of the Northern Range. Following government approval to import East Indians to Trinidad in 1844, planters brought the first sanctioned boatload of 225 East Indians aboard the *Fatel Rozack* to Port of Spain in May 1845. A small number of the East Indians from this ship were sent to La Reconnaissance. The 1851 census for La Reconnaissance lists fifty-nine people, mostly of Spanish-Venezuelan and East Indian extraction. The former estate was once at the forefront of a thriving cacao industry. In fact, La Reconnaissance was the largest cacao plantation in Trinidad during the early nineteenth

Figure L.4. Lopinot estate, Trinidad. Courtesy of Neal Lopinot.

century. Unfortunately, there is little known about the estate after that period. However, it can be assumed that the estate continued to emphasize the production of surplus cacao, particularly during the late nineteenth and very early twentieth centuries, when prices remained high and cacao eventually surpassed sugar cane as the island's leading agricultural export crop.

As currently understood, the archaeological component of the La Reconnaissance estate is estimated to have dimensions of about 260 meters north-south by 180 meters east-west. This area encompasses the former central compound of residential and agricultural buildings, but it does not include the larger agricultural landscape (193.4 hectares). Before emancipation, the buildings consisted of the estate house (which was originally about four times larger than the current version; see Figure L.4), probably four cocoa houses or service buildings (of which two remain standing), an unknown number of fermentation houses, an overseer's house, and twenty-five tapia cabins for the enslaved. By the middle nineteenth century, the cabins for the enslaved had been replaced by a barracks with twenty-four rooms (twelve on either side of a central hallway) that was 30–36 meters long. To date, archaeological investigations have delineated the foundations for the original estate house, two former cocoa houses, and one fermentation house. Refuse deposits are scattered about the slopes. A large cellar associated with the original estate house has also

been discovered. The array of historic artifacts that date to the nineteenth century includes many iron artifacts and dark olive bottle glass fragments (Figure L.5). The recovered ceramics include porcelain, stoneware, and a wide variety of earthenwares, including some examples of low-fired Afro-Caribbean ware, the first of its kind reported for Trinidad. Fragments of numerous styles of nineteenth-century pipes produced in Glasgow, Scotland, also occur in abundance throughout the site. Alcohol and tobacco consumption were apparently prevalent throughout the nineteenth century.

The La Reconnaissance site also includes the remains of an Amerindian village (SGE34B) that measures about 140 × 85 meters. Four AMS radiocarbon ages have been obtained from various contexts in this village: AD 550–650, AD 610–660, AD 640–680, and AD 770–900/1020–1050. Despite relatively limited excavations (a grid of shovel tests and three 1 × 1 meter units), this site has produced a large sample of pottery and a variety of lithic artifacts, including worked pieces of local schist and chert flakes, some of which are suspected of being cassava grater chips. The pottery assemblage is largely utilitarian and includes several different wares with three primary temper inclusions—grog, crushed quartz, and micaceous materials. Flat-bottomed bowls exhibiting a variety of rim forms are common, and cassava griddles are also represented. Some of the bowl rims have strap handles. Others have zoomorphic adornos. Black or

Figure L.5. Dark green glass bottle fragments found at Lopinot estate. Courtesy of Neal Lopinot.

red paint or slip and incised motifs are rare. The chert is almost certainly from a source on the island located in the west-central portion of the Central Range. Although bone and charcoal preservation is poor, the economy of the people living at SGE34B was probably based on farming supplemented by hunting and gathering.

Unfortunately, the landscape of the site has been altered by recent residential, recreational, and tourism developments. These have negatively and irrevocably impacted the archaeological record. Since 2003 alone, the historic component of the site has suffered from the construction of new bathroom facilities, the emplacement of attendant sewer and electrical lines, the construction of a track around the savanna and a gazebo, the construction of new pads for picnic tables, the replacement of support posts beneath the estate house, the enlargement of a turnaround and emplacement of guard posts, and much more. The prehistoric site also has been impacted by the construction of a house and drainage ditches and the ongoing use of the south part of the site as a village cemetery. It is hoped that future tourism interests will be balanced by a new attitude toward archaeological preservation, which can augment tourism if given a chance. This attitude should be one that confronts new development with an understanding of the importance of preserving the archaeological record of the past for the future.

Further Reading

Boomert, A. 2010. "Crossing the Galleons' Passage: Amerindian Interaction and Cultural (Dis)Unity between Trinidad and Tobago." *Journal of Caribbean Archaeology* (Special Issue 3): 106–21.

Brereton, B. 1981. *A History of Modern Trinidad, 1783–1962.* Portsmouth, NH: Heinemann Educational Books.

Chauharjasingh, A. S. 1982. *Lopinot in History.* Port of Spain, Trinidad: Columbus Publishers.

Reid, B. A. 2009. *Myths and Realities of Caribbean History.* Tuscaloosa: University of Alabama Press.

See also Afro-Caribbean Earthenwares; Clay Tobacco Pipes (Bowls and Stems); Drax Hall Estate (Jamaica); Magens House Compound, Kongens Quarters (Charlotte Amalie, St. Thomas); Rum; Trinidad and Tobago.

Loyola (French Guiana)

Anne-Marie Faucher and Allison Bain

Introduction

Archaeological research in the Département de la Guyane française, or French Guiana, remains virtually unknown to the broader archaeological community. Archaeologists from the Institut national de recherches archéologiques préventives (INRAP), the Service regional d'archéologie de Guyane (SRA Guyane), and the Association pour la protection et l'étude de l'archéologie et de l'architecture en Guyane (APPAAG) have excavated sites from the precolonial and colonial periods. However, the majority of their work consists of unpublished reports or is compiled in annual reports that circulate primarily within francophone research networks. Most research-based archaeological excavations (as opposed to salvage projects) focus on sugar plantations from the historic period, and specialized analyses are often limited to architecture and material culture. The Jesuit sugar plantation known as the Habitation Loyola is the only long-term archaeological project in French Guiana (Figure L.6). The site contains the remains of impressive structures from the colonial period and the remains of one of the few windmills in the *département*.

Historical Background

In 1494, the Treaty of Tordesillas awarded Spain the region of South America west of Belem, which today is found in Brazil. Spain did not actively invest in the region between Belem and Venezuela and this area was colonized by the British, Dutch, and French creating the colonies of Guyana, Suriname, and French Guiana respectively. From 1604 to 1674, there were several attempts to settle French Guiana, but with the exception of a brief Dutch occupation of the area from 1654 to 1663, French Guiana remained a French territory.

Figure L.6. Map of French Guiana showing the location of the Loyola archaeological site. Courtesy of Anne-Marie Faucher.

While large plantations developed elsewhere in the French Caribbean, primarily in Guadeloupe, Martinique, and Saint-Domingue (Haiti and the Dominican Republic), French Guiana's location at times hindered its prosperity. Early plantation owners settled primarily on high ground (*les terres hautes*), which had poor soils. They quickly exhausted the soil's nutrients as they grew sugar cane, rocou (*Bixa orellana* L., or annatto, a plant used in making red dye), indigo, tobacco, cotton, and cocoa, among other crops. They did not develop lowland agriculture, a system they learned from the Dutch in Suriname, until the late eighteenth century. Most colonists were not prepared for farming in the tropics. Colonists were often vagabonds, penniless nobles, and, before slavery was introduced, soldiers and indentured laborers, who were commonly called *les 36 mois* (thirty-six months). The latter were hired to work for an average of three years, at the end of which they would receive a parcel of land or a sum of money. Adding to these challenges was the erratic nature of the colony's contact with France. Trade winds hindered the arrival of many vessels, those over 300 tons had to anchor offshore, and the wide, shallow rivers around the capital, Cayenne, required expert navigators. These factors discouraged maritime traffic which was erratic at best, according to Mam-Lam-Fouck (1992).

Finally, few enslaved Africans worked the small farms of the *petits colons*. Unlike colonies with absentee land owners in France, French Guianese plantation owners generally lived on their estates, even participating in manual labor on the smallest plantations. In 1690, there were around a dozen large plantations with over 100 enslaved Africans. These were by far the minority, as most plantations had only three or four enslaved Africans. Colonists and their enslaved African populations shared the territory with the native Amerindian population, who after initial enslavement, were freed by the king of France after Jesuit missionaries intervened on their behalf.

In 1664, one year after France took the colony back from the Dutch, Jesuit priests arrived with members of an expedition of the Compagnie de la France équinoxiale. The Jesuits quickly established a monopoly over the spiritual life of the colony. Soon they owned several plantations, including Maripa in Kourou and Loyola in Rémire. The largest plantation, Loyola, was founded by Father Grillet in 1668. It was primarily a profitable sugar plantation, but it also produced coffee in the first half of the eighteenth century. An estimated 400 enslaved Africans provided the labor that operated the plantation. Loyola also served as a place for both physical and spiritual convalescence for priests returning from missionary work in isolated parts of the colony or in neighboring Brazil. The plantation ceased production and was abandoned in 1763, when the Jesuit order was dissolved.

Archaeological Research

Loyola settlement, which covered 1,500 hectares by the 1760s, was divided into different activity areas and terraces. Today, the site contains many well-preserved and highly diverse features, including an aqueduct, building foundations, and a well. The residential sector, which was laid out around the master's house, dominated the landscape, overlooking both the cane fields and the ocean. A building on its south-west side served as both a kitchen and hospital while a chapel and an adjacent cemetery were located to the southeast (Figure L.7). The enslaved village has never been identified archaeologically, but archival sources suggest its presence on the west side of the settlement. The economic sector of the site contained many buildings used for sugar production, such as the *purgerie* (curing room), the *sucrerie* (boiling house), and a windmill. Craft and storage buildings included a smithy, a warehouse, and a pottery workshop for producing the sugar cone and drip jars (*poterie sucrière*) that were needed in huge quantities for sugar produc-

Figure L.7. Loyola archaeological site with the kitchen/hospital building to the left. Courtesy of Anne-Marie Faucher.

tion. Other structures point to Loyola's diversified economy, including the *indigoterie* for processing indigo, the *caféterie-cacaoterie* for drying coffee and cacao, and the *vinaigrerie* (rum distillery). The remains of an aqueduct and a well have also been identified.

Thanks to successful collaborations between Université Laval (Québec), APPAAG, and SRA Guyane, Loyola has been excavated each year since 1994. Studies have been undertaken by both French and Québécois researchers and students. Many features are partially or completely excavated, including the master's house, the chapel, the cemetery, and the kitchen and hospital. Other buildings and features related to sugar and pottery production, and storage were investigated; these include the smithy, the windmill, and the *indigoterie*.

While thousands of ceramic and glass sherds and metal artifacts were recovered and analyzed, no systematic archaeoenvironmental studies have ever been done at Loyola. In order to better understand the daily lives and consumption patterns of those who lived at this Jesuit site, a systematic archaeobotanical sampling program began at Loyola in the summer of 2010. Prior

investigations by INRAP at other sites in the *département* suggest the presence of carbonized layers, charcoal remains, and, at times, carbonized seeds from all cultural occupations. However, this material has not been systematically analyzed. The archaeobotanical studies to date in French Guiana include a few analyses of prehistoric phytoliths and charcoal.

Ironically, botanists as early as the eighteenth century were fascinated by the flora of the region. Botanists and modern French institutions such as the Office national des forêts de Guyane, the Herbier de Guyane, and the Centre technique forestier tropical have been studying this flora since the eighteenth century, providing exemplary reference collections and archival sources. While historical documents and encyclopedias describe the vegetation, including size, leaf shape, color, and medicinal or poisonous properties, little is known about human/plant interactions in the historic period, including the use of plants and trees for food, construction materials, and tools. Many questions will remain unanswered unless archaeobotanical data are systematically studied.

Université Laval's archaeobotanical project examined

the potential for the preservation of seed macroremains and charcoal from Loyola. Analyses from this project concentrated on samples recovered from the kitchen/hospital building. The kitchen's main features, which include an oven, a hearth, and a bread oven with a paved floor, were sampled for botanical remains in 2010. The southern end of the hospital was also excavated with soil samples taken for archaeobotanical studies, as there was evidence suggesting the presence of a privy feature that may reveal important information about lifestyle and diet on the site. To establish the potential for archaeobotanical analyses, a consistent volume of soil was tested from all contexts. Initial results suggested that only carbonized or burned materials were preserved, though carbonized seeds and charcoal were found in almost all the contexts sampled. Seed remains were uncommon and represent almost exclusively wild plant species, even in the kitchen area. Unfortunately, they do not suggest food processing or meal preparation and their presence is probably due to accidental carbonization. Similar results were recovered from the area adjacent to the hospital wall. This evidence, combined with the evidence from artifact analyses, does not support the hypothesis of a privy at this location, as no seed species associated with human consumption (e.g., fruits or cereals) were recovered. However, the continuation of a wall from a nearby terrace was found, providing further information about this area of the site.

Conclusion

In 2009, Loyola was acquired by the Conservatoire du littoral, a nonprofit organization working in France and overseas whose mission is to protect and restore natural habitats and endangered shoreline environments. This new status ensures that archaeological work will continue at Loyola and that the site will be protected from urban development. Furthermore, there are currently discussions with local partners to establish an archaeological management plan. The archaeobotanical information gathered in 2010 is significant, as it provides rare data on human/plant interactions from the colonial period. It may shed light on commercial activities and trade networks and may also provide information about how Jesuit priests interacted with and adapted to their tropical home.

Further Reading

Fusée-Aublet, J. C. 1775. *Histoire des plantes de la Guiane françoise, rangées suivant la méthode sexuelle, avec plusieurs mémoires sur différens objets intéressans, relatifs à la Culture & au Commerce de la Guiane françoise, & une Notice des Plantes de l'Ile-de-France.* 4 vols. Paris: Pierre-François Didot.

Le Roux, Y. 1994. "L'Habitation guyanaise sous l'Ancien Régime: Étude de la culture matérielle." Vol. 3. PhD diss., École des Hautes Études en Sciences Sociales, Paris.

Le Roux, Y., A. Réginald, and N. Cazelles. 2009. *Les jésuites et l'esclavage: Loyola L'habitation des jésuites de Rémire en Guyane française.* Québec: Presses de l'Université du Québec.

Mam-Lam-Fouck, S. 1992. *La Guyane française, de la colonisation à la départementalisation: La formation de la société créole Guianaise.* Paris: Désormeaux.

Sagot, P. A. 1885. "Plantes de la Guyane française." *Annales des Sciences Naturelles: botanique et végétale* 20: 198–216.

Touchet, J. 2004. *Botanique et Colonisation en Guyane française (1720–1848): Le Jardin des Danaïdes.* Cayenne, French Guiana: Ibis Rouge Editions.

See also Betty's Hope Plantation (Antigua); Drax Hall Estate (Jamaica); Environmental Archaeology; La Reconnaissance Site (Trinidad); Magens House Compound, Kongens Quarters (Charlotte Amalie, St. Thomas); The Seville Sugar Plantation (British Colonial Jamaica).

Luna Calderón, Fernando (1945–2005)

Clenis Tavárez María

Fernando Luna Calderón was trained in modern physical anthropology and osteopaleopathology techniques at the Smithsonian Institution. His previous experience as a medical student assisted him greatly in his physical anthropology studies. He also taught at various Dominican universities. Luna Calderón was a founding member of the Museo del Hombre Dominicano (MHD) and its prestigious team of researchers. During his time at the MHD, he served as director of the Department of Physical Anthropology, subdirector of the museum, and, eventually, as general director. He also served as general director of the Museo Nacional de Historia Natural.

He was a member of the Academia de Ciencias de la República Dominicana and other national and international scientific associations.

His work as an anthropologist in the Dominican Republic included both archaeology and physical anthropology. He conducted excavations and studied indigenous cemeteries throughout the country. His work in colonial archaeology included excavations at the sixteenth-century Diego Caballero sugar mill in Nigua, San Cristóbal; at Pueblo Viejo en Azua; at the Monasterio de San Francisco; at the first Spanish aqueduct in the Americas; and at the cemetery of the Santa Bárbara church in the colonial zone of Santo Domingo. Luna Calderón conducted joint research projects with Marcio Veloz Maggiolo, Renato O. Rimoli, Elpidio J. Ortega, José G. Guerrero, Bernardo Vega, Clenis Tavárez María, Mario Sanoja, Iraida Vargas, Alfredo Coppa, C. Roschild, Andrea Cucina, and Andrea Drussini, among others.

He also worked as a visiting professor at Harvard University, Universidad Central de Venezuela, Sapienza Università di Roma, and Universidad de Oriente in Santiago, Cuba. His research led him to work in all of the Greater Antilles, in many of the Lesser Antilles, and in Venezuela. He participated in national and international scientific events and his articles were published in prestigious national and international journals. His most important work may have been the *Atlas de patología ósea* (1976).

Luna Calderón reported the first cases of syphilis in the Caribbean in human remains from Samaná. This find is of great importance because it confirmed the existence of syphilis in the Americas before the arrival of Europeans. He identified a new type of burial, which he named residual (details are found in Veloz Maggiolo et al. 1977). He also reported for the first time the presence of cranial deformation and pseudocircular deformation among Caribbean Preceramic groups. Luna Calderón discovered osteological evidence for tuberculosis in the María Sosá cave. He also uncovered the earliest case of amputation (left leg of a young woman) among the precolonial people of the Caribbean on the remains of an individual from Gonave Island, Haiti (details are found in Luna Calderón 1980).

He also discovered the only reported case of the ritual of *athebeanequen* in his excavations of the cemeteries of La Cucama, San Pedro Macorís. This ritual involved interring the chief's favorite wife alive with her dead husband after she was likely drugged with a hallucinogen. This find confirmed reports of this ritual in the Spanish chronicles. In another cemetery, El Atajadizo, located in La Altagracia province in the eastern part of the country, Calderón found evidence of violence in Amerindian human remains, although he was not able to determine whether the conflict was intertribal or with Europeans.

At La Isabela, he conducted excavations with José G. Guerrero that provided interesting results. For example, they found evidence of the first Spanish women in the continent that was later confirmed with ethnohistoric sources. Other finds included an individual with his hands tied behind his back and isolated from the rest of the burials, a man and a woman who were buried together at the same time, an infant who probably was one of the first European children born in the Americas, a female Amerindian, and Amerindian offerings accompanying many of the burials. He also discovered prehistoric mucopolysaccharidosis on human remains in Quibor, Venezuela. This condition includes a group of hereditary diseases that produce progressive cellular damage that affect appearance, physical abilities, the functioning of organs and systems, and, in most cases, mental development. Throughout his professional career he also worked in rescue archaeology and in the identification of the remains of national heroes and other renowned individuals. Luna Calderón had a passion for physical anthropology, and he dedicated his life to the field until his death.

Further Reading

Luna Calderón, F. 1976. *Atlas de patología ósea*. San Pedro de Macorís, R.D.: Ediciones de la UCE.

———. 1980. "Estudio de un caso de amputación de Isla Gonaive—Haití." *Boletin del Museo del Hombre Dominicano* 13: 46–52.

Veloz Maggiolo, Marcio, Elpidio Ortega, Joaquín Nadal, C. Fernando Luna, y Renato Rimoli. *Arqueología de la Cueva de Berna*. Republica Dominica: Universidad Central dl Este San Pedro de Macorís, 1977.

See also La Isabela (Dominican Republic); Museo del Hombre Dominicano.

Magens House Compound, Kongens Quarters (Charlotte Amalie, St. Thomas)

Douglas V. Armstrong

The Magens archaeological project is the first phase of an investigation of a series of housing compounds in the nineteenth-century port town of Charlotte Amalie, St. Thomas, United States Virgin Islands (USVI) (formerly Danish West Indies). The project provides insights into urban life in the Danish West Indies (Armstrong, Williamson, and Knight 20010; Armstrong, Williamson, and Armstrong 2013). The Magens house compound includes the main house, the cook house, and outbuildings that were occupied by property owners, enslaved laborers, servants, and midlevel managers. The study examines a cross-section of life and social interaction in an urban residential compound. The entire urban house compound has remained intact but the primary owner's residence was destroyed by Hurricane Marilyn in 1995. Researchers are examining the main house foundation and ruins and outbuildings that are distributed on the ten terraces that make up the compound (Armstrong and Williamson 2011a, 2011b) (Figure M.1).

St. Thomas, which was initially settled as early as 1672 by Danish colonists, remained under Danish control until 1917 (excluding two brief periods of British

Figure M.1. Magens House compound. The main house was destroyed by Hurricane Marilyn in 1995. The walled compound includes the main house, slave/servant quarters, and two houses that were rented out. Courtesy of Douglas V. Armstrong.

occupation), when the Danish West Indies were officially sold to the United States (Dookhan 1994). The scale of settlement remained rather small until the latter part of the eighteenth century, when trade patterns in the hemisphere and colonial financial interests in the region changed (Dookhan 1994). By the late eighteenth century, Charlotte Amalie had become a major port town, replacing other ports such as the port at St. Eustatius in both volume and breadth of global trade. Although St. Thomas was officially under Danish control, the island developed into a cosmopolitan island that attracted merchants and sailors from the Caribbean and Europe.

The residential compound is located in a National Register District on the east side of 99 Steps, a path that leads up to Skytsborg Tower (also known as Blackbeard's Castle). The findings from this site are being incorporated into a broader study of the historic district on Blackbeard's Hill (Skytsborg), St. Thomas. The project involves excavations, public interpretation, and the development of a research center and museum (Armstrong 2011). Archaeological research at sites on and near Blackbeard's Hill is being incorporated into public interpretation programs and historic tours of the hill. The archaeological field work is designed to engage the public through formal tours for visitors and educational tours for residents.

J. M. Magens is listed as the owner of the combined plot as early as 1805 (Freiesleben 2001). By 1818, his children were co-owners, and in 1827, 1834, and 1837 they were listed as full owners. Scottish merchant Duncan McDougal is listed as owning the property in 1867 (Freiesleben 2001). He was an importer and exporter of a wide variety of goods, including iron ornamentation for construction. He had several warehouses on the Charlotte Amalie waterfront.

Structures on the hill were built on a series of terraces, and each terrace was sampled. Study findings included detailed information about building construction and construction sequences. The deposits yielded well-stratified remains spanning the early nineteenth through twentieth centuries. Units on the upper terraces included evidence of a bone button workshop; evidence included dozens of cow bone fragments from which buttons were cut. This cottage industry probably provided an extra source of income for servants and/or enslaved laborers on the property (see Klippel and Schroedl 1999). Research continues on this site and will form the base of a dissertation being completed by Christian Williamson of Syracuse University, New York.

Further Reading

Armstrong, A. 2011. "Archaeology, Historic Preservation, and Tourism in the Kongens Quarter, Charlotte Amalie, St. Thomas (formerly Danish West Indies)." In *Actes de XVIII Congrès International d'Archéologie de la Caraibe (Proceedings of the XVIII International Congress for Caribbean Archaeology)*, ed. G. Richard, 185–99. Basse-Terre, FWI: l'Association Internationale d'Archéologie de la Caraibe, Région Guadeloupe.

Armstrong, D. V., and C. Williamson. 2011a. "The Magens House, Charlotte Amalie, St. Thomas, Danish West Indies: Archaeology of an Urban House Compound and its Relationship to Local Interactions and Global Trade." In *Islands at the Crossroads: Migration, Seafaring, and Interaction in the Caribbean*, ed. L. A. Curet and M. W. Hauser, 137–63. Tuscaloosa: University of Alabama Press.

———. 2011b. "19th Century Urban Port Town Merchant's Residence in Charlotte Amalie, St. Thomas, Danish West Indies." In *Actes de XVIII Congrès International d'Archéologie de la Caraibe (Proceedings of the XVIII International Congress for Caribbean Archaeology)*, ed. G. Richard, 2:276–91. Basse-Terre, FWI: l'Association Internationale d'Archéologie de la Caraibe, Région Guadeloupe.

Armstrong, D. V., C. Williamson, and A. Armstrong. 2013. "Networked Interaction: Archaeological Exploration of Walled and Terraced House Compounds in the Danish Colonial Port Town of Charlotte Amalie, St. Thomas." In *Scandinavian Colonialism and the Rise of Modernity: Small Time Agents in a Global Arena*, ed. Magdalena Naum and Jonas M. Nordin, 275–95. New York: Springer.

Dookhan, I. 1994. *History of the Virgin Islands*. Kingston: Canoe Press.

Freiesleben, B. 2001. *The History of Haagensen's House on St. Thomas*. Denmark: Forlaget ACER.

Klippel, W. E., and G. Schroedl. 1999. "African Slave Craftsmen and Single-Hole Bone Discs from Brimstone Hill, St. Kitts, West Indies." *Post-Medieval Archaeology* 33: 222–32.

See also Drax Hall Estate (Jamaica); La Reconnaissance Site (Trinidad); The Seville Sugar Plantation (British Colonial Jamaica).

The Magnificent Seven Mansions (Port of Spain, Trinidad)

Rudylynn De Four Roberts

The seven Queens Park Savannah mansions, affectionately known in Trinidad as "The Magnificent Seven," are part of a single historic district that was designated a "Monument of the Greater Caribbean" by the Caribbean Council of Monuments and Sites (CARIMOS) in 1998. The government of Trinidad owns four of these mansions and is now beginning restoration work on them.

According to architect John Newel Lewis (1983), these mansions, which were all constructed in the period 1902–1910, were well built and sensibly engineered. They reveal a full understanding of good construction practices in a tropical climate and were originally intended for Trinidadians of diverse origins (French, German, Indian, Corsican, and Scottish). The highly cultivated individuality of the Trinidadian is reflected in the style and elegance of these façades. These characteristics radiate happiness and celebrate the work of craftsmen who were able to exercise their skills at every turn. The skills and technological knowledge of the architects involved in the construction of these buildings are of the highest order (Lewis 1983). Lewis described these mansions as a crazy defiant architecture of romanticism that is as gorgeous as the exotic birds, butterflies, and flowers of Trinidad and Tobago.

The population of Trinidad was highly diverse at the turn of the twentieth century as it is today. It included Spanish, French, and English colonial settlers; descendants of enslaved Africans; Portuguese, Scottish, Chinese, and Middle Eastern immigrants; and Indian indentured laborers. This and the fact that Trinidad is located outside the region's hurricane belt encouraged the architects and builders on the island to develop freely, rejecting the Georgian style that is so typical of other West Indian Islands. The architects who designed these seven buildings produced very different buildings, mixing details of different architectural styles. Each one is a masterpiece.

At the time these mansions were built, cocoa was the main export Trinidad produced, and the cocoa barons built massive urban residences that proclaimed their wealth to all. These mansions have survived in spite of years of neglect in a country where historic preservation has not been a priority.

The first to be constructed was Killarney, the home of the Stollmeyer family. The building, which was designed by Scottish architect Robert Gillies, was inspired by Balmoral Castle. The Stollmeyers still own vast tracts of cocoa estates in Santa Cruz. The building is now owned by the government of Trinidad and Tobago.

Rosenweck, known as Whitehall today, was built in 1904 by Joseph Agostini, who was the owner of large cocoa estates in the Caura Valley. Whitehall, the largest of the homes in this historic district, is built primarily of Barbados coral and timber. It was sold to Robert Henderson, who lived there with his family until his death in 1918. During World War II, the U.S. military commandeered Whitehall from the heirs of Robert Henderson. Over the years it has also been the home of the British Council, the Trinidad Central Library, the Trinidad Art Society, and the offices of the prime minister of Trinidad and Tobago.

Archbishop's House, which was completed in 1904, was constructed by Scottish architect George Brown. It is the home of the Roman Catholic Archbishop of Port of Spain and the center of administration of the Catholic Archdiocese.

Ambard's Residence, which was designed in the French baroque colonial style, was the home of Lucian Ambard, the owner of an estate in Erin. The ornate renaissance ironwork manufactured by McFarlane's of Glasgow is one of the signature features of the building. It was purchased in 1940 by Timothy Roodal and is occupied by Roodal's heirs, the family of Dr. Yvonne Morgan, who renamed it Romoor.

Mille Fleurs, with its iron fretwork and refined setting, is another typical town house of its day. It was built by architect George Brown for Mrs. Virginie Prada as a gift for her husband, Dr. Enrique Prada, mayor of Port-of-Spain from 1914 to 1917. Mrs. Prada (née Blanc) was the daughter of a Venezuelan Cocoa baron. The house was sold to Joseph Salvatori in 1923, to George Matouk in 1973 and to the government of Trinidad and Tobago in 1979.

Hayes Court was constructed as the home of the bishop of the Anglican Church. The building was completed in 1910 by Taylor and Gillies. It was named after Bishop Hayes, the first occupant. It is a grand house that

Figure M.2. Queens Royal College. Photo by Geoffrey MacLean.

combines the English country style with cast-iron columns and brackets on the ground floor veranda, adding a little playfulness to the otherwise sober façade.

Queen's Royal College was built in the German Renaissance style. It was constructed of concrete and is faced with blue limestone from a local quarry and colored lime render (Figure M.2). Designed by D. M. Hann, it originally had six classrooms and a lecture hall that accommodated 550 persons. The building was opened on March 25, 1904 by Sir Alfred Maloney. In 1913, a King Edward VII memorial clock was presented to the college by William Gordon Gordon. This clock, which has contributed greatly to the building's landmark status, chimes on the quarter hour and holds fond memories for persons living in the St. Clair area and for the residents of Port of Spain who use the Queen's Park Savannah for recreation.

Further Reading

Ali, A., ed. 2000. *Trinidad and Tobago: Terrific and Tranquil.* London: Hansib.

Lewis, C. A., and H. E. Shepard. 1988. *Three Monuments of Trinidad: Proposed to the Organization of American States for the Selection of Monuments of the Greater Caribbean.* Gainesville: Preservation Institute Caribbean, College of Architecture, University of Florida.

Lewis, J. N. 1983. *Ajoupa: Architecture of the Caribbean; Trinidad's Heritage; Republic of Trinidad and Tobago.* [Port of Spain]: J. N. Lewis,

Mavrogordato, O. 1977. *Voices in the Street.* Port of Spain: Inprint Caribbean.

See also Falmouth (Jamaica); Port Antonio (Jamaica); Spanish Town (Jamaica); Willemstad (Curaçao).

The Maroons

Cheryl White

Introduction

In the past twenty years, Maroon archaeology has emerged as an interesting genre of historical archaeology. The growing interest in the material remains of runaway slave descendants and their communities has refashioned how historical archaeologists approach and discuss African Diaspora material culture. Maroons are descendants of the enslaved who developed structured societies during the height of colonialism. Maroon communities were documented during the sixteenth through the nineteenth centuries in isolated regions of the Caribbean's Greater and Lesser Antilles and continental America. Maroons are distinguished by their place of habitation, language, customs, and unique history in relation to plantation enslaved. Because Maroon sites are often well hidden for obvious reasons, Maroon archaeology presents a unique set of challenges. Traditional archaeological survey and excavation techniques are not always applicable or sufficient to "address [the] recognition of sites, conducting excavations, construction of typologies and development of models that incorporate oral history and ethnoarchaeology" (Ngwenyama 2007, 273).

Maroon archaeological theory includes the traditional themes of rebellion, resistance, and retention and presents the innovation of a broader and more inclusive theory: ethnogenesis, the formation of a new ethnic group. The methods of explaining Maroon ethnogenesis include oral history, ethnoarchaeology, archaeometry, and creative techniques for surveying and excavating in dynamic terrains and environments. These methods, when combined, present a challenge for researchers of Maroon archaeology, but this challenge also marks a pivotal and perhaps a new way to discuss and understand a history that goes beyond a reliance on distant associations. The theory and methods place the focus on Maroons, a distinctly New World group with a material culture that speaks to its historical development among Europeans and indigenous peoples. The pertinent issues for the field of Maroon archaeology can be organized into four themes: site locations and geographical features; theory; method; and archaeological evidence.

Maroon Archaeological Sites

Maroon archaeological sites have been identified in present-day Jamaica, Cuba, Brazil, Suriname, and St. Croix. Geographical features, such as dense neotropical forests, wetland swamps, and mountainous terrains and terraces, presented environments where runaway enslaved could hide from colonial pursuers and flourish in relative isolation. Indigenous peoples also used these types of environments, and these locations offer the possibility of a range of material remains for recovery.

In the Maroon Ridge area of northwestern St. Croix, natural features such as inaccessible rock shelters of coves, caves, and overhangs provided quick, ready-made, indestructible shelters for transient Maroon camps in the seventeenth and eighteenth centuries (Norton and Espenshade 2007). In contrast, in Cuba, Maroons used naturally stepped mountainous regions for permanent settlements (La Rosa Corzo 2003). The viewshed from the stepped mountains allowed Maroons to detect the whereabouts and distance of invading militias and to respond accordingly. In either setting, Maroons were able to determine how to use their short- or long-term place of residence for maximum defense in case of a colonial attack. According to historical records, seventeenth- and eighteenth-century Maroon settlements in the dense tropical forest of Suriname (South America) boasted jutting spikes. These spikes were positioned in a moat formation which afforded Maroon inhabitants a defensive advantage (White 2009).

Theories and Methods Relating to Maroon Archaeology

The theories applied to Maroon research include cultural transformation, hybridity, creolization, and ethnogenesis. In addition, a range of methods are often employed to identify and analyze archaeological evidence from Maroon sites, including archaeology, ethnography and ethnoarchaeology, soil sampling, archaeometry, archival data, and oral history. These approaches provide researchers with the tools needed to identify, explore, and discuss the most definitive Maroon archaeological finds.

Creolization and hybridity theories that originated in African Diaspora cultural anthropology and plantation archaeology, have traditionally sought to dissect the nuances of African Diaspora cultural transformation. These paradigms are interchangeable and are used to explain recently developed ethnicities in the New World. Each term suggests that cultural transformation is a by-product of interaction under duress. In addition, the concept of cultural transformation emphasizes the retention of Africanisms. However, ethnogenesis also allows archaeologists to consider the material influences of indigenous peoples and Europeans, and this process is better suited for understanding Maroon archaeological finds.

Archaeology, aided by ethnography and oral history, is the primary method applied to the study of Suriname Maroon ancestral communities. White's (2009) research focused on detecting architectural arrangements vis-à-vis kinship relations, named places, and domestic and specialized material culture in contemporary and traditional Maroon villages in Suriname. Radiocarbon dating and artifact analysis shed light on the relationship Maroons had with indigenous peoples (Ngwenyama 2007). Archaeometry and ceramic analysis are only a few of the methods used in Maroon site interpretation.

Norton and Espenshade (2007) suggested that research methods at Maroon Ridge and subsequent Maroon settlements in St. Croix should include oral history interviews, soil surveys, and digital elevation models. These research methods may create a signature approach for locating potential shelters and caves. The major defining Maroon archaeological discoveries include long-term ancestral settlements and unique Maroon ceramic technologies. Other findings that will aid archeologists include distinct Maroon patterns of settlement, the fact that historical European vessels have been located in association with Maroon artifacts, earthwork features, architectural forms, and indigenous ceramics and earthworks that Maroons appropriated and reinterpreted.

In Cuba, long-term settlements called *palenques* are defined by subsistence plots, but they are more commonly found in the vast and rugged terrain in the southeastern part of the country. Cuba's historical documentation of Maroons also notes ephemeral settlements known as *rancheria*. These temporary settlements offered shelter to armed bands during bouts of guerrilla warfare. More than thirty *palenques* are recorded, the first and largest of which is El Portillo, which was recorded in 1731. These settlements also supported animal husbandry and subsistence horticulture. A stable farming community is also noted in the archaeological record of eighteenth-century Maroons in Jamaica, where two regions of Maroon settlements have been archaeologically studied: the Windward Maroons of the Blue Mountains region and the Leeward Maroons of the Cockpit country. The first is Nanny Town, which is named after Jamaica's only national heroine, Nanny of the Windward Maroons. Archaeological research found that Nanny Town is composed of three dispersed settlements where approximately 200 occupants engaged in subsistence farming. The Leeward community of Accompong Town has been studied both historically and archaeologically. In both cases, ethnoarchaeology was the primary method used.

Ethnoarchaeological research in Suriname has revealed a long-term Maroon settlement called Kumako, located in the dense tropical forest of the Upper Suriname River Basin (White 2009). The excavations at Kumako revealed earthwork features in the form of a man-made mound approximately one mile in circumference. Radiocarbon dates situate the mound in the prehistoric era, AD 560; in the seventeenth century, during the *gran marronage*; and in the mid-eighteenth century, when stable Maroon settlements developed. In addition to the settlement features, earthenware objects were recovered that featured technology similar to the Yabba and Colonoware ceramics excavated at plantation sites in the circum-Caribbean and southeastern United States. The features that distinguish Colonoware vessels—low-fired utilitarian earthenware pots—are similar to the features of Maroon vessels in Suriname. But the interpretation of how these vessels were used differs because of the different ethnospace in which Suriname Maroons used ceramics.

According to White's (2009) research in Suriname, current ethnoarchaeological research findings demonstrate that Maroons used low-fired earthenware vessels primarily for rituals and not for subsistence-related activities, as is the common interpretation in plantation archaeology. Saramaka Maroon ceramic vessels called *aghbangs* are found in sacred shrines strategically placed in contemporary and traditional villages with customary arrangement patterns (White 2009). Their origin, however, as ethnographic and archival research has demonstrated, lies in the reciprocal relationship Saramaka Maroons had with their seventeenth- and eighteenth-century indigenous neighbors.

Interactions between Maroons and Natives

The notion that Maroons had an enduring relationship with their indigenous counterparts has long been suggested in the historical literature of New World Blacks. However, it was thought that Maroons relied on their native neighbors in only peripheral ways until Scott Allen's (2001) work in Brazil offered a more revealing look at exactly how Maroons were using indigenous ceramics. Allen's work at Quilombos dos Palmares in Brazil contested the long-held belief that Maroons were the makers of their own ceramic vessels. Allen (2001) and Funari (2006) both surmised that ceramic sherds were either of indigenous origin or not solely Maroon. Their research could not identify a distinct Maroon ceramic tradition.

Conclusion

The foregoing discussion offers only a small portion of what remains to be uncovered in Maroon archaeology. Archaeological data have made a significant contribution to the growth of historical archaeology and to our understanding of Diaspora cultural transformation and development. The methodological concerns of Maroon archaeology include recognizing sites, conducting excavations, constructing typologies, and developing models that incorporate oral history and ethnoarchaeology. Maroon material culture is relevant at the local, regional, and international levels, and as interest in research on this topic increases, it has the potential to provide a more dynamic perspective on the lives of New World Maroons.

Further Reading

Allen, S. 2001. "Zumbi Nunca Vai Morrer: History, the Practice of Archaeology, and Race Politics in Brazil." PhD diss., Department of Anthropology, Brown University.

Funari, P. 2006. "Conquistadors, Plantations, and Quilombo: Latin America in Historical Archaeological Context." In *Historical Archaeology*, ed. M. Hall and S. W. Silliman, 209–29. Oxford: Blackwell.

La Rosa Corzo, G. 2003. *Runaway Slave Settlements in Cuba: Resistance and Repression.* Trans. Mary Todd. Chapel Hill: University of North Carolina Press.

Ngwenyama, Cheryl. 2007. "Material Beginnings of the Saramaka Maroons: An Archaeological Investigation." PhD diss., Department of Anthropology, University of Florida.

Norton, H., and C. Espenshade. 2007. "The Challenge in Locating Maroon Refuge Sites at Maroon Ridge, St. Croix." *Journal of Caribbean Archaeology* 7: 1–17.

White, C. 2009. "Archaeological Investigation of Suriname Maroon Ancestral Communities." *Caribbean Quarterly* 55 (1): 65–88.

See also Afro-Caribbean Earthenwares; Archaeometry; The Nanny Town Maroons of Jamaica.

Martinique

Benoît Bérard, Ryan Espersen, and Cheryl White

Martinique, which is administered directly by France, is located in the volcanic arc of the Lesser Antilles. The island has an area of 1,128 square kilometers. The French government's archaeological maps of Martinique identify more than 100 Amerindian sites. The evidence for the earliest human occupation on Martinique found thus far dates to the first century BC at the Vivé site. In 1937, J. B. Delawarde was the first archaeologist to publish research based on research in Martinique (Delawarde 1937). Delawarde's work focused on the excavations at the Anse Belleville prehistoric site. Since that time, Martinique has been a major center of precolonial archaeology in the Lesser Antilles. This work relies heavily on the work of local volunteers. Local support enabled Martinique to host the first Congress of the Association for the Studies of the Lesser Antilles Pre-Columbian Civilizations (the predecessor of the International Association for Caribbean Archeology), which the Société d'histoire de la Martinique held at Fort-de-France in 1961.

Precolonial Archaeology

Knowledge of Martinique's precolonial archaeology revolves around work conducted on a few major sites. In the 1970s, M. Mattioni conducted large excavations at early Cedrosan Saladoid sites, including Fond-Brûlé and Vivé. The latter site was also excavated by J. P. Giraud and B. Bérard (Bérard 2004) for several years in the 1990s.

The Vivé site was abandoned quickly at the beginning of the Mount Pelée volcanic eruption around AD 350–400, making it a Caribbean precolonial version of Pompeii. The exceptional preservation conditions have made Vivé a major attraction for archaeologists for decades. The many publications based on their research have made the Vivé site a primary reference for West Indian early ceramic occupation. The main middle-late Saladoid phase reference site is Dizac au Diamant. The site has been excavated by several researchers since the 1960s. N. Vidal conducted the most recent operation in the 1990s. The primary reference publication on post-Saladoid occupation in Martinique remains L. Allaire's dissertation (1977), which is based on his work at the two major sites of Paquemar (Troumassan Troumassoid) and Macabou (Troumassan Suazoid). New sections of the Macabou site were excavated under S. Grouard's direction in the period 2005–2009. The precolonial cultural chronology of Martinique is thus based on numerous recent and large excavations and is one of the major references for the Windward Islands.

The Colonial Period

Several colonial archaeology programs that combine archaeological, ethnoarchaeological, and archival research have been initiated in Martinique over the last two decades. Martinique was settled in 1635 by the French. Pierre Belain d'Esnambuc took possession of the island in the name of the Compagnie des Isles d'Amérique, although the island was still inhabited by the Island-Carib. This first French settlement in the town of Saint-Pierre began with the construction of the Saint-Pierre fort. Soon the first tobacco plantations were set up; they relied primarily on the labor of white indentured servants. A major change in the island occurred in 1654 with the arrival of between 300 and 400 Dutch Jews from Brazil. These immigrants introduced new techniques that significantly improved sugar production on Martinique. Because the Dutch Jews used enslaved labor, there was also an increase in the number of enslaved Africans on Martinique during this period. The first African enslaved arrived in the mid-1600s, and by 1700 the enslaved population numbered some 16,000, eclipsing the enslaved population of Saint-Domingue, which at the time was 9,000. Sugar was the island's primary commercial resource from the 1690s to 1800, and the profitability of this crop made Martinique the most valuable French colony in the Lesser Antilles. After France lost Saint Domingue at the beginning of the nineteenth century because of the Haitian Revolution, Martinique became even more important. Over the next two centuries, Martinique was one of the most strategically valuable colonies during France's conflicts with England in the West Indies.

Saint-Pierre was the island's economic center until its complete destruction by the eruption of Mount Pelée on May 8, 1902. Several academic and contract archaeological research programs have been conducted at Saint-Pierre, primarily by S. Veuve, over the two last decades. These projects have focused on the first church (*l'église du Fort*), the first cemetery (*le cimetière du fort*), the cathedral, the psychiatric hospital (*la maison coloniale de santé*), the theater, the combat engineer house (*la maison du genie*), and several small private house blocks. The results of this research have been synthesized in a monograph publication that analyzes Saint-Pierre's architectural and urban history, including the results of underwater excavations in Saint-Pierre Bay (Veuve 1999). A diachronic study of the Martinique strategic military defense has been conducted by Laurence Verrand, combining archaeological surveys and archival research (Verrand 2004). Verrand divided the island's military history into four periods, each associated with a distinctive strategic military defense site pattern.

In 1672, during the first period (1635–1700), King Louis XIV ordered the construction of Fort Saint Louis in Baie de Fort-Royal. Two defensive batteries were maintained at Fort-Royal to protect the island from raids launched by buccaneers and Martinique's indigenous population. During the second period (1700–1750), Martinique's population doubled. The growth in the number of colonists and enslaved Africans and a shift from a tobacco-based economy to self-sustaining sugar plantations brought an increase in revenue and wealth. Batteries could now be found along the island's coastal rim where natural barriers of toxic foliage (such as *Hippomane mancinella*), cliffs, reefs, and swamps were also used as defense mechanisms. Lime kilns made during the first three periods have been examined using ethnoarchaeological, historical, and archaeological techniques. Researchers have determined that lime, a local natural resource, was used to construct garrisons and a purifier for the sugar distillation process (the so-called claying process for making white sugar).

During the third period (1750–1802), which included the Seven Years' War, Martinique resisted capture by the English in 1759 but fell to them in 1762/1763. Britain returned Martinique to France in the Peace of Paris treaty that ended the Seven Years' War. In 1784, the French constructed a naval base in Martinique in order to make the island the center of their Caribbean operations. Following the institution of laws recognizing equal rights for free blacks across the French colonies in 1791 and 1792, unrest ensued in Martinique, pitting republicans in favor of those laws against the monarchists. The British, who sided with the monarchists, captured Martinique, Guadeloupe, Tobago, and Saint Lucia in 1794 in response to this unrest. However, Martinique was returned to France in the Peace of Amiens in 1802, and slavery was maintained as an institution in Martinique. In response to these invasions and occupations and an increase in slave revolts, the first landlocked fort was built to defend against land attacks. Slavery was finally abolished in Martinique in 1848. The fourth and final period (1803–1848) marked a shift in French military strategy. In the years leading up to the abolishment of slavery, there was increased concern about inland slave revolts. To remedy the issue, military installations were built on high ground to moderate the onset of tropical illnesses among vulnerable European soldiers. These fortifications provided a quick visual survey of surrounding areas as protection against potential threats.

After Saint-Pierre town and fortifications system, another well-developed research focus of colonial archaeology in Martinique is plantation and slavery archaeology. It began in the 1980s with industrial archaeology research led by the Université des Antilles et de la Guyane. To date, around fifteen masters' theses have been written about plantations in Martinique, using classic historical approaches and analyses of the standing buildings and ruins. The first real archaeological excavations were conducted in the 1990s on the Crève Coeur, Fond Saint Jacques, and Dizac sugar plantations. These excavations were associated with a temporal analysis of the variability and evolution of sugar production. During the later 1990s, S. Veuve conducted an important excavation program at the Saint-Pierre plantation of the Jesuits (Veuve et al. 1999). As a result of Veuve's work, the great house was completely excavated; as was the nineteenth-century village that housed slaves and, after emancipation, free workers.

Kenneth Kelly's (2008) investigations complement plantation archaeology research in Martinique. To better understand French colonial slavery during the French Revolution, Kelly conducted research at plantation Crève Coeur, located in the southern region of Martinique. His excavations focused on the enslaved village site. His finds included low-fired earthenware ceramics that are commonly referred to as Afro-Caribbeanware. In addition, he identified and excavated house floors, wrought-iron nails, and midden deposits with faunal remains.

Although a large quantity of articles, books, and field reports have been published in French, there are few English publications about Martinique's archaeological record. Since 1994, the French Ministry of Culture and Communication has published an annual review of archaeological work undertaken on Martinique entitled *Bilan Scientifique de la Région Martinique*. This governmental body identifies, records, and oversees archaeological sites on the island.

Further Reading

Allaire, L. 1977. "Later Prehistory in Martinique and the Island-Caribs: Problems in Ethnic Identification." PhD diss., Yale University.

Bérard, B. 2004. *Les premières occupations agricoles de l'arc antillais migration et insularité: Le cas de l'occupation saladoide ancienne de la Martinique*. Oxford: Archaeopress.

Delawarde, Jean-Baptiste. 1937. *Préhistoire Martiniquaise, Les gisement du Prêcheur et du Marigot*. Fort de France: Imprimerie officielle.

Kelly, K. 2008. "Creole Cultures of the Caribbean: Historical Archaeology in the French West Indies." *International Journal of Historical Archaeology* 12 (4): 388–402.

Verrand, L. 2004. "Fortifications Militaires de Martinique, 1635–1845." *Journal of Caribbean Archaeology* (Special Issue 1): 11–28.

Veuve, S., en collaboration avec M. Delacourt-Léonard, M. Guillaume, and L. Verrand. 1999. *Saint-Pierre de la Martinique, suivi M. de Guillaume—Saint-Pierre et la mer*. Paris: Ministère de la culture et de la communication.

See also Afro-Caribbean Earthenwares; Brimstone Hill Fortress National Park (St. Kitts); Guadeloupe (Eastern); Historical Archaeological Sites (Types); Island-Carib.

Matapi

Lesley-Gail Atkinson

A *matapi* is a plaited sieve used to press poisonous juices out of cassava root to make the plant edible (Figure M.3). Yuca, also known as cassava or manioc (*Manihot esculenta*), was the most important staple for many of the indigenous people in the Americas. Cassava is said to have been domesticated in South America and later introduced into the Antilles. There are two types of cassava, sweet and bitter. Cassava, particularly the bitter cassava, was used to make *casabe* (cassava bread), which was produced in the Americas from as early as 2000 BC. The bitter cassava, however, has a toxic prussic acid, and thus an important part of making cassava bread is extracting these poisonous juices. Traditionally, the *matapi* is used. The term *matapi* (tipiti, or Carib snake), is associated with the Kalinago (Island-Carib). The *matapi* technique, however, is used by many cultures in the Americas, such as in Venezuela, Guyana, Brazil, Suriname, and the Caribbean. The *matapi* is called *cibucán* by the Taíno, and the Lokono refer to it as *yoro*. It is called *coulevre* by the French, because the diamond weave and shape reminds them of the skin of a grass snake in France by that name.

The *matapi* is a woven cylindrical basket made of palm or plant fibers that has either two loops at both ends or a fastening at the top and a bottom ring. The top end is used to suspend the *matapi*, in most cases from a tree branch, while the other end allows the use of weights. The size of the *matapi* varies according to the culture; it can be up to or more than 15 centimeters (5.9 inches) in width and as large as three meters (9.84 feet) in length. After the cassava is grated, the wet pulp is placed into the *matapi*. The prussic acid is extracted by using stones to pull the basket downward or a stick to turn and twist the *matapi*. Prussic acid can also be extracted by having children sit on a large pole that serves as a seesaw, forcing the *matapi* to expand and contract, a process that squeezes and strains the grated cassava. The cassava flour is then removed from the *matapi* and is shaped, dried, and baked on a *burén* (a circular clay griddle).

Figure M.3. Open house used to process manioc in Lower Oyapock, French Guiana. Two *matapis* are hanging from the roof. Courtesy of Stéphen Rostain.

Further Reading

Keegan, W. F. 2001. "The Caribbean Including Northern South America and Lowland Central America: Early History." In *The Cambridge World History of Food*, ed. F. Kiple and K. C. Ornelas, 1260–78. Cambridge, UK: Cambridge University Press.

Petitjean Roget, J. 1976. "A propos des Platines a Manioc." In *Proceedings of the Sixth International Congress for the Study of Pre-Columbian Cultures of the Lesser Antilles, 1975*, ed. R. P. Bullen, 76–81. Gainesville, FL: R. P. Bullen.

Veloz Maggiolo, M. 1999. The Daily Life of the Taíno People." In *Taíno: Pre-Columbian Art and Culture from the Caribbean*, ed. F. Bercht, E. Brodsky, J. A. Farmer, and D. Taylor, 34–45. New York: Monacelli Press.

See also Cassava (Manioc); Griddles.

The Meillacan Ostionoid Subseries

L. Antonio Curet

The Meillacan Ostionoid subseries, originally known as the Meillacoid series (Rouse 1964), was first defined by Rouse (1992) in Hispaniola. This subseries is characterized by thin, hard, and fine pottery mostly in the form of incurving bowls with roughed surfaces (Figure M.4). Paint is completely missing from these ceramics, and the main forms of decoration consist of parallel rectilinear incisions that form hatching and cross-hatching designs in panels above the shoulder and extend horizontally around the vessel. Punctated ridges below the rims and appliqués sometimes accompany these incisions. Small geometric, zoomorphic, and strap handles are also common. In addition to pottery, Meillacan assemblages include clay griddles, *zemíes*, and, in some cases, Courian (Archaic) flint blades. Meillacan pottery is more prevalent along the northern to the western coasts of Hispaniola, in a number of regions of Cuba, in Jamaica, and some islands of the Bahamian archipelago. Dates for this subseries range from AD 600 to 1500, depending on the region.

Because of similarities between the decoration of Meillacan pottery and that of the Casimiroid, several scholars have argued that the former was the result of interaction or transculturation between the Casimiroid and the Saladoid or Ostionoid communities (Chanlatte 1990; Keegan 2000; Rouse 1992). In other words, the Meillacan Ostionoid were descendants of Casimiroid people who adopted their ceramic technology from groups such as the Ostionan Ostionoid. However, other researchers (e.g., Veloz Maggiolo, Ortega, and Caba 1981) have suggested that the Meillacan groups represented another migration or diffusion of ceramic attributes from South America.

Interestingly, because early European settlements

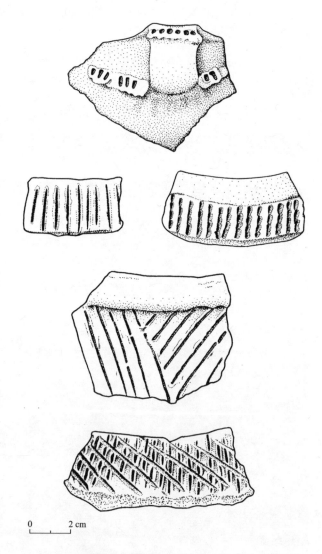

Figure M.4. Examples of Meillacan pottery. Drawings by Jill Seagard after Veloz Maggiolo, Ortega, and Caba (1981). Courtesy of L. Antonio Curet.

concentrated on the northern Hispaniola coast, where Meillacan assemblages predominate, many scholars have related these latter groups with the historical Macorix groups mentioned in Columbus's journals. The Meillacan Ostionoid used an intensive agricultural technique called *montones*, a hillock of gathered topsoil to promote the growth of tubers. It is likely that they were organized in stratified societies. In general, however, this subseries is poorly studied and little is known about their social and political organization, settlement patterns, and subsistence strategies.

Further Reading

Chanlatte Baik, L. A. 1990. "Cultura Ostionoide: un desarrollo algroalfarero antillano." In *Proceedings of the XI Congress of the International Association for Caribbean Archaeology*, ed. A. G. Pantel Tekakis, I. Vargas, and M. Sanoja, 295–311. San Juan: Fundación Arqueológica, Antropológica e Histórica de Puerto Rico.

Keegan, W. F. 2000. "West Indian Archaeology. 3. Ceramic Age." *Journal of Archaeological Research* 4: 265–94.

Rouse, I. 1964. Prehistory of the West Indies. *Science* 144: 499–513.

———. 1992. *The Tainos: Rise and Decline of the People Who Greeted Columbus.* New Haven, CT: Yale University Press.

Veloz Maggiolo, M., E. Ortega, and A. Caba. 1981. *Los Modos de Vida Meillacoides y sus Posibles Orígenes.* Santo Domingo: Museo del Hombre Dominicano.

Wilson, S. M. 1990. *Hispaniola.* Tuscaloosa: University of Alabama Press.

See also The Casimiroid; The Chican Ostionoid Subseries; Chiefdoms (*Cacicazgos*); *Conucos*; The Elenan Ostionoid Subseries; The Palmettan Ostionoid Series; The Saladoid.

Mines

R. Grant Gilmore III

The volcanoes on many Caribbean islands and other geological phenomena have given rise to a wide variety of mineral resources in exploitable quantities, including but not limited to gold (Au), silver (Ag), lead (Pb), sulfur (S), bauxite, limestone (Ca) and salt (NaCl). Prehistoric peoples in the Caribbean recovered chert, salt, and precious metals such as gold and silver from small-scale mining operations. Chert (composed primarily of microcrystalline, cryptocrystalline, and microfibrous quartz) was targeted for its qualities that were useful in making stone tools. In the northern Antilles, both Antigua and Barbuda produced chert that was exported throughout the Antilles by Saladoid peoples. Precious metals were primarily obtained on the Greater Antilles and became an immediate target for European explorers when they arrived in 1492. Europeans enslaved native peoples to work in mines, and the exploitation of mineral resources became the primary economic focus for several decades after contact. Once native populations had been decimated by disease and overwork, Europeans began importing enslaved Africans to recover precious minerals in mining operations.

Few archaeologists have studied these mining activities. Kathleen Deagan and her team at La Isabela (Cristóbal Colón's first settlement in the Americas) recovered evidence of smelting, including slag, crucibles, a furnace, and mercury. The slag recovered from the site was previously thought to have been from Hispaniola, but it has recently been determined to be of Iberian origin and was likely used in assaying recovered galena deposits. Pierre Rostan has studied the lead mining operations conducted on Saint Barthélemy during the nineteenth century. The salt works on Bonaire have been examined in some detail, although their "shelters for the enslaved" have often been misinterpreted as enslaved laborers' housing in popular publications. Sulfur mines were active on Dutch Saba well into the nineteenth century.

Further Reading

Deagan, K., and J. M. Cruxent. 2002. *Archaeology at La Isabela: America's First European Town.* New Haven, CT: Yale University Press.

Knippenberg, S. 2001. "Lithic Procurement during the Saladoid Period within the Northern Lesser Antilles." In *Actes de XVIII Congrès International d'Archéologie de la Caraibe* (*Proceedings of the XVIII International Congress for Caribbean Archaeology*, ed. G. Richard, 1:262–71. Basse-Terre,

FWI: l'Association Internationale d'Archéologie de la Caraibe, Région Guadeloupe.

Rostan, P. 2005. "L'activité minière de l'île de Saint Barthélemy."
*Proceedings of the Twenty-First Congress of the International
Association for Caribbean Archaeology*, ed. Basil Reid, Henry
Petitjean Roget, and Antonio Curet, 2:623–32. St. Augustine,
Trinidad and Tobago: School of Continuing Studies, Uni-
versity of the West Indies.

Thibodeau, A. M., D. J. Killick, J. Ruiz, J. T. Chesley, K. Deagan,
J. M. Cruxent, and W. Lyman. 2007. "The Strange Case of
the Earliest Silver Extraction by European Colonists in the
New World." *Proceedings of the National Academy of Sciences* 104 (9): 3663–66.

See also Elite Exchange in the Caribbean; Lapidary Trade.

Montserrat

John F. Cherry and Krysta Ryzewski

Montserrat is a relatively small (ca. 102 square kilometers) pear-shaped island situated near the southern end
of the Leeward Island chain in the Lesser Antilles. Antigua, Nevis, and Guadeloupe are its closest neighbors.
Though the island was sighted and named by Christopher Columbus on his second voyage in 1493, its first European occupation was by English and Irish settlers who
arrived from nearby St. Kitts in 1632. Aside from two
brief periods of French control, Montserrat has always
remained in British hands, and it is currently governed
as a British overseas territory. Located on the inner arc of
the boundary between the Atlantic and Caribbean tectonic plates, Montserrat is of volcanic origin. Its topography is dominated by three volcanic dome complexes of
decreasing age from north to south: Silver Hill, Centre
Hills, and Soufrière Hills. Wherever it has not been disturbed by the land clearances of the plantation era or
by more recent activities, the natural landscape consists
of very steep mountain slopes that are clothed in dense
rainforest and are drained by numerous deep ravines, or
ghauts, some with a continuous flow of water. The coastline is generally rocky and precipitous, and the hills rise
sheer from the sea along many stretches. The island has
few bays or beaches and no deep sheltered harbors, but it
has a number of resource-rich, shallow-water reefs that
lie off the leeward coast.

To describe Montserrat as it is today and to understand
the current state of its archaeology, one must appreciate
the enormity of the catastrophes that have befallen the
island over the past two decades. It was still recovering
from the devastating effects of Hurricane Hugo in 1989
when the Soufrière Hills volcano abruptly resumed activity on July 18, 1995. This activity has continued to the
present. A series of major eruptions, dome collapses, and
pyroclastic flows led to the loss of the capital Plymouth
in 1997 and forced the abandonment of the entire south
of the island (Figure M.5), formerly the most densely
settled region of Montserrat but now a strictly policed
exclusion zone. Two-thirds of the island's population of
approximately 12,000 have emigrated, mainly to England and the United States, and the remaining residents
have moved to new settlements in the north (which is
relatively safe from direct volcanic impacts). This area
is currently the focus of increasingly ambitious development projects designed to accommodate resettlement
and recovery efforts. These activities are directly impact-
ing archaeological sites and cultural heritage resources.

The Soufrière Hills eruptions have had disastrous effects on sites that are now in the exclusion zone. Some
prehistoric sites have been deeply buried, while standing
structures at some historic sites have been flattened. A
recent assessment of the loss of the archaeological record offers a grim picture. Sites can be "lost" in different ways. They can be totally destroyed by high-velocity
pyroclastic flows over the site; they can be entombed
(but not necessarily destroyed) by volcanic mud flows;
or they can be rendered inaccessible, even if they are still
intact, because they are located in the exclusion zone.
Amazingly, some eighteenth-century windmill towers
on former sugar plantations have survived far better
than most other more recent structures around them,
and they stand out as lonely sentinels in landscapes that
are otherwise scenes of utter devastation.

Compared to the archaeological research that has
been done on the nearby islands of St. Kitts, Nevis, Antigua, and Guadeloupe, that on Montserrat has been quite
limited. The first systematic archaeological exploration
of Montserrat did not occur until David Watters did

Figure M.5. Devastation of the Montserratian landscape by pyroclastic flows from the Soufrière Hills volcano, seen from the northeast. Photo by K. Ryzewski. Courtesy of John F. Cherry and Krysta Ryzewski, 2012.

the fieldwork for his doctoral dissertation in 1978 and 1979. He conducted a stratified random transect survey of circa 8 square kilometers of the island with the goal of discovering prehistoric sites, and he documented several settlements, all located on the coast. Around the same time, the most sustained fieldwork project on Montserrat began: the mapping and excavation of the Galways Plantation estate in the south of the island, undertaken by Lydia Pulsipher and Conrad "Mac" Goodwin. A few salvage excavations have taken place in advance of or as a consequence of construction work. These include the excavation of an eighteenth-century cemetery for the enslaved at the Harney Site near Bransby Point, the westernmost tip of the island; prehistoric deposits at Dagenham Beach, just north of Plymouth; and locations near the major prehistoric and historic-era site at Trants, in connection with a proposed extension of the runway at the former Bramble Airport. Chance finds have been made in many different parts of the island, as has become clearer from a systematic inventory in 2011 of the material stored at the Montserrat National Trust in Olveston.

The pace of field research has increased in the past several years with the inception of two major projects. One is the excavation (by Mary Beaudry and Lydia Pulsipher in 2005–2007 and 2010–2011 and by Jessica Striebel MacLean in 2012) of the Little Bay estate originally thought to be that of planter William Carr, a site of particular importance to Montserrat's heritage, as it is perhaps the oldest known European settlement on the island. The other is the Survey and Landscape Archaeology on Montserrat (SLAM) project, which has been co-directed by the present authors since January 2010. Its objectives include locating and documenting archaeological sites and features in the accessible area outside the exclusion zone and assessing the risks to these resources that environmental or cultural threats pose. This inventory should serve as a much-needed resource for heritage managers and developers on Montserrat, but it is also the basis for an archaeological research program that examines the nature of cultural development and human-environment interaction in the long term (Figure M.6).

Figure M.6. Map of Montserrat showing the location of archaeological sites located and documented by the Survey and Landscape Archaeology on Montserrat project in 2010 and other sites mentioned in the text. Map by Sarah Craft. Courtesy of John F. Cherry and Krysta Ryzewski, 2012.

How far back human occupation of Montserrat extends is at present uncertain. Small quantities of chert artifacts found by chance in Centre Hills led to the discovery during survey activities in 2012 at Upper Blake's of a chipped-stone assemblage earlier than anything hitherto encountered. It is the product of a percussion blade technology that is quite unlike the expedient flake industries that are characteristic of the lithic assemblages at all Saladoid and post-Saladoid age prehistoric sites on the island. However, these artifacts are comparable to those reported from the more than forty Archaic sites known on nearby Antigua, some with dates older than 2000 BC. There is no doubt that horticulturalists using Saladoid-style pottery were established on Montserrat soon after circa 500 BC. Trants, on the east coast near the former airport, is the best example. Numerous test pits have revealed a 200 × 300 meter oval midden that ranged around a central plaza, a configuration that probably reaches back to the period of the earliest deposits at the site, which is radiocarbon dated to circa 480–440

BC. This long-lived site yielded large samples of Saladoid ceramics (including examples of both zone-incised-crosshatched and white-on-red pottery that was consistently found together); chert from Long Island, Antigua (there is none on Montserrat); animal and fish bones; shell, bone, and coral tools; and evidence that the site was a center for lithic bead and pendant manufacture, specializing in carnelian beads. Unfortunately, Trants was destroyed by pyroclastic flows in February 2010.

Watters's fieldwork located several other prehistoric sites (Windward Bluff near Spanish Point, Farnsworth, Radio Antilles, Dagenham Beach just north of Plymouth, Belham Valley, and Little Bay), all located on the coast, and all now likewise destroyed. Material from test pits at some of these sites (not fully published) is also Saladoid—early in the case of Radio Antilles (with C-14 dates of 760–380 BC) but mostly late or post-Saladoid. This general picture is confirmed by new evidence from the SLAM survey, which has documented post-Saladoid prehistoric sites around the northern coast at the Woodlands, Bunkum, and Rendezvous Bays; Valentine Ghaut; Thatch Valley; and Margarita Bay, as well as numerous modest scatters of prehistoric sherds and lithics. At the Valentine Ghaut site, which is being damaged by coastal erosion, targeted rescue excavations in 2010, 2011, and 2012 recovered many restorable post-Saladoid vessels associated with several precise C-14 dates that average to AD 1020. An exception to this generally coastal pattern is the Glendon Hospital site, which is located well inland. Surface collection and brief test-pitting have recovered many hundreds of sherds at this site, including zone-incised-crosshatched and white-on-red styles that are indicative of an early date. Overall, it appears that Montserrat was a target for horticultural colonization at a very early stage of the Saladoid period but that widespread settlement (primarily along the coast and near watercourses) did not become common until a millennium later.

In the absence of relevant archaeological evidence, it is not known whether there was Amerindian settlement on Montserrat at the time the first Europeans arrived. Sir Henry Colt, who visited in 1631, leaves the matter undecided. He reported that "We arrived att Montserrat ye land . . . with noe inhabitants; yet weer ye footstepps seen of some naked men" (Hutson 2002, 30). Standing ruins, windmill towers, and other remains of the historic period remain visible across much of the island's landscape, hinting at the intensity with which agricultural resources and human labor were exploited, especially in the seventeenth through nineteenth centuries. To date, however, only a handful of historic-period sites and communities have been studied in detail by archaeologists. These include Delvins Plantation, Galways Plantation, the Trants Estate, and the Little Bay Plantation (formerly believed to be the Carr Estate). Except for the Little Bay Plantation, all these sites are now located in the exclusion zone. The remains of these plantation sites can be set in the context of the results of a rapid visual assessment of fifty such sites throughout the island that was undertaken in 1995 by David Miles and Julian Munby, shortly before the first major eruption. Only sixteen of the fifty sites they identified remained accessible in 2010.

The most extensive historical archaeological investigation was of Galways Plantation estate, conducted from 1981 to 1995 by Pulsipher and Goodwin. David Galway first constructed Galways in the 1660s, when it was worked by Irish indentured servants and enslaved Africans. However, the excavated remains and industrial ruins of a large sugar-processing complex and the associated residential areas appear to date to post-1750. Galways was unfortunately an early victim of the volcanic eruptions that began in 1995, and it is now entirely destroyed. The Little Bay Plantation, possibly the location of the William Carr Estate (ca. 1639), has been the focus of research by Beaudry and Pulsipher since 2005. Excavations have examined the Manor House, enslaved laborers' dwellings, industrial buildings, and other outbuildings. The resulting findings will be of special interest for Caribbean historical archaeologists, especially since they provide data about the initial periods of colonization, vernacular architecture, interactions in a plantation-based community, and evidence of changing agricultural and industrial practices over time.

To date, historical archaeological research on Montserrat has centered on individual sites and historic periods (post-1632). This focus has not yet allowed for investigations of longer-term land use over time, interactions between European settlers and Island-Carib/Kalinago peoples, Maroon communities, and cultural landscapes beyond immediate settlement loci—research topics that have been productively examined by archaeologists on Dominica, Guadeloupe, Haiti, St. Eustatius, and Jamaica. Early results from the SLAM project's surveys from 2010 to 2012 have identified and recorded over thirty historic-period sites and over two hundred landscape features in the island's north, all but one of which were previously unknown and/or undocumented. This information holds the potential to address many of the questions that these new data raise through a focus on connections between Montserrat's landscape, people, and environment.

Because so much of the central and southern portions of the island's landscape are destroyed or are inaccessible for the foreseeable future, Montserrat's archaeology is destined to remain incomplete. This places a premium on the thorough exploration of what still remains relatively intact in the north and the sensitive curating of known cultural heritage resources there. Part VI of Montserrat's Physical Planning Act (January 2002) sets out detailed regulations about listing, preservation, and management of historic buildings and sites; authorizing excavations; penalties for illicit artifact collection; restrictions on the export of artifacts; and other related matters. Implementation is challenging, however, in the absence of an archaeological officer or trained cultural heritage manager. Nonetheless, archaeology on Montserrat may have a brighter future now than since the volcanic eruptions began. The SLAM project is producing a thorough database of all known archaeological sites and features in the north. Artifacts at the Montserrat National Trust are in process of being properly catalogued and given better storage conditions. The core area of the Little Bay Plantation is under excavation in readiness for its presentation as a heritage site at the very heart of the Little Bay Development Plan, and a new museum adjacent to the site opened in March 2012.

Further Reading

Cherry, J. F., K. Ryzewski, and T. P. Leppard. 2012. "Multi-Period Landscape Survey and Site Risk Assessment on Montserrat, West Indies." *Journal of Island and Coastal Archaeology* 7 (2): 282–302.

Cherry, J. F., K. Ryzewski, T. P. Leppard, and E. Bocancea. 2012. "The Earliest Phase of Settlement in the Eastern Caribbean: New Evidence from Montserrat." *Antiquity* 86 (333).

Fergus, H. A. 1994. *Montserrat: History of a Caribbean Colony*. London: Macmillan.

Hutson, J. E., ed. 2002. *The Voyages of Sir Henry Colt to the Islands of Barbados and St. Christopher, May–August 1631*. St. Michael, Barbados: Barbados National Trust, 2002

Miles, D., and J. Munby. 2006. "Montserrat before the Volcano: A Survey of the Plantations Prior to the 1995 Eruptions." *Landscapes* 2: 48–69.

Pulsipher, L. M. 1986. *Seventeenth-Century Montserrat: An Environmental Impact Statement*. Norwich: Geo Books.

Watters, D. R. 1980. "Transect Surveying and Prehistoric Site Locations on Barbuda and Montserrat, Leeward Islands, West Indies." PhD diss., University of Pittsburgh, 1980.

Watters, D. R., and G. E. Norton. 2007. "Volcanically Induced Loss of Archaeological Sites in Montserrat." In *Proceedings of the Twenty-First Congress of the International Association for Caribbean Archaeology*, ed. B. Reid, H. P. Roget, and C. Antonio, 1:48–55. St. Augustine, Trinidad: School of Continuing Studies, University of the West Indies.

See also Antigua and Barbuda (Archaic Sites); Guadeloupe (Eastern); Nevis.

Morban Laucer, Fernando (1921–2007)

Clenis Tavárez María

Fernando Morban Laucer was a Dominican dentist who successfully combined his interest in archaeology and training in dentistry. He taught at the Universidad Autónoma de Santo Domingo and eventually became its academic vice-chancellor and director of its Instituto de Investigaciones Antropológicas. He taught courses in archaeology, physical anthropology, anthropology, and ethnology at educational institutions throughout the country. He worked at the Museo del Hombre Dominicano in the mid-1970s and became its director from 1986 to 1996. He was member of the Academia de Ciencias de la República Dominicana and other national and international scientific associations. From 1996 until the time of his death, Morban Laucer was an associate researcher at the *museo*.

Morban Laucer's interest in archaeology began in his youth when he traveled across the Dominican Republic looking for tangible evidence of the indigenous people of Hispaniola. During his research expeditions, he was accompanied by Manuel A. García Arévalo, Manuel Mañón Arredondo, Luis Chanlatte Baik, and the brothers Emil and Rafael Kasse Acta, among others. He participated in archaeological projects at La Caleta and Boca Chica in collaboration with René Herrera Fritot. In 1968, Morban Laucer studied the rock art of Cueva de las Maravillas near San Pedro de Macorís.

His work focused on diverse anthropological topics, particularly rock art and physical anthropology. Within the field of rock art, he discovered a number of new sites and studied their designs, the pigments used in their pictographs, and their artistic expressions. His interest in physical anthropology led him to study indigenous teeth, and he also made an effort to find indigenous genetic dental features in modern Dominican populations. In general, his work focused on the study of the indigenous people of Hispaniola, a topic that ranged from their art and culture in general to mythological themes and archaeology. He also conducted excavations in Puerto Rico.

Morban Laucer participated in a large number of national and international conferences and other scientific events. He also published widely in national and international journals. His research can also be found in newspapers and books. His most important work includes *El arte rupestre y petroglifos de la República Dominicana: Petroglifos de la Provincia de Azua* (1979a); *Petroglifos de Santo Domingo* (1970); *El Arte rupestre de la Sierra de Bahoruco* (1995); *Antropología y arqueología Quisquellana* (co-authored with Mañón Arredondo and Manuel de Jesús; 1968), and *Ritos funerarios: acción del fuego y medio ambiente en las osamentas precolombinas* (1979b). Many of his essays are published in the *Boletín del Museo del Hombre Dominicano*. At the time of his death, he was preparing a book on the rock art of the Dominican Republic.

Further Reading

Mañón Aredondo, Manuel de Jesús, and Fernando A. Morban Laucer. 1968. *Antropología y arqueología Quisquellana*. Santo Domingo: Universidad Autónoma de Santo Domingo.

Morban Laucer, Fernando. 1970. *Petroglifos de Santo Domingo*. Santo Domingo: Universidad Autonoma de Santo Domingo.

———. 1979a. *El arte rupestre y petroglifos de la República Dominicana: Petroglifos de la Provincia de Azua*. Santo Domingo: Fundación García Arévalo.

———. 1979b. *Ritos Funerarios. Acción de fuego y medio ambiente en las osamentas precolombinas*. Santo Domingo: Editorial Taller.

———. 1995. *El Arte Rupestre de la Sierra de Bahoruco*. Santo Domingo: Editorial Taller.

See also Museo del Hombre Dominicano; Rock Art.

Museo del Hombre Dominicano

Clenis Tavárez María

The Museo del Hombre Dominicano (MHD) is located in the Plaza de la Cultura Juan Pablo Duarte in Santo Domingo, Dominican Republic (Figure M.7). This institution houses the most important collection of pre-Hispanic cultures of the island of Hispaniola. The richness of its collections range from Archaic utilitarian artifacts made of chert and other stones, shell, wood, and bone to the more elaborate ones, especially ceramics made by later agricultural groups. True masterpieces associated with the Taíno, Macorix, and other groups from Hispaniola, Venezuela, and the rest of the Caribbean form part of this collection.

The MHD, which opened its doors on October 12, 1973, is under the Ministerio de Cultura and is also responsible for the conservation of archaeological sites in the Dominican Republic. This institution, which was designed and organized by its first director, José A. Caro Alvarez (1973–1978), became a model to be followed by similar institutions in the Caribbean. Mario Veloz Maggiolo, who was also involved in this project since its inception, became the head of a prestigious research team that included Elpidio J. Ortega, Plinio Pina, Renato O. Rímoli, Fernando Luna Calderón, Joaquín Nadal, and Carlos Esteban Deive.

In addition to its pre-Hispanic collections, this institution exhibits other aspects of the Dominican culture that date from its inception to the present. The *museo* also conducts anthropological research in Dominican Republic. By law, the MHD's mission is to preserve, protect, exhibit, and disseminate aspects of Dominican culture. The results of the MHD's research are published regularly in its main periodical, *Boletín del Museo del Hombre Dominicano*. To date, forty-five bulletins have been published. The MHD also publishes books and monographs on many topics relating to archaeological and anthropological work. Some of this research has

Figure M.7. Museo del Hombre Dominicano, Santo Domingo, Dominican Republic. Reproduced by permission of Museo del Hombre Dominicano, Ministerio del Cultura.

been organized in scientific research series, catalogs, lectures, and occasional papers. Examples include *Los cacicazgos de la Hispaniola* (Vega 1980); *El Precerámico de Santo Domingo, nuevos lugares y su posible relación con otros puntos del área antillana* (Veloz Maggiolo and Vega 1973); *Vodú y magía en Santo Domingo* (Deive 1980); and *Voces del purgatorio* (Davis 1981).

As part of its educational mission, the MHD also organizes seminars, workshops, symposia, conferences, congresses, and scientific events that contribute to the dissemination of anthropology and archaeology among the Dominican people. The *museo* has twice hosted the International Congress for Caribbean Archaeology, in 1980 and 2003. As an institution, the MHD has become an important cultural icon in the Caribbean.

Further Reading

Davis, Martha Ellen. 1981. *Voces del purgatorio. Estudio de la Salve dominicana*. Santo Domingo: Museo del Hombre Dominicano.

Deive, Carlos Esteban. 1980. *Vodú y magía en Santo Domingo*. Santo Domingo: Museo del Hombre Dominicano.

Vega, Bernardo. 1980. *Los Cacicazgos de la Hispaniola*. Santo Domingo: Museo del Hombre Dominicano.

Veloz Maggiolo, Marcio, and Elpidio Ortega. 1973. *El Precerámico de Santo Domingo, nuevos lugares y su posible relación con otros puntos del área antillana*. Santo Domingo: Museo del Hombre Dominicano.

See also Morban Laucer, Fernando (1921–2007); Taíno Museum at White Marl (Jamaica).

The Museum of Antigua and Barbuda

Reg Murphy

The Museum of Antigua and Barbuda was established in the Old Court House in St. John's in 1984 (Figure M.8). The building was designed and built by architect Peter Harrison in 1750 and functioned as the seat of government, justice, and social life for colonial Antigua. It was severely damaged by earthquakes in 1842 and 1974. After restoration in the early 1980s, the Historical & Archaeological Society was given the building to establish a national museum. The museum focuses on the Amerindian, African, and European heritage of Antigua

Figure M.8. The Old Court House in St. John's, Antigua, that houses the Museum of Antigua and Barbuda. Courtesy of Reg Murphy.

and Barbuda and holds extensive collections from these periods and cultures, as well as rocks and fossils representative of the natural history of the island. It has an excellent reference library and an extensive computerized database on Antigua and Barbuda.

From its conception, the first president and director, Desmond Nicholson, placed great emphasis on computerization and created a database that was accessible to the public. Today, the librarians of the museum continue to add relevant information to the database daily. It is a popular site for visitors and students, and many academics visit for research annually. Its most recent goal is to establish a digital archive of its documents, photographs, and artifacts. It works closely with the Nelson's Dockyard Museum and manages the Betty's Hope Estate conservation site. The museum is managed as an NGO working in partnership with the government of Antigua and Barbuda.

Nelson's Dockyard and Its Museum

Nelson's Dockyard, which is located in English Harbour, Antigua, was established as a British naval dockyard in the late 1720s. It was dedicated to repairing and servicing naval warships. Many famous British naval heroes visited and worked there, including Hood, Rodney, Vernon, Collingwood, and Nelson. In 1895, the British navy abandoned the facility, which had become obsolete after the birth of steam-driven iron warships. In 1949, Commander Vernon Nicholson sailed into the derelict port with his family and began to charter his yacht *Mollihawk* to anyone who wanted to cruise through the islands of the Eastern Caribbean. Restoration of the dockyard was begun by the Friends of English Harbour, a nongovernmental organization that supported his enormously successfully activities, and the yacht-chartering industry of the Caribbean was born. Antigua Dockyard was renamed Nelson's Dockyard in 1961 in honor of Admiral Horatio Nelson, who served as senior captain of the facility in 1784–1787.

The Dockyard Museum is dedicated to researching and exhibiting the life and times of the dockyard. Its research mandate includes the fifteen fortifications; the barracks of the British army, engineers, and artillery; cemeteries on the hills surrounding the dockyard; and underwater archaeology. It operates an active field research facility and manages archaeological and environmental impact assessments for National Parks Antigua. The Dockyard Museum opened in 1961 and is the oldest museum on Antigua.

See also Betty's Hope Plantation (Antigua); Nicholson, D. V. (1925–2006).

The Museums Association of the Caribbean (MAC)

Alissandra Cummins

The Museums Association of the Caribbean (MAC) was formed in 1987 by museum officials from Antigua and Barbuda, Barbados, Dominica, Jamaica, Martinique, Nevis, and Trinidad and Tobago. The inaugural meeting took place in Dominica in 1989, and the first president elected was Alissandra Cummins (Barbados). The MAC's primary objectives are:

- To develop a common policy on the role of museums and duties of curatorial staff and common practices with regard to exhibitions, conservation, preservation, legislation and regulations to protect national patrimony.

- To act as an advisory board to government and public and private institutions on matters pertaining to museum development.
- To serve as a forum for the exchange of information and ideas on a regional basis.
- To develop links with international and other regional and national museum-related organizations and agencies.

The highlight for the MAC is the Annual General Meeting, which includes themed presentations and training or professional development sessions. Members count on this special forum to voice their concerns, share their expertise, and establish strategic partnerships. It has been hosted in recent years by Saint Lucia, the Turks and Caicos Islands, St. Croix, St. Maarten, Santiago de Cuba, the Dominican Republic, St. Kitts and Nevis, and Barbados. The present MAC board generally includes representatives from the English, French, Dutch and Spanish Caribbean. Throughout MAC's existence, there have been numerous training sessions and joint projects. From 1999 to 2001, many museums in the region took part in the UNESCO/WTO Slave Route Sites of Memory Project. In addition, a risk preparedness survey of Caribbean Museums was conducted in 2010–2011 in preparation for a regional capacity-building program in 2012.

The MAC has proposed that common action be taken to protect the region's cultural heritage. It advises governments of the Caribbean to promote and enforce legislation designed to protect museums as well as historical, natural, and cultural sites. The MAC also consults with museums, universities, and other institutions around the world to identify and inventory tangible artifacts, records of intangible heritage, and research records that relate to the Caribbean. This is being undertaken to benefit future researchers and for the economic and cultural benefit of the Caribbean.

Further Reading

Green, Patricia. N.d. "Caribbean Monuments and Sites Inventory: On the Trans-Atlantic Slave Trade (The UNESCO Slave Route Project. UNESCO-WTO Joint Caribbean Programme of Cultural Tourism)." ICOMOS-CIIC Web site. http://www.icomos-ciic.org/CIIC/pamplona/PROYECTOS _Patricia_Green.htm. Accessed 23 April 2013.

MAC. 2013. Web site of the Museums of the Caribbean. http://www.caribbeanmuseums.com/. Accessed January 14, 2013.

UNESCO. 2008. "Places of Memory for the Slave Route in the Caribbean." http://portal.unesco.org/culture/en/ev.php-URL_ID=32149&URL_DO=DO_TOPIC&URL_SECTION=201.html. Accessed January 24, 2013.

See also The Institute of Jamaica; The International Association for Caribbean Archaeology (IACA); The International Council of Museums (ICOM); Museo del Hombre Dominicano; The Museum of Antigua and Barbuda; Taíno Museum at White Marl (Jamaica).

The Nanny Town Maroons of Jamaica

Cheryl White

Historical Background

Enslaved Africans were introduced to Jamaica when Spain established New Seville in 1509. By 1655, after more than a century of colonial instability, Jamaica was acquired by England and the *gran marronage*—the large-scale flight of slaves from plantations—was at its height. This led to the establishment of settled communities of Maroons comprised of runaway enslaved Africans and their descendants. Two Maroon strongholds emerged: the Leeward Maroons of the Cockpit country and the Windward Maroons of the Blue Mountains region (Bilby 1996). A significant Maroon site is the seventeenth- and eighteenth-century Windward Maroon settlement in the parish of Portland, historically known as Nanny Town.

Named after its founding heroine "Grandy Nanny," it is strategically situated along a bend of the Stony River. The village was surrounded by Abrahams Ridge in the foothills of the Blue Mountains (Figure N.1). The extended Nanny Town settlement is located roughly 2,000 meters above sea level at the foothills of the peak of the Blue Mountains.

Jamaican folklore and Caribbean literature perpetuate the history and myth of "Queen" Nanny and her penchant for militarism, which set the stage for years of guerilla warfare between the British and Maroons. To end the conflict, the British conceded with a "Land Patent to Nanny" (1739/1740), which functioned as a peace treaty between the Maroons and the British. The terms of the treaty created the conditions for the Maroon cul-

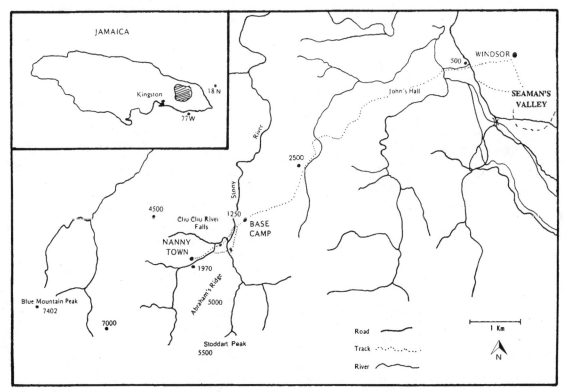

Figure N.1. Nanny Town in the Blue Mountains of Jamaica. Reproduced by permission of E. Kofi Agorsah.

tural development that is now being explored through archaeological investigations at Nanny Town.

Archaeological Research

Reconnaissance and later surveys of Nanny Town began in the late 1960s and early 1970s. The survey results helped build a predictive model for identifying historical sites in the area (Bonner 1974). In 1974, Anthony Bonner did exploratory excavation that confirmed that the settlement was a type of garrison. Kofi Agorsah launched a full-scale excavation in 1993. Research at Nanny Town sought to explain the functional adaptation of Maroons in relation to migration routes, settlement patterns, food procurement, resource acquisition, and locally manufactured objects. This research used archaeological survey methods (including excavation), artifact analyses, and radiocarbon dating. Ethnographic accounts from descendants have also helped researchers interpret archaeological finds. To date, Nanny Town is the most extensively excavated Maroon site.

According to Agorsah's (2001) research, Nanny Town had three settlement phases (Figure N.2). Phase I is distinguished by a preponderance of locally made anthropomorphic earthenware sherds and stone and shell artifacts. This phase may represent Maroon acculturation through brief interaction with remaining local Taíno groups who would also have escaped from colonial people. Many ceramic artifacts exhibit indigenous construction techniques and decoration. The end of Phase I is marked by the appearance of Spanish coins with 1668 dates.

During Phase II, or what is commonly referred to as the Maroon Phase, a period spanning the 1650s to the early 1730s (Agorsah 2001), the folkloric/historic figure of Nanny emerges as an embattled heroine, mystic, and herbal healer. Part of this legend has some basis in the archaeological record: Agorsah's survey of botanical remains revealed the presence of non-native curative plants. Agorsah describes the "town" as a sedentary community of around 200 occupants who were subsistence farmers at several dispersed settlements. By the early 1700s, Nanny and her fellow Maroons had declared war on the British.

The Maroon Phase offers the cultural markers of Nanny Town's formative development. This second period of Maroon material development was characterized by the acquisition of household items and combat equipment during a period of repetitive battles with British settlers. Artifacts representative of this phase include "local ceramics, grinding stones and a considerable quantity of charcoal, gun flints, fragments of gun bar-

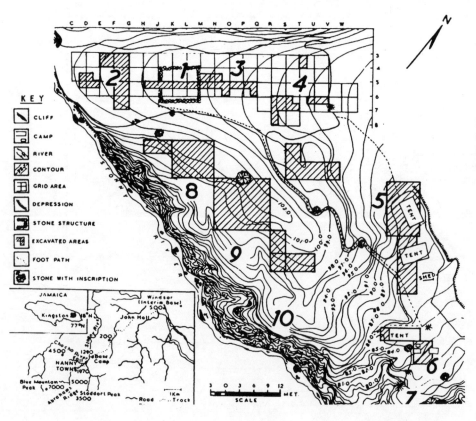

Figure N.2. Archaeological map of Nanny Town. Reproduced by permission of E. Kofi Agorsah.

rels, musket balls, iron nails, a red clay and several kaolin smoking pipe bowls and stems, [and] green and clear glass bottle fragments" (Agorsah 2001, 5).

In Phase III, the time of Maroons' direct and open military encounter with British forces, a shift occurred in material culture toward a pattern that more closely resembled European consumerism than native or African traditions. The artifacts of Phase III include stone fortifications with and without petroglyphs. One engraved stone records the date of Nanny Town's conquest by British officers as December 17, 1734 (Agorsah 1994). Domestic items that include medicine bottles, imported ceramic bowls, plates, and cups and scissors are artifactual indicators of Phase III (Agorsah 2001, 5).

The idea of Nanny as a Maroon combatant figure is an intrinsic part of Jamaican historiography. She is viewed as a reflection of the strength of character for which Jamaicans are known. Although historians question the archival evidence that supports the notion that "Queen" Nanny possessed the militaristic abilities as claimed by traditional oral history, their skepticism has not hindered ongoing efforts to recognize Nanny as a real historical figure. Because currently available primary sources do not indicate the spatial dimensions of Nanny Town, historians have no choice but to turn to archaeological evidence, as archaeology has unveiled material intricacies about Nanny Town that situate the village geographically. Archaeological research at Nanny Town has found evidence of three occupational phases that demonstrates Maroon use of Jamaica's Taíno material culture, new cultural lifeways in the Blue Mountains, and the presence of European strongholds. Equally important, the archaeology of Nanny Town is essential to the management of Jamaican cultural heritage today.

Further Reading

Agorsah, E. K., ed. 1994. *Maroon Heritage: Archaeological, Ethnographic, and Historical Perspectives*. Kingston, Jamaica: Canoe Press.

———. 2001. *Freedom in Black History and Culture*. Middletown, CA: Arrow Point Press.

Bilby, K. 1996. "Ethnogenesis in the Guianas and Jamaica: Two Maroon Cases." In *History, Power, and Identity: Ethnogenesis in the Americas, 1492–1992*, ed. Jonathan D. Hill, 119–41. Iowa City: University of Iowa Press.

Bonner, A. 1974. "The Blue Mountain Expedition." *Jamaica Journal* 8 (2–3): 46–50.

See also Historical Archaeological Sites (Types); The Maroons.

The National Archaeological Anthropological Memory Management Foundation (NAAM)

Ieteke Witteveen

Founded in 1998, the National Archaeological Anthropological Memory Management Foundation (NAAM), formerly called the Netherlands Antilles Archaeological and Anthropological Institute (AAINA), disseminates knowledge about the tangible and intangible heritage of Bonaire, Curaçao, St. Maarten, Saba and St. Eustatius/Statia. Its goal is to reinforce the Caribbean cultural identities of peoples in these countries. While the foundation is headquartered in Curaçao (Figure N.3), its board members are from the five islands of the Dutch Caribbean.

The NAAM's main tasks are as follows:

(1) Preserve, register, document, and digitize artifact collections, including those of the Archaic, African, and colonial periods
(2) Manage heritage
(3) Educate the public, especially youngsters
(4) Conduct archaeological and anthropological research
(5) Provide advice about heritage legislation

The NAAM is currently involved in developing teaching materials for primary schools. It also publishes bimonthly articles on cultural heritage in newspapers in the Leeward and Windward Islands. Its publications are in the three national languages, Papiamentu, English, and Dutch. The NAAM has also staged exhibits on the Heritage of Slavery (2006), Freetowns of the Caribbean (2008), and the Afro-Caribbean spiritual heritage in Altars of Curaçao (2009).

One of the NAAM's primary tools for policy and legislative advisement is a digital map of cultural/historic sites called *Mapa Kultural Históriko di Kòrsou*. The

Figure N.3. Headquarters of the National Archaeological Anthropological Memory Management Foundation, Curaçao. Photo by Prince Victor/ Prince Imaging.

map includes information about Amerindian, colonial, maritime, and Afro-Caribbean heritage and places of memory. Much of the tangible and intangible heritage of the Dutch Caribbean has disappeared as a result of colonization and slavery. Because this heritage was not protected, much has been destroyed and even forgotten. This is why the NAAM seeks to reconstruct and preserve the collective memory and heritage of the Dutch Caribbean through advocacy, research, and digital mapping, particularly whenever heritage sites are being threatened. In order to achieve its objectives, the NAAM often works collaboratively with regional organizations such as the Museums Association of the Caribbean (MAC) and the International Association of Caribbean Archaeology (IACA).

Further Reading

National Archaeological Anthropological Memory Foundation. 2012. "Safeguarding Our Shared Memory." http://www. naam.an/. Accessed January 14, 2013.

See also The International Association for Caribbean Archaeology (IACA); The Museums Association of the Caribbean (MAC).

The National Trust of Trinidad and Tobago

Basil A. Reid

The National Trust of Trinidad and Tobago is the premier government agency responsible for heritage in the twin island republic. The organization was established through the assiduous efforts of many dedicated persons and interest groups, including the Citizens for Conservation. The efforts to establish the National Trust were precipitated in part by the UNESCO draft plan for Educational Development in Trinidad and Tobago (1968–83), part of which specifically dealt with the conservation and preservation of our national heritage (Reid and Lewis 2011).

Under the National Trust Act (2000), the National Trust Council is empowered to prepare lists of buildings and sites of particular national, historic, archaeological, or architectural interest that should be preserved. Developers are constrained by the minister of town and country planning, who can block development in areas with significant archaeological remains until the developer makes proper arrangements to organize the survey and excavation of these areas. The National Trust of Trinidad and Tobago offers some measure of protection to archaeological sites if the land is listed as a "property of interest."

Further Reading

Reid, B., and V. Lewis. 2011. "Trinidad and Tobago." In *Protecting Heritage in the Caribbean*, ed. Peter E. Siegel and Elizabeth Righter, 125–33. Tuscaloosa: University of Alabama Press.

See also The Archaeological Committee of Trinidad and Tobago; Archaeological Heritage Management; The Jamaica National Heritage Trust; Trinidad and Tobago.

Nevis

Marco Meniketti

Introduction

Nevis is part of the Independent Federation of St. Christopher (St. Kitts) and Nevis, located in the northern end of the Lesser Antilles (Figure N.4). The island was first inhabited by Archaic peoples who probably arrived 3,000 years ago from South America or elsewhere in the Caribbean. European knowledge of the island began in 1493 when Columbus sighted the islands during his second voyage. The island was colonized by English adventurers in 1627 for the purposes of establishing plantations for tobacco, indigo, and ginger. Early experiments with sugar cane were not profitable and unsustainable. When a community of Sephardic Jews who had been expelled from Brazil arrived in the 1650s, they brought expertise in sugar production. From this period until emancipation in 1834, sugar crop monoculture was the mainstay of the economy. At first Irish, Indian, and indentured English workers performed the labor on sugar plantations; ultimately, enslaved Africans did this work. Ruins from close to 200 sugar estates cover the landscape from sea level to over 365 meters elevation. Most of these are not mapped or archaeologically documented.

Water on Nevis is intermittently abundant in the higher elevations, which have a tropical climate tempered by the northeast trade sea winds. The island has no marked rainy season, although torrential rainfall occurs. The temperatures are relatively constant throughout the year. From July to September, the island is affected by hurricanes. From the northwest shores of Nevis, the islands of Saba, St. Eustatius, and St. Kitts are visible. The islands of Montserrat and Redonda can be seen from the southeast shore. Because the intensive cultivation of sugar cane ruined the island's inland and offshore ecosystem, it is difficult to accurately reconstruct precolonial flora. It is known that manioc, coconut, papaya, arrowroot, and mamey apple, among other plants, were introduced to the island and to the Antilles region by precolonial societies that first settled the different islands in different periods, and that their diets were complemented by seafood and terrestrial animals (Crosby 2003).

Archaeology on Nevis has followed two main tracks: prehistoric settlement patterns and colonial landscapes. Surveys of prehistoric sites of Preceramic Ostionoid and Ceramic Saladoid periods were initiated by Samuel Wilson (University of Texas) in the 1980s. Wilson located

Figure N.4. Map of Nevis showing major precolonial and colonial sites. Courtesy of Marco Meniketti.

and mapped numerous sites along the southeast Atlantic side and a few isolated sites near natural springs on the western coast. Since the 1990s, this work has been expanded by Elaine Morris (Southampton University) as a facet of the Nevis Heritage Project (Morris et al. 1999). Several historic and prehistoric sites have also been recorded by historian David Small (Bristol University). Morris's current research agenda entails completing the documentation of later prehistoric ceramics and figurines that are emerging from eroded sites in several coastal sites. Morris also documented what is possibly the earliest extant seventeenth-century English redoubt in the Caribbean before it was demolished to allow for the expansion of the island's airport runway.

Prehistoric Archaeology

The archaeological sites of Nevis are concentrated mostly on the windward coast and reflect three major periods: the Archaic culture, which dates to the last millennia BC; the Saladoid culture (AD 200 to AD 600); and the Ostionoid culture (AD 600 to the period of European contact). The fact that the western side of the island presents almost no archaeological sites may be the result of site destruction through beach formation processes, tectonic activity, and/or storms.

The Archaic Age is represented on Nevis by two settlements located close to large reefs and a stream bed that supplied fresh water. The Archaic people were hunter-gatherers involved in some level of plant manipulation. Archaeological data indicate that their subsistence was primarily based on marine animals such as mollusks, a variety of shallow reef fish, land crabs, and terrestrial animals, complemented by foraging for wild edible plants and fruits on the island. The artifact assemblage indicates that these first inhabitants made chert tools (grindstones and hammerstones), petaloid celts, conch-scrapers and gougers.

In the first century AD, a small group of sedentary horticultural people from the northeast coasts of South America settled on Nevis. They brought a distinctively decorated ceramic style of red and white painting known as Saladoid pottery. The Saladoid people adapted their mainland culture to the island's environment and lived in agricultural villages close to the shore where they were involved in fishing and shell-fishing activities. The Saladoid culture came to an end on Nevis around AD 600 and is followed by the Ostionoid/Taíno period, which lasted until AD 1600. This period of transition from Saladoid to Ostionoid/Taíno is reflected especially in the new pottery style of the latter, which shows a progressive discontinua-

tion of the Saladoid decorative feature of white paint over red paint and an increased use of modeled incision decorative technique of the Ostionoid/Taíno culture.

The Ostionoid pottery of Nevis bears strong affinities with contemporary pottery in the Virgin Islands, eastern Puerto Rico, and other nearby Leeward Islands. Because of this, it can be classified as part of the Elenan Ostionoid subseries that is found throughout these islands. Changes are also evident in the subsistence and settlement pattern of the Elenan/Ostionoid, possibly as a result of technological change and/or overexploitation. During this period, occupation of the island was denser and more widely distributed than it had been previously, indicating a considerable increase in the size and number of sites, which were mainly located at the mouths of streams. These inhabitants used the island's environment to practice horticulture and also exploited inshore, offshore, and reef marine species.

Ceramic, technological, and stylistic preferences did not change significantly through time in the Elenan Ostionoid period. There is no evidence of a different ceramic phase that supplanted the Elenan Ostionoid culture. In this sense, the island was inhabited by the Elenan Ostionoid culture that developed autochthonously around AD 600. Although the island seems to have been abandoned for a brief period around AD 1300, Ostionoid culture returned shortly before contact. Both archaeological and historical data imply that Nevis was sparsely inhabited shortly before European contact (Crosby 2003).

Historic Sites Archaeology

Archaeological research of the historic period gained momentum after the mid-1990s. Michelle Terrell did groundbreaking research in an effort to locate the remains of a synagogue that served the Sephardic Jewish community from the late seventeenth through the early eighteenth centuries. Her research comprehensively documented the Jewish cemetery in Charlestown using a rigorous systematic electrical resistivity study. She detailed the results of her research in an award-winning book (Terrell 2005).

Excavations at the New River and Coconut Walk estates were conducted by James Chiarelli in collaboration with Earthwatch. Chiarelli addressed complex social development issues stemming from the transition period surrounding emancipation by excavating a village site on the Coconut Walk property that chronologically straddles that period (Chiarelli 1999).

Extensive fieldwork carried out at the Montravers Estate, the home of John Pinney, one of the wealthiest

Nevis colonial planters of the eighteenth century, was directed by Roger Leech in conjunction with the Nevis Heritage Project. This multi-phase project served as a field school for Southampton University. Leech (2002, 2003) excavated at numerous other sites around the island, including the highest recorded sugar works, the Upper Rawlins site, and documented the oldest extant wooden structure on Nevis at the Hermitage.

The site of Jamestown on the western side of the island, traditionally considered the earliest English settlement, was subjected to geophysical survey by researchers from Southampton University and excavation by Eric Klingelhofer. Jamestown was destroyed by an earthquake in 1690. Although the site did not sink into the sea, it was ruined and was eventually covered over by a swampy forest. In the nineteenth century, a coconut plantation occupied the site. Klingelhofer's excavations revealed several phases of construction dating to the early seventeenth century and structures that postdated the 1690 disaster. Various foundations exhibited distortions that were possibly brought about by the earthquake episode. The evidence suggests that Jamestown did not disappear, as is related in local legend, but declined economically for several years. The Jamestown site is split by the island's main road, and much of it lies beneath a new condominium complex and former equestrian center.

Marco Meniketti has directed annual systematic landscape surveys and excavations at several sugar estates as part of the Historic Colonial Landscape Project (Meniketti 2006). Regular updates are available at www.caribbeanarchaeology.com. Work included documenting a possible customs house and adjacent sugar facilities at Indian Castle on the rugged south coast. Surveys from 2001 to 2004 recorded twenty-two mill complexes. Meniketti currently directs research for San Jose State University at the site of Bush Hill Estate, a sugar plantation that operated from the late seventeenth through the early twentieth centuries. All archaeology on the island falls under the jurisdiction of the Nevis Field Study Centre and the Nevis Historical and Conservation Society, which operates within the purview of Nevis Island Administration. These agencies have developed guidelines and permit procedures for conducting fieldwork and have been proactive in encouraging research. Several ruins have never been archaeologically documented, including many prominent sites. Nelson's Lookout, a high-elevation fort that was built in the early 1700s and was substantively enhanced under direction of Horatio Nelson, awaits documentation. In places the walls stand thirty feet tall. Charleston Fort overlooking Gallows Bay has received only cursory attention from archaeologists.

Cannon, ceramics, gunflints, and other eighteenth-century artifacts lay scattered about the site. Some of the cannon at Fort Charles were transported there from the fort at Indian Castle by the Royal Navy during a goodwill tour at the conclusion of the Falklands War.

A project of considerable scope that significantly contributes to an understanding of broad regional issues of slavery was undertaken by the Digital Archaeological Archive of Comparative Slavery (DACCS). Jillian Gale, Fraser Neiman, and Anna A. Davies extensively documented the Jessups Estate plantation sites beginning in 2006. They also recorded the remains of an African village near the Coconut Walk and New River estates. The associated Web site (www.daccs.org) is a valuable asset to scholars and is updated regularly.

In 2010 Scott Fitzpatrick and colleagues initiated fieldwork at the Coconut Walk Estate focused on the pre-Columbian component of the landscape. Results of the initial season included documentation of pottery, food remains, and evidence of Saladoid-era settlements.

Maritime Archaeology

Marine archaeology in Nevis is in its infancy, despite the likelihood that over 200 historic vessels lie buried in the waters surrounding the island. Meniketti documented the last remaining traditional Nevisian sailing lighter in 2001, and the Nevis Historical and Conservation Society is using line drawing from that project in an effort to build a replica. The Nevis Historical and Conservation Society initiated underwater surveys in 2007, and B. Foster-Smith has completed a magnetometer survey of The Narrows. Several vessels are known to have been lost because of natural disasters, and a small number were lost in war or to pirates. Nevis lacks protected harbors and serves more as a safe anchorage on a lee shore. To the north are The Narrows, a relatively shallow stretch that separates Nevis from St. Kitts by 3.2 kilometers. In places, the bottom shoals are close to the surface, creating invisible navigation hazards. Shifting sands along the western shore alternately expose and rebury the remains of defensive works, batteries, and fortifications. The hurricane of 1999 scoured the shores and revealed several eighteenth-century cannon at a depth of eight feet in the immediate vicinity of the Four Seasons Hotel beachfront. This was documented by Tessa Machling.

The 1690 earthquake sank ships in the harbor. Meniketti conducted underwater surveys off the shore of the Jamestown site but did not locate any structures. Surveys offshore from Indian Castle located a badly corroded seventeenth-century cannon, possibly from the fort that once stood on the cliffs overlooking the anchorage. Documents in the Nevis Archives, housed in the Horatio Nelson Museum in Charlestown report the loss of several ships in Charlestown roadstead during hurricanes. Wrecks during hurricanes are recorded for 1747, 1772, 1779, 1790, 1792, and on through the nineteenth century. The naval engagement between British and French forces in the waters of St. Kitts known as the Battle of Frigate Bay (1782) scattered several damaged vessels into The Narrows, and some came to rest on the northern shores of Nevis in the area of Newcastle. In 2010, the island signed articles with UNESCO for the protection of underwater cultural resources and historic sites. Underwater reconnaissance undertaken in 2011 by a joint team from San Jose State and Texas A&M universities in partnership with the Nevis Historical and Conservation Society located the remains of the frigate HMS *Solebay*, which was damaged during the Battle of Frigate Bay. Chris Cartellone of Texas A&M University initiated a systematic documentation of the site in 2011. Several cannon and ship debris were recorded. A Web site on Nevis maritime archaeology is available at http://www.nevis-maritime-archaeology.org. The Museum of Underwater Archaeology also maintains a frequently updated Web site at http://themua.org.

Further Reading

Chiarelli, J. 1999. "Archaeological Field Work Continues at Coconut Walk Estate, New River." *Nevis Historical and Conservation Society Newsletter* (August 6–7).

Crosby, A. 2003. "Further Investigations at Hickman, Nevis: The Nevis Heritage Project." Unpublished report, University of Southampton.

Davis, D. 1982. "Archaic Settlement and Resource Exploitation in the Lesser Antilles: Preliminary Information from Antigua." *Caribbean Journal of Science* 17: 107–22.

Hubbard, V. 1996. *Swords, Ships, and Sugar: History of Nevis to 1900.* Corvallis, OR: Premiere Editions International.

Leech, R. 2002. "Impermanent Architecture in the English Colonies of the Eastern Caribbean: New Contexts for Architectural Innovation in the Early Modern Atlantic World." In *Building Environments: Perspectives in Vernacular Architecture,* ed. Kenneth A. Breisch and Alison K. Hoagland, 153–68. Knoxville: University of Tennessee Press.

———. 2003. "The Early Colonial Settlement and Landscape of Nevis–St Kitts." *Nevis Historical and Conservation Society Newsletter,* No. 67.

Meniketti, M. 2006. "Sugar-Mills, Technology, and Environmental Change: A Case Study of Colonial Agro-Industrial Development in the Caribbean." *Journal of the Society for Industrial Archaeology* 32 (1): 53–80.

Morris, E., R. Read, E. James, T. Machling, D. Williams, and B. Wilson, eds. 1999. "'The old stone ort at Newcastle . . .': The Redoubt, Nevis, Eastern Caribbean." *Post-Medieval Archaeology* 33: 194–221.

Terrell, M. 2005. *The Jewish Community of Early Colonial Nevis.* Gainesville: University Press of Florida.

Wilson, S. 1989. "The Prehistoric Settlement Pattern of Nevis, West Indies." *Journal of Field Archaeology* 16 (4): 427–50.

See also The Archaic Age; Brimstone Hill Fortress National Park (St. Kitts); The Elenan Ostionoid Subseries; Geoinformatics; The Saladoid.

Newton Burial Ground (Barbados)

Kevin Farmer

The Newton burial ground for enslaved individuals is located on the Newton Plantation in southern Barbados. It is the only known and excavated communal enslaved burial ground on a plantation setting in the region. Jerome Handler and Frederick Lange, who investigated and excavated it in the 1970s, published the seminal source on the enslaved experience within the plantation setting (Handler and Lange 1978), and the plantation has become the normative case study from which the enslaved experience is defined in the region. In the second half of the seventeenth century Samuel Newton, an Englishman, purchased several small parcels of land in Christ Church and developed two plantations (both called Newton) that were in operation by the 1660s. Mayo's map of Barbados in 1717–1721 identifies one plantation called Newton in Christ Church

Figure N.5. Newton Burial Ground for the Enslaved looking south toward the Newton factory yard. Courtesy of the Barbados Museum and Historical Society.

that occupied 581 acres. Newton was occupied by enslaved Africans and their descendants during the period 1660–1834. The enslaved persons on the plantation numbered approximately 200–300 persons up to the period of emancipation.

The enslaved persons on this plantation used a sloping pasture area of 3,600 square meters for their burial ground (Figure N.5). The cemetery site has shallow soil and numerous rock outcroppings and was unsuitable for agricultural production. Some 1,000 enslaved individuals died on Newton plantation from 1670–1833, and it is believed that an estimated 570 are interred at the Newton Burial Ground, some in low earthen mounds and others in nonmounded burials. Excavation of these mounds has allowed researchers a glimpse into the diet of the enslaved; religious practices associated with the burial of the deceased, including the placement of grave goods such as necklaces, pipes, and bracelets in graves; and age at death, cause of death, and the work practices of the enslaved individuals at the Newton plantation. Individuals in earlier burials at Newton that were enslaved Africans were interred with their heads facing west, while those who were buried later were interred with their heads facing east. The latter burial pattern suggests that over time the enslaved population on the plantation became creolized.

Newton Burial Ground is unique not only because it contains a communal burial site but also because it conveys much about the history of the African and African-descended enslaved of Barbados. The Barbados Museum and Historical Society acquired the land in the 1990s and is committed to protecting the site and preserving it for the people of Barbados and the region.

Further Reading

Handler, J. S., and F. W. Lange. 1978. *Plantation Slavery in Barbados*. Cambridge, MA: Harvard University Press.

See also Barbados; Barbados Museum and Historical Society; Historical Archaeological Sites (Types).

Nicholson, D. V. (1925–2006)

Reg Murphy

Desmond Vernon Nicholson (Figure N.6) arrived on Antigua in 1949 as a young man with a strong sense of adventure and humor. Living among the historical relics and ruins of the old naval yard and sailing throughout the Caribbean Islands created in Desmond a strong respect and love for the islands and their peoples. In the late 1950s, he worked closely with Dr. Fred Olsen to establish the Antigua Archaeological Society. After Nicholson conducted numerous excavations in partnership with Yale University, he learned the basics of field archaeology and the issues and theories of Caribbean archaeology. His motto was that knowledge must be shared if it is to be of any use, and he began a lifelong voluntary campaign of research, documentation, publication, and preservation. Nicholson served as the president of the Antigua Archaeological Society from 1971 until the late 1990s.

He was deeply disturbed by the facts that Antigua's treasures were hidden away in storerooms and boxes in various overseas universities and that Antiguans never had the chance to learn about or enjoy these artifacts. Because of this concern, he founded the Museum of An-

tigua and Barbuda. This organization generated many voluntary projects, including the Betty's Hope Restoration Project and the Environmental Awareness Group. He served on the National Archives Committee and the Historic Sites Commission. He was a director of the Caribbean Conservation Association and a founding member of the Museums Association of the Caribbean and the International Association of Caribbean Archaeology. Following a series of hurricanes, he worked on rebuilding the Dockyard Museum and served as its director from 1996 until his retirement.

One of his most amazing accomplishments was his writing and documentation. He produced over twenty-five publications, hundreds of articles, and a massive database on the history and natural history of Antigua and Barbuda. Under his leadership, the Museum of Antigua became the first in the region to computerize its information database and cataloguing and search systems. He also developed a "please touch system" of museum management, and his personal collection of more than 6,000 books established the initial collection of the libraries in the Dockyard Museum and at the Museum of Antigua and Barbuda.

In recognition of his solid contributions to Antigua and Barbuda, Desmond Nicolson received the Antigua Order of Honour (Silver Class) for Heritage Preservation, the Rotary International Lifetime Service Award, and the UNESCO Honour Award for his outstanding contribution to the improvement of literacy and literary arts in Antigua and Barbuda.

Further Reading

Nicholson, D. V. 1994. *Heritage Landmarks: Antigua and Barbuda.* St. John's, Antigua: Museum of Antigua and Barbuda Publications.

———. 2002a. *English Harbour: The First 2,000 Years.* St. John's, Antigua: Dockyard Museum, Nelson's Dockyard National Park.

———. 2002b. *Shipwrecks and Other Marine Disasters.* Antigua: Museum of Antigua and Barbuda.

See also Antigua and Barbuda (Archaic Sites); Betty's Hope Plantation (Antigua); The International Association for Caribbean Archaeology (IACA); The Museum of Antigua and Barbuda.

Figure N.6. Desmond Vernon Nicholson. Courtesy of Reg Murphy.

Nidhe Israel Synagogue and Mikvah (Barbados)

Alissandra Cummins

Documentary evidence indicates that Jews were settled in and transacting business in Barbados as early as 1628. Richard Ligon (1657/1673) records their presence in his 1640s account of the island. The Nidhe Israel Synagogue was established in Bridgetown in 1654 by Kahal Kadosh Nidhe Israel (Holy Congregation of the Scattered of Israel). The congregation were Sephardic Jews who had fled Catholic persecution in Recife, Brazil, bringing with them mercantilist networks and expert knowledge of sugar production, skills that were highly valued in the frontier colony of Barbados, which sought to nurture Atlantic trade networks and expand its economic potential (Schreuder 2004, 181–84). The original synagogue was destroyed by a hurricane in 1831. The building that replaced it was constructed on the original foundation of the seventeenth-century edifice, occupying an area of 2,000 square feet (Figure N.7). It was consecrated on March 29, 1833, and was described in detail in the *Barbados Globe* on April 1, 1833:

It is thirty-seven feet high, and receives considerable strength from the rounding of the angles, which are capped with large antique censers uniting a balustrated [*sic*] parapet all round, the roof being so little elevated as not to be perceived. The windows are lancet-shaped, and tastefully harmonize with the proportions of the building; . . . the whole of the exterior is lightly tinged of stone-colour, and scored out in blocks, and the appearance altogether is classical and chaste. . . . The court-yard around this edifice is well-drained and neatly paved, and a handsome marble fountain occupies a niche within the inner court. . . . It is computed to hold almost three hundred persons.

Cemeteries

The cemetery associated with the synagogue is considered the oldest Jewish *beth haim* (cemetery) in the Eng-

Figure N.7. Nidhe Israel Synagogue, Bridgetown, Barbados, with principal *beth haim* (cemetery) in the foreground. © 2012 by William St. James Cummins.

lish Americas. Burials there date from 1654 onward. In stark contrast to Jewish tradition, probably due in part to the restrictive laws of Barbados, the cemetery was placed directly around the synagogue within its main yard. The two oldest grave ledgers that have been recorded date from 1658 and are among the oldest in the New World (Watson 2004, 197). Inscriptions on various gravestones are in Hebrew, Portuguese, Ladino, and English, and some depict remarkable iconography (ibid., 208).

The Mikvah

In early 2008, excavations by The University of the West Indies, Cave Hill, led to the unearthing of a mikvah on the Synagogue's grounds. A structure adjacent to the cemetery that researchers had assumed was the former rabbi's house was in fact the *bañadeira* (or *baño*), the building that housed the congregation's ritual bath. The structure had been hidden by a parking area since the mid-1850s. Excavations eventually revealed a flight of steps covered with a combination of marble, granite, and slate tile that led to a spring-fed pool twelve feet deep, eight feet long, and four feet wide. The bath is floored with red granite tiles and flanked by three alcoves that may have accommodated lamps for illumination. The pool was built over a natural spring that is still active.

Archaeological evidence points to the mid-1600s as the date of construction of the mikvah, based on the rubble stone, the method used to line the bath with bricks, and the artifacts recovered from the structure. Fragments of bellarmine jugs, delft earthenware, and clay pipe stems date to the seventeenth century. The architectural debris includes coarse red earthenware bricks and fragments of yellow bricks that clearly predate the British Navigation Acts of the mid-seventeenth century that would have banned their importation from Holland. Window glass recovered at the site points to the evolving nature of the building project. Locally manufactured plain red earthenware water jars and cooking vessels and artifacts of a more intimate nature that include glass beads, ceramic marbles, and white clay tobacco pipes have also been recovered from the yard (Miller 2010, 97).

The Pathway

More recent archaeological research has focused on the original seventeenth-century pathway leading to the synagogue. Three test units were dug during the summers of 2009 and 2010. Excavations revealed a high concentration of ceramics, including creamware that dated

as early as 1762, deposited in a dense layer of sandy loam and resting on a solid layer of crushed marl. The marl layer contained sherds of white salt-glazed stoneware (1730s) that was not found in the coral rubble and sand layer that dates ca. 1700 or in the earliest occupation layers below (mid-1600s). The dates for the original burial ground wall, which runs adjacent to the pathway, are also consistent with the mid-1600s. High percentages of faunal remains, mainly cow bones but also fish, bird, and other remains, were present (80 percent). Architectural remnants including iron nails (8 percent) and slate (approximately 3 percent) were deposited in the layer that rests atop the original coral stone pathway. High concentrations of ash and charcoal were also found in this layer, evidence of the many fires that struck Bridgetown in the late seventeenth and early eighteenth centuries (Bowden 2003, 92–94). These layers were dated using several techniques to establish a terminus post quem for each layer. The mean ceramic date for the bottom layers is 1700 (Miller 2010, 92–95).

These excavations have provided new insights into the material culture of Jews in Bridgetown and their communal and religious practices (Miller 2010, 102). The Nidhe Israel Museum opened in 2008 in the former synagogue school building. It tells the fascinating story of the history of Jews in Barbados through colorful panel displays and interactive and multimedia presentations. Perspex-covered alcoves that are embedded into the museum floor display artifacts on layers of sand that were recovered from the excavation, mimicking their location in the stratigraphy of the site.

Further Reading

Bowden, M. 2003. "The Three Centuries of Bridgetown: A Historical Geography." *Journal of the Barbados Museum and Historical Society* 49: 1–137.

Ligon, R. 1657/1673. *A True & Exact History of the Island of Barbadoes.* 2nd ed. London: Peter Parker and Thomas Guy.

Miller, D. 2010. "The Bridgetown Synagogue Pathway Archaeological Project: A Preliminary Report." *Journal of the Barbados Museum and Historical Society* 56: 87–104.

Schreuder, Y. 2004. "A True Global Community: Sephardic Jews, the Sugar Trade, and Barbados in the Seventeenth Century." *Journal of the Barbados Museum and Historical Society* 50: 166–94.

Watson, K. 2004. "The Iconography of Tombstones in the Jewish Graveyard, Bridgetown, Barbados." *Journal of the Barbados Museum and Historical Society* 50: 195–211.

See also Barbados; The Jodensavanne and Cassipora Cemetery (Suriname).

Origins of Indigenous Groups in the Northern Caribbean

L. Antonio Curet and Basil A. Reid

When Europeans arrived in the Caribbean, diverse cultural groups occupied the Greater Antilles. These groups appear to have developed over thousands of years as a result of migration, colonization, interaction, and creolization. Throughout time, archaeologists have proposed the following explanations for these developments: 1) the Saladoid-to-Chican lineal model; 2) the Archaic-Saladoid–La Hueca-Ostionoid-Taíno model; and 3) the Archaic-to-Chican model.

The Saladoid-Archaic-Ostionoid-Taíno Model

The Saladoid-to-Taíno linear model, which Rouse (1992) proposed, theorizes that the historical indigenous groups of the Greater Antilles were the result of a linear sequence of cultures by which a new one replaces an old one (Figure O.1). In Rouse's model, the sequence begins around 4000 to 5,000 BC with the first Archaic (Ortoiroid and Casimiroid) migrations, which were replaced in the Lesser Antilles and Puerto Rico by fully horticultural pottery-making Saladoid groups. As the Saladoid immigrated to the Caribbean region around 500 BC, they eradicated, displaced, or absorbed preexisting Archaic groups. However, this migration wave stopped once they arrived in Puerto Rico and did not resume until around AD 600. According to this model, the pottery vessels and designs of the Saladoid were simplified during the 1,000-year pause in Puerto Rico. For example, the distinctive characteristic of Saladoid pottery—the elaborate white-on-red painting—was abandoned in favor of simpler decorative styles. These changes eventually led to the development of the Elenan and Ostionan Ostionoid subseries, whose people around AD 600 began moving westward and eastward to Hispaniola, Jamaica, Cuba, the Bahamas, and the Lesser Antilles. In the Greater Antilles, these series, possibly with some influence of Archaic (Casimiroid) groups, continued to evolve and eventually led to the development of the Chican and

Meillacan Ostionoid subseries. The general assumption is that the Ostionoid culture had spread east, west, and north to the other islands by AD 600, eventually leading to the emergence of the historic indigenous groups of the Greater Antilles, whom many scholars refer to as Taíno. While more than one series were present in the same island at one time, the premise of this theory is that they occupied different territories.

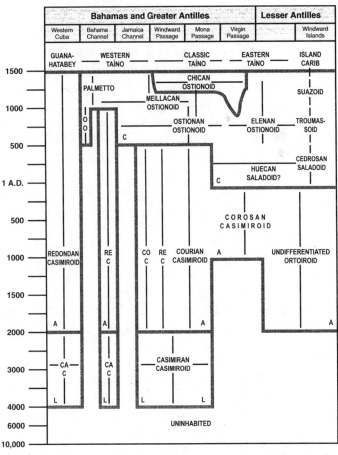

Figure O.1. Benjamin Irving Rouse's time-space systematics showing the cultural evolution of indigenous groups in the Caribbean. Reprinted from Rouse (1992, adapted from fig. 8) by permission of Yale University Press.

One problem with this model is the matter of chronology. The model has the Ostionoid subseries developing first in Puerto Rico around AD 600 and then expanding west to the other Greater Antilles. However, in reality the dates when the Ostionoid populated Puerto Rico, the rest of the Greater Antilles, and the Bahamian archipelago differ very little. They populated the whole island of Hispaniola and began populating the Bahamian archipelago and parts of Cuba in less than 200 years. For example, the occupation of the Bahamian archipelago has been dated as early as AD 685 to AD 700; some Ostionoid deposits in Cuba have been dated to AD 700, AD 700–800, and AD 620 (Keegan 2000); and dates as early as AD 650 have been obtained from Jamaica (Rouse and Allaire 1978).

The Archaic-Saladoid–La Hueca-Ostionoid-Chican Model

Rouse's unilinear model has been questioned since the 1970s, when Chanlatte Baik (1986) discovered a new culture, La Hueca (or the Huecoid series), that coexisted contemporaneously with the Saladoid at the same site. This raised questions about the traditional model in two ways: it refuted the idea that the Saladoid were the only people that migrated from South America after the Archaic people and it disproved the premise that only one culture existed in a region at a time.

To explain these discoveries, Chanlatte Baik proposed a model that we call the Archaic-Saladoid–La Hueca-Ostionoid-Chican model. Unfortunately, although this model is important, it has generally received insufficient attention in Caribbean archaeology (Curet 2005; Chanlatte Baik 1986; Reid 2009). The model does not assume that the Archaic peoples or cultures were eradicated from Puerto Rico once the Saladoid–La Hueca people arrived on the island. On the contrary, it proposes that they came in contact with each other and established a relationship that lasted for some time (Reid 2009). It proposed that two main Ostionoid subseries, the Ostionan Ostionoid and the Elenan Ostionoid, emerged as products of this period of cultural interaction between the Archaic and Saladoid–La Hueca peoples (Curet 2005; Reid 2009). The model suggests that the Ostionan subseries developed from interactions between the Saladoid and Archaic groups, while the Elenan subseries arose from contacts between La Hueca and the Archaic groups (Curet 2005; Reid 2009). It further suggests that shortly after their emergence, the Ostionoid in Puerto Rico colonized neighboring islands in the northern Caribbean, evolving

into the Chican and Meillacan Ostionoid by AD 1200. There is some archaeological evidence from Ostionoid deposits in Puerto Rico that supports this model. While large amounts of seashells, which are characteristic of many Archaic deposits, have been found in Ostionoid deposits in Puerto Rico, much smaller quantities of seashells have been identified in Saladoid–La Hueca assemblages (Curet 2005; Reid 2009). It is also significant that in Puerto Rico the lithic technology of the Ostionoid is more similar to the one used by their Archaic forerunners than to the stone technology practiced by the Saladoid–La Hueca. This suggests a strong Archaic contribution to the development of the Ostioniod cultures. A major shortcoming of the Archaic-Saladoid–La Hueca-Ostionoid-Chican model is that Chanlatte Baik presented it in very general terms (Chanlatte Baik 1986) without giving any specific details about the dynamics of Saladoid–La Hueca-Archaic interactions (Curet 2005).

More recently, some researchers have taken some of Chanlatte Baik's suggestions and developed more specific models. Curet (2005) and Keegan and Rodríguez Ramos (2007) have argued that the interactions between farmer/ceramist groups and Archaic communities were not limited to the island of Puerto Rico, as Chanlatte Baik's model proposes, but that these interactions happened simultaneously across as the Greater Antilles. According to these researchers, this multivector and intense relationship is responsible for the development of the Ostionoid series almost coincidentally throughout the region, explaining at the same time the near-contemporaneity of the earliest dates for the series in all the Greater Antilles.

The Archaic-to-Chican/Meillacan Model

The last school of thought seriously challenges the notion that the late groups of the Greater Antilles evolved out of interactions between the Saladoid and the Archaic. This theory argues that pottery was in fact being produced by the Casimiroid peoples of Cuba and Hispaniola and their descendants about 2,000 years before the arrival of the Saladoid in the Caribbean and by Ortoiroid peoples in the Lesser Antilles and Puerto Rico before the Ostionoid expansion (Reid 2009). The theory further argues that the pottery-making Casimiroid descendants in both Cuba and Hispaniola evolved into Ostionoid and that the Ostionoid on these islands subsequently colonized neighboring Caribbean territories.

There is considerable evidence for pottery-making by Archaic peoples in the Caribbean. In Haiti, there is pottery at the Archaic Couri 1 site (Reid 2009). As early as 1921, mention was made of pottery at Archaic sites in Cuba. Twelve Archaic sites in Cuba bearing pottery were identified in the 1980s. Sites in the Dominican Republic include El Caimito (La Caleta) and Musié Pedros, which date to as early as 300 BC, and others found at Honduras del Oeste and El Barrio. Pottery at Archaic sites on Puerto Rico was reported for Playa Blanca and Jobos. This wide distribution of pottery at Archaic sites prior to the arrival of the Saladoid suggest that pottery was not originally introduced in the Greater Antilles by Saladoid colonists (Keegan and Rodríguez Ramos 2007; Reid 2009).

The features of the Late Archaic ceramics of Haiti, Hispaniola, and Puerto Rico bear a strong resemblance to early Ostionoid pottery but also reflect a period of experimentation with different pastes and decorative techniques. Sherds are not common at these sites, and when they are present they exhibit a high degree of variability. Despite this, there are some general patterns: the main vessel forms include boat-shaped forms and globular bowls with round or flat bottoms. The most common decorations use red, pink, white, or black paint and incised and modeled designs (Reid 2009). In addition, the flaked-stone artifacts and shell tools at Ostionoid sites look more similar to Archaic artifacts than to tools found in Saladoid sites. These cultural similarities suggest that the Ostionoid people, who later became the Taíno, may have in fact evolved from Archaic peoples rather than from the Saladoid. The extensive Archaic presence in the Greater Antilles, which later gave rise to the Ostionoid people, probably explains the rapid expansion of the latter across Hispaniola, Cuba, Jamaica, and the Bahamas after AD 700, when they seemed to have been stuck in Puerto Rico/eastern Hispaniola for 1,000 years, if we are to subscribe to the Saladoid-Archaic-Ostionoid-Taíno model (Reid 2009).

Conclusion

In summary, the current evidence more strongly supports modified versions of the Archaic-Saladoid–La Hueca-Ostionoid-Chican and Archaic-to-Chican/Meillacan models, at least for Cuba and Hispaniola. However, the Taíno in western Puerto Rico appeared to have been a product of cultural interactions between the Saladoid in Puerto Rico and Archaic peoples. A modified version of the Archaic-Saladoid–La Hueca-Ostionoid-Taíno model is also a plausible explanation for the origins of the Ostionoid in Puerto Rico (Reid 2009). Essentially, the historical native groups of the Greater Antilles, which Caribbean archaeologists commonly referred to as Taíno, did not migrate from South America but evolved indigenously in the Caribbean, emerging around AD 1200 as a product of distinct types of ancestral societies and multiple historical processes (Keegan and Rodríguez Ramos 2007).

Further Reading

Chanlatte Baik, L. A. 1986. "Cultura Ostionoide: Un desarrollo agroalfarero antillano." *Homines* 10: 1–40.

Curet, L. A. 2005. *Caribbean Paleodemography: Population, Culture History, and Sociopolitical Processes in Ancient Puerto Rico.* Tuscaloosa: University of Alabama Press.

Keegan, W. F. 2000. "West Indian Archaeology. 3. Ceramic Age." *Journal of Archaeological Research* 8 (2): 135–67.

Keegan, W. F., and R. Rodríguez Ramos. 2007. "Archaic Origins of the Classic Taínos." In *Proceedings of the Twenty-First Congress of the International Association for Caribbean Archaeology*, ed. B. Reid, H. Petitjean Roget, and L. Antonio Curet, 1:211–17. St. Augustine, Trinidad and Tobago: School of Continuing Studies, University of the West Indies.

Reid, B. A. 2009. *Myths and Realities of Caribbean History.* Tuscaloosa: University of Alabama Press.

Rouse, I. 1992. *The Tainos: Rise and Decline of the People Who Greeted Columbus.* New Haven, CT: Yale University Press.

Rouse, I., and L. Allaire. 1978. "Caribbean." In *Chronologies in New World Archaeology*, ed. R. E. Taylor and C. W. Meighan, vol. 1. New York: Academic Press.

See also Arawak versus Taíno; The Archaic Age; The Chican Ostionoid Subseries; The Elenan Ostionoid Subseries; The Meillacan Ostionoid Series; The Ortoiroid; The Ostionan Ostionoid Subseries; The Palmettan Ostionoid Series; The Saladoid.

The Ortoiroid

Basil A. Reid and Richard T. Callaghan

The Ortoiroid people were Archaic colonists who originated from northwest Guyana. Their name derives from the shell midden of Ortoire in southeast Trinidad. The Ortoiroid first settled Banwari Trace and St. John in Trinidad approximately 7,000 years ago, eventually colonizing the entire eastern swath of the eastern Caribbean region right up to Puerto Rico. Ortoiroid has also been called Banwaroid after the site of Banwari Trace of the same culture. However, computer simulations suggest that some Ortoiroid groups may have jumped directly from South America to the Greater Antilles. The artifacts from Banwari Trace and St. John include tools made of bone and stone related to fishing and collecting, canoe building, plant processing, and general cutting and scraping. Many of the ground stone tools appear to have been used for pounding and processing hard and fibrous vegetable matter. There is mounting evidence that the Ortoiroid were among the first farmers and potters of the Caribbean (Reid 2009).

The Ortoiroid series is difficult to define and divide into subseries because its sites contain small artifact counts that are all simple types, because few traces of manufacture have been found, and because the number of diagnostic features is insufficient (Rouse 1992). In the northern Leeward Islands, two local cultures, Coroso in Puerto Rico and Krum Bay in the Virgin Islands, have been grouped into a Corosan subseries. Jolly Beach on Antigua, Boutbois on Martinique, and Ortoire on Trinidad are the only other recognizable cultures, and none of these can be assigned to subseries. However, Callaghan (2010) is of the view that sites classified as Ortoiroid in the Leeward Islands may possibly be misidentified outliers of Casimiroid sites.

Further Reading

Callaghan, R. T. 2010. "Crossing the Guadeloupe Passage in the Archaic Age." In *New Perspectives on the Prehistoric Settlement of the Caribbean*, ed. Scott M. Fitzpatrick and Ann Ross, 127–47. Gainesville: University Press of Florida.

Reid, B. A. 2009. *Myths and Realities of Caribbean History*. Tuscaloosa: University of Alabama Press.

Rouse, I. 1992. *The Tainos: Rise and Decline of the People Who Greeted Columbus*. New Haven, CT: Yale University Press.

See also Antigua and Barbuda (Archaic Sites); The Archaic Age; Banwari Trace (Trinidad); The Casimiroid; The First Caribbean Farmers; Kabakaburi and Wyva Creek Shell Mounds (Northwest Guyana); St. John Site (Trinidad).

The Ostionan Ostionoid Subseries

L. Antonio Curet

The Ostionan Ostionoid subseries (originally known as the Ostionoid series [Rouse 1964]) was first defined by Rouse (1992) as the first post-Saladoid subseries for western Puerto Rico. Today, this subseries has been identified by Rouse in Hispaniola, Jamaica, and Cuba. However, while in Puerto Rico this subseries seems to have spanned from AD 600 to 1200 or later, their presence in the other islands was short lived (AD 600–900). According to Rouse, the Ostionan Ostionoid is represented by at least eight styles: in Puerto Rico by the Pure (AD 600–900) and Modified (AD 900–1200) Ostiones styles; in Hispaniola by the Anadel style (AD 600–900) in the east and the Macady style in the west; in eastern Cuba by the Arroyo del Palo style (AD 600–900); and in Jamaica by the Little River style (AD 600–900) (Figure O.2). In Puerto Rico this subseries is known as Pre-Taíno and in Cuba as Sub-Taíno.

A general trend in the simplification of pottery aesthetics began toward the end of the Saladoid series, a process that led to the Ostionan Ostionoid subseries. However, some of the Saladoid craftsmanship was retained. During the early styles of this subseries, some of the technology and vessel forms of the final Saladoid pottery persisted, including looped handles and red-painted and slipped ceramics, but a limited number of other kinds of decoration were added, including smudging. The persistence of a few Saladoid traits into the early part of the Ostionoid period makes the assignment of this pottery to one or the other series very difficult, since there is no clear break in the ceramic trend. The distinction between these series becomes clearer at a later date, when the Pure Ostiones style is characterized by large amounts of red-slipped (or Redware) pottery and simpler vessel forms. Further, the late Saladoid practice of limiting red paint/slip to interior bases, shoulders, and rims continued. The pottery is thin, hard, and smooth surfaced. Common forms are straight-sided, open bowls.

Because of his assumption that the Ostionan Ostionoid subseries evolved from the Saladoid series, Rouse argues that the former developed first in Puerto Rico and resumed the westward migration movement the Saladoid had begun centuries earlier, reaching Hispaniola, Cuba, Jamaica, and the Bahamas. However, taking in consideration the almost synchronic beginning of this subseries in all these islands, some have questioned this statement and have suggested that a process of intensive interaction and transculturation between groups from different islands is responsible for the development and widespread nature of this subseries.

Despite the similarities that characterize the Ostionan Ostionoid across the Greater Antilles, strong local variants are present. For example, Ostionan Ostionoid ceramics from western Puerto Rico is especially characterized by the presence of a lilac/pinkish slip in addition to the red slip. In addition, the most common type of zoomorphic handles on ceramics found in Puerto Rico is bat heads, while other animals such as birds are more often represented on other islands. Finally, Puerto Rico is the only island that shows a much later survival of the Ostionan Ostionoid than any of the other islands. The main difference between the early (Pure Ostiones) and late (Modified Ostiones) styles is that in the latter style there is an increase in the use of incisions in red- or lilac-slipped vessels. Interestingly, toward the end of the Modified Ostiones style some of these incised designs have some similarity to the ones found in the later Chican Ostionoid (e.g., circles with a central dot, lines ending in dots, and triangles).

Although many Ostionan sites have been excavated in Puerto Rico and Hispaniola, very few have been investigated intensively. Moreover, no intensive regional studies have been conducted in any of the islands, and therefore little is known about settlement patterns, site types, and site distribution. One important aspect of Ostionan sites is their preference for coastal lowlands, valleys, and mountains. Furthermore, in Puerto Rico and in contrast to the Elenan Ostionoid further east, the Ostionan Ostionoid shows very little evidence of the presence of ball

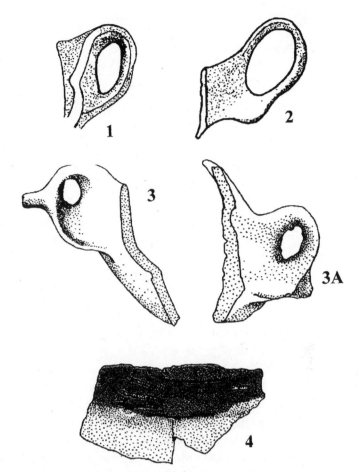

Figure O.2. Types of Ostionan Ostionoid (Redware) handles in Jamaica according to James Lee's handle typology: *1*, plain; *2*, with flared base; *3*, with flared base and tab or spur; *3a*, identical to 3 but occurring placed below rather than on the rim; *4*, horizontal loop. Reprinted from Allsworth-Jones (2008, fig. 20) by permission of the University of Alabama Press.

courts, plazas, or ceremonial centers. As a matter of fact, only one has been identified for western Puerto Rico, at the El Batey del Delfín site, in contrast to the hundreds found on the eastern side of the island. Evidence for agricultural intensification has been reported in the form of terraces in the mountain area of Puerto Rico and *montones* (mounds of loose topsoil for the production of tubers) in both Puerto Rico and Hispaniola.

Because of the dearth of intensive and extensive research on the Ostionan Ostionoid, it is difficult to identify patterns in the archaeological record relating to the size and role of household units, mortuary practices and the distribution of burials, relationships between settlements, population estimates and structure, ritual traditions, human–environment interactions, and interactions between regions and islands. This problem has limited our ability to identify and study aspects of their social, political, and economic organizations.

Further Reading

Allsworth-Jones, P. 2008. *Pre-Columbian Jamaica*. Tuscaloosa: University of Alabama Press.

Lee, J. W. 1980. "Jamaican Redware." In *Proceedings of the Eighth International Congress for Study of Pre-Columbian Cultures of the Lesser Antilles*, ed. S. Lewenstein, 597–609. Tempe: Arizona State University.

Rouse, I. 1964. "Prehistory of the West Indies." *Science* 144 (3618): 499–513.

———. 1992. *The Tainos: Rise and Decline of the People Who Greeted Columbus*. New Haven, CT: Yale University Press.

Wilson, S. M. 2007. *The Archaeology of the Caribbean*. Cambridge, UK: Cambridge University Press.

See also The Chican Ostionoid Subseries; The Elenan Ostionoid Subseries; Jamaica (Prehistory of); The Meillacan Ostionoid Series; The Ortoiroid; The Palmettan Ostionoid Series; The Saladoid.

The Ostionoid

Basil A. Reid and Richard T. Callaghan

The Ostionoid is a cultural tradition that indigenously developed in the Greater Antilles around AD 600 to AD 1200 (Figure O.3). It is named after the Ostiones type site in Puerto Rico that developed out of the Saladoid-period Cuevas culture in eastern Hispaniola around AD 600. Local types that are considered subseries of the Ostionoid tradition include the Ostionan Ostionoid, the Elenan Ostionoid, the Meillacan Ostionoid, the Chican Ostionoid, and the Palmetto pottery subseries of the Bahamas (Reid 2009). The relationship between these subseries is not sequential, since the Ostionan, Meillacan, and Chican were contemporarily present in Hispaniola, as were the Ostionan and Elenan Ostionoid on the western half of Puerto Rico.

There is much debate about the origins of the Ostionoid. The first school of thought argues that the culture directly evolved from the Saladoid-Huecoid peoples who inhabited Puerto Rico. However, recent research has shown that the Ostionoid culture, particularly in Hispaniola and Cuba, evolved from the pottery-making cultures of the Casimiroid (Keegan and Rodríguez Ramos 2007). Features of Late Archaic ceramics and tools from Cuba, Puerto Rico, and (especially) Hispaniola bear strong resemblances to early Ostionoid artifacts, further suggesting that Archaic groups laid the foundation for the emergence of the Ostionoid tradition, which is characterized by a variety of local styles and interaction spheres. In many ways, the Ostionoid were the precursors of cultural diversification in the Greater Antilles and neighboring islands, where the development of a variety of local types represented movements of pottery-making and fully agricultural peoples throughout the Greater Antilles, the Bahamas, and the northern Leeward Islands. Ostionoid from Hispaniola probably migrated to Jamaica and the Bahamas, and they were the first population to colonize both Caribbean territories around AD 600/650 (Keegan 1992; Callaghan 2008).

The Ostionoid lived in sedentary agro-ceramic villages on the coast, near rivers, and at the foot of the mountains. They were organized in socially complex societies. They practiced manioc agriculture as their economic mainstay, though retaining their traditional practices of exploiting marine and freshwater resources. By AD 1200, the Ostionoid had evolved into the Taíno people Columbus encountered in the northern Caribbean in 1492.

Further Reading

Callaghan, R. T. 2008. "On the Absence of Archaic Age Sites on Jamaica." *Journal of Island and Coastal Archaeology* 3 (1): 54–71.

Keegan, W. F. 1992. *The People Who Discovered Columbus*. Gainesville: University Press of Florida.

Keegan, W. F., and R. Rodríguez Ramos. 2007. "Archaic Origins of the Classic Tainos." In *Proceedings of the Twenty-First Congress of the International Association for the Caribbean Archaeology*, ed. Basil A. Reid, Henry Petitjean Roget, and Antonio Curet, 1:211–17. St. Augustine, Trinidad and Tobago: University of the West Indies School of Continuing Studies.

Reid, B. A. 2009. *Myths and Realities of Caribbean History*. Tuscaloosa: University of Alabama Press.

See also The Chican Ostionoid Subseries; The Elenan Ostionoid Subseries; The Meillacan Ostionoid Series; Origins of Indigenous Groups in the Northern Caribbean; The Ostionan Ostionoid Subseries; The Palmettan Ostionoid Series.

Figure O.3. The Ostionoid in the northern Caribbean (AD 600–1200). Reprinted from Reid (2009, fig. 4.7) by permission of the University of Alabama Press.

P

Pagán Perdomo, Dato (1921–2000)

Clenis Tavárez María

Dato Pagán Perdomo was a Dominican geographer who worked in archaeology from his youth, focusing primarily on rock art. He taught at the Universidad Autónoma de Santo Domingo (UASD), where he became the director of its Department of Geographic Sciences and of its main library. He worked in the Department of Archaeology of the Museo del Hombre Dominicano (MHD) from 1973, later becoming the director of the divisions of speleology and rock art. He was the general director of the museum from 1996 to 2000.

Pagán Perdomo was a founding member of the Sociedad Dominicana de Geografía (1970); the founding president of the speleology group Los Haitises (1974), which was affiliated with the UASD and the MHD; the founding president of the Sociedad Dominicana de Espeleología (1977); and vice-president of the Federación Espeleológica de America Latina y el Caribe (1983). He was a member of the Academia de Ciencias de la República Dominicana and other national and international scientific organizations.

Pagán Perdomo reported many archaeological sites, caves, and locations with rock art throughout the Dominican Republic. His interest in rock art led him to publish a complete bibliography on that topic in the Caribbean islands: *El arte rupestre en el Caribe*, published by the Fundación García Arévalo in 1978. His interest in indigenous rock art was not limited to forms and techniques; he also viewed this type of art as an expression of culture that can be used to assess the society of the people who made it.

Pagán Perdomo's book *Nuevas pictografías en la Isla de Santo Domingo, Las Cuevas de Borbón* (1978) became a landmark in the study of rock art in the Dominican Republic. This book features three caves of Borbón (Pomier), San Cristóbal, and many examples of rock art, including images of *cohoba* rituals. Pagán Perdomo is also credited with the re-discovery, in 1976, of a cave in the Borbón system that was described in the nineteenth century by English consul Sir Robert Schomburgk. In 1979, he published the first rock art inventory for the Dominican Republic (Pagán Perdomo 1979b). This publication is essential reading for any researcher of Dominican rock art. It provides the locations, coordinates, and topographic forms of rock art clusters (stations). The quality of his research made it possible for Pagán Perdomo to participate in scientific events in and outside his homeland and to organize the Seventh Simposio de Arte Rupestre Americano in Santo Domingo in 1987.

Pagán Perdomo was also interested in compiling research on geology, paleontology, and rock art, which he eventually published in *Bibliografía geológica y paleontológica de la Isla de Santo Domingo* (1976) and *Bibliografía general de la Isla de Santo Domingo* (1979a). He also published a number of articles in national and international newspapers and scientific journals.

Further Reading

Pagán Perdomo, Dato. 1976. *Bibliografía geológica y paleontológica de la Isla de Santo Domingo*. Santo Domingo: Universidad Autónoma de Santo Domingo.

———. 1978. *Nuevas pictografías en la Isla de Santo Domingo: Las Cuevas de Borbon*. Santo Domingo: Museo del Hombre Dominicano.

———. 1979a. *Bibliografía general de la Isla de Santo Domingo*. San Pedro de Macorís, RD: Universidad Central del Este.

———. 1979b. "Inventario del Arte Rupestre en Santo Domingo." *Boletín Museo del Hombre Dominicano* 12: 119–36.

See also *Cohoba*; Museo del Hombre Dominicano; Rock Art.

Paleodemography

L. Antonio Curet

Demographic issues related to the ancient Caribbean have commonly been dealt with superficially in a way that considers only the number of people and their spatial distribution (Curet 2005). However, while useful for a number of purposes, these levels of study obscure considerable variability, especially in the structure of local populations. The internal structure and nature of local populations play a major role in shaping the economic, social, and (in some instances) political organization and dynamics of human societies. In other words, how many people compose a society is not the only salient point; who is included in that population is also important. For example, a relatively young or old population with large number of "unproductive" members can experience economic problems because of the low number of young or middle-aged adults who normally compose the labor force of a society. The same is true if one gender is disproportionately represented, since males and females tend to have different social and biological roles in society. Thus, in studying the role of population variables, it is necessary to take into consideration not only the number of people but also the age and sex distribution of that population and issues such as fertility and mortality rates.

In archaeology, issues of population structure are studied by a multidisciplinary branch of the field called paleodemography. Richard Meindl and Katherine Russell describe paleodemography as "more than the study of mortality and fertility of archaeological populations. It also includes the estimation of the distribution, density, and age composition of prehistoric peoples. It considers intrinsic rates of growth or decline, and it may include migration and the age and sex structure of migration as well" (Meindl and Russell 1998, 376). Paleodemography also attempts to study issues related to paleopathology and paleoepidemiology such as diseases, frailty, and morbidity.

Assumptions and Principles of Paleodemography

Paleodemography uses techniques, methods, and theories from archaeology, biological anthropology, osteology, pathology, demography, and epidemiology. It focuses on ancient populations mainly through the study of skeletal remains. Sometimes researchers use other sources of information, such as historical documents. In general, paleodemography can be divided into two areas of interests. The first one deals with more pure demographic variables, such as population growth, fertility and mortality rates, sex distributions, and life expectancy. The second area focuses more on pathological issues such as frailty and morbidity and the role and/or impact of diseases on populations and cultural and social processes. Andrew Chamberlin (2006), L. Antonio Curet (2005), Mary Jackes (1992), Clark Larsen (2002), Richard Meindl and Katherine Russell (1998), and Lori Wright and Cassadi Yoder (2003) provide more information about paleodemography.

Paleodemography in the Caribbean

Migration

Migration is an alluring topic for students of island cultures, and the Caribbean archipelago has been a particularly fertile ground for developing theories about population movements. Since the beginning of the twentieth century, archaeologists and historians have worked to identify the origins and the routes of migration of the early inhabitants of the Caribbean. Migration has become the favored explanation for a number of phenomena, including social and cultural change. The standard model of migration has been a simplistic one: migration of relatively large populations as a unitary, one-way event with a termination and an endpoint that is followed some time later by another unitary, one-way event, each case involving the resumption of the migration (hence the wave theory of migration). Today, modern anthropological theory considers most migrations as processes that involved many steps and decisions and not necessarily a one-time event. It is believed that migrations involve multiple social, spatial, and temporal dimensions that may shape the structure of the migrant group, the destination of the group, and the conditions of settling in a new setting.

In the case of the Caribbean, archaeologists and historians have proposed at least five major migrations or colonizations: 1) the Archaic colonizations; 2) the Saladoid/La Hueca migration, mostly to the Lesser Antilles and Puerto Rico; 3) the Ostionoid expansion from Puerto Rico to the Greater Antilles and the northern

Lesser Antilles; 4) the colonization of the Bahamas; and 5) the probable Island-Carib migration before 1492. Discussion and debates on these migrations have normally focused on two issues: identifying the place of origin and (in a few cases) identifying the reasons for migrating. For the first issue, most of the discussion concentrates on stylistic similarities between artifacts from the migrant communities and those from potential parent communities. Discussions about the reasons for migrating have generated push or pull models in a few cases, where either a strong attractor, such as a better food supply pulls, the population toward a new settlement site, or a strong detractor, such as warfare or resource exhaustion, pushes the population into migrating.

Of these five major migrations, only the Saladoid–La Hueca migration and the Ostionoid expansion have been discussed beyond the simple identification of the place of origin and the proposition of reasons for migration. Analytical discussion of these two migrations has included considerations of interethnic interactions between Saladoid and La Hueca groups and between either or both of these and Archaic groups. Anthropological studies (Anthony 1990) on migrations suggests that movements such as the early Saladoid and La Hueca migrations probably involved gathering information, making decisions, and engaging in prior social interactions with the Archaic groups into whose territory they moved and with whom they thereafter cohabited. In addition, available information now suggests alternative hypotheses of population movement that replace the traditional unidirectional replacement hypotheses. In the case of the so-called Ostionoid migration, or the Ostionoid expansion, which chronologically followed the Saladoid migration, the archaeological data are open to conflicting interpretations. A tentative conclusion offered here is that the Ostionoid expansion may have involved one or more complex processes of interaction and transculturation between the Archaic and Saladoid societies that are normally not considered by the traditional view. These two major migration issues, which still await complete understanding, highlight the inadequacy of conventional population-replacement theories for explaining social developments during and after contact and suggest that researchers might do better to locate an account of population movements in social factors.

Population Issues

Paleodemographic studies based on osteological remains in the Caribbean are difficult, especially because of the way osteological samples are traditionally collected. As Edwin Crespo Torres (2000) argues, in the Caribbean, most samples of human remains have been the product of accidental discoveries, and few studies have been designed to recover skeletal samples appropriate for population and statistical analysis. For this reason, assemblages of archaeological human remains in the Caribbean tend to be too small to reach significant results or conclusions. Even in the cases where samples are large enough, many of them have not been studied appropriately or the results of the studies have not been published, at least not in a format that can be used by other researchers. These difficulties in obtaining the appropriate data have significantly hindered the furthering of paleodemographic goals in the study of the history of the Caribbean.

Although there are recent exceptions to these general problems in the study of skeletal populations for the Caribbean (e.g., Crespo Torres 2000), until we build a number of regional data sets about population structures at local levels, we will not be able to test many models or understand the factors involved in the decision-making process at the community level. Another goal is to show the importance of considering the sex and age structure of a population as well as aspects of fertility and mortality when studying their material remains. A population that is experiencing marked negative growth rates tends to behave differently than populations that are growing. Also, the social and cultural behavior in populations that are dominated numerically by one of the sexes or by only a few age categories will be different from populations that are not experiencing these things.

Few studies in the Caribbean have studied skeletal populations from this perspective. Antonio Curet (2005) compared population structure and demographic tables from three sites in Puerto Rico. Although the results of this study are equivocal, they demonstrate that the internal structure and demography of a local population can affect social and cultural processes. Furthermore, he was also able to discuss aspects of population growth, fertility and mortality rates, sex distributions, and life expectancy. This type of thorough methodology and analysis can also help evaluate the representativeness of skeletal samples for demographic and pathological studies. In another study, Gabino La Rosa Corzo and Rafael Robaina (1994) examined the age distribution of remains from a mortuary cave in Cuba. Their findings showed a large number of infants, suggesting the possibility of infanticide in ancient times. However, this may also be the product of the high infant mortality that was common among preindustrial populations. Finally, Edwin Crespo Torres (2000) compared age at death and pathologies from remains at two sites in Puerto Rico to determine aspects of diseases and malnutrition. However, because of the condition of the remains he was unable to deal with issues such as morbidity and frailty. In conclusion, even though little has been done in terms of paleodemographic studies in the Caribbean, the few projects that are available and the data that are beginning to accrue over time are expected to help researchers detect demographic trends in the structure of archaeological populations and help us understand past social processes.

Further Reading

Anthony, D. W. 1990. "Migration in Archaeology: The Baby and the Bathwater." *American Anthropologist* 92: 895–914.

Chamberlin, A. 2006. *Demography in Archaeology*. Cambridge: Cambridge University Press.

Crespo Torres, Edwin. 2000. "Estudio comparativo biocultural entre dos poblaciones prehistóricas en la isla de Puerto Rico: Punta Candelero y Paso del Indio." PhD diss., Instituto de Investigaciones Arqueológicas, Universidad Nacional Autónoma de México, México City.

Curet, L. A. 2005. *Caribbean Paleodemography: Population, Culture History, and Sociopolitical Processes in Ancient Puerto Rico*. Tuscaloosa: University of Alabama Press.

Jackes, M. 1992. "Paleodemography: Problems and Techniques." In *Skeletal Biology of Past Peoples: Research Methods*, ed. Shelley R. Saunders and M. Anne Katzenberg, 189–224. New York: Wiley-Liss.

Larsen, C. S. 2002. "Bioarchaeology: The Lives and Lifestyles of Past People." *Journal of Archaeological Research* 10: 119–66.

La Rosa Corzo, G., and R. Robaina. 1994. *Infanticidio y costumbres funerarias en aborígenes de Cuba*. Havana: Multigraf.

———. 1995. *Costumbres funerarias de los aborígenes de Cuba*. Havana: Editorial Academia.

Meindl, R. S., and K. F. Russell. 1998. "Recent Advances in Method and Theory in Paleodemography." *Annual Review of Anthropology* 27: 375–99.

Wood, J. W., G. R. Milner, H. C. Harpending, and K. M. Weiss. 1992. "The Osteological Paradox: Problems of Inferring Prehistoric Health from Skeletal Samples." *Current Anthropology* 33: 343–70.

Wright, L. E., and C. J. Yoder. 2003. "Recent Progress in Bioarchaeology: Approaches to the Osteological Paradox." *Journal of Archaeological Research* 11: 43–70.

See also Environmental Archaeology; Origins of Indigenous Groups in the Northern Caribbean.

The Palmettan Ostionoid Series

Jeffrey P. Blick, Emma K. Bate, and Charlene Dixon Hutcheson

Palmettan Ostionoid pottery (or Palmetto Ware) was first defined by Charles A. Hoffman Jr. (Hoffman 1967) at the type site, Palmetto Grove, located on the northwest corner of San Salvador, Bahamas. Palmetto Ware is recorded from the Bahamas and the Turks and Caicos Islands. Although it is classified as "Unaffiliated" in Rouse's ceramic chronology (1992, 52, Fig. 14), today it is best described as Palmettan Ostionoid and has both Chican Ostionoid (e.g., curvilinear incised designs, some of which terminate in dots, and molded and appliquéd lugs with human and animal heads) and Meillacan Ostionoid traits (e.g., rectilinear incisions, appliqué work, and punctations). Palmettan Ostionoid pottery is dated to approximately AD 600–1500 on San Salvador and approximately AD 700–1200 in the Turks and Caicos Islands. Palmetto Ware appears to be one of the ceramic types in the Bahamian Archipelago that was still in use just before the arrival of the Europeans in 1492. Palmetto pottery continued in use until (and perhaps just slightly after) the arrival of the Spaniards on San Salvador, as in-

dicated by mixed late Lucayan Palmetto Ware and early colonial Spanish ceramics in the same archaeological strata at the Long Bay site on San Salvador, Bahamas, which was also excavated by Hoffman.

Taíno ceramicists working in the Meillacan style on the island of Hispaniola and Cuban potters working in the Ostionan style introduced Meillacan and Ostionan/Baní trade wares to the Bahamian Archipelago around AD 600 and AD 800, respectively (ca. AD 700 in the Turks and Caicos Islands). Ceramic-temper and thin-section analyses suggest that the ceramics of the central Bahamas have connections to both Cuba and Hispaniola (Winter and Gilstrap 1991). Local Bahamian wares borrowed from Meillacan and Ostionan styles, becoming the local Palmettan ceramic subseries that today includes Abaco Redware, Crooked Island Ware, and Palmetto Ware (plain variety) styles (Granberry and Vescelius 2004, 43–47). A 1978 study by William H. Sears and Shaun Sullivan divided Palmetto Ware into four types: Palmetto Plain, Palmetto Mat Marked, Palmetto Punctate Incised, and Palmetto Molded Appliqué. All of these ceramic types are generally classified as low-fired earthenwares or terra-cottas. The typology used below relies heavily upon the descriptions in Granberry et al. (1998). The doctoral dissertation by Emma K. Bate (2011) is one of the most recent and thorough reviews of the ceramics of the Bahamian Archipelago to date.

Abaco Redware

Abaco Redware (Figure P.1) has a paste made of Bahamas red loam and typically has no inclusions other than small- to medium-sized pieces of crushed shell temper, believed to include *Strombus* (queen conch), *Codakia* (tiger lucine), and/or *Lucina* sp. This ware is usually manufactured with the coil technique and is fired in a 60–70 percent oxidizing atmosphere at the relatively low temperatures that might be generated in a campfire or a pit using wood or palm fronds (ca. 600–850/1,000°C). At these temperatures, the interior paste turns light to dark gray. Abaco Redware is moderately soft and measures between 3.5 and 5.5 on the Mohs scale of hardness, averaging 4.5. The texture of the ceramic is slightly granular with minor temper exposure, and the surfaces are usually polished to a moderate degree and covered with a fine buff or reddish slip on both interior and exterior surfaces. Abaco Redware vessel forms are not well known, but curved sherds indicate the likelihood that small hemispherical rounded bowls (ca. 20 centimeters in diameter) of unknown base configuration were a common form of Abaco Redware. Vessel shoulders may be narrow, they typically are not

Figure P.1. Example of Abaco Redware from the Long Bay site (SS-9), San Salvador, Bahamas. Reprinted from Bate (2011, fig. 7.14).

thick, and they are sometimes incurvate. The rim and lip are typically rounded, are tapered near the lip, and may be beveled on the inside; beveled rims may sometimes flare outward. Occasionally, folded or appliquéd rims may occur. Vessel thicknesses are reported to range from 6 to 14 millimeters, averaging 7–10 millimeters, although vessel thicknesses may be highly variable depending upon vessel form. Decoration on Abaco Redware is reported to be relatively common (25 percent of known examples) and includes cutting, straight-line incision with lines usually widely spaced, and/or punctations, all made when the clay was likely leather hard (i.e., still somewhat moist). Designs include nonintersecting cross-hatching; parallel, diagonal, or oblique lines; and half-diamond motifs. Linear series of punctations may occur just below the rim (a common location if any design is present). Abaco Redware vessels may also be characterized by small incised lugs or handles that usually occur in pairs or, rarely, singly. Abaco Redware appears to be restricted to the northern and north-central Bahamas and has been reported from Grand Bahama, Great Abaco, and San Salvador.

Crooked Island Ware

The paste of Crooked Island Ware (Figure P.2) is made of Bahamas red loam with frequent inclusions of medium-sized limestone particles. Like Abaco Redware, the temper is composed of what is thought to be *Strombus*, *Codakia*, and/or *Lucina* sp. and makes up about 10 percent of the paste. Crooked Island Ware was also made using the coiling technique and was fired in an oxygen reduction environment that caused the core of the paste to be very dark or black. This ware is slightly softer than Abaco Redware, ranging from 0.5 to 5.5 on the Mohs scale, with an average hardness of 4–4.5. The texture of Crooked Island Ware is moderately to finely granular with small inclusions of limestone, and the surfaces are typically well polished and covered with a thick shell-tempered dark reddish slip that appears to have been applied before the firing of the vessel. As in Abaco Redware, this slip is firmly united to the exterior of the paste but may wash off or scrub off with vigorous washing. Crooked Island Ware vessel forms are not well known, but curved sherds and other vessel fragments suggest rounded, semi-hemispherical bowls about 30 cm in diameter, possible navicular (or boat-shaped) bowls, and some straight-sided forms.

Necked bowls are suggested by a minority of Crooked Island sherds. Shouldered vessels are found only on necked jars, which were likely vessels for storing water or serving vessels for liquids. Flat rims and rounded rims

Figure P.2. Example of Crooked Island Ware from the Long Bay Site (SS-9), San Salvador, Bahamas. Reprinted from Bate (2011, fig. 7.12).

with some beveling occur, and lips are slightly tapered. The form of the base is unknown, but as in many coiled vessels the base is a circular structure with a flattened or slightly rounded bottom. The wall thickness of Crooked Island sherds range from 6–14 millimeters with an average of about 10–14 millimeters, although wall thickness may vary with vessel form. According to published sources, approximately 10 percent of Crooked Island Ware is decorated with cutting, straight-line incisions, engraved incisions, or punctated designs. Linear designs are generally wide and fairly rough, as on Abaco Redware, and appear to have been applied to leather-hard clay. Lugs, rim horns, or peaks and low-placed handles occur, along with sigmoid appliquéd strips. As with most of the Palmettan subseries, decoration occurs frequently on the upper portions of the vessel and near the rim. Crooked Island Ware is most often found in the central islands of the Bahamian Archipelago on San Salvador, Long Island, and Crooked Island. Recent identification of Crooked Island Ware in the lowest levels at the Minnis Ward site and in deposits at the Three Dog site, San Salvador (M. J. Berman, personal communication) suggests that Crooked Island Ware is a good chronological marker for early components (ca. AD 600–900) in the Bahamian Archipelago.

Palmetto Ware

Palmetto Ware (Figure P.3) proper is made of a paste consisting of Bahamas red loam with limestone inclusions.

The tempering agents of Palmetto Ware are thought to include small to large particles of pulverized *Strombus*, *Codakia*, and/or *Lucina*, which comprises about 10–25 percent of the paste. Specific identification of this shell temper is questionable and complicated, but it is based on the frequency of species encountered in archaeological sites, gross inspection, and a magnification of around 10X. The texture of Palmetto Ware is medium to fine grained with a hardness of 2.5 on the Mohs scale. Thus, it is one of the softest, most friable ceramic types in the Bahamian Archipelago. Palmetto Ware and the related Palmettan Ostionoid wares are highly recognizable by their brick-red color and their often incompletely oxidized dark cores. Inner surfaces of Palmetto Ware vessels are often highly to mildly polished; the exteriors are less expertly polished. Vessel forms of this ware include rounded and navicular bowls about 20–40 centimeters in diameter and 5–20 centimeters in height. A common Palmetto Ware form is the ceramic griddle or *budare* (aka *burén*), like a Mexican comal, which is typically used to cook manioc (*Manihot esculenta*) or other breads, for example, corn-based flatbreads such as tortillas. These ceramic griddles could be from 30–60 centimeters up to almost 1 meter in diameter and around 2.5–5.0 centimeters in thickness and probably were extremely heavy and cumbersome to move. Palmetto ceramic griddles usually had rounded unraised lips and flat bottoms that were often impressed with mat markings.

The shoulders of Palmetto Ware vessels were straight or slightly incurvate but are recorded as rarely or never curving inward. Bowl forms had rounded or thickened flat rims, sometimes beveled on the inner side, and some vessel walls were tapered toward the lip. Bowls most often had rounded bases, although sometimes flat-based bowls are found with mat-impressed bottoms. Vessel thicknesses ranged from 5–16 millimeters, although griddles were substantially thicker. The decoration on Palmetto Ware included mat impressions on the lower portions and bases of bowls and griddles. Some taller vessels, however, had sporadically placed impressions throughout the exterior, rim to base, and many of these also have charring on the interior (Berman and Hutcheson 2000). These patterns were once thought to be the by-product of manufacturing ceramics on woven mats, but recent work by Charlene Dixon Hutcheson (2013) suggests these mat impressions are likely also decorative. Other decorations included incised parallel lines, punctation, and nonintersecting or cross-hatched lines, typically on or just below the rim of the vessel. Palmetto molded appliqué ware has appliquéd strips that may be applied on or below the

Figure P.3. Examples of Palmetto Plain rim sherds excavated in 2005 from the North Storr's Lake site (SS-4), San Salvador, Bahamas. Photo by Jeffrey P. Blick.

vessel rim on the vessel exterior. Appliquéd designs may also appear on lugs with zoomorphic, anthropomorphic, or other designs, handles, and sigmoid strips. The percentage of decoration on Palmetto Ware sherds appears to be very low, ranging from around 4 percent to less than 1 percent at various sites such as Pigeon Creek and Minnis Ward on San Salvador. If mat marking and slipping are included as forms of decoration in future analyses of Palmetto Ware, the percentage of decorated sherds may increase significantly (Bate 2011; C. D. Hutcheson, personal communication). Palmetto Ware appears to be relatively late in the Bahamian ceramic sequence. It is found at sites with later radiocarbon dates and is mixed with Spanish artifacts at some sites (e.g., Long Bay). Mat-impressed pottery, which is not typically found on early types such as Crooked Island Ware, appears to be much more common on later sites as well.

Conclusion

Palmetto Ware is distributed throughout the Bahamian Archipelago and appears to be the primary locally manufactured ceramic ware of the prehistoric Lucayans of the Bahamas and the Turks and Caicos Islands. Recent work by Emma Bate and M. J. Berman is refining the chronology of Bahamian ceramics using a large variety of ceramic traits. These traits (vessel thickness, rim form, lip treatment, slip, oxidation patterns, decoration, etc.) may serve as sensitive chronological indicators to better clarify what has for long been considered a monotonous corpus of seemingly unchanging ceramic types in the Bahamian Archipelago.

Further Reading

Bate, Emma K. 2011. "Ceramic Technology and Spanish Contact: Analysis of Artifacts from the Long Bay Site, San Salvador Island, the Bahamas." PhD diss., Indiana University, Bloomington.

Berman, Mary Jane, and Charlene Dixon Hutcheson. 2000. "Impressions of a Lost Technology: A Study of Lucayan-Taíno Basketry." *Journal of Field Archaeology* 27 (4): 417–35.

Granberry, Julian, Mary Jane Berman, Donald T. Gerace, Kathy Gerace, Perry L. Gnivecki, Charles Hoffman, Grace Turner, and John Winter. 1998. *Standards for the Analysis of Bahamian Prehistoric Ceramic Wares*. 2nd rev. ed. San Salvador: Bahamian Field Station Ltd. of The College of The Bahamas.

Granberry, Julian, and Gary S. Vescelius. 2004. *Languages of the Pre-Columbian Antilles*. Tuscaloosa: University of Alabama Press.

Hoffman, Charles A., Jr. 1967. "Bahama Prehistory: Cultural Adaptation to an Island Environment." PhD diss., University of Arizona.

Hutcheson, Charlene Dixon. 2013. "Decoration or Happenstance: Experimental Archaeology and Basketry Impressed Palmetto Ware." In *Proceedings of the Fourteenth Symposium on the Natural History of the Bahamas*, ed. C. Tepper and R. Shaklee, 213–28. San Salvador, Bahamas: Gerace Research Centre.

Rouse, I. 1992. *The Tainos: Rise and Decline of the People Who Greeted Columbus*. New Haven, CT: Yale University Press.

Sears, W. H., and S. D. Sullivan. 1978. "Bahamas Prehistory." *American Antiquity* 43 (1): 3–25.

Winter, J., and M. Gilstrap. 1991. "Preliminary Results of Ceramic Analysis and the Movements of Populations into the Bahamas." In *Proceedings of the Twelfth International Congress for Caribbean Archaeology*, ed. L. S. Robinson, 371–86. Martinique: International Association for Caribbean Archaeology.

See also The Chican Ostionoid Subseries; Columbus's Landfall; The Elenan Ostionoid Subseries; The Meillacan Ostionoid Series; The Ostionan Ostionoid Subseries.

Palo Seco (Trinidad)

Alexandra Sajo

Palo Seco, located on the southwestern coast of Trinidad, is one of the most extensively studied sites of the island. It is the type site of the Palo Seco complex, the second of the two subsequent ceramic assemblages that characterize the development of the Cedrosan Saladoid subseries in Trinidad. The geographical vicinity of Trinidad to the South American mainland is considered to have played an important role in this sequence, as it was one of the first islands that Saladoid people settled after taking off from the coastal area of Venezuela around 350 BC. The colonization of Trinidad involved a complex adjustment of Saladoid settlement patterns and subsistence strategies in order to adapt to the island environment. The oldest Saladoid assemblage of Trinidad is known as the Cedros complex. This can be dated to 350 BC; at the time of Christ it gave way to the Palo Seco complex.

The Palo Seco site is a multicomponent midden deposit associated with a series of Amerindian burials that is packed with shells of various species and interspersed with layers of earth and cultural materials. The site occupies part of the Palo Seco beach camp, located southwest of Los Bajos on the shore of the Columbus Channel. It was excavated by John A. Bullbrook in 1919 and by Irving Rouse in 1946 and yielded cultural materials of three subsequent cultural complexes: Cedros and Palo Seco, both belonging to the Saladoid series, and the Barrancoid Erin complex. The radiocarbon dates of the Palo Seco assemblage range from the time of Christ to AD 650. From AD 350 onward this style reflects an increasing Barrancoid influence. Palo Seco ceramics characterized various sites distributed throughout most of Trinidad, with slight local differences in the motifs of pottery decoration. In the south and central parts of the island, Palo Seco ceramics are tempered with fine crushed shell and/or medium to coarse grog. However, in north Trinidad it is tempered with fine to medium-coarse sand temper containing quartz and mica particles combined with grog. Palo Seco illustrates certain elements that are characteristic of the previous Cedros style, but its motifs and designs are quite distinctive.

Palo Seco pottery vessels come in a variety of shapes and sizes. The common forms are bowls with a wide range of rims, from thick to elaborate compound rims. Other vessel shapes include asymmetrical bottle-like vessels, spouted vessels, almost pear-shaped jars, and dou-

ble-spouted jars. The functions of these vessels included storage, cooking, and food preparation. Vessels such as hammock-shaped bowls may have been used in both ceremonial and domestic contexts. Decoratively, Palo Seco pottery show painted, incised, punctated, and modelled motifs. Painted decoration is defined especially by white-on-red painting sometimes combined with black-painted designs and black painted lines separating white- and red-painted areas. Painting is also used to accentuate certain applied elements such as particular features of anthropozoomorphic head lugs. Incised lines in white-painted areas and the later Barrancoid-influenced motifs in red- and black-painted designs are also present (Figure P.4).

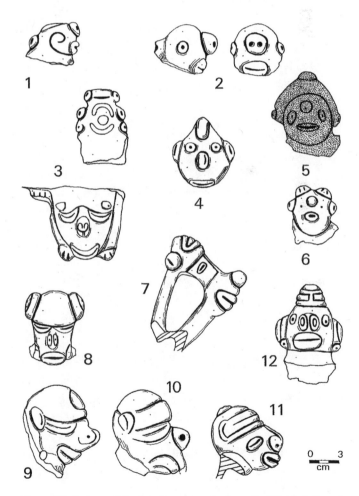

Figure P.4. Pottery of the Palo Seco complex from the Trinidad sites of Whitelands (*1*), Blanchisseuse (*2*), Erin (*3, 5, 8–10*), Atagual (*4, 6, 11*), and Blue River (*7, 12*). Reprinted from Boomert (2000) by permission of Arie Boomert.

Incised decoration consists of straight and curvilinear designs; engraved designs of single or multiple narrow lines, parallel wavy lines and semicircles, spirals, and stepped lines. Also present are simple modelled elements such as buttons-and-bar motifs applied to vessel rims or vessel bellies and triangular side lugs surmounting D-shaped strap handles that are considered to represent traits that continued from the Cedros complex. In contrast, four-lobed or dimpled vessel rims and trapezoidal side lugs appear as a new element of Palo Seco pottery. Anthropomorphic and zoomorphic adornos of the Palo Seco episode are more elaborate and varied and were placed on rims of bowls, bottle spouts, and stoppers. Although the animal species the adornos portray are difficult to identify, some seem to represent monkeys, bats, birds, felines, parrots, armadillos, turtles, frogs/toads, caimans, king vultures, and unidentified reptiles. Some of these biomorphic head lugs are hollow and contain small clay or stone pellets that produce a rattling sound when moved.

Further Reading

Boomert, A. 2000. *Trinidad, Tobago, and the Lower Orinoco Interaction Sphere*. Leiden: Alkmaar Cairi Publications.

———. 2009. "Between the Mainland and the Islands: The Amerindian Cultural Geography of Trinidad." *Bulletin of the Peabody Museum of Natural History* 50 (1): 63–73.

Boomert, A., B. Faber-Morse, and I. Rouse. 2012. *The Yale University Excavations in Trinidad of 1946 and 1953*. New Haven, CT: Department of Anthropology, Yale University Press.

See also Bullbrook, John A. (1881–1967); The Saladoid; Trinidad and Tobago.

The Peabody Museum of Natural History (Yale University)

Roger H. Colten

Yale University's Peabody Museum of Natural History curates one of the largest and most comprehensive prehistoric Caribbean archaeological collections in the world. These collections were assembled over a 70-year period by several researchers affiliated with Yale University, primarily Irving Rouse, Cornelius Osgood, and Froelich Rainey, as part of a comprehensive research program to document the prehistory of the greater Caribbean region from northern South America to the Greater Antilles. Many other archaeologists were involved in the project, including Ricardo Alegría, José Cruxent, Patrick Gallagher, John Goggin, Paul Hahn, George Howard, Marshall McKusick, Fred Olsen, and Gary Vescelius. The Peabody Museum's Caribbean collection includes over 142,000 catalog entries under 76 accession numbers, totaling a minimum of 360,000 individual objects. The bulk of the artifacts are ceramic sherds (nearly 90 percent), although stone, bone and shell artifacts, and unmodified faunal remains (bones and shells) are also represented.

The Peabody Museum of Natural History was founded in 1866 when it was informally called the Yale College Museum. Initial funding for the museum was provided by George Peabody, for whom the museum is named.

The museum's first curator was Othniel Charles Marsh, professor of paleontology at Yale University. Although the primary focus of the museum in the nineteenth century was vertebrate paleontology, anthropological objects have always been among the collections. After George Grant MacCurdy became the first anthropology curator in 1902, the anthropological collections from throughout the museum were united under a single division. MacCurdy's active research in Europe and the presence of an archaeologist in the museum contributed to the growth of the anthropological collections.

Under the direction of Cornelius Osgood, systematic collection of Caribbean archaeological material began in 1933, when the Caribbean Anthropological Program was established, co-sponsored by Yale University's Department of Anthropology (see DaRos and Colten 2009). The program was initiated "as an attempt to improve the methodology of archaeology through intensive research in a particular area, as well as to resolve the historical problems of the aboriginal populations of the West Indies and related peoples in North and South America" (Osgood 1942, 5). Two of Osgood's graduate students, Froelich Rainey and Benjamin Irving Rouse, were instrumental in establishing this program. The Caribbean program at the Peabody was very active from 1933 through the mid-1960s. The final field project was the excavations at the Indian Creek Site in Antigua in 1973 (see Rouse and Morse 1999). Field work seems to correspond with Cornelius Osgood, who was curator of anthropology at the Peabody Museum from 1934 to 1973. Although the program is widely known for its contributions to archaeology, it also included ethnographic research (Mintz 1960).

The first field seasons were in Florida and Venezuela in 1933. During the later 1930s, field work was focused in Haiti, the Dominican Republic, and Puerto Rico, although Rainey acquired a small but important archaeological collection in the Bahamas in 1934. The 1930s collections from Puerto Rico are the largest of the Caribbean assemblages in the Peabody Museum. The archaeological research in Puerto Rico was the basis for the publication *Scientific Survey of Porto Rico and the Virgin Islands* published by the New York Academy of Sciences in 1940 and 1952. The Haitian collections were the basis of Rouse's dissertation and his pioneering research in ceramic analysis.

In the early 1940s, excavations were completed in Cuba and Venezuela. Rouse conducted major excavations at five sites at Trinidad in 1946. From 1942 to 1949, most of the program's field research was focused on Florida in part because of the complexity of travel during World War II. During the 1950s, many projects produced small collections from Aruba, British Guiana, Cuba, Dominica, Florida, Jamaica, Martinique, St. Croix, Saint Lucia, and Venezuela. In the 1960s, research continued in Venezuela.

The largest Caribbean archaeological collections at the Peabody Museum in terms of volume or the number of catalog records in the database are from Venezuela, Trinidad, Haiti, Puerto Rico, and Cuba. Other important collections are from Antigua, the Bahamas, Jamaica, and several smaller islands. The museum also houses large archaeological collections from Florida because the program initially included that state. Because the Peabody's Caribbean archaeology collections were assembled as part of a systematic program of survey and excavation, they have great research potential. The focus of the initial studies was chronology and culture history with an emphasis on stylistic analysis of artifacts, primarily ceramics. Modern methods of compositional analysis of ceramics and various studies of faunal remains have become more common in recent years.

The focus of the Caribbean archaeological program at Yale University has shifted to the management of collections and facilitating research at the Peabody Museum.

In 1993, the museum received funding from the National Science Foundation to transfer the paper catalog records to an electronic database. More recent projects have focused on upgrading the physical storage of the collections and organizing and digitizing archival and photographic material.

Until about 2003, the collections were stored primarily in cardboard boxes. Using surplus museum storage cabinets acquired from another part of the Peabody Museum, the anthropology division staff began a pilot project in which collections were transferred from the boxes to new archival-quality specimen trays in drawers inside cabinets. This greatly improved physical access to the collections. As the collections were moved, they were inventoried and more precise storage locations were added to the database, further improving access to the material. In 2005, the museum received funding from the Institute for Museum and Library Services to continue rehousing the Caribbean archaeological collections. With those funds, the museum purchased 54 state-of-the-art storage cabinets and hired a part-time museum assistant to continue to inventory, clean, and move the collections.

In 2008–2009, all of the Caribbean archaeological collections were moved to a recently renovated climate-controlled facility at Yale University's new West Campus. All of the Peabody Museum's Caribbean archaeology materials are now stored in modern museum storage equipment using appropriate archival packaging. The collections and associated archival and photographic material are available for scholarly use and are frequently studied by archaeologists, physical anthropologists, zoologists, and other scientists from around the world.

Further Reading

DaRos, M., and R. H. Colten. 2009. "A History of Caribbean Archaeology at Yale University and the Peabody Museum of Natural History." *Bulletin of the Peabody Museum of Natural History* 50 (1): 49–62.

Mintz, S., comp. 1960. *Papers in Caribbean Anthropology*. New Haven, CT: Yale University Press.

Osgood, C. 1942. *The Ciboney Culture of Cayo Redondo, Cuba*. New Haven, CT: Yale University Press.

Rouse, I., and B. Faber Morse. 1999. *Excavations at the Indian Creek Site, Antigua, West Indies*. New Haven, CT: Yale University Press.

See also Alegría, Ricardo E. (1921–2011); Cruxent, José María (1911–2005); Rainey, Froelich G. (1907–1992); Rouse, Benjamin Irving (1913–2006).

Petersen, James B. (1954–2005)

John G. Crock

James B. Petersen, professor of anthropology at the University of Vermont (Figure P.5), was an American archaeologist who earned his PhD from the University of Pittsburgh in 1981. He was a leading authority on the archaeology of northeastern North America, the Caribbean, and lowland South America and was an expert in the study of ceramics and perishable fiber industries. Petersen was first introduced to Caribbean archaeology by David R. Watters of the Carnegie Museum of Natural History through analysis of ceramic assemblages from Watters's excavations at pre-Columbian sites in Anguilla, Barbuda, and Montserrat. He subsequently co-directed excavations with Watters at the Early Saladoid site of Trants in Montserrat and later, with former student John G. Crock, led field schools and the investigation of numerous sites on Anguilla.

Petersen also engaged in a long-term study of fabric-impressed ceramics and colonial-era Afro-Caribbean wares. His publication record is notable for its geographic scope and extensive list of collaborators. In addition to his careful study of material culture, which led to important insights into social interaction and ethnic identity, Petersen made substantial contributions to the understanding of cultural connections between the Caribbean and the South American mainland. He was murdered in 2005 during a robbery at a family restaurant in Iranduba, Brazil. At the time of his death, Jim was co-directing the Central Amazon Project, a groundbreaking archaeological study of the past societies that once thrived near the confluence of the Rio Negro and the Amazon.

Figure P.5. James B. Petersen. Courtesy of John G. Crock.

Further Reading

Petersen, J. B. 1996. "Archaeology of Trants, Montserrat. Part 3. Chronological and Settlement Data." In *Annals of the Carnegie Museum* 63: 323–61.
———. 1997. "Taino, Island-Carib, and Prehistoric Amerindian Economies in the West Indies: Tropical Forest Adaptations to Island Environments." In *The Indigenous People of the Caribbean*, ed. S. M. Wilson, 118–30. Gainesville: University Press of Florida.

See also Afro-Caribbean Earthenwares; Anguilla; Montserrat.

Plazas and *Bateys*

Joshua M. Torres and Samuel M. Wilson

Taíno, the native people of the Greater Antilles, used the word *batey* to refer to the ball game, the ball court, and the ball itself. The term *batey*, which is broadly defined in archaeological contexts, refers to open spaces delimited by stones or earthen embankments used for ballgames. In English publications, these features are commonly referred to as ball courts or ceremonial plazas. Las Casas offers a general description of the plazas:

> The towns of these islands are not organized by streets, but rather the house of the king or cacique of the town was located on the best site. In front of the royal house there was a large plaza, level and well swept, longer than it was wide, that they call in the language of these islands "batey," with the middle syllable long, which also means the ball game, which, God willing, I will describe later. There are also other houses near this plaza, and if it were a big town, they would have other plazas or ball game courts that were smaller than the main one. (Las Casas 1967, 1:244)

Las Casas describes the courts as being three times longer than they were wide and bounded by earthen berms 20–40 centimeters high (1967, 2:350). These dimensions are often applied as standard measurements for classifying stone-lined enclosures in archaeological sites in Puerto Rico and Hispaniola (Curet and Torres 2010). In contrast, other stone or earthen enclosures that are square or circular are generally referred to as plazas.

Archaeological research in conjunction with ethnographic documentation presents strong evidence that in addition to the ball game, these features were used for ritual performances known as *aryetos*, ceremonial dances that were associated with ancestor veneration and promoting communal memories.

The origin of these features on the island is currently a matter of speculation. Alegría (1983) suggests they were likely the result of Mesoamerican influences that diffused through lower Central America to northeastern South America, eventually reaching the Greater Antilles. Recent research has alluded to morphological and structural similarities between Puerto Rican stone enclosures and stone pavements registered in Costa Rica (Wilson 2007). However, the nature of these relationships and their influence on the development of stone enclosures and political organization in Puerto Rico remain unknown.

Jesse Walter Fewkes was one of the first scholars to report the presence of plazas or ball courts in the Greater Antilles. However, J. Alden Mason was the first to formally document these structures in any detail, based on his research in Puerto Rico (Mason 1919). Mason excavated and mapped the structures at the site of Caguana (Figure P.6), where he documented a long history of construction and reconstruction of these ceremonial structures. Other early documentation of *batey*/plaza features was done by Gudmond Hatt of the Danish National Museum in the 1920s at the Salt River site on St. Croix. Hatt uncovered a stone row consisting of nine upright slabs with petroglyphs.

So far, the *bateys*/plazas have been found on Cuba, the Bahamas, Hispaniola, Puerto Rico, and the Virgin Islands. Europeans described people playing the ball game in Jamaica, so it is likely that *bateys*/plazas also existed there as well. Puerto Rico has the largest number of these features; over 150 have been documented for the island. The earliest known *batey*/plaza features in the Caribbean are located on the south-central coast of Puerto Rico at the sites of El Bronce, Tibes, and Las Flores. Based on pottery and radiocarbon dates of associated middens from these sites, it appears that *batey* features emerged sometime around the seventh century AD. The highest frequency of these features on the island dates from approximately AD 900 to 1500.

Current archaeological data from many of the earliest documented stone enclosures on Puerto Rico indicate that these spaces were used as burial grounds in which the stone enclosures were built to delimit the extent of existing Saladoid cemeteries. While there is some debate regarding the continuity of this practice through later times, current research indicates that these practices were regionally variable. These spaces served to solidify communal relationships by linking the worlds of the living and the dead, the sacred and profane, in particular places on the landscape.

Recent research has suggested that the burials documented in many Saladoid cemeteries may provide evidence that community members who had relocated to locations outside the immediate locality at marriage were brought back to their natal community for interment after death. While this hypothesis has yet to be tested, the idea is compelling. Whether or not this was indeed the case, the later plazas and *bateys* and the performative

Figure P.6. Ceremonial center of Caguana, Puerto Rico. *Above*, photo of Caguana plaza features looking northeast. Courtesy of Sam Wilson. *Below*, plan view of plaza/*batey* features. After Mason and Rouse (1941, fig. 2).

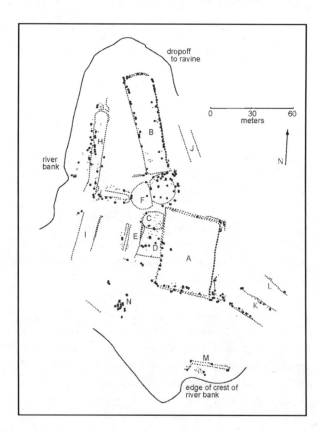

ritual practices tied to ancestor veneration purportedly associated with them likely served as a central component of communal identity and regional politics in the ancient past of the region.

There is considerable variability in the shape and size of *bateys*/plazas. Many sites in Puerto Rico and eastern Hispaniola have multiple rectangular plazas, but single plazas are more common in central Hispaniola, where they might be circular, oval, square, or have other shapes (Alegría 1983). Although Hispaniola's large plazas share features with rectangular plazas, such as stone boundaries and raised stone pavements or walkways on perimeters, they may have been used in different ways (Wilson 1990, 22–26). The largest of these, Corral de los Indios in San Juan de la Maguana, is circular and over 80 meters in diameter. The flat interior is surrounded by a cobbled pavement 6.4 meters wide. As with many Taíno plazas, it was connected to a nearby stream by a pathway, or *calzada*, that is also bounded by cobbled embankments (Alegría 1983, 33–35).

Elaborate stone-etched petroglyphs are perhaps some of the most significant features at these sites, particularly in Late Ceramic Age Puerto Rico. In Puerto Rico, petroglyphs assume a variety of zoomorphic and anthropomorphic forms. The most well-known of these is the "Frog Lady," a design that was originally documented at the Ceremonial Center of Caguana and more recently has been documented at the site of Jácanas (PO-29) in the south-central part of the island (Figure P.7).

Batey and plaza features have been a key component in the interpretation of the sociopolitical organization of the precontact Caribbean. The time and labor invested in the construction of these features provides evidence of the formalization of centralized authority and of a certain level of political and decision-making power (Alegría 1983, 118). Typically, the presence of these features is considered evidence for the emergence of regional "chiefdom" type political organizations that emphasized differences in power through control over ritual activities.

Since the work of Alegría was published in 1983, analysis of the function of these features has focused on the role of both vacant and occupied ceremonial centers. While there is clear evidence that ties small plaza/*batey* features to long-term residential settlements, larger sites, particularly in Puerto Rico (e.g., Caguana and Tibes), do not present evidence that indicates substantial residential populations. Recent interpretations of these sites presented by Jose Oliver suggest that they were likely occupied by a small number of households that maintained the sites and associated features.

The spatial distribution of these sites has been examined in the context of central place theory whereby a hierarchy of social rituals and power is based on the size and number of features at a given site. A somewhat different (yet not necessarily conflicting) interpretation, presented by the late Gary Vescelius, is that these features were constructed at the peripheries or boundaries

Figure P.7. *Left*, photo of in situ north wall of Jácanas site (PO-29) looking east-northeast, Ponce, Puerto Rico. *Top right*, stone 5 from north wall (*A*). *Bottom right*, stone 9 from north wall (*B*). Photos by David Diener. Courtesy of New South Associates. Archaeological investigations were conducted under a contract administered by the U.S. Army Corps of Engineers.

of sociopolitical territories (personal communication in Rouse 1992, 15). From this perspective, *bateys*/plazas would have served as liminal spaces where social differences and conflicts between competing social groups were negotiated through ritual feasting and, perhaps, through competitive gift giving and bride exchange.

Recent research indicates that these features served various functions at both local and regional levels in the region's ancient past (Curet and Torres 2010). Conventional functional interpretations of political centers posit that these features were also used in local village-based rituals that did not necessarily involve the entire supra-village community. They have also been interpreted as physical manifestations of lineage groups that imply heritable property rights and communal histories that linked peoples and places with broader social and political landscapes.

Further Reading

Alegría, R. E. 1983. *Ball Courts and Ceremonial Plazas in the West Indies.* New Haven, CT: Yale University Press.

Curet, L. A., and J. M. Torres. 2010. "Plazas, Bateys, and Ceremonial Centers: The Social and Cultural Context of Tibes in the Ancient History of Puerto Rico." In *Tibes: People, Power, and Ritual at the Center of the Cosmos,* ed. L. A. Curet and L. Stringer, 261–86. Tuscaloosa: University of Alabama Press.

Las Casas, B. de. 1967. *Apologética historia sumaria.* 3 vols. Mexico City: Universidad Nacional Autónoma de México, Instituto de Investigaciones Históricas.

Mason, J. A. 1919. "A Large Archaeological Site at Capá Utuado, with Notes on Other Porto Rico Sites Visited in 1914–1915." *Scientific Survey of Porto Rico and the Virgin Islands* 18 (2). New York: New York Academy of Sciences.

Mason, J. A., and I. Rouse. 1941. *A Large Archaeological Site at Capá, Utuado: With Notes on Other Porto Rican Sites Visited in 1914–1915.* New York: New York Academy of Sciences.

Oliver, J. R. 1998. *El Centro Ceremonial de Caguana, Puerto Rico.* Oxford: Archaeopress.

Rouse, I. 1992. *The Tainos: Rise and Decline of the People who Greeted Columbus.* New Haven, CT: Yale University Press.

Vescelius, G. S. 1977. "Ballcourts and Boundaries in the Eastern Antilles." Unpublished manuscript, Department of Anthropology, Peabody Museum, Yale, New Haven, CT.

Wilson, S. M. 1990. *Hispaniola: Caribbean Chiefdoms in the Age of Columbus.* Tuscaloosa: University of Alabama Press.

———. 2007. *The Archaeology of the Caribbean.* Cambridge, UK: Cambridge University Press.

See also Alegría, Ricardo E. (1921–2011); Arawak versus Taíno; Caguana/Capa Site (Puerto Rico); Chiefdoms (*Cacicazgos*); Zemíes (*Cemís*).

Port Antonio (Jamaica)

Elizabeth Pigou-Dennis

Port Antonio is located on the eastern end of Jamaica along the coast, like most of Jamaica's main towns (Figure P.8). It reached its historic peak as a port, first for exports related to sugar-cane plantations in the eighteenth century and then as a banana port in the late nineteenth and early twentieth centuries. The history of Port Antonio and its environs provide a microcosm of the sociocultural and geopolitical history of Jamaica. The terrain was occupied by the Taíno prior to 1494, then it was occupied by the Spanish during the sixteenth and seventeenth centuries. African and Taíno Maroons lived there during those centuries, and the city was occupied by the British after 1660. The conquest of the island by the British had a far-reaching and long-standing impact; colonial rule lasting until 1962. In 1723, when the parish of Portland was organized in the eastern section of the island, Port Antonio was its capital. The treaty between the Windward Maroons and the British government in 1739 and the establishment of a military presence in barracks in 1730 solidified the prospects for British colonial settlers. The barracks and Fort George, located on the promontory called Titchfield Hill, disclosed the colonial occupiers' intentions of using force to contain internal threats and external threats from other European navies.

The sugar monoculture based on slavery that was established by the British in Jamaica became the mainstay of the Portland economy. During the eighteenth century there were twenty-nine sugar estates in the parish. The plantation economy contributed to the growth of the small town of Port Antonio. When sugar production declined sharply after emancipation, Portland played a significant role in the diversification of agriculture for the locality. The new economy was based on banana cultivation and export, first through the initiatives of

Figure P.8. Port Antonio, Jamaica, 1899. Albert Tomson Photo Album, National Library of Jamaica. Courtesy of the National Library of Jamaica.

peasant farmers (former enslaved Africans), and then by the United Fruit Company, which was based in New England. During this phase of banana prosperity in the second half of the nineteenth century, key elements of Port Antonio's townscape were constructed.

In the nineteenth and early twentieth centuries, the town hugged the coastline, with the Blue Mountains rising in the background. Thus, in terms of materials and configuration, the building designs in the town were very well adapted to the tropical location. Roofs were high and steeply pitched to facilitate both interior cooling and water runoff. Public streets featured covered arcades fronting the buildings to facilitate the comfort of pedestrians. Closely cropped eaves helped prevent roofs from lifting off buildings during strong winds.

Vernacular houses, mainly built of timber on stone-pile foundation, were also highly adapted to climate and context, featuring the ubiquitous tropical element of the veranda; high, steep-pitched roofs; shutters; louvers; cooler boxes; and fretwork details. By the end of the nineteenth century, there was a distinctive residential area on Titchfield Hill. The town had a few nota-

ble examples of civic, public, and religious structures: Christ Church, the parish church (1840), the court house (1895), the railway station (1896), De Montevin Lodge (ca. 1900), and Titchfield Hotel (1897).

Each of these structures reflected contemporary themes in local, British, and American architecture. The parish church was Romanesque Revival, the court house was late Jamaican Georgian, while De Montevin Lodge, the railway station, and Titchfield Hotel were generally Victorian. Despite these stylistic labels, it should be pointed out that the late nineteenth century was an era of eclecticism and revivalism that challenged any attempts at architectural purism. Within the Jamaican context, the tropical climate and local materials produced creolized interpretations. For example, the railway station, which was built of timber with cast-iron brackets, fretwork, and lattices, is a very Jamaican creation. The hotel has Renaissance Revival characteristics in its round arched elevations and features a wrap-around veranda. However, what is most significant is not the stylistic labels but the fact that this small town, which had a population of no more than a few thousand, was a participant in a global economy. It was the exit point for local agricultural produce and its residents consumed ideas and images from abroad, including architectural trends.

The banana boom that fueled the economy of the port town and its architectural embellishment in the late nineteenth century stalled in the early twentieth century due to a combination of factors, including plant disease, hurricanes, and the expansion of Jamaica's capital, Kingston, as a port facility. However, the banana trade had opened Port Antonio to tourism and to a social "winter season" that revolved around the Titchfield Hotel. Up to the mid-twentieth century, Port Antonio retained its mystique as a celebrity hideaway and film location. The most famous association of the town was with the late actor Errol Flynn, who purchased Navy Island, off the Western harbor.

During the past several decades, Jamaica's economy has shifted from plantation crops to mineral extraction (bauxite) and all-inclusive tourist packages on the north coast. The island has struggled with phases of low economic growth and high national debt. Within this general context, Port Antonio has remained a modest and quiet town that is currently attempting to revive its local tourist economy. Attractions include its beaches and yachting facilities, the unique ecology of the nearby Blue Mountains, and its rich Maroon culture and colonial architectural heritage. Heritage markers have been placed at Fort George and Christ Church under the sponsor-

ship of the telecommunications company Digicel. The waterfront and yachting facilities have been redesigned as the New Marina by the architecture firm Marvin Goodman and Associates. The significance of Port Antonio's architecture is its incorporation of contemporary versions of vernacular architectural elements. The town has great potential as a heritage site. Fort George, for example, is a potential site for a modest museum of the history of the town. Because Port Antonio has not been subjected to rapid development, its walkable scale has been preserved, making it potentially interesting for heritage walking trails.

Further Reading

Massa, A., C. Easton, T. Spence, and Portland Parish Council, Jamaica, eds. 2000. *The Parish of Portland: A Sustainable Development Plan*. Portland: Portland Parish Council.

Padron, M. F. 2003. *Spanish Jamaica*. Trans. Patrick Bryan. Kingston: Ian Randle.

Phillips, A. 1993. *Jamaican Houses: A Vanishing Legacy*. Kingston: De Sola Pinto.

Senior, O. 2003. *Encyclopedia of Jamaican Heritage*. Kingston: Twin Guinep.

Tortello, R. 2007. *Pieces of the Past*. Kingston: Ian Randle.

See also Falmouth (Jamaica); Spanish Town (Jamaica); Willemstad (Curaçao).

Port Royal (Jamaica)

R. Grant Gilmore III and Basil A. Reid

Port Royal was established by the Spanish but was developed by the English starting in 1655 (Figure P.9). The town occupies a 21-hectare site on a sand spit known as Palisadoes at the entrance to Kingston Harbour in Jamaica. It evolved rapidly as a commercial center, attracting the typical range of merchants, privateers, and pirates. It soon earned a reputation that caused it to be known as the "Sodom of the New World." Rent prices skyrocketed as the population grew rapidly during the latter part of the seventeenth century. Boston, Massachusetts, was the only other English town with an equivalent population (around 7,000–8,000). Taverns, brothels, homes, and warehouses were crammed together to form a bustling city that served the greater Caribbean as a trading post and a haven for pirates.

Port Royal's significance as a trading center continued

to grow until 11:43 a.m. on June 7, 1692, when a strong earthquake and a series of tsunamis resulted in the destruction and submergence of a good portion of the city. These disasters, coupled with the spread of contagious diseases, killed the majority of the population. What remained of the city continued to survive through the eighteenth century, when additional earthquakes, fires, and hurricanes further reduced the functional capacity of the town. An earthquake in 1907 was the final blow to the town's economic survival.

Archaeological work on the site began in 1959 when famed underwater explorer, aviation pioneer, and inventor Edwin A. Link brought a team co-sponsored by National Geographic and the Smithsonian Institution. They began to map underwater Port Royal using scuba technology and recovered artifacts from several locations.

During the 1960s, Robert F. Marx began to excavate extensively in response to the threat of imminent development. Marx recovered thousands of artifacts, which induced government officials to delay further development and to focus instead on the preservation and display of the history of seventeenth-century Port Royal. The artifacts Marx recovered eventually formed the core collection for a museum located at the Old Naval Hospital.

During the 1980s, additional work was completed by Donny Hamilton of the Institute of Nautical Archaeology, based at Texas A&M University. Full conservation laboratories were set up and reports were produced for much of the work undertaken. The archaeological work resulted in one of the largest collections of seventeenth-century English material culture to be found anywhere in the world.

Because individual homes and businesses were destroyed within minutes in 1692, a cross-section of life in the colonial world that has no equal has been preserved at Port Royal. For example, Maureen Brown's (2011) analysis of the New Street Tavern site assemblage (1692–1703), probate inventories, and historical data, has provided some very useful insights into Port Royal's British colonial merchant class. The tavern, or victualing house, was the most common type of shop in Port Royal and an important meeting place for merchants. Brown found that the New Street Tavern assemblage (which consists of ceramics, glass, pipes, and vessels for storing beverages, food, condiments, spices, and apothecary goods) suggests that the tavern catered to a clientele that had considerable social standing. This interpretation is supported by an abundance of desirable goods, the presence of decorated wares and vessel forms, individual drinking and eating vessels, and forms that were associated with expensive foods.

The Jamaica National Heritage Trust, the agency responsible for protecting, preserving, and promoting Jamaica's material cultural heritage, has been working over the years to bring new life to the old city. The trust may consider the work of noted architect, the late Oliver Cox, in its plan to develop historic Port Royal.

Further Reading

Brown, M. 2011. "Evidence for Port Royal's British Colonial Merchant Class as Reflected in the New Street Tavern Site Assemblage, Port Royal, Jamaica." In *Out of Many, One People: The Historical Archaeology of Colonial Jamaica*, ed. J. A. Delle, M. Hauser, and D. V. Armstrong, 3–100. Tuscaloosa: University of Alabama Press.

Hamilton, D. L. 2008. "Port Royal, Jamaica: Archaeological Past, Present, and Future." In *Underwater and Maritime Archaeology in Latin America and the Caribbean*, ed. Margaret E. Leshikar-Denton and Pilar Luna Erreguerena, 259–69. Walnut Creek, CA: Left Coast Press.

Link, M. C. 1960. "Exploring the Drowned City of Port Royal." *National Geographic* 117 (2): 151–83.

Marx, R. F. 1973. *Port Royal Rediscovered*. New York: Doubleday.

See also Underwater Archaeology.

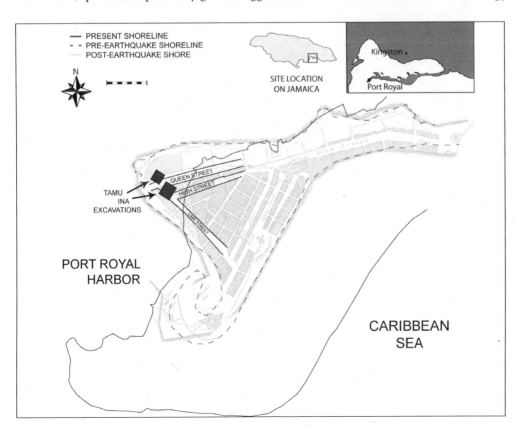

Figure P.9. Port Royal, Jamaica. Drawn by R. Grant Gilmore III and Katrien Janin.

Puerto Real (Haiti)

Gifford J. Waters

Puerto Real, located on the northern coast of what is today Haiti (Figure P.10), was founded just ten years after Columbus made his first voyage to the Americas. It was one of seventeen towns established as part of an island-wide colonizing effort from 1502 to 1506. The goals of this project were to control and exploit the native peoples and natural resources of Hispaniola and to firmly establish Spanish town life. It was in Puerto Real and the other earliest towns that the first experiments with establishing the New World Spanish colonial system took place.

Puerto Real was established in 1503 by Captain Rodrigo de Mexía after he and his forces vanquished the Taíno people living in the vicinity. It was never a large town and was often economically marginal. The number of initial settlers is unknown, but many of them were adventurers and men-at-arms in Mexía's forces who were looking for wealth and adventure. By 1514, there were probably some 200 to 250 Spaniards living in the town, among them a barber, a blacksmith, a schoolmaster, public officials, clergy members, merchants, a cassava planter, and shipmasters. The wives of five *vecinos* (land-owning citizens) were listed in 1514; two were Indians and three were Spaniards. Thirty-four Spaniards controlled 504 native Taíno workers, many of whom labored away from the town on farms and ranches.

Copper mines were discovered near Puerto Real during the first years of settlement that garnered the interest and support of the Crown. Early in 1505, King Ferdinand sent a caravel of tools, supplies, a German mining expert, and sixteen enslaved Africans. This was one of the first arrivals of enslaved Africans in the Americas. Despite royal support and foreign expertise, the copper mine never produced the riches that were expected.

By the 1520s, the economy of Puerto Real was based on cattle ranching and cattle hide production, most of which was sold illegally to foreign ships that traded regularly with the isolated Spanish towns of northern Hispaniola. Despite attempts by officials in Santo Domingo and Spain to end this regularized trade, they could not control the colonists of Puerto Real. In 1578, the Crown decreed that Puerto Real was to be abandoned and merged with the town of Lares de Guahaba in a new location that could be more closely controlled. Puerto Real was forcibly evacuated and destroyed by Spanish officials in 1579.

In 1975, Dr. William Hodges, a medical missionary and founder of the Hôpital le Bon Samaritain in Haiti, discovered the ruins of Puerto Real while searching for La Navidad. After documenting the find, Hodges contacted Dr. Charles Fairbanks of the University of Florida. Through the concerted efforts of the Haitian Institut de Sauvegarde du Patrimoine National; the Organization of American States; the National Endowment for the Humanities; the Musée de Guahaba in Limbé, Haiti; and the Florida Museum of Natural History at the University of Florida, a seven-year interdisciplinary study of Puerto Real was launched that was led by Fairbanks and Dr. Kathleen Deagan.

In 1978, all that remained of Puerto Real had been buried. The organization of the Puerto Real community was revealed only through archaeology. Archaeology has clearly shown that the town's builders incorporated the principles that were later formalized as the ideal design for urban life in the Spanish Americas. Regular linear organization, the concentration of governmental and religious authority in the central plaza, and the spatial segregation of the residences of differing status groups and production activities can all be documented in the

Figure P.10. Puerto Real, northern Haiti. Courtesy of the Florida Museum of Natural History, Historical Archaeology Collections.

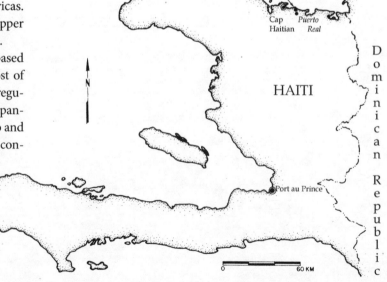

archaeological record of early sixteenth-century Puerto Real. Subsurface surveys of the site revealed that the town was laid out parallel to the east side of the now-extinct Fossé River. Its maximum extent covered a regular rectangular about 500 meters north-south by 400 meters east-west (≈20 hectares). The densest concentrations of all types of European artifacts and structural remains occur in a more restricted area in the center of the site, which covers an area of about 290 meters north-south and 230 meters east-west (≈17 hectares). The size of the town's population varied considerably through its life, and the areas of occupation changed accordingly.

The orientation of Puerto Real's built environment was extremely regular, suggesting a linear, grid-like organization. The town's church, which was located on the plaza at the center of the town, measured 7 by 27 meters. A cemetery was to the west, and the plaza was to the east. To the north of the church was another massive stone structure thought to be the *audiencia* (seat of government) or possibly the *convento* (the residence of the religious at Puerto Real). These buildings were made of stone, tile, and flat brick, and were massive. They featured pillared colonnades, stone gargoyles, and decorative tiles that were found only in these public areas of the town. Private homes and commercial enterprises were located around and expanding outward from the central area. Surveys located evidence for at least forty-nine masonry construction areas (probably not all occupied simultaneously). To date only masonry structures have been excavated at Puerto Real, though there were undoubtedly many more as-yet-undocumented wood and thatch buildings there.

Floor plans were typically based on multiple rooms laid out in a linear arrangement around or alongside a patio. Stone footings, tiled patios or floors, brick drains, and brick pavements were used in combination with trench walls and post walls. All of the excavated structures incorporated flat *ladrillo* bricks in walls and floors and curved-barrel roof tiles (*tejas*). The domestic structures excavated at Puerto Real showed evidence for lot boundary walls. In some cases these walls formed part of the structures in addition to serving as a boundary. These enclosed occupation complexes probably contained not only the living areas for the inhabitants but also animal corrals, gardens, and possibly areas where commercial or light industrial activities took place. One excavated complex that was probably a commercial area related to the cattle hide industry contained a remarkable assemblage of cattle remains and hide-working tools.

As in any colonial community, the conditions of life varied widely for residents of Puerto Real according to a household's status, power, and access to resources. Race and origin were paramount considerations, and those who were (or were perceived to be) Taíno and enslaved Africans were relegated to inferior positions. In Puerto Real, most people of Taíno or African heritage were enslaved laborers on ranches, farms, docks, and public constructions or were domestic servants. Archaeology has so far provided few insights into the life of these residents of Puerto Real beyond their contributions to the domestic foodways of the community and the documentation of their exploitation and decline. People of European origin controlled the social, political, and economic hierarchies at Puerto Real, although a wide range of status and prestige was found within this group. Factors contributing to elite status in the community included pure Castilian background, membership in the founding group of Puerto Real, *vecindad* (official citizenship), office-holding in the colonial administration of the town, possession of large land grants, an allocation (*repartimiento*) of Indian laborers, and the presence of a Spanish woman in the household. All of these factors were also associated with wealth.

The presence of numerous non-European household servants and possibly family members was reflected in the kitchens of Puerto Real's Spanish households, where cooking was done more often than not in Taíno- or African-made pottery vessels. Archaeological research has shown that cooks of both Spanish and Amerindian origin were instrumental in shaping the emerging foodways of Puerto Real. The Spanish colonial diet in the earliest years of settlement was the result of a complex interplay among tradition, environment, preference, adaptation, and cultural interaction. The archaeological data indicate that people were flexible and creative in the way they maintained ideal Iberian food preferences as they adjusted to local ecological conditions. They also incorporated unfamiliar local foods, such as turkeys, turtles, and manioc, developing a cuisine that was distinct from both indigenous American and Iberian diets but had some traits in common with each.

Further Reading

Deagan, K. 1995. *Puerto Real: The Archaeology of a Sixteenth-Century Spanish Town in Hispaniola.* Gainesville: University Press of Florida.

Ewen, C. R. 1992. *From Spaniard to Creole: The Archaeology of Culture Formation at Puerto Real, Haiti.* Tuscaloosa: University of Alabama Press.

Hodges, W. 1979. "How We Found Puerto Real." Unpublished manuscript, Musée de Guahaba, Limbé, Haiti.

See also La Isabela (Dominican Republic).

R

Rainey, Froelich G. (1907–1992)

Gifford J. Waters

Froelich Gladstone Rainey conducted archaeological excavations and ethnographic fieldwork around the world. He served as director of the Museum of Archaeology and Anthropology at the University of Pennsylvania from 1947 to 1977. Rainey first became interested in archaeology while taking a college course taught by Ralph Linton, a Sterling Professor of Anthropology at Yale University. Though Rainey is most well known for his archaeological and ethnographic research in the Arctic, he also conducted research throughout the world, including the Caribbean.

Rainey's research in the Caribbean began in the 1930s while at still a student at Yale University. He first focused on the islands of the Bahamas and Hispaniola, then moved to Haiti and Puerto Rico. During his research on Haiti, he introduced Irving Rouse, then an undergraduate student, to Caribbean archaeology in Haiti. While conducting some of the earliest stratigraphic excavations

in Puerto Rico, Rainey discovered distinct differences in the materials found in the lower and upper stratigraphic levels of the middens. In his PhD dissertation, Rainey hypothesized that the remains excavated in the Puerto Rican middens indicated the presence of two distinct and temporally separate cultures that he termed the Crab and Shell Cultures. While this dichotomy was discredited by Rouse and others, it is still debated today and at the very least represents one of the earliest discussions of the possibility of Saladoid and Ostionoid settlements in Puerto Rico.

Further Reading

Rainey, F. G. 1992. *Reflections of a Digger: Fifty Years of World Archaeology*. Philadelphia: University Museum of Archaeology and Anthropology, University of Pennsylvania.

See also Crab/Shell Dichotomy.

Rescue Archaeology

Quetta Kaye

Rescue archaeology, otherwise known as salvage archaeology, is archaeological work undertaken in advance of an imminent threat to or destruction of a site or area where archaeological remains have been positively identified or where there is a potential for archaeological remains to be recovered based on historical documentation. By nature, rescue archaeology rarely involves full-scale excavation. The remit of rescue archaeology is to partially excavate or record a site before it disappears. At the minimum, this means carrying out a "watching brief"—that is, gathering as much information as possible by collecting and recording any obvious archaeological remains (by photography and written record) before they are destroyed.

In the Caribbean, threats to archaeology take four main forms: 1) looting, which has the potential to destroy sites and remove valuable contextual information; 2) land development, which is increasingly part of a burgeoning tourism industry; 3) intensified agricultural use, where more intrusive mechanical equipment than was used in earlier periods plows deeper into the soil, destroying any archaeological remains in the process; and

4) the forces of nature. Particularly in vulnerable coastal areas, archaeological remains are vulnerable to threats from changing weather patterns (perhaps accelerated by climate change) that can lead to destruction by erosion. An example of this can be seen at the archaeologically rich coastal site of Grand Bay, Carriacou, where measurements taken since 1999 show that the site has been eroding at roughly one meter per year.

Unfortunately for investigators of precolonial Caribbean archaeology, the early inhabitants of the islands constructed their dwellings from organic materials and did not create monumental stone architecture, with the exceptions of petroglyph carvings, ball courts, and plazas. As a result, the majority of archaeological remains of previous settlements lie beneath the surface. However, they are frequently revealed by surface scatters of material or middens, which sometimes require full-scale excavation. The use of geoinformatics can help identify sites and facilitate targeted excavations.

Additionally, precolonial settlements on most Caribbean islands tend to be found in the fertile but vulnerable coastal areas. These areas were attractive to settlers in prehistory, but they are also attractive to current inhabitants and to developers seeking to boost local economies by expanding the tourist industry. Without enforced legislation, sufficient funding, and trained local personnel, it is often difficult to conduct archaeological surveys of these areas of interest in order to identify and register archaeological remains. All too often, the location of an archaeology site is revealed only after the construction of a road, a hotel complex, a marina, or a golf course has already started. Even when archaeological help is available, the financial considerations of slowing down the development mean that any archaeological intervention will be limited to rescue or salvage. However, rescue archaeology has had a few successes in the region. A prime example is the work of the Jamaica National Heritage Trust to document and survey archaeological sites in Jamaica prior to the Jamaican government's Highway 2000 project.

Without protective legislation, development on most Caribbean islands is invariably permitted without consideration of archaeological issues. Where rescue archaeology can be conducted, the final development rarely incorporates any archaeological features, as was the case with the large marina construction at Port St. Charles, Barbados, which was built over one of the largest archaeological sites on that island.

Further Reading

Drewett, P. L. 2000. *Prehistoric Settlements in the Caribbean.* Barbados: Archetype.

Kaye, Q. P., S. M. Fitzpatrick, and M. Kappers. 2005. "Continued Archaeological Investigations at Grand Bay, Carriacou, West Indies (May 23rd–July 22nd, 2005), and the Impact of Hurricanes and Other Erosive Processes." *Papers from the Institute of Archaeology* 16: 108–14.

Oliver, J. R. 1998. *El Centro ceremonial de Caguana, Puerto Rico: Simbolismo itiosnary, itiosnary y el itios caciquil Taino de Boriquen.* Oxford: Archaeopress.

See also Archaeological Heritage Management; Barbados; Geoinformatics; The Jamaica National Heritage Trust.

Rock Art

Michele H. Hayward and Michael A. Cinquino

Definition and Distribution

Rock art in the form of petroglyphs (carved images) and pictographs (painted designs) is found on a number of different rock surfaces throughout the Caribbean island arc and on near-continental landforms. Amerindians executed most of this substantial body of visual expression, with native and African groups continuing to produce this art into the early historic period on certain islands, including Cuba and Hispaniola. Although geoglyphs and large-scale rock arrangements have not been reported, small-scale compositions and rock layouts for astronomical observation may have been constructed. The region's rock art exhibits a high percentage of anthropomorphic or human-like images as well as a high degree of assemblage variability. The latter suggests that image-makers selected from a common canon of figure elements, motifs, and layouts to affect design sets for particular places, times, and events.

Anthropomorphic images, including human-animal combinations, range from minimal facial features to fully detailed head and body figures. Unenclosed, partial, or fully enclosed facial elements rendered as pits, dashes, and ovals that are interpreted as eyes and mouths make up a significant design category (Figures R.1A, B). Facial elaboration is also common, involving the addition of internal and external features that include noses, ears, enclosed eyes and mouths, rays above and below the face, headdresses, and multiple enclosures (Figure R.1C, D). Attached body forms frequently include simple outlines, stick figures, and enclosed images in which the torso either lacks or has diverse internal design features that lack appendages or indicate enfolded arms and legs (Figure R.1E). Fully detailed figures, though rare, normally display complex heads and torsos with arms, hands, legs, feet, and sex indicated (Figure R.1F). Zoomorphs, which are often rendered realistically, include birds, fishes, bats, owls, turtles, snakes, and spiders (Figure R.2A, B), while geometric and abstract designs include spirals, crosses, and varying arrangements of lines, circles, and pits (Figure R.2C, D).

Characterizations of the images and sites are ongoing, as systematic site surveys and documentation efforts for the Lesser and Greater Antilles are incomplete. The continued discovery of rock art sites is likely to alter our current understanding of these visual remains and their patterns of distribution. At present, rock art is found on all the major islands of the Greater Antilles

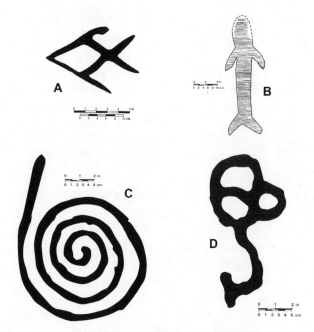

Figure R.2. Zoomorphic and geometric images from Puerto Rican rock art sites. *A*, fish petroglyph, Maisabel, beach rock. Reprinted from Roe (1991). *B*, shark pictograph, Cueva de Mora. Reprinted from Roe, Meléndez, and DeScioli (1999). *C–D*, spiral and abstract petroglyphs, La Piedra Escrita, river boulder. Reprinted from Hayward, Meléndez, and Ramos Vélez (1992b).

and tends to be found only on islands greater than 85 square kilometers in the Lesser Antilles. Image numbers per site vary from one to the low hundreds for petroglyphs and into the low thousands for pictographs. Sites can be found at five general locations: caves and rock shelters, waterways, open-air rock formations, ball courts, and beach rocks. Sites and images are not evenly distributed throughout the region; particular islands have higher concentrations of image numbers or images at particular locations. For example, petroglyphs are almost exclusive to the Lesser Antilles, while pictographs predominate on the near-continental islands of Aruba, Bonaire, and Curaçao.

Dating

Opportunities for the direct dating of petroglyphs or pictographs remain rare in a Caribbean context. Instead, advancement in chronological control has largely come through the integration of indirectly dated sites based on dateable associated materials, sites, and similar rock art assemblages and through the development of local and regional relative frameworks. Even though issues such as contemporaneity, where multiple occupational phases are present at or near rock art sites, and validity, where

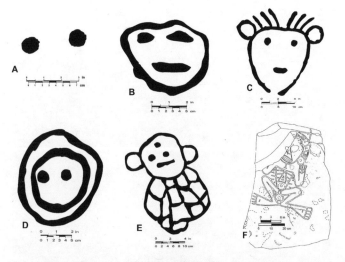

Figure R.1. Anthropomorphic petroglyphs from Puerto Rican rock art sites. *A*, Río Guacio, river boulder. Reprinted from Hayward, Meléndez, and Ramos Vélez (1992a). *B*, Cueva del Indio; *C*, Quebrada Maracuto, river boulder; *D–E*, Piedra Escrita, river boulder. Reprinted from Hayward, Meléndez, and Ramos Vélez (1992b). *F*, Jácana, ball court slab. Reprinted from Loubser et al. (2010).

datable elements from different rock art assemblages are unclear, may affect the soundness of these approaches, certain chronological statements can nonetheless be made. Rock art was executed during three broadly defined periods: the Preceramic (7500/4000–400/250 BC), the Ceramic (400/250 BC–AD 1500) and the early historic (AD 1500). Primary production occurred during the Ceramic period, and a discontinuous pattern is suggested or present in many areas.

Rock art linked to Preceramic Archaic period groups is found in the Greater Antillean islands of Cuba and Hispaniola and the islands of Aruba, Bonaire, and Curaçao. The emphasis in these assemblages is on geometric and abstract pictograph designs. The succeeding major migration into the region of Early Ceramic Saladoid populations was apparently not marked by the immediate production of rock art. Two proposed relative dating frameworks place the start of rock art near the end of the Early Ceramic (400 BC–AD 300/500) for the Lesser Antilles and at the beginning of the Late Ceramic (AD 600–1500) for the Greater Antilles. Ceramic period rock art assemblages display an increased emphasis on petroglyphs and a diverse range of forms and elaboration. Chronological refinement is ongoing as new sites become known and as dating frameworks are tested.

Interpretation

Examples of interpretation in the literature vary from simple identifications and descriptions of figures to well-developed proposals about the roles and functions of particular rock art assemblages or rock art in general. Interpretations normally rest on a combination of ethnohistoric accounts of natives at European contact (especially Taíno groups), ethnographic analogies from the culturally cognate lowland South American natives, and theoretical approaches from the fields of archaeology and allied disciplines. While rock art is frequently considered to have functioned primarily in the religious sphere, the images most likely had multiple meanings and roles in intersecting sociopolitical, economic, and religious contexts.

The proposed functions of rock art include the theory that the images regulated mythic or actual earthly extremes in cases where the location of the rock art identifies which extremes or opposing states were involved. Rock art located near water sources may have been intended to protect humans from too much water (floods) or too little water (droughts), while figures in caves may have been intended to mediate the multiple opposing states of male and dry exterior from female and humid interior. Rock art at ball courts or plazas may have provided a visual reinforcement of stone alignments that partitioned interior sacred space from the everyday exterior world. Images located on the boundaries of islands delimit the dry world of land from the wet world of the ocean.

The images have also been conceived as one class of objects that possess cemí, or spiritual potency. Certain spiritual forces and entities might make known their character or their presence to humans in a number of ways that would require their transformation into a variety of media that included ceramics, shells, and the rock surfaces of boulders, caves and ball courts. Carved and painted figures that were imbued with cemí potency were more than mere representations; they were transformed into active and engaged members of the spirit world who interacted with the living.

Rock art has also played an important role in forming the boundaries of ethnicities and groups. Prehistoric petroglyphs and pictographs at particular cave locations on Puerto Rico exhibit a discrete spatial and stylistic pattern. Petroglyphs are located at the entrances to the cave systems, while larger and more detailed pictographs are located in the central chambers. Researchers have theorized that the petroglyphs acted as outer guardians and supplicants to the inner and primary pictographs. Within the emerging ranked sociopolitical order of the Late Ceramic, this pattern may have reflected status differences; the outer, more accessible petroglyphs may have been available to commoners and the inner central pictographs may have been reserved for the elite. Rock art continues to function to form ethnic boundaries in modern Puerto Rican and Dominican societies that use actual or reinterpreted design elements and forms taken from the Late Ceramic—particularly petroglyphs, pictographs, and large-scale sculptures—to symbolize the native foundation of their tri-partite Spanish-, Native-, and African-formed cultures. The new designs and forms are found on a variety of popular artisan objects, prominent public murals, and civic monuments.

Preservation

As with other site types in the Caribbean, rock art is under pressure from development, vandalism, and natural processes of weathering and decay. The knowledge that rock art sites are arresting visual elements on the landscape and are critical for our understanding of past cultural development within the region is increasing.

Site preservation has become a priority for the region's researchers, and a number of sites have been listed as national monuments and are owned or managed by governmental agencies. Future efforts should include site surveys and assessments for the purpose of conservation and the establishment of new or the strengthening of existing conservation laws that specifically target rock art sites.

Further Reading

Dubelaar, C. N. 1995. *The Petroglyphs of the Lesser Antilles, the Virgin Islands, and Trinidad.* Amsterdam: Foundation for Scientific Research in the Caribbean.

Haviser, J. B., and M. Strecker. 2006. "Caribbean Area and North-Coastal South American." In *Rock Art of Latin American and the Caribbean*, 43–83. Paris: International Council on Monuments and Sites.

Hayward, M. H., L. Atkinson, and M. A. Cinquino. 2009. *Rock Art of the Caribbean.* Tuscaloosa: University of Alabama Press.

Hayward, Michele H., Marisol J. Meléndez, and Marlene Ramos Vélez. 1992a. *Informe final. Documentación del sitio LM-4 arte rupestre, Río Guacio, Las Marías.* San Juan: División de Arqueología, Instituto de Cultura Puertorriqueña.

———. 1992b. *Informe preliminar I. Documentación de tres sities de arte rupestre: Piedra Escrita, Jayuya; Cueva del Indio, Las Piedras; Quebrada Maracuto, Carolina.* División de Arqueología, Instituto de Cultura Puertorriqueña, San Juan, Puerto Rico.

Loubser, Johannes, Eva Yi-Hua Weng, Christopher T. Espenshade, and Hernan Bustelo. 2010. "Batey Borders/Rock Art," in "The Cultural Landscape of Jacana: Archaeological Investigations of Site P0-29, Municipio de Ponce, Puerto Rico (Draft Report)," compiled by Christopher T. Espenshade. New South Associates, Stone Mountain, Georgia, submitted to Jacksonville District, U.S. Army Corps of Engineers, Jacksonville, Florida.

Roe, Peter G. 1991. "The Petroglyphs of Maisabel: A Study in Methodology." In *Proceedings of the Twelfth Congress of the International Association for Caribbean Archaeology,* ed. Linda S. Robinson, 317–70. Martinique: A.I.A.C.

Roe, Peter G., José Rivera Meléndez, and Peter DeScioli. 1999. "The Cueva de Mora (Comerío, PR) Petroglyphs & Pictographs: A Documentary Project." In *Proceedings of the Seventeenth Congress of the International Association for Caribbean Archaeology,* ed. John H. Winter, 20–59. Rockville Centre, NY: Molloy College.

Sanz, Nuria. 2008. *Rock Art in the Caribbean: Towards a Serial Transnational Nomination to the UNESCO World Heritage List.* World Heritage Papers no. 24. Paris: UNESCO World Heritage Centre.

Stevens-Arroyo, A. M. 1988. *Cave of the Jagua: The Mythological World of the Taínos.* Albuquerque: University of New Mexico Press.

See also Bonaire (Dutch Caribbean; Former Netherlands Antilles); Curaçao (Former Netherlands Antilles); Plazas and *Bateys*; *Zemíes* (*Cemís*).

Roth, Vincent (1889–1967)

Mark G. Plew and Jennifer Wishart

Vincent Roth, the son of Walter E. Roth, was born in 1889 in Australia and was educated in Tasmania. He followed his father to British Guiana in 1907. After working as a newspaper reporter, he began work as a surveyor and the warden/magistrate for the Department of Lands and Mines, a position he held for some twenty-five years. During this time, he offered proposals regarding development of the Guyanese interior. From 1919 to 1962, he published a number of papers and short notes on Amerindian arts and crafts, most notably, papers on basketry, bead making, and celts. In addition, he published *Tales from the Trails* (1960), a personal account of his experiences in Guyana. Roth's most lasting contribution was the rebuilding of the Guyana Agricultural and Historical Society following the Georgetown fire of 1945 and the founding of the national zoo. Following his death in 1967, his diaries were edited by his son-in-law, Michael Bennett. They appeared in two volumes as *Vincent Roth, A Life in Guyana. Volume 1: A Young Man's Journey, 1889–1922* and *Volume 2: The Later Years, 1922–1936.*

Roth, Walter E. (1861–1933)

Mark G. Plew and Jennifer Wishart

Walter Roth was born in England in 1861. Though he trained as a physician, Roth served for many years as a colonial administrator in Australia and Guyana. He was appointed Northern Protector of Aborigines in 1898 and assumed the position of Chief Protector in 1904. In this capacity, Roth authored a series of bulletins on North Queensland ethnography in the period 1901–1906. In 1906, he was named protector of Indians in the Pomeroon district of British Guiana. During his time as an administrator, he wrote and published extensively on Amerindian culture and lifeways, including papers pertaining to animism, folklore, medicinal practices, and linguistics. His most noted works include: *An Introduction to the Study of Arts, Crafts, and Customs of Guiana Indians* (1924) and *Additional Studies of the Arts, Crafts, and Customs of Guiana Indians with Special Reference to those of Southern Guyana* (1929), which were published as Bulletins 38 and 91 of the Bureau of American Ethnology. Roth also undertook the first study of prehistoric ceramics in the Northwest district. Following his retirement from government service in 1928, he served as curator of the Museum of the Royal Agricultural and Commercial Society and as a government archivist. The Walter Roth Museum of Anthropology in Georgetown, Guyana, is named in his honor.

Further Reading

McDougall, R., and I. Davidson. 2008. *The Roth Family, Anthropology, and Colonial Administration*. Walnut Creek: Left Coast Press.

Rouse, Benjamin Irving (1913–2006)

Basil A. Reid and Roger H. Colten

Benjamin Irving Rouse, a pioneer in Caribbean archaeology, helped identify the origin of the indigenous people and the general prehistoric chronology of the region (Figure R.3). Rouse's stellar career was characterized by the publication of many books and articles on Caribbean archaeology and on general archaeological theory. Rouse's most notable publications include *Prehistory in Haiti: A Study in Method* (1939), *Introduction to Prehistory: A Systematic Approach* (1972), *Migrations in Prehistory: Inferring Population Movement from Cultural Remains* (1986), and *Excavations at Maria De La Cruz Cave and Hacienda Grande Village Site (Loiza, Puerto Rico)* (1990). His most recent major publications were *The Tainos: Rise and Decline of the People Who Greeted Columbus* (1992) and (with Birgit Faber-Morse) *Excavations at the Indian Creek Site, Antigua, West Indies* (1999).

Rouse was born in Rochester, New York, in 1913. He began his career at Yale University in 1930 as an undergraduate in plant science and switched to archaeology while a student employee of the Anthropology Division of the Peabody Museum of Natural History. Rouse changed his academic focus partly due to financial reasons; in the aftermath of the 1929 stock market collapse, his bank failed and he lost all his money. Rouse took a variety of jobs on campus, but eventually Cornelius Osgood hired him to catalog archaeological collections in the Peabody Museum. He completed his BS in plant science in 1934 and his PhD in anthropology in 1938, after which he joined the faculty in anthropology and became a member of the Peabody Museum staff.

In college, Ben Rouse had been drawn toward taxonomy in botany, a mature field of study, but he shifted to the much younger discipline of anthropology in part because he saw a more urgent need for classification there. "As I look back," he said, "I am impressed by the fact that archaeology by the 1960s had reached the same state of maturity in classification that biology had reached when I was an undergraduate only 30 years earlier" (Siegel

Figure R.3. Benjamin Irving Rouse. Reproduced by permission of the Division of Anthropology, Yale Peabody Museum.

1996, 672). Professor Rouse himself was largely responsible for that transformation. His breadth of perspective equipped him to devise ways of organizing archaeological evidence that would serve researchers and theorists well for many years.

Professor Rouse quickly became a pioneer in circum-Caribbean archaeology and a major contributor to the development of archaeological methods, particularly the analysis, typology, and chronology of ceramics. Many of Rouse's students completed investigations in the Caribbean that complemented the early projects of Yale's Caribbean Archaeology Program, and some of them acquired collections that are now housed at the Peabody Museum. Some of these students were Robert Howard (who did a survey in Jamaica), Marshall McKusick (who worked on Saint Lucia), Paul Hahn (who excavated in Cuba), and Louis Allaire (who worked in Martinique).

A firm believer in cultural history (the reconstruction of the history of peoples through detailed cultural data such as ceramics and lithics), Rouse developed a time-space systematics for the Caribbean that used characteristic modes of pottery at a site to identify a style that usually bore the name of the first site at which it was described. For example, "Saladoid" was named after

the site of Saladero in Venezuela, where its pottery characteristics were first described. Local pottery styles that shared sufficient similarities were grouped into subseries (denoted by an -an suffix), and subseries were grouped into series (denoted by an -oid suffix). The concept of subseries was first proposed by Gary S. Vescelius, the territorial archaeologist for the United States Virgin Islands, in 1980. Rouse used this classification to identify peoples and cultures, which in his view were two sides of the same coin, one consisting of a local population group and the other of the cultural traits that define the group. For example, Ostionoid is the name of a series and Meillacan and Ostionan are the names of subseries within the Ostionoid series. Rouse recognized that while it might have been possible to name certain Caribbean cultural groups that existed at the time of European contact (such as the Taíno of the northern Caribbean), it was virtually impossible to accurately name cultural groups that existed deep in time. Therefore, his series and subseries were designed to bring order to the classification of pre-Columbian peoples and cultures in the Caribbean.

Despite minor adjustments through the years, this system of classification remains an intrinsic part of scholarly research in the Caribbean to this day. In subsequent years Rouse and José M. Cruxent extended this Caribbean chronological scheme to embrace the several archaeological regions of Venezuela, a scheme that was subsequently validated by radiocarbon dates (Rouse and Cruxent 1963).

During his field expeditions to Trinidad in 1946 and 1953, Rouse visited the Archaic (Ortoiroid) sites of St. John and Ortoire, the Ceramic Age (Saladoid) sites of Cedros and Palo Seco, the Ceramic Age (Barrancoid) site of Erin, the Ceramic Age (Arauquinoid) site of Bontour, and the Ceramic Age (Mayoid) sites of St. Joseph and Mayo. His archaeological expeditions in Trinidad led to the creation of a number of series and subseries for the wider Caribbean, for example Ortoiroid (named after Ortoire in eastern Trinidad) and Cedros (named after Cedros in southwestern Trinidad). Rouse also produced some publications on Trinidad's archaeology, including the notable *Prehistory of Trinidad in Relation to Adjacent Areas* (1947).

From an archaeological standpoint, Rouse did for the Caribbean what Donald Lathrap did for the Amazon—he brought scholarly attention to a region that was considered peripheral to mainstream archaeology in the New World. While inordinate focus was being placed on the so-called high cultures of the Mayas and Aztecs of Central America, the Incas of Peru, and the large chiefdom societies of the American southeast and southwest,

Irving Rouse dared to concentrate his academic energies on the "inconspicuous" yet important pre-Columbian societies of the Caribbean. Willey and Sabloff (1993) described his contributions to modern archaeological theory in great detail in their discussion of the classificatory-historical period in American archaeology.

In honor of his unswerving dedication to service, Irving Rouse was the recipient of many prestigious awards, including the Viking Fund Medal of the Wenner-Gren Foundation for Anthropological Research in 1960, the Franz Boas Award for Exemplary Service to Anthropology in 1984, and an award from the International Association for Caribbean Archaeology in 1995. He was a member of the National Academy of Sciences, held important roles in national anthropological and archaeological organizations, and helped found the Archaeological Society of Connecticut.

Rouse was affiliated with Yale University and the Peabody Museum of Natural History throughout his more than 70-year academic career. At various times from 1938 through his retirement in 1984, Professor Rouse was curator, assistant curator, research associate, and faculty affiliate of the Peabody Museum. Rouse held an academic appointment in the Department of Anthropology at Yale University from 1939 until he retired in 1984.

Rouse continued to correspond and meet with scholars and students throughout his life, even after retirement. He was the principal investigator for the Peabody Museum's first grant-funded project to create an electronic database of its anthropology catalog records, a project that began in 1993 and served as the foundation for the anthropology division's collections management and publicly searchable databases.

Further Reading

Keegan, W. F. 2009. *Benjamin Irving Rouse (1913–2006): A Biographical Memoir.* Washington, DC: National Academies Press.

Rouse, I. 1947. "Prehistory of Trinidad in Relation to Adjacent Areas." *MAN* old series 47 (103): 93–98.

———. 1992. *The Tainos: Rise and Decline of the People Who Greeted Columbus.* New Haven, CT: Yale University Press.

Rouse, I., and J. M. Cruxent. 1963. *Venezuelan Archaeology.* New Haven, CT: Yale University Press.

Siegel, Peter F. 1996. "An Interview with Irving Rouse." *Current Anthropology* 37 (4): 671–89.

Willey, G. R., and J. A. Sabloff. 1993. *A History of American Archaeology.* New York: W. H. Freeman.

See also The Florida Museum of Natural History; The Peabody Museum of Natural History (Yale University); Trinidad and Tobago.

Rum

Frederick H. Smith

Rum has been a key commodity of Caribbean economies and an integral part of modern Caribbean identities. Historical archaeologists have investigated the production, transport, consumption, and use of rum at a number of Caribbean sites. This work has helped shed light on the contributions rum made to the emerging Atlantic economy and to the social lives of Caribbean peoples. Alcohol distillation was known in Europe as early as the 1200s. The first distillers were physicians and apothecaries who distilled spirits for medicinal purposes. The large-scale commercial distillation of alcohol expanded globally in the mid-seventeenth century, driven, in part, by the expansion of sugar production in the Caribbean, which provided an enormous amount of base material (molasses) for local Caribbean distillers and distillers in Europe and North America.

Historical archaeologists have investigated rum distilling at a number of sites in the Caribbean. For example, Conrad Goodwin (1994) surveyed Betty's Hope Plantation, an eighteenth- and early nineteenth-century sugar estate in Antigua, and recorded the central placement of the estate's rum distillery in the larger sugar plantation complex. Betty's Hope had an unusual double windmill system that underscores the immense scale of sugar production on the estate. The low elevation at which the windmills were set, however, probably required workers to develop a complex system of troughs and gutters for getting the freshly squeezed sugarcane juice to the sugar cauldrons and fermentation vats in the main factory. Indeed, the process of rum distilling and the layout of the natural terrain dictated the location of structures on Caribbean sugar estates. For example, at St. Nicholas Abbey Plantation in Barbados, the estate owner constructed the main factory downhill from the estate's windmill so that the sugar-cane juice squeezed from the rollers in the windmill could flow quickly and easily down gutters into the estate's copper sugar boilers and fermentation vats (Smith 2008). In Tobago, Christopher Clement conducted an extensive survey of sugar estates in the island and recorded details about the location of rum distilleries on the plantation landscapes. According to Clement, the need for water, a key ingredient of rum-making, determined the placement of sugar factories on plantations in Tobago. Clement wrote, "Of the 22 sugar factories encountered during the survey, 19 were located adjacent to a water source sufficient to provide water for rum production. . . . This reliance on water for rum-making resulted in the confinement of factories to valley bottoms, broad vales, or locations that could be reached by canal in areas of high topographic relief" (Clement 1997, 95).

Archaeological and architectural surveys of sugar estates in the Caribbean have produced plan drawings of plantation boiling houses and rum distilleries. Rum distilleries have also been investigated at colonial and post-revolutionary sites in North America, where rum was produced from imported Caribbean molasses. Unlike the factory-in-the-field operations found in the Caribbean, rum distilling in early North America, especially in New York and New England, was an urban industrial enterprise.

Rum also played a crucial role both the social and spiritual lives of Caribbean peoples, and historical archaeologists have examined these uses of rum in the region. In particular, researchers have interpreted the presence of glass and stoneware bottle fragments at the dwelling sites of enslaved peoples in the Caribbean as evidence of alcohol drinking. In Jamaica, the large number of glass and stoneware bottle shards recovered from an area of the enslaved village at Drax Hall Plantation indicated that one structure at the site was probably the remains of a "village bar or liquor shop" (Douglas 1990, 135).

A historical archaeological study of Mapps Cave, a cavern and sinkhole complex in rural Barbados that was used by enslaved peoples from the seventeenth to the nineteenth centuries, found that alcohol-related materials were a significant proportion of the site's artifact assemblage and indicated that rum drinking was one of the primary activities that occurred at the site. Drawing on the work of alcohol studies researchers, Frederick Smith (2008) argued that Mapps Cave, a liminal space on the plantation landscape, provided a temporary refuge from the rigors of plantation life for enslaved peoples from surrounding sugar estates and that the use of alcohol at Mapps Cave enhanced those feelings of escape.

Theresa Singleton (2006) contends that bottle glass recovered from the El Padre village of enslaved people in Cuba was evidence that enslaved peoples at the site were engaged in illicit alcohol consumption. In Montserrat, a Turlington Balsam of Life bottle recovered from the Harney slave burial ground may have once contained rum and may been a grave good buried with one of the individuals interred at the site. Although a number of historical documents refer to the placement of bottles filled with alcoholic beverages in the graves of deceased slaves, the Harney cemetery represents the strongest archaeological evidence to date of such practices. The detrimental effects of rum are also evident in the archaeological record. Jerome Handler et al. (1986) found evidence of lead toxicity in the human skeletal remains of enslaved peoples buried at Newton Plantation, Barbados, from the seventeenth through the nineteenth centuries. According to Handler and colleagues, enslaved people in Barbados were frequently exposed to lead, but the particular cause of lead toxicity in this enslaved population may have been the consumption of rum that was tainted by lead during the distilling process.

Further Reading

Armstrong, Douglas. 1990. *The Old Village and the Great House: An Archaeological and Historical Examination of Drax Hall Plantation, St. Ann's Bay, Jamaica*. Urbana: University of Illinois Press.

Clement, C. O. 1997. "Settlement Patterning on the British Caribbean Island of Tobago." *Historical Archaeology* 31 (2): 93–106.

Goodwin, C. M. 1994. "Betty's Hope Windmill: An Unexpected Problem." *Historical Archaeology* 28 (1): 99–110.

Handler, J. S., A. C. Aufderheide, R. S. Corruccini, E. M. Brandon, and L. E. Wittmers Jr. 1986. "Lead Contact and Poisoning in Barbados Slaves: Historical, Chemical, and Biological Evidence." *Social Science History* 10 (4): 399–425.

Singleton, T. A. 2006. "African Diaspora Archaeology in Dialogue." In *Afro-Atlantic Dialogues: Anthropology in the Diaspora*, ed. K. Yelvington, 249–87. Santa Fe, NM: SAR Press.

Smith, F. H. 2008. *The Archaeology of Alcohol and Drinking*. Gainesville: University Press of Florida.

See also Betty's Hope Plantation (Antigua); Bottles (Colonial); Newton Burial Ground (Barbados).

S

Saba

Corinne L. Hofman and Menno L. P. Hoogland

In 1923, Dutch anthropologist J. P. B. de Josselin de Jong, then a curator at the Leiden Museum of Ethnology, was the first to conduct archaeological excavations on the island of Saba, at The Bottom. In the 1980s, Jay Haviser made an inventory of the precolonial and colonial sites of Saba as part of a survey of the islands of the Netherlands Antilles by the Archaeological-Anthropological Institute of the Netherlands Antilles. Using this work as a point of departure, Leiden University carried out excavations from 1987 to 2006 at the sites of Spring Bay, Kelbey's Ridge, The Bottom, and Plum Piece.

As on many other islands in the Lesser Antilles, many isolated stone tools dating to the Archaic age are known from the interior mountainous parts of the island of Saba. The small campsite of Plum Piece, which dates to 3883–3528 BP, is situated in the northwestern part of the island. Remains at the site suggest that hunter-fisher-gatherers occupied the site seasonally. The surface area of the site is around 200 square meters and has been preserved, in part, by slope wash, which covered archaeological deposit(s). These deposits were found after a local farmer began planting crops in the area. A dense midden and a number of archaeological features suggest that the area was used intensively at least 3,500 years ago. The midden consists of a thick layer of unusually well-preserved food remains. Multifunctional tools appear to have been repeatedly abandoned in the midden as well. A clear phase of abandonment marks the end of the occupation. During this phase, grinding stones, shell, coral, and ground stone tools were deposited on top of the midden layer. In addition, a number of shallow postholes, stake holes, and pits were uncovered, pointing to the construction of light wooden shelters.

The Plum Piece midden is rich in mountain crab (*Gecarcinus ruricola*) remains, bird bones (particularly Audubon's shearwater [*Puffinus lherminieri*]), and pelagic and reef fish (chiefly *Epinephelus* sp., *Acanthurus* sp., *Lutjanus* sp., *Sparisoma* sp., and *Haemulon* sp.). Mollusks are virtually absent, but the meat of conchs

(*Strombus* or *Lobatus gigas*) may have been extracted down at the beach at Well's Bay in order to supplement the diet. Adzes made of conch shell have been used to work wood, probably for making canoes. Antigua flint, which is abundantly present at the site and is used to cut plants, provides evidence of the existence of an early network for procuring raw materials. The seasonal diet and the toolkit of the campsite at Plum Piece suggest that the site was occupied contemporaneously with coastal sites of surrounding islands.

There is a settlement gap on Saba, as it is not until 1400 BP that sites such as Spring Bay and Kelbey's Ridge, both situated in the northeastern part of Saba, were inhabited by the Saladoid people. Around 1000 BP, early native settlements on Saba increased and locales such as St. Johns and The Bottom became inhabited. During this time, all sites on Saba are characterized by Mamoran Troumassoid pottery and the presence of exotic lithic materials such as Antigua flint, St. Martin greenstone, calcirudite, and jadeite. This suggests that at that time the inhabitants of Saba were part of a dynamic web of social relationships that included a wide range of communities on neighboring islands.

At about 800 BP, Saba may have become a vital hinge in the network that linked the chiefdoms, or *cacicazgos*, of the Greater Antilles with those of the South American mainland. The island's steep topography and its rich fishing grounds at the Saba Bank must have attracted many seafarers. Excavations at Kelbey's Ridge have uncovered features relating to a number of small round wooden dwellings. The dead were buried under the floors of houses. There are indications that the grave pit was left open after the deposition of the dead and that bones were taken away when the body was desiccated. These bones (often long bones or skulls) were probably used in ritual practices, underscoring the exceptional ties the island inhabitants had with their ancestors. Early chronicles also mention this custom among the early seventeenth-century Island-Carib of the Lesser Antil-

Figure S.1. Manatee bone snuff inhaler from the Kelbey's Ridge site, Saba (AD 1350–1450). Excavations by Corinne Hofman and Menno Hoogland 1989. Photo by Jan Pauptit.

les. The dead were buried with ritual paraphernalia such as a snuff tube in the shape of a fish. The fish is made of manatee bone (*T. m. manatus*) and has a y-shaped connection between the mouth and the gills. A powder made from the seeds of the hallucinogenic cohoba (*Anadenanthera peregrina*) was inhaled through hollow bird bones (Figure S.1).

Strontium isotope analysis shows that the individuals at this site had heterogeneous origins, suggesting that the inhabitants of Kelbey's Ridge came to Saba at an adult age to found the settlement. Material culture remains show affiliations with the Chican Ostionoid subseries of the Greater Antilles, an indication that the late prehistoric Saban may have come from the larger islands to the north in a period when the Greater Antillean *cacicazgos* were expanding. The large amounts of fish waste in the settlement, which were found in a number of large hearths, indicate that the villagers at Kelbey's Ridge were involved in intensive fishery. The predominance of pelagic species points to the exploitation of the Saba Bank, and the extensive drying and smoking of fish at the settlement could be an indication of the site's importance in regional exchange networks. The settlement at Kelbey's Ridge was abandoned around AD 1400, providing us with an end date of precolonial occupation of the island. Kelbey's Ridge is also the location where the remains of the earliest colonial occupation of the island were found.

Leiden University is also excavating at the abandoned village site of Mary's Point, which was occupied from the eighteenth century until the 1920s. Over a dozen house sites have been identified. The material culture and site location of these houses indicate clear status levels. Furthermore, excavations are currently going on at the small free black village of Middle Island and the plantation sites of Flat Point and Spring Bay Flat. In 2011, a joint project by the Sint Maarten Archaeological Center (under Jay Haviser) and the St. Eustatius Center for Archaeological Research (under Grant Gilmore) exhumed and reburied five nineteenth- and twentieth-century burials on the windward side. The excavations revealed an interesting burial custom whereby flat stones were used to construct an underground burial vault. Cracks between the stones were chinked with clay and mud, sealing the chambers so that they replicated a cave environment for the skeletons.

Further Reading

Espersen, R. 2009. "From Folklore to Folk History: Contextualizing Settlement at Palmetto Point, Saba, Dutch Caribbean." RMA thesis, Leiden University.

Haviser, J. B. 2001. "Historical Archaeology in the Netherlands Antilles and Aruba." In *Island Lives: Historical Archaeologies of the Caribbean*, ed. P. Farnsworth, 60–81. Tuscaloosa: University of Alabama Press.

Hofman, C. L. 2007. "The Caribbean: Lesser Antilles." In *Encyclopedia of Archaeology*, vol. 3, ed. D. M. Pearsall. Amsterdam: Elsevier.

Hofman, C. L., A. J. Bright, and M. L. P. Hoogland. 2006. "Archipelagic Resource Mobility, Shedding Light on the 3,000-Year-Old Campsite at Plum Piece, Saba (Northern Lesser Antilles)." *Journal of Island and Coastal Archaeology* 1 (2): 145–64.

Hofman, C. L., and M. L. P. Hoogland. 2003. "Plum Piece: Evidence for Archaic Seasonal Occupation on Saba, Northern Lesser Antilles around 3300 BP." *Journal of Caribbean Archaeology* 4: 12–27.

Hoogland, M. L. P., and C. L. Hofman. 1999. "Taino Expansion towards the Lesser Antilles: The Case of Saba." *Journal des Américanistes* 85: 93–113.

See also The Dutch Caribbean.

Saint Lucia

Corinne L. Hofman

Saint Lucia played a central role in the earliest systematic study of Caribbean prehistory. The Saint Lucia Archaeological and Historical Society was one of the first heritage organizations in the islands, and it still functions today as the main archaeological authority on Saint Lucia. It cooperates with other organizations such as the Saint Lucia National Trust and the Saint Lucia National Archives. Despite its early role in stimulating archaeological research in the West Indies, very little formal archaeological work has been conducted on the island in the past twenty-five years. Notable exceptions include research undertaken by researchers from the University of Vienna in the 1980s at the precolonial site of Saltibus Point and the historical archaeology excavation at the Balenbouche Estate by Dan Hicks. Prior to these, the last major field investigations were conducted by Marshall B. McKusick in 1956 and 1957 and Ripley and Adelaide Bullen in the 1970s.

The last major summary of Saint Lucia's archaeology was written by Rev. C. Jesse in 1960 and revised in 1968. From 2002 to 2004, a team that included representatives from Leiden University and the Florida Museum of Natural History, Gainesville, carried out an extensive survey project in southern Saint Lucia in an effort to develop a more complete understanding of the precolonial settlement history of Saint Lucia. In 2009, rescue excavations were conducted by the same team at the site of Lavoutte on the northeast coast of the island. Increased land erosion over the years has had a negative impact on the remains of the prehistoric Lavoutte community. Fieldwork was done to salvage information from the most vulnerable parts of the site and to expand on previous knowledge of this aspect of Saint Lucian history.

Archaeologically, Saint Lucia can be divided into three main areas: the interior, the leeward coast, and the windward coast. The interior is very densely vegetated and therefore very difficult to prospect. Only a few precolonial sites are known from that area. Most of the known sites are situated along the coast or along rivers. Approximately 159 precolonial sites have been inventoried to date. Among the major known sites on the island are Grande Anse, Giraudy, Troumassée, Lavoutte, Comerette Point, and Pigeon Island. The Saint Lucia Archaeological and Historical Society continues to add archaeological sites to the island's inventory as they are

discovered. It also provides excellent care of archaeological collections recovered on the island.

Early work on the island established a chronological sequence that is still in use today. The sequence starts with Rouse's Period IIb (AD 150), which includes the Cedrosan Saladoid subseries. Cedrosan ceramics are characterized by their thinness, hardness, and overall quality. This highly decorative series is found at the site of Grande Anse, among others. A Troumassoid series, divided into Troumassée A and B, follows the Cedrosan Saladoid series during period IIIa (AD 350) and a late Troumassée during period IIIb (AD 750). Troumassoid ceramics are thick with relatively soft, grit-tempered paste that splits rather easily. Vessel shapes are varied and include boat shapes, kidney shapes, and pedestal, bottomless, double, hemispherical, and inverted bell-shaped bowls. Rims tend to be thickened with a variety of forms that include flanges and rim bevels. Painted decoration is common, including bichromes and polychromes with red, white, and black. Some modeled-incised motifs are present. Over time, the painted decoration disappeared, as did fine-line cross-hatching. Tripod griddles were introduced in the Troumassoid, and modeled-incised decorations became more elaborate. The type site for the Troumassoid series is the site at Troumassée River. Period IV (AD 1150) is characterized by a Micoid series, which includes Choc and Fannis style ceramics. Dominant characteristics of the Micoid series are the introduction of leg bases, clay pestles, and a construction that is thick and crude. Decoration tends to be garish, and heavy incised lines and complicated model-incised lugs, often with human figures, are typical. Red paint is common and bichrome is rare. Finger-notched rims become predominant in the later phase of the series. The Choc style is named after the site with the same name in the northwestern part of the island, and Fannis is named after the proprietor of a property at Micoud.

The Late Ceramic Age site of Lavoutte (AD 1000–1500) has been known to local governmental and historical authorities and (through reports of previous research) to the international archaeological community for a number of decades. The site is situated on the northern side of the bay of Cas-en-Bas, Saint Lucia, and was discovered by Harold Devaux and Mr. B. H. Easter of the Saint Lucia Archaeological and Historical Society in 1958. The site's midden was extensively excavated by the Bullens in collaboration with Eric Branford of the Saint Lucia Archaeological and Historical Society. During the 1980s, a small scale excavation was carried out by the University of Vienna under Dr. Hedwig Friesinger that uncovered three human burials. The site is especially known for the famous Lavoutte statue, to which some scholar attribute Taíno influences.

The construction of a hotel in the bay and increased tourist activity in the area has accelerated land erosion and uncovered skeletal remains of numerous individuals in the eastern part of the site, south of the Bullens' excavations. The excavations revealed a habitation area in the southern part of the site where structures and burials were found and a garbage dump to the north that also has a few burials underneath it. The size of the dump is estimated as 350 square meters and is comprised of refuse material at a depth of more than 40 centimeters, covered by a layer of large broken pots of the Suazan Troumassoid subseries. Other ceramic artifacts include loom weights, spindle whorls, body stamps, and fragments of figurines. In addition, artifacts of shell, coral, and stone found in the garbage dump include celts, grinders, axes, and ceremonial paraphernalia. The lithic assemblage consists of a variety of local rock types.

The habitation area is distinguished by a number of features such as postholes and cooking features that indicate the presence of a house and auxiliary structures. It also features a large number of burials. Both the diameter and size of the posts suggest the construction of fairly heavy structures that offered protection from the heavy Atlantic winds. The carbonized core of some posts and evidence of a burned house floor suggest that the structures were burned. A few postholes still contained remains of wood. In the southern part of the excavation, an area with burned patches of clay was uncovered; these were interpreted as burned house floors. A total of fifty burials were excavated (Figure S.2). Great consistency is found in the orientation of the burials. More than 90 percent of the individuals face east.

The Lavoutte site represents the settlement of a small Amerindian community on a dynamic coastal landscape. From AD 1000, this community exploited the marine and littoral resources of the surrounding area, which is slightly more sheltered from the Atlantic winds than the exposed woodlands on the other sides of the bay. The poor condition of the dentition of many of the individuals suggests a reliance on plant carbohydrates and marine proteins, which are well represented in midden deposits. A range of domestic ceramics for cooking and food preparation, flake tools of local stone, and pottery figurines and artifacts of nonlocal stone varieties

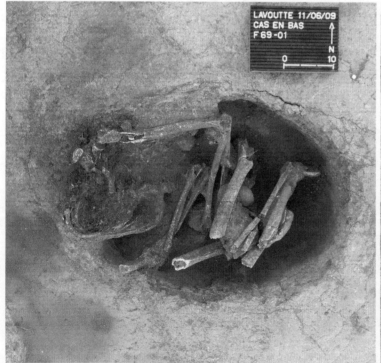 

Figure S.2. Burial F69-01 at Lavoutte, Saint Lucia. Adult male found in seated position. The upper part of the torso including the cranium and the knee joints are missing, probably due to traffic and erosion. Two tools (one of stone and one of coral) with clear use marks were found on both sides of the body close to the pelvis. In addition, a fragment of very weathered manatee rib was found on the right tibia. Photo by Corinne L. Hofman.

provide evidence of a full range of quotidian and ritual activities at the site. This illustrates that the Lavoutte community was tied into local subsistence and wider social networks.

Further Reading

Bright, A. J. 2011. *Blood Is Thicker than Water: Amerindian Intra- and Inter-insular Relationships and Social Organization in the Pre-Colonial Windward Islands.* Leiden: Sidestone Press.

Bullen, A. K., and R. P. Bullen. 1970. "The Lavoutte Site, Saint Lucia: A Carib Ceremonial Centre." In *Proceedings of the Third International Congress for the Study of Pre-Columbian Cultures of the Lesser Antilles,* 61–86. St. George: Grenada National Museum with the International Association of Caribbean Archaeology.

Hicks, D. 2007. *The Garden of the World: An Historical Archae-ology of Sugar Landscapes in the Eastern Caribbean.* Oxford: Archaeopress.

Hofman C. L., and E. M. Branford. 2009. "Lavoutte Revisited: Preliminary Results of the 2009 Rescue Excavations at Cas-En-Bas, Saint Lucia." Paper presented at the Twenty-Third Congress of the International Association for Caribbean Archaeology, Antigua.

Hofman, C. L., M. L. P. Hoogland, and W. F. Keegan. 2004. "Archaeological Reconnaissance at Saint Lucia, West Indies, 4-18-2004 to 5-12-2004: Annual Report." http://www.flmnh.ufl.edu/caribarch/stlucia2004.pdf. Accessed January 14, 2013.

Hofman, C. L, M. L. P. Hoogland, H. L. Mickleburgh, J. E. Laffoon, J. D. Weston, and M. Field. 2012. "Life and Death at Lavoutte, Saint Lucia, Lesser Antilles." *Journal of Field Archaeology* 37 (3): 209–25.

See also The Saint Lucia Archaeological and Historical Society (SLAHS); The Suazan Troumassoid (Suazey); The Troumassan Troumassoid.

Saint Lucia Archaeological and Historical Society (SLAHS)

Winston F. Phulgence

The Saint Lucia Archaeological and Historical Society (SLAHS) is a nongovernmental organization on the island of Saint Lucia. The society has been a strong advocate for the protection and preservation of the island's cultural heritage, which includes early native sites, estates, colonial architecture, and historical fortifications. The organization was founded in 1954 by Fr. Charles Jesse, Harry Simmons, Wilfred St. Clair-Daniel, and B. H. Easter, who each had an avid interest in the archaeological heritage of the island. Professor Irving Rouse, a visiting archaeologist from Yale University who was on Saint Lucia that same year, also lobbied for the formation of the society. The SLAHS is one of the oldest heritage organizations in the Anglophone Caribbean.

Since its inception, the society has staged lectures and exhibitions and has facilitated projects by many leading Caribbean archaeologists. From 1955 to 1969, the SLAHS facilitated excavations by William Haag, Marshall B. McKusick, Robert Pinchon, Irving Rouse, and Ripley and Adelaide Bullen. These excavations produced the ceramic series Troumassan Troumassoid and thus had a major impact on the development of Caribbean archaeology. The Saint Lucia Archaeological and Historical Society helped found the International Congress for the Study of Pre-Columbian Cultures in the Lesser Antilles and hosted the fourth congress in 1971.

Excavations conducted on Saint Lucia over the years have produced a large archaeological collection that is presently managed by the society. In 1964, the SLAHS sponsored an exhibition of prehistoric and historical materials in its possession. The success of this exhibition led to the establishment of a small part-time museum in 1965. In 1975, the museum became a fully established organization, housed in historic military barracks at Morne Fortune in Castries. In 1981, it was relocated to Pigeon Island, which also contains historic military buildings and fortifications. The exhibition at Pigeon Island was officially opened to the public in 1984. In 1993, the society started a traveling exhibition that helped expose Saint Lucia's schoolchildren to their cultural heritage. While the society no longer exhibits its large collection, it is still a strong advocate for the establishment of a national museum for Saint Lucia.

In the 1970s, the government of Saint Lucia recognized the SLAHS as the official custodian of the island's cultural heritage. In 1974, the government appointed the society "Preserver of Records" for Saint Lucia. This expanded role enabled the society to receive official government documents as well as several private collections. Advocacy by the SLAHS eventually led to the founding of the National Archives of Saint Lucia, the sole custodian and preserver of national records on the island. In 1971, the Saint Lucia Archaeological and Historical Society laid the legislative framework for the establishment of a National Trust for Saint Lucia. The legislation was eventually passed in 1975, leading to the establishment of the Saint Lucia National Trust, a statutory body with a mandate to preserve architectural heritage, historical objects, and natural heritage, including flora and fauna. The organization is also responsible for national parks and nature reserves.

The work that was begun in 1954 with the establishment of the Saint Lucia Archaeological Society has had considerable impact on the protection and preservation of the cultural heritage of Saint Lucia. The SLAHS's advocacy has also led to the creation of the National Archives and the National Trust, whose roles are critical to the protection and preservation of Saint Lucia's cultural heritage. The organization celebrated half a century of service to Saint Lucia in 2004 and continues to fulfill its mandate as it moves toward its sixtieth anniversary.

See also The Archaeological Society of Jamaica; Barbados Museum and Historical Society; Rouse, Benjamin Irving (1913–2006); Saint Lucia; The Troumassan Troumassoid.

The Saladoid

Corinne L. Hofman and Basil A. Reid

Saladoid, named after the site of Saladero in Venezuela, refers to a pottery series that was first identified along the Lower Orinoco. For many years, the people responsible for making this pottery were thought to be horticulturists who island-hopped to the Caribbean islands from South America sometime between 800 BC and 200 BC. This migratory model has been modified in light of emerging archaeological data. Apart from some early dates from the sites of Cedros and Palo Seco in Trinidad (Boomert 2000) and Lovers' Retreat in Tobago (Reid 2005), the majority of the radiocarbon dates for the early presence of Saladoid ceramics in the Antilles are from the northern Lesser Antilles and Puerto Rico. Dates from the sites of Trants (Montserrat), the Hope Estate (St. Martin), and Sorcé (Vieques) would suggest direct jumps from the South American mainland to the northern Caribbean, however new radiocarbon data from the southern Lesser Antilles may change this view. During this time, the Saladoid shared the islands with Archaic and La Hueca peoples, with whom they interacted.

Multiple local groups apparently entered the Antilles around this time or simultaneously developed locally. A diversity of cultures and peoples from different continental areas settled the islandscape, socializing and interacting with one other in a process that continued until European contact. The exploitation of the

Long Island flint sources near Antigua may have been an important impetus for the formation of a northeastern Caribbean interaction sphere. These flint materials were first exploited by Archaic age communities, and then later by the Saladoid and Huecoid.

The main Saladoid expansion, however, took place between 200 BC and AD 100. During this period, the region shows an increase of settlements. More islands became inhabited, and an array of lithic sources was exploited. Competition for lithic resources among Archaic, Saladoid, and Huecoid communities is evidenced by the fact that settlements were strategically located near main quarries. Trants (Montserrat), for instance, yielded a great number of stone beads and numerous pendants made of twenty-nine varieties of rocks and minerals, not one of which appears to be endemic to Montserrat. Sorcé/La Hueca (Vieques) yielded several thousand complete micro-lapidary artifacts, while its Huecan locus yielded more than 1,000 ornaments and inlays made of shell and mother-of-pearl and some pieces of decorated bone and petrified wood. The number of finished stone and shell beads and pendants from Punta Candelero (Puerto Rico) has been estimated to exceed 2,500; the unfinished pieces number several thousand. Frog-shaped pendants are numerous throughout the Caribbean. In addition, a small number of pendants representing jaguars, dogs, bats, raptorial birds, frigate birds, caimans, turtles, sharks, manatees, and possibly rodents such as hutias (Indian coneys; *Isolobodon portoricensis*) have been identified.

Radiocarbon dates suggest that the majority of the southern Lesser Antilles were settled around the time of Christ at sites such as Vivé and Fond Brûlé on Martinique and other sites on St. Vincent, Grenada, and Trinidad and Tobago. No Huecoid sites were recorded after AD 400, but nearly all the islands from Trinidad to Puerto Rico show Saladoid occupation. The production and exchange of semi-precious materials slowly faded away as more emphasis was placed on procuring local materials and exploiting local environments. An intensive interaction network existed among the islands of the Lesser Antilles, where these materials and objects were traded.

The initial Saladoid communities were first believed to have lived predominantly on the northern and eastern sides of volcanic islands in areas that were distant from the coast, near rivers, or surrounded by forest. However, it is clear now that a variety of environments were used for habitation and that a variety of locations were settled, including on beaches near reefs and mangrove areas and on hilltops. Ghandi Village in Trinidad is an example of a Saladoid hilltop settlement. Perched on the top of a hill approximately 26 m above sea level, Ghandi Village, with its commanding view of the surrounding countryside of southwestern Trinidad, was apparently an important defensive hilltop settlement (Reid 2008). Saladoid communities practiced a mixed economy in which they grew root crops, hunted land animals, fished, and collected mollusks (shellfish). The presence of clay griddles suggests that bitter manioc but also other root crops such as sweet potato and zamia were cultivated and processed. Many of these cultigens had been introduced into the islands during the Archaic age, as recent botanical studies have demonstrated. Horticultural practices, landscape modifications, and the increased exploitation of natural resources altered island habitats very rapidly and disrupted their ecological balance.

Pottery is perhaps the most distinctive feature of the Saladoid. During its earlier phase, it is generally characterized by white-on-red painted decorations, bell-shaped vessels, small nubbins, modeled-incised adornos, and zone-incised cross-hatching. Saladoid pottery is now considered to be much more heterogeneous than was previously thought in terms of style, morphology, and technology. Saladoid pottery can be distinguished from contemporary Huecoid pottery. The latter has different vessel shapes, lacks painting, and is character-

ized by a different type of modeled figures, and particular types of curvilinear zone-incised designs that are filled with punctations or cross-hatchings. During its later phase (AD 400–600/900), Saladoid pottery is heavier; bears polychrome painting of white, red, black, and orange; has many modeled incised anthropozoomorphic and zoomorphic adornos; many incised motifs; and few zone-incised cross-hatched designs.

The Saladoid belief system was based on South American cosmology and was profoundly polytheistic and animistic. It revolved around a belief in a vast number of spirits related to nature, including the forest, the sky, rivers, and mountains. Symbols and mythological themes depict a dynamic relationship between humans and animals in which human transformation into animal forms was the norm rather than the exception. After AD 400, Saladoid communities transformed their mainland lifeways to suit an island environment, an adaptation that was expressed in their material culture remains. Mainland iconography was replaced by island imagery that included more generalized and occasionally fantastic creatures, such as bats, birds, frogs, or lizards. The Late Saladoid is associated with the appearance of cult sites with petroglyphs. In the Lesser Antilles, petroglyphs are situated mostly along creeks or rivers, along the coast, in river valleys or ravines, on top of low wooded hills, and in rock shelters. Only a small proportion of petroglyphs are found in caves. A classic example is the site of Trois Rivières in Basse Terre, Guadeloupe, where more than 300 petroglyphs have been documented.

Saladoid social organization was formerly described as egalitarian or "tribally based." In this interpretation, Saladoid villages did not provide evidence of the size-rank hierarchy that was characteristic of Late Ceramic Age Taíno in Puerto Rico and Hispaniola. However, new data have led to several alternative interpretations, including theories about Big Man collectivities and models in which the social processes of complex tribes included public ceremonies of competitive emulation. The basis for these models is the wealth of material culture associated with Huecoid and Saladoid sites and the high numbers of social valuables buried in their middens. In addition, archaeological investigations at the site of Trants in Montserrat have revealed data about the size and longevity of Saladoid villages that demonstrates their complexity. The Trants village itself has a circular or ring pattern and is about 60,000 square meters in area. The artifact distribution area (including outlying areas) is 600,000 square meters. This makes Trants one of the largest Saladoid sites in the

Figure S.3. Saladoid white-on-red vessel from the site of Morel, Guadeloupe (AD 200–400). Photo by Corinne L. Hofman.

insular Caribbean. The site may have been occupied by as many as 200–300 people for 800 years. It is possible that Trants was one of the regional centers for Saladoid communities on nearby islands in the Lesser Antilles, comparable to the contemporaneous Huecoid/Saladoid site of La Hueca/Sorcé on Vieques Island. Other large Saladoid sites in the area include Indian Creek and the Royall's site on Antigua, Morel on Guadeloupe (Figures S.3 and S.4), and Hope Estate on St. Martin, which were all inhabited for multiple centuries. These large settlements may have been nodes in a multi-island Saladoid settlement system. Dog burials are also characteristic of this period. On both Puerto Rico and Guadeloupe, numerous dogs have been found buried among the humans with shell and stone paraphernalia as burial goods.

After AD 400, Saladoid villages became highly structured places. They are usually discerned archaeologically by the presence of middens arranged around a large space that was carefully cleared of refuse. This cleared space was the central plaza and was the venue for ritual displays and ceremonial feasts. At the late Saladoid site of Maisabel in Puerto Rico, deceased individuals were interred in this central place, which was considered to be the axis mundi. Ancestor veneration took place in this plaza during ceremonies. The plaza

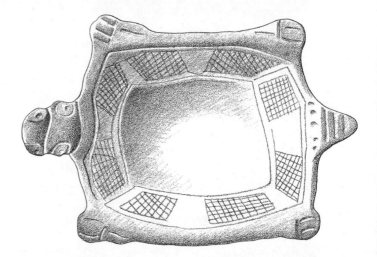

Figure S.4. Saladoid vessel with zoned-incised cross-hatched decorations from Morel, Guadeloupe (AD 200–400). Image by Corinne L. Hofman.

burials may have illustrated social solidarity among widely scattered villages and that the individuals buried in these spaces were returned to be buried with their original clan members after postmarital residence elsewhere.

Other examples of Saladoid villages are encountered throughout the Lesser Antilles. The most salient examples are from the Golden Rock Site on St. Eustatius and

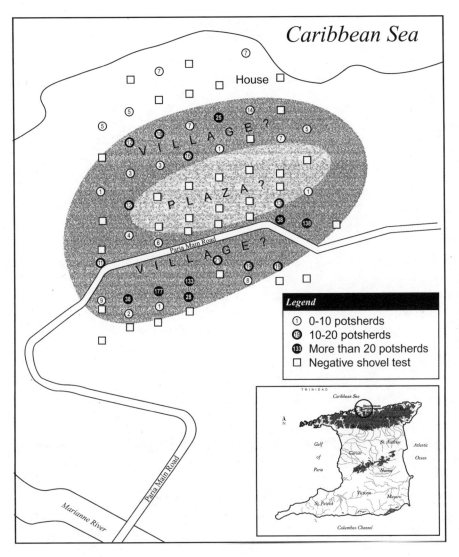

Figure S.5. Layout of Saladoid village at Blanchisseuse, north Trinidad (based on pottery densities). Reproduced by permission of Anne V. Stokes and David W. Steadman.

the two-hectare site of Marianne Estate in Blanchisseuse in northern Trinidad (Figure S.5). Numerous house plans of various sizes have been uncovered at Golden Rock. The largest, which has a diameter of nineteen meters, has been compared to the *maloca* of the Tropical Lowlands and may be related to the presence of successful shaman-leaders in late Saladoid and post-Saladoid society.

Further Reading

Boomert, A. 2000. *Trinidad, Tobago, and the Lower Orinoco Interaction Sphere: An Archaeological/Ethnohistorical Study.* Alkmaar: Cairi Publications.

Fitzpatrick, S. M. 2012. "The Southward Route Hypothesis." In *Oxford Handbook of Caribbean Archaeology*, ed. W. F. Keegan, C. L. Hofman, and R. Rodríguez Ramos, 198–204. Oxford: Oxford University Press.

Hofman, C. L., A. Bright, A. Boomert, and S. Knippenberg. 2007. "Island Rhythms: The Web of Social Relationships and Interaction Networks in the Pre-Columbian Lesser Antilles." *Latin American Antiquity* 18 (3): 243–68.

Keegan, W. F. 2009. "Central Plaza Burials in Saladoid Puerto Rico: An Alternative Perspective." *Latin American Antiquity* 20 (2): 375–85.

Reid, B. A. 2005. Archaeological Excavations of Lovers' Retreat (TOB-69), Tobago (Phases 2&3), Final Report." Conducted for Island Investment Limited.

———, ed. 2008. *Archaeology and Geoinformatics: Case Studies from the Caribbean.* Tuscaloosa: University of Alabama Press.

Wilson, S. M. 2007. "The Saladoid Phenomenon." In *The Archaeology of the Caribbean*, ed. S. M. Wilson, 59–94. Cambridge, UK: Cambridge University Press.

See also Anguilla; Golden Rock Site (St. Eustatius); Lapidary Trade; Montserrat; Origins of Indigenous Groups in the Northern Caribbean; Palo Seco (Trinidad); Trinidad and Tobago.

The Santa Rosa Carib Community, or Santa Rosa First People's Community (Trinidad)

Tracy Assing

The Santa Rosa Carib Community (SRCC, sometimes referred to as the Santa Rosa First People's Community) in Trinidad is an organization made up of descendants of the First People (Amerindians) who were settled at the Roman Catholic mission in the town of Arima in eastern Trinidad. The organization, which initially registered as a limited liability company led by Ricardo Bharath Hernandez, has played a key role in keeping some elements of Trinidad's indigenous culture alive. Members conduct regular workshops on basket weaving and roof thatching and the preparation of traditional foods, which they also trade (cassava bread, cassava farine, cassareep). The Santa Rosa Carib Community is closely associated with parang, a popular music form in Trinidad and Tobago that is heard primarily during the Christmas season and is thought to be closely connected to or to have derived from the native *arietos* (songs that were used during Taíno ceremonies). The Santa Rosa Carib Community Centre at Paul Mitchell Street in Arima has often hosted students and researchers who are interested in the medicinal uses of plants and herbs and aspects of indigenous life that are still being practiced.

In 1757, Capuchin monks built a church and established a mission at Arima. It was one of several established by the monks around the island, as the monks believed that converting the natives to Catholicism was one of the key tasks related to conquering the New World. The church was dedicated to the first canonized saint of the New World, Rosa of Lima, Peru, and celebrating the Santa Rosa Festival in August was part of life on the Arima mission. The feast of Saint Rose, which

Figure S.6. Members of the Santa Rosa Carib Community in Arima, Trinidad, celebrate the Santa Rosa Festival, 2009. Photo by Tracy Assing.

today is celebrated on August 23, continues to be celebrated by descendants of those Arima mission "Carib" (Figure S.6).

By 1786, Arima was the last surviving mission town on the island of Trinidad. Amerindians of various missions (and various native groups) were gathered there to cultivate cocoa and placed under the supervision of a Catholic priest. The baptismal registers at the Santa Rosa Roman Catholic Church show mission residents with Spanish names that have religious associations (names of saints or names found in the Bible). Some names were entered with the classification "Carib" or "indio."

In the early decades of the nineteenth century, the first British governor of Trinidad, Ralph Woodford, made several moves to reserve Arima as a place for the country's "Amerindians," going so far as to order non-Amerindians to leave the Arima Mission. However, none of his edicts were enforced after his death in 1828.

On May 19, 1990, the government of Trinidad and Tobago officially recognized the SRCC as the sole legitimate representative of Trinidad's retained community of Amerindians. In 2007, an Amerindian Project Committee was appointed to advise the government about the development of the community. On August 31, 1993, the Santa Rosa Carib Community received the Chaconia Medal (Silver) for Culture and Community Service from President Noor Hassanali. The work of the Amerindian Project Committee has also resulted in the establishment of a Day of Recognition, which takes place each year on October 14.

Bharath Hernandez continues to run the SRCC, although membership has dwindled over the years, leaving a core group of just about 200 men and women. The average age of the group is 60. A committee comprised of elders; the Carib Queen; and the community's *paiman* (medicine man), Cristo Adonis, assists Bharath Hernandez in administrating the SRCC. The current Carib Queen is Jennifer Pile-Cassar (elected in 2011).

The Santa Rosa Carib Community has been largely dependent on the state and private contributions for funding, but Bharath Hernandez has lobbied successive governments for land for the community with the intention of constructing a model village/botanical park, setting up a cassava-processing industry, and creating a research and documentation center.

Although no archaeological sites of note have yet been located in Arima, this may be due to the fact that the town of Arima has developed rapidly. Some members of the community regularly conduct tours to the Caurita Stone in Maracas, St. Joseph, where some hieroglyphics have been identified. In recent times, members have begun conducting smoke ceremonies at the sites of other former missions and at Banwari Trace.

Further Reading

Forte, M. C. 2005. *Ruins of Absence, Presence of Caribs: (Post) Colonial Representations of Aboriginality in Trinidad and Tobago.* Gainesville: University Press of Florida.

Reid, B. A. 2009. *Myths and Realities of Caribbean History.* Tuscaloosa: University of Alabama Press.

See also Banwari Trace (Trinidad); Kalinago Descendants of St. Vincent and the Grenadines; The Kalinago Territory (Dominica); Trinidad and Tobago.

Seafaring Simulations

Richard T. Callaghan

Researchers have conducted computer simulations of ancient voyaging and maritime contacts since work was done in the early 1970s on the Polynesian dispersal. These simulations have included investigations into the routes of initial colonization of islands and the effects of El Niño on eastward Pacific crossings. Other investigations have considered the translocation of domestic species to new lands and problems associated with historic European voyages of discovery. Other simulations have considered the potential for ancient maritime interaction spheres. The majority of these and other simulations have been used in the Pacific Ocean, but several were used to investigate archaeological questions in the Caribbean Sea and Gulf of Mexico.

Two types of simulation models have been developed to date: deterministic and statistical. In deterministic models, vessel movement is calculated using data about daily winds and currents provided by numerical models. Deterministic models can make use of several data sources. These data sets are produced from models based on direct observations to produce best estimates of atmospheric and oceanic conditions at a particular time. The period of length for winds and currents determines the duration of the simulation, or how long the simulated voyage will last in days.

Statistical simulations are based on data collected from ship's logs over an extended period of time. The six seafaring simulation studies conducted in Caribbean archaeology are all statistically based. In these studies, the wind and current data were compiled by the U.S. Navy. The field for the simulation, the Caribbean Sea and adjacent waters, is divided into one-degree Marsden squares (one degree of latitude by one degree of longitude).

Four main variables are considered in these seafaring simulations: current patterns of flow, wind patterns of flow, vessel type, and method of propulsion. The simulation is structured by factors that include how data are selected and the percentage of simulated voyages reaching a selected target. Parameters include such factors as the starting position of the vessel, downwind (vessels are sailing before the wind) or directed voyage (attempts are made to sail in a particular direction), duration at sea, and whether a vessel reaches a selected target within the limits of crew survival calculated from historical records.

Ocean currents affect any objects that are caught in them in a 1:1 ratio. That is, the object will have the same speed and set (direction) as the current unless other forces are operating. For example, any object floating with an appreciable part above the water will be more affected by wind than by currents unless the current is exceptionally strong. Traditional navigators in Kiribati, for example, used the effect of the wind on objects floating high in the water to determine the direction of land when recent winds differed from the flow of the current.

The type of vessel and how it is propelled make up the final variables of any simulation, as the shape of an object both above and below the waterline will respond to the effects of wind. Several different types of traditional circum-Caribbean canoes were used in these simulations, although given equivalent size they vary little in performance. The program randomly selects wind and current data contained in each Marsden square that are frequency-weighted according to the compiled observations from ships' logs. These forces are then allowed to operate on vessels for a 24-hour period before a new selection is made.

In the computer simulations, the actual distance and direction a vessel traveled is based on the wind; current frequencies, directions, and speed from the U.S. Navy database; and on the speed a particular vessel type can make in relation to the wind. Researchers chose two strategies in their simulations. One was to allow vessels to drift before winds and currents. Figures S.7 and S.8 show computer simulations of drift voyages from the Canary Islands to the Americas under November and January conditions, respectively. The other research strategy was to set a specific heading for intentional travel. The heading can be adjusted during a simulation, or researchers can instruct the computer program to allow vessels to sail downwind. This ability to choose between setting headings or having a vessel sail downwind in the simulation allows for some assessment of the level of skill required for a particular sea crossing. The speed of drifting or paddled vessels is derived from field experiments conducted in Central and South America. The result of the simulations is expressed as the percentage of times that a particular vessel type reached a defined target from selected points. Survival rates for voyagers were calculated from data compiled during World War II.

One of the first Caribbean seafaring simulations (Callaghan 2001) was a study of seafaring by Ceramic Age peoples between the South American mainland and the islands of the Caribbean. In this study, two dugout canoe designs were assessed. One design was based on a canoe recovered from the Bahamas. The other was a style found widely around the Caribbean that is similar to those depicted in Spanish documents.

The simulation asked two questions. One was how likely it was that the Saladoid peoples from South America discovered the Antilles by chance. Canoes of both styles were set adrift from several locations along the northern South American coast. The times of year for the simulations were January, April, July, and October. One thousand simulations were run from each position. Success ranged from 0.3 percent in April to 0.1 percent in October. The second question was whether technology and the environment limited voyagers to traveling in a stepping-stone fashion along the Lesser Antilles. It was noted that the earliest Saladoid dates are in the north of the Lesser Antilles and Puerto Rico. In this scenario, canoes were simply paddled in a northerly direction. All canoes in the successful simulations made landfall in the north in about one week with no significant crew loss. The simulations also revealed that traveling north or south to the west of the Lesser Antilles could be a safer strategy than traveling between the channels or near the lee shores of the islands.

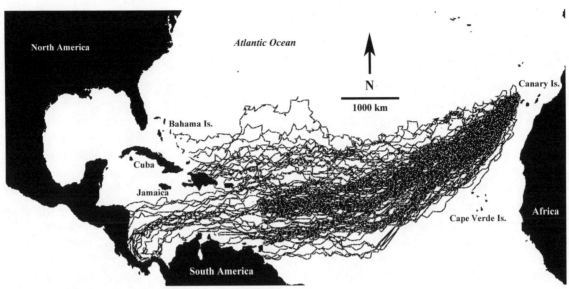

Figure S.7. Computer simulations of drift voyages from the Canary Islands to the Americas in the month of November. Courtesy of Richard T. Callaghan.

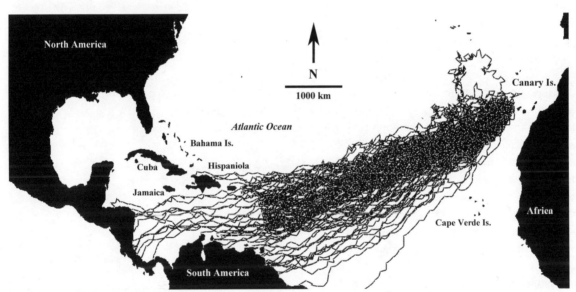

Figure S.8. Computer simulations of drift voyages from the Canary Islands to the Americas in the month of January. Courtesy of Richard T. Callaghan.

In a subsequent study (Callaghan 2003), seafaring simulations were used to examine the likely origins of the early Archaic cultures in the Greater Antilles and to evaluate the level of navigation skill that the island colonizers would need. The early Archaic cultures of the Greater Antilles are dated to between 4000 and 2000 BC. They are found in Hispaniola, Cuba, and Puerto Rico. Two mainland areas, South America and Central America, have artifact assemblages bearing resemblance to those found in early contexts in the Greater Antilles, but with important differences. Callaghan's study considered both chance discoveries by drifting and intentional voyaging by paddling toward the islands. Chance discovery

of the Greater Antilles was possible from three mainland areas: southern Florida, northern Central America, and northern South America. In Callaghan's simulations, the success rate for intentional voyages from all three areas was high. But in terms of the navigational skill required and the risk involved, voyaging from northern South America was more likely. Voyaging from southern Florida involved considerable risk of being swept into the Gulf Stream, while voyaging from northern Central America required foreknowledge of the islands in order to make course changes out of sight of land.

In a study that was not directly related to the Caribbean islands but had implications for interaction throughout the region, simulations were conducted to investigate possible direct seaborne contacts and possible migration between the Colombian Caribbean coast (Tairona) and Costa Rica (Callaghan and Bray 2007). Evidence for contacts between the Tairona coast and Costa Rica is seen archaeologically between about AD 200 and 800 and from the ninth century to Spanish conquest. Similarities in the archaeological data are not as strong in the intervening mainland areas between the two points. The simulation shows that drift voyages from the Tairona region to Costa Rica are possible. Round trip intentional voyages are also possible year round. The simulations suggest that strong contact between the two regions was possible but that there may have been minor contact in the areas between Tairona and Costa Rica.

Simulations were also used to explain the apparent absence of human colonization of Jamaica until the Ostionoid period, circa AD 600 (Callaghan 2008), when other islands of the Greater Antilles had already been occupied for thousands of years. This research involved simulations of travel between Cuba, Hispaniola and Jamaica in conjunction with evaluations of hurricane patterns and changes in sea level. Neither of the two latter factors could explain the absence of early sites through erosion or submersion. However, the sea conditions on the north coast of Jamaica are unusually rough and may have discouraged colonization until the increased social complexity of the Ostionoid period fostered the ability to organize labor for the construction of very large canoes.

In another case, simulations were used in part to understand the absence of Archaic Ortoiroid sites from an area that began south of the Guadeloupe Passage in the Lesser Antilles and extended to Trinidad and Tobago (Callaghan 2010). The simulations revealed that there were no significant navigational difficulties involved with crossing the passage. Other factors that could obscure early sites, particularly volcanism, were also examined but could not be credited with causing sampling bias. The results of this study suggested that the Archaic sites north of the Guadeloupe Passage are in fact outliers of the Casimiroid peoples in the Greater Antilles, as the only diagnostic tools found at these sites appear to be Casimiroid.

The most recent simulation to date examines the issue of contacts between Caribbean Island peoples and mainland populations other than those in northern South America (Callaghan 2011). Some suggestions of contacts between the islands and the southeastern United States and Mesoamerica do exist, but have for the most part they not been investigated. Simulations were run from northern Cuba, western Cuba, southern Jamaica, southern Hispaniola, southern Puerto Rico, and Antigua. In simulations, virtually all drift voyages made safe landfall, although many landed on intervening island coasts rather than the mainland. Figure S.7 shows simulation results that illustrate that drift voyages are so easily successful that it stands to reason that intentional ones would been even easier because they would have been considerably shorter. The simulations do suggest that direct sea crossings without stopping at intervening coasts were unlikely. However, they also raise a question: If contacts with other mainland areas were not difficult, why is there such little evidence for it? The answer may lie in the patterns of trade that had already established. It may be that the personal contacts, patterns of coastal movement, and goods desired shaped trade networks and kept island trade focused on South America, precluding its expansion elsewhere.

Seafaring simulations are useful tools for establishing most the likely routes, what the risks and skill requirements are, and where to look for evidence to support various cultural contacts. They are also useful for suggesting reasons why some things did or did not happen. However, they cannot be used to identify precise locations of landfall. They also do not prove that a particular event happened; they can only provide information about the probability of an event.

Further Reading

Callaghan, R. T. 2001. "Analysis of Ceramic Age Seafaring and Interaction Potential in the Antilles." *Current Anthropology* 42 (2): 308–13.

———. 2003. "Comments on the Mainland Origins of the Preceramic Cultures of the Greater Antilles." *Latin American Antiquity* 14 (3): 323–38.

———. 2008. "On the Absence of Archaic Age Sites on Jamaica." *Journal of Island and Coastal Archaeology* 3 (1): 54–71.

———. 2010. "Crossing the Guadeloupe Passage in the Archaic Age." In *New Perspectives on the Prehistoric Settlement of the Caribbean,* ed. S. M. Fitzpatrick and A. Ross, 127–47. Gainesville: University Press of Florida.

———. 2011. "Patterns of Contact between the Islands of the Caribbean and the Surrounding Mainland as a Navigation Problem." In *Islands in the Stream: Migration, Seafaring, and Interaction in the Caribbean,* ed. Antonio Curet and Mark Hauser, 59–72. Tuscaloosa: University of Alabama Press.

Callaghan, R. T., and W. Bray. 2007. "Sea Contacts between Costa Rica and Colombia." *Journal of Island and Coastal Archaeology* 2 (1): 4–23.

See also The Casimiroid; The Ortoiroid; The Saladoid.

The Seville Sugar Plantation (British Colonial Jamaica)

Douglas V. Armstrong

Archaeological studies at the Seville Sugar Plantation in Jamaica have provided a large body of data about the conditions of slavery and enslavement in Jamaica. The Seville study examined two temporally discrete settlements of African laborers and three levels of managerial residences (owner, manager, and timekeeper) (Armstrong 2011; Armstrong and Kelly 2000). In addition, the study located and examined the residence of an East Indian (Armstrong and Hauser 2004; Kelly, Hauser and Armstrong 2011). In addition to generating a series of publications, the study was useful in the development of interpretive materials for Seville National Historic Park, a property on Jamaica's north coast that is eligible for UNESCO world heritage status.

Surveys of the African Jamaican settlements on the property were initiated in 1980 and 1981, and formal excavations were carried out by Syracuse University in cooperation with the Jamaica National Heritage Trust from 1987 to 1993. Key findings included residential data from a series of well-defined house sites located in two spatially and temporally distinct areas. The early village was established by the third quarter of the seventeenth century as part of an early sugar estate founded by the Heming family. Houses in this village were organized in two tightly spaced parallel rows. Archaeological findings revealed a range of activities in the yard areas behind the house indicated by the presence of hearths, work areas, and burials in the house yard (Digital Archaeological Archive of Comparative Slavery 2007; Armstrong and Kelly 2000).

The data from Seville provided evidence about the power relations on the estate. For example, the scale of housing differentiated between planters and laborers: planters' residences were large and expansive stone structures, while housing for laborers were much smaller wattle-and-daub and wood frame structures. The spatial layout of these structures facilitated managerial surveillance and control by the planter and later managers of the estate. However, these power relations changed through time. By the fourth quarter of the eighteenth century, when the village was moved after a hurricane damaged plantation structures, labor relations had changed and the new village was built at some distance from the planter's residence. The new village allowed laborers to construct their residences as they pleased,

and they reconfigured their community with clusters of houses and large yard areas to reflect social dynamics in their community. From the new location of the village, enslaved workers could more freely move to the fields instead of having to pass by the planter's residence on the way to work. Still, a strong element of control is expressed in the construction of a new overseer's house immediately adjacent to the works. This was to ensure supervision of the processing of cane in the mill and boiling house (Armstrong and Kelly 2000).

The Seville data point to the importance of multiple uses of space. This is reflected in a pattern of house-yard usage at laborers' residences that is tied to African patterns of household and community space (Figure S.9). The pattern of spending much time outside in the yard is a practical response to a hot and tropical environment. In fact, by the late eighteenth century we find that when the planter rebuilt his house, he had a large porch built that allowed his household to live in a cooler outdoor environment. A significant feature of the early African Jamaican village was the presence of four burials in the house yard. These graves were located very near the houses and all contained objects related to the lives of those who had died, including a calibrated spacer that suggests the presence of an individual who had been a carpenter.

The Seville study provides one of the most clearly defined examples of a large-scale sugar plantation in Jamaica. The several living-area contexts that were excavated provide a basis for distinguishing between material evidence linked to ethnic identity and ethnic preferences in the choice and use of material goods (Armstrong 1999, 2011; Kelly, Hauser, and Armstrong 2011). Often, interpretation of the reasons enslaved peoples chose certain goods is limited by the very nature of the poverty and lack of options slavery involves. However, at Seville we see not only the broad and enveloping impact of the economic and social conditions of slavery but also the expression of ethnic cultures in the goods enslaved people selected. This is made possible by the presence of the household of an East Indian laborer at the site and the fact that the African Jamaican and East Indian Jamaican assemblages are quite distinct, particularly within groupings of artifacts associated with foodways (food preparation, dietary remains, and food consumption). Distinct differences in

Figure S.9. House yard site at Seville Plantation (1670s–1880s), Jamaica. Photo by Douglas V. Armstrong.

the assemblage of these two laborer groups are also seen in the array of personal possessions and products related to health and hygiene practices.

The Seville study has been integrated into interpretive programming at Seville National Historic Park. The individuals who were found in the house-yard burials at the site have been reburied in a place of honor in a secure location on the plantation grounds. The direct results of the project include the reconstruction of a house and garden site to represent lifeways associated with African Jamaicans who were enslaved on the property.

Further Reading

Armstrong, D. V. 1999. "Archaeology and Ethnohistory of the Caribbean Plantation." In *I, Too, Am America: Archaeological Studies of African-American Life*, ed. T. Singleton, 173–92. Charlottesville: University of Virginia Press.

———. 2011. "Reflections on Seville: Rediscovering the African Jamaican Settlements at Seville Plantation, St. Ann's Bay." In *Out Of Many, One People: Historical Archaeology in Jamaica*, ed. James Delle, Mark Hauser, and Douglas V. Armstrong, 77–101. Tuscaloosa: University of Alabama Press.

Armstrong, D. V., and M. W. Hauser. 2004. "An East Indian Laborers' Household in 19th-Century Jamaica: A Case for Understanding Cultural Diversity through Space, Chronology, and Material Analysis." *Historical Archaeology* 38 (2): 9–21.

Armstrong, D. V., and K. Kelly. 2000. "Settlement Patterns and the Origin of African Jamaican Society." *Ethnohistory* 47 (2): 368–97.

Digital Archive of Comparative Slavery. 2007. "Seville House 16." Data compiled by Douglas Armstrong and Jillian E. Galle. http://www.daacs.org/sites/seville-house-16/#background. Accessed January 17, 2013.

Kelly, K. G., M. W. Hauser, and D. V. Armstrong. 2011. "Identity and Opportunity in Post-Slavery Jamaica." In *Out of Many, One People: Historical Archaeology in Jamaica*, ed. James Delle, Mark Hauser, and Douglas V. Armstrong, 243–57. Tuscaloosa: University of Alabama Press.

See also Drax Hall Estate (Jamaica); The Jamaica National Heritage Trust.

Sint Maarten (Former Netherlands Antilles)

Jay B. Haviser

Sint Maarten is the southern Dutch half of the northeast Caribbean island. It is shared with the French Territory, St. Martin. At the time of initial historic contacts with St. Martin/Sint Maarten, it was reported that no peoples were living on the island. The Amerindian names for the island are somewhat confusing; the name "Soualiga" can be traced only to more recent historical sources that relate to the seventeenth-century salt industry in St. Martin. The name "Oualichi" was first mentioned for St. Martin by Father Breton in his 1665 Carib-French dictionary (Breton 1665/1892).

The earliest archaeological survey of Sint Maarten was written by J. P. B. de Josselin de Jong as his field notes during a ten-day visit to the island in 1923. He did not record any archaeological sites for the island. In the early 1950s, local amateur archaeologist Hyacinth Connor recorded prehistoric archaeological sites at Pic Paradise, Mount William, and Billy Folly. In 1958, John and Dorothy Keur discovered two more sites at Red Bay and Cupecoy Bay. Although there are no published reports of these findings, some of the artifacts are at the Smithsonian Institute in Washington, DC. In 1966, Ripley and Adelaide Bullen published results of a 1961 archaeological survey they conducted in Sint Maarten. During their short stay on the island, they made test excavations at the Cupecoy Bay site and located a new site at Point Terres Basses (Long Bay Point) (Bullen and Bullen 1969, 1985). Comments on the Bullens' investigations can be found in the *Encyclopedie van de Nederlandse Antillen* (De Palm 1985) and in Johan Hartog's history of the island (1981). In 1976, E. H. J. Boerstra and Elis Juliana conducted a brief inventory of archaeological, anthropological, and folkloric materials from Sint Maarten, at which time they noted a prehistoric site on Great Bay in downtown Philipsburg. In 1982, an unpublished manuscript was written by Menno Sypkens Smit of a survey he conducted at St. Martin/Sint Maarten's archaeological sites in 1979–1980. Sypkens Smit presented an inventory of artifacts from private collections on the island and evidence he recorded from excavations at Red Bay and Philipsburg. In 1988, Sypkens Smit and Aad Versteeg published a brief inventory of archaeological materials known from St. Martin/Sint Maarten, based on Sypkens Smit's earlier fieldwork (Sypkens Smit and Versteeg 1988).

In 1986, Jay Haviser conducted salvage archaeological excavations at the Cupecoy Bay site on behalf of the Archaeological-Anthropological Institute of the Netherlands Antilles (AAINA); he presented a written report in 1987. Also in 1987, Haviser conducted an archaeological survey of both sides of St. Martin/Sint Maarten. This was the most thorough identification of sites for the entire island until that time (Haviser 1988). A listing and description of all the known prehistoric sites for St. Martin/Sint Maarten can be found in Haviser's 1988 publication, a later edition of which was published by House of Nehesi Publishers (Haviser 1995).

In 1986, an underwater archaeological survey was conducted around the Fort Amsterdam peninsula by Wil Nagelkerken (Nagelkerken 1987). In 1988, systematic excavations were undertaken at the Early Ceramic Age site of Hope Estate on the French side. This work was done by Haviser, representing the AAINA, and by Henry Petitjean Roget, representing the Direction des Fouilles et des Antiquites, Guadeloupe. Archaeologists from the Direction Regionale des Affaires Culturelles of Guadeloupe assisted with this project. The results were presented in 1989 at the IACA congress on Curaçao. In 1987, the first historical archaeology was conducted at Fort Amsterdam on the Dutch side by Amsterdam city archaeologist Jan Baart (Baart, Knook, and Lagerwey 1989). In 1993 and 1994, more extensive excavations at the Hope Estate site were conducted by an international team of archaeologists that included Haviser, Menno Hoogland, Corrine Hofman and numerous students from Leiden University, Christophe Henocq of the Association Archeologique Hope Estate, Nicolas Weyden, Dominique Bonnissent, Anne Bouille, and Philippe Pannoux. Artifacts from the 1988, 1993 and 1994 excavations are now in the possession of the Association Archeologique Hope Estate in Marigot, on the French side. Hofman and Hoogland published an extensive edited volume on this Hope Estate research (Hofman and Hoogland 1999), and Bonnissent has conducted more extensive research on the site's inventory for the French side.

In 1991 and 1992, researchers from the College of William and Mary, Williamsburg, Virginia, conducted a historical sites survey of the Dutch side under the direction of Norman Barka (Barka 1993). As a student of Barka, S.

Sanders conducted a rescue excavation of several graves uncovered at the Bishop Hill plantation site during road construction in 1992. She reported on the results the same year. Starting in 1994 and 1995, Kathryn Bequette conducted an underwater survey and excavations at the *Proselyte* shipwreck in Great Bay, Sint Maarten (Bequette 1995). In 1995, historical archaeology surveys were conducted at the Belvedere Plantation by Jay Haviser for AAINA; this research identified several settlement areas of enslaved African on the plantation grounds (Haviser 1996). In 2004, Haviser conducted a rescue archaeological excavation at the Vineyard Burial Ground site, located in a free African settlement area on the Dutch side (Haviser 2004). In 2005, Corinne Hofman, Menno Hoogland, and R. Grant Gilmore conducted an archaeological survey and mapping of the Bethlehem Plantation site on the Dutch side (Hoogland, Hofman, and Gilmore 2006). In 2006, Haviser conducted an archaeological survey and test excavations at the Emilio Wilson Estate on the Dutch side, a site that consists of two eighteenth- and nineteenth-century sugar plantation complexes (Haviser 2006b). This work was conducted in collaboration with the Sint Maarten Archaeological Center Foundation (SIMARC) youth and science stimulation program, which Haviser created on Sint Maarten in 2005. Also in 2006, Haviser and the SIMARC students conducted an exhumation of a nineteenth-century Dutch priest on Sint Maarten (Haviser 2006a).

In 2007, Haviser conducted two archaeological projects with the cooperation of the SIMARC Foundation students: a nineteenth-century burial ground at the Great Bay Bridge, where nine graves were investigated, and the Cay Bay development area, where remains of a Dutch attack on the island in 1644 were found (Haviser 2007a, 2007b). In 2007 and 2008, Haviser did an inventory of historic trees on the Dutch side with the help of SIMARC Foundation students. Over 280 trees with base diameters over 100 centimeters were recorded for the Dutch side. This information (which included GPS coordinates) was given to the government planning office for incorporation into its computer systems for the purpose of controlling permits. In 2008, Haviser and the SIMARC Foundation students conducted archaeological excavations at the Over-the-Bank free African settlement on the Dutch side (Haviser 2008)

In October 2010, St. Maarten became an autonomous entity within the Kingdom of the Netherlands, and the Netherlands Antilles as a country ceased to exist.

Further Reading

Baart, J., W. Knook, and A. Lagerwey. 1989. "Fort Amsterdam: Archeologisch onderzoek op Sint Maarten, Nederlandse Antillen." *KNOB Bulletin* 87 (6): 1–15.

Barka, N. F. 1993. *Archaeological Survey of Sites and Buildings, St. Maarten, Netherlands Antilles. I.* Williamsburg, VA: Department of Anthropology, College of William and Mary.

Bequette, K. 1995. "Report of the 1994 Maritime Archaeology and Research of the HMS Proselyte, St. Maarten." Report submitted to the Archaeological Anthropological Institute of the Netherlands Antilles, Curaçao.

Breton, R. 1665/1892. *Dictionaire Caraibe-Francais.* Leipzig: B. G. Teubner.

Bullen, R. P., and A. Bullen. 1966. "Three Indian Sites on St. Martin." *Nieuwe West-Indische Gids* 45 (2–3): 137–47.

———. 1974. "Inferences from Cultural Diffusion to Tower Hill, Jamaica, and Cupecoy Bay, St. Martin." In *Proceedings of the Fifth International Congress for the Study of Pre-Columbian Cultures of the Lesser Antilles*, edited by D. Nicholson, 48–60. Antigua: Antigua Archaeological Society.

De Palm, Julius Philip. 1985. *Encyclopedie van de Nederlandse Antillen.* Netherlands Antilles: De Walburg Pers.

Farnsworth, P., ed. 2001. *Island Lives: Historical Archaeologies of the Caribbean.* Tuscaloosa: University of Alabama Press.

Hartog, J. 1981. *History of Sint Maarten and Saint Martin.* Philipsburg, St. Maarten: Sint Maarten Jaycees.

Haviser, J. B. 1988. *An Archaeological Survey of St. Martin–St. Maarten.* Curaçao: Institute of Archaeology and Anthropology of the Netherlands Antilles.

———. 1995. *In Search of St. Martin's Ancient Peoples: Prehistoric Archaeology.* St. Martin: House of Nehesi Publishers.

———. 1996. "An Archaeological Survey of the Belvedere Plantation Parcels I, II and III, St. Maarten." Report submitted to the Archaeological Anthropological Institute of the Netherlands Antilles, Curaçao.

———. 2004. "Vineyard Burial Ground, St. Maarten: Emergency Archaeological Observations and Recovery." Mission Report for the Island Territory of St. Maarten and the National Archaeological-Anthropological Museum, Curaçao.

———. 2006a. "Archaeological Excavation of a 19th century Dutch Priest of the Dominican Order, Buried on St. Maarten." SIMARC Technical Reports submitted to the Island Territory of St. Maarten.

———. 2006b. "An Archaeological Survey of the Emilio Wilson Estate." SIMARC Technical Report for the Island Territory of St. Maarten.

———. 2007a. "An Archaeological Survey of Cay Bay: Specific Areas of Proposed Development." SIMARC Technical Report submitted to the Cay Bay Development Company, St. Maarten.

———. 2007b. "Emergency Archaeological Excavation of Human Remains, Buried Adjacent to the Great Bay Bridge, St.

Maarten." SIMARC Technical Report submitted to the Island Territory government of St. Maarten.

———. 2008. "Archaeological Testing of a Free-African Settlement Site at Over-the-Bank, St. Maarten." Technical Report prepared for Reza Amjad McSood and the Island Territory Government of St. Maarten.

Hofman, C., and M. L. P. Hoogland, eds. 1999. *Archaeological Investigations of St. Martin (Lesser Antilles)*. Leiden: Leiden University.

Hoogland, M., C. Hofman, and R. G. Gilmore. 2006. "Archaeological Assessment of the Bethlehem Plantation Complex, St. Maarten, Netherlands Antilles." Technical Report submitted to the Bethlehem Real Estate Development Company, St. Maarten.

Nagelkerken, W. 1987. *Preliminary Report of an Underwater Archaeological Survey around the Fort Amsterdam Peninsula, St. Maarten*. Curaçao: Institute for Archaeology and Anthropology of the Netherlands Antilles.

Sypkens Smit, M., and A. Versteeg. 1988. *An Archaeological Reconnaissance of St. Martin*. Amsterdam: N.p.

See also The Dutch Caribbean; Sint Maarten Archaeological Center (SIMARC).

Sint Maarten Archaeological Center (SIMARC)

Jay B. Haviser

The Sint Maarten Archaeological Center, called SIMARC, was founded by Jay B. Haviser in 2005. It is a nonprofit foundation that is assisted by the government of Sint Maarten. Its mission is to develop policy concepts for scientific research and educational programs initiated for the people of St. Maarten. The SIMARC Center seeks to work directly with the population of St. Maarten, in particular teenage youth, to provide education and training in scientific methods and to conduct professional scientific research about the culture and history of St. Maarten. It is important that Antillean youth pursue careers in the sciences so that they can eventually be local leaders in the scientific aspects of ecotourism and heritage/nature conservation on the islands. One of the more important characteristics of this project is that around twenty students from various St. Maarten high schools contributed to all aspects of the planning, research, and archaeological work. SIMARC's research priority is to investigate the science, history, and culture of St. Maarten from the perspective of St. Maarteners. This program concept has become a model for the broader Caribbean region; exemplifying the potential of individual islands to conduct their own cultural heritage research and reduce the intervention of foreign specialists.

The SIMARC Foundation provides an after-school program for study credits from the various high schools of St. Maarten. The program is supported by the government of St. Maarten and the Ministry of VROMI (Public Housing, Spatial Development, Environment, and Infrastructure) of St. Maarten. The foundation also receives funds from organizations such as the Stichting Antilliaanse Medefinancierings Organisatie (AMFO) and the Prince Bernhard Culture Funds.

The SIMARC program teaches both theory and practical applications. The theoretical and informative aspects of classroom lectures, group discussions and presentations, including some practical work relating to archaeology, history, geography, anthropology, and other fields are conducted during the regular school academic year at the SIMARC facility. Field projects in archaeology, history, geography, biology and anthropology are conducted for students and sometimes for other community members. The SIMARC center has become a focal point for the St. Maarten community for heritage research. It is a place where heritage artifacts from both public and private collections can be examined, identified, and stored. In 2011, the St. Maarten government recognized SIMARC as the official facility for archaeological research and collections depository for St. Maarten.

See also Bonaire Archaeological Institute (BONAI); Sint Maarten (Former Netherlands Antilles).

Sint Maarten National Heritage Foundation

Jay B. Haviser

The Sint Maarten National Heritage Foundation was founded in 1993 when the National Parks Foundation (STINAPA; founded in 1982) and the Sint Maarten Museum Foundation (founded in 1988) merged. It is a nonprofit, nongovernmental organization. The foundation aims to promote, protect, and investigate every aspect of the history, archaeology, culture, and natural environment of the island of Sint Maarten/Saint Martin and its surroundings. Two of its primary functions have been to make the Sint Maarten Museum a focal point for awareness in the community of the cultural, historical, archaeological, and natural heritage of the Dutch side of the island; and to conduct limited inventories of and research and monitor heritage monument sites on the island.

Further Reading

St. Maarten Heritage Foundation. N.d. Web site of the St. Maarten Heritage Foundation. http://www.museumsintmaarten.org/. Accessed January 28, 2013.

Sloane, Sir Hans (1660–1753)

James Robertson

Sir Hans Sloane, a British physician and scientist, visited the West Indies from 1687 to 1689 (Figure S.10). He later wrote major studies on Jamaican natural history and accumulated material on the West Indies. After his death, his collections were purchased by Parliament and became one of the foundation collections of the British Museum.

Sloane was born in Ulster, the youngest son of an Anglo-Scottish family. He trained as a physician in London, where he met several leading botanists. After studying at the Jardine de Plants in Paris, he took his MD in 1683 at the Huguenot University of Orange. On his return to England, he worked with the leading London physician Thomas Sydenham. This impressive start to his career combined botanical fieldwork with patient-centered medicine. He was elected a fellow of the Royal Society in 1685 and of the College of Physicians in 1687.

Later in 1687, he accepted the post of physician to Christopher Monk, second duke of Albemarle, after James II appointed him governor of Jamaica. Sloane accompanied the duke to the West Indies and used the opportunity to learn about cures that local physicians had developed

Figure S.10. A mid-eighteenth-century engraving of Sir Hans Sloane by Johann-Martin Bernigeroth (1713–1767) after Gottfried Kneller (1646–1723).

and gather natural history specimens. However, he could not keep his client alive. In 1689, he returned to London with the widowed countess and his specimens. He became active in scientific circles and was elected secretary of the Royal Society in 1693, the year he published his Latin *Catalogus plantorum quae in insula Jamaica sponte proveniunt*. He proved an effective administrator, securing unpaid subscriptions, encouraging correspondence with international researchers, and reviving (and then editing) the Royal Society's *Philosophical Transactions*. In 1727, Sloane succeeded Sir Isaac Newton as president of the Royal Society. From 1719, he was president of the Royal College of Physicians. Sloane remains the only individual to have combined these roles. Alongside all these activities Sloane became a highly successful London physician and was physician-in-ordinary to several members of the royal family. George I made him a baronet in 1716.

Dr. Sloane's fee income, along with his wife's revenue as the widow of her first husband, a Jamaican planter-physician, funded his passion for collecting, which he extended to books, manuscripts, coins, and medals. He published *A Voyage to the Islands Madeira, Barbados, Neves, S. Christophers, and Jamaica, with the Natural History . . . of the Last of These Islands* in two volumes in 1707 and 1725. In his efforts to describe unfamiliar West Indian plants to his fellow botanists, his descriptions drew parallels with plants known in Europe or reported by botanists and travelers in North and South America, Asia, and elsewhere. Sloane's research on the West Indies contributed to keeping the region at the center of eighteenth-century botanical research.

Further Reading

Churchill, W. D. 2005. "Bodily Differences? Gender, Race, and Class in Hans Sloane's Jamaican Medical Practice, 1687–1688." *Journal of the History of Medicine and Allied Sciences* 60 (4): 391–444.

de Beer, G. R. 1953. *Sir Hans Sloane and the British Museum*. London: Oxford University Press.

MacGregor, A., ed. 1994. *Sir Hans Sloane: Collector, Scientist, Antiquary, Founding Father of the British Museum*. London: British Museum.

Walker, A., A. MacGregor, and M. Hunter, eds. 2012. *From Books to Beozars: Sir Hans Sloane*. London: British Library.

See also Environmental Archaeology; The Institute of Jamaica; Jamaica (Prehistory of).

Spanish Colonial Ceramic Types

R. Grant Gilmore III

As with other aspects of colonial Spanish culture (architecture, cuisine, etc.), ceramics in the Spanish colonies were an amalgamation of old and new, local production and imports, and included a diversity of forms reflecting the various cultures that were incorporated into the Spanish colonial world. Islamic influences, Native American ideas, and Roman legacies were all combined to form a unique Iberian material culture in the Americas and the Caribbean in particular (Figure S.11). Iberian or locally made ceramic types include coarse earthenwares and majolica in a variety of forms. Common coarse earthenware varieties include both redware and grayware.

A *hidroceramo* is a water jug with a spout and a strap handle that is often unglazed and is made from grayware or redware. It was likely used for storing and cooling water and may have been produced primarily in Mexico. This vessel dates to the eighteenth century primarily, although there is some evidence that the form may be as old as the sixteenth century. They are also known as *botijos*. An *orza* is a bulbous vessel form with a flat base and an opening that is smaller than the fullest body diameter. Generally made from redware, it was used for storage. Small versions were used as drug pots. Very large examples (sometimes over one meter high) were used to store water outside homes.

Grayware, which consists of a fine gray paste and a sand temper, is a distinctive ceramic type that was often used in the production of *hidroceramos*. The type has been found primarily on post-1750 sites. In addition to Puerto Rico, Santo Domingo, and Cuba, the type is also found regularly on St. Eustatius. Majolica is a tin-glazed ceramic type in the same family as the French *faïence* and other misnamed "delftwares." The body is yellow and its glazed decoration includes distinctive geometric and floral motifs. Its Moorish influence is clear. "Majoli-

Figure S.11. Spanish earthenwares recovered from various late-eighteenth-century sites on St. Eustatius. *Clockwise from upper left*: internally glazed olive jar, unglazed olive jar, a *hidroceramo* jar top, and sherd from a very large *orza* used as a water jar. Courtesy of R. Grant Gilmore III and SECAR.

cas" were also produced in the Netherlands by potters influenced by Spanish imports. They are found quite commonly on both Dutch and Spanish islands.

The origins of olive jars are traceable to the Phoenicians and the Romans (most notably to the amphora). Olive jars could be glazed or unglazed, depending on what was to be stored. The vessel form evolved over the centuries. Early-style jars (sixteenth century) are bulbous and include two strap handles and everted mouths. Middle-style jars (from the seventeenth and

eighteenth centuries) are also bulbous but lack strap handles and instead have a ring neck. Although the style is found throughout the Caribbean, additional research is needed to discern its temporal changes more precisely. A thinner neck with a ring form, sometimes a simple donut shape attached to the body, is indicative of many late-style olive jars. Dating to the end of the eighteenth century on into the early nineteenth century, late-style jars closed out the development of olive jar forms in the Hispanic world. Some middle and late olive jars may be elongated in shape and more reminiscent of the amphora produced by earlier Mediterranean cultures. The *plato* was a plate/saucer or shallow dish that is expressed by both majolica and coarse earthenware manufacturers. The Spanish chamber pot, or *bacin*, was often made from red coarse earthenware. The cylindrical form with everted rim is distinctive.

Further Reading

Deagan, K. 1987. *Artifacts of the Spanish Colonies of Florida and the Caribbean, 1500–1800*. Vol. 1, *Ceramics, Glassware, and Beads*. Washington, DC: Smithsonian Institution Press.
Fairbanks, C. 1972. "The Cultural Significance of Spanish Ceramics." In *Ceramics in America*, ed. I. Quimby, 141–74. Charlottesville: University of Virginia Press.
Goggin, J. 1960. *The Spanish Olive Jar: An Introductory Study*. New Haven, CT: Yale University Press.
———. 1968. *Spanish Majolica in the New World*. New Haven, CT: Yale University Press.

See also Dutch Colonial Ceramic Types; French Colonial Ceramic Types.

Spanish Town (Jamaica)

James Robertson

Spanish Town, also known as St. Jago de la Vega, Jamaica's former capital, is a long-established town founded by the island's Spanish colonists (Figure S.12). It was retained as the island's seat of government after the English conquest in 1655 until 1872. It is still an administrative and marketing hub today. In addition, it holds substantial physical remains that offer the potential to document the successive stages of its archaeological and architectural heritage.

In 1534, the town's Spanish founders established a grid when they laid out their new settlement on a hillside sloping down to a ford across what the Spaniards called

the Caguaya River (today the Rio Cobre). The town is located where the north-south route that traverses Jamaica's central mountains joined the east-west trail that links the island's southern coastal plains. A sugar plantation and water mill were already established on the site; the key feature of the new town's plan was the lane up from the ford. There had been some earlier human use of the site. For example, scraps of a Taíno bowl located during excavations at the Old King's House probably originated from burials at the Taíno settlement at White Marl (Mathewson 1972, 4). The Spaniards' selection of a site for a European-planned town in the vicinity of a ma-

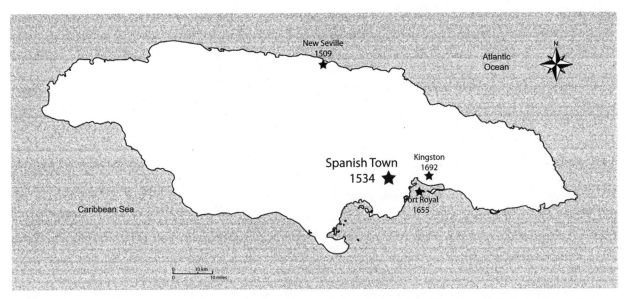

Figure S.12. Location of Spanish Town, Jamaica. Reproduced by permission of Thera Edwards; redrawn by R. Grant Gilmore III.

jor existing indigenous settlement paralleled the choices Spanish colonists made elsewhere in the New World.

Spanish Town was initially called New Seville, but it remained the sleepy capital of an undeveloped colony. Most of its initial residents moved there from the earlier Spanish port of the same name on the island's north coast. This site was abandoned when the Spaniards failed to find gold mines there. Shifts in Spanish sailing patterns left the site a backwater. Unlike its predecessor, the new inland town was neither a port nor a mining or manufacturing center, though a kiln stood near the river bank on the eastern side of the town and some tanneries were located downstream. In 1534, when Spanish Town was founded, there were no royal subventions for constructing elaborate stone chapels or hospitals. The island of cattle ranches had unimpressive public buildings, although the Spaniards placed them on an ambitious grid plan. To the south of this grid lay small huts that housed surviving Taíno and the enslaved Africans who worked in the town. By the late sixteenth century, the Taíno were no longer a distinct urban population. Spanish Jamaica's principal town in the mid-seventeenth century was described as "well proportioned and symmetrical, with streets, squares and public places," with "houses [that] were for the most part built of plaster" (Colón de Portugal 1992, H). (Figure S.13). The compounds, lining its narrow streets, were primarily one-story wooden-framed structures with hardwood corner posts, thick walls, and tile or palmetto thatch roofs. Its principal church, the church of the abbot of Jamaica on the main plaza, was constructed of canes plastered over with clay.

Today, one of the two names used for the town, St. Jago de la Vega; the choice of an inland rather than a seaside site; the town's two principal squares; the ground plan of the brick-built friary; and the widths of individual streets all remain from the Spanish period, which lasted from 1534 to the English invasion in 1655. Foundations for at least two Spanish-era sites still lie just below modern surfaces: one, a residence on the road up from the ford, was observed during work on the parking lot at the St. Catherine Public Library; the other is on Emancipation Square's south side, where into the 1930s townspeople claimed that when heavy rain washed away the gravel road surface, the foundations of the abbot's "White Church" were revealed.

Although no Spanish buildings stand today, many lasted long despite the English invaders' lack of appreciation of the townspeoples' single-story low-ceilinged houses and the narrow streets those structures lined. These buildings were well suited to Jamaica's geology and weather; they rode out the earthquakes and hurricanes that over the next sixty years toppled all the tall brick English-style residences that the newcomers erected. The island's public buildings—those that were not demolished in the takeover—were also part of what the English inherited from the Spaniards. The newly reconstructed brick Dominican friary on the southern edge of the town became "the red church" and, from 1660, the Anglican parish church. On the western side of the *plaza mayor* stood the townspeoples' municipal council chamber, the *casa cabilde* next to the wooden *audiencia*. The invading English commander requisitioned both buildings, which later became the gover-

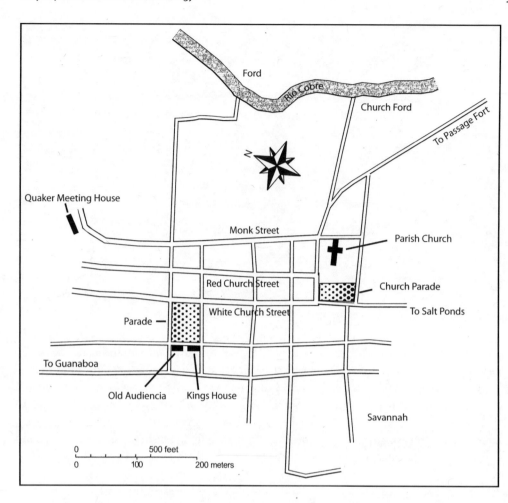

Figure S.13. Layout of Spanish Town, Jamaica, in the 1660s. Reproduced by permission of Thera Edwards; redrawn by R. Grant Gilmore III.

nor's residence, known as the King's House. These structures continued in use through the 1750s. The location of the Spanish governor's house is unidentified, though a Victorian commentator proposed a site near the Infirmary Gardens, a block to the east of the former *plaza mayor*, perhaps primarily because of a "magnificent avenue" of long-lived tamarind trees there. The physical continuities of route and width that shape the town's narrow streets struck visitors and contrasted with the buildings and wide streets of Port Royal and Kingston, where town planners followed English styles.

Under English rule, Spanish Town ceased to be the island's primary urban settlement. The town became the seat of government of a rich colony and a thriving local market center. Excavations by the Jamaican National Heritage Trust in 1995 at a late-seventeenth-century site at 15½ White Church Street located a kiln used for manufacturing clay pipes from the local red clay. A visiting Englishman noted that "the negroes make Tobacco pipes with" this commodity (Buisseret 2008, 179). The town's showpiece public buildings date from the eighteenth into the early nineteenth centuries, as do many of the substantial houses and shops on Spanish Town's older streets. The public buildings included the parish church, which was rebuilt after a hurricane in 1712 destroyed the brick-built Spanish friary, and the site of today's Emancipation Square, where a combined armory and archives building was authorized in the early 1740s. The old *audiencia* was demolished in 1759 so a new King's House could be built, and a House of Assembly was built across from the King's House. Both were completed in 1762. In the 1780s, the assembly authorized a building to house the island secretary's office, and an adjoining colonnade housed an expensive imported statue of Admiral George Rodney by John Bacon. In 1819, the square was completed when a new court house was built on its southern side. The town also gained a barracks in the early 1760s, expensive marble monuments in the parish church, and, as an innovative solution to the flood-prone ford across the Rio Cobre, a prefabricated iron bridge imported from England in 1802 (Francis-Brown and Francis 2005). Despite the fact that fires gutted the old King's House in 1925 and the court house in 1986, the facades surrounding the square remain impressive, displaying the skills of local building workers, both free and enslaved. Excavations by Mathewson at the old King's House site from 1971 to 1974 exceeded expectations and generated two interim reports and extensive finds (Mathewson 1970, 1972).

Eighteenth- and early nineteenth-century Spanish Town housed a large number of private buildings that a mid-eighteenth-century French report characterized as "très-bien bâties" (very well built). These provided permanent residences for senior government officials and lawyers and elite shops and properties that were leased out when the law courts were in session and during the accompanying social season. The buildings that have survived form one of the largest collections of domestic buildings from this period on the island, even though individual structures are vulnerable to dilapidation and alteration (Concannon 1970). This important group has received little archaeological study, though test excavations of the Neveh Shalom Synagogue site in 1998 and 1999 demonstrated the potential for further work at the site of one eighteenth-century brick structure (Allsworth-Jones, Gray, and Walters 2003). Further architectural studies of old houses in Spanish Town, photographic surveys by the Jamaica Georgian Society in the late 1970s, and surveys by students at the University of Technology, Jamaica, in 1994 all generated useful data. The society's photographs are now at the National Library of Jamaica and other data are held at the University of Technology, Jamaica (Harrison, 1982). In the eighteenth century, the assembly sought to control the urban compounds that the enslaved occupied. Laws were passed that said that fences had to be too tall to leap over, and houses of the enslaved could have only one door. These measures were intended to deter running away from patrols, but at the same time they offered residents some privacy.

The buildings of nineteenth-century Spanish Town have received less attention, overshadowed by both their splendid eighteenth-century predecessors and by the relocation of the colony's seat of government to Kingston in 1872. During this century, several substantial buildings were added to the town. Churches include the Wesleyan Methodist and Baptist chapels that were constructed in the 1820s. The Anglicans erected a chapel in 1844, and another Baptist chapel was built in 1852. After the town's parish church was elevated to an Anglican Cathedral in 1844, it endured substantial "restorations" to make it appear suitably medieval (Robertson 2011). In 1872, falling property prices permitted the town's Roman Catholics to construct a brick chapel. Further public commissions include the Sligo Water Works, which opened in 1834,

part of whose works are still standing; the Jamaica Railway Company, which opened in 1846; the Rio Cobre Dam and associated irrigation canals, which begun in the 1870s; and the St. Catherine District Prison, which was erected over the protests of local civic leaders in the 1890s. Extensive plans at the Jamaica Archives record these projects, which were among the island's most substantial public works. The town's late Victorian covered market complex still provides a facility for farmers and craftspeople from a sizable catchment area.

The relocation of the governor's office from Spanish Town to Kingston prompted an abrupt transition. Landlords demolished large houses that stood empty after the pool of tenants who came for the assembly terms and social season disappeared. The rubble was reused in the new Rio Cobre Canal's irrigation system. Spanish Town still served as a regional market center, however. In addition, when the new irrigation works began to operate in 1880s and 1890s, it became a hub for a thriving economy of banana and sugar plantations. This led to further changes in the townscape as farm laborers and small shopkeepers settled its streets. In the late nineteenth and early twentieth centuries, new one- and two-story shops were built with cast-iron pillars on cement foundations, along with sizable numbers of small wooden houses built with imported lumber on balloon frames. The carved barge boards on some of these cottages and the fretwork tracery that decorates transoms over front doors display the pride of the local artisans who built them. The potential for studies of this vernacular architecture is remarkable.

The town continued to change after Jamaica secured its independence from Britain in 1962. Proposals for heritage preservation exist, but since tourism is centered on the north coast, the absence of free-spending visitors in Spanish Town may undermine residents' appreciation of preservation. New building continues. The town has added sizable suburbs while streetscapes in the old center have changed; now three-story buildings constructed from cement blocks occupy lots that originally held smaller structures. Older houses are transformed by concrete extensions, steel roofs, aluminum louvers, plate-glass windows, and vivid paint colors. There is still plenty to see, and some African craft traditions survive. Careful studies in the 1980s of the coiled clay pottery constructed by the late Mrs. Louisa Jones, "Ma Lou," and her family just outside the town highlighted continuities with African potters' practices (Ebanks 1984). Spanish Town may project a modern face, but the historic city is not far below its modern surface.

Further Reading

Allsworth-Jones, P., D. Gray, and S. Walters. 2003. "The Neveh Shalom Synagogue Site in Spanish Town, Jamaica." In *Towards an Archaeology of Buildings: Contexts and Concepts*, ed. G. Mala, 77–88. Oxford: Archaeopress.

Buisseret, D., ed. *Jamaica in 1687: The Taylor Manuscript at the National Library of Jamaica*. Kingston, Jamaica: University of the West Indies Press.

Colón de Portugal, Pedro Nuño. 1992. *The Columbus Petition Document of Don Pedro Colón de Portugal y Castro . . . for the Island of Jamaica, 1672*. Kingston, Jamaica: Mill Press.

Concannon, T. A. L. 1970. "Our Architectural Heritage: Houses of the 18th and 19th Century with Special Reference to Spanish Town." *Jamaica Journal* 4 (2): 23–28.

Ebanks, R. C. 1984. "Ma Lou and the African-Jamaican Pottery Tradition." *Jamaica Journal* 17 (3): 31–37.

Francis-Brown, S., and P. Francis. 2005. *The Old Iron Bridge*. Kingston, Jamaica: Caribbean School of Architecture, University of Technology.

Harrison, D. "19 White Church Street." *Jamaican Historical Society Bulletin* 8 (7): 167–78.

Mathewson, R. D. 1970. "The Old King's House Archaeological Project." *Jamaican Historical Society Bulletin* 5 (11): 140–50.

———. 1972. "History from the Earth: Archaeological Excavations at Old King's House." *Jamaica Journal* 6 (2): 3–11.

Robertson, J. 2005. *Gone Is the Ancient Glory: Spanish Town, Jamaica, 1534–2000*. Kingston: Ian Randle Publishers.

———. 2011. "Victorian Restorations: Reconfiguring the Cathedral in Spanish Town." *Jamaica Journal* 33 (3): 36–43.

See also Falmouth (Jamaica); The Magnificent Seven Mansions (Port of Spain, Trinidad); Port Antonio (Jamaica); Taíno Museum at White Marl (Jamaica); Willemstad (Curaçao).

St. Eustatius

R. Grant Gilmore III

St. Eustatius possesses the densest concentration of archaeological sites in the Americas. Archaeological data from St. Eustatius was first obtained by the eminent Dutch geologist/volcanologist, Gustaaf Mollengraf. Mention of the prehistoric peoples on St. Eustatius was made in his 1886 book *De geologie van het eiland St. Eustatius* (The Geology of the Island of St. Eustatius). However, it was not until the arrival of an ethnographer from Leiden University, Jan Petrus Benjamin de Josselin de Jong, that sites were identified and recorded using archaeological methods. He recorded in some detail a Saladoid site near the St. Eustatius airport that has come to be known as the Golden Rock Site (SE 88/89). This site was extensively excavated in the mid-1980s, when it was threatened by a runway extension, by a team from Leiden University led by Aad Versteeg and Kees Schinkel. The layout of the village, burials, faunal remains, and carbon dates for occupation all provided essential information on this centrally located village site. The St. Eustatius Historical Foundation Museum in Oranjestad has exhibitions about this excavation as well as a model *maloca* (a large peaked housing structure) on display.

The European settlement of St. Eustatius began during the 1620s, when French settlers occupied a cliff-top site overlooking Oranje Bay. Within a few years, Dutch colonists had taken over and established tobacco and cotton plantations and a rudimentary trading station under the Dutch West Indies Company. By the 1660s, St. Eustatius had developed enough to garner the attention of marauding privateers, including Edward Morgan from Jamaica. In 1665, Morgan died from a heart attack during an assault, but this did not stop his men from sacking Statia in the name of the English King. During the next few decades, Statia became better known as a trading station. During the first few decades of the eighteenth century, Statia developed into one of the primary slave-trading depots in the northern Caribbean. Tens of thousands of slaves were bought and sold here.

Through the middle decades of the eighteenth century, sugar plantations and rum distilleries were established across the island. At least one indigo plantation was also built and operated there. In contrast to other islands in the Caribbean, these plantations were not built for profit from local sugar crops. Instead, they were used to "launder" sugar to avoid taxes charged in England, France, Spain, and the Netherlands. Massive quantities of raw sugar from other islands, including Jamaica, St. Kitts, and Antigua, were brought clandestinely to St. Eustatius to be refined or processed into rum. The increased profit margin was then shared between planter and merchant. During the Seven Years' War (1756–1763), known in North America as the French and Indian War (1754–1763), Statia cemented its position as the preeminent Atlantic World trading hub, a position it held for the next fifty years.

As a neutral nation, The Netherlands (through St. Eustatius and to a lesser extent Curaçao) took advantage of trading opportunities with both sides in the conflict. Warehouse construction along Oranje Bay expanded so rapidly that by the time Britain's North American colonists had declared their independence in 1776, Statia had no equal as an entrepôt for war matériel and every essential item a colonial household needed. For the first few years, St. Eustatius almost single-handedly supplied the American colonists in their bid to establish a new nation. French, Dutch, Spanish, and even English merchants threw their buying and selling power into the fray. In 1781, the English sacked Statia, which shut down trade for a few months, until the French retook the island later that year. English admiral G. B. Rodney auctioned the warehouse contents, as was customary at the time. The resulting bounty illustrates the sheer wealth on the island; over 5 million pounds sterling were realized, the equivalent of 10–15 percent of England's GDP at the time.

Contrary to popular belief, Rodney's sacking of St. Eustatius did not spell the end of the island's meteoric rise. The post-war period was Statia's heyday. During the 1790s, over 3,400 ships a year landed in Statia, bringing trade from all nations. Disaster, however, came with the French occupation of the island. France implemented a tax policy, something that had not been seen on St. Eustatius for many decades. Merchants, who were accustomed to a free trade environment, fled in droves to St. Thomas, Saint Barthélemy, and New England. The decline of Statia's fortunes was heightened during the Napoleonic period, when the island switched hands between the French and the English several more times. When the Netherlands was finally able to gain control of St. Eustatius permanently in 1816, it was already too late. Economic recovery was impossible because most merchants had moved on to other islands and the United States to reestablish their businesses. Although it has been traditionally said that the resulting stagnation caused great suffering for Statia's inhabitants throughout the nineteenth century and into the mid-twentieth century, documentary evidence held in Curaçao indicates that some trade continued at least the 1860s, but not at the levels there were seen at the end of the eighteenth century. After slavery ended in 1863, Statia's economic decline truly began. The positive result of this predica-

ment (at least for archaeologists) was that Statians had little economic power to rebuild or take down old structures. The consequences are seen on the landscape today in an incomparable collection of eighteenth-century wooden buildings and numerous archaeological sites. While positive economic development on other Caribbean islands resulted in a wholesale destruction of the colonial fabric, on Statia the colonial heritage has been preserved virtually untouched for almost two centuries.

In many ways, Statia's cultural heritage is unique. As Adam Smith has noted, the foundations of capitalism can be found in the free trade economy that was developed on St. Eustatius (Smith 1869, 151). This permitted an extravagant lifestyle that is reflected in archaeological and architectural remains today. The architecture on the island is a combination of French, Dutch, and English aesthetic and engineering styles. Documentary records and archaeological remains indicate extravagantly appointed homes that commonly featured marble floors, crystal chandeliers, and silk wallpaper. Ceramics are perhaps the most interesting evidence of extreme wealth. For example, hand-enameled porcelain (the most expensive ceramic) is commonly found at slave-occupied sites. Creamware found on the island, especially pearlware forms and types, is also diverse and extravagant. The decline of Statia's economy is also reflected in its material culture—virtually no whiteware or ironstone products are found here. Trade declined significantly after the 1820s, and the dearth of new material culture entering the island is a direct reflection of this fact. Ceramics were reused, as Ivor Noël Hume attested in his account of a 1972 visit to the island, during which he was served tea with a completely intact set of engine-turned redware!

Historical archaeologists Edwin Dethlefsen and Norman Barka visited St. Eustatius in the late 1970s. As a result of their visit, they established an ongoing research program on the island through the College of William and Mary that lasted for twenty years. Dozens of William and Mary undergraduate and graduate students encountered Caribbean fieldwork for the first time through this program. In addition, a number of St. Eustatius residents attended the College of William and Mary, resulting in closer ties between the university and the island. Barka excavated a range of sites, including the Government Guest House, which was formerly a barracks; the Honen Dalim Synagogue (the second oldest in the Americas); several warehouses on Oranje Bay; Battery de Windt, Governor de Graff's Concordia plantation, and a number of additional urban sites. In all, Barka identified over 600 archaeological sites on the island, making it the most densely concentrated archaeological area in the

Americas. The work he completed on St. Eustatius was not published extensively. However, his students' work became his legacy. Over thirty MA theses and several PhD theses were based on his research on St. Eustatius.

In 1997, R. Grant Gilmore III worked on Statia with Norman Barka to investigate areas around the Simon Doncker house (now the site of the St. Eustatius Historical Foundation Museum) and what was then called the Voges house. By the summer's end, plans were drawn up to try to bring a permanent archaeological presence to the island in the form of the St. Eustatius Center for Archaeological Research (SECAR). Plans did not come to fruition until 2004, when Gilmore became the founding director of the research center. Since then, a number of sites have been excavated, including further work at the Honen Dalim Synagogue, where a mikvah was found. Several sites on Oranje Bay, including what may have been the headquarters for the Dutch West Indies Company and what may have been a ceramic production site, have also been identified. Joanna Gilmore led a team that excavated a leprosy hospital site for the first time in the Americas. SECAR has also identified numerous new enslaved village sites in addition to a possible free black village adjacent to what is traditionally known as the Congo Burial Ground, a cemetery for the enslaved. SECAR has also completed a geographic information system for the island and is currently working on one for Saba. Close to 1,000 archaeology sites have been identified thus far, representing over 12 percent of the known archaeological sites in the entirety of The Netherlands. In October 2010, St. Eustatius became a special entity of The Netherlands, which has around 15,000 archaeological sites.

The changing political status of St. Eustatius in 2010 has resulted in significant changes for archaeology and the development of monuments policy on the island. In May 2008, a monuments ordinance was finally passed by the island's Executive Council. However, there is still no protection for archaeological heritage on the island, although SECAR has spearheaded efforts to change this situation.

Further Reading

Dethlefsen, E., and N. F. Barka. 1982. "Archaeology on St. Eustatius: The Pompeii of the New World." *Archaeology* 35 (2): 8–15.

Gilmore, R. G. 2006. "All the Documents Are Destroyed! Documenting Slavery for St. Eustatius." In *African Re-Genesis: Confronting Social Issues in the African Diaspora*, ed. J. Haviser and K. MacDonald. London: Routledge.

———. 2008. "Geophysics and Volcanic Islands: Resitivity and Gradiometry on St. Eustatius." In *Archaeology and Geoinformatics: Case Studies from the Caribbean*, ed. Basil A. Reid, 170–83. Tuscaloosa: University of Alabama Press.

———. 2013. "St. Eustatius—The Nexus for Colonial Caribbean Capitalism." In *The Archaeology of Interdependence*, ed. D. Comer, 41–60. New York: Springerlink.

———. In press "Vernacular Architecture in the Caribbean." In *Archaeology, Syncretism, Creolisation*, ed. T. Clack. Oxford: Oxford University Press.

Smith, Adam. 1869. *An Inquiry into the Nature and Causes of the Wealth of Nations*. Vol. 2. Oxford: Clarendon Press.

See also Bonaire (Dutch Caribbean; Former Netherlands Antilles); Curaçao (Former Netherlands Antilles); The Dutch Caribbean; Sint Maarten (Former Netherlands Antilles).

St. Eustatius Center for Archaeological Research (SECAR)

R. Grant Gilmore III

The St. Eustatius Center for Archaeological Research, a not-for-profit foundation, was originally conceived in 1997 by Norman F. Barka (College of William and Mary, Virginia), R. Grant Gilmore III, Siem Dijkshoorn (Historical Core Renovation Project), and Gay Soetekouw (then at the St. Eustatius Historical Foundation). In 2004, a budget was obtained from the government of St. Eustatius. R. Grant Gilmore was its first director. SECAR's mandate includes the following:

• To educate the local, regional, and international public about the prehistoric and historic archaeological history of St. Eustatius and the Caribbean.
• To develop innovative technologies and methods of improving the recording of underwater and terrestrial archaeological sites, site identification, artifact recording, and artifact identification.
• To protect underwater and terrestrial cultural heritage resources.

- To enhance the interpretation of underwater and terrestrial cultural heritage resources.
- To help local, regional, and international governments reach their goals for protecting underwater and terrestrial cultural heritage resources.
- To help local, regional, and international nongovernmental organizations reach their goals for protecting underwater and terrestrial cultural heritage resources.
- To help local, regional, and international governments develop goals for underwater and terrestrial cultural heritage tourism.
- To help local, regional, and international nongovernmental organizations develop goals for underwater and terrestrial cultural heritage tourism.

To fulfill these goals, SECAR has brought several hundred volunteers and professionals to the Caribbean and St. Eustatius to participate in what it calls an "Excavation Experience." Recent discoveries have included the first mikvah (ceremonial bath) to be excavated in the Caribbean, a free black village settlement, burials of enslaved individuals and executed criminals, what is likely

the headquarters for the Dutch West Indies Company on Statia, a pottery production site, and dozens of slave quarters on plantations in the northern quarter of St. Eustatius. SECAR spearheaded efforts in the islands of Bonaire, St. Eustatius, and Saba to enhance legislative and community protection of archaeological heritage on these islands as they rejoined the country of the Netherlands in 2010.

Further Reading

Gilmore, R. G. 2006. "Urban Transformation and Upheaval in the West Indies: The Case of Oranjestad, St. Eustatius, Netherlands Antilles." In *Cities in the World, 1500–2000*, ed. A. Green and R. Leech, 83–95. London: Maney.

Gilmore, R. G., and S. Dijkshoorn. 2005. "St. Eustatius Monuments and Heritage—Preservation: History and Archaeology on the Historical Gem." In *Archeology in the Caribbean and the World Heritage List: An Archeological Approach towards the Global Strategy*, ed. Nuria Sanz, 200–205. Paris: UNESCO.

Gilmore, R. G., and J. B. Haviser. 2011. "Cultural Heritage Management and Legislation in the Netherlands Antilles." In *Protecting Heritage in the Caribbean*, ed. P. Siegel and E. Righter, 134–46. Tuscaloosa: University of Alabama Press.

The St. Eustatius Historical Foundation

Joanna K. Gilmore

In 1972, students from the Netherlands and Prof. Temminck Grol made an inventory of the historical buildings in Oranjestad. This inventory was made as part of a direct appeal to the authorities to preserve the historical character of the island. The increased awareness that resulted of the island's unique historical remains from its prosperous colonial past and the construction of a pier in 1973 that uncovered many artifacts encouraged a group of dedicated citizens—Statian, Dutch, and American—to establish the St. Eustatius Historical Foundation in March 1974. The aims of the St. Eustatius Historical Foundation include encouraging historical study of and interest in St. Eustatius, promoting excavations and investigations of archaeological/historical sites on St. Eustatius, and ensuring that historical finds of any kind are kept on the island.

The island government provided the foundation with a building in Oranjestad to house artifacts and conduct meetings. In the beginning, the historical foundation

provided historical walking tours of Oranjestad and used donkey carts to take tourists around the historical sites. Another early project was the Island Beautification Plan, which involved landscaping along the Bay Road.

Starting in 1979, the historical foundation played a key role in coordinating archaeological field schools with Dr. Norman F. Barka from the College of William and Mary in Virginia. Barka and his students excavated at a number of plantation, military, warehouse, and urban sites during his almost twenty years of fieldwork on the island. The entire island was surveyed, and John Eastman recorded and mapped all known archaeological sites in 1995. Many masters' theses were written by students at the College of William and Mary after they completed fieldwork on Statia. Dr. Aad H. Versteeg and other archaeologists from Leiden University in the Netherlands and at the Archaeological-Anthropological Institute of the Netherlands Antilles began work at the Golden Rock prehistoric site on Statia in 1984. The excavation continued until 1987; a total of 2,800 square meters of earth were uncovered.

The Golden Rock prehistoric site is the largest and most important Saladoid period site (dating from fifth to ninth centuries AD) on St. Eustatius. The community of possibly 75–100 individuals lived on a flat agricultural plain, a central location from which they could access marine resources, clay sources, coral, wood, and groundwater. Zooarchaeological evidence suggests that the group's diet mainly consisted of protein from marine resources and was supplemented by iguanas, rice rats, agoutis, birds, and land crabs. The inhabitants also cultivated cassava. Archaeologists found postholes from a number of circular structures that may have been similar to the *malocas* seen in Venezuela today. Artifacts found at the site include a wide variety of tools and decorative items made of bone, shell, stone, and coral and earthenware pottery with red and white slip designs, incisions, and rims that were modeled into human and animal forms.

In 1983, Queen Beatrix of the Netherlands purchased the eighteenth-century house of a wealthy merchant, Simon Doncker, for the St. Eustatius Historical Foundation. Restoration and furnishing of the building took place over the next two years, and the official opening took place in September 1985. The final shipment of eighteenth-century furniture from Holland arrived in 1987. The completed exhibits were displayed at an open house in November 1987. In 1991, the museum won an American Express award as the best example of historic preservation in the Caribbean area. A major renovation of the building was completed in 1999, and a complete renovation of the documents in the main exhibit room was completed in 2005.

The island government gave the historical foundation the authority to manage a number of historical structures in Oranjestad, such as the Dutch Reformed Church (consecrated in 1755) and the Honen Dalim Synagogue. These two buildings have been restored by the Dutch government. Since 1998, the historical foundation has also operated a small gallery on Oranje Bay, which displays and sells local arts and crafts. This gallery provides a small income for the St. Eustatius Historical Foundation and is staffed entirely by volunteers.

The St. Eustatius Monuments Foundation, formed under the St. Eustatius Historical Foundation, was established in April 1990. Its purpose is to protect, renovate, and reconstruct cultural goods (particularly historic structures) on the island. In 2004, the St. Eustatius Historical Foundation also established SECAR, the St. Eustatius Center for Archaeological Research, which was founded to take over the archaeological research on the island. R. Grant Gilmore was the director of SECAR from 2004 to 2011. The St. Eustatius Center for Archaeological Research was established as a separate foundation in February 2008. In 2005, Gilmore and his students located an eighteenth-century mikvah at the Honen Dalim Synagogue (built in 1739). Other excavations and surveys have been conducted at a number of sites across the island.

The St. Eustatius Historical Foundation has published books relating to local cuisine and a guide to walking tours on the island. A multiyear project that re-created an eighteenth-century blacksmith shop, which demonstrates the tools used in the blacksmithing trade and exhibits handmade iron artifacts from the museum collection, was completed in 2011. The historical foundation also has a relationship with the Cooperstown Graduate Program in History Museum Studies (part of the State University of New York), whereby students work as interns on museum projects each summer.

Further Reading

St. Eustatius Center for Archaeological Research. N.d. "The St. Eustatius Center for Archaeological Research." www.secar.org. Accessed January 17, 2013.

St. Eustatius Historical Foundation. 2010. "St. Eustatius Historical Foundation Museum." www.steustatiushistory.org. Accessed January 17, 2013.

See also Golden Rock Site (St. Eustatius).

St. John Site (Trinidad)

Basil A. Reid

St. John is located south of the Godineau River in Trinidad in close proximity to the South Oropouche mangrove swamp. The site is a relatively deep shallow shell midden about 1.2 meters (4 feet) deep, with a maximum diameter of 38.1 meters (125 feet). At the western end, exposed strata show that each is characterized by a predominance of different mollusk species. In 1924, J. A. Bullbrook collected shells and mammal bones at the site. In 1953, Bullbrook and Irving Rouse relocated the site, and Rouse, Bullbrook, and colleagues excavated a trench that yielded Arauquinoid ceramics in the uppermost level. Materials retrieved from these 1953 excavations are housed at the Peabody Museum, Yale University. Over the years, hammerstones and celts have been discovered at St. John. A radiocarbon assay of the site in 1994 yielded a C14 date of 6672±48 BP, which, when calibrated, is 5470–5290 BC. This agrees well with its classification as an Archaic Age Ortoiroid site, making St. John virtually contemporary with Banwari Trace, also in southwestern Trinidad.

In February and March 2009, October 2009, March and April 2010 (Reid 2011), and February, March, and April 2013, surveys and excavations were undertaken at the St. John site (SPA-11) in southwestern Trinidad. Spearheaded by the Archaeology Unit in the Department of History at The University of the West Indies, St. Augustine, the project was made possible by the involvement of UWI undergraduate history/archaeology students and a handful of volunteers. Of major significance was the retrieval of four grindstones and three pestles from 2009 to 2013 (Figure S.14). These artifacts clearly intimate that plant materials were processed at this site and, by extension, the existence of early Ortoiroid farming (Reid 2011). Many of the ground stone tools appear to have been used for pounding and processing hard or fibrous vegetable material.

An abundance of shells, mammal bones, and stone artifacts (including flakes, pestles, and grindstones) were recovered from the site. This suggests that the Ortoiroid, who inhabited St. John approximately 7,000 years ago, used a judicious combination of strategies for getting food and exploited a range of resource habitats in close proximity to the site. Like Banwari Trace, the archaeological remains at St. John suggest that there was little use of deep sea resources. In addition, there was a general shift from the use of terrestrial animals toward the use of

Figure S.14. Jesse Ramdeo, a history/archaeology student at The University of the West Indies, St. Augustine removing a large grindstone from the St. John, Trinidad, site in March 2010. Courtesy of Basil A. Reid.

foods from marine environments, particularly inshore and estuarine species (Boomert 2000). Bone tools, primarily sharpened bone tips for hunting or fishing spears, have been preserved at St. John in large numbers. They range from about 2 to 15 centimeters in length (Wilson 2007). Similar to Banwari Trace, the artifacts from St. John include bone and stone tools relating to fishing and collecting, canoe building, plant processing, and general cutting and scraping (Wilson 2007).

Further Reading

Boomert, A. 2000. *Trinidad, Tobago, and the Lower Orinoco Interaction Sphere: An Archaeological/Ethnohistorical Study.* Alkmaar: Cairi Publications.

Reid, B. A. 2011. "Interim Report on the St. John Archaeology Project." In *Archaeology and Anthropology, Journal of Walter Roth Museum of Anthropology* 1 (17): 39–54.

Wilson, S. M. 2007. *The Archaeology of the Caribbean.* Cambridge, UK: Cambridge University Press.

See also The Archaic Age; Banwari Trace (Trinidad); The Ortoiroid.

St. Vincent

Richard T. Callaghan

St. Vincent is located in the Eastern Caribbean. It is one of the four large islands of the Windward Island group. It is located to the north about 46 kilometers from Saint Lucia. Between St. Vincent and the island of Grenada (about 72 kilometers to the south) lie the thirty-two small islands of the Grenadines. The mountainous center of the island is covered in forest that is usually shrouded in cloud. The La Soufrière volcano is the most prominent topographic feature. This active volcano is 1,220 meters high and has had historic eruptions in 1718, 1812, 1902, and 1979 (Sigurdsson and Carey 1991). Prehistorically, there was a massive eruption of Soufrière around 2700 BC, and there have been fairly regular eruptions since about AD 700 to historic times. These eruptions are likely to have had as much or more impact on prehistoric populations as they have had on historic ones. There are numerous permanent and intermittent rivers and streams on the island, but the courses of these have often been altered by volcanic activity.

St. Vincent is a fertile island (Caribbean Conservation Association and Island Resource Foundation 1991, 1). The native vegetation patterns have undergone considerable modification in some areas. Much of this is due to historical agriculture practices, but some of the modifications began with the earliest human occupation of the island. Below 300 meters above sea level, much of the island has been under cultivation for some time. However, cultivation also is practiced above this zone, and in some cases even steep slopes have been cleared. Despite this, large areas of primary forest remain, including rain forests in the interior and along the northwest coast. These forests exist in part due to the lack of road access and the designation of much of them as protected.

Archaeological Research

Reports of Archaic cultures occupying St. Vincent have been made, but the evidence for such occupations is questionable (Keegan 1994). The prehistoric chronology of the island, as it is known, is largely based on ceramic styles and a small number of radiocarbon dates. Human occupation of the island appears to have begun about AD 200 or slightly earlier (Bullen and Bullen 1972). The prehistoric cultural periods of the Lesser Antilles in general are Cedrosan Saladoid (500 BC–AD 500), Barrancoid (AD 350–800), Troumassan Troumassoid (AD

500–1000), and Suazan Troumassoid (AD 1000–1500). The overlap in the dates for these periods is because of the continuation of ceramic traits from earlier time periods into succeeding periods.

The reporting of prehistoric archaeology (see Callaghan 2007 for a summary research on the island prior to 2005) seems to have started on St. Vincent with Branch's article in *The St. Vincent Handbook, Directory and Almanac for 1911*, which provided some locations and information on sites. In 1913 and 1914, J. Walter Fewkes conducted a survey on St. Vincent. In his report, Fewkes described over 3,000 ground stone artifacts, many of which would be classified as axes. None of these artifacts is easily assigned to a specific prehistoric culture or period. In *Origins of the Tainan Culture*, Sven Lovén (1935) included some discussion of Vincentian archaeology. Dr. Earle Kirby and the St. Vincent Archaeological and Historical Society conducted considerable survey work (see Kirby 1969, 1970), and work by the National Trust continues today.

Archaeological investigations were conducted in 1969 and 1970 on St. Vincent and the Grenadines by Ripley and Adelaide Bullen (1972). Their work is the most extensive publication on the archaeology of these islands to date. Dr. Earl Kirby and the St. Vincent Archaeological and Historical Society continued to collect information on prehistoric sites. In the 1990s, Dr. Louis Allaire began to investigate sites on St. Vincent with the goal of identifying Island-Carib pottery associated with early evidence of European contact. Two of Dr. Allaire's students, David Duval and Iosif Moravetz, conducted research focused on Saladoid ceramics and the Saladoid iconography expressed in ceramic adornos. More recently, transect surveys were conducted across the island in order to locate archaeological sites in an east-west direction of the Cross-Island Highway. The results were negative.

In 1999, Richard Callaghan of the University of Calgary began a site survey of St. Vincent (Callaghan 2007). The goals of the long-term project were to locate deeply buried sites that might still be largely undisturbed and to investigate settlement patterns on St. Vincent. Thirty new sites were discovered and three previously unreported sealed components that were dated by ceramic chronology to the Cedrosan Saladoid period were discovered. This brought the number of known habitation sites on the island to eighty-three (Figure S.15). The sites

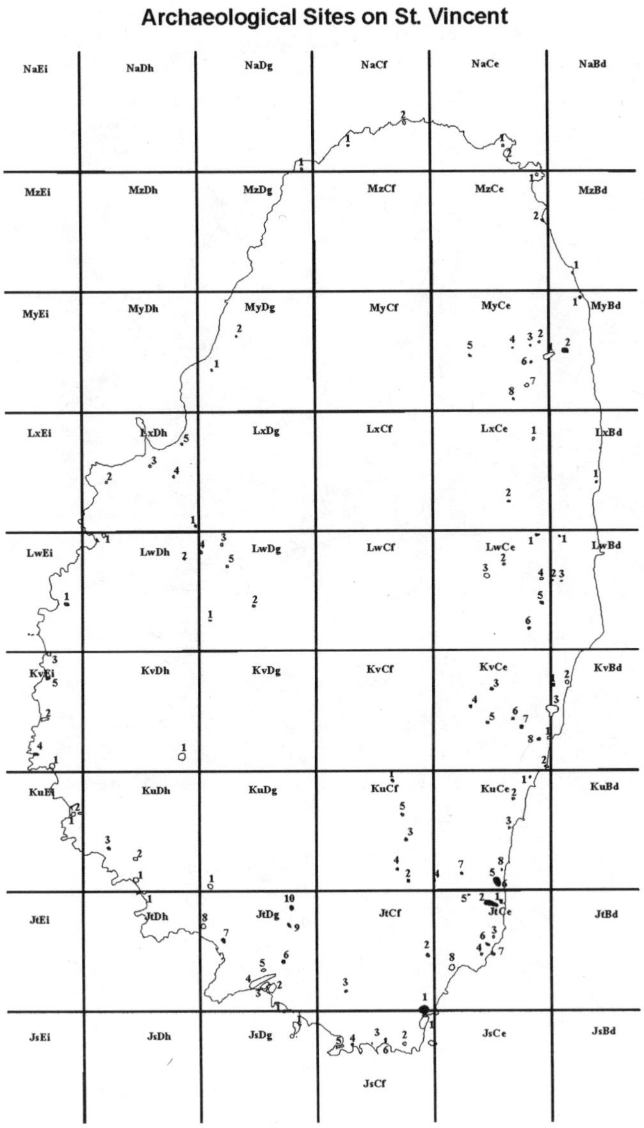

Archaeological Sites on St. Vincent

Figure S.15. Archaeological sites on St. Vincent. Courtesy of Richard T. Callaghan.

were mapped for a number of features, such as elevation, distance from the coast, vegetation type, windward versus leeward locations, and distance to reefs. Of the three previously undocumented and deeply buried occupation levels located by this survey, one of the most interesting is the Escape site, located on the windward coast, an area with many prehistoric habitation sites that is one of the few relatively flat areas on the island. It became the preferred location for a new international airport.

Escape Site

In 2004, the International Airport Development Company officially announced development plans for the new Argyle International Airport. Concerns over the potential impact to heritage resources in the area were raised, and through the efforts of a number of people, particularly members of the St. Vincent and the Grenadines National Trust, funds were made available for some mitigation of the impact of the airport on the Escape site and other heritage resources. While it is unfortunate that the Escape site and others will be buried under the airport tarmac, with the assistance of the International Airport Development Company, a great deal was learned by carefully stripping the overburden from the site. Iosif Moravetz of Bison Historical Services Ltd. of Calgary, Canada, and Richard Callaghan of the University of Calgary (Moravetz and Callaghan 2011) conducted the work. At the time, this was the largest excavation to take place on St. Vincent. A total of thirty-six human burials were identified during excavations. Burials include both primary and secondary interments, but all remains are extremely fragile and utterly friable because of an unfavorable soil matrix. Long bones were better preserved and provided the only data on body position and orientation. The majority of the burials were clustered in an area of 20–25 meters. Three of the primary burials were extended and one was in a seated position. All the other primary burials were in flexed positions, but there was no consistency in terms of cardinal orientation or which side the individual was laid on. One flexed burial was positioned on its back, and a child interment was found in a pot. Secondary burials were haphazardly distributed in the central area. In some cases, only incomplete remains were buried. Determining sex and age was not possible because of the very poor condition of the remains.

Several of the burials contained personal adornments such as pendants and beads. In one burial, a Saint Lucia zoned-incised bowl (Figure S.16) was placed next to the skull, and in another burial, bowl griddle fragments were found placed on top of the skull. All diagnostic materials with the burials indicate a Saladoid date. One burial was particularly noteworthy for its grave offerings. This was an extended burial with lithic tools and personal adornment. Four axes and an assortment of lithic flakes were placed between the feet of the individual. Both local and nonlocal cherts were used to produce the flakes. In addition to these artifacts, two carnelian beads, two small zoomorphic pendants, and one large quartz pendant were placed near the head. The style of the zoomorphic pendants suggests a late Saladoid date.

Over 700 features were recorded at the Escape site. Most of these were postholes. At least seven structures (Figure S.17) were identified. One is associated with

Figure S.16. Saint Lucia zoned-incised bowl found at the Escape site on St. Vincent. Courtesy of Richard T. Callaghan.

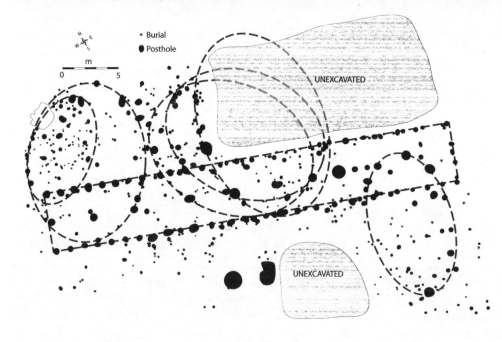

Figure S.17. Eastern part of Escape site, St. Vincent. Courtesy of Richard T. Callaghan.

Suazan Troumassoid pottery, and four are associated with Saladoid pottery, including early Saladoid. All of these structures are oval in shape. Two long rectangular structures are likely to be historic. They have an outline similar to tobacco-drying sheds, but there are a few puzzling aspects. One is the very large size of one of the structures (36 meters × 5.5 meters) and the techniques that were used to construct the structures. The roof of both of these structures was supported with center posts rather than rafters, as would be more common in colonial-era construction. The placement of the larger structure makes it susceptible to sea spray, which would not be conducive to proper drying of tobacco. Subsequently, researchers from the University of Leiden excavated at the far east end of the Escape site beyond the area excavated by Bison Historical Services Ltd. More pits, burials, and postholes were identified by Don van den Biggelaar and Arie Boomert (2010). The report also includes a lithic analysis by Sebastiaan Knippenberg.

Argyle Site

A second site that was impacted by airport construction is the Argyle site. It is a single-component Suazan Troumassoid site associated with the Island-Carib. This is the most poorly understood group in Caribbean archaeology. Work at the Argyle site continued under the direction of Corinne Hofman, Menno Hoogland, and Ari Boomert from Leiden. The archaeological excavations revealed structures and evidence of European contact. Reports of work conducted by the Leiden teams are on file with the St. Vincent and the Grenadines National Trust in Kingstown.

Further Reading

Bullen, R. P., and A. K. Bullen. 1972. *Archaeological Investigations on St. Vincent and the Grenadines, West Indies.* Orlando: William Bryant Foundation.

Callaghan, R. T. 2007. "Prehistoric Settlement Patterns on St. Vincent." *Caribbean Journal of Science* 43 (1): 14–26.

Caribbean Conservation Association and Island Resource Foundation. 1991. *St. Vincent and the Grenadines Island Profile.* St. Michael, Barbados: Caribbean Conservation Association and Island Resource Foundation.

Keegan, W. 1994. "West Indian Archaeology. 1. Overview and Foragers." *Journal of Archaeological Research* 2: 255–84.

Kirby, E. 1969. *Pre-Columbian Monuments in Stone.* Kingstown, St. Vincent: St. Vincent Archaeological and Historical Society.

———. 1970. "The Pre-Columbian Stone Monuments of St. Vincent." In *Proceedings of the Third International Congress for the Study of the Pre-Columbian Cultures of the Lesser Antilles,* 114–28. Grenada: Grenada National Museum.

Lovén, S. 1935. *Origins of the Taínan Culture.* Göteborg: Elanders boktyrckeri aktiebolag.

Moravetz, I., and R. T. Callaghan. 2011. "Archaeological Impact Mitigation at Escape, St. Vincent and the Grenadines." In *Proceedings of the XXIII Congress of the International Association for Caribbean Archaeology,* ed. S. A. Rebovich, 640–54. Antigua: International Association for Caribbean Archaeology.

Sigurdsson, H., and S. Carey. 1991. *Caribbean Volcanoes: A Field Guide.* Sudbury, Ont.: Geological Association of Canada.

van den Biggelaar, D., and A. Boomert. 2010. "Rescue Excavations at the Site of the Future Argyle International Airport, Southeast St. Vincent (June 2009)." Report on file with the St. Vincent and the Grenadines National Trust.

See also The Cayoid Pottery Series; Island-Carib; Kalinago Descendants of St. Vincent and the Grenadines; Kirby, I. A. Earle (1921–2005); Rescue Archaeology.

Strombus gigas (Queen Conch)

Peter L. Drewett

Strombus gigas is a marine gastropod that provided a major source of protein for humans in the prehistoric and historic Caribbean. In prehistory, its shell was widely used for tool manufacture and the manufacture of exotic goods, some of which were used as social status markers.

Strombus gigas was originally described by Linnaeus in 1758, although earlier records exist. The family Strombidae has recently undergone some taxonomic revision; Petuch and Roberts renamed it *Eustrombus gigas* in 2007, and Landau, Kroneberg, and Herbert renamed it *Lobatus gigas* in 2008. The average *Strombus gigas* grow to 15–30 centimeters with a maximum length of some 35 centimeters. The shell is solid and heavy with spines, and adults develop a flared outer lip. They are found throughout the tropical West Atlantic coasts and the Caribbean on sandy sea beds with depths of 0.3–25 meters. They are herbivorous and eat mainly sea grass and algae. Humans extracted meat from the shells by perforating the shell near the apex to force the animal to release its hold on the shell. In prehistory, this was generally done with the spine of another conch, thus producing a circular perforation, while in the historic period an iron knife was often used, producing an elongated narrow slit.

Conch meat was the main source of protein on many small islands with no land mammals. Small islands such as those in the Los Roques archipelago off Venezuela

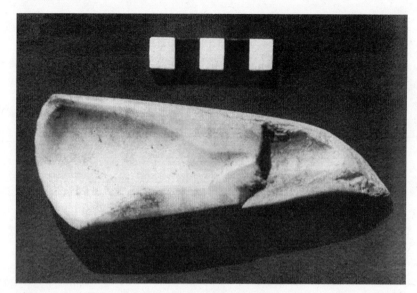

Figure S.18. Ax adze made of conch (*Strombus gigas*), Silver Sands, Barbados. (Scale 5 cm). Reprinted from Drewett (1991) by permission of Peter L. Drewett.

supplied conch meat to mainland South America. The result was very large conch shell middens on the islands. Similar middens are found elsewhere in the Caribbean on islands such as Anegada. Meat from these islands was probably exported in salted or dried form, although fresh meat can be consumed raw, boiled, or roasted.

The shell of *Strombus gigas* was a significant raw material for manufacturing tools and ornaments on Caribbean islands that had no good stone resources. Prehistoric residents of Barbados, for example, used shell as a major raw material. The earliest type of shell axe/adze on Barbados was simply the detached lip of the conch with a polished cutting edge. The earliest on the island has a date of 2530–2220 BC. After Saladoid-influenced peoples came to Barbados, the columella of the shell was used to manufacture finely ground petaloid axes similar to those of stone on other islands (Figure S.18). The final and distinctively Barbadian type of shell axe/adze, which has a distinctive twist and a scoop-like reverse, developed around AD 1000. In addition to tools, conch was also used to manufacture a wide variety of ornamental and ritual objects (for example carvings of frogs, geckos,

and humans), beads, teeth plates, and eyes to inlay in wooden effigies. Fish lures and fish hooks were made of conch, and it may be presumed that conch meat was used as fish bait in prehistory, as it still is on some islands today. Conch shell was infrequently used to manufacture artifacts in the historic period, and until the very recent past, whole shells were often used to mark graves on islands without stone.

Further Reading

Drewett, P. L. 1991. *Prehistoric Barbados*. London: Archetype Publications.

Humfrey, M. 1975. *Sea Shells of the West Indies: A Guide to the Marine Molluscs of the Caribbean*. London: Collins.

Landau, B., G. C. Kronenberg, and G. Herbert. 2008. "A Large New Species of Lobatus (Gastropoda: Strombidae) from the Neogene of the Dominican Republic, with Notes on the Genus." *The Veliger* 50 (1): 31–38

Petuch E. J., and C. E. Roberts. 2007. *The Geology of the Everglades and Adjacent Areas*. Boca Raton, FL: CRC Press.

See also Barbados.

The Suazan Troumassoid (Suazey)

Mark C. Donop

The Suazan Troumassoid ceramic subseries (AD 1000–1500) is the culmination of indigenous pottery production in the southeastern Caribbean. Suazan pottery is the principal archaeological material from which the history of an enigmatic Amerindian culture has been reconstructed. Suazan Troumassoid pottery is generally considered to be simple and crude, and its origins and the reasons for its abandonment remain controversial. Relatively little research has been devoted to the archaeology of the Suazan peoples, compared to the research that has been done on their northern Ostionoid neighbors and Saladoid predecessors.

The history of Suazan archaeology is strongly connected to the narrative of an Island-Carib invasion from the mainland. Early historical accounts suggest that South American Carib strongly interacted with the Arawakan Igneri of the southeastern Caribbean during the late prehistoric and early historic periods, resulting in the ethnogenesis of the Island-Carib, or Caraïbes. Archaeologists have expended considerable effort to establish an archaeological connection between Suazan pottery and a number of ethnic groups. Marshall B. McKusick was the first archaeologist to systematically study and identify both the Troumassoid and Micoid series through his work on Dominica and Saint Lucia in the 1950s. He came to the conclusion that the Micoid series and the late prehistoric finger-indented Fannis style represented a Carib invasion from Venezuela and Suriname. Ripley and Adelaide Bullen supported McKusick's hypothesis of a gradual mainland Carib invasion from the Guianas based on their work on numerous Windward Islands in the 1960s and 1970s. The Bullens renamed the Micoid series the Suazey series after the Savanne Suazey site they excavated on Grenada. However, archaeological and ethnohistoric research by Louise Allaire on Martinique and St. Vincent in the 1970s and 1980s strongly suggested that Suazey pottery, referred to as Suazoid pottery, was not made by Island-Carib but was instead an in situ devolution from the earlier Troumassoid period. The Suazoid series has since been reclassified as the Suazan Troumassoid subseries.

The Suazan Troumassoid subseries was the climax of a gradual trend of ceramic simplification that occurred throughout the southeastern Caribbean. Suazan ceramics were produced from approximately AD 1000 to AD 1500 from Guadeloupe to Tobago. Although it displays considerable heterogeneity, Suazan pottery is generally believed to be devolved, sloppy, and artistically destitute and is recognized for its thick walls, rough finish, mineral temper, legs, scratched or scraped surfaces, and finger-indented rims (Figure S.19). A minority of finer pottery pieces were burnished and decorated with red paint, linear and curvilinear incisions, rim lugs and pegs, and modeled anthropomorphic and zoomorphic adornos. Suazan fineware was often assumed to have been from an earlier time period, and it is sometimes associated with the Bullens' Calivinoid series, or the Caliviny style, known primarily for its polychrome painting. A variety of ceramic artifacts, including legged griddles, snuff pots, incense burners, pestles, spindle whorls, loom weights, body stamps, female figurines, and pot support rings, have been recovered from Suazan archaeological sites.

The limited evidence available suggests that the Suazan people were not as unsophisticated as their ceramics might seem to indicate. Although the Suazan did not often produce ceramics that were as finely executed as those of their Saladoid predecessors, they should not

Figure S.19. Suazan Troumassoid vessel. Courtesy of the Anthropology Division of the Florida Museum of Natural History, 98008-09.

be considered crude or degenerate. The simple vessel forms and surface treatments that dominate most Suazan assemblages appear to have been intentionally designed to serve utilitarian functions for a minimal cost of production and replacement. Ceramic aesthetics are not reliable indicators of societal complexity. Decorative simplification may indicate a shift in emphasis toward more perishable means of expression that are difficult to detect archaeologically such as weaving or woodworking.

The Suazan peoples seem to have developed a regional exchange network during the Late Ceramic Age. Some Suazan Troumassoid artifacts share iconographic similarities with Ostionoid artifacts, suggesting that the southeastern Caribbean interacted significantly with the Leeward Islands and Greater Antilles during late prehistory. The increased number of spindle whorls during this time period suggests that the Suazan may have been middlemen in a trade network with both South America and the Greater Antilles that exchanged perishable items such as cotton.

The Suazan culture is believed to have collapsed between AD 1450 and AD 1500. The large Suazan population, whose size is roughly indicated by the abundance of sites throughout the southeastern Caribbean, suddenly collapsed shortly before or after the arrival of the first Europeans. Definitive archaeological evidence to support the precolonial Carib invasion narrative remains elusive, and it is not known what connection the Suazan had with the Arawakan-speaking Island-Carib found on the same islands in the 1600s. If the Suazan culture continued into the historic period, European contact proved disastrous for it and left the islands of the southeastern Caribbean sparsely populated by Amerindians.

Further Reading

Allaire, L. 1977. "Later Prehistory in Martinique and the Island-Caribs: Problems in Ethnic Identification." PhD diss., Yale University.

Bullen, R. P. 1964. *The Archaeology of Grenada, West Indies.* Gainesville: University of Florida.

McKusick, M. B. 1960. "Distribution of Ceramic Styles in the Lesser Antilles, West Indies." PhD diss., Yale University.

Petersen, J. B., C. L. Hofman, and L. A. Curet. 2004. "Time and Culture: Chronology and Taxonomy in the Eastern Caribbean and the Guianas." In *Late Ceramic Age Societies in the Eastern Caribbean*, ed. A. Delpuech and C. L. Hofman, 17–32. Oxford: Archaeopress.

See also Bullen, Ripley (1902–1976), and Adelaide Bullen (1908–1987); The Cayoid Pottery Series; Island-Carib; Trinidad and Tobago; The Troumassan Troumassoid.

Taíno Museum at White Marl (Jamaica)

Lesley-Gail Atkinson

White Marl, formerly known as Caymanas, is one of the most significant Taíno sites in Jamaica. The village site located atop White Marl Hill in St. Catherine was discovered in the early nineteenth century. To date, White Marl is the largest and longest-occupied prehistoric site on the island. The site spans thirty-three acres and has eighteen middens that produced a date range of AD 877 ± 95 to 1490 ± 120 (uncalibrated). In 1944, during the construction of the road from Kingston to Spanish Town, a portion of the site was cut through, exposing skeletal remains and a considerable amount of artifacts. The site was later excavated by Dr. Howard in 1958, 1961, 1963, and 1964. He was hoping to continue excavations at the site until his sudden death in 1965.

The Taíno Museum at White Marl was opened in memory of Dr. Robert Randolph Howard on July 19, 1965. It is administered by the Institute of Jamaica. The museum building has an octagonal shape with a high conical roof that was inspired by a Taíno *caney* (dwelling). Mr. Ronald Vanderwal, a former graduate student of Dr. Howard, continued research at White Marl from 1965 to 1968. In 1968, a burial cave was discovered about 500 yards from the White Marl village site that contained twelve burials. A total of sixteen burials, three of which were infants, were unearthed at White Marl. The exhibits at the museum highlight different aspects of Taíno life, including subsistence practices, religion, burial practices, technology, and art, and includes features and artifacts from sites across the island. The museum was severely damaged by Hurricane Gilbert in 1988 and closed until May 2002. In 1992, the Taíno Museum at White Marl was declared a National Monument by the Jamaica National Heritage Trust.

Further Reading

Allsworth-Jones, P. 2008. *Pre-Columbian Jamaica*. Tuscaloosa: University of Alabama Press.

Howard, R. R. 1961. "The Arawak Village Site at White Marl." *Jamaican Historical Society Bulletin* 3 (4): 59–63.

Vanderwal, R. L. 1968. *The Prehistory of Jamaica: A Ceramic Study*. MA thesis, University of Wisconsin–Milwaukee.

See also Barbados Museum and Historical Society; The Institute of Jamaica; The International Council of Museums (ICOM); Jamaica (Prehistory of); The Museum of Antigua and Barbuda.

Taíno Settlement Ethnohistory

Jeremiah Kaplan and R. Grant Gilmore III

Ethnohistory involves using historical written accounts that describe another human cultural group to assist in understanding their social, economic, religious, and spatial development. These accounts may contain structural and factual biases as the result of a filtering of gathered information through the authors' (or their editors') particular worldview, including politics, religion, and social class. These biases aside, the ethnohistorical approach has been successfully applied in understanding the contact period in the Spanish Caribbean of the fifteenth century.

Although the first Spanish settlers in the Caribbean were concerned with recording the names of individual

Taíno *caciques*, they did not record many fundamental aspects of Amerindian life, especially detailed ethnohistoric information on topics such as village structures and house construction. Most existing accounts are basic and reflect a European bias. For example, they describe Taíno homes as crude compared to European homes. However, a few useful in-depth descriptions do exist in the early historic record pertaining to what domestic life was like for the Amerindians during the early contact period in the Caribbean.

Peter Martyr D'Anghera recounts how a Taíno village was structured on Guadeloupe (Lovén [1935] believes that this quote may actually refer to Espanola) at the time of Columbus's second voyage to the Americas. As this description contains detailed information, it is valuable for understanding pre-Columbian settlement and structures. D'Anghera writes details such as "While exploring the island, numerous villages, composed of twenty or thirty houses each, were discovered; in the centre is a public square, round which the houses are placed in a circle." He also describes in detail the construction of a Taíno house from a builder's perspective:

> It seems that they are built entirely of wood in a circular form. The construction of the building is begun by planting in the earth very tall trunks of trees; by means of them, shorter beams are placed in the interior and support the outer posts. The extremities of the higher ones are brought together in a point, after the fashion of a military tent. These frames they then cover with palm or other leaves, ingeniously interlaced, as a protection against rain. From the shorter beams in the interior, they suspend knotted cords made of cotton or of certain roots similar to rushes, and on these they lay coverings. (D'Anghera 1970, 1:71)

D'Anghera also provides the name he believes the Taíno used to describe their houses—"*boios*"—giving us one of the few European references to the indigenous names used to describe a dwelling. Today the term *bohios* is the accepted term for a home with peeled bark walls and a thatched roof—with palm or other materials.

Another descriptive passage relating to the construction techniques of Taíno houses comes from Haiti and has been translated and compiled from previous Spanish accounts by Sven Lovén (1935). He writes: "For the most part, the posts were of such wood as did not rot easily. . . . The construction and the walls also must have been very resistant, for not even a hurricane destroyed the *bejucos*. On the other hand the roof rotted and had to be replaced each second or third year. The middle post was rammed securely into the earth . . . and the radial rafters

of the roof were bound fast to its point" (345). Lovén also believes that "there [are] sufficient grounds for the belief that originally the Taíno only had round houses. Columbus and Las Casas mentioned only round houses" (349). Still, Lovén cautions that "although there is great probability that the rectangular Indian house with roof having a roof-beam first appeared in Espanola due to Spanish influence, still we must not forget that this form of [house] already [existed] in Indian times, must have a tendency to advance from western regions and probably also from more southern ones nearer to the Amazon, to the northeastern part of South America. To judge from the oldest accounts, the round house was much more predominant there in primitive days than in more recent times" (341).

Curet (1992) adds that although most ethnohistoric accounts indicate a general similarity between houses of the various islands in terms of building materials and construction techniques, documentary evidence supports the idea of regional variations across the Caribbean. Curet also notes that Columbus mentioned in his *diario* some differences between Lucayan Taíno housing and housing in Cuba, both in quality and shapes.

On his first voyage, Columbus writes about a house

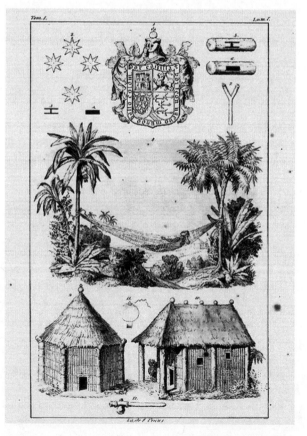

Figure T.1. Depictions of Taíno houses in Oviedo and Valdés (1851).

that had "*dos puertas, porque asi son todas*" (two entrances, one for men and the other for women). Lovén argues that this is still customary in the houses of the Arawak tribes on the large interior savanna of British Guiana. Lovén also writes that the houses of the Arawak Cauixana and Uainuma in the Yapura region have also two rectangular entrances placed opposite one another and that Taíno house entrances had no doors. Oviedo has provided illustrations, among other things, of two Taíno houses: one round and the other rectangular (see Figure T.1). As historians and archaeologists comb archives around the world, additional ethnohistorical information will continue to come to light. These documents, in combination with archaeological data, provide a richer understanding of past people's lifeways, including the contact period in the Caribbean.

Further Reading

Curet, L. A. 1992. *The Development of Chiefdoms in the Greater Antilles: A Regional Study of the Valley of Maunabo, Puerto Rico*. PhD diss., Arizona State University-Tempe.

D'Anghera, P. 1970. *De Orbe Novo: The Eight Decades of Peter Mártyr D'Anghera*. 2 vols. Trans. Francis Augustus MacNutt. New York: Burt Franklin.

Lovén, S. 1935. *Origins of the Tainan Culture, West Indies*. Goteborg: Elanders Bokfryckeri Akfiebolag.

Oviedo, F., and G. Valdés. 1851. *La Historia General y Natural de Indias, 1478–1557: Islas y Tierra-firme del Mar Océano*. Madrid: De la Real Academica de la Historia.

Pané, F. R. 1999. *An Account of the Antiquities of the Indians: Chronicles of the New World Encounter*. Trans. Susan C. Griswold. Durham, NC: Duke University Press.

See also Chiefdoms (*Cacicazgos*).

Trinidad and Tobago

Arie Boomert

Trinidad and Tobago are continental islands that originally formed part of the mainland of South America, from which they became detached due to the global rise in sea level in the late and post-Pleistocene. In prehistoric times, they served as a link between the continent and the Caribbean archipelago that was crucial for human migration and the exchange and diffusion of cultures. Both islands formed part of an extensive Amerindian interaction sphere, which also included the lower Orinoco Valley, the coastal zone of eastern Venezuela, and the western littoral of the Guianas. These areas were interconnected during prehistoric and contact periods by an intricate system of sea channels, rivers, lagoons, and estuaries.

Lithic and Archaic People

Wandering groups of Lithic hunters/foragers visited Trinidad infrequently around 8000 BC when it still a part of the South American continent. However, Archaic (Meso-Indian) hunters, fishers, and food collectors who arrived ca. 6000 BC were the first inhabitants of the island. This first wave of colonization took place after Trinidad had become fully detached from the mainland. These Indians, who belonged to the Ortoiroid series, followed highly diversified subsistence strategies that exploited a wide range of environmental niches. Three successive Archaic complexes have been identified in Trinidad: Banwari Trace (6000 BC–4000 BC); Poonah Road (3500 BC–2500 BC); and Ortoire (1200 BC–800 BC). Both Banwari Trace and Poonah Road have been assigned to the Banwarian subseries, while Ortoire relates to the Ortoiran subseries. Shell midden sites such as Banwari Trace (Figure T.2) and St. John in southwestern Trinidad have yielded a distinctive toolkit consisting of stone, bone, and antler artifacts, including bone fishhooks and grooved ground stone axes, pestles, and side ("faceted") grinders used to process plant foods. At Banwari Trace, a primary burial of the flexed skeleton of a young-adult woman was found; a smooth pebble was placed near the skull and a needle point near the hip. These remains are the oldest human burial in the Caribbean.

By 3000–1000 BC, the southwestern portion of Tobago was colonized by Archaic settlers of the Milford complex, who originated in Trinidad. Using large dugouts, Archaic migrants from the eastern littoral of Venezuela and Trinidad eventually reached the Leeward and Virgin Islands, where they may have encountered other

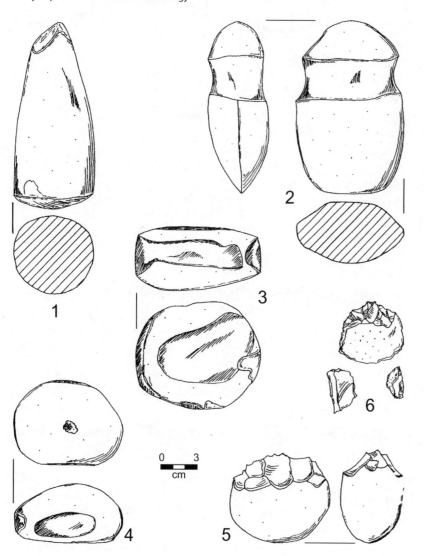

Figure T.2. Stone artifacts from Banwari Trace: *1*, conical pestle; *2*, grooved ax; *3–4*, side ("faceted") grinders; *5*, chopper; *6*, utilized flakes. Reprinted from Boomert (2000) by permission of Arie Boomert.

Archaic colonists who came from the Greater Antilles. It is likely that the Warao Indians of the Orinoco delta and Northwest Guyana are the present-day descendants of the Archaic Age Ortoiroid Indians. In fact, Warao groups from the Orinoco delta paid regular trading visits to Trinidad as recently as the mid-twentieth century.

Saladoid People

Around 200 BC, settlers of the Saladoid series moved into Trinidad from eastern Venezuela. These pottery-making Amerindians who had migrated to the Venezuelan coast from the lower Orinoco Valley subsisted on a combination of root crop horticulture (bitter cassava and sweet potatoes), hunting, fishing, and the gathering of edible animal and plant foods. The Saladoid colonists were able to adapt very successfully to their local environment. They interacted well with the last Archaic survivors of the Venezuelan coastal zone (of

the Manicuaran subseries), from whom they learned about maritime technology and the navigational skills they needed to reach the southern Windward Islands In all, two successive Saladoid ceramic complexes are known from Trinidad: Cedros (200 BC–AD 1) and Palo Seco (AD 1–750). Tobago has three Saladoid complexes: Courland (100 BC–AD 350); Mount Irvine (AD 100–350); and Friendship (AD 350–750). Attracted by the favorable conditions for settlement in the Antillean archipelago, adventurous young men in the local communities of the mainland and Trinidad probably initiated the Saladoid expansion into Tobago, the Windward Islands, and beyond.

Across the Caribbean archipelago, the Saladoid presence is clearly represented in the remarkable uniformity of the earliest pottery of the Cedrosan subseries, named after Trinidad's Cedros site. Cedros pottery is characterized by small- to medium-sized bowls and jars that exhibit a variety of bichrome and polychrome painted, incised, and modeled designs. The local evolution of Cedrosan Saladoid ceramics in Trinidad reflects regional stylistic developments during Early Palo Seco times. The typically Cedrosan zoned-incised-crosshatched designs disappeared rapidly on Trinidad's southern shore, whereas elsewhere in the Lesser Antilles they remained in fashion for some time. On Trinidad's north coast, a specific type of thin-line incised (or rather engraved) designs eventually developed out of Cedros incisions. These designs bear a strong resemblance to the Mount Irvine pottery motifs of Tobago, the Cedrosan ceramics of the Windward Islands, and the Río Guapo pottery of the central Venezuelan coast.

Saladoid-Barrancoid Interactions

The makers of the Cedrosan pottery of Trinidad and Tobago gradually adopted some pottery styles of the Barrancoid people of the lower Orinoco Valley, who arrived in Trinidad around AD 350. Interactions between the Barrancoid and Saladoid communities of Trinidad and Tobago and Venezuela had been growing. Pottery and small amounts of bone and stone ornaments were apparently important trade items during this period. Among the ceramics traded were Barrancoid vessels with elaborately modeled-incised biomorphic head lugs, suggesting representation of spirit-related messages and strong shamanic associations. These Barrancoid exchange items reached as far as Tobago, where they served as mortuary gifts, a demonstration of their value in the eyes of the local Saladoid population.

Other exchange items during the Saladoid/Barrancoid period were turquoise, chlorite, and serpentinite beads. Unworked pieces of amethyst were probably used to manufacture amethyst ornaments. From the late Cedrosan period onward, Tobago was an important center of diorite bead manufacturing and distribution. Mother-of-pearl pendants made of nacreous freshwater mussels found in Saladoid contexts in south Trinidad are another category of social valuables. These were used as exchange items throughout the West Indies, as far north as the Leeward and Virgin Islands. These interactions conceivably promoted information exchange in the forms of myths, tales, songs, dances, and knowledge, thus strengthening political alliances based on kinship ties and rituals between communities.

Saladoid-Barrancoid Ceramics

The Saladoid and Barrancoid ceramics of Trinidad and Tobago are decorated with an abundance of anthropo-

zoomorphic head lugs that reflect the animistic religion of their makers. These ceramics also provide insights into the high value natives placed on ritualistic communication with the spirit world in order to ensure health, fertility, social order, and group survival. Shamanic paraphernalia include double-spouted "nostril bowls," which were used to pour tobacco or pepper juice into the nose in order to induce an ecstatic visionary trance. There were also vessels with hollow biomorphic head lugs containing small clay pellets or tiny pebbles that obviously functioned as rattling devices during curing ceremonies, ceremonial pottery cylinders or incense burners, and stone three pointers. Tobago yielded a three pointer made of calcirudite, which may have been brought to the island through down-the-line exchange from St. Martin. The variety of forms of Saladoid/Barrancoid pottery suggests that it was principally destined for the public display of food and was an active expression of status, rank, or kinship affiliation. Such displays could have been part of ceremonies involving competitive demonstrations of wealth, gift giving, or even property destruction during ceremonial feasts. These ceremonies were hosted by local headmen, or "big men," who could attract a large following through gift giving. As a result of their personal qualities, these headmen also became important arbiters of war and trade in their communities.

Regular interactions between Saladoid and Barrancoid communities of the region culminated in the establishment of a local Barrancoid ceramic complex called Erin in south Trinidad. Erin pottery has been consistently found in association with Palo Seco ceramics, indicating the largely simultaneous manufacture and use of both wares. All of this suggests that people of Barrancoid cultural affiliation (who had originated in the lower Orinoco Valley) moved to Trinidad and intermarried with the Saladoid inhabitants of the island. Erin settlement in Trinidad began around AD 350, but a substantial portion of Trinidad's Erin pottery appears to be affiliated with the Arauquinoid-influenced Barrancoid ceramics of the lower Orinoco, which date from AD 650 to 800. It is clear that the settlement of the Erin people in south Trinidad was partially connected with the downstream movement of the Arauquinoid Indians in the Orinoco Valley.

Arauquinoid Settlers

Arauquinoid domination eventually stretched as far as the east Venezuelan littoral and Trinidad, where the Arauquinoid-influenced Barrancoid pottery led to the emergence of ceramics of the Bontour complex in AD 750/800. Bontour belongs to the Guayabitan subseries of the Arauquinoid series and is characterized by ceramics with very minimal decoration. Apparently, Arauquinoid ceramics had less ceremonial significance than the ceramics of the Saladoid-Barrancoid period, suggesting that the transition from Saladoid/Barrancoid to Arauquinoid in Trinidad and elsewhere represented a genuine cultural break. This does not mean that the previous Saladoid-Barrancoid population of the island was completely replaced by the Arauquinoid newcomers. On the contrary, a steady cultural transition that primarily involved a locally based population characterized Trinidad throughout the Ceramic Age. These natives lived in villages characterized by circular house structures surrounded by shell midden deposits in which they buried their dead, as was customary in the Saladoid/Barrancoid period.

An increasing population density throughout Trinidad is suggested by a large increase of the number of sites during the Arauquinoid period. Regular communication and interactions between Trinidad's Arauquinoid people and their counterparts on the mainland are evidenced by the presence of exchange objects from the lower Orinoco. Prime examples are griddles and ceramic roller stamps. Following Trinidad's extensive Arauquinoid habitation, Tobago was drawn into the Troumassoid interaction sphere, which was centered on the Windward Islands and Barbados. On Tobago, Bontour pottery has been found in association with the ceramics of the Golden Grove complex (AD 750–1100), which is considered to be a local Troumassan Troumassoid assemblage.

From the Arauquinoid period onward, the islands of Trinidad and Tobago were increasingly incorporated into a number of major interaction networks that were characterized by pottery complexes that expressed various cultural and perhaps ethnic loyalties. Contacts across the Galleons' Passage did not cease; for example, diorite beads made in Tobago continued to be exported to Trinidad. Nevertheless, the cultural resemblances between the post-Saladoid Tobagonian pottery assemblages and those of the Windward Islands and Barbados point to much more intensive interaction between the Troumassoid communities of Tobago and the southern Caribbean than between the former and the Arauquinoid villages of the mainland. This is suggested also by the presence of Caliviny exchange pottery or imitations of such pottery from the Windwards in Tobago's Plymouth complex (AD 1100–1450).

Mayoid Ceramic Tradition

The Mayoid series was the final Amerindian ceramic tradition of Trinidad before European contact. It emerged in AD 1300, about two centuries before Columbus encountered the island on his third journey to the West Indies in 1498. Mayoid pottery may have been manufactured until the mid-eighteenth century. The exclusive use of *caraipe* (burned tree bark) as a tempering material was one of its defining characteristics. The strong resemblance between Mayoid cooking jars and the "buck-pots" (pepper pots) of the Arawak (Lokono) in the Guianas suggests strong cultural affinities between the two groups. This connection is further bolstered by the rare occurrence of a typically Koriabo-Cayo necked vessel in Mayoid archaeological sites. Mayoid ceramics of Trinidad were apparently manufactured by both the Nepoio and Arawak (Lokono) Amerindians. While several socially complex multiethnic and multilingual native groups emerged during the Mayoid period in Trinidad, Tobago at this time was predominantly inhabited by Suazan Troumassoid and, after AD 1450, by Island-Carib.

Further Reading

Boomert, A. 1996. *The Prehistoric Sites of Tobago: A Catalogue and Evaluation*. Alkmaar, The Netherlands: Boomert.

——. 2000. *Trinidad, Tobago, and the Lower Orinoco Interaction Sphere: An Archaeological/Ethnohistorical Study*. Alkmaar, The Netherlands: Cairi Publications.

Boomert, A., B. Faber-Morse, and I. Rouse. 2013. *The Yale University Excavations in Trinidad of 1946 and 1953*. New Haven, CT: Yale University Press.

Harris, P. O. 1976. "The Pre-Ceramic Period in Trinidad." In *Proceedings of the First Puerto Rican Symposium on Archaeology, Santurce, Puerto Rico 1973*, ed. L. S. Robinson, 33–65. San Juan: Fundacíon Arqueológica, Antropológica e Historica de Puerto Rico.

——. 1991. "Amerindian Trinidad and Tobago." In *Proceedings of the Twelfth Congress of the International Congress for Caribbean Archaeology*, ed. L. S. Robinson, 259–67. Martinique: Association Internationale d'Archéologie de la Caraïbe.

Reid, B. A. 2010. *Archaeology, GIS, and Cultural Resource Management in Trinidad*. Saarbrücken, Germany: Lambert Academic.

See also Banwari Trace (Trinidad); Elite Exchange in the Caribbean; La Brea Pitch Lake (Trinidad); Palo Seco (Trinidad); St. John Site (Trinidad).

The Troumassan Troumassoid

Corinne L. Hofman and Basil A. Reid

Caribbean archaeologists have traditionally made a distinction between the early Troumassoid ceramic series, called Troumassan Troumassoid, and the later Troumassoid series referred to as Suazan Troumassoid. Troumassan Troumassoid pottery, which was named after the site of Troumassée in Saint Lucia and has a timeline of AD 500 to 1000, seems to have been influenced by the Saladoid series in the Lesser Antilles. The Troumassan Troumassoid subseries is found throughout the southern Lesser Antilles (Figure T.3) and is characterized by boat-shaped, kidney-shaped, round bottomless, inverted bell-shaped, and hemispherical bowls; double bowls; effigy bowls; and cylindrical pot stands. This series features polychrome painting with curvilinear incisions (Donop 2005; Hofman 2013) (Figure T.4).

The Troumassoid series developed differently in the northerly Leeward and Virgin Islands than in the more southerly Windward Islands (Boomert 2003). In the for-

mer, the Mamoran Troumassoid subseries developed between AD 800 and 1200 after Saladoid ceramics disappeared (Hofman 2013; Murphy 2004). Mamoran Troumassoid pottery, which was named after the Mamora Bay site on Antigua, reflected some Cedrosan Saladoid elements, although these became less prominent over time. Red-slipped surfaces gradually replaced bicolor and polychrome painting. Incisions were broad-lined with curvilinear designs. Cedrosan Saladoid–style modeled appliqués and handles disappeared, and lugs were rare (Hofman 2013; Reid 2009).

In the Virgin Islands, the pottery was characterized by the Magens Bay style, named after the Magens Bay site in St. Thomas (United States Virgin Islands). Because Magens Bay ceramics display striking similarities with those of eastern Puerto Rico, where the Ostionoid series emerged, this style is generally classified as part of the Elenan Ostionoid series. There is evidence of trade

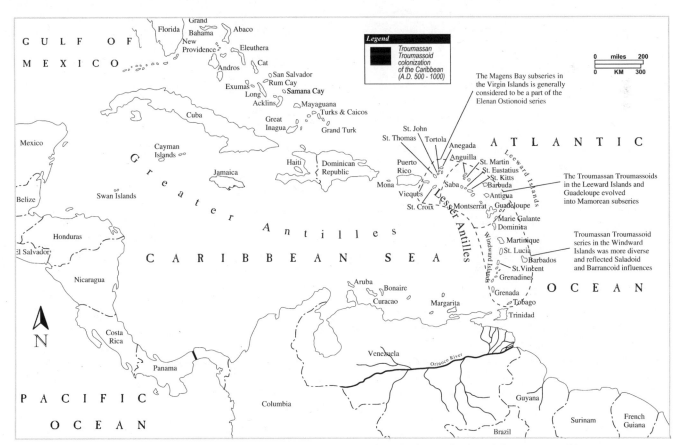

Figure T.3. Troumassan Troumassoid colonization of the Caribbean. Reprinted from Reid (2009, fig. 2.17) by permission of the University of Alabama Press.

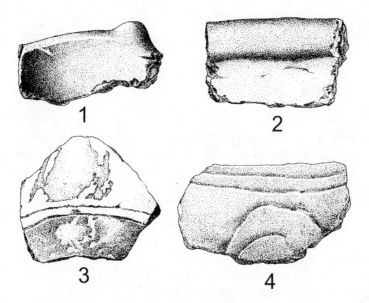

Figure T.4. Troumassan Troumassoid pottery: *1*, wedge-shaped lug on a triangular rim; *2*, red-painted ridge inside a rim; *3*, white design on badly worn red slip; *4*, curvilineal incised design. Reprinted from Rouse (1992, fig. 33) by permission of Yale University Press.

and cultural exchanges between the developing societies in the Greater Antilles and the late precolonial settlers of the Virgin Islands. By AD 1200, both the Magens Bay style pottery in the Virgins Islands and Mamoran Troumassoid pottery in the Leewards were heavily influenced by the Ostionoid series in Puerto Rico to the east to the extent that some archaeologists have classified them as Eastern Taíno (Rouse 1992).

The Troumassan Troumassoid series in the Windward Islands differs considerably from the Marmoran Troumassoid in the north, especially in terms of pottery style. Troumassan Troumassoid pottery is characterized by painted red, black, and white paint and is often outlined with curvilinear incised lines. It also has unpainted curvilinear incision and, like the pottery of the Saladoid, has wedge-shaped lugs. The pottery is cruder and plainer than the pottery of previous time periods, and the Saladoid zoomorphic and anthropozoomorphic adornos and loop handles have for the most part disappeared. Vessels are fitted with legs, pedestals, or annular (or ring-shaped) bases. The Barrancoid influence of stylistic modeling has disappeared as well. Beginning in the eight century, the quality of the pottery decreased markedly and decorations became more simplified.

Troumassan Troumassoid ceramics display many stylistic features that are similar to the later ceramic styles of coastal Venezuela. The large number of clay spindle whorls in Troumassan Troumassoid assemblages suggests an increase in cotton cultivation and perhaps trade in fabricated cotton items. Local communities adapted to the islands' environments in ways that allowed them to expand territorially. In Martinique, an increased production of salt and cotton may explain why communities of the late precolonial period on the island spread out

from the humid and fertile northeastern part of Martinique to occupy the more arid southeastern section (Allaire 1991). To date, one of the best-known Troumassan Troumassoid sites in the Caribbean is Paquemar on Martinique (Allaire 1977; Reid 2009).

Further Reading

Allaire, Louis. 1977. "Later Prehistory in Martinique and the Island-Caribs: Problems in Ethnic Identification." PhD diss., Yale University.

———. 1991. "Understanding Suazey." In *Proceedings of the Thirteenth International Congress for Caribbean Archaeology*, ed. E. N. Ayubi and J. B. Haviser, 2:715–28. Curaçao, Netherlands Antilles: AAINA.

Boomert, A. 2003. "Agricultural Societies in the Continental Caribbean." In *General History of the Caribbean: Autochthonous Societies*, ed. J. S. Badillo, 1: 134–94. Paris: UNESCO.

Donop, M. C. 2005. "Savanne Suazey Revisited." MA thesis, University of Florida. http://etd.fcla.edu/UF/UFE0013281/donop_m.pdf. Accessed January 17, 2013.

Hofman, C. L. 2013. "The Post-Saladoid in the Lesser Antilles." In *The Oxford Handbook of Caribbean Archaeology*, ed. W. F. Keegan, C. L. Hofman, and R. Rodriguez Ramos, 205–20. Oxford: Oxford University Press.

Murphy, R. 2004. "Life in an Insular Environment: The Case of Antigua." In *Late Ceramic Age Societies in the Northeastern Caribbean*, ed. A. Deluech and C. L. Hofman, 205–13. Oxford: Archaeopress.

Reid, B. A. 2009. *Myths and Realities of Caribbean History*. Tuscaloosa: University of Alabama Press.

Rouse, I. 1992. *The Tainos: Rise and Decline of the People who Greeted Columbus*. New Haven, CT: Yale University Press.

See also Martinique; The Suazan Troumassoid (Suazey); The Virgin Islands.

U

Underwater Archaeology

Margaret E. Leshikar-Denton and Della A. Scott-Ireton

Introduction

Underwater archaeology is archaeology performed in a submerged environment. The goal of research into the human past and the methods of excavation and interpretation are the same as for other types of archaeology; only the tools are different. Underwater archaeologists work in often-challenging environments, including oceans, seas, bays, lakes, rivers, springs, marshes, and cenotes and their adjacent landscapes. Specialized tools and technology enable scientists to work from the interface of land and water to the deepest oceans. Although shipwrecks are the most commonly studied type of site, many other maritime cultural heritage sites offer opportunities for research and interpretation as heritage tourism attractions. These include remains of watercraft and aircraft, survivors' campsites, fishing areas, bridges, lighthouses and other navigational aids, anchorages, careening places, ports, harbors, coastal settlements, towns, wharves, shipbuilding sites, and coastal forts and defenses. Sites of catastrophic events, terrestrial erosion, or inundation and locations where cultural material was lost or intentionally put in the water are also locations where underwater archaeologists work.

Underwater archaeology, which emerged as a science in the mid-twentieth century, has evolved into the next great archaeological frontier and has the potential to reveal artifacts at exceptional levels of preservation in many cases. The Caribbean region has incredible potential for research, from evidence of early habitation and interisland relations to evidence of the European discovery of the New World, colonization, and the development of modern nations. Recurring themes emerge as island nations work to develop research and preservation programs to promote heritage tourism, including proper uses of heritage, how to respond to approaches from commercial salvors and treasure hunters, heritage legislation, underwater cultural heritage

(UCH) management, scientific research, the meaning of archaeological finds to descendent communities, and preservation for the future. Some countries are more advanced in undertaking protection and management of UCH, but there is a growing concern in the region that commercial exploitation is not beneficial and should be stopped. Creativity in managing cultural resources and cooperation in sharing knowledge, technical skills, and professional expertise are important concepts that Caribbean peoples are exploring and adopting. While assistance is welcomed from outside of the region, there is a growing awareness that sustainability must come from within it.

To date, the following Caribbean countries have ratified the 2001 UNESCO Convention on the Protection of the Underwater Cultural Heritage: Antigua, Barbados, Barbuda, Cuba, Haiti, Grenada, Jamaica, St. Kitts and Nevis, Saint Lucia, St. Vincent and the Grenadines, and Trinidad and Tobago. These countries are also discussing the benefits of establishing compatible national legislation. The following presents short synopses of underwater archaeological work undertaken in the Caribbean.

Anguilla

In Anguilla, the Historic Wrecks Advisory Committee was created in the mid-1990s to advise the government on how to respond to proposals from groups that wanted to do commercial salvage work on the 1772 inbound Spanish merchantmen *El Buen Consejo* and *Jesús, María y José*. The committee sought advice from individual members of the International Committee on Underwater Cultural Heritage of the International Council on Monuments and Sites and the Advisory Council on Underwater Archaeology. Archaeologists from East Carolina University surveyed the two shipwreck sites and produced a map and site analysis for the government.

Figure U.1. Lillian Azevedo documenting a site with nine cannon during a comprehensive survey of Anguilla's waters by a team from the University of Southampton. Photograph by Raymond Hayes. Reproduced by permission of the Anguilla Shipwreck Survey.

Since 2009, Lillian Azevedo and a team of graduate students from the University of Southampton have been conducting a comprehensive survey of Anguilla's waters (Figure U.1). They have located seven historic wrecks, a site with nine cannon, another with four anchors, a nineteenth-century site, a twentieth-century barge, and isolated anchors and cannon. The Anguilla Archaeological and Historical Society and Azevedo are also creating a land-based Heritage Trail.

Bahamas

In 1995, a ceremonial Lucayan canoe found in Stargate blue hole (a submerged cenote) on Andros Island was investigated by the University of South Carolina's Institute of Archaeology and Anthropology at the request of the government of the Bahamas. In the 1980s, the Institute of Nautical Archaeology (INA) investigated an early sixteenth-century site, the Highborn Cay Wreck, in the Bahamas. In 1991, another sixteenth-century vessel, the

St. Johns Bahamas Wreck, was discovered on the Little Bahama Bank.

Barbados

During the 2008 UNESCO meeting in Saint Lucia, a representative from Barbados related that no UCH activities will be undertaken in Barbados until the proposed Preservation of Antiquities and Relics Bill is passed, which includes UCH. The Barbados Museum and Historical Society is the principal contact for issues related to heritage matters. Over 200 documented wrecks are located in the waters of Barbados.

Cayman Islands

At the invitation of the Cayman Islands government, Roger Smith and a team from the INA surveyed the islands' waters from 1979–1980 and documented seventy-seven sites. They test-excavated the Turtle Bone Wreck, which is believed to be an English turtle-fishing sloop that was burned in 1670 by Spanish privateer Manuel Rivero Pardal, and the Duck Pond Careenage, which was used for overhauling vessels for three centuries. In the 1990s, Margaret Leshikar-Denton investigated HMS *Convert* and nine ships of her merchant convoy (1794), known collectively as the Wreck of the Ten Sail. These ships were lost together on the East End reefs of Grand Cayman during the French Revolutionary Wars. Under the auspices of the Cayman Islands National Museum, her team worked to enlarge the country's shipwreck inventory to over 140 sites, including early sites such as HMS *Jamaica* (1715) and the Spanish brigantine *San Miguel* (1730), both of which are worthy of special protection. They test-excavated a turtle-fishing encampment that dates to about 1700 and excavated an early historic stepwell on the waterfront. In the 1990s, researchers from the University College London and the Florida Museum of Natural History surveyed for prehistoric sites with negative results. *Geneva Kathleen*, a three-masted schooner loaded with lumber that wrecked in 1930, was documented by researchers from Ball State University in the 1990s. With the assistance of Leshikar-Denton and Della

Scott-Ireton, a Maritime Heritage Partnership launched a land-based Maritime Heritage Trail in 2003. It consists of thirty-six sites located around the coastlines of three islands and highlights a range of themes, including early explorers, maritime place names, historic anchorages, shipwrecks, wrecking practices, lighthouses, seaside forts, shipbuilding, turtle fishing, and hurricanes. Bert Ho and a team from Florida State University helped the Cayman Islands National Museum document the Norwegian-flagged *Glamis*, which was lost in 1913, providing the foundation for creating a future shipwreck preserve on the shipwreck site (Figure U.2).

Cuba

Although little information has been reported on UCH research in Cuba, the country is developing site inventories, undertaking excavations, conserving remains, and establishing museums. Early colonial shipwrecks are known to exist in Cuban waters, for example at the Cayo Ines de Soto site, where a ship is thought to have sunk in 1555–1556, but difficulties in sharing data and conducting scientific research limit the information available.

Figure U.2. An anchor on the Norwegian-flagged *Glamis*, which was lost in 1913, provides an interesting feature that can be interpreted in a future shipwreck preserve. Photograph by Alexander Mustard. Reproduced with permission of the *Glamis* Project.

Dominica

During the 2008 UNESCO meeting in Saint Lucia, a representative from Dominica pointed out that Hurricane Dean had uncovered a shipwreck and that various interests exist that may assist the government in finding ways to protect and manage this and other sites. A harbor survey of Roseau was reported by Wil Nagelkerken, Dennis Knepper, and Raymond Hayes.

Dominican Republic

The Dominican Republic's Comisión de Rescate Arqueológico Submarino, which was established in 1979 under the auspices of the Dominican Navy to salvage, conserve, and exhibit underwater cultural heritage, conducted excavations in cooperation with commercial interests on the *Nuestra Señora de la Pura y Limpia Concepción* (1641), the *Nuestra Señora de Guadalupe* (1724), and the *Conde de Tolosa* (1724); the French warship *Scipión* (1782); and the French ships *Diómedes* and *Imperial* (1806). The Museo de las Reales Atarazanas, the Museo de Arqueología Submarina del Faro a Colón, and the Museo de las Casas Reales display artifacts from these shipwrecks. In 1998 and 1999, after working with commercial interests for twenty years, the Dominican government headed the meetings of the Latin American and Caribbean Group, a Technical Commission on Underwater Cultural Heritage created by the Forum of Ministers of Culture and Officials Responsible for Cultural Policy of LAC, and wisely announced that it preferred to work with universities and to keep 100 percent of artifacts that were recovered within the country. The National Office for the Protection of the Underwater Cultural Heritage was created in June 1999, replacing previous authorities, although political changes have influenced success. The first scientific projects undertaken in the Dominican Republic include the INA's search in the 1980s for Columbus's *Santa María* and the caravels *Mariagalante, Gallega, San Juan,* and *Cardera*. Researchers from Indiana University and Panamerican Consultants investigated a prehistoric plaza and a cenote containing Taíno artifacts at Manantial de la Aleta in the 1990s. The Monte Christi Shipwreck (1652–1656) was excavated by the Pan-American Institute of Maritime Archaeology in the 1990s. In 2002, with assistance from Indiana University under the direction of Charles Beeker, the Dominican Republic established an underwater museum featuring artifacts from two galleons, *Guadalupe* and *Tolosa*. The artifacts were stored away from public view for years until they were replaced on the sea floor and interpreted for divers and snorkelers. A second underwater museum, Guaraguao Reef Cannons Preserve, was opened in 2004 with artifacts from other Spanish shipwrecks replaced to resemble a shipwreck site. In 2007, pirate captain William Kidd's ship *Quedagh Merchant* was discovered by a team from Indiana University. This wreck will be scientifically investigated and ultimately will be interpreted for the diving and snorkeling public.

Dutch Caribbean

The Archaeological-Anthropological Institute of the Netherlands Antilles (AAINA), in cooperation with the College of William and Mary, investigated the historical anchorage at Orange Bay, Saint Eustatius, in the 1980s, identifying seventeenth- and eighteenth-century Dutch, French, and English artifacts. In 2007, a Leiden University student completed a survey of both underwater and terrestrial cannon and anchors. An estimated 200 ships have wrecked around St. Eustatius, once one of the busiest ports in the world.

In 1994 and 1995, archaeologists mapped HMS *Proselyte*, a captured Dutch frigate that wrecked in 1801, under the auspices of the Sint Maarten National Heritage Foundation, the Ministry of Culture, the Department of Planning and Environment, and Maritime Archaeology and Research, in preparation for developing a management plan. Under the auspices of AAINA, Wil Nagelkerken, Raymond Hayes, and volunteers with the Maritime Archaeological and Historical Society surveyed the historical anchorage adjacent to Fort Orange and Kralendijk at Bonaire, recovering 600 artifacts from Holland, England, France, and Germany. They also identified the Dutch warship *Sirene*, which was lost in 1831. In the 1980s, AAINA surveyed the Dutch frigate *Alphen* in Curaçao, which exploded and sank in 1778 in Santa Anna Bay. In 1994 and 1998, excavations were conducted on the site. In 1993, in response to dredging during repair of the commercial wharf at the entrance to Santa Anna Bay, a survey and surface collection yielded artifacts from the seventeenth through nineteenth centuries. SS *Mediator*, which was lost in 1884 in the Willemstad harbor, has been mapped, and protected from damage caused by ship traffic. The site is to be interpreted in situ for the public. Museum displays about the site have been developed at the nearby Curaçao Maritime Museum, and education, resource management, and promotional activities were planned by a partnership of heritage organizations. In 2000, as a result of this work, Nagelkerken and Hayes formed the Foundation for Marine Archaeology of the Netherlands Antilles (STIMANA) for the purpose of underwater research in the Dutch Caribbean and other islands.

Grenada

Grenada has begun a listing of sites that suggests that at least 174 wrecks may be located in the island's waters. In January 2009, a historical shipwreck site was reported to the government, and discussions are under way with the dive operation that reported it about ways to protect and manage the site. Grenada also has a project in place with France to develop protected areas.

Haiti

In 1995, the Haitian government created the National Office of Marine Archaeology, although delays and changes have stalled its establishment. In the past, Haiti has made agreements with the French Nautical Archaeological Research Group to identify sites in Haitian waters.

Jamaica

In 1692, a catastrophic earthquake devastated the thriving English colonial city of Port Royal, Jamaica, a great portion of which subsided into Kingston Harbour. Underwater excavations were conducted by Edwin Link and the National Geographic Society in the 1950s that resulted in a pre-1692 map of Port Royal. In the 1960s, Robert Marx excavated caches of artifacts. Philip Mayes began terrestrial excavations at Port Royal in 1969. The first scientific underwater archaeology excavations were undertaken by Texas A&M University and the INA, under the direction of Donny Hamilton, and in association with the Jamaica National Heritage Trust (JNHT). From 1981 to 1990, Hamilton led field schools in excavations of eight buildings and a ship that wrecked as it rammed through a building during the 1692 earthquake (Figure U.3). Dor-

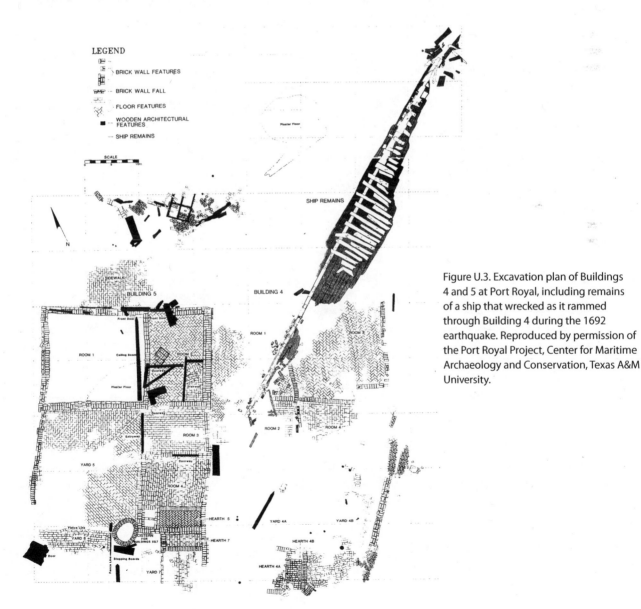

Figure U.3. Excavation plan of Buildings 4 and 5 at Port Royal, including remains of a ship that wrecked as it rammed through Building 4 during the 1692 earthquake. Reproduced by permission of the Port Royal Project, Center for Maritime Archaeology and Conservation, Texas A&M University.

rick Gray, technical director of archaeology at the JNHT, was the first Jamaican to be trained in underwater archaeology at Hamilton's field schools. Port Royal's rich body of archaeological data represents all aspects of life in seventeenth-century Port Royal, although much remains to be excavated. Today, museums interpret this remarkable world heritage. During the 1980s and 1990s, INA teams sought to discover the remains of Columbus's caravels *Capitana* and *Santiago de Palos*, which both ran aground in 1503 in St. Ann's Bay. Unsuccessful in the quest for the Columbus sites, they found instead six eighteenth-century merchant vessels. One was a British sloop known as the Reader's Point Wreck, which was investigated in the 1990s by Greg Cook and a team from the INA/JNHT. The INA also assisted the government in the 1980s in surveys on the Pedro Banks for early shipwreck sites, but little scientific work has been carried out because of remoteness of locations, complicated logistics, and nominal funding. In 1983, the Institute of Jamaica sponsored work by Leshikar-Denton to document the building of a traditional Jamaican dugout canoe using hand tools.

Martinique and Guadeloupe

France ratified the UNESCO Convention on the Protection of the Underwater Cultural Heritage on February 7, 2013. Because Martinique and Guadeloupe are departments of France and are subject to French laws, this convention applies to them. These two countries have begun a project to inventory their shipwrecks and have established a Web site that describes archival and archaeological work that has been done. The site lists 90 ships that were lost from the seventeenth through the twentieth centuries (www.archeonavale.org/martinique). The list identifies 73 archaeological sites, 19 of which are known by the ship's name. Among the sites are *Notre Dame de Bonne Espérance* (1687), HMS *Raisonable* (1762), and *Le Cygne* (1808).

Puerto Rico

In Puerto Rico, the Underwater Archaeology Office of the Consejo para la Conservación y Estudio de Sitios y Recursos Arqueológicos Subacuáticos has compiled an inventory of over 200 shipwrecks. Puerto Rican archaeologists have recorded two Spanish steamships, *Alicante*, which wrecked in 1881, and *Antonio López*, which was lost in 1898 during the Spanish-American War, as well as the seventeenth-century *Rincón Astro-*

labe wreck. They have recorded an eighteenth-century English warship wrecked on the Laurel Reefs of La Parguera, Lajas; verified sites reported at Mona Island; and documented the Cerro Gordo sites in Vega Alta, a shipyard of the seventeenth to nineteenth centuries. With the help of Jerome Hall and Richard Wills, they recorded a PT boat (a small fast patrol vessel used by the U.S. Navy in World War II) in Desecheo Island and two aircraft—a B-29 in Aguadilla and a PBY Catalina flying boat in La Parguera—for the U.S. Navy. They also assessed Buoy 4 in San Juan to investigate the *Manuela* and the *Cristobal Colon*, both of which were lost during the Spanish-American War. An international team recently assisted in a survey of sites off Mona Island that features thirty-one historical anchors that date from the sixteenth century to the present day. Richard Fontánez, Gustavo García, and Consejo personnel Juan Vera and Amilcar García recently conducted an inventory of the Cayo Ratones in Cabo Rojo, where a semi-submerged indigenous archaeological site was investigated. In 2008, the Puerto Rican Instituto de Investigaciones Costaneras, the Center for Maritime Archaeology and Conservation at Texas A&M University, and the INA surveyed the northern coast of Puerto Rico between Loíza and San Juan Bay. The team, which included Fontánez, Filipe Castro, and Gustavo García, located sites in an area where pre-Columbian settlements existed and over sixty-six ships were lost.

Saint Lucia

Saint Lucia was the first Caribbean country to ratify the 2001 UNESCO Convention on the Protection of the Underwater Cultural Heritage. The country hosted regional UNESCO meetings in 2003 and 2008 to assist and inform Eastern Caribbean countries about the benefits of this international legal instrument. The Saint Lucia Archaeological and Historical Society has a long history of professionally addressing the island's terrestrial archaeological heritage and is a leader in ethical underwater and maritime archaeology in Saint Lucia and the subregion.

St. Kitts and Nevis

At the 2008 UNESCO meeting, which was held in Saint Lucia, a representative from St. Kitts and Nevis pointed out that while previous archaeological emphasis in St. Kitts and Nevis has been on land sites, the waters that surround the island contain at least 200 wrecks that should be protected and managed. The Nevis Maritime

Archaeological Group, which includes both local and international members, has recently been formed and in 2011 conducted research on HMS *Solebay*, lost in January 1782 during the Battle of Frigate Bay.

St. Vincent and the Grenadines

During the 2008 UNESCO meeting in Saint Lucia, a representative from St. Vincent and the Grenadines pointed out that although many wrecks are located in the islands' waters, an inventory has yet to be developed. In 1997–1998, with the cooperation of the government of St. Vincent and the Organization of American States, a joint team of researchers and students from Florida State University and the Institute of Maritime History carried out a project in Kingstown Harbour that included remote sensing, surface mapping, artifact recovery, and limited excavations on a shipwreck from the late eighteenth century.

Trinidad and Tobago

During the 1998 meeting of the Latin American and Caribbean Group, Vel Lewis, a representative from Trinidad and Tobago and the director of the Trinidad National Museum and Art Gallery, noted that French shipwrecks lost in a 1677 battle with the Dutch had been discovered during dredging in a harbor in the island of Tobago. In response, Trinidad and Tobago introduced the United Kingdom–based Protection of Wrecks Act (1994). In 1997, a Technical Advisory Committee was appointed to advise the government minister on site designation and license approvals and to consider conservation and artifact disposition. Plans are under way to compile an inventory of sites with the help of the local Military Museum, to review the 1994 legislation, and to develop a set of guidelines to approve requests from international bodies who wish to work in the twin island republic.

Turks and Caicos Islands

At the request of the government of the Turks and Caicos Islands, a team from INA under the direction of Donald Keith excavated the Molasses Reef Wreck from 1982 to 1985 and began conservation treatments on the artifacts. Keith established a nonprofit organization, Ships of Discovery, which continued the conservation from 1988. This sixteenth-century site, which treasure hunters first incorrectly proclaimed was Columbus's *Pinta*, dates from the 1520s and may be the earliest shipwreck discov-

ered to date in the Western Hemisphere. The Molasses Reef Wreck is the first shipwreck in the Caribbean to be fully excavated by scientific archaeological methods, and it provides substantial information about a ship type known as the caravel, thus joining the Highborn Cay Wreck in the Bahamas and the Bahía Mujeres wreck in Mexico in providing such clues. Another important research project under way today is the search for the slave ship *Trouvadore*, a Spanish ship that was lost in 1841. The ship was carrying a human cargo of 193 people who were intended for slavery in Cuba but who were freed after the ship wrecked in the Turks and Caicos Islands. In 2008, a Ships of Discovery team located remains of the U.S. navy brig *Chippewa*, lost in 1816 while patrolling the Caribbean on a mission to counter the African slave trade and piracy. In 1996, a Lucayan paddle dating to about AD 1100 was discovered in North Creek, Grand Turk. It is one of only two found in the Bahamian Archipelago and is considered to be related to a nearby archaeological site that was used as an outpost of the Taíno from Haiti. Today, both the Molasses Reef Wreck and the Lucayan paddle are displayed and interpreted in the Turks and Caicos National Museum.

Further Reading

Catsambis, A., B. Ford, and D. L. Hamilton, eds. 2011. *Oxford Handbook of Maritime Archaeology*. New York: Oxford University Press.

Delgado, J. P., ed. 1997. *Encyclopedia of Underwater and Maritime Archaeology*. London: British Museum Press.

Grenier, R., D. Nutley, and I. Cochran, eds. 2006. *Underwater Cultural Heritage at Risk: Managing Natural and Human Impacts*. Paris: ICOMOS.

International Council on Monuments and Sites. 1996. "ICOMOS International Charter on the Protection and Management of Underwater Cultural Heritage." http://www.international.icomos.org/charters/underwater_e.pdf. Accessed January 30, 2013.

Leshikar-Denton, M. E. Forthcoming. "Caribbean Maritime Archaeology." In *The Encyclopedia of Global Archaeology*, ed. Claire Smith. New York: Springer.

Leshikar-Denton, M. E., and P. Luna Erreguerena, eds. 2008. *Underwater and Maritime Archaeology in Latin America and the Caribbean*. Walnut Creek, CA: Left Coast Press.

Leshikar-Denton, M. E., and D. A. Scott-Ireton. 2012. "Creativity in Maritime Heritage Management in the Cayman Islands." In *Caribbean Heritage: A Source Book*, ed. Basil Reid. Trinidad and Tobago: University of the West Indies Press.

Ruppé, C., and J. Barstad, eds. 2002. *International Handbook of Underwater Archaeology*. New York: Kluwer Academic/Plenum Press.

United Nations Educational, Scientific, and Cultural Organization. 2001. "UNESCO Convention on the Protection of the Underwater Cultural Heritage." www.unesco.org/new/en/culture/themes/underwater-cultural-heritage/2001-convention/. Accessed January 17, 2013.

———. 2004. *Patrimonio Cultural Subacuático: América Latina y el Caribe*. Havana: UNESCO.

See also Archaeological Heritage Management; Foundation for Marine Archaeology of the Netherlands Antilles (STIMANA); The Jamaica National Heritage Trust; The National Archaeological Anthropological Memory Management Foundation (NAAM); Port Royal (Jamaica); Rescue Archaeology.

V

The Virgin Islands

Brian D. Bates

The Virgin Island group is located approximately 35 miles east of Puerto Rico. Currently, the Virgin Islands are divided into three political units: the United States Virgin Islands (USVI); the British Virgin Islands (BVI); and the islands of Vieques and Culebra, which belong to Puerto Rico. The USVI are principally composed of St. Thomas, St. John, and St. Croix. The BVI are composed of nearly seventy islands and islets; the four major islands are Tortola, Virgin Gorda, Anegada, and Jost Van Dyke. The USVI occupy an area of 216 square kilometers (135 square miles), while the BVI's total land mass is 95 square kilometers (59 square miles) (Figure V.1).

Evidence for human occupation in the Virgin Islands dates to as early as 1680 BC at Krum Bay, St. Thomas. This Ortoiroid period is described on both St. Thomas and St. John as the Krum Bay subseries and is characterized by flake tools, hammerstones, shell tools, and ground celts. Archaeological and paleobotanical evidence from Krum Bay and other sites on St. Thomas and St. John indicate that these locations were occupied semi-permanently by seasonal foragers and fishers who settled near the shores, arriving in canoes directly from South America. They exploited the ecological diversity of the islands, and their economy was primarily based on coastal fishing and shellfish. This was augmented by bird and tortoise hunting and cultivation of roots, wild grains, and fruit trees between 1000 BC and 100 BC (Lundberg 1989). The first settlers of the smaller islands of the Lesser Antilles were accomplished seamen who had a well-developed sense of navigation. Their maritime adaptation did not, however, appear to dull their knowledge of inland pursuits.

Arriving around 400–500 BC, the Saladoid settled these islands for an extended period. The Saladoid settlers appear to have continued much of their South American subsistence activities, as reflected in their reliance on horticultural sources of nourishment, sup-

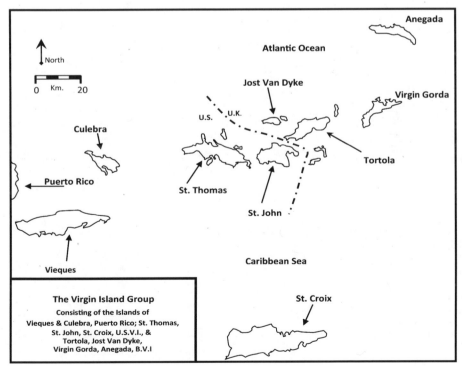

Figure V.1. The Virgin Island group. Courtesy of Brian D. Bates.

plemented by inshore and reef marine resources. This adaptation contrasts with the practices of the Ortoiroid groups, for whom marine resources provided the bulk of subsistence, and the practices of the post-Saladoid groups, who shifted their energies toward marine exploitation while also maintaining horticultural productivity. The Saladoid inhabitants of the Virgin Island group established most of their principal settlements in the northern and western quadrants of the islands. They used all areas of the islands for temporary campsites and for gathering and processing resources. Their subsistence activities shifted over time from a horticultural and inshore and reef marine economy to a horticultural and offshore marine economy.

The Saladoid period came to an end around AD 650 in the Virgin Islands. It was followed by the Ostionoid period. Ceramics from this new period are known in the Virgin Islands as Elenan Ostionoid (Rouse 1992). Elenan Ostionoid ceramics can be divided into two styles: the earlier Monserrate style (AD 600–900) and the later Santa Elena (AD 900–1200). The evidence that is emerging of more complex ritual behavior is suggestive of a shift in social organization over time in the Virgin Island group. The data from Cape Wright, Jost Van Dyke, British Virgin Islands (Bates 2001) suggest that the apparently egalitarian communal system that was descended from the Saladoid period changed to a more socially ranked system just after AD 900. The evidence of ritually deposited symbolic artifacts points to an emerging social elite.

During the Elenan Ostionoid period, the number of sites in the Virgin Island group and Puerto Rico proliferated and populations exploited a variety of resource habitats. Throughout the Saladoid and Elenan Ostionoid periods, the inhabitants of the Virgin Islands primarily exploited the coastal plain areas of the islands, although some inland sites are also known from this period. The coastal plain is characterized by broad expanses of land that extend from the coastal interface inland. The coastal plain would have provided the most appropriate environment for horticulture, particularly cassava cultivation, and easy access to the inshore and reef marine species that they were exploiting for subsistence.

Around AD 1200, the Elenan subseries gave way to the Chican subseries. Chican ceramics are prominently decorated with curvilinear incised designs and modeled-incised lugs (Rouse 1992, 125) and are known in the Virgin Islands as the Esperanza pottery style. It is during this last precolonial period that the culture known as the Taíno emerged. Also during this period the inhabitants began extending their predation into the coastal

strand—generally long and rather narrow strips of land at the coastal interface and in the coastal plain areas. In addition, they located their temporary campsites in the drier marginal southern and eastern quadrants of the islands. The marine resources they exploited appear to have shifted late in this period from the inshore and reef species to offshore species. This change suggests that populations may have expanded to the point of overexploitation of the more fragile inshore and reef ecosystems.

During the Elenan Ostionoid period, ball courts emerged and spread throughout Puerto Rico, Hispaniola, and the Virgin Island group (Rouse 1992, 112–13). Peter L. Drewett and Brian D. Bates recently excavated a ball court at the Belmont site on Tortola (Drewett 2003). The evidence from Belmont of multiple episodes of house construction, a change in structure type, and the presence of a ball/dance court, is indicative of Classic Taíno social organization. This was characterized by a paramount chief whose authority and power was legitimized by his claim to be the closest living descendant of the prime deity in the ancestor cult. During the expansion of population that accompanied this shift in social organization, the environment around villages such as Belmont was overexploited, necessitating the late prehistoric practice of establishing temporary campsites such as Paraquita Bay in areas that had been ignored or avoided throughout the earlier occupation periods on these islands. Ultimately, overexploitation of resources may have led to the abandonment of the islands in the Virgin Islands in favor of the larger islands such as Puerto Rico, where populations may have been consolidating shortly before the arrival of Columbus.

Further Reading

Bates, B. D. 2001. Ceramic Period Prehistoric Settlement of the Virgin Island Group, United States, and British Virgin Islands. PhD diss., University of London.

Drewett, P. L. 2003. "Belmont: Ball Games in the Prehistoric Caribbean." *Current World Archaeology* 2: 46–50.

Lundberg, E. 1989. Pre-Ceramic Procurement Patterns at Krum Bay, Virgin Islands. PhD diss., University of Illinois, Champaign-Urbana.

Rouse, I. 1992. *The Tainos: Rise and Decline of the People Who Greeted Columbus.* New Haven, CT: Yale University Press.

William, K. 2000. "West Indian Archaeology. 3. Ceramic Age." *Journal of Archaeological Research* 8: 135–67.

See also The Chican Ostionoid Subseries; Chiefdoms (*Cacicazgos*); The Elenan Ostionoid Subseries; The Ortoiroid; Plazas and *Bateys*; The Saladoid.

Willemstad (Curaçao)

Gertrudis J. M. Gehlen

Willemstad was founded by the Dutch in the seventeenth century. It is a unique historical urban landscape because most of the urban structures that were built between 1650 and 1900 still exist. The city contains a large number of monuments. Because it is a remarkable example of a former Dutch colonial city in the Caribbean, Willemstad was successfully nominated as a UNESCO world heritage city in 1997. Historic Willemstad consists of four quarters: Punda, Pietermaai and Scharloo on the eastern side, and Otrobanda on the western side of the St. Anna Bay, the deep channel that divides Willemstad into two parts (Figure W.1).

The oldest quarter, Punda, owes its name to Dutch "*de punt*" (the point), which was the name given to the peninsula on which Fort Amsterdam was built. This name became Punta in Spanish and was later changed to Punda. Fort Amsterdam was constructed by the Dutch West India Trading Company to protect the entrance of the St. Anna Bay in 1635, a year after the island was conquered. The fortress marks the beginning of the city and is the oldest structure on the island.

During the seventeenth century, the settlement called Willemstad gradually spread north of Fort Amsterdam. On three sides, the city was walled in, but the city was

Figure W.1. Willemstad, Curaçao, 2009. Photo by Michael A. Newton.

open on the waterfront of St. Anna Bay. The city grew rapidly, especially in the last quarter of the seventeenth century. By the beginning of the eighteenth century, the walled-in town had become too small to accommodate the increasing population and people started to build beyond the city walls. Punda was so densely populated that some areas were dark and close; they remained this way even after the walls were demolished at the end of the nineteenth century.

The first houses of the district of Pietermaai were built half a kilometer to the east. The district was separated from Punda by an open space that was the length of the field of fire of the cannon at Fort Amsterdam. Pietermaai featured a linear urban development along the road that led to the eastern part of the island. After the demolition of the ramparts of Punda in 1866, colourful mansions filled in the open area between Punda and Pietermaai.

The Scharloo quarter developed on a former plantation. The first mansions of Scharloo were constructed along the northern shore of the inland bay of Waaigat. In the second quarter of the nineteenth century, Scharloo developed into a residential district of great prominence. Many of the luxurious Neoclassical villas were inhabited by Jewish merchants.

In Otrobanda, some houses had already been built before 1707. In this year, the Dutch West India Company gave permission to parcel out the first lots in the area on the western shore of St. Anna Bay for new settlers. From the point of view of those living in Punda, this was the "other side," so it was called Otrobanda in Papiamentu. Because this suburb was not restricted by city walls, it expanded rapidly. Half a century later it was larger than Punda. On the southern edge, Otrobanda bordered on a large reef, called the Rifwater (reef water). This area was filled in during the twentieth century so that it could be built upon. The northern part of Otrobanda, which is situated on a hill, was not developed until well into the nineteenth century. Except for Brionplein (the large square in Otrobanda) and the Breedestraat, the main shopping street, Otrobanda has always been a residential area.

The oldest architecture of the city is derived from seventeenth-century Dutch architecture. The houses in Punda are similar to the houses in walled-in cities in Holland. The tall and narrow houses are joined with a high façade on the street side. However, from the beginning, houses in Willemstad displayed a typical character of their own. Over time, local architectural styles adapted to local conditions that included climate, available building materials, and local craftsmanship. Shops and warehouses were located on ground floors, and the second and third floors were used as dwellings and ware-

houses. Galleries were introduced in the first half of the eighteenth century, mainly to create a buffer between the hot climate and the interior of the house so that the inside temperature would be more agreeable. Wooden galleries (and later, stone galleries) were added to the original fronts of dwellings. In new houses, the gallery was incorporated in the design. Some old galleries that were later additions to existing houses can still be found.

Until the first decades of the eighteenth century, houses were characterized by tall façades with small triangular pediments on top. Because of the Amsterdam influence, this architecture is called the Curaçao Dutch style. Underneath the pediment, the date of construction was often displayed in a rectangular frame. The oldest known dwelling with a date in the top of the gable is the building that now houses the Postal Museum in Curaçao, which was constructed in 1693. The Curaçao Monument Foundation restored the building in the early 1990s. The finest examples of Curaçao architecture were built in the eighteenth century. This architecture, which is called Curaçao Baroque, is characterized by curved lines. Some very fine examples can be found in the center of Punda, for example, the Penha building and the Sephardic synagogue. The Curaçao Baroque style was also used in houses in Scharloo and Otrobanda and in some plantation houses.

At the beginning of the nineteenth century, the architecture became rather plain. A modest gable with a small ornament on top was typical of this period. All over the island, houses were built in this style. At the beginning of the second half of the nineteenth century, the Neoclassical architectural style was introduced to Curaçao. Houses that were built in this style have prominent cornices, hipped roofs, and typical classical elements, such as pediments and columns. Until the first decades of the twentieth century, both very luxurious and rather modest buildings were created in this style. Examples of Neoclassical monuments can be found in the inner city and on former plantations.

A conspicuous feature of the traditional architecture of Willemstad is the color of its buildings. This is because a government act of 1817 ordered that the façades, which were normally finished in white lime, be painted in colors other than white.

During the twentieth century, a few extraordinary examples of Functionalism and Art Deco were added to the diverse architectural styles of the old city.

Historic Willemstad is an exceptionally well-preserved example of a Dutch colonial trading settlement. The government of Curaçao has put policies in place to preserve the city for future generations. The monument legislation and the zoning acts for the inner city have ensured the conservation of monuments and the historic urban area. In the 1990s, about half the buildings in historic Willemstad were proclaimed protected monuments by the island government. New developments in the historic area continue to be done within the context of governmental heritage protection.

Further Reading

Buddingh, B. R. 1994. *Onstaan en groei van Willemstad Curaçao vanaf 1634. De Willemstad tussen 1700 en 1732 en de bouwgeschiedenis van de synagoge Mikve Israel-Emanuel 1730–1732* [Establishment and Growth of Willemstad Curaçao since 1634, the City of Willemstad between 1700 and 1732 and the Building History of Synagogue Mikve Israel-Emanuel 1730–1732]. 's-Hertogenbosch: Aldus Uitgevers.

Coomans, H. E. 1990. *Building Up the Future from the Past.* Zutphen, Netherland: De Walburg Pers.

Ozinga, M. D. 1959. *De Monumenten van Curaçao in Woord en Beeld* [The monuments of Curaçao in text and illustrations]. 's-Gravenhage: Staatsdrukkerij en Uitgeverijbedrijf.

Pruneti Winkel, P. 1987. *Scharloo: A Nineteenth-Century Quarter of Willemstad, Curaçao: Historical Architecture and Its Background.* Florence: Edizione Poligrafico Fiorentino.

Temminck Groll, C. L. 1990. *Curaçao: Willemstad, a City of Monuments.* The Hague: SDU-Gary Schwarz.

See also Falmouth (Jamaica); The Magnificent Seven Mansions (Port of Spain, Trinidad); Port Antonio (Jamaica); Spanish Town (Jamaica).

Williams, Denis (1923–1998)

Jennifer Wishart and Mark G. Plew

Noted Guyanese artist, writer, and archaeologist Denis Williams was born in Georgetown, Guyana. After he graduated from high school in 1941, Williams was awarded a British Council scholarship to attend the Camberwell School of Arts in London (1946–1948). In 1949, he returned to Guyana, where he focused on a series of locally based works that were shown in private exhibitions. Returning to England in 1950, he taught at the Central School of Fine Arts in London. During this period, his noted artwork *Human World* was reproduced in *Time* magazine.

Leaving London, Williams spent ten years in Africa—lecturing first at the Institute of African Studies in Khartoum and later at the Universities of Ife (1962) and Lagos (1966) in Nigeria. In Khartoum, he visited numerous archaeological sites, an experience that fostered a developing interest in archaeology. While in Sudan, he published *Other Leopards*, his first novel, now a classic work in Caribbean literature; *Icon and Image: A Study of Sacred and Secular Forms of African Classical Art*; and *The Third Temptation*. His literary works of this period reflect the alienation he felt as a colonial artist.

Returning home in 1968, Williams spent a number of years in Issano on the Mazaruni River, where he developed a serious interest in the prehistory of Guyana. Though not formally trained in archaeology, Williams initiated a series of important excavations that served as a foundation for ongoing regional investigations. In 1974, he moved to Georgetown to become the director of art for the new Republic of Guyana. In 1978, he served as chair of the nation's newly founded National Trust. Following his return to Guyana, he founded the E. R. Burrowes School of Art in 1975 and the Walter Roth Museum of Anthropology in 1977. Another important contribution was the founding of *Archaeology and Anthropology*, the journal of the Walter Roth Museum of Anthropology, which is the first English-language anthropology journal in the Caribbean.

During this time, Williams initiated a series of archaeological surveys and excavations in areas near the Mazaruni, Berbice, and Essequibo Rivers and in the Rupununi savannahs of southern Guyana. This work was facilitated by time Williams spent as a visiting research scholar at the Smithsonian Institution in 1980 (Figure W.2). These investigations formed the basis of Williams's attempts to develop a broad chronology of the region. Perhaps because of his background in art, Williams developed a serious interest in the rock art of Aishalton. In "A Report on Preceramic Lithic Artifacts in the South Rupununi Savannahs" (1979), he argued that the Aishalton rock art reflected a system of enumeration that was common among hunter-gatherers in

Figure W.2. Denis Williams in his office at the Smithsonian Institution. Courtesy of Jennifer Wishart.

which different combinations and directional orientations of motifs identified the location of raw materials and the ranges of edible plants and animals. Williams was among the first to suggest that such rock art was produced by shamans. Notably, he was the first archaeologist in the region to excavate near rock panels in search of the tools used in its production—an element of his 1979 paper. His major synthesis appeared as "Petroglyphs in the Prehistory of Northern Amazonia and the Antilles" (Williams 1985).

An important aspect of Williams's work is his consideration of artifact (type) correlations to functionally discrete activities. In a number of papers he relates changes in faunal remains and artifacts to alterations in coastal environments, for example, in his analysis of how sharper grooves related to tool sizes in the context of climatic fluctuations. Though he was a dedicated culture historian, his work often transcended common archaeological thinking and practice. This is well reflected in his fisheries management hypothesis, which posits that Amerindian peoples identified the seasonal availability of fish resources (and required fishing technologies) in differing contexts, particularly during periods of environmental stress. Following this theme, his more recent work used paleoenvironmental data to argue that early horticulture evolved in response to new environmental conditions that emerged at the end of the Archaic (7000–8000 BP). Especially important in this regard is Williams's "recharacterization" of the horticultural Mabaruma phase in which he argues that pottery-making horticulturalists appear much earlier than was originally thought. The later discussion is prominent in

Prehistoric Guiana (Williams 2003), the first major synthesis of the prehistory of Guianas, which was published posthumously. To some extent, Williams spent his archaeological career working in scholarly isolation. Remarkably, much of his work uses analytical frameworks that are common outside Amazonia and the Caribbean. A good example is his calculations of the nutritional value of shellfish harvests as a means to measure potential environmental productivity.

Williams's contributions to the study of Guyana prehistory, the prehistory of northern Amazonia, and the southern Caribbean were acknowledged by his receipt of an honorary doctorate from The University of the West Indies (1989) and a series of awards that included the Cacique Crown of Honor (1989) from the Republic of Guyana, the Gabriel Mistral Award of the Organization of American States (1994), and the Cowrie Circle Award (1998) from the Commonwealth Association of Museums.

Further Reading

Williams, D. 1979. "A Report on Preceramic Lithic Artifacts in the South Rupununi Savannahs." *Journal of Anthropology and Archaeology* 2 (1): 10–53.

———. 1985. "Petroglyphs in the Prehistory of Northern Amazonia and the Antilles." In *Advances in World Archaeology*, vol. 4, ed. F. Wendorf and A. E. Close, 335–87. New York: Academic Press.

———. 2003. *Prehistoric Guiana*. Kingston; Miami: Ian Randle Publishers.

See also Kabakaburi and Wyva Creek Shell Mounds (Northwestern Guyana).

Z

Zemíes (Cemís)

Alexandra Sajo and Peter E. Siegel

Traditionally, the term *zemíe*, or *cemí*, referred to sacred objects that represented deities in a wide range of forms, some anthropomorphic or zoomorphic. *Zemíes* are associated with the Taíno people and their ancestors, who created them from a variety of materials including wood, stone, shell, pottery, bone, and cotton. There is good archaeological evidence that the use of deity icons in the Caribbean has a long antiquity, dating to approximately 400 BC. Recently, José Oliver (2009, 59) argued that "*cemí* refers not to an artifact or object but to an immaterial, numinous, and vital force." In Taíno culture, *zemíes* were considered to be spirits that represented and, with proper treatment, delivered cosmological power. The degree of *zemíe* power and sacredness depended on the combination of elements, which included form, material, production process, and the values ascribed to these elements. The world was animated by forces derived from nature and by Taíno ancestral spirits that resided in specific domains of their physical environment (trees, rocks, caves, rivers, volcanoes, and other landscape features) and their social world.

Social life revolved around the veneration, capture, and manipulation of these powerful, ever-present, and ambivalent spirits. Through physical characteristics and symbolic associations, *zemíes* embodied distinct powers that ranged from domestic (such as fertility and successful childbirth) to political, economic, and religious spheres (such as success in war and the fertility and abundance of crops). Shamanism was fundamental to Taíno society and the preference for wood in manufacturing *zemíes* may have been linked to close spiritual relationships people had with trees. For instance, community members believed that trees had spiritual, medicinal, and curative proprieties that were transferrable to *zemíes* carved from wood. *Zemíes* played an important role in furthering chiefly or shamanistic status and power and were included with elite and religious paraphernalia such as *duhos* (ceremonial seats), which were reserved for caciques and shamans. Wooden *zemíes* have been found throughout the Greater Antilles.

All members of Taíno society possessed at least one *zemíe*. *Zemíes* probably appear most frequently in the form of distinctively carved three-pointed objects (made of stone, bone, or shell), often with anthropomorphic or zoomorphic imagery. Many of these three-pointers represented Yucahú, the cassava god. Three-pointer *zemíes* have been found throughout the Antilles. Ethnographic, ethnohistoric, and archaeological data reveal numerous commonalities between the cosmological views of the natural and spiritual worlds of the Taíno and lowland Amazonian cultures. There is evidence too that caciques used the tradition of lineage-based ancestral *zemíes* in their quest for political power; caciques venerated and consulted *zemíes* as their supernatural allies. In the *cohoba* ceremony, the shaman or cacique demonstrated his or her ability to link a range of issues and concerns of individuals or the community at large with the spirit realm through active engagement with *zemíes*.

Further Reading

Alegría, R. 1997. "An Introduction to Taino Culture and History." In *Taíno: Pre-Columbian Art and Culture from the Caribbean*, ed. F. Bercht, E. Brodsky, J. A. Farmer, and D. Taylor, 18–33. New York: El Museo del Barrio and the Monacelli Press.

Moscoso, F. 2003. "Chiefdoms in the Islands and the Mainland: A Comparison." In *A General History of the Caribbean: Autochthonous Societies*, ed. J. Sued-Badillo, 1:292–315. Paris: UNESCO.

Oliver, J. R. 2009. *Caciques and Cemí Idols: The Web Spun by Taíno Rulers between Hispaniola and Puerto Rico*. Tuscaloosa: University of Alabama Press.

Rouse, I. 1992. *The Tainos: Rise and Decline of the People Who Greeted Columbus*. New Haven, CT: Yale University Press.

Saunders, N., and D. Gray. 1996. "Zemies, Trees, and Symbolic Landscapes: Three Taino Carvings from Jamaica." *Antiquity* 70: 801–12.

See also The Chican Ostionoid Subseries; Chiefdoms (*Cacicazgos*); *Cohoba*; *Duhos* (*Dujos*); Jamaica (Prehistory of); Rock Art.

Glossary

abolition. The cessation of the slave trade. The United Kingdom abolished the slave trade in 1807, although slavery was still legally practiced in the Anglophone Caribbean until emancipation in August 1834, which was followed by an extended period of unpaid "apprenticeship" that ended in 1838. See also **emancipation**.

adorno. Modeled and incised (anthropomorphic, zoomorphic, or anthropozoomorphic) ornamentation on the rims or handles of ceramic pieces.

African Diaspora. The dispersal of Africans after their forcible removal from their homes and communities in Africa. The term also applies to descendants of the Africans who were removed from their homes and did not return to the original African location.

Amerindian. The peoples associated with the pre-Columbian settlement of the Americas. See also **indigenous**.

ancient DNA (aDNA). Any genetic material recovered from ancient samples (usually more than fifty years old) or from biological remains that have not been preserved with the intention of genetic analysis. Analysis of aDNA can reveal information about individuals (genetic profiles), at the within-group level (kinship relations, biological distance, within-group diversity), and at the between-group level (comparisons between distinct populations, evolutionary and phylogenetic relationships) of ancient populations. See also **mitochondrial DNA**.

anthropology. The study of human beings, including behavior, biology, linguistics, and social and cultural variations. In the United States, anthropology is divided into four subdisciplines: archaeology, biological/physical anthropology, cultural anthropology, and linguistics. All of these subdisciplines study aspects of past or present humans. Archaeologists generally study the physical and material remains of ancient societies. Physical anthropologists study human skeletons and other bodily remains. Biological anthropologists deal primarily with the evolution of humans and primates. Linguists study languages, especially their development and their function within human culture.

anthropomorphic. Resembling the form or attributes of humans in abstract or literal ways. See also **biomorphic; zoomorphic**.

anthropophagy. Human cannibalism. The word is derived from Greek *anthropos* (man) and *phagein* (to eat.)

anthropozoomorphic. Having both human and animal characteristics and forms.

appliqué. A French term that means "applied." An example would be a motif or design made separately, then affixed to a ceramic vessel.

Arawakan. Speakers of languages of the Arawakan language family, which developed among ancient indigenous peoples in South America. Branches of these peoples migrated to Central America and the Lesser/Greater Antilles in the Caribbean and the Atlantic, including what is now called the Bahamas.

archaeobotany. The study of preserved plant remains from archaeological sites. Such remains include wood, charcoal, seeds, phytoliths, starch granules, and pollen grains.

archaeological conservation. The documentation, examination, and analysis of the processes of deterioration and the practices that mitigate those processes through stabilization and treatments by conservation professionals.

archaeological heritage. According to Article 1 of the Charter for the Protection and Management of the Archaeological Heritage of the International Council on Monuments and Sites, "archaeological heritage comprises all vestiges of human existence and consists of places relating to all manifestations of human activity, abandoned structures, and remains of all kinds, together with all the portable cultural material associated with them."

archaeological theory. A research paradigm archaeologists use to define methods, data collection, and data interpretation. Processual archaeology, postprocessual archaeology, and Marxist archaeology are examples.

archaeologist. A trained professional who researches, analyzes, and interprets material remains to better understand human behavior in the ancient and recent past. See also **avocational archaeologist**.

archaeology. The systematic study of past human life and culture through the recovery and examination of remaining material evidence, such as graves, buildings, tools, and pottery.

archaeology field school. A relatively short teaching period often led by professional archaeologists to instruct future archaeologists on excavation techniques and site and artifact interpretation. Caribbean archaeological field schools are a primary labor source for basic research and for rescue archaeology.

archaeometry. The term archaeologists use for the application of scientific methods from the physical sciences and engineering to archaeological problems. Radiocarbon dating techniques, remote sensing, and trace element analysis are all classified as archaeometric methods.

Archaic. A term used to describe a Caribbean cultural developmental stage characterized by marine-oriented subsistence followed by a terrestrial hunting and incipient-horticulture economy. The absence of pottery was until recently considered a defining characteristic of Archaic peoples. However, evidence of pottery making among the Casimiroid and Ortoiroid has now invalidated this idea. It is sometimes confused with and/or used synonymously with "aceramic" or "preceramic."

areito or *areyto* **(pl.** *areitos***).** A Taíno ceremony associated with ancestor worship. *Areitos* involved dance and music and were important in Taíno social, political, and religious life. The main village plaza or the area in front of the chief's house was used for these ceremonies. The dance area was often bounded by an earthen embankment or by a series of standing stones that were often decorated with carved images of *zemíes* (mythological beings or ancestral spirits).

arquebus. An early European firearm with a serpentine firing mechanism; the predecessor of the musket. It was used around 1450–1550.

artifact. An object made or modified by humans.

Ashkenazim/Ashkenazi Jews. A Jewish religious, ethnic, and cultural group that originated in the Rhine area of Germany. By the colonial period, the vast majority of European Jews were Ashkenazi; thus, the majority of Jews who left Europe for the Caribbean belonged to this group. Colonial Ashkenazi and Sephardic Jews often remained separate because of strong religious, ethnic, and cultural differences, except in locations where there was no other choice but to worship together, such as on St. Eustatius.

assemblage. A group of artifacts found in the same archaeological context (locus, matrix, stratum).

assimilation. A process by which a minority group is absorbed into a majority population, during which the less powerful group takes on the values and norms of the dominant culture. See also **creolization**.

Atlantic World. A conceptual paradigm that encompasses all the peoples that border the Atlantic Ocean. It emphasizes their social, economic, and religious interconnectedness, especially during the colonial period, although recent archaeological work is beginning to show strong prehistoric connections across similar geographical distances. The Caribbean is an essential element in Atlantic World studies.

avocational archaeologist. A person who participates in archaeological projects but does not derive his/her primary livelihood from practicing archaeology. In the Caribbean, avocational archaeologists provide much-needed assistance to professional archaeologists and contribute to archival research, excavation, analysis, reporting, and public engagement. See also **archaeologist**.

axis mundi. In cosmology, that which ties or connects the celestial realm to the earth and/or the underworld. This "center of the world," or world axis, is often symbolized by a cave, a mountain, a tree or vine, or some other object.

ball court. A largely ceremonial stone and earthen structure built by Caribbean and neighboring Mesoamerican prehistoric peoples. Games played on ball courts used a small rubber ball that was moved by teams that most often used only their hips.

Baní. A zone of northeastern coastal Cuba near modern Banes, east-northeast of Holguín. Also a type of ceramic ware called Baní Ware.

battery. A military fortification that is not completely enclosed by protective walls. Batteries were often smaller than forts and were garrisoned with a small contingent of soldiers and enslaved individuals. They were sometimes used for surveillance. Batteries can be found throughout the Caribbean islands in geographical locations that required some form of defense, but not large military fortifications.

biomorphic. A term used to describe objects that resemble animals or plants in abstract or literal senses. See also **anthropomorphic; zoomorphic**.

Blue Mountains. The highest mountain range in Jamaica, famous for its coffee and as a historical refuge for Jamaica's Maroons.

bohío **(also** *buhío***).** A domestic vernacular architectural form derived from indigenous peoples that is commonly found in the Hispanic Greater Antilles. The walls of these post-built and/or timber-framed structures were often covered with the inner bark of palm trees, and the roofs were covered in thatch made of palm fronds or banana leaves. These materials were directly tied to the local indigenous peoples and are what differentiates the *bohío* from other colonial vernacular architectural forms in the Caribbean. Straw, grass, reeds, thatch or similar material and wattle-and-daub or clay mortar were also sometimes used on roofs and walls.

The Bottom. A late Ceramic Age site that produced Mamoran Troumassoid ceramics. It is the current capital of the island of Saba. The site was first discovered by de Josselin de Jong in 1923.

brass. An alloy of copper and zinc that is resistant to corrosion; sometimes confused with bronze. Brass artifacts such as nautical instruments, candlesticks, and containers are often found on historical archaeological sites in the Caribbean.

bronze. An alloy of copper and tin that is resistant to corrosion and is easily cast. Bronze is often used in maritime applications for instruments and equipment (e.g., cannon, oarlocks) and is sometimes confused with brass. On terrestrial sites, the oxidation of bronze artifacts may be relatively advanced and may present challenges in conservation. Bronze cannon are commonly associated with early colonial shipwrecks in the Caribbean.

budare. A ceramic griddle typically used to cook manioc or other breads; also known as *burén*.

buhío. See *bohío*.

canoe. Derived from the Taíno word *canoa*, the canoe is an open-decked boat form used by indigenous and immigrant peoples in the Caribbean. Canoes of indigenous peoples were most often dugouts (large logs hollowed and shaped using a combination of slow-burning fire and stone or shell tools). Colonial canoes were also built this way, but the term can also refer to a similarly shaped vessels constructed using a plank-on-frame technique. The canoe is also referred to as a pirogue, from the Cariban word *piragua*, a term adopted by the Spanish.

capitalism. An economic system whereby labor and natural resources are exploited to produce goods of more value than their constituent parts so that profits are realized. These profits are often reinvested in the exploitation process so that ever-greater efficiency through production and resource exploitation must be found to maintain the economic system. In the Caribbean, labor was provided by African and African-descended enslaved individuals and later by East Indian indentured workers. Historical archaeology is often defined as the archeology of capitalism.

Cariban. The Cariban languages are an indigenous language family of South America. They are widespread across northernmost South America, from the mouth of the Amazon River to the Colombian Andes, but they also appear in central Brazil. Cariban languages are relatively closely related and number two to three dozen, depending on what is considered a dialect. Most are still spoken, though often by only a few hundred speakers.

Caribbean literature. A body of indigenous and foreign written stories and records that often describe lifeways from a Caribbeanist perspective. As with many literary forms, this genre may be helpful for interpreting prehistoric and historical archaeological sites as long as the author's biases are understood.

Cassipora Cemetery. A Jewish Sephardic cemetery established in the 1660s on the Suriname River, two miles upstream of Jodensavanne.

cast iron. An iron alloy that contains up to 5 percent carbon. The alloy is melted and poured into a mold to obtain a usable shape. Common cast iron objects found by Caribbean archaeologists include cannon, cannon balls, and kettles. Although easy to form, cast iron is more prone to breakage than other alloys, and thus artifacts are often fragmented. See also **wrought iron**.

ceramic. An artifact made with clay-based material. Ceramics are heated to stimulate the formation of microscopic crystalline structures that give the objects strength and rigidity. These traits permit ceramic objects to survive relatively well in the archaeological record and therefore form the basis of many archaeological assemblages. Ceramics include cooking, ceremonial, and art objects.

Ceramic Age. The period when ceramics were first produced and used by cultural groups in the Caribbean. It was initially believed that the Ceramic Age in the Caribbean began with the advent of the Saladoid in 500–250 BC. However, this school of thought is no longer supported by the evidence, as the Ortoiroid (5000–200 BC) and the Casimiroid (4000–400 BC) were the region's first potters.

ceramic classification. The process of placing ceramics into groups on the basis of material, aesthetic, and form traits. Groups with trait similarities are referred to as ceramic types. Ceramic classification can facilitate intersite and intrasite comparisons, including the delineation of interaction spheres in the Caribbean.

Chatoyer, Josef. The first national hero of St. Vincent and the Grenadines; the Paramount Chief of the Carib in the late 1700s. For years, Chatoyer fought to prevent the English from settling in his native land. As many groups have done in wars between unequal foes, he used guerilla warfare. His leadership was so effective that it was only after his death in 1795 that the English were able to round up and banish his Black Carib people to Roatan Island, the largest of the Bay Islands in Honduras. From there, survivors relocated to mainland Honduras and Belize to form Garífuna communities.

Chican. The Chican subseries developed in the Dominican Republic, then spread to Puerto Rico and St. Croix and perhaps to the rest of the Virgin Islands, where it strongly influenced the cultures of the northern Leeward Islands. Usually associated with the Classic Taíno, Chican pottery, especially the Boca Chica style, is characterized by more highly burnished surfaces and more refined modeled incisions than the other Ostionoid and Taíno pottery subseries found elsewhere in the northern Caribbean.

chiefdom. A ranked or hierarchical society conventionally defined by the emergence of institutionalized social inequality and the formation of multivillage political units (or polities) under a centralized political authority. See also **polity**.

circum-Caribbean. The circum-Caribbean area includes the zone along the Caribbean coast that extends south from Honduras through Central America, along the north coast of South America, northward up the Lesser Antilles, and northwestward to the Greater Antilles and the Bahamian Archipelago.

clay. A mineral deposit formed by erosive hydraulic action consisting of metal oxides and organic matter. Water combined with clay's colloidal particles produces a plastic mineral fabric that can be shaped into various forms. It is the primary constituent, with various organic and inorganic tempers, of ceramic. Caribbean clay deposits are more frequently found in the geologically older Greater Antilles and in the outer arc of the Lesser Antilles.

coastal plain. A low-lying and often fertile area immediately adjacent to the ocean or sea. This fertile zone was attractive for agricultural pursuits in prehistoric and historic periods.

cognate. Having a common linguistic ancestor. For instance, English and Danish, both of which are Germanic, are cognate languages. Every language in the Indo-European language family has lexical items that are related to lexical items in another language in the family.

colonial period. A historical era in world history that refers to the global expansion of European cultures, religions, economies, and militaries that lasted from the 1400s to the post–World War II period. The exploitation of resources during the colonial period propelled the industrial revolution and the expansion of capitalism. See also **capitalism; historical archaeology**.

colony. An outpost of European powers that was settled to establish a beachhead for exploiting labor, natural, mineral, and agricultural resources. In the Caribbean, European colonies were engaged in the wholesale destruction of most indigenous communities and virtually all endemic flora and fauna on many islands.

commercial salvage. The search for and recovery of materials from shipwrecks and archaeological sites for profit (i.e., looting). The practice was known as wrecking in the colonial period, but today it is considered a type of treasure hunting. Recovered artifacts usually are sold into private collections or are given to investors, thus becoming unavailable for study or for public viewing. Commercial salvage of historic shipwrecks is considered unethical within the archaeological community. It results in the loss of heritage information and the destruction of heritage sites.

comparative collection. A collection of objects or specimens that are used to identify fragmentary remains from archaeological sites through comparison. An example would be the excellent comparative collection of Caribbean fish at the Florida Museum of Natural History.

context. The physical location of an artifact or artifact assemblage. Objects without context lose much of their archaeological meaning because they cease to provide information about the people who occupied a particular site. In the Caribbean, however, artifacts can retain some contextual information about the presence or absence of particular artifact types even at island-wide or regional levels.

cosmology. A philosophical or religious explanation of the origin and structure of the universe.

Creole. The concept of a *crioulo*, creole, or *créole* identity began with fifteenth-century Portuguese settlers in West Africa and the Cape Verde islands. Locally born Europeans first used the concept as part of an attempt to describe the unique situation they found themselves in with regard to language, society, religion, material culture (including architecture), and foodways. This group experienced profound psychological changes related to identity formation. Far-flung European outposts produced exceptional societies that drew upon indigenous and European archetypes. Over time, the term was used across the Atlantic World to identify many unique groups that resulted from the mixing of Africans, Amerindians, and Europeans.

Creole architecture. In the Caribbean, Creole people adapted local building materials and methods to their own conception of architectural forms in perhaps what is the most overt manifestation of the creolization process.

creolization. The process by which imported or foreign cultural forms became indigenous, with special but not exclusive reference to the fusion of Amerindian, African, and European cultural forms in the Caribbean and elsewhere in the Americas. Also the process through which creole peoples are created.

cultural evolution. The development of cultures and societies over time. Although cultural evolutionary models typically provide an understanding of the relationship between technologies, social structure, the values of a society, and how and why these elements change with time, they vary in their explanations of social change.

cultural heritage. The legacy of physical cultural property and the intangible heritage of prior generations that provides a sense of identity, historical context, and orientation for current and future generations. Cultural heritage includes buildings, art, artifacts, archaeological sites, culturally significant landscapes, folklore, traditions, languages, and songs.

cultural heritage management. The conservation and protection of tangible and intangible human heritage through (written or oral) recordings, museums, educational outreach, public awareness, and legislation.

cultural history. An archaeological method by which archaeologists use artifacts to determine the who, when, and where of past cultures. Describing and classifying finds into groups is an important part of culture history, and classification can be done using design styles, geographic distributions, or chronological periods. An example of the application of culture history in Caribbean archaeology is the series and subseries approach, which relates to cultures and peoples, respectively.

cultural landscape. See **landscapes (cultural, environmental).**

cultural resource management. Formal legislative measures or grassroots efforts to consider, conserve, or mitigate the adverse effects of modern development on heritage resources.

curate. To maintain, manage, and preserve collections; to establish and develop long-term repositories for collections so that they are available to researchers, scientists, historians, scholars, and the general public in perpetuity.

curator. In archaeology, a person who facilitates the long-term preservation and interpretation of artifacts. Curators are often based in museums or other heritage institutions.

debitage. An assemblage of debris resulting from flint knapping or jewelry manufacturing (e.g., debris from stone tools, shell tool, or bead making). In the Caribbean, such assemblages are indicative of the production of local stone tools or shell artifacts in prehistoric (e.g., stone points or knives and shell beads) and historical (e.g., gun flints) contexts.

descendant communities. People related by culture or genetics to prehistoric or historical groups who self-identify with these past peoples (e.g., the Kalinago/ Carib in Dominica or the Garífuna in Honduras). These peoples may be used as ethnographic resources by archaeologists to supplement other data.

diet. In a Caribbean archaeological context this often refers to the material culture of food storage and food preparation practices as well as to particular consumables. The full nutrient intake of an individual or group is analyzed through such data as butchery marks, isotope analyses, faunal remains, and seeds recovered from flotation analyses.

Early Lucayan period. The archaeological time period, ca. AD 900–1200, when the Lucayan culture becomes evident in the Bahamian Archipelago.

Early Ostionoid period. An archaeological time period, dated to ca. AD 600–900, during which pottery of the Ostionan style becomes common.

egalitarianism. A sociopolitical system in which members of a society have equal access to resources, with some exceptions determined by gender, age, and special personal or physical characteristics. Egalitarian societies contrast with ranked sociopolitical systems, in which a small elite group controls most, if not all, of the resources of a society.

El Buen Consejo. A ship carrying Spanish missionaries to Mexico that wrecked off Anguilla's south coast in 1772.

elite exchange. Gift-giving among elite groups. Elite exchange was characteristic of Taíno chiefdoms, for example, and was designed to build both local and regional alliances.

emancipation. The end of slavery. In the Anglophone Caribbean, all enslaved individuals were emancipated in August 1834, but full freedom was not achieved until the end of the apprenticeship system in 1838. In 1804, Haiti was the first Caribbean nation to end slavery, while Cuba was the last to end slavery in the Caribbean, in 1886. See also **abolition**.

encomienda. A system the Spanish Crown instituted in 1503 in which conquistadors, soldiers, colonists, and notable Amerindians were granted a tract of land and an allocation of native inhabitants of the area, including the benefits of the labor of those individuals. The grantee was expected to protect the Amerindians from their enemies, instruct them in the Spanish language, and convert them to Catholicism in return for their labor or goods. Most grantees, however, exploited the natives and treated them as enslaved people.

estate. See **plantation**.

ethnography. A method used by researchers in many social science fields whereby participant observation of a people, an ethnic group, or settlement patterns permits the collection of (mostly empirical) data that is used to interpret various aspects of social, economic, and material culture.

ethnohistory. The study of (often non-Western) cultures of the recent past using documentary sources such as the accounts of explorers, missionaries, and traders and collections of oral histories and other archival materials, often supplemented with archaeological data.

excavation. The exposure, recording, recovery, processing, and analysis of buried cultural material using specialized techniques, skills, and careful preparation. See also **large-scale excavation**; **test excavation**.

farming. Farming, or agriculture, has been defined as the practice of cultivating the land or raising stock. It can also be defined as production that relies heavily on growing and nurturing plants and animals, especially for food, usually with land as an important input. Precolonial societies in the Caribbean and elsewhere can be properly be described as farmers, even though agriculture may have been part of a larger network of other food-getting strategies such as collecting, fishing, and hunting.

Fatel Rozack. A holiday celebrated by East Indians of Trinidad on Indian Arrival Day (May 30th), named after the first ship to bring indentured laborers from India to Trinidad. The reported numbers of East Indians who departed from Calcutta in February 1845 varies from 217 to 237. Six individuals apparently died at sea during the 103-day voyage. The ship was named after a Calcutta merchant named Abdool Rozack Dugman, and the voyage to Trinidad was captained by an Englishman named Cubit S. Rundle.

Finspång Foundry. A Swedish ironworks considered to be the highest-quality producers of cannon during the colonial period. Many cannon from this foundry may be found across the Caribbean region.

flaking. The removal of stone chips by striking a source rock or other object, such as a partially formed tool, with a hammer or percussor. The source object can also be struck against a stationary anvil stone using a method known as bipolar percussion. Percussors are traditionally stone cobbles or pebbles, often referred to as hammerstones, or a billet made of bone, antler, or wood. Often flakes are struck from a core using a punch, in which case the percussor never actually makes contact with the core. The latter technique is referred to as indirect percussion. See also **debitage**.

foraging. Strictly interpreted, foraging refers to the search for food. However, in behavioral ecology, it also refers to predator-prey interactions and other phenomena.

fort. A fully enclosed military structure, often with higher and larger walls than those found at batteries. Forts may be constructed of earth, wood or masonry. In the Caribbean they were often armed with cannon. See also **battery**; **cannon**.

free black. A formerly enslaved individual of African descent who has become free through escape, emancipation, or self-purchase. Free blacks constituted a significant proportion of the Caribbean population in the colonial era.

free black village. A settlement of domestic structures that housed free blacks. Although there were many, few have been located for excavation in the Caribbean. The Congo Free Black Village that Grant Gilmore excavated on St. Eustatius and the free black community Douglas Armstrong examined on St. John's East End are notable exceptions.

fretwork. A Caribbean colloquial term for the fenestrated timber that decorated architecture. Free Africans used it on eaves, veranda balustrades, door transoms, and interior room dividers. Traditional fretwork patterns are linked directly to African symbolism. The term gingerbread is sometimes used generically to describe this form.

gallery. The upper piazza of the second story on Jamaica Georgian building. Sometimes the terms gallery and piazza are used interchangeably.

geoarchaeology. An interdisciplinary archaeological subdiscipline that uses geological methods and tools to understand past human behavior. Ground-penetrating radar and petrography are two examples that are used commonly in the Caribbean.

geochemical analysis. The analysis of the chemistry of geological materials to provide information about their age, nature, and physical structure.

gran marronage. The banding together of free blacks to

form a self-governing community that was often set apart from the general population to obscure its existence. See also *petit marronage*.

Greater Antilles. The geologically older and larger Caribbean islands, including Cuba, Jamaica, Hispaniola and Puerto Rico.

grinding stone. A tool used to reduce grains, nuts, seeds, and spices into flour or another usable consistency. The stone may be artificially or naturally shaped and is often flat and broad with a slight depression in the center to consolidate the ground food items. Grinding stones have been found in both prehistoric and historical contexts. See also **metate**.

hammerstone. A natural or artificially shaped stone tool used to pound seeds and nuts or to assist in shaping other stone tools such as blades, adzes, and axes. They are often fist-sized with peck marks on one end and are found most commonly on prehistoric sites in the Caribbean. See also **debitage**; **flaking**.

horticulture. The cultivation of plants using simple garden tools such as hoes and digging sticks. Archaeologists are increasingly making little or no distinction between horticulture and what is generally described as agriculture. See also **farming**.

house trajectories. The material pathways houses create and how they reproduce themselves. It can also be defined as spatiotemporal units made up of a sequence of houses reproduced over time that expressly refer to the first house. House trajectories are not only more durable than their inhabitants but encompass the worldview of inhabitants through social and cultural reproductions and through formal, structural, and explicit renewal of house architecture and house practices.

hybridity. A noun used to describe linguistic, genetic, and cultural mixing and the social, economic, and religious ramifications of this mixing. In the Caribbean, the term can be used in both prehistoric and historical contexts. One of the defining characteristics of Caribbean culture today is its hybridity (also known as *mestizaje*).

inclusions. Mineral, shell, sand, and other particles intentionally added to or found naturally within paste used for ceramic manufacture. See also **paste**.

indentured servant. A person who exchanged his or her labor for a set period of time in exchange for passage to a new settlement or colony. Colonial entrepreneurs and plantation owners used indentured servants before and after the slavery period. In the Caribbean, indentured servants were often from Europe, but after the abolition of slavery, they were imported from China and India.

indigenous. Originating and living or occurring naturally in an area or environment. The term can be applied to peoples, plants, and animals.

intangible heritage. The immaterial legacy of prior generations, including oral histories, customs, belief systems, and languages. See also **tangible heritage**.

landscapes (cultural, environmental). A term used by archaeologists to describe the land area defined by certain specific cultural or environmental traits. For example, the boundaries of plantation landscapes are determined by plantation agricultural practices, while a volcanic landscape is defined through the environmental impacts of volcanic activity. See also **viewscape**.

lapidary. An artisan who practices the craft of working, forming, and finishing stones, minerals, gemstones, and other suitably durable materials (including amber, shell, jet, pearl, copal, coral, horn, bone, and glass) into functional, decorative, or wearable items (e.g., cameos, cabochons, and more complex faceted designs). Lapidary trade relates to the trading of those items. Indigenous groups such as the Saladoid practiced lapidary work and trade.

large-scale excavation. archaeological excavation of a large area to reveal many archaeological features on a particular site. The entirety of a domestic site or even a village may be revealed through this process, thus providing greater insights into past human activity than the excavation of test excavations. The excavation of the Golden Rock site on St. Eustatius is an example. Also known as open-area excavation. See also **excavation**.

Lavoutte. A late Ceramic Age site at Cas en Bas in the northeastern part of Saint Lucia.

Lazaretto leper colony. The first leprosy hospital to be excavated in the Americas. It is located on St. Eustatius. The Lazaretto site was located by researchers from the College of William and Mary. The site's cemetery was mapped and partially excavated by Joanna K. Gilmore.

Leeward Islands (Dutch and English). The islands that were affected by the Northeast Atlantic trade winds in the "lee" of the Windward Islands. In English colonial parlance, this term refers to all the Lesser Antilles north and northwest of the Windward Islands. In Dutch colonial parlance, it refers to all of the Caribbean islands east of St. Eustatius, including the islands along the South American coast and Trinidad and Tobago. The French and Spanish generally followed the English tradition. See also **Windward Islands**.

Lesser Antilles. A long arc of smaller, mostly volcanic

islands in the Caribbean Sea that extend in a north-south direction from the Virgin Islands to Trinidad and in an east-west direction from Margarita to Aruba.

limestone. A geological term used to describe calcium carbonate deposited by sedimentary activity such as mechanical destruction of coral or by chemical precipitation from sea water. The outer arc of the Lesser Antilles is built primarily of limestone laid down over millennia from the buildup and subsequent death of coral reefs. Prehistoric and historical peoples used limestone to make tools and construct buildings.

liminal phase. A liminal phase is an intermediary or transitional period. This phase is typically experienced during a ritual, when an individual passes between two states of being, such as the hallucinatory experience of the *cohoba* ritual. Individuals in the liminal phase are often considered to be extremely holy, sacred, dangerous, powerful, or spiritually contaminating.

Lucayans. The indigenous inhabitants of the Bahamas and the Turks and Caicos Islands. The name "Lucayan" is an Anglicization of the Spanish Lucayo or Lucaya, which is derived from the Arawakan words *lukku kaíri* ("island men"), meaning "people of the islands." The Lucayans shared a common ancestry with the Taíno of the Greater Antilles through the Ostionoid peoples who originally settled the islands between ca. AD 600 and 1200. They are the people of the Americas who met Columbus in 1492.

lug. A handle-like protuberance or knob on a ceramic pot that is used to lift, support, or turn the pot.

Maisabel. A multicomponent (Saladoid through Ostionoid) site on the north-central coast of Puerto Rico.

maker's mark. A mark left by an object's maker that is stamped, incised, or impressed upon a ceramic or metallic object. The information contained in this mark may lead archaeologists to a better understanding of the artifact's origin, its production date, and perhaps its symbolic meaning. European ceramics and bronze, brass, pewter, silver, and gold artifacts often have identifiable maker's marks.

maloca. An ancestral longhouse originating in lowland South America.

mano. A cylindrical or oval-shaped grinding stone used by hand, often in conjunction with a smooth metate or quern. *Manos* are used for grinding vegetable material such as maize, seeds, nuts, and pigments. See also **metate**.

Maroons. From the Spanish word *cimarrón*, meaning fugitive or runaway (literally "living on mountaintops," from the Spanish *cima*: top, summit). Maroons were runaway enslaved persons in the West Indies, Central America, South America, and North America who formed independent settlements, usually in remote areas. Primary examples are the Maroon communities of Colombia, Jamaica, Trinidad, Suriname, and Venezuela. See also *petit marronage* and *gran marronage*.

Mary's Point. A colonial settlement located in northwestern Saba. The village was abandoned in the twentieth century when its inhabitants moved to The Bottom. See also **The Bottom**.

material culture. The body of evidence archaeologists use to form an understanding of past human lifeways. Material culture consists primarily of artifacts.

mean artifact date (or mean date). A date for an archaeological deposit calculated from the known production dates of all the artifacts found in a particular deposit. The formula for the mean artifact date is derived from the formula for the mean ceramic date.

mean ceramic date. A date for an archaeological deposit calculated from the known production dates of the ceramic types found in a particular archaeological deposit.

metate. A flat or basin-shaped stone (e.g., a mortar) that has a shallow depression in the upper surface for holding maize or other grains to be ground with a *mano*. Metates are found in many shapes and sizes and are made from any coarse-grained rock that will work well as an abrasive surface. See also *mano*.

midden. A refuse deposit left from past human activities, especially in relation to habitation areas. In the Caribbean, lengthy exploitation of a particular location's natural resources may result in significant deposition of refuse such as conch shells, fish, and other remains together with fragments of pottery or artifacts of stone or bone. Archaeologists look for middens in their search for new habitation sites in order to better understand foodways and other aspects of past human history. Also called a trash pit or trash pile.

mitochondrial DNA (mtDNA). A circular genome found in the mitochondrion of eukaryotic cells. Because mtDNA has a matrilineal inheritance pattern, it is not subject to recombination. mtDNA can be used to study the genetic origins of ancient populations and to postulate migration routes. See also **aDNA**.

morbidity. The rate of death caused by natural and human events that impact the average lifespan of a particular human population. European disease and enslavement greatly increased morbidity among indigenous and African populations. Archaeologists look for evidence in human skeletal remains and cemeteries to gain an understanding of this process.

multicomponent site. A single archaeological location with multiple, culturally distinct settlement periods that offers direct comparisons between peoples of different time periods and/or cultures within the same geographical, geological, and natural landscape.

musket balls. Lead (or sometimes stone) spheres used as projectiles in many firearms used throughout the colonial period. Early Europeans in the Caribbean were usually heavily armed, and archaeologists often find these artifacts in the region.

neotropical. Having to do with the ecozones associated with South America, Central America, the Bahamas, Florida, and the Caribbean (also known as the New World tropics).

New World. An historical Eurocentric term still often used to differentiate the Americas from Europe and Asia (the Old World). The term has been supplanted by others such as "the Americas" and "Western Hemisphere."

Orange Bay (Oranjestad). A bay on the lee side of St. Eustatius that is relatively deep compared to other similar bays in the Caribbean. It thus offered better near-shore shelter for larger ships, which led to the establishment of the most extensive warehouse district in the Caribbean during the 1700s. By the 1790s, the anchorage at Orange Bay was the busiest in the world. The ruins of these warehouses, their accompanying artifacts, and over 200 shipwrecks constitute one of the Caribbean's archaeological treasures. The anchorage is now used by the world's largest oil tankers to transship oil stored at St. Eustatius's oil terminal.

oral history. Data collected by archaeologists and anthropologists from living persons or from live recordings in order to gain insights into past human history or perceptions of this history for a particular site or region. See also **intangible heritage**.

ordnance. The totality of weaponry available to a military or one of its units, including but not limited to ammunition, firearms, and cannon and associated logistical supplies.

origin myth. A myth that purports to describe the origin of some feature of the natural or social world. See also **cosmology**.

paleobotany. The study of plant remains (phytoliths, seeds, and carbonized plant structures such as branches, leaves, and fruits) to reconstruct past botanical landscapes. See also **phytoliths**.

Palmetto Ware. A pottery series made by the Bahamian Lucayans. Palmetto pottery is distributed throughout both parts of the archipelago, the Turks and Caicos Islands, and the Bahamian Archipelago. Palmetto pottery is technologically inferior to the rest of the Ostionoid pottery in the northern Caribbean, primarily because of the poor quality of the clay in the Bahamian Archipelago. Palmetto pottery is thick, crude, and mostly shell-tempered and is highly friable or fragile. However, similar to the Meillacan styles, this pottery type has examples of appliqué work and punctation. While this ware is predominately plain, some pottery is decorated with incised lines and basket impressions.

paste. The soft, smooth, plastic material, typically derived from clay, that is used in the manufacture of ceramics. See also **inclusions**.

peccary. A general term for three genera (*Tayassu*, *Dicotyles*, and *Catagonus*) of pig-like hoofed mammals of North and South America. Also called javelina.

pecking. A method of shaping the surface of natural stones to fashion tools, to modify the form of the stone, or to create patterns of various sorts (such as petroglyphs). It involves hitting the surface of the stone, thus fashioning it in a controlled way by using a harder stone of appropriate size (e.g., a hammerstone) that pulverizes the surface of softer stone and removes small portions with each blow. See also **hammerstone**.

periphery. The outer edge of a relatively culturally homogenous area. Those who live at this boundary may acquire cultural traits associated with adjacent cultures. Geographers refer to the Caribbean periphery as the rimland, in contrast to the mainland of South and Central America.

pestle. A club-shaped tool used for crushing or pounding material in a mortar. See also *mano*; **metate**.

petit marronage. The escape of an individual from slavery, often with little or no external support during the period of freedom.

petroglyphs. Images made by humans on relatively stationary rock surfaces (boulders, caves, rock shelters, rock formations, ball courts) produced by pecking, grinding, abrading, scratching, or other means; a type of rock art. See also **pictograph**.

petrographic analysis. Microscopic analysis of the mineralogical composition of archaeological materials and objects. A polarizing microscope is used to match mineral patterns in the object of interest (e.g., a fragment of pottery) to known materials, thereby facilitating an understanding of the elemental and mineralogical structure of the object.

phytoliths. Siliceous microscopic plant remains that are studied to reconstruct past vegetation and past domestication of plants. See also **paleobotany**.

piazza. The fenestrated timber shed or enclosed veranda on the principal floor of a structure built in the Jamaica-Georgian style. The piazza functioned as an indoor-outdoor space that was added to the masonry core of the structure. Classical Palladian design principles and architectural detailing are reflected in the piazza.

pictograph. A painted image on relatively stationary rock surfaces (boulders, caves, rock shelters, rock formations); a type of rock art. See also **petroglyph**.

Pigeon Island. A precolonial and historical site in northern Saint Lucia.

plantation (estate). A large farm that implemented methods developed for maximizing agricultural production (and profits) through the more efficient use of labor and mechanization. African enslaved people and indentured servants were often the predominant labor force on plantations. Plantations transformed the Caribbean landscape by clearing the natural forests of most islands so crops could be planted, primarily sugar cane, tobacco, cotton, and indigo. Caribbean plantations constitute a significant research area for archaeologists.

plantocracy. A ruling class comprised of planters that had substantial influence in local, regional and international politics. Members of this class could and did act as a kind of aristocracy living abroad. The plantocracy assembled social and material cultural traits into a powerful mechanism for reinforcing their position in Caribbean society.

Plum Piece. An Archaic Age site in northwestern Saba.

polity. A politically organized unit (e.g., a chiefdom, town, or city).

Post-Saladoid period. An archaeological time period dated to ca. AD 600–900 that followed the Saladoid period (ca. 500 BC–AD 600). It is roughly coeval with the Early Ostionan period.

power relations. The division of power among human actors based on economic and social status. In the Caribbean, archaeologists look for expressions of these relationships in the material culture and landscapes they are investigating, especially with regard to enslaved individuals and their owners.

precolonial. Of or relating to the time before colonization of a region or territory. In the Caribbean, the precolonial period generally preceded the arrival of Christopher Columbus in 1492. See also **precontact**; **precolonial**; **Spanish contact**.

pre-Columbian. Of or relating to the time that preceded the arrival of Christopher Columbus in the Americas. See also **precontact**; **precolonial**; **Spanish contact**.

precontact. Refers to the many millennia that predate the arrival of Columbus or any other European in the Americas. This term is rapidly becoming less concrete as more archaeological evidence from across the Americas is building a picture of significant human contact from Europe for many centuries (if not millennia) prior to Columbus's arrival. Archaeologists use the term to refer to peoples that they believe have not been influenced by European visitors. See also **pre-Columbian**; **precolonial**; **Spanish contact**.

projectile point. A point made of stone, bone, or metal to strengthen the tip of a spear or an arrow. The point is usually made from a different material than the shaft.

punctate. A type of design found on pottery that consists of small squarish, roundish, or wedge-shaped impressions, usually created by pressing the end of a stick or reed into the leather-hard body of a pot before it is fired.

radiocarbon dating. A scientific method developed by W. F. Libby and colleagues in 1949 to measure the age of material of biological origin, such as bone and shell and artifacts made of wood and charcoal, based on the rate of radioactive decay of carbon 14 to nitrogen 14. Currently, radiocarbon dates are most commonly obtained through accelerator mass spectrometry (AMS), which counts the atoms of the carbon-14 isotope in the specimen that is being dated. Also known as carbon-14 or 14C dating.

raised fields. Large artificial platforms of soil created to protect crops from flooding. They are generally found in areas with a high water table or seasonal flooding. In the Guianas, for example, four types of ancient raised fields have been identified: ridged fields (Spanish: *eras*), large raised fields, medium-sized raised fields, and small fields of rounded earthen mounds (*conucos*).

rock shelter. A rock or cliff overhang or cave used to provide temporary or long-term shelter from the elements. Rock shelters are often associated with prehistoric peoples, but they were also often occupied by colonial peoples. Some rock shelter sites may have multicomponent occupations.

root crops. Food plants that are raised primarily for their roots. In the Caribbean, such agricultural products include cassava (manioc) and various types of potatoes (e.g., sweet potatoes) that provided carbohydrates for both prehistoric and historic peoples.

Archaeological evidence for these crops include the tools used to plant and manage them, starch grains on stone tools, and plaque deposits on excavated human teeth that were produced by a diet that included these plant resources.

Saint-Domingue. The name used for the western third of Hispaniola prior to 1804; an area colonized by the French. In 1804, it was renamed Haiti. By the late 1700s and before the slave rebellions of the 1790s, Saint-Domingue was France's most profitable possession; it produced more coffee and sugar than any other colony in the French and British empires. Also called La Perle des Antilles.

Santo Domingo. The capital and largest city of the Dominican Republic, located in the southeast part of the island of Hispaniola on the Caribbean Sea. It was founded in 1496 by Christopher Columbus's brother Bartholomew and is the oldest continuously inhabited European settlement in the western hemisphere. The name has also been used for a Spanish colony on Hispaniola and for the Dominican Republic.

Savanne Suazey. An archaeological site on Grenada that yielded the ceramic assemblage that was used to define Suazoid ceramics.

Sephardim (Sephardic Jews). A common name for the descendants of Jews from the Iberian Peninsula; often used to refer to Portuguese Jews. The Sephardim settled in many communities throughout the Caribbean region.

settlement pattern. The distribution of archaeological sites across the landscape. The concept includes areas where resources were procured and other special-purpose locations.

shot. The ammunition used in cannon or other firearms that may include cannon balls, musket balls, bar shot, chain shot, and grape shot. All of these are found on Caribbean archaeological sites.

sigmoid. Shaped like the letter "S."

slash-and-burn agriculture. A horticultural practice that involves cutting vegetation and burning the cuttings. The process clears land for crops and produces ash, which is used as a fertilizer. Also known as swidden farming or shifting cultivation.

slip. A thin, watery, clay-based wash used as a functional or decorative addition to the exterior of a ceramic vessel (e.g., to increase the impermeability of a vessel or to add color or design).

social inequality. A condition resulting from a hierarchical power relationship that may involve the oppression and control of a less powerful social group or class. See also **power relations**.

soil survey. A systematic study of the soil of an area that includes classification and mapping of properties, crop adaptations, and the distribution of various soil types.

Sorcé/La Hueca. The type site for the Huecoid ceramic series; located on Vieques Island, Puerto Rico.

Spanish contact. The period after Columbus's initial arrival. It is characterized by significant social, economic, and ecological upheaval across the Caribbean region because of the Spaniards' exploitation of natural and human resources.

Spring Bay. A bay on the northeastern coast of Saba where there was continuous occupation by Amerindians from AD 450 to 1450.

stable isotope analysis. An analytic technique used with skeletal remains of humans and animals that provides information about diet and population movements. The relative ratio of radioactive isotopes (e.g., carbon/nitrogen, calcium/strontium, etc.) varies naturally across the geological landscape, and thus animals (including humans) may build up a "fingerprint" of these elements that may be matched to a specific diet (e.g., terrestrial carnivore) or geographic locale. See also **diet**.

starch grain analysis. The analysis of starch grains, tiny granules that operate in plants as the main mechanism for food storage. This has become an important tool that archaeologists use to identify the diets of past peoples. See also **diet**.

stratigraphic excavation. The careful documentation and excavation of soil strata so as to not destroy context or provenience.

subseries and series. In Caribbean archaeology, pottery and lithic styles that share sufficient similarities are grouped into subseries (denoted by -an suffix), and subseries are then grouped into series (denoted by an -oid suffix). Irving Rouse used this classification to identify peoples and cultures. For example, Saladoid is a series and Cedrosan Saladoid is a subseries.

subsistence farming. Agriculture undertaken to provide food for personal or family consumption; virtually no surplus is produced for trade. In the Caribbean, the majority of prehistoric peoples practiced this type of agriculture. In contrast, in the historic period, farming was largely done for the profits derived from surpluses. African enslaved individuals also commonly practiced subsistence farming for household or family consumption. See also **farming; horticulture**.

tangible heritage. The terrestrial or underwater material legacy of prior generations, including artifacts, documents, archaeological sites, shipwrecks, monuments, and abandoned villages and sites. See also **cultural heritage**.

tapia. A construction technique that uses a mixture typically of mud and straw that often includes other additives such as animal dung or pebbles. The mixture is beaten and kneaded together and then pressed into a latticework of pliable branches, vines, or other woody strips. See also **wattle-and-daub**.

temper. An organic or inorganic ingredient added to clay to provide additional structural integrity and to reduce shrinkage in the clays used to construct objects and vessels. Organic tempers may include moss, straw, grass, and seeds. Inorganic tempers may include sand, pebbles or crushed rocks, crushed shell, and grog (small fragments of fired clay). Variations in clay temper help archaeologists differentiate between some low-fired earthenwares, such as those produced by many Caribbean cultures.

terminus ante quem (Latin: time before which). The time before an artifact or archaeological deposit was laid down; that is, the latest possible date of an archaeological deposit. Usually indicated by an artifact of known date (e.g., a coin) or an archaeological deposit beneath the foundation of a building that was demolished in a known year.

terminus post quem (Latin: time after which). The time after an artifact or archaeological deposit was laid down; that is, the earliest possible date of an archaeological deposit. Usually indicated by an artifact of known date.

terra preta **(Portuguese: black earth).** A type of very dark, fertile anthropogenic soil found in the Amazon Basin and elsewhere. Also known as *terra preta do indio*, "Indian black soil." Such black soil is often indicative of intensive human occupation of an archaeological site.

test excavation. Shovel testing or excavation of small exploratory units (e.g., 50 × 50 centimeters); often the second phase of an archaeological investigation after an initial walk-over or field survey. Small test excavations (sometimes trenches) are conducted to determine the integrity, extent, and age of a particular archaeological site for the purposes of heritage management. The results can also be used to guide large-scale excavations.

transculturation. Constant interaction between two or more cultural components that produces a third cultural identity. It can also refer to the ways that subordinate or marginal groups select and invent from dominant cultures. Although subordinate groups cannot control what emanates from the dominant culture, they determine in varying degrees what they absorb into their own cultures and what they use it for. The term was coined in 1947 by Fernando Ortiz Fernández. See also **creolization**.

Trants. An early Saladoid site on the east coast of Montserrat.

Troumassée. The type site of the Troumassan Troumassoid subseries; located on Saint Lucia. Two phases (Troumassée A and B) were identified by Marshall McKusick in the 1960s.

UNESCO. The United Nations Education, Science and Culture Organization, founded in 1945, is a specialized agency of the United Nations. Its mission is to use dialogue and cooperation to build peace through knowledge, social progress, education, and mutual respect and understanding among peoples. In the field of heritage resource management, UNESCO is involved in the development and application of various international conventions that seek to promote, protect, conserve, and preserve many aspects of the world's tangible and intangible heritage.

várzea. A seasonally flooded forest/woodland that grows along rivers in the Amazon.

vernacular architecture. An architectural form that is most commonly used by non-elites. In the Caribbean, these would include enslaved individuals, free persons, indentured laborers, and common laborers.

vessel form. The shape of a ceramic or glass container that often determines its function as a tool or decorative item. Archaeologists look at this shape as an important stage in artifact identification, after determining the material from which an artifact was made.

viewscape. The visual range of a person or community across the local setting. An understanding of the viewscape of enslaved people may help archaeologists understand such issues as agency and power relations. The term may also be used to describe the view from a military installation for defensive purposes.

vomit spatula. A tool that precolonial Amerindians thrust down their throats to induce vomiting as a means of purifying themselves before ritual activities.

ware. A particular kind or type of pottery, e.g., Palmetto Ware, Palmettan Ostionoid ware, or Afro-Caribbean ware. See also **ceramic**.

wattle-and-daub. A vernacular building technique. Wattle consists of the mesh of woven sticks placed between the timber posts of a building to serve as the support for a wall. Daub refers to the mud or clay that is sometimes mixed with lime and other organic material to form an earthen mortar that was plastered on both sides of the wattle as a weatherproof barrier.

If maintained, a building thus constructed could last several decades. See also **tapia**.

white-on-red. A polychrome painting style typical of Saladoid pottery.

Windward Islands. A term used primarily by the Dutch and English that refers to the islands that were affected by the Northeast Atlantic trade winds south of the Leeward Islands. In English colonial parlance, the term refers to all of the Caribbean Lesser Antilles to the south of the Leeward Islands. In Dutch colonial parlance, it refers to St. Eustatius, Saba, Sint Maarten, and all the Caribbean Islands west of this group. See also **Leeward Islands**.

wrought iron. An iron alloy or low-carbon steel containing less than 0.5 percent carbon that was used to produce a wide range of tools, weapons, and structural and decorative items. It derives its name from the process of hammering raw iron by hand or with mechanical means into a desired shape on an anvil. In the Caribbean, iron may quickly develop an oxidized coating that creates a barrier that inhibits further degradation. However, submerged and buried archaeological contexts are often harmful to wrought iron. Also called forged iron.

zone-incised cross-hatching. A ceramic design composed of zones that are etched into a vessel's surface, outlined with incisions, and filled in with fine cross-hatching made using lighter incisions.

zoomorphic. Representing or resembling animal forms. See also **anthropomorphic**; **biomorphic**.

Notes on Contributors

E. Kofi Agorsah is professor of Black studies and international studies at Portland State University, Oregon. He was formerly keeper of the board of Ghana Museums and Monuments (1973–1978) and served as lecturer/senior lecturer at the University of Ghana (1983–1987). He pioneered the archaeology program at The University of the West Indies, Mona, Jamaica, where he was the first Edward Moulton-Barrett Lecturer in Archaeology (1987–1992). He has served as director and vice-president of the International Association for Caribbean Archaeology and is a U.S. Senior Fulbright Scholar. He is a leading authority on the archaeology of Maroon heritage and serves as a specialist on the board of the African Burial Ground Project of the City of New York. He has written many books, book chapters, and journal publications on African and African Diaspora archaeology.

Douglas V. Armstrong is the Laura J. and L. Douglas Meredith Professor of Anthropology at Syracuse University, Syracuse, New York, where he is a Maxwell Professor of Teaching Excellence. His academic interests include historical archaeology, public policy archaeology, archaeology of the African Diaspora, ethnohistory, cultural contact and cultural change, and the prehistoric archaeology of the Americas. His publications on Caribbean archaeology include *The Old Village and the Great House: An Archaeological and Historical Examination of Drax Hall Plantation, St. Ann's Bay, Jamaica* and a chapter in *Archaeology and Geoinformatics: Case Studies from the Caribbean.*

Tracy Assing is a writer, photographer, and filmmaker based in Trinidad. Her work on indigenous culture has been published in the *Caribbean Review of Books* and *Caribbean Beat* magazine. She has also served as a contributing editor to *Caribbean Beat* and as the editor of *Discover Trinidad and Tobago* and *Energy Caribbean.* She is currently a contributing editor for *ARC (Art. Recognition. Culture).* Her documentary film *The Amerindians,* which explores her identity as a member of Trinidad's indigenous community, premiered at the Trinidad and Tobago Film Festival in 2010. She is currently at work on a documentary that focuses on the use of herbs for medicine. Her research interests include pre-Columbian history, archaeology, anthropology, culture, religion, and botany.

Lesley-Gail Atkinson is an archaeologist with the Jamaica National Heritage Trust. In 2010–2011, she was a lecturer in archaeology at The University of the West Indies, Mona, Jamaica. She obtained her MPhil in archaeology at the University of Glasgow and is currently pursuing a PhD in anthropology at the University of Florida, specializing in Caribbean prehistory. Her academic interests are Taíno and Afro-Jamaican archaeology, rock art, cultural contact studies, and ceramic analysis. She is the editor of *The Earliest Inhabitants: The Dynamics of the Jamaican Taíno* and the co-editor (with Michele H. Hayward and Michael A. Cinquino) of *Rock Art of the Caribbean.* She has also written several publications on Jamaican prehistory and rock art.

Allison Bain is professor in the History Department at Université Laval in Québec. She is a specialist in environmental archaeology and paleoeconomy and studies prehistoric and historic landscapes through the lenses of anthropogenic change and past human ecodynamics. She has collaborated on projects in Canada, France, the United States, Greenland, and Iceland. In the Caribbean region, she works with Brooklyn College in Antigua and Barbuda and with Université Laval in French Guiana. At Université Laval, she directs the Environmental Archaeology Laboratory, which specializes in the study of archaeologically preserved plant and insect remains. She also directs the university's field school in historical archaeology at the Intendant's Palace Site in Québec. Her recent publications include an edited volume for the journal *Historical Archaeology* and articles in *Post-Medieval Archaeology* and *Journal of the North Atlantic.*

Emma K. Bate is a member of the Karen D. Vitelli Center for Archaeology in the Public Interest at Indiana University. Her research focuses on the technology and variability of Palmettan ceramics, and her research interests include ceramic technology and analysis, the relationship between material culture and social status, the

Spanish contact period, and trade and exchange in the prehistoric Caribbean. She has worked in the Bahamas, the Dominican Republic, Greece, and Indiana.

Brian D. Bates is currently associate professor of anthropology in the Department of Sociology, Anthropology, and Criminal Justice at Longwood University, Farmville, Virginia, where he is the department chair. He is also the director of the Longwood Archaeology Field School. He has conducted field work in the British Virgin Islands since 1996 and has excavated in Barbados and in Virginia. His research interests include settlement patterns, the Ceramic period in the Caribbean and Virginia, complex societies, and the transition from Big Man social organization to chiefdoms.

Zachary J. Beier is a graduate student in anthropology at Syracuse University. His research interests include the African Diaspora and trans-Atlantic studies, war and slavery, British social history, consumption and identity relations, materiality and memory, and cultural heritage management. In 2010, he completed a Fulbright on the island of Dominica, where he investigated the material and spatial patterns of enslaved laborers and soldiers at the Cabrits Garrison (1763–1854). His dissertation combines this archaeological data with extensive archival research in order to better understand the role of military labor in Afro-Caribbean society. In 2011, he was a fellow at the International Centre for Jefferson Studies/Digital Archaeological Archives of Comparative Slavery.

Benoît Bérard is currently associate professor of Caribbean Archaeology at the Université des Antilles et de la Guyane at the Martinique campus, where he is head of the History Department and vice-director of the Archéologie industrielle, histoire et patrimoine de la Caraïbe EA 929 laboratory. He also served for several years as a guest professor at the Ecole normale supérieure in Haïti. He has conducted excavations and research programs on many Lesser Antillean islands. He has edited or coedited several books and published numerous book chapters and journal articles on subjects that include the early Ceramic occupation of the Caribbean, pre-Columbian navigation techniques, the Amerindian/European contact period in the West Indies, and the incorporation of Amerindian heritage by the modern West Indian French creole populations. He chaired the Twenty-Fourth Congress of the International Association of Caribbean Archaeology (IACA) in 2011. He is currently the IACA's vice-president.

Jeffrey P. Blick is professor of anthropology and interdisciplinary studies and coordinator of the anthropology program at Georgia College & State University, Milledgeville, Georgia. He has written numerous reports, articles, and chapters in books about archaeology in Latin America, especially the circum-Caribbean. He has been awarded grants from agencies such as the National Science Foundation, the H. John Heinz III Charitable Trust, the Tinker Foundation, and the Council on Undergraduate Research. He is currently working with students on his long-term project, the osteometry and paleopathology of prehistoric dogs.

Arie Boomert worked as an archaeologist at the Surinaams Museum, Paramaribo, Suriname; Leiden University; the University of Amsterdam; and The University of the West Indies, St. Augustine, Trinidad. He has been a desk editor at PlantijnCasparie Heerhugowaard (1988–2004) and assistant professor and senior researcher at the Faculty of Archaeology, Leiden University (2004–2011). He also functioned as a director of the International Association for Caribbean Archaeology (1983–1987) and as a member of the Advisory Board of *Antropológica*, Fundación La Salle, Caracas, Venezuela (1983–1999). He is the author of over sixty publications, including *The Prehistoric Sites of Tobago: A Catalogue and Evaluation* and *Trinidad, Tobago and the Lower Orinoco Interaction Sphere: An Archaeological/Ethnohistorical Study*. His research interests include the archaeology, ethnohistory, and historical linguistics of the Caribbean and Amazonia, more specifically Trinidad and Tobago, the Windward Islands, the Orinoco Valley, and the coastal zone of Venezuela and the Guianas.

Bridget Brereton is emerita professor of history at the St. Augustine, Trinidad, campus of The University of the West Indies. She has served as head of the Department of History, as deputy principal, and as interim principal, all at St. Augustine. She has also been a visiting professor at Johns Hopkins University, Baltimore, Maryland. She is a past president of the Association of Caribbean Historians and a past editor of the *Journal of Caribbean History*. In 1996, she won the Vice-Chancellor's Award for Excellence in Teaching, Research and Administration, the first woman to do so. She has been chair of the board of the National Library and Information System Authority and chaired the committee appointed by Cabinet to consider the nation's highest award (the Trinity Cross) and other national symbols and observances. She is the author of several books, including *Race Relations in Colonial Trinidad, 1870–1900* and *A History of Modern Trinidad, 1783–1962*, and many published journal articles and book chapters. She is the editor of volume V of the UNESCO General History of the Caribbean, *The Twentieth Century*, and is the coeditor of several other books.

Richard T. Callaghan is professor in the Department of Archaeology at the University of Calgary in Alberta, Canada. His specializations include the archaeology of the Caribbean and Lowland South America, global water transport and navigation, and human ecology. Much of his research has been focused on maritime migrations and voyages of discovery using computer simulations. He has published on these topics in the Caribbean, the North and South Pacific, the Indian Ocean, and the Mid-Atlantic. Since 1999 he has been conducting research on the island of St. Vincent. Recent Caribbean publications include chapters in *Island Shores, Distant Pasts: Archaeological and Biological Perspectives on the Pre-Columbian Settlement of the Caribbean* and *Islands at the Crossroads: Migration, Seafaring, and Interaction in the Caribbean*.

John F. Cherry is the Joukowsky Family Professor of Archaeology and professor of classics and anthropology at Brown University in Providence, Rhode Island. He previously taught archaeology at the University of Michigan, where he directed the Interdisciplinary Program in Classical Art and Archaeology, and at the University of Cambridge in England, where he was also fellow and tutor at Fitzwilliam College. His research interests include Mediterranean prehistory, archaeological survey, island archaeology, the emergence of complex societies, and lithic technology, on all of which he has published extensively. He has conducted archaeological survey–based fieldwork in Great Britain, the United States, Italy, Armenia, and (especially) Greece and is currently co-director of the Caribbean project Survey and Landscape Archaeology on Montserrat. He is the coauthor of *Landscape Archaeology as Long-Term History: Northern Keos in the Cycladic Islands from Earliest Settlement to Modern Times* (winner of the Cotsen Prize), the editor of *Colonization of Islands*, and the coeditor of *Side-by-Side Survey: Comparative Regional Studies in the Mediterranean World*. He was the coeditor of *World Archaeology* from 1988 to 1997 and has coedited the *Journal of Mediterranean Archaeology* since 1990.

Michael A. Cinquino received his doctorate from the State University of New York at Stony Brook in 1986 and is presently the director of the Buffalo, New York, office of Panamerican Consultants, Inc. He has conducted documentary studies and archaeological fieldwork in Mexico, the United States, and the Caribbean and has served as the state archaeologist for the Puerto Rican State Historic Office. His involvement in Caribbean rock art studies includes field documentation, coauthorship of *Rock Art of the Caribbean*, and preparation of articles for publication and presentation at conferences.

Roger H. Colten is the senior collections manager for the Division of Anthropology at the Peabody Museum of Natural History at Yale University, New Haven, Connecticut. His research interests include ecological adaptations to coastal environments, the emergence of social complexity among hunter-gatherers, and faunal analysis. While much of his research is focused on prehistoric hunter-gatherers of the Santa Barbara Channel region of southern California, he has recently analyzed and published articles on archaeological faunal collections from Oregon, British Columbia, France, and Cuba. Dr. Colten has archaeological field experience in California, Germany, Israel, Italy, Malta, Michigan, Mississippi, and Nevada.

Ivor Conolley is the director of external affairs at Falmouth Heritage Renewal in Falmouth, Jamaica. He has been engaged in field excavation projects in Jamaica and Nevis and is president of the Archaeological Society of Jamaica. He was a part-time lecturer in archaeology at The University of the West Indies, Mona, in 2010–11 and in 2010 was an International Centre for Jefferson Studies/Digital Archaeological Archives of Comparative Slavery Fellow. His publications include *Taíno Sites in Trelawny*, articles for the *Jamaica Historical Society Bulletin*, and (with Parris Lyew-Ayee) a chapter in *Archaeology and Geoinformatics*.

John G. Crock is associate professor of anthropology at the University of Vermont, Burlington, and the director of the UVM Consulting Archaeology Program. He has published numerous articles on the archaeology of the northern Lesser Antilles, including the results of work at numerous sites in Anguilla. In addition to ongoing investigations in the Caribbean, he is actively involved in research projects and cultural resource management studies in northeastern North America. He is the associate editor of *Caribbean Connections* and is on the editorial board of *North American Archaeologist*. His research interests include maritime adaptations, interregional trade and exchange, the development of inequality, and heritage management.

Alissandra Cummins is director of the Barbados Museum and Historical Society and a lecturer in Heritage and Museum Studies at The University of the West Indies, Cave Hill, Barbados. She was the founding president of the Museums Association of the Caribbean and was president of the International Association for Caribbean Archaeology and the International Council of Museums. She has served as vice chairperson and rapporteur of the World Heritage Committee and has chaired UNESCO's Intergovernmental Committee for Promoting the Return of Cultural Property to Its Country of Origin or Its Restitution in Case of Illicit Appropriation (ICPRCP) and the International Advisory Committee of UNESCO's Memory of the World Programme. Her research interests include Caribbean art history, museum history and theory, heritage studies, and heritage resource management. She is the author of articles and chapters in various publications, including *Art and Cultural Heritage: Law, Policy and Practice* and *History Workshop Journal*. She is the coeditor of *Plantation to Nation: Caribbean Museums and National Identity* and *Curating in the Caribbean*. She is editor-in-chief of the *International Journal of Intangible Heritage*.

L. Antonio Curet is curator at the National Museum of the American Indian in Washington, D.C. His main interest is the study of social and cultural changes in pre-Columbian Puerto Rico, specifically those leading to social stratification. Currently he is conducting an excavation project at the site of Tibes, Ponce (Puerto Rico), one of the earliest ceremonial centers in the Caribbean. He has published several books, including *Caribbean Paleodemography, Dialogues in Cuban Archaeology*, and *Tibes: People, Power, and Ritual at the Center of the Cosmos*. He also has published articles in *Latin American Antiquity, Journal of Field Archaeology, Journal of Anthropological Archaeology, Journal of Archaeological Science, El Caribe Arqueológico*, and *Revista de Arqueología del Área Intermedia*.

Kathleen Deagan is Distinguished Research Curator of Archaeology emerita and the Lockwood Professor of Florida and Caribbean Archaeology at the Florida Museum of Natural History, Gainesville, Florida. She has taught at Florida State University and the University of Florida. She has directed archaeological field schools in the Spanish colonial sites of St. Augustine, Florida, since 1972 and has concurrently directed ongoing excavation programs in Haiti and the Dominican Republic at several sites associated with Christopher Columbus. She is the author of many scholarly articles and books, including *Columbus's Outpost among the Tainos: Spain and America at La Isabela, 1493–1498* (with José M. Cruxent), *Puerto Real: The Archaeology of a Sixteenth-Century Spanish Town in Hispaniola*, and volumes 1 and 2 of *Artifacts of the Spanish Colonies of Florida and the Caribbean*. She has served as a consultant to UNESCO on cultural heritage development in Panama, Peru, Jamaica, and Haiti.

Rudylynn De Four Roberts is a fellow of the Trinidad and Tobago Institute of Architects and is a registered architect in Trinidad and Tobago. She has devoted much of her life to restoring historic buildings and lobbying for the preservation of the built heritage in Trinidad and Tobago. She established and served as director of Trinidad and Tobago's Government Historic Restoration Unit for twelve years. As a founding member of Citizens for Conservation, she was actively involved in researching and drafting the National Trust Act of Trinidad and Tobago and was a member of the first three executive councils of the trust. Her experience in the field of preservation enabled her to serve on several government committees, such as the Queen's Park Savannah Management Committee, the Archaeology Committee, and the Restoration Action Committee. She has represented her country at several conferences and symposia, delivering lectures and networking for the heritage preservation movement.

Maaike de Waal is partner at ARGEOgraph, an archaeological company that specializes in Caribbean archaeology, archaeology in the Netherlands, and geoinformatics in archaeology. She has been a lecturer in archaeology at The University of the West Indies, Cave Hill, Barbados. Since 1992, she has participated in various Caribbean archaeological research projects in St. Martin, Guadeloupe, and Saint Lucia. She has directed several field projects in Barbados and Guadeloupe. Her research interests include the Late Pre-Columbian period, Amerindian inland settlement and settlement patterns, and pre-Columbian ceramics. In 2013 she was appointed lecturer in archaeology at Leiden University.

Mark C. Donop is a doctoral candidate in anthropology at the University of Florida in Gainesville, Florida. He has worked as an anthropologist in Florida, California, North Carolina, Brazil, Peru, Tobago, and Guyana and conducted research based on an analysis of archaeological materials from Grenada. His research interests include maritime adaptation, archaeological ceramics, and cultural heritage management.

Peter L. Drewett was emeritus professor of archaeology at the University of Sussex, United Kingdom. He taught field archaeology at the Institute of Archaeology, University College London, for thirty-four years. At the invitation of the Barbados Museum and Historical Society, he set up the Barbados Archaeological Survey in 1984. He excavated a range of threatened prehistoric sites on the island, culminating in the extensive area excavation of the Heywoods site prior to the construction of the Port St. Charles Marina. He also worked on excavations on Tortola, British Virgin Islands, and on the Cayman Islands. He was the author of *Prehistoric Barbados*; *Prehistoric Settlements in the Caribbean: Fieldwork in Barbados, Tortola and the Cayman Islands*; and *Above Sweet Waters: Cultural and Natural Change at Port St. Charles, Barbados, c. 1750 BC–AD 1850*. He also wrote the undergraduate text *Field Archaeology: An Introduction*.

Ryan Espersen is a PhD candidate at Leiden University. His MA thesis focused on determining motivations for settlement and the socioeconomic status of individuals who lived at the abandoned colonial-era village of Mary Point, Saba, Dutch Caribbean. His research interests include the Dutch colonial era in the Caribbean, colonial ceramics and glassware, historical/archaeological method and theory, and colonial- and precolonial-era Oaxaca, Mexico.

Kevin Farmer is the curator of history and archaeology at the Barbados Museum and Historical Society. He is currently pursuing doctoral studies in archaeology at the University of Sussex in the United Kingdom. He contributed to *Archaeology and Geoinformatics: Case Studies from the Caribbean*. From 2010 to 2011, he was assistant lecturer in archaeology in the Department of History at The University of the West Indies, St. Augustine, Trinidad. He is currently deputy director of the Barbados Museum and Historical Society.

Anne-Marie Faucher is a PhD candidate in archaeology at Université Laval, Québec, Canada. She is presently continuing her studies in archaeobotany in the Caribbean region, mainly in Barbuda and French Guiana. Her research interests include long-term vegetation evolution, human impacts on the landscape, and the study of introduced species from the pre-Columbian and Columbian periods.

Scott M. Fitzpatrick is currently associate professor of archaeology at the University of Oregon. He specializes in the archaeology of islands and coasts, particularly the Pacific and Caribbean. His primary areas of interest include colonization strategies, exchange systems, chronometric techniques, and historical ecology. He is the founder and coeditor of the *Journal of Island and Coastal Archaeology*. He has published more than eighty journal articles and book chapters and edited several volumes, including *Voyages of Discovery: The Archaeology of Islands and Island Shores* and *Distant Pasts: Archaeological and Biological Perspectives on the Pre-Columbian Settlement of the Caribbean*, which was nominated for the 2013 Society for American Archaeology Scholarly Book Award. He currently has several active field projects on islands in the southern Lesser Antilles and western Micronesia.

Georgia L. Fox is professor in the Department of Anthropology at California State University, Chico, where she also directs the Heritage Resources Conservation Laboratory and co-directs the Museum of Anthropology and Museum Studies Program. Her academic interests and specializations include underwater archaeology and the historical archaeology of New World Caribbean colonization, museum and material culture studies, and the preservation and conservation of archaeological and ethnographic materials. Her work in the Caribbean includes research into preindustrial consumerism at Port Royal, Jamaica, and she is currently principal investigator of excavations at Betty's Hope Plantation on Antigua. She is working on a book about the British plantation system in relation to the environment and sustainability.

Gertrudis J. M. Gehlen studied the history of art and classical archeology at the University of Leiden, Netherlands. In 1999 she began working at the Monument Bureau of the island of Curaçao, Netherlands Antilles, and was division head of the Bureau from 2006 to 2013. She is the author of several publications on the architectural and social history of monuments on Curaçao and is presently a guest lecturer at the University of the Netherlands Antilles.

Joanna K. Gilmore is currently a freelance museum consultant. Her work has been published in the *International Journal of Osteoarchaeology*. Her primary research interests are leprosy history, human remains in archaeology, public archaeology, and museum studies.

R. Grant Gilmore III is a freelance heritage management consultant. He was the founding director of the St. Eustatius Center for Archaeological Research. His excavation experience includes work on a wide variety of colonial period sites in Williamsburg, Jamestown, Yorktown, Appalachia, and tidewater Virginia in the United States and on St. Eustatius, St. Maarten, and Saba in the Netherlands Caribbean. He serves on the board of the International Committee for Archaeological Heritage Management of the International Council on Monuments and Sites. Dr. Gilmore has authored book chapters and articles on the topics of public archaeology, slavery, the archaeology of capitalism, and heritage management.

Patricia E. Green is an architect and heritage professional. She was engaged in the 1990s as community architect for the historic town of Falmouth in Jamaica, where she initiated the Falmouth Façade Improvement Program. The program culminated with a community exhibition in 1993. She is a distinguished member of La Cathedra de Gonzalez de Cardenas, which studies and promotes vernacular architecture in Cuba, the Caribbean, and internationally and has published in various journals and books, including contributions to the *Encyclopedia of Vernacular Architecture of the World*. She was editor-in-chief of the ICOMOS publication *National Monuments and Sites: Jamaica.*

José G. Guerrero is a historian and educator. He directed the Archaeology Department and was assistant director of the Museo del Hombre Dominicano in Santo Domingo. At present, Mr. Guerrero directs the Instituto Dominicano de Estudios Antropologicos in Santo Domingo. From 1983 to 1986 he carried out archaeological excavations in La Isabela and reconstructed the Columbian route to the interior of the country. He has published several books, including *Los Inicios de la Colonización en América: La Arqueología como Historia*, and essays about pre-Columbian archaeology, Indo-European contact, and colonial history. He currently teaches at Universidad Autónoma de Santo Domingo and Instituto Tecnólogico de Santo Domingo.

Jay B. Haviser is currently the archaeologist for the Urban Planning and Environment Ministry of St. Maarten. He is on the Leiden University Faculty for Archaeology. He has served as president of the International Association for Caribbean Archaeology, as the senior regional representative for the Caribbean in the World Archaeological Congress, and as president of the Museums Association of the Caribbean. In 2008, he was granted a knighthood by Queen Beatrix for his archaeology work in the Netherlands Antilles. His publications include

African Sites: Archaeology in the Caribbean and over eighty international publications. He is currently directing youth and science programs called SIMARC on St. Maarten and BONAI on Bonaire and at the University of St. Martin.

Michele H. Hayward graduated with a doctorate from The Pennsylvania State University in 1986 and is currently a senior archaeologist with Panamerican Consultants, Inc. She has been involved with a variety of archaeological projects in the United States and the Caribbean. Her interest in Caribbean rock art began with her first postgraduate position at the Institute of Puerto Rican Culture and has grown to include documentation of rock art sites and organizing and participating in national and international sessions on Caribbean rock art. She coedited *Rock Art of the Caribbean.*

Ainsley Henriques, a businessman, chaired the Jamaica National Heritage Trust from 1991 to 1999. He is a member of the Archaeological Society of Jamaica and was appointed an Honorary Life Member in 2007 for his services to the society and to archaeology in general. He chaired the World Archaeological Congress Inter-Congress in Jamaica that year. He has served on the National Archives Committee and is currently a member of Council of the Institute of Jamaica. He has written on cultural resource management and has presented papers at the Archaeological Society of Jamaica's annual symposia. His articles include "The Jamaica National Heritage Trust: Reflections on the First 50 Years" (*Jamaica Journal*). He was the founder and creator of Jamaica's Jewish Heritage Centre, which opened in 2006. His other interests include many aspects of Jamaican heritage, genealogy, and antiquities.

Corinne L. Hofman is currently professor of Caribbean Archaeology and Dean of the Faculty of Archaeology at Leiden University, The Netherlands. Since the 1980s she has been conducting archaeological research on many islands of the Lesser and Greater Antilles, for which she was awarded prestigious grants (ASPASIA, VIDI, VICI) from the Netherlands Organisation for Scientific Research, HERA from the European Science Foundation, and Synergy from the European Research Council. She directs the Caribbean Research Group at Leiden composed of PhD and postdoctoral researchers from all over the world. Her current research themes are mobility and exchange, colonial encounters, intercultural dynamics, ceramic technology, and sociopolitical organization in the precolonial and early colonial Caribbean. She has published on Caribbean archaeology in international peer-reviewed journals. In addition, she has coedited several books, including *Archaeological Investigations on St. Martin* (with Menno Hoogland), *Late Ceramic Age Societies in the Eastern Caribbean* (with André Delpuech), *Communities in Contact* (with Anne van Duijvenbode), and *The Oxford Handbook of Caribbean Archaeology* (with William F. Keegan and Reniel Rodríguez Ramos). She is also a member of the editorial boards of the Paris Monographs in American Archaeology (BAR Series), *El Caribe Arqueológico*, the *Journal of Caribbean Archaeology*, and *Taboui*.

Lennox Honychurch is a Dominican anthropologist whose research focuses on the period of contact and cultural exchange between the Carib/Kalinago people of the Lesser Antilles and new arrivals from Europe and Africa. Dr. Honychurch has conducted fieldwork in the Caribbean with Henry Petitjean Roget and Benoît Bérard of Martinique. He is curator of Dominica's archaeology storage unit at Fort Shirley. He has identified the majority of the sixty pre-Columbian archaeological sites on Dominica and continues to work with and provide local support for visiting archaeologists.

Menno L. P. Hoogland is associate professor at the Faculty of Archaeology at Leiden University in the Netherlands. He has been conducting archaeological research in the Caribbean since the mid-1980s. In 2004 he was awarded a grant by the Netherlands Foundation for Scientific Research for the program Houses for the Living and the Dead, which is carried out in cooperation with the Museo del Hombre Dominicano. His academic interest centers on settlement archaeology. He has carried out extensive excavations on settlement sites on Saba and Guadeloupe. His bioarchaeological research, which focuses on the study of mortuary practices, includes archaeometric techniques such as isotope analysis and analysis of a-DNA. He is the author of numerous articles on Caribbean archaeology and bioarchaeology and has coedited two volumes: *Archaeological Investigations on St. Martin* and *Crossing the Borders: New Methods and Techniques in the Study of Archaeological Materials from the Caribbean.*

Naseema Hosein-Hoey holds an MA in artifact studies from the Institute of Archaeology, University College London. She has worked on various pre-Columbian and historical sites in Trinidad and Tobago and Guadeloupe. From 2004 to 2007, she was a research assistant at the Archaeology Centre in the Department of History at The University of the West Indies, St. Augustine, Trinidad.

Charlene Dixon Hutcheson is an independent archaeologist in Roanoke, Virginia. She began working in the Bahamas on Lucayan basketry-impressed ceramics as a graduate student in 1995 and has continued to work with these ceramics to the present. She has presented numerous papers on basketry-impressed ceramics at national and international conferences on Caribbean and Bahamian archaeology. Hutcheson has published articles in conference proceedings, coauthored an article in the *Journal of Field Archaeology*, and has a chapter in *Crossing the Borders: New Methods and Techniques in the Study of Archaeological Materials from the Caribbean.* Hutcheson has excavated in the United Kingdom since 1994, and since 2002 she has worked principally with the Llangynidr Local History Society on several sites in the Brecon Beacons mountain range.

Jeremiah Kaplan began his career in Caribbean archaeology in Anguilla in 2001 under the direction of James B. Petersen. Since that time, he has worked extensively on sites in Anguilla, Puerto Rico, Curaçao, the Dominican Republic, and the eastern United States and Hawaii. His current research focuses on pre-Columbian structural patterning in south-central Puerto Rico, the Caribbean, and South America.

Quetta Kaye currently co-directs excavation projects in Carriacou and Nevis, where she oversees students from the Institute of Archaeology of University College London. She has also excavated in Barbados, Mustique, and Cuba and at various sites in the United Kingdom. She has been secretary of the International Association for Caribbean Archaeology since 2003. She has authored and coauthored a number of papers emanating from excavation projects in Carriacou and Nevis and her PhD research. Her research interests are the prehistory of the Caribbean and the circum-Caribbean area, the ancient use of hallucinogens and altered states of consciousness, and the archaeobotanical and chemical analysis of prehistoric materials for evidence of intoxicants.

K. O. Laurence was appointed lecturer in history at The University of the West Indies at Mona, Jamaica, in 1959, where he taught Caribbean and European History. In 1972 he was appointed professor of history at the university's campus at St. Augustine, Trinidad. He was a member of the Trinidad and Tobago Archaeological Committee from its establishment in 1979 until 2009 and served as its chair from 1981 to 2009. In the mid-1980s, Professor Laurence chaired the Board of Management of the National Museum of Trinidad and Tobago.

In 2007 he was granted a Lifetime Achievement Award by the National Trust of Trinidad and Tobago in recognition of nearly four decades of consistent involvement in promoting and preserving the country's national heritage.

Elise V. LeCompte is registrar and assistant department chair at the Florida Museum of Natural History. She also serves as adjunct faculty in the University of Florida Museum Studies Program and associate faculty in the Johns Hopkins University Museum Studies Program. Her professional interests include collections management, artifact conservation, museum administration, museum ethics, and archaeology. Ms. LeCompte is also a professional archaeologist and has been a member of many archaeological excavations in the mid-Atlantic, Florida, and the Caribbean, serving as excavator, field supervisor, lab assistant, and lab director. She has published articles and reports on collections management, standards for computer collections databases, artifact conservation, and archaeological exhibits and field projects.

Stephan Lenik is presently at St. Mary's College in Maryland. He was lecturer of archaeology in the Department of History and Archaeology at The University of the West Indies, Mona, Jamaica from 2011 to 2013. His research focuses on how religious communities enacted missionization programs on frontiers and in colonies in the Caribbean. He has worked on archaeological projects in Dominica, St. John, St. Croix, St. Thomas, Jamaica, Guadeloupe, and Cuba and in eastern North America. His publications include articles in *Ethnohistory*, the *International Journal of Historical Archaeology*, and the *Journal of Social Archaeology*, as well as contributions to the proceedings of the International Association of Caribbean Archaeology.

Margaret E. Leshikar-Denton is director of the Cayman Islands National Museum. Her research interests include seafaring, ships, and shipwrecks in the Caribbean. She has worked in the Cayman Islands, Jamaica, the Turks and Caicos Islands, Mexico, the United States, Spain, and Turkey. She is chair of the Society for Historical Archaeology's UNESCO Committee and is a research associate with the Institute of Nautical Archaeology and Ships of Discovery. She also serves on the International Committee on Underwater Cultural Heritage of the International Council on Monuments and Sites and as an emeritus member of the Advisory Council on Underwater Archaeology. She writes on the protection and management of the Caribbean's underwater cultural heritage.

She co-edited (with Pilar Luna Erreguerena) *Underwater and Maritime Archaeology in Latin America and the Caribbean* and contributed to the *Oxford Handbook of Underwater Archaeology*.

Neal H. Lopinot is director of the Center for Archaeological Research and research professor at Missouri State University, Springfield, Missouri. He has authored or co-authored publications in such journals as *American Antiquity*, *Geoarchaeology*, *Illinois Archaeology*, the *Journal of Archaeological Science*, the *Journal of Geology*, and *Southeastern Archaeology*. He has also published articles in a number of edited books, including *Foraging and Farming in the Eastern Woodlands*; *Cahokia: Domination and Ideology in the Mississippian World*; and *Hunter and Gatherer Lifeways of the Early Holocene*. Since 2006, he has served as secretary of the Missouri Archaeological Society and as the editor of the *Missouri Archaeological Society Quarterly* and the *Missouri Archaeologist*. His major research interests include archaeobotany, cultural resource management, experimental archaeology, and early hunter-gatherer behavior. He is also interested in colonial archaeology and has conducted research on the La Reconnaissance site in Trinidad.

George M. Luer has spearheaded a multidisciplinary archaeological research program in peninsular Florida since the 1970s. He has worked with many colleagues to produce numerous scientific publications, popular texts, and exhibitions and to preserve many endangered sites. He has worked extensively with ceramics, shell tools, canoe canals, early contact period metal artifacts, zooarchaeology, shell midden formation, and radiocarbon dating. Luer knew Ripley and Adelaide Bullen and was inspired by their dedication to the Florida Anthropological Society, its journal the *Florida Anthropologist*, and its monograph series. Over the years, he has worked hard to support those vehicles of archaeological progress.

Onika Mandela is a former research assistant in the Archaeology Centre in the Department of History, The University of the West Indies, St. Augustine, Trinidad.

Kathy Martin assumed the role of Chair of the St. Vincent and the Grenadines National Trust after a career in education. She developed a special interest in prehistoric cultures as she undertook the curating and permanent exhibition of the National Archaeological Collection. In this capacity, she was responsible for managing site registers and inventorying the country's many petroglyphs. She involved the National Trust in raising awareness of the heritage sites at the Argyle International Airport and joined with the Airport Board and overseas archaeologists to mitigate the impact of construction on these sites. Her experience in heritage management and education prepared her to serve on the boards of a number of government statutory bodies, including the National Parks Authority and the Tourist Board. Her publications include *Set in Stone: the Rock Art of St. Vincent and the Grenadines*; *St. Vincent and the Grenadines*; and numerous articles on the patrimony of St. Vincent and the Grenadines.

H. Gregory McDonald is the senior curator of natural history in the Museum Management Program of the U.S. National Park Service. He is also adjunct professor in the Department of Anthropology at Colorado State University, where he teaches zooarchaeology. He has worked extensively on extinct ground sloths and their relatives and on other Pleistocene fauna in North and South America and the Caribbean. His research focuses on the biogeography and paleoecology of Pleistocene fauna and how these may be related to their extinction. Over the years he has collaborated with archaeologists on identifying faunal remains for various sites, including Warm Mineral Springs in Florida. He is currently working on recently discovered ground sloths from a cave site in the Dominican Republic.

Marco Meniketti is currently associate professor and senior archaeologist in the Anthropology Department at San Jose State University, California, and is director of the nonprofit Institute for Advanced Interdisciplinary Caribbean Studies. Each summer Dr. Meniketti directs a field school that focuses on plantation settlement and maritime history on the island of Nevis. He is also a National Fellow in the Explorers Club.

Reg Murphy is director of heritage resources for National Parks Antigua, the secretary-general for the National Commission for UNESCO Antigua, and the chair of the Betty's Hope Trust. His work includes planning and developing heritage sites, parks, and protected areas and supervising field research projects on Antigua and Barbuda. He chaired the Twenty-First Congress of the International Association of Caribbean Archaeology in Antigua in 2009. In 2011, he was elected president of the International Association for Caribbean Archaeology.

Lee A. Newsom is associate professor with the Department of Anthropology and a member scientist of the Institutes of Energy and the Environment at the Penn-

sylvania State University, University Park. Her research emphasizes environmental archaeology in theory and practice, drawing especially on insights from paleoethnobotany and island biogeographic theory to consider issues involving biotic resources and human social organization, plant and animal domestication, the evolution and transformation of Caribbean garden systems, and the so-called Columbian exchange. Her research focuses on the study of later sites associated with the more socially complex groups of the Caribbean Ceramic Age, South Florida's Calusa Indians, and the contact era. She coauthored *On Land and Sea: Native American Uses of Biological Resource in the West Indies*. In 2002, Newsom was named a MacArthur Fellow, and she has since used that award to foster a variety of projects and initiatives in the Caribbean.

Maria A. Nieves-Colón is a graduate student in physical anthropology specializing in molecular anthropology and ancient DNA at Arizona State University. She has done archaeological fieldwork in Puerto Rico, Mexico, and the United States and has studied osteological collections from Portugal and Puerto Rico. She received a National Science Foundation Graduate Research Fellowship in 2010 and is currently conducting research on the genetic heritage of modern Caribbean populations in collaboration with Juan C. Martínez Cruzado of the University of Puerto Rico, Mayagüez.

Winston F. Phulgence is lecturer in history at the Sir Arthur Lewis Community College in Saint Lucia. His research interests include Caribbean prehistory, archaeology, and cultural heritage management. He recently coauthored a contribution to *Protecting Heritage in the Caribbean*.

Elizabeth Pigou-Dennis is currently senior lecturer in the Caribbean School of Architecture at the University of Technology, Kingston, Jamaica. She also teaches part-time at Mico University College in Kingston, Jamaica, where she has developed and delivered a course in the history of Caribbean architecture. She has served on the Board of Directors of the Museums of History and Ethnography of the Institute of Jamaica. She has published several articles and book chapters on various themes in architectural history and theory, including Rastafari spatial and iconographic expressions, the history of bungalows in Jamaica, and interpretations of urban spaces. She is currently working on a book on class identity, spatial experience, and architecture during the interwar years in Jamaica.

Mark G. Plew is professor of anthropology at Boise State University, Boise, Idaho, where he also serves as director of the Center for Applied Archeological Science. His primary research interest is the human ecology of hunter-gatherers. He has conducted numerous archaeological projects in North and South America. During the past eighteen years he has worked cooperatively with the Amerindian Research Unit of the University of Guyana and the Walter Roth Museum of Anthropology. He serves as an associate editor of *Archaeology and Anthropology* and as a member of the museum's Scientific Advisory Board. He is director of the Archaeological Field School program of the Denis Williams School of Anthropology, a cooperative program between the Walter Roth Museum of Anthropology and the University of Guyana. He has published numerous books, including *The Archaeology of Guyana* and has contributed to numerous edited collections, including *Proceedings of the National Academy of Natural Sciences* and *Anthropologies of Guayana*.

Basil A. Reid is senior lecturer in archaeology in the Department of History at The University of the West Indies, St. Augustine, Trinidad. He is currently the senior representative for Central America and the Caribbean at the World Archaeological Congress. His major research interests are the pre-Columbian archaeology of the Caribbean, archaeology and geoinformatics, landscape archaeology, and historical geography. He has published in a variety of peer-reviewed publications, including the *Journal of Caribbean History, Caribbean Quarterly, Caribbean Geography*, and *Archaeology and Anthropology*. He edited *Archaeology and Geoinformatics: Case Studies from the Caribbean; A Crime-Solving Toolkit: Forensics in the Caribbean*; and *Caribbean Heritage* and is the author of *Myths and Realities of Caribbean History* and *Archaeology, GIS and Cultural Resource Management in Trinidad*. He is a member of the editorial boards of the *Historic Environment* and the *Archaeological Society of Jamaica*. Reid was the lead archaeologist for the Red House Restoration Project (Trinidad) from July 1, 2013, to January 31, 2014.

Andrea Richards has worked in the field of cultural resource management in Jamaica for more than ten years. Her research interests include public attitudes toward the past, trade in cultural objects, and cultural heritage legislation. She has served as the marketing and events manager of the Devon House heritage site, where she was responsible for monitoring the historic mansion's restoration program of 2008. She coordinated the Caribbean's first staging of the World Archaeological Inter Congress (2007) and is vice-president of the Archaeological Society of Jamaica and project coordinator of the Institute of Jamaica's movable cultural property program. She works as a consultant with the Latin America and the Caribbean Unit of the UNESCO World Heritage Centre. Her most recent publication is "Cultural Resource Management: A Study of Jamaica," in *Protecting Heritage in the Caribbean*.

James Robertson is senior lecturer in history at the Department of History and Archaeology, University of the West Indies, Mona, where he has taught since 1995. He is the author of *Gone Is the Ancient Glory: Spanish Town, Jamaica, 1534–2000* and is the coeditor of *Caribbean Quarterly*'s first issue on Caribbean Archaeology and Material Culture (2009). He has published on Jamaican history, archives, and architectural history and on early modern Britain. He has served as vice-president of the Jamaican Historical Society, vice-president of the Archaeological Society of Jamaica, and was a member of the board of the Museums Division of the Institute of Jamaica. He is currently writing a book on the Western Design.

Stéphen Rostain was employed as an archaeologist in French Guiana from 1985 to 1994. He co-directed the archaeological project Tanki Flip in Aruba, which led to the publication of a large monograph. From 1996 to 2001 he lived in Ecuador, where he was co-director of the archaeological project Sangay-Upano and director of the Rio Blanco project. He is presently director of research at the CNRS (National Center for Scientific Research) of French Guiana. In 2008, he received the Paris Clio award for French projects in foreign countries. His research focuses on the Amazonian and Caribbean Lowlands.

Krysta Ryzewski is assistant professor in the Department of Anthropology and an affiliated faculty member of the Department of Chemical Engineering and Materials Science at Wayne State University in Detroit, Michigan. She has participated in terrestrial and underwater archaeological projects in the United States, Great Britain, and the Caribbean and is currently co-director of the Greene Farm Archaeology Project (Rhode Island) and of the project Survey and Landscape Archaeology on Montserrat. Her primary interests are in the craft and production of materials, the transfer of technology, industrial ecology, and multimedia archaeology. She is the author of several forthcoming book chapters and of articles published in the *Journal of Archaeological Method and Theory, Archaeological and Anthropological Sciences*, the *Journal of Island and Coastal Archaeology*, and *Archaeologies*.

Alexandra Sajo has worked for the Venezuelan Cultural Heritage Institute in various archaeological projects in different Venezuelan archaeological sites. She has worked with the Proyecto Arqueológico de la Región de Sicarigua Los Arangues project in the northwest region of Venezuela and has published on the topic of pre-Hispanic agricultural systems.

Brinsley Samaroo is senior research fellow at the Academy of the University of Trinidad and Tobago, Trinidad. Prior to this position, he taught history at The University of the West Indies, St. Augustine, where he chaired the Department of History. He has published widely on the history of Trinidad and Tobago, particularly on the Indian Diaspora. Currently, he is a member of Trinidad and Tobago's National Commission for Higher Education and chair of the Sugar Museum and Heritage Village committee, which is developing a large swath of Caroni lands at Brechin Castle in central Trinidad.

Gerald F. Schroedl is professor of anthropology at the University of Tennessee, Knoxville. His research interests in the Caribbean are focused primarily on the British military and their use of enslaved Africans to further their objectives in the region. From 1996 through 1999 and again from 2004 to 2008 he excavated at the Brimstone Hill Fortress National Park, St. Kitts, with the goal of documenting archaeological evidence for enslaved Africans and of making comparative studies of contexts relating to British army officers and enlisted men.

Della A. Scott-Ireton worked with the Pensacola Shipwreck Survey; West Florida Historic Preservation, Inc.; and the Florida Bureau of Archaeological Research before joining the Florida Public Archaeology Network, where she serves as associate director. She is certified as a Scuba Instructor with the National Association of Underwater Instructors. Her interest in public interpretation of maritime resources led her to work with Dr. Margaret Leshikar-Denton on the creation of a Maritime Heritage Trail in the Cayman Islands. Scott-Ireton is an officer and elected board member of the Advisory Council on Underwater Archaeology, a board member of the Society for Historical Archaeology, and a member of the Register of Professional Archaeologists and is appointed to the Marine Protected Areas Federal Advisory Committee. Her research interests include public interpretation of maritime cultural heritage, both on land and under water, and training people with an avocational interest in archaeological methods and practices.

Peter E. Siegel is professor of anthropology and serves on the steering committee of the Center for Heritage and Archaeological Studies at Montclair State University, Montclair, New Jersey, where he has been teaching since 2006. Before that, he worked for fourteen years in heritage management. His major interests include Caribbean and lowland South American archaeology and ethnography, the archaeology of eastern North America, heritage studies, and historical ecology. Siegel has conducted archaeological studies throughout much of eastern North America, Puerto Rico, the United States Virgin Islands, the Lesser Antilles, and eastern Bolivia. He has conducted ethnoarchaeological research among the Waiwai in Guyana and the Shipibo in the *montaña* region of eastern Peru.

Harrold Sijlbing has been engaged in the rehabilitation of the Jodensavanne settlement and Cassipora cemetery in Suriname since 1998. He is the current chairman of the Jodensavanne Foundation. He is also a cultural heritage tourism consultant at the Suriname Alliance for Nature Conservation and Sustainable Tourism and lectures on tourism at several institutes in Paramaribo, Suriname.

Sherry-Ann Singh is lecturer in the department of history at The University of the West Indies, St. Augustine, Trinidad. She specializes in the social, religious, and cultural transformation among Indians in Trinidad and in the Indian Diaspora; Hinduism and the Ramayana tradition in the Indian Diaspora; and on the Indian indenture system. She teaches courses in South Asian history and Indian Diaspora studies. She has held fellowships at the Centre for the Study of Culture and Society in Bangalore, India, and at the University of Warwick. Her recent publications include *The Ramayana Tradition and Socio-Religious Change in Trinidad, 1917–1990*, a chapter in *Bindi: The Multifaceted Lives of Indo-Caribbean Women*, and articles in the *Journal of Caribbean History, Man in India: A Quarterly International Journal of Anthropology*, and *ICFAI: Journal of History and Culture*.

Theresa Singleton is associate professor in the Department of Anthropology at Syracuse University, Syracuse, New York. Her areas of expertise include African Diasporas, slavery and plantations, museums, the southern United States, and the Caribbean, particularly Cuba. She was introduced to historical archaeology in the Caribbean in 1990, when she participated in excavations of an enslaved village site at Galways Sugar Plantation on Montserrat, West Indies. In 1999, she began archaeological investigation at the coffee plantation Santa Ana de Biajacas, a project that is still ongoing. She is the editor of *The Archaeology of Slavery and Plantation Life* and *"I, Too, Am America": Archaeological Studies of African-American Life* and has written over forty articles and book chapters. She has consulted on numerous museum exhibitions.

Frederick H. Smith is associate professor of anthropology at the College of William and Mary, Williamsburg, Virginia. He is the author of *Caribbean Rum: A Social and Economic History* and *The Archaeology of Alcohol and Drinking*. He has published numerous journal articles. Since 1995 Smith has regularly conducted historical archaeological investigations in Barbados. He has investigated the lives of early British colonists and enslaved peoples in the urban context of Bridgetown, Barbados, and in rural sugar plantation contexts.

Ruud Stelten has since 2009 been involved in historical archaeological research and cultural resource management on St. Eustatius and Mauritius. He has also conducted fieldwork in Greece and the Netherlands, where he has an appointment at a commercial archaeology firm. He was formerly employed as an archaeologist at the St. Eustatius Center for Archaeological Research.

Clenis Tavárez María is head of the Department of Human Biology of the Museo del Hombre Dominicano, Santo Domingo, Dominican Republic. She has taught courses in social sciences at the Universidad Nacional Pedro Henríquez Ureña and the Universidad Católica, Santo Domingo. Her research has focused mainly in archaeology, physical anthropology, and ethnohistory. She has contributed to a number of research projects in the Dominican Republic and Martinique. Her research has been published in journals, volumes, and proceedings. She has participated in and organized a number of national and international conferences and congresses and was one of the main organizers of the International Congress for Caribbean Archaeology in Santo Domingo in 2003.

Joshua M. Torres is a project archaeologist with Southeastern Archaeological Research in Gainesville, Florida. His research focuses on geographical information systems applications in archaeology, social landscapes, settlement patterns, and the organization and development of pre-Columbian polities in the New World.

Marcie L. Venter is currently a Visiting Scholar at the University of Kentucky in Lexington. She specializes in the archaeology of social interactions, particularly in Mesoamerica. Her primary research interests are identity, colonialism/imperialism, ceramic technological styles, culture change, and ethnohistory in Latin America and the Caribbean. She is currently collaborating on a study of tourist facilities and their appropriation of archaeological heritage in Veracruz, Mexico. She is also working with colleagues at the La Reconnaissance archaeological site in Lopinot, Trinidad. She has published book chapters, reports, and articles in peer-reviewed journals, including the *Journal of Archaeological Science* and *Mexicon*.

Gifford J. Waters is the collections manager for historical archaeology at the Florida Museum of Natural History, Gainesville, Florida. His academic interests include identity, culture contact studies, Spanish colonial archaeology, the impact of missionization on Native Americans, and museum and material culture studies. He has conducted archaeological research throughout Florida and the southeastern United States and in the Caribbean at the sites of La Isabela in the Dominican Republic and Nueva Seville in Jamaica.

Cheryl White is a historical archaeologist with a special focus on the African Diaspora communities of the circum-Caribbean. Her recent research focuses on applied anthropological research among tribal communities, including the topics of social development and infrastructural heritage management. She has published several book chapters and journal articles on the topic of historical archaeology and heritage management. Her primary work is in Suriname in South America.

Samuel M. Wilson is professor and chair of the Department of Anthropology at the University of Texas in Austin, Texas. He is interested in the ethnohistory and archaeology of the Caribbean, particularly the emergence of complex forms of social and political organization over time.

Jennifer Wishart is director of the Walter Roth Museum of Anthropology, Georgetown, Guyana, and the editor of *Anthropology and Archaeology*. A longtime associate of Denis Williams, she has participated in archaeological excavations throughout Guyana and has published on the Abary Phase at the site Recht-door-Zee. She is the founder of Guyana's Junior Archaeology program